ALSO BY THOMAS J. SCHOENBAUM

The New River Controversy

Islands, Capes, and Sounds

WAGING PEACE AND WAR

Thomas J. Schoenbaum

DEAN RUSK
IN THE TRUMAN,
KENNEDY, AND
JOHNSON YEARS

SIMON AND SCHUSTER
New York London Toronto Sydney Tokyo

PUBLISHED BY SIMON AND SCHUSTER
A DIVISION OF SIMON & SCHUSTER INC.
SIMON & SCHUSTER BUILDING
ROCKEFELLER CENTER
1230 AVENUE OF THE AMERICAS
NEW YORK, NY 10020
SIMON AND SCHUSTER AND COLOPHON ARE REGISTERED TRADEMARKS OF
SIMON & SCHUSTER INC.
DESIGNED BY KAROLINA HARRIS
MANUFACTURED IN THE UNITED STATES OF AMERICA
1   3   5   7   9   10   8   6   4   2
LIBRARY OF CONGRESS CATALOGING-IN-PUBLICATION DATA
SCHOENBAUM, THOMAS J.
WAGING PEACE AND WAR.
BIBLIOGRAPHY: P.
INCLUDES INDEX.
1. RUSK, DEAN, 1909–   . 2. STATESMEN—UNITED
STATES—BIOGRAPHY. 3. UNITED STATES—FOREIGN RELATIONS
—1945–   . I. TITLE.
E748.R94S36 1988   973.92'092'4   88-3134
ISBN 0-671-60351-5

PHOTO CREDITS FOR CHAPTER OPENINGS:
PROLOGUE: DEPARTMENT OF STATE, VISUAL SERVICES SECTION, DEAN RUSK
COLLECTION, UNIV. OF GEORGIA
CHAPTER 1: DEAN RUSK COLLECTION, UNIV. OF GEORGIA
CHAPTER 2: DEAN RUSK COLLECTION, UNIV. OF GEORGIA
CHAPTER 3: DEAN RUSK COLLECTION, UNIV. OF GEORGIA
CHAPTER 7: WIDE WORLD PHOTOS
EPILOGUE: LEANNE TURNER, SCHOOL OF JOURNALISM, DEAN RUSK COLLECTION,
UNIV. OF GEORGIA

For my sons and daughters

CONTENTS

P R E F A C E

THE story of this book began in 1983, when I took a new job as executive director of the Dean Rusk Center for International and Comparative Law at the University of Georgia. At that time I became a colleague of Dean Rusk, the Sibley Professor of International Law at the school and, of course, the person for whom the center was named.

For me, Rusk fairly typified the office of Secretary of State. He had held this position for eight momentous years in the 1960s, which, in my own life, spanned the time I was a college undergraduate, a graduate student in Europe, a law student, an attorney practicing in Chicago, and a young professor at the University of North Carolina. I respected him and thought that on the whole he had served his country well, but like so many of my generation, I had disagreed profoundly with his and President Johnson's decisions to send American troops into battle in Vietnam.

Thus when I took up my duties, I felt as if I had just been assigned a part in *The Big Chill,* a movie about the sixties generation twenty years later. I soon found, however, that there was an immense difference between the public image of Dean Rusk and the reality. In person he was witty, eloquent, and self-deprecating, qualities that had escaped me when he was Secretary of State. I also sensed that he had been deeply wounded by the reaction of his countrymen to his prosecution of the war, but that he had not fundamentally changed his view of the justice of the American cause.

Still, I did not set out to write a book about Dean Rusk. The idea came to me only after several months of conversation with him that I found fascinating. Through his words and stories, I realized that he was a man who had not merely witnessed but had exercised an enormous influence over the major historical events of our time. It also came to me that Rusk—almost alone among his contemporaries—had never written his memoirs. Thus I was conscious of the fact that if someone did not collect his stories and recollections, much of historical importance would be lost with his passing. And that would be an irretrievable loss.

So one day I marched into his office with the proposition that I write the story of his professional life and asked for his cooperation. He readily agreed, although it meant an invasion of his privacy and a substantial infringement on his free time. Soon I was joined by his son Richard, who was also fascinated by Rusk's career and realized the importance of recounting his place in our history.

Although I have benefited immensely from my access to Rusk, my task was of course much more complicated than merely recording his recollections. I went to the public record as well, as it exists in the National Archives, the Department of State, and the Kennedy and Johnson presidential libraries. I endeavored to interview everyone who was associated with Rusk through the years and consulted the available oral histories in the presidential libraries and the Princeton University archives. I also consulted the immense literature of the period, consisting of both eyewitness accounts and secondary renditions of events.

Thus I offer this account of the life and career of one of the most dominant, and least known, figures of American history in the twentieth century. It is in no way an authorized account. Rusk has not seen the manuscript, nor did I offer it to him. The interpretations, conclusions, and opinions expressed are mine alone.

I acknowledge the indispensable assistance of several persons who have been involved in this project: Savanna Jackson Mapelli, my research assistant; Nelda Parker, who typed and retyped the manuscript; my excellent editors Fred Hills and Burton Beals; and Maria Carvainis, my agent, who first recognized the importance of this project.

THOMAS J. SCHOENBAUM
Athens, Georgia
January 1988

"The Best Man Available"

President-elect John F. Kennedy announces Dean Rusk as his choice for Secretary of State on December 12, 1960.

T HROUGHOUT the turmoil of the 1960s in the United States, one man served as Secretary of State in the administrations of both John F. Kennedy and Lyndon B. Johnson. That man was Dean Rusk, who, as the preponderant force in the presidential councils of the time, is above all remembered for the prosecution of the war in Vietnam. He made himself the rock against which crashed the successive waves of dissent. To many he was like the Bourbon kings of France who seemed to have learned nothing and forgotten nothing. Urbane, calm, and almost maddeningly patient, he explained over and over again the premises behind our involvement in Vietnam: we have a solemn commitment to defend South Vietnam from aggression; all we want is for North Vietnam to "leave its neighbors alone"—a phrase he repeated so often at his press conferences that it evoked nervous laughter. Rusk willingly took on the difficult burden of being the principal public defender of American policy, until Vietnam became known in Wash-

ington as "Dean Rusk's war." Widely regarded as the chief hawk in
the aerie of Vietnam advisers, he was subjected to enormous vilification, and the tarnish has persisted with the bitter recollections of
Vietnam as the "only war America ever lost."

The portrait historians have drawn of the man who was Secretary
of State for more years than anyone in American history save Cordell
Hull is too one-dimensional to do him justice. For the image fails to
take into account that during his long career in government service
Rusk exerted an enormous and at times decisive influence on many
questions of great national and international importance, quite apart
from the conflict in Vietnam. His voice was heard in both the Oval
Office of the White House and in the capitals of world power. He,
quite literally, dealt almost daily with matters of war and peace. Yet
he remains one of the least understood public figures of his time, a
man the press called even during his term in office "an enigma," "a
mystery," and "the anonymous Mr. Rusk."

That the real Dean Rusk has eluded historians is not accidental.
Hiding his inner self is part of his character. Unlike most occupants
of high office, he has never written his memoirs, nor has he ever kept
a diary or an organized record of events. He wanted to assure the
Presidents whom he served as well as his other associates that he
would not later disclose intimacies that might violate their privacy or
cause embarrassment. When Rusk left the State Department after
eight years as Secretary of State, he not only refused to take any
papers or documents with him, but systematically destroyed records
of confidential conversations with Presidents Kennedy and Johnson.

Even at the time, his penchant for extreme confidentiality was considered odd. A story making the rounds during the Kennedy administration was that one day President Kennedy and Dean Rusk were
chatting alone together in the Oval Office and Kennedy asked him for
his advice on an important matter of foreign policy. After nervously
looking around the empty room, Rusk finally whispered, "I would be
glad to give you my advice, Mr. President, but it is a very sensitive
matter, and I think we should discuss it in a slightly smaller meeting."

President Kennedy himself used Rusk's preoccupation with confidentiality to play a practical joke on his Secretary of State. Early in
the new administration, a high-level appointment was being discussed, and the names of those being considered were known only to
the President, Rusk, and a few advisers in the State Department.
Despite all efforts to maintain secrecy, the *Washington Post* ran a
story disclosing the matter and the names of those under consideration. On the morning the story appeared, Rusk was at home eating

breakfast when the telephone rang. President Kennedy was on the line; Rusk had never heard him so irate. The President scolded at length about how such leaks were unacceptable, complained bitterly about the State Department, and ordered Rusk to find the culprit. Profoundly disturbed, Rusk conducted the investigation himself. He called in the reporter who wrote the story and told him bluntly, "You have to make your living around here, and if you know what's good for you, you'll tell me who leaked that story." It turned out that the source of the leak was none other than Kennedy himself. When Rusk came to Kennedy with the news, the President laughed and said with a twinkle in his eyes, "Mr. Secretary, I just wanted to see if you were on your toes."

The period during which Rusk was Secretary of State, 1961–69, almost exactly spans the 1960s, and his career is a prism through which we can view this tumultuous and difficult decade. It was a unique time in our national life—a period of idealism, hopes, and dreams; of upheaval and change; of crushing disillusionment, failure, and assassination. The events of this decade and the Vietnam experience haunt us still, and define to a great extent what America has become. As a nation we have not yet totally cast off our emotional numbness and come to terms with these years.

In the 1960s Dean Rusk was a figure larger than life. Most Americans looked upon him as the quintessential representative of the "establishment" of the country. His spiritual lineage passed through such men as Truman, Marshall, Stilwell, Pershing, Wilson, and Robert E. Lee. In the Kennedy administration he seemed a bit too old and stuffy to be a member of the New Frontier. Later he would quietly boast that he had never been tossed—as had so many others—into Ethel Kennedy's swimming pool. In the Johnson administration Rusk became an LBJ intimate to an extent not generally known at the time. His power was such that, subject to the President's general judgment, he exercised the final decision over the whole of our foreign policy. (In 1967 he was also thrust into the national consciousness in a different role: as a proud father giving away his daughter in marriage to a black man.)

Yet those who knew him remarked that Rusk was rather humble, even ordinary. When he returned home in the evening from his duties as Secretary of State, he dismissed his security guards and, even when told that his personal safety was in danger, refused Secret Service protection. One Saturday morning at the height of the Vietnam War, things were going badly at the Rusk household, and on top of everything, the washing machine would not work. Dressed in old clothes and a favorite battered hat, Rusk put the basket of laundry in his car and drove to a coin-operated laundromat. There he spent a quiet morning, unrecognized, reading newspapers and patiently doing the family wash.

Rusk's rapid rise from obscure origins to a position of enormous power seems to smack of driving ambition, yet no one ever accused him of bureaucratic knife-wielding, and many thought he lacked a certain zest for competition. He never appeared to have his eye on the "next" job, and he did not try very hard even to become Secretary of State. The secrets to Rusk's advancement were loyalty, intelligence, a Victorian devotion to duty, and dogged hard work. He also exhibited an unusual ability to get along with other people as part of a team.

Ironically, Rusk's greatest weakness grew out of these very strengths. His unswerving and limitless loyalty to the men he served meant that he sometimes did not present his own views forcefully enough, especially when they differed from those of his superiors. Indeed, some even wondered if he had any views of his own; like a lawyer working for a favorite client, Rusk advanced the cause of those in power. He was always conscious of the fact that he did not quite belong in the world of the elite. He had risen above his hardscrabble boyhood in Cherokee County, Georgia, by getting along well with those who held power. All his life he would instinctively support those in charge and protect those who, as he put it, "had the burden of decision." He became the consummate insider, secretive and distrustful of those who dared question the authority of their betters. His early religious training gave Rusk a theological bent that carried over into politics and made him somewhat rigid and inflexible in his views. His ability to work well with people caused him to seek harmony and cooperation; he shied away from confrontation and controversy.

Rusk's dour manner masked a streak of messianic idealism about the place of the United States in the world. Cautious and judicious by temperament, he was nevertheless impatient with theory and abstract debate; he prided himself on avoiding the pitfall of the intellectual who is comfortable only with constant study of a problem. He often quoted Dean Acheson's maxim, "We think correctly only in action." And from Harry Truman, Rusk took the idea that a decision-maker, to be successful, must be capable of oversimplification at the critical moment of decision.

Some questioned Dean Rusk's judgment, but no one who knew or worked with him questioned his character. He was a man of deeply held principles and beliefs, and he adhered to them scrupulously. His friends adored him and considered him a man apart, or as one commented, a "man transcendent." Men as disparate as Lyndon Johnson and George Ball used the word "love" when speaking of him. His selflessness, dedication, and strength of will were remarkable. He never seemed to lose control no matter how great the pressure. In his personal life he exhibited an austerity rare for the times. Except for official or obligatory functions, he avoided the Washington cocktail party circuit, and was a devoted family man.

It would be a mistake to call him a drudge, however. He has a lively, wry wit that is often turned on himself. Many years after his retirement from public life, an elderly woman eyed him intently while he was waiting for a plane at the Atlanta airport. She obviously recognized him as someone she had seen before. Finally she could contain herself no longer and walked up to him and said, "You're in television, aren't you?" Rusk looked at her and said, "Oh, you remember Hoss Cartwright, don't you?" The woman walked away with a satisfied smile on her face.

Another characteristic remarked by those who know him is Rusk's eloquence. In his speeches to small groups, many find him mesmerizing, with a rich, mellifluous voice, crisp, logical thought, and ready wit. But those qualities rarely came across in his television appearances in the 1960s; viewers saw only a bald, round-faced man who appeared tightly controlled, nervous, and laconic.

When he was appointed Secretary of State, it was a surprise to virtually everyone. On a gray December day in 1960, Rusk, who was then president of the Rockefeller Foundation, was presiding over a meeting of the board of trustees in Williamsburg, Virginia, when he was handed a message asking him to come to the telephone. The caller was the President-elect, John Fitzgerald Kennedy, who, just the month before, had defeated Richard M. Nixon by a narrow margin in a bitterly fought campaign. Rusk was startled and surprised. On his right sat Chester Bowles, who he knew had been close to Kennedy during the campaign. Rusk showed Bowles the telephone slip. "What do you think he wants?" he whispered.

"He wants you to be his Secretary of State," Bowles replied.

Rusk got up and walked to another room to the phone. He had never met Kennedy or talked with him before. A few days earlier, Sargent Shriver, the President-elect's brother-in-law, had called to ask Rusk for some biographical information. But Rusk, unfamiliar with the Kennedy family, thought little about this; he assumed he was talking to one of Kennedy's *military* aides. Of course Rusk had voted for Kennedy; he was a lifelong Democrat. But he was a Stevenson man. In fact, Rusk had organized a group called "Scarsdale Citizens for Stevenson" in the New York suburb where he lived. After Kennedy was nominated, Stevenson had come to Scarsdale to speak at a rally in support of Kennedy and his running mate, Senator Lyndon Johnson. The hall was packed, and Stevenson gave a witty, erudite speech that received a standing ovation. The only problem was that Stevenson never once even mentioned Kennedy or Johnson. After the applause died down, Rusk had to remind the crowd that Kennedy was running for President and needed their votes.

Rusk picked up the phone, not knowing what to expect, and when Kennedy came on the line his voice was jovial and relaxed. "I need your advice about some appointments for my administration over at the State Department," he said. "Can you come up to Georgetown for a talk?"

A few days later Rusk, conservatively dressed in a dark wool flannel suit, was admitted to the Kennedys' elegant Georgetown townhouse at 3307 N Street after pushing past the reporters and identifying himself to the single Secret Service agent on guard outside. A maid showed him into the library, where Kennedy rose in greeting. The President-elect was casually dressed; books and papers were spread out on his desk and on the floor around his chair.

Seeing Kennedy face to face, Rusk had a sense of his youth and inexperience. He had been around Presidents before. Truman had been unprepared for the job, but from Rusk's perspective he had always seemed presidential—decisive, firm, correct. Eisenhower had been very businesslike, running the government as he ran his Army staff. Kennedy, in contrast, seemed vaguely unsure of himself. The mess of papers on the floor did not endear him to Rusk; neither did his air of easy informality. Rusk suddenly felt his status as a professional in the presence of an amateur, and foreign policy was no place for amateurs or those with untidy minds. The meeting confirmed Rusk's view of Kennedy as an upstart who had no business wresting the presidency away from Stevenson, who, after all, had been anointed by Harry Truman. Yet he suppressed his negative feelings. Kennedy was going to be the President, and Rusk owed him the fealty and loyalty due the occupant of that high office.

The meeting was not a formal job interview. The two men talked for a while about Rusk's experience in government. His first job in the State Department, in 1946, was as assistant chief of the Division of International Security Affairs, and Kennedy chuckled when Rusk reminded him that his boss at State had been "a man named Alger

Hiss." Thereafter, Rusk had risen rapidly through the State Department ranks, eventually becoming Deputy Under Secretary in 1949 and Assistant Secretary for Far Eastern Affairs in 1950.

Then Kennedy asked for his general views on American foreign policy since World War II, and Rusk replied, characteristically, in terms of the nobility of the American purpose. The United States had come out of the war with enormous power and, in disproof of the dictum of Lord Acton—that power tends to corrupt and absolute power tends to corrupt absolutely—the American postwar record was one of "restraint, responsibility, and generosity." "We did not set out to establish an American empire," he reminded Kennedy; rather, our purposes had been "simple and decent."

Kennedy and Rusk chatted comfortably and superficially, but Kennedy made no mention of a job in the new administration. Rusk began to feel uneasy; he wondered exactly why he was there. Kennedy then commented that Rusk knew the State Department very well and asked him what kind of a man would make a good Secretary of State.

Rusk replied by saying that he had served two excellent Secretaries, Marshall and Acheson, and each of them had done a good job in his own way. Marshall's position was unique, he reflected. President Truman considered him the greatest living American and delegated a great deal to him. Acheson did not quite have that status, but he grew into the job. And both of them were extremely loyal to their chief. Rusk recalled that Truman's first Secretary of State, James Byrnes, got into trouble because he had the idea that he, not Truman, should have been Roosevelt's last running mate and succeeded to the presidency. That was a fatal error, and Byrnes eventually paid the price when Truman asked for his resignation. Loyalty is the most important quality in a Secretary of State, Rusk explained.

Kennedy only smiled and asked another question: "Who do *you* think would make a good Secretary of State?"

Rusk immediately suggested Stevenson, but he could see from the look on Kennedy's face that the former Illinois governor and twice-defeated Democratic presidential candidate had no chance. Despite public harmony between Kennedy and Stevenson, the President-elect still resented Stevenson for remaining open to a draft at the convention and for refusing to nominate him as Kennedy had done for Stevenson in 1956. He also wondered whether Stevenson as Secretary of State might not be given to public pronouncements on foreign policy that differed from his own. Kennedy joked that "Adlai might even forget who's the President and who's the Secretary of State."

Rusk then suggested Robert Lovett, who was a nominal Republican, but that was all right. He had served with distinction at State as Marshall's Under Secretary. Kennedy told Rusk he had already talked to Lovett, but his ulcers made it impossible for him to accept any job in the new administration. They also discussed Senator William Fulbright, who Kennedy agreed was intelligent and able, and would accept the job. But Kennedy was worried about his record on civil rights. Rusk told him that if Fulbright did not have to run for reelection in Arkansas every six years, he would have a pro–civil rights record in Congress. Kennedy agreed, but talked about the necessity of finding someone with unquestioned liberal credentials. He asked Rusk what he thought of Chester Bowles. Rusk replied that Bowles was not ready for the top job but would make a splendid Under Secretary.

Kennedy thanked him for coming, and Rusk left the room feeling rather strange. On the table in plain view while the two men had been talking was a copy of an article Rusk had written, titled "The President," in the journal *Foreign Affairs*. In it he had called for a strong President who could take the lead in foreign affairs and in making the constitutional system work. Kennedy had obviously read the article, but did not mention it. He neither asked for Rusk's substantive advice nor discussed his availability for the post of Secretary of State.

Rusk went back to New York and told his colleagues at the Rockefeller Foundation not to pay any attention to the press speculation about him as the next Secretary of State. Kennedy had not broached the subject. He would be staying on as president of the foundation.

But, in fact, Kennedy had been sizing Rusk up, quietly making his own assessment. He had already consulted widely about who should be his Secretary of State, and Rusk's name was prominent on every list. Robert Lovett, in turning down the job, had recommended him. (Robert Kennedy later said that Lovett's recommendation was decisive with President Kennedy.) At State in the Truman administration, Rusk had been Marshall's fair-haired boy and had risen fast in the bureaucracy without making enemies. Dean Acheson had also recommended Rusk. "All the Presidents I have known are uneasy about the State Department," he told Kennedy. "You want someone over there who is not only competent and experienced, but also loyal, and who will close ranks with you when there is trouble." Rusk was that kind of person.

Kennedy also asked some of his key aides, men he had known for a long time, for their assessment of Rusk. McGeorge Bundy recalled a conference at Harvard in the late 1950s concerning academic and cultural exchanges with the Soviet Union, then a very controversial subject. Rusk had presided over the meeting and made a deep impression, particularly for his qualities of judgment and fairness.

Kennedy asked Walt Rostow who should be Secretary of State, saying there were three candidates, David Bruce, William Fulbright, and Dean Rusk. Rostow had just ghostwritten an article for Kennedy in the *Saturday Review* about the criteria for selecting a Secretary of State. "You remember what I said," he told Kennedy. "The most important thing is that the President must feel comfortable with him." "Yeah," said Kennedy, "it's a bit like getting married, isn't it?" Then he thought for a moment and told Rostow that the man he was most comfortable with was Fulbright. The two had been colleagues in the Senate and had worked side by side on foreign aid bills and other matters. "He's humanly comfortable," said Kennedy, "but he's lazy." If that's the case, Rostow said, it's not enough, because the Secretary of State works harder than the President. Rostow added that he knew and liked David Bruce, but did not know Rusk except by reputation.

It was a surprisingly casual and superficial search for a job many considered the most important in the cabinet. Kennedy checked out Rusk's speeches and writings and found nothing objectionable. Kennedy's staff was pleased that Rusk received high marks from his associates for his performance at Far Eastern Affairs and had not been touched in the least by the McCarthyite attacks on the State Department.

For Kennedy, however, the personal meeting with Rusk seems to have been the real test. He must have liked Rusk's thoughtful, judicious manner. Rusk would not seek the limelight, and that was good. He would be loyal to the President, and was also a proven administrator who could cope with the growing bureaucracy at State. Kennedy knew the appointment would be well received in diplomatic circles and in foreign capitals. He may have thought it was an advantage that no one knew much about Rusk. It would free the new administration from the past and provide the flexibility to look at new approaches. Kennedy may also have liked the fact that Rusk did not push himself for the job. Yet he was smart enough not to push Bowles either. Unknown to Rusk, Kennedy had asked Bowles a few days before what kind of an organization he would set up if he were Secretary of State. Bowles had said he would start by naming Rusk his Under Secretary.

So it would be Rusk for the job. He seemed the ideal choice for a vigorous and self-confident young President who, if he did not intend to be his own Secretary of State, certainly wanted to retain foreign policy decisions in his own hands. Rusk would be the wise counselor who would be the instrument of the President, a professional who would see that the President's will was carried out. Kennedy called him the very next day in New York and offered him the post. Rusk was surprised, and hesitated. Characteristically he said, "Now wait a minute. There are lots of things we ought to talk about before you make that decision."

Kennedy, somewhat taken aback by his reluctance, said, "All right, come on down to Palm Beach tomorrow, and we'll talk things over."

Rusk was genuinely shaken by the prospect of becoming Secretary of State. He remembered talking with John Foster Dulles just after Eisenhower had asked him to be his Secretary of State. Dulles had wanted the job very badly, but once he had it, he was unsure, even afraid. Just after his appointment, he told Rusk that he would rather have a job in the White House making policy recommendations for presidential action. Now Rusk felt the same way, in sudden awe at the weight of the responsibility.

Of course, he had had plenty of experience watching other Secretaries of State. He had known Byrnes and worked intimately with Marshall and Acheson. Dulles had called him frequently for advice. But Rusk saw what the office had done to their lives and how intractable the problems were. Even Marshall, his great hero, had had a difficult time. Rusk did not share the boisterous enthusiasm of some of the people around Kennedy, who seemed to think that by the mere application of their superior brain power and new ideas the problems the nation faced would melt away. Rusk had more modest goals. All that a President or Secretary of State could do was to manage problems so that when it came time for them to leave office, the world would be a somewhat safer place.

Why serve this young and inexperienced new President at all? At the age of fifty-one, Rusk had already attained a position of power, money, and status. As president of the Rockefeller Foundation, his annual salary was more than twice the amount paid to the Secretary of State. His job at the foundation was to range over the entire world to attack the evils that afflict mankind: poverty, hunger, ignorance, and disease. He had the use of a good measure of the financial fortune of the wealthiest family America had ever known. This family and its aged patriarch, John D. Rockefeller, Jr., urged him forward and gave him a free hand. In eight years Rusk had disbursed over $240 million to eradicate smallpox, to develop better varieties of wheat and corn, to improve universities, to support the arts, and to further an endless variety of other noble efforts.

Rusk moved freely in the world of brains and wealth that was the Eastern aristocracy. The bankers, government officials, lawyers, and university presidents whose decisions set the tone for the nation eagerly sought his counsel. He was the president of the Council on Foreign Relations, out of whose deliberations came the ideas for America's relationships with the rest of the world. He was the chairman of a Rockefeller-sponsored reexamination of American foreign policy written by elite academics like Henry Kissinger.

Yet Rusk's admission to this rarefied atmosphere had been far from automatic. He was born and grew up in Georgia, and although he had lost most of his Southern accent as a Rhodes scholar at Oxford, the culture and outlook of his region left an enduring mark. He had a deep religious faith that had remained simple and elemental in spite of his outward sophistication. As a Presbyterian, a dissenter, descended from the Scotch-Irish stock who settled the backcountry of the South, he was set apart from the Irish Catholic culture of the Kennedys, the big cities of the East, and even the Anglican Protestant, old-money establishment. Nor was he competitive or combative by nature, like the Kennedys. He was intensely proud, but it was morally wrong to be ambitious, to strive for personal gain. He had instead a sense of the guiding hand of Providence and the elect operating in human affairs. Human nature and the world were beset by evil and original sin. The good man must lead a life of self-abnegation to work for his salvation and for all mankind. Self-control and devotion to duty were the hallmarks of the good life. By fulfilling one's duty, one would attain prosperity and success, if that was the will of God, or at least justification in the next life.

This intensely moral vision of human behavior produced paradoxes and contradictions in his personality. He was proud and even somewhat vain, yet humble and selfless. His most important goal in life was to work for world peace, but he had a deep sympathy for the military and for the professional soldier. When asked about the seeming inconsistency of his attitudes toward war and peace, Rusk explained that the eagle in the Great Seal of the United States has two claws, one bearing arrows, the other an olive branch. It is a mistake, he said, to believe that one is sufficient without the other. He told this to Kennedy, who would borrow it for one of his speeches.

Another article of faith for Rusk was the system of American democracy. He was intensely patriotic. He believed in America, not as a kind of happy historical accident, but as a quasi-religious creed of values and institutions. For Rusk the Constitution, like the Bible, was something to be read and pondered over again and again. Respect for the values embodied in the Constitution was the glue holding society together, and he was convinced that America had a mission to share these values with the other nations of the world. Were Kennedy and the men around him motivated by that same idealism?

Another concern of Rusk's was money. Although he lived in the affluent suburb of Scarsdale and was responsible for giving away millions, he had no great personal wealth. He had managed to put aside only a few thousand dollars in savings, which he planned to use for his children's college education. Later, in the Senate hearings on his nomination as Secretary of State, Senator George Aiken of Vermont questioned Rusk closely on his connections with the "Rockefeller–Chase Manhattan–Standard Oil family." "Did I understand you to say," Aiken asked Rusk, "that you have divested yourself of securities in corporations?" Rusk replied, "I have never held securities in corporations." Aiken, obviously taken aback, then asked, "What do you do with your money?" Rusk grinned and said, "Well, I begin, sir, by paying my taxes." Rusk knew that as Secretary of State he would have to dip into his savings. Shortly after he was confirmed, he wrote to the president of Davidson College, his alma mater, and asked to be "quietly relieved" of his pledge to give money to the school.

Thus Rusk had many misgivings as he left New York for his meeting in Palm Beach. Kennedy seemed to have no such misgivings. When Rusk arrived, Kennedy told him that he wanted to settle the matter that day and that a news conference was scheduled for noon. Still Rusk hesitated, and at this, only the second meeting between the two men, they talked again about the role of the Secretary of State and Rusk's views about the world. Kennedy was relaxed and tanned and seemed to Rusk supremely self-confident. And in the tranquility of the sumptuous oceanfront home, which belonged to Kennedy's father, the problems of the world seemed far away.

Walking on the beach with swaying palm trees in the distance and the gentle sounds of the surf in their ears, they continued their conversation. Kennedy, who had his own ideas about foreign policy and had no reluctance to make his own decisions, was not seeking specific advice. The role of the Secretary of State, he and Rusk agreed, was to advise the President and to carry out presidential decisions and policies. "When the President is making a decision," Rusk assured Kennedy, "he should know what the alternatives are, and he should not be confronted with simply a monolithic recommendation." Kennedy seemed pleased. He also liked Rusk's approach to the newly emerging countries of the world: "Part of the problem," Rusk said, "is that we have not kept our contact with some of the national movements and the demands for change which are part of the democratic revolution of our own tradition."

Kennedy asked Rusk whether he felt qualified for the job of Secretary of State. Rusk replied that he would leave that judgment to Kennedy; his previous experience was at least relevant to the job, but "there is no way to be adequately prepared to become the Secretary of State." Kennedy smiled and added, "The same is true for the job of President."

When they returned to the house, Rusk noticed a copy of the *Washington Post* on the living room table. A large headline read: "Rusk to be Secretary of State." The news was already out even before he had accepted the job.

"Is there anything I ought to know about you before I ask you to take this post?" Kennedy asked. Rusk said there was nothing embarrassing in his personal life to be worried about. Politically, he added, he had been in the center all his life; he expected to be criticized on both the left and the right. Then Rusk wryly commented, "Mr. Kennedy, is there anything about you that I should know before I take this job?" Kennedy just laughed. "If you still want me, then," Rusk said, "I will accept." Kennedy nodded, the two men shook hands, and it was done.

Rusk told Kennedy frankly that the job of Secretary of State would put him "on a thin financial margin.'" He was making $60,000 at the Rockefeller Foundation and his salary as Secretary would be only $25,000. His friends at the foundation were helping him out by setting up a trust fund in the form of severance pay at the Chase Manhattan Bank. He would receive payments from the fund over a number of years, but nevertheless it would be difficult for him to serve more than one term. Kennedy replied that he understood.

Rusk also disclosed to the President-elect that he had been a Stevenson man during the campaign. In fact, he had sent a telegram to Averell Harriman, who headed the New York delegation at the convention in Los Angeles: "Don't be a damn fool. Support Adlai Stevenson." "I wanted you to hear that from me," Rusk told Kennedy, "rather than from someone else." Kennedy simply threw back his head and roared with laughter.

Then Kennedy said he intended to name Chester Bowles as Under

Secretary. Bowles, a former advertising executive who had been
elected to Congress from Connecticut, had been one of Kennedy's
principal advisers in the campaign. He was in many ways the opposite
of Rusk, voluble and garrulous by nature, but Rusk said that he could
work well with Bowles. He hoped to have an "alter ego" relationship
with him like the one Marshall had had with his Under Secretary,
Robert Lovett.

Kennedy also told Rusk he intended to name Adlai Stevenson as
Ambassador to the United Nations. He knew this would be regarded
as a major appointment that would emphasize the administration's
commitment to the world body. Rusk approved of the choice and said
he would have no trouble working with Stevenson. At that, Kennedy
got Stevenson on the phone, and Rusk was amazed at the selling job
he did to convince Stevenson to take the job. Both men knew Stevenson was temperamental by nature and suffering from wounded pride.
As Kennedy told Stevenson in glowing terms about how large a role
the U.N. ambassador would play, Rusk wondered, half seriously, if
there would be anything left for the Secretary of State. Finally Stevenson agreed to accept the appointment, and Rusk took the phone to
congratulate him. "The country needs you, and I need you," he said.

Kennedy was pleased that everything seemed to be settled—at least
in the foreign policy area. He and Rusk went out onto the sunlit patio,
where the President-elect announced all three appointments to the
waiting press. Dean Rusk, he said, was "the best man available" for
Secretary of State.

Late that evening Rusk arrived home utterly exhausted. His son Richard would always remember the sight of his father, white as a ghost,
entering the house, and his job had not yet begun. During the busy
time of the first two weeks after his appointment, Rusk lost fifteen
pounds. The constant questioning of the press unnerved him, bringing
home the magnitude of his task. He discussed with Kennedy the necessity of not making any pronouncements or getting involved with
policy before the inauguration. There could be, he felt, only one President and one Secretary of State at a time.

During the transition before he took office, Rusk spent long days at
the State Department talking with Acting Secretary Christian Herter
and with desk officers and staff. He read endless briefing papers. He
felt at home in the department and knew many of the senior officers
personally because of his prior service there or through his work on
the Council on Foreign Relations. The major decisions to be made

involved the staffing of key positions in the department and the appointment of new ambassadors. Rusk fought to retain the professionals and career Foreign Service officers. He clashed with Robert Kennedy, the Attorney General–designate, who wanted to appoint "Kennedy men" to key positions. It was not the last time he would have his differences with the President's brother.

There would be no differences between Rusk and the President, however. Rusk's sense of loyalty would not allow it. Theodore Sorensen, who was supervising the transition, remembers calling on Rusk for the first time—in his Washington hotel room at the Statler Hilton —with a practical joke in hand. Sorensen's sister, who was living in Costa Rica at the time, had sent him a newspaper clipping which had superimposed a picture of President-elect Kennedy on a picture of someone else meeting with President Jiménez of Costa Rica. The caption read: "President-elect Kennedy on his way from Washington to Palm Beach stopped off in Costa Rica where in a meeting with President Jiménez he pledged $200 million"—an enormous sum at the time—"in economic aid." Sorensen showed the article to Rusk and with a totally straight face told him that he ought to know about the pledge Kennedy had just made to Costa Rica. Rusk merely nodded his head gravely and said, "Well, if it's a commitment, we will honor it." Sorensen then laughed, and Rusk looked relieved when he explained that it was only a joke.

Rusk also spent time during the transition visiting the key members of Congress on Capitol Hill. He worked long hours answering questionnaires on everything from his personal and family background to anticipated foreign policy issues. He went through an intensive investigation by the FBI. A question on one form was, "Have you or any member of your family ever tried to overthrow the government of the United States by force or violence?" In a playful mood, Rusk answered "yes" and listed the names of his two grandfathers, a matter which caused consternation among the FBI investigators until it was realized that they had fought in the Civil War as officers of the Confederacy. The Senate Foreign Relations Committee approved Rusk unanimously on January 18, and on January 21, 1961, he was confirmed by the full Senate by unanimous voice vote.

A few days before the inauguration, Kennedy asked Rusk to look over a draft of his Inaugural Address. He made one small but significant contribution. His suggestion was to change the line that read "My fellow citizens of the world, ask not what America can do for you, but what you can do for the freedom of man" to "what we together can do for the freedom of man." This was characteristic of

Rusk, who believed that the task of assuring freedom in the world was the central responsibility of the United States.

On the eve of the inauguration, at the height of the busy preparations, Kennedy and Rusk met with President Eisenhower and Christian Herter for a final review of the crisis points that Kennedy would have to deal with immediately on taking office. Eisenhower's mood was glum. Southeast Asia was in chaos; Kennedy would have to act right away if a Communist takeover was to be prevented. Laos, Eisenhower said, was the key. "You are going to have to put troops in Laos," he told Kennedy, "with other nations if possible—but alone if necessary." Kennedy asked why, if the situation was so critical, Eisenhower himself had not acted. "I would have," Ike responded, "but I did not feel I could commit troops with a new administration coming to power." This was a portent of things to come. The nation faced elemental crises of war and peace at every turn: in Cuba, in the Congo, over Berlin, in the Dominican Republic, in the Middle East, and above all, in Southeast Asia.

But Rusk went to the inauguration on January 20, 1961, in an optimistic mood. Thoughts of crisis were forgotten on that day of new beginnings. The weather in Washington was extremely cold, with heavy snow on the ground, but it was crystal clear. Rusk sat on the podium, feeling privileged and proud. He noted the reaction of the crowds to the youthful President and his glamorous family. He had never seen anything like their adulation and respect. There was a real sense of Kennedy's generation—and his own—coming of age to assume its responsibilities; Kennedy was the first President to be born in the twentieth century. In his eloquent Inaugural Address, one passage in particular struck his Secretary of State:

> Let every nation know, whether it wishes us well or ill, that we shall pay any price, bear any burden, meet any hardship, support any friend, oppose any foe, to assure the survival and the success of liberty.

That night, Rusk and his wife, Virginia, sloshed through the snow, she in long evening dress and he in white tie and tails, to put in the mandatory appearance at each of the six presidential balls before they finally returned to their hotel. Rusk was back in Washington at least for the length of Kennedy's first term of office. The youthful President would not complete even that term, but Rusk would remain Secretary of State for Lyndon Johnson, Kennedy's Vice President and the shrewd and seasoned Texas politician who would succeed him.

PART ONE

THE EDUCATION OF A SECRETARY OF STATE

Georgia Boyhood

Dean Rusk as a schoolboy in At-
lanta, Georgia

E VEN today, Americans like their leaders to come from humble origins. The Rusk family into which the future Secretary of State was born on February 9, 1909, in Cherokee County, Georgia, was indeed humble. If the Kennedys were a mere three generations—and several million dollars—removed from their humble beginnings, the Rusks were what Southerners call an "old family": stay-put people who had lived in the same area for a long time. They were also what is known as a "good family": ordinary folks—well behaved, steady, hard-working, and poor. In a remarkable parallel with Lyndon Johnson's family origins in the Texas hill country, Dean Rusk sprang not from the plantation South, but from the "small farmer" South (Lyndon Johnson's great-grandfather, John Johnson, was in fact a small farmer from Georgia).

The Rusk family had emigrated from Northern Ireland to Charleston, South Carolina, in 1791 and settled in the Pendleton District of that state, near present-day Clemson. The country here was infertile and hilly, unlike the rich plantations near the coast, and three Rusk brothers grew up to farm the land: David (born 1773), James (born 1775), and John (born 1778). Their father was a stonemason who found work helping to build churches in the staunch Scotch-Irish community in the district.

The revelation of something extraordinary in this apparently ordinary family appeared in the next generation of Rusks. Thomas Jefferson Rusk, the first son of one of the brothers, John Rusk, showed such brilliance of mind that he attracted the attention of John C. Calhoun, the Secretary of War under President Monroe (and later a legendary senator from South Carolina) and the largest landowner in the Pendleton District. Calhoun became the young boy's mentor and helped him to study law. In 1835 Thomas Jefferson Rusk emigrated to Texas, where he met Sam Houston, helped organize the independence movement, and was one of the signers of the Texas Declaration of Independence.

Dean Rusk loved to regale Lyndon Johnson with his Texas kinsman's exploits. At the battle of San Jacinto against the Mexicans, Thomas Jefferson Rusk took over as commander in chief of the Texas forces when Sam Houston was wounded. After independence, he served as Secretary of War, chief justice of the Texas Supreme Court, and president of the convention of 1845, which wrote the Texas constitution and brought Texas into the Union. He was later elected to the United States Senate and was even mentioned as a presidential candidate in 1856, but he refused to run. A mysterious malaise tugged at his soul. Affected with melancholy, he committed suicide in 1857. After Dean Rusk became Secretary of State, his colleagues in the department dug up a letter that President Polk's Secretary of State had written to Thomas Jefferson Rusk, protesting his intrusion into Louisiana with an armed band. Rusk had retorted: "I wasn't invading Louisiana, I was just chasing a bunch of Indians."

Dean Rusk was descended from the eldest Rusk brother, David, who with his wife Jane moved down to Cherokee County, Georgia, which was then still Indian country, and staked out some land on which to farm and raise a family. There they lived out their lives and had seven children, the youngest of whom was James Edward Rusk (1822–93), the grandfather of Dean Rusk. In a little family cemetery in Cherokee County are the graves of David and Jane Rusk, as well as many of their descendants. Dean Rusk remembers looking at the gravestones and reflecting that his "great-grandmother was born in 1776, the year of the Declaration of Independence, and just four generations of my family have spanned the entire history of the United States as an independent nation."

James Edward Rusk married Margaret Susanna Brooke (1837–1912), a local girl, and settled down to keep the old homeplace going. They had eleven children, of which Dean Rusk's father, Robert Hugh (1868–1944), was number nine. Robert was "the smartest member of the family" and was encouraged to enter the ministry. He attended Davidson College in North Carolina, where he graduated in 1894, and went on to the Louisville Presbyterian Theological Seminary in Louisville, Kentucky. In 1896 he returned to Cherokee County an ordained Presbyterian minister, the first of his family to achieve higher education. He was widely considered the most accomplished man in the county and, Dean Rusk recalls, "could even play the violin."

But Robert Rusk's career as a minister was short-lived. It seems that he could not preach, at least in the emotional, shouting manner demanded at the time. The precise reason was somewhat of a puzzle. The story is told that he had something wrong with his throat, but no specific illness was ever diagnosed. His oldest daughter, Margaret, thought that he suffered an inferiority complex. In any case, he drifted from job to job, taught school, then decided to try to make a living at farming back in Cherokee County.

In 1899, Robert married Elizabeth Frances Clotfelder, a schoolteacher from Rockdale County, an intelligent young woman with coal-black hair and rosy cheeks who had gone to the Normal School in Milledgeville, Georgia. Unlike his brothers and sisters, Robert had not received any land from his father's estate, because he had gone to college. Now he was the poor relation, and had to rent forty acres of red-clay farmland owned by his sister Mary and her husband. On this land Robert built with his own hands a three-room house for his family. It had a porch and glass windows—one of the first houses in the neighborhood to have glass panes. The well was in the front of the house, and the privy was located about fifty yards in back. The Rusks lived at a subsistence level, making or raising almost everything they needed. They kept a cow for milk, and chickens for eggs; a few hogs butchered in the fall, after the first hard freeze, were the yearly supply of meat. They raised corn for the animals and for grinding and baking into cornbread. They ate bacon, fatback, ham, milk, and cornbread, with sorghum syrup candy for dessert. The only cash crop was cotton; each year they sold a few bales to pay the rent on the farm and to buy the necessities at the country store about three miles away. Their world was a tightly knit, isolated society of farm families who lived as they did and knew each other very well.

Dean was the fourth of five children born to Robert and Elizabeth Rusk. He was named David Dean—David for his great-grandfather and Dean for the horse that had carried the doctor several miles on a stormy night to preside at his birth. From the first he was called simply Dean.

The family left the farm and moved to Atlanta when Dean was four years old. The move was prompted by the rigors and hopelessness of farming a small plot of land that the family could never hope to own. It was backbreaking work, and his mother became sickly and discouraged. There was no way to make any money, and yet the toil was unceasing. In the spring of 1912 floods ravaged their land. In despair Robert Rusk went off to Atlanta to look for a job, and on his forty-fifth birthday, the last day before he would be too old to qualify, he found work at the post office as a letter carrier. (He filled out the application only ten minutes before the post office was to close for the day.) The family moved into a little house on Fifth Street that still had an outdoor privy, though it was in the center of the city. A few months later they were able to find a larger house on Whitehall Street in the West End section of Atlanta.

It was a modest, middle-class neighborhood of single-family homes about two miles from downtown. Nearby was the Wren's Nest, a children's library which had been the home of Joel Chandler Harris, the author of the Uncle Remus stories. And not far away were the tracks of the Central of Georgia Railroad, which marked the boundary of the "Dip," the black section of town. The Rusks' frame house had no electricity, but there was an indoor flush toilet, and the children used to pull the chain just for the fascination of seeing how this marvelous invention worked. The house had a small yard with two huge cottonwood trees, and a large porch on which to sit and watch the passing parade out on the sidewalk and the cobblestone street. It was also fun to watch the trains; a half-block away was a railroad switching tower where a man sat pulling the routing levers.

In Atlanta the Rusks were subjected to slights and taunts because of their poverty and their country ways, and because they lived in the "wrong" neighborhood, too close to the railroad tracks and the Negro part of town. Rusk's mother sewed all his clothes, including drawers she made out of flour sacks. He remembers learning to read and write at home from his mother and his older brother, and when it came time to send him to school, it was decided to give him a test to see whether he should start in the first or the second grade. He spelled the word "girl" *g-a-l,* but everything else was right, so the teacher just smiled and admitted him to the second grade.

Rusk attended the Lee Street School a few blocks from his home, a strange, experimental school designed to teach children in the open air, on the theory that this prevented disease. The school building was bizarre: it had a roof and a floor but no walls, only canvas curtains, which were lowered in bad weather. There was no heat, and in winter the children and teachers kept warm, Rusk recalls, by "wearing heavy clothing and drinking lots of hot chocolate."

However, a benefit of attending the Lee Street School was that, because it was experimental, the best teachers were selected to teach there, and Rusk and his classmates received an excellent basic education. He is remembered for having a "superior brain" and for his outgoing, buoyant personality. As a boy he had a round, moonlike face, "snapping brown eyes," dark curly hair, and fat rosy cheeks with a few freckles. He enjoyed reading adventure stories like *The Swiss Family Robinson* and *Robinson Crusoe,* and each year, Rusk remembers, he studied a volume of Carpenter's *Geographic Reader* devoted to a particular area of the world: Asia, Europe, Africa, and Latin America.

Although he was smart, Rusk was not bookish or reticent. On the contrary, everything fascinated him, especially the sights and sounds of his neighborhood. The railroad by his house was a continual source of interest, and he and his friends learned to anticipate how far away a train was by putting an ear to the track and listening to the sounds. Coal was very expensive at the time, and they found, to their delight, that if they waved and threw stones at the men on the trains, they would throw back pieces of coal, which were then gathered up in buckets to take home or sell.

The Negroes in the "Dip" across the railroad tracks were poor and uneducated, but everyone took their miserable condition and the separation of the races for granted. The white Protestant community of the West End where Rusk grew up was "distrustful and prejudiced against the blacks as well as Catholics, Jews, and foreigners." Black and white children would cross over the tracks and play with each other, but in games of cops and robbers or cowboys and Indians, the sides were invariably chosen along racial lines.

When Rusk was eight years old he went to work for three dollars a week at a little grocery store run by a man named Leatherwood, delivering groceries on both sides of the tracks in a red wagon. He recalls that he would often sit on the porch of a house in the black neighborhood listening to the people talk among themselves. "I knew then that black people lived in a separate world that I as a white boy could not know much about."

Later, in high school, he made deliveries of another sort. Answering an ad in the newspaper, he took a part-time job working for the Knights of the Mystic Kingdom, an offshoot of the Ku Klux Klan, at their offices in the Flatiron Building in downtown Atlanta. He was given packages to deliver all over town. He remembers that at the time working for the Klan did not bother him, but he quit when one of the recipients of the mysterious packages told him that he was delivering bootleg liquor.

The Civil War was very much a part of the fabric of life in Atlanta. Rusk joined other children in collecting shell fragments and other Civil War relics, which could still be easily found, and they played war games in old Civil War trenches. On hot summer evenings he listened to stories about the burning of Atlanta and Sherman's cruel march to the sea. Rusk recalls that he "did not question the licking the South had received, but that didn't prevent me from idolizing the Confederate leaders, especially Robert E. Lee." Studying Lee's battles and tactics, he admired his "patient courage, patriotism, and his love for his men." Lee was a great man, Rusk believed, "because he did not seek war, but he fought nobly and well when required by circumstances to do so." Rusk's father reinforced this thought, telling him "never to be ashamed of someone who fought for what he believed in."

Military service in fact was part of the tradition of the Rusk family. Both of Rusk's grandfathers had fought in the Civil War. One was a colonel in the Confederate Army who earned his commission because when he volunteered he brought a hundred men with him. His other grandfather was a bugler who, wounded in the war, talked with pride about "the Yankee bullet he carried in his body." Years later no one was sure exactly what battles the two had fought in, but young Rusk had no doubt that his grandfathers had served honorably in Lee's army.

World War I also made a strong impression. On May 21, 1917, Atlanta's Great Fire broke out, laying waste to a large area of the city, and the rumor was that it had been caused by a German warplane. At the Candler Warehouse in the West End, German prisoners of war were kept behind a chain link fence. Rusk watched them exercise and work around the yard. With a child's curiosity he engaged them in conversation and even invited them home to his house, where his mother served them dinner.

Shortly after the end of the war, General John "Black Jack" Pershing came to Atlanta and paraded right past Lee Street School. Rusk also went to see Woodrow Wilson when he came to Atlanta in 1918 on his campaign for the acceptance of the League of Nations. Wilson had just returned from Versailles convinced that a collective security arrangement was necessary to safeguard peace in the world. The President's manner and idealistic rhetoric captured the imagination of the ten-year-old Rusk. When Wilson rode by, he carried a placard in support of the League and marched proudly through the crowds.

Religious belief held a special place in the Rusk household. Both of Dean's parents were very pious, and Robert Rusk was a teaching elder at the West End Presbyterian Church. The approach to religion was quiet and unemotional. Rusk remembers his mother reading the Bible to the family and his father chanting the Psalms in Hebrew in his soft, high-pitched voice. The family had their own pew at church and attended services regularly. Rusk went to Sunday school and learned by heart the Westminster Catechism and what were called "pearls"—special passages of the Bible. When he was fourteen Rusk became one of the leaders of a society called Junior Christian Endeavor and was called on to give talks at other churches around the state. He learned to drive his father's old Model T Ford and, in a time when there were no drivers' licenses (and little traffic), he "traveled from church to church, at the unbelievable speed of forty miles an hour, like an itinerant preacher."

After seventh grade Rusk enrolled in Boys' High School, one of four public high schools in the city for white pupils. Boys' High was a college preparatory school, and there Rusk continued to compile a record of considerable achievement: he was an honor student with grades consistently in the 90s in difficult courses that included Greek, Latin, French, mathematics, and science; he was president of his senior class, editor of both the school newspaper and the yearbook, and cadet commander of the school ROTC battalion: A teacher remembered him as "one of the few students I came across in forty-five years of teaching who seemed to be born mature and adequate to any situation."

In high school Rusk continued to work part-time to supplement his family's meager finances, holding a variety of jobs as a delivery boy and selling electrical appliances for the Western Electric Supply Company. He was the school-page editor for the *Atlanta Journal,* where he edited letters and articles from the city's elementary schools for publication each week in the newspaper. The job paid forty dollars a month, a large sum for the time, especially since it took him only one day a week.

Rusk's favorite in high school was his Greek teacher, Preston Epps. The quality of his instruction must have been remarkable, for Epps went on to become the Kenan Professor of Greek at the University of North Carolina at Chapel Hill. Rusk took Greek for four years, and the class read and translated the major Greek authors such as Plato, Homer, and Xenophon. Epps remembered Rusk especially for his maturity and the thoughtful way he responded in class. He also recalled buying a toaster from Rusk which seems to have had a remarkable history. The Eppses used it as the family toaster until 1945, when they gave it to their daughter as a wedding present. It continued to work perfectly until the 1960s, when it was given as a present to their granddaughter when she went to college. To Professor Epps, the longevity of this device was not surprising. The explanation was that "Dean Rusk would never sell anything unreliable"; in the Epps household, this humble appliance was always referred to as the "Dean Rusk toaster."

When he graduated from Boys' High in 1925, Rusk was voted the most popular boy in the class and shared the *Atlanta Journal* cup given to the best all-around student. He hoped to attend Davidson College in North Carolina, where his father had studied, but it was a private school and his finances did not permit it. Still desperately poor, he was the only boy in his graduating class who still wore knickers, because he could not afford the customary suit with long pants. In a quandary, he decided to get a job and try to save money so that he could go to Davidson. The day after graduation, he went to work for a young lawyer named Augustus Roan, where he was expected to do everything from filing papers to interviewing witnesses.

The work was dull, and he had plenty of time to think about what he wanted to do with his life. He was only sixteen, but he had a strong sense of fate, of being in the hands of God. He also saw himself against the background of his father's life of failed prospects and ambitions and became determined not to let that happen to him. He had excelled in everything he attempted. He felt called to a high destiny; he would make a difference in the world. His Christian faith made him think about studying for the ministry and going off as a missionary to China. But another plan increasingly dominated his thoughts: he would "get a job in the Foreign Service and work for world peace."

But how was he to realize this ambition? He had heard about the Rhodes scholarship program at Oxford University. If he did well at Davidson College he might have a chance to win one of these scholarships. But he knew that the Rhodes program also demanded "interest and skill in athletics." So Rusk decided that he had better learn how to play basketball in order to qualify. For regular practice, he joined a team at the Luckie Street YMCA, played almost every evening, and became reasonably good at the sport.

Two years went by, and still he had not saved up the money necessary for college because most of what he earned was needed at home. He talked things over with his parents, and they agreed that if he was ever going to college he had better enroll, money or no money. He wrote to Davidson, asking for admission and financial aid. He was accepted, and because his father was a minister, he received a small scholarship to pay for his tuition. He would have enough to make ends meet, and at the age of eighteen it was time to leave home for the wider world.

When his brother Parks drove him up to the college that fall, Rusk was conscious of a new beginning. In later years, however, he readily acknowledged the abiding influence of his upbringing: the hard work, poverty, quiet religious faith, love of country, and high idealism had made their mark. In the corridors of power at the State Department and the White House, he retained an image of himself as "a freckle-faced boy from Cherokee County."

"The Most Pleasant Existence I've Ever Run Across"

*Rusk (back row, second from left) on the tennis team
as a Rhodes scholar at Oxford*

A SORT of poor man's Princeton" is how Rusk remembers Davidson College, his alma mater. The comparison is apt. The Davidson campus is beautiful and spacious, shaded by giant oak trees, and the school has a strong intellectual tradition in the liberal arts and classical studies. But in Rusk's time the atmosphere was intensely religious—the college was supported and run by the Presbyterian Church. The Presbyterians believed in education and learning, and Davidson was their showplace. But it was a very different world from the elite Eastern universities that were the training grounds for most of Rusk's contemporaries who attained great power and influence.

Located about twenty miles north of Charlotte, North Carolina,

Davidson had about six hundred students, all male and all white. Most were bright and capable; many of Rusk's classmates went on to leadership positions in business, the diplomatic service, the professions, and in universities. People on campus still talked about Davidson's most important "alumnus," Woodrow Wilson—everyone called him Tommy—who had spent a year at Davidson in the 1880s. There was youthful idealism and emphasis on service to Mankind (with a capital *M*) and on duty to God and to country. There was no agitation for change or reform. The existing social order and its values went unquestioned.

When Rusk arrived at Davidson in the fall of 1927, it was a quiet time in American life, especially in the South. The nation was relatively prosperous and at peace. A decade before, the world had fought the "war to end all wars," and much to Rusk's sorrow, the United States had rejected Wilson's plea to join the League of Nations. But what would become the chimerical Kellogg-Briand Pact was being negotiated by the statesmen of the world, to outlaw war "as an instrument of national policy" and to enjoin nations to "resolve all disputes by peaceful means." Sixty-two nations signed this treaty in 1928, including Germany and Japan, and it was ratified by the U.S. Senate by a resounding vote of 85 to 1. So much for war. America's mood was isolationist, and people settled down to take life easy, to indulge and enjoy themselves, free of worry about any national or international crisis.

Rusk had to find work to stay in school. It so happened that every four years the small bank in town hired an entering freshman as bookkeeper and assistant teller. This position came open in the fall of 1927, and Rusk got the job. Throughout his college days, he arrived at the Bank of Davidson at one o'clock in the afternoon and worked until five o'clock or later. On Saturdays he put in at least half a day, and summers he worked full-time, except after his junior year, when he worked in a bank in Greensboro, North Carolina, because he wanted to live in a bigger city than tiny Davidson. He became a familiar sight sitting in the teller's cage, a green eyeshade covering already thinning hair. Rusk was known to be scrupulously honest, and his accounting was invariably correct. Sometimes the black tenant farmers came in and asked him to check over their accounts, and Rusk incurred the displeasure of some of their landlords when he found discrepancies.

Rusk's classmates remember him for his energy, intelligence, and a maturity beyond his years. He joined the Kappa Alpha fraternity and was elected president of the freshman class. He also took Army

ROTC for all four years, which not only paid him a small salary but provided a free room at the armory. Each summer he went to a two-week training camp at Anniston, Alabama. In his "spare" time, he was manager of the student store and waited on tables at the fraternity. He purchased a car on credit and paid for it by renting it out by the mile to church groups in the area. With three friends he drove up to visit Washington, D.C., and then on to New York City, his first visit to the North. His friends remember him stopping the car as soon as they got to New York and gawking at all the tall buildings. In time, he would become a member of the inner circles of power in both cities, but there was always something of the awe of a country boy in his quiet, reserved manner.

While many of the men with whom he would share that power were testing their athletic mettle at tennis, polo, football, and crew, Rusk tried out for basketball, and his years practicing at the YMCA paid off when he made the team. As starting center his sophomore, junior, and senior years, he was a steady but unspectacular team player. According to the rules at that time, there was a center jump after every basket, and Rusk was chosen primarily for his size: six feet tall and over two hundred pounds. His teammates called him "Elijah" and "Old Folks" because of his maturity and rapidly receding hairline. The highlight of his basketball career was a victory over the University of North Carolina, 17 to 12, a game in which Rusk was the high scorer with six points. "Now this sounds like a slowed-down game," he commented years later, "but it wasn't at all. Both sides were trying like the dickens, but in those days it was a different game—no hook shots, jump shots, or the like." (On a visit to Davidson when he was Secretary of State, someone handed Rusk a basketball and asked him to have a go. For the first time in years he shot the ball and, to the delight of the crowd—and his own surprise—it went in. They gave him the ball again, and again it swished through the basket. Lefty Driesell, the Davidson coach, was suitably impressed; he told Rusk that if he ever wanted to come back, there was a scholarship waiting for him.)

By his senior year at Davidson, Rusk was a Big Man on Campus and was offered his choice of student leadership offices. The two he selected are revealing of the man. He became cadet colonel of the ROTC, the top student military office of the school, and president of the YMCA, the chief religious and social organization. Chapel was compulsory at the college, and a typical day began for Rusk at dawn, when he filed into Sherer Hall for services along with the other students. Afterward there would be a meeting of the student body, and Rusk often spoke about YMCA activities or an upcoming ROTC exercise. He was also a member of the court of control, which enforced student discipline for "infractions" such as the failure of the freshmen students to wear their black beanies or to carry matches to light cigarettes for the upperclassmen.

In the small-town atmosphere of Davidson everyone knew each other, and friendships were easy and strong. By all accounts, Rusk commanded a truly extraordinary respect, bordering on adulation. A natural leader and a young man of deeply held principles and beliefs, he was always at the head of any organization or activity involved with religious or social action. "In those days at Davidson," he recalled, "I was running to the bank, then running to basketball practice, and back to wait on tables. It was a kind of breathless experience." Because of his work, he could not devote long hours to studying, and his classmates were amazed by his ability to read and digest material in a short time and do well on a test. His roommate remembers that he used to come back from work, stand up against a wall, and intently speed-read the pages of a book for an exam the next morning.

Rusk excelled in his studies as he did in everything else. He took a liberal arts curriculum that also included science courses in physics and biology. He was gifted in languages, and studied Greek and Latin as well as German and French. But a professor of political science named Archibald Currie was his favorite teacher, and Rusk decided to major in that field. Professor Currie was a lawyer by training, and Rusk took his courses on international law and international relations. He studied in detail the tragedy of World War I, which seemed to him a senseless waste, and he was fired anew by the idealism of Woodrow Wilson, who had tried to achieve a peace that would forever eliminate war. For the first time in history, legal machinery—the Covenant of the League of Nations—had been established to resolve disputes among nations, much as quarrels were settled among neighboring landowners. It seemed to Rusk that if all nations would accept the principles of the League, mankind could abolish the scourge of war.

Rusk's newfound passion for politics and international relations opened up a window in his soul. He thought less and less about a career in the ministry, much to the disappointment of his father, and considered becoming a college professor. Many of his friends, however, thought he was headed for a career in business because of his work at the bank. Moreover, he was in love with a girl named Sarah

Withers, whom he had met shortly after coming to Davidson his freshman year. She lived in town, the daughter of the bank's president. By all accounts their relationship was rather innocent, but very intense. Sarah's mother adored Rusk, and he became almost a part of the family. He could marry Sarah and continue his work at the bank. It would all be so easy.

But Rusk was still pursuing his dream: a Rhodes scholarship at Oxford. In his senior year he applied to the Rhodes committee for the State of North Carolina and was called to Raleigh for an interview. The committee was chaired by Josephus Daniels, Secretary of the Navy under President Wilson and publisher of the *Raleigh News and Observer*. Daniels was a sharp-eyed, white-haired man with an intimidating manner, and during the interview Rusk noticed that he was leafing through his dossier with a scowl on his face. Something was wrong. Finally Daniels looked up and said, "Mr. Rusk, I see from your papers here that you live down in Georgia. Why in the world should we give a North Carolina appointment to someone from Georgia?"

Rusk was taken aback, but somehow he came up with an answer. "Well, Mr. Chairman," he said, "I have lived in North Carolina for four years and I have spent not only the school year here but the summers too. I worked in a bank in Greensboro and in the Bank of Davidson. And I have even paid the poll tax here in North Carolina."

Daniels's brow remained deeply furrowed until he heard the last statement. "Oh," he said, "you paid the poll tax in North Carolina? Then it's all right. You are one of us."

Rusk gave a sigh of relief. Paying the poll tax had been just an accident on his part. It happened that the teller of the Bank of Davidson, a Mr. Thompson, was the town treasurer and the man who collected the poll tax for the state. Whether out of fun or sentiment, Rusk had paid him a dollar for the poll tax each year.

It was an excellent investment. A few weeks later Rusk received the good news that he had won a coveted Rhodes scholarship and could attend Oxford in the fall. Years later he reflected about the role that fate or circumstance had played in his life. He knew that if he had not paid that poll tax during his years in North Carolina, he never would have been chosen a Rhodes scholar.

On May 31, 1931, Rusk graduated from Davidson with a B.A. in political science, a Phi Beta Kappa pin, and the Rhodes scholarship to boot. At the age of twenty-two he felt as if he were the luckiest man alive. Curiously, only his parents, who drove up for the graduation ceremony, were uneasy. To them the prospect of their son spending the next three years at Oxford seemed a needless luxury. Didn't he see the necessity of getting on with his life, finding a job or going to graduate school? His friends were surprised when at a reception his mother suddenly pointed to his older brother Roger and said, "You see that one over there? *He's* the smartest boy in the family."

The Rhodes scholarship meant the end of Rusk's relationship with Sarah Withers. She was happy for him, and they promised to write, but the Oxford experience and Rusk's absence would put too much distance between them for their love to survive. Sarah Withers married Dan Currie, another Davidson graduate. She would later say that she had had two ardent suitors in her life, Dean Rusk and Dan Currie, and she could have married either one; she married Dan Currie because he needed her the most. If the story wasn't exactly true, Dean Rusk was too much of a gentleman to deny it.

In October 1931, Rusk began the journey to Oxford and, even more significant, a spiritual journey that was to transform his life. He sailed from New York on the R.M.S. *Berengaria*. Too excited to sleep, he waited up past midnight to watch the ship cast off and slowly make its way out of New York Harbor. The night was dark and cloudy, but he remembers the thrill of seeing in the distance the blazing torch of the Statue of Liberty.

The sea voyage was an adventure for the young Rusk. He was confronted with new and exotic experiences, and he soaked them up with the enthusiasm of a child. The people he met on board were of particular fascination to a country boy. There was a dignified English-woman of about forty whom he dubbed "Miss Prim." When she heard he was from Georgia, she playfully exclaimed, "Oh, that's where you butcher your Negroes, now don't you?" Not to be outdone, Rusk replied, "Oh, yes, and we consider them rare delicacies." There was a Canadian doctor traveling to Edinburgh to study public health whom Rusk derisively called "the sot," because he spent almost all his time in the bar and ate only one meal a day, mostly as a base for the evening's beverages. There was a redheaded girl he took up with when he found her sitting in his deck chair one morning. The two of them sneaked into the first-class section to mix with the rich and famous and watch Bill Tilden, the tennis champion, play a game of Ping-Pong. All in all, the crossing was a fascinating experience; in his first letter home he called it "about as interesting a thing as I ever did in my life."

Rusk was probably of equal interest to his fellow passengers. He was very self-conscious about his Georgia accent, and he wrote his mother that he was going to "have to modify my speech a little so that they can understand me." In the course of his three years at Oxford, he abandoned most of his Southern drawl and incorporated a slight British inflection into his speech.

At Oxford, Rusk settled into St. John's College, one of the oldest and most prestigious of the famous Oxford schools. His rooms looked out on the Canterbury Quadrangle, a quiet cloister of arches and pilastered towers surmounted by a battlement, built in the early 1600s. He loved to walk along the gentle curve of "the High" (High Street), past All Souls, St. Mary's, and Queen's, all the way down to the Magdalen College tower, which was reflected in the river near the Magdalen Bridge. He wandered over the surrounding hills, where he could gaze upon the yellow stone city with its battlements and spires. How different this was from everything he had known before! As beautiful as Davidson was, it had nothing that compared to this.

Rusk's roommate during his first year was Grady Frank, another Rhodes scholar, who had graduated from the University of North Carolina the year before. They shared a living room and had separate bedrooms. It was unusual to have roommates at Oxford; Rusk noticed that all the English boys were assigned single rooms, and he asked the warden about this. Rusk roared with laughter at the reply: "You see," the warden told him, "with you Americans there is not the presumption of homosexuality that attends the English boys."

According to the custom at Oxford at the time, Rusk and his roommate were assigned a pair of "scouts," manservants who cleaned up their rooms, waited on them, and in general attended to their needs. Rusk's scout, Dudley, was tall and as thin as a crane, with thick, mobile eyebrows that often provided the only clue to what he was thinking. Each morning Dudley would wake up his charge, light a fire in the fireplace, and put the kettle on to boil water for tea. Then Dudley brought an English breakfast—eggs, bacon, fried tomatoes, and bread. For Rusk, who generally despised English food, it was the best meal of the day, after which he would go about his academic work—attending lectures, meeting with his tutors, and working on the written essays he was required to present each week. At noon Dudley brought in a lunch that was prepared in a basement kitchen known as the "buttery."

On one occasion Rusk had some American friends over for breakfast and asked Dudley to serve cantaloupe as the first course. Dudley raised his eyebrows and rolled his eyes before leaving, but after a minute he reappeared and said to Rusk, "Sir, the master of the buttery wants to know if you really mean that you want cantaloupe." Rusk looked at him and said, "Yes, of course, that is what I would like to have." So Dudley served the cantaloupes, and they were quite good. At the end of the term Rusk was presented with the bill, and he learned that the cantaloupes had cost five pounds, or about twenty-five dollars, each. Only then did it dawn on him that a cantaloupe, which cost less than a nickel in Georgia, had to be hothouse grown in England.

Rusk adapted quickly to life at Oxford, and before long he wrote home that he was leading "about the most pleasant existence I've ever run across." His first college report called him "an excellent, sensible fellow." There was no such thing as working one's way through Oxford. The scholarship took care of his needs, and for the first time in his life he could take a rather leisurely approach to his studies. "At Oxford," Rusk remembers, "I was accepted as an honorary gentleman from the very beginning since Oxford undergraduates were of that class." He spent a great deal of time in social activities, sports, and old-fashioned "bull sessions" with his fellow students. Afternoons were generally reserved for sports—lacrosse, tennis, and rugby. At four o'clock it was time for tea, conversation, and a rubber of bridge. It was Rusk's first contact with games of cards; they were strictly forbidden at Davidson College. Bridge, and then poker, became lifelong passions.

In his first term at St. John's, Rusk was appointed to chair a committee of the Junior Common Room (the student organization at the college) to petition the president of the college to provide a ladies' room. There was no such facility at St. John's, and women guests had to go out on the square into an underground privy outside the college. Rusk took his assignment quite seriously and made an appointment to see the president, Dr. James. As Rusk made his presentation, James, a bearded man in his eighties, stared at him incredulously and at the end said simply, "What a *monstrous* proposal!" Rusk and his committee members quietly withdrew.

Social life at Oxford included many invitations to dances, parties, and dinners given by English families or sponsored by the Rhodes Trust. At one dinner dance Rusk was to meet the members of the British cabinet. He was somewhat apprehensive, and in a letter home he wrote that he hoped "I won't make a fool of myself and spill my soup in some Duke's hat."

He was also invited to the homes of the English gentry whose sons were studying at St. John's. They lived in the biggest houses he had ever seen, on spacious estates with manicured lawns. On one such occasion Rusk took his first drink, a glass of sherry. When it was set before him, he stared at it for a full thirty minutes pondering what he should do. Finally he drank it down, rationalizing that he owed it to his hosts. It must have agreed with him. He became a regular social drinker, and developed a renowned fondness for scotch. At Oxford, Rusk lost his scruples about liquor; he wrote his parents that there was "less drunkenness in England than in the United States." He also observed that St. John's had a marvelous wine cellar, "one of the best in all of Oxford."

Each week the students at St. John's received a list of events and activities—plays, concerts, and lectures. Professors often held open house for any student who wished to drop in, especially if a well-known visitor was in town. Oxford was very much a part of the world, and important political and academic figures came almost every week. Rusk met Edvard Beneš, who later became the President of Czecho-slovakia, and George Bernard Shaw, the playwright. In the fall of 1931 Mahatma Gandhi, who was attending the second Indian Round Table Conference in London, came to Oxford. The Lotus Club, the society of Indian students, allowed each member to bring a non-Indian guest, and Rusk attended with a friend from St. John's. Gandhi, who had just been released from an English prison, sat cross-legged in his loincloth on a table at the front of the room to answer questions. With him were two goats that he kept for the milk that was his principal nourishment. Rusk was deeply moved by Gandhi's speech. At one point Gandhi said, "I've always expected the best of the other fellow, including British leaders, because people tend to try to live up to your expectations of them." But at another point he said, "You know, people will talk about me in spiritual terms. That is because of the way I dress, the way I live, and many of the things I say. And they will forget"—and here his voice became rather harsh—"they will forget that I have discovered the secret of power in India. We Indians cannot expel the British by returning their fire gun-for-gun, cannon-for-cannon. We simply don't have the means. But we can drive them out of India because they can't stay there without us. All we have to do is sit down. Now some of us may starve; some of us may die. But the British will have to leave. That," he added, "is raw power." This remark and his later insistence that the Japanese had to be defeated led Rusk to be skeptical about whether Gandhi was the complete pacifist that many people thought him to be.

Rhodes scholars at Oxford were expected to participate in sports, and Rusk was known as an excellent athlete. There was no basketball, but he played lacrosse, soccer, cricket, rugby, and tennis. In every sport, the biggest game of the year was always against Cambridge. The honor of being chosen to play Cambridge was especially coveted, because for this game the student would receive a "half-blue," the equivalent of a varsity letter. Rusk was chosen to play the wing defense position on the Oxford lacrosse team for the big game against Cambridge. He earned his "blue," and was proud that Oxford beat Cambridge two of the three years he played. He also tried out for the tennis team, but narrowly missed being chosen when he was beaten by an English boy. Five of the six chosen for the Oxford team were Americans from North Carolina. He was disappointed not to make it an all–North Carolina team, although he later described his tennis ability as "a high level of mediocrity."

At first Rusk was perplexed by the fact that at Oxford each student was left on his own to pursue his studies as he saw fit. But he soon began to enjoy his newfound freedom. The only compulsory appointments were the sessions with his tutors, usually two per week, and at these meetings he would go over his written assignments, receive comments and criticisms, and decide on a topic for the next week's essay. His academic life was centered in the college, and his tutors were all members of St. John's, but he was free to attend any lecture course in the university that he thought would aid his studies.

Rusk chose to study for the degree of M.A. in philosophy, politics, and economics, known as PPE or Modern Greats. It was up to him when he might take his examinations for the degree; he could do it after one year, two, or three—the college was indifferent. At Oxford the tutorials were merely exercises, designed to prepare the student for the final examinations.

At St. John's, Rusk was a free spirit, and he read widely and eclectically. It was a marvelous educational program that encouraged creativity, speculation, and new ideas. He found that his prior education with its seven years of Greek and eight years of Latin was comparable to an English classical education, and his tutors admired and respected him. He concentrated on works of history, law, politics, and philosophy; he studied biographies of Bismarck and other important nineteenth-century political leaders. He stumbled on Holdsworth's multivolume *History of the English Law* and read it from start to finish. His fascination with international law deepened. John Brierly, author of *The Law of Nations* and perhaps the leading scholar of this subject, was at Oxford at the time, and Rusk eagerly attended his lectures. Under Brierly's tutelage he saw international law as a key concept in ordering affairs between nations and in the peaceful resolution of disputes. More than ever he was convinced that world peace depended upon the acceptance of international law by the nations of the world.

In the United States at the time the public mood was what is loosely called "isolationism," the conviction that the nation could stay out of war by avoiding foreign entanglements. Rusk's experience and training at Oxford ran counter to this view, and he became firmly international in his outlook. War, he believed, could be avoided only by "collective action by the democratic states of the world."

He also developed a strong admiration for British political institutions. He studied the evolution of democracy and human rights in Britain and their influence on the United States and other countries. To Rusk, American civilization was essentially British in character, with its respect for the individual, its reliance on law and institutions, and its capacity for slow change and growth instead of precipitous reaction and reform.

To be sure, there were some things about England he did not like. The food was atrocious; he grew very tired of overcooked lamb and beef. His letters to his parents were often about the food he missed at home. He asked his mother to send him things, and wrote that when he returned to Atlanta he expected to "have some butterbeans in the pot, and some fried chicken, and some buttermilk, and some cornbread, and some sweet potato pie, and—well, that'll be enough for the first meal anyhow!" He couldn't believe the lack of heating, bath, and toilet facilities "in the country that launched the industrial revolution." He was also surprised and somewhat amused by the English class system. Almost all the undergraduates at Oxford were gentlemen by origin, a fact they took for granted. The scouts, tradesmen, and others of the lower classes took their status for granted as well. Since everyone accepted the system and did not presume to be anything else, daily friction was avoided, but it still struck Rusk as somehow "inconsistent with the British libertarian tradition."

He also noticed a relative indifference among the British to other cultures and countries of the world. As far as many of them were concerned, Rusk was a man from "out there in the colonies." Few people knew or cared much about the United States. On one occasion his law tutor made a nasty crack to Rusk that "most of the Justices of the Supreme Court in the United States were political appointees who had little notion of law." His patriotism aroused, Rusk went off to the library and researched the background of the British law lords of the past two hundred years and confronted his tutor with evidence that 90 percent of them came from political backgrounds as well. His tutor was surprised, but congratulated Rusk and admitted his error.

At Oxford Rusk studied the legal structure governing the British Empire and was acutely aware of the developing cracks in the system. The self-governing colonies of the Commonwealth—Canada, Australia, New Zealand, and South Africa—had already attained a great measure of autonomy, further enhanced by the Statute of Westminster in 1931, which gave this constitutional force. As for the rising nationalism among the colonies, it struck Rusk that when the British built their empire, they took along with them the seeds of its destruction—the notions of freedom and democracy, and the strong English political system. He became convinced that the empire must eventually be dissolved and replaced by some other collective grouping such as the League of Nations.

There was a good deal of antiwar sentiment at Oxford. The memories of World War I were fresh; almost everyone Rusk met had a family member who had been killed in the war. His friends at Oxford were acutely conscious of the whole generation of Oxford men who had gone off to fight and had not returned. The Great War was dirty and unheroic, devoid of gallantry and glory. The foremost thought on everyone's mind was "never again."

The focal point of political discussion was the Oxford Union, an undergraduate social club with a number of comfortable rooms, including a dining room and a bar. But it was especially famous for its debating hall, called at that time the "womb of Prime Ministers" because of the many political figures who had debated there as undergraduates. Debates were held periodically on all manner of questions and were rather formal affairs; the debaters wore white tie and tails and conducted themselves accordingly. At times, however, they were humorous; Rusk attended one debate entitled "Resolved, That This House Regrets Christopher Columbus," a rip-roaring spoof of the Americans.

For a brief moment in February 1933 worldwide attention was directed to the Oxford Union when the debate topic was "Resolved, That This House Will in No Circumstances Fight for Its King and Country." Rusk was there; it was a tumultuous occasion. The philosopher C. E. M. Joad led the pacifist side, the forces in favor of the proposition. He was witty, erudite, and brilliant, much to the delight of the crowd of onlookers, and those who opposed the question were quite inadequate to respond. At one point in the debate one of them asked Joad, "What would you do, sir, if someone were going to rape your sister?" Joad, in the squeaky little voice for which he was famous, said, "I would simply step in between them." The crowd hooted and clapped. At the end the vote was taken; by 275 to 153 the resolution was carried. The pacifists marched out of the hall singing and triumphant. Less than two weeks before, the fanatical Adolf Hitler had come to power in Germany; he would later refer to this incident as evidence that Britain would not go to war over his aggressive policies.

How Rusk voted is not recorded, but a friend who was with him claims that he voted with the pacifists in favor of the resolution. This is highly unlikely. Throughout his long career Rusk cited the Oxford pacifist movement as proof that only strength and determination can deter aggression. "We must be prepared to go to war," he often said, "in order to prevent war."

In his first year at Oxford, Rusk watched with rapt attention the unfolding of the Manchurian drama—the first international military and political crisis that he studied in detail. The Japanese Army had moved on September 18, 1931, in a carefully planned strike designed to take over and occupy the whole of the North China district of Manchuria. The military planners viewed this as a necessary action to secure Japan's resources and strategic location, and to block the northward expansion of Chiang Kai-shek's Kuomintang, who were attempting to unify a strife-torn China still in the throes of revolution. Civilian Japanese authorities quietly capitulated, and on December 10, 1931, the government in Tokyo was taken over by the militarist Seiyukoi party.

Rusk carefully studied every step of the international diplomatic activities that resulted from the Japanese move. The invasion came as a surprise and threw into question the whole structure of peace in the postwar world. The Kellogg-Briand Pact outlawing aggressive military action and the Nine-Power Far Eastern Settlement of 1921–22 had been blatantly violated, and according to the Covenant of the League of Nations, it was up to the League members to come to China's aid. With high emotion Rusk watched the newsreels of the Chinese delegate Wellington Koo pleading with the League for help.

After three weeks of debate the League Council appointed a five-member fact-finding body, the so-called Lytton Commission, to visit Manchuria. One of the members was an American, General Frank R.

McCoy. Rusk was glad to see that an American was involved in the League's work. He had been strongly in favor of American membership in the League; this was not to be, but Rusk thought the United States should do the next best thing: participate actively in League matters.

Rusk applauded when on January 7, 1932, Secretary of State Henry L. Stimson sent identical notes to Tokyo and Nanking stating that the United States would not recognize any territorial changes in the Far East brought about in violation of recognized international agreements. This was Rusk's first acquaintance with the idea of nonrecognition as a political weapon, a concept he himself would later apply to Communist China. He was disappointed that the British and the French would not join in a multilateral declaration of nonrecognition. To Rusk at the time it looked as if Stimson's desired policy of firmness and collective economic and even military pressure on the Japanese was being frustrated by, first of all, the Europeans and second by President Herbert Hoover, who wanted to rely on moral suasion alone. The nonrecognition doctrine had no effect on the Japanese. They formed a puppet state out of Manchuria that they called Manchukuo. Rusk instinctively felt that it had been a mistake not to do something when China was first invaded by Japan and that this would lead to further trouble.

The parallel diplomatic effort of the League to make the Japanese retreat also failed. The Lytton Commission report, adopted by the League in 1933, condemned the Japanese action as aggression but, bending over backward to be neutral, conceded that Tokyo had acted under provocation. The League, however, refused any action to enforce the report, and Japan's response was simply to withdraw from the Covenant. Rusk was extremely disillusioned by the lack of effectiveness of the League and its failure to stand up for its own principles. His friends at St. John's remember him talking about the indivisibility of peace in the world and the ominous implications of violating international law.

Rusk's views changed and evolved on several other issues while he was at Oxford, one being the very important matter of race. Before Oxford, his attitude toward Negroes was about the same as that of other educated whites at that time in the South (or the North). He bore them no malice, to be sure, but he came in contact with them only in inferior positions, which, like everyone else, he took for granted. At Oxford he met African as well as American blacks as students—as equals and individuals. He began to see the injustice of the condition of the American Negro, particularly in his native South. He wrote to his mother: "I've changed a good bit in my attitude toward the Negroes. . . . It'll be interesting to see how I'm affected by a 'Yas-suh boss' when I get home again. But it just seems like something's wrong when you realize there are 84 blacks in our American Who's Who, who wouldn't be able to get a decent hotel room in Atlanta."

He had frank discussions with his friends about ethnic and racial differences. One humorous exchange came when he noticed that the Indians from India "have a very peculiar odor—it's rather like dusty velvet curtains with lavender talcum powder sprinkled in them." He mentioned this to an Indian friend at Oxford, who told him that this was their racial odor and that whites to the Indian nose have a most distinct odor themselves. Rusk got to thinking about this, and he wondered in a letter home: "It seems that members of the same race can't detect this racial odor in each other. Do you suppose we smell bad to the niggers at home?"

Rusk also thought a great deal about the economic depression and politics in the United States. His letters home were full of requests for copies of American newspapers. He was personally very lucky, he felt, although he worried about getting a job at the end of his three-year scholarship. His family was not among those most severely affected. His father kept his job at the post office and was looking forward to retirement and his pension. The Rusks were poor but were not desperate. Rusk regularly sent home a few dollars a month that he saved out of his scholarship.

But he pondered the causes of the Depression, which had brought so much misery to the world, ascribing it to an unrestrained capitalistic system that made all values subservient to private gain and individual profit. In a letter home he wrote: "We must begin to look for our freedom in culture, thought, religion, leisure time, art, invention, but not in economic victory over other people." He was firmly in favor of Roosevelt's proposals for reform and, though he rejected a socialist state, he believed it would be "madness to turn down an economic organization on socialistic lines." He saw his own generation as "heir to organizations completely changed by force of circumstances, both in politics and economics." He called his a "disinherited and 'soul-sick' generation dispirited by the war and the post-war period." But he believed that "these frivolous young folks are going to rebuild America." Later on he became even more convinced that Roosevelt was on the right course and called the pre-Roosevelt era "the Rule of the Belly." He wrote home that "Roosevelt must not let the chance slip to convince the American people that the interests of the . . . people have got to come first, and that special interests like farmers, auto manufacturers, industrial workers, and all the rest of them have got to make sacrifices in order to put the whole thing in gear again. He's got to go further with his state control or give way to general chaos."

Another of Rusk's preoccupations was his Christianity. He was absorbing many new ideas in philosophy and politics, and he found them at some variance with his religious views. After reading moral philosophy and various theories of good and evil, he came to the conclusion that skeptical philosophers like Hume and Hobbes left him in a "hopeless muddle." He pronounced their thought sterile and wanting, without a sense of "the ultimate to fall back on. If," he wrote, "philosophers would accept a religious answer to their questions, they would find a way out." He decided to apply this to his study of politics and began to work "privately," as he put it, on "the politics of Christ." He reread the Bible and asked his father to send him a statement of his conception of predestination. As he progressed with this line of inquiry, he became more and more uncomfortable. He retained his faith in God and Christianity, but he appears to have come to the conclusion that theology was not much use to the kinds of questions he was asking: how to effect social reform and "think earnestly and fruitfully about the problems of the postwar world." He regretted that the church had been perverted into a conservative force in the world. He feared that "a Christian politician would be too far from the actual facts to be of any use if he took his material from the Bible." He seems to have made his own private discovery of the principle of separation of church and state. His religion became an artifact of his interior life; he would never allow it to be a litmus test of a course of action or decision.

One benefit of the gentlemanly pace of life at Oxford was the opportunity for travel. Rusk had never known so much vacation time. There were summers and generous stretches between terms at Christmas and Easter. On his very first vacation, at Christmas 1931, he took a trunkful of books and went off to the Channel island of Guernsey, where he thought he would relax, study, and do some deep-sea fishing. He got a fair amount of work done, but he felt somewhat isolated and lonely among the fishermen and farmers on the island.

On his next vacation, at Easter 1932, he went to Paris and lived at a little hotel on the Left Bank just across from Notre Dame. Paris was lovely and seemed prosperous—the Depression was not as severe as in Britain and the United States. He saw the museums and churches, and spent a lot of time browsing at the sidewalk bookstalls along the Seine. He wanted to perfect his French and enrolled in some classes at the Sorbonne, but there was not enough time to become comfortable with the spoken language.

One evening Rusk was walking around the Place de la Concorde when a shabbily dressed little man approached him and said, "Do you want to buy some French postcards?" He looked around very nervously as if making sure they were not being watched. Pornographic photographs were illegal at the time, but Paris was famous for their easy availability.

"How much are they?" Rusk asked.

"Ten francs."

Rusk reached into his pocket and gave him the ten francs, and the man hurried off. Rusk put the packet in his pocket and went back to his hotel. When he opened it, he found they were indeed French postcards—pictures of the Arc de Triomphe, Notre Dame, the Place de la Concorde, and the Eiffel Tower. He could only laugh at his own foolishness.

Rusk returned to Paris once again for his Easter vacation in 1934, a memorable trip because it was his first airplane ride. He booked a flight from London because the trip by boat across the Channel always made him seasick. But most of his travels were in Britain itself, and he came to feel at home among the English. London was only a short distance from Oxford by train, and he liked to attend plays and concerts and browse in the fine shops. "London doesn't seem like a foreign city," he wrote; I feel "perfectly at home now, thinking in terms of chemist's shop instead of drug store, hairdresser's for barber shop, bootery for shoe shop, and cinema for picture show." The English girls he met were eager to show him around, and he was invited to stay for weekends with English families. He bought a camera and started a hobby of taking pictures of old churches. When he was in Oxford on weekends, he took long bicycle rides into the countryside.

During one summer vacation Rusk joined a group of ten Oxford students to go on a "reading party" to the Lake District of northern England. There they read the poetry of Wordsworth and Coleridge, visited Dove Cottage, where Wordsworth and De Quincey had lived and worked, and hiked around the Derwent Water and Windermere. Rusk grew a beard, which turned out to be very red and bushy. One afternoon he rented an old motorbike and set out to explore the countryside. To the staid English he must have been quite a sight. At a petrol station he noticed a large, black, chauffeured limousine and a well-dressed woman in the backseat looking at him intently through her lorgnette. When he returned to the camp where he and his friends were staying, they told him that the lord and lady of the local manor house had kindly invited the entire party to tea the next afternoon. Everyone cleaned up for the occasion, showering and shaving off their beards and dressing in their finest clothes.

The next day, the minute Rusk walked in the door of the manor he recognized the lady of the house as the woman in the black limousine. The tea was lovely, served with plenty of fruit and sweet breads in the spacious garden. During a lull in the conversation their hostess commented, "Oh, young gentlemen, I must tell you that yesterday I saw the most horrible creature I have ever seen in my life!" She proceeded to describe Rusk's appearance the afternoon before in great detail. Rusk grimaced, but his fellows recognized the description and he had no choice but to own up and admit that he was the "horrible creature" on the motorbike. He was very relieved when everyone just laughed. The lady was a good sport and thought the incident was very amusing.

Rusk had other encounters with British nobility, many of them more felicitous. Among his friends at Oxford was the second son of the fifth Earl of Donoughmore. Rusk was invited several times to stay at Lord Donoughmore's estate in Clonmel in southern Ireland, and he enjoyed playing golf on Donoughmore's private nine-hole course. One of the holes was a challenging 450-yard par 4 with a dogleg to the right. On his second shot Rusk hit a screaming, low line drive. The ball hit the ground and kept rolling, up onto the green and into the hole. Later, he described this shot as a 200-yard "eagle putt."

While he was at Oxford, Rusk was interested in working on his German, which he considered his best language. He was told that the purest form of German was spoken in Hannover, so in the summer of 1932 he went there and enrolled in a German-language course. Rusk's mother was half German, and he felt a special affinity for the German people.

It was a momentous time to be in Germany. With over five million wage earners out of work, the country was in the grip of economic chaos. Rampant inflation and high taxes impoverished the middle classes. Farmers could not meet their mortgage payments. The country owed a huge external debt and chafed under the payment of reparations required by the Treaty of Versailles.

There was political chaos as well, and the Weimar Republic seemed unable to deal with the situation. The parliament was paralyzed; no government could achieve a majority in the Reichstag to carry out any policy. The President of the republic, the World War I Field Marshal Paul von Hindenburg, was eighty-four years old and drifting into senility. In 1932 his seven-year term was scheduled to end, and there would be a new election for President. In the forefront of those maneuvering for power was Adolf Hitler, the ruthless chieftain of the National Socialist Party, the Nazis.

On February 22, 1932, while Rusk was still at Oxford, Hitler announced his candidacy for President. It was a large gamble, and Hitler came up short, polling 30.1 percent of the vote to Hindenburg's 49.6 percent. Since Hindenburg failed to win an absolute majority, however, a second election was scheduled for April 10. Again Hindenburg won, with 53 percent, but Hitler gained in the total share of the vote, with 36.8 percent. This did not end matters, however. The fragile democratic government soon fell under Nazi pressure; the Reichstag was dissolved and new elections were scheduled for July 31.

Rusk was studying at Hannover during this election campaign, and he saw the political violence of the Nazis at first hand. Hitler's storm troopers took to the streets, breaking up the rallies of the democratic parties. Rusk was in Hamburg on Sunday, July 17, the day of a Nazi march through the suburb of Altona, when 19 persons were killed and 285 wounded in clashes between the Nazis and the Social Democrats. He thought it ironic that the democratic state was extending its freedoms to the Nazis, a party that wished to destroy it. In the July 31 election the Nazis won an astounding and frightening victory, their 230 seats making them the largest party in the Reichstag. Still, they had polled only 37 percent of the total vote and did not command a majority of the 608 seats.

After Rusk went back to Oxford for the fall term, Germany continued along its tragic course. A succession of coalition governments was tried and another general election was held on November 6, which reduced the number of Nazi deputies in the Reichstag. Finally, in desperation, the ailing President Hindenburg offered the chancellorship to Hitler on January 30, 1933.

The Nazis held only three of the eleven positions in the new government, but Hitler had the important one, the chancellorship. The government lacked a majority in the Reichstag, and Hitler shrewdly played upon the weakness of his coalition partners to attain his ends. The fire which gutted the Reichstag on the night of February 27, almost certainly set by Nazi storm troopers, provided him with an excuse for suspending civil liberties. Finally, on March 23, 1933, the Nazis, through a combination of terror and deceit, pushed through the Reichstag a law granting Hitler full dictatorial powers. The Weimar Republic was no more; parliamentary democracy was over in Germany. It was the beginning of the Third Reich.

Rusk understood that something extraordinary was happening, and he decided to return to Germany, to stay for a longer period so that he could learn German well and get to know the country and its politics. Berlin, the German capital, especially fascinated him—that was where everything was happening. He would go to see for himself. He had just finished his second year at Oxford, and his exams were still a year away. If he spent the last year of his scholarship in Berlin, he could take his books along and prepare for his exams as well. He went to his tutors to ask their permission. They reviewed the lecture courses for the coming term, and there was nothing useful listed that Rusk had not already taken. He received permission and left for Berlin as soon as classes ended in the summer of 1933.

Like most people, Rusk did not yet perceive the Nazi state as a threat to peace. The period of his residence in Germany—from mid-1933 to February 1934—was well before any of Hitler's foreign adventures. Hitler had yet to consolidate his power, and he was on his best behavior. Rusk saw that the German people largely supported him—for the most part out of idealistic motives. They just did not believe what he had written in *Mein Kampf* and disregarded his notions of war and conquest.

On May 17, 1933, Hitler gave a "peace speech," calling war "unlimited madness" and announcing that Germany was willing to renounce all offensive weapons together with other nations. He embraced President Roosevelt's call for a conference on disarmament and peace, and the speech drew very favorable comment in England and the United States. Hitler even adopted a conciliatory tone toward Poland, one of Germany's most hated enemies and a symbol of the imposed Versailles settlement. Negotiations with Poland led to the signing of a ten-year nonaggression pact on June 26, 1934. On July 20, 1933, Hitler had also signed a concordat with the Vatican, guaranteeing the freedom of the Catholic religion and the right of the Church "to regulate her own affairs."

Looking back at this time, Rusk recalled a story about Robert D. Murphy, later the U.S. Ambassador to Germany. As a young Foreign Service Officer, Murphy served in Germany in the 1930s and got to be friendly with the young Monsignor Eugenio Pacelli, who conducted the Vatican's negotiation with the Hitler regime. After World War II, Murphy visited Pacelli—now Pope Pius XII—in the Vatican, and together they recalled their optimistic view of Hitler's intentions.

"Well, we were sure wrong about that one, weren't we?" Murphy said to Pacelli.

"Yes, we were," agreed Pacelli. Then he smiled and said, "But now I'm infallible."

Like Murphy and Pacelli at the time, Rusk wasn't quite sure what to make of Hitler. "It's hard to know what to say about Germany," he wrote his mother just after he arrived in Berlin. "The change has been tremendous, although from my personal point of view, it hasn't made much change in the situation for me. I live just about like I lived in Germany last summer. The University is giving me plenty to do, and is intensely interesting."

Rusk found lodgings with a family named Kemmerer in a suburb of Berlin called Neubabelsberg, near Potsdam, a beautiful area of castles, lakes, and forests. The father of the family was a bookbinder and was well enough off to own a small motorboat. On Saturdays and Sundays Rusk often joined them on cruises on the lakes. He continued to study German and became quite fluent. On visits to museums, especially the Greek, Roman, and Egyptian collections in the Kaiser Wilhelm Museum, he thought that the bust of Nefertiti was the most beautiful art object he had ever seen. It was a very pleasant time— the calm before the storm.

In the fall Hitler reverted to form and announced that since the Allied powers were refusing equality of treatment, Germany was immediately withdrawing from the Geneva Disarmament Conference as well as the League of Nations. The implications of his action were clear: Germany would rearm in violation of the disarmament provisions of Versailles. He was daring the League to stop him. Playing upon the raw exposed nerve in the German body politic—the dishonorable Peace of Versailles—he dissolved the Reichstag and scheduled a new election for November 12, 1933. Voting would be limited to a single slate of Nazi deputies. Germany was henceforth a one-party state.

Rusk followed the election campaign closely and attended Nazi rallies and lectures. His report to his tutor at St. John's revealed the character and appeal of the Nazi cause:

I attended the open meeting of the latest propaganda campaign last night, this campaign in preparation for the "plebiscite" on November

12. Dr. Goebbels spoke very well for two hours and a half and indicated the general lines on which the campaign would be conducted. "National Honour and Freedom" will form the various battle-cries and the "Geneva School" of statesmen will be subjected to the usual fascist ridicule. I am very glad that jingoism will not be tolerated and that the campaign will accept as fundamental the necessity for preserving peace. The will to peace in Germany is as certain as the methods by which it is to be preserved are uncertain. People here are generally optimistic and in a very good humor over the recent events. From the standpoint of pure humor, Dr. Goebbels' detailed description of the German action at Geneva was a masterpiece.

But soon Rusk began to be appalled by some of what he saw and experienced. He witnessed the harsh Nazi crackdown against the universities. At the Berlin Hochschule für Politik he enrolled in a seminar on international law taught by a Professor Bruns. On the first day of the seminar, as the professor was discussing the subjects to be studied, two brown-shirted Nazis stood up and said that there was only one subject to study—the illegality of the Treaty of Versailles. Soon afterward the Nazis took over the university and turned it into a leadership training school. Rusk moved to the University of Berlin, but even that was affected by Nazi indoctrination. One day he attended a lecture by a well-known German historian on the subject of how best to incorporate the Germans in the United States into the Third Reich. The lecturer proposed that Germany set up a party organization and demand territorial enclaves in Milwaukee and St. Louis. Rusk spoke out and said that the idea that Americans of German blood were a kind of colony in the midst of a strange people was nonsense. "The Nazis get furious," he wrote in a letter home, "when, having boasted of German culture and such figures as Kant, Goethe, Lessing, etc., they're told that these gentlemen belong to us just as much as to the people who happen to be living in the present boundaries of the place called Germany."

But on the whole, Rusk enjoyed the lectures he attended on foreign policy, international law, and colonial policy. He wrote St. John's asking to extend his stay, adding—very undiplomatically—that the lectures and seminars "are much fresher than anything I have had on those subjects from my tutors in Oxford." Not surprisingly, his request was turned down, and he was told to report back at the beginning of the next term.

Soon Rusk had to watch what he said in front of the Nazi brownshirts, who seemed to be everywhere. In a letter to his mother he said he could not write frankly about what was happening because he thought his letters were being opened and read. "Foreigners don't make many remarks, even in letters, that might be misunderstood by our friends the Nazis," he wrote, a clever phrasing designed to let his family know what was happening while giving no offense to the "friendly" censors.

At Nazi rallies he sometimes had to give the "Sieg Heil" salute to avoid trouble with the brown-shirts. On one occasion he went to the Tempelhof Airport to hear Hitler speak. It was the biggest crowd he had ever seen: hundreds of thousands of frenzied, adoring Germans cheering the Führer. Long afterward he remembered the "deep, guttural roar of the crowd—the larger the crowd, the deeper its tone." At one point, listening to a bugle corps playing some martial music, he turned to a friend and said, "They sound like a bunch of geese." A man standing in front of Rusk thought he had insulted the Führer and called over one of the brown-shirts. Rusk was taken away for questioning, held briefly, and released.

Another run-in with the authorities came when an Indian student, a friend from Oxford, came for a visit. Rusk showed him around the city, and the two friends went to a Hitler Youth rally at the Sportspalast. At the gate they were stopped by a brown-shirt who looked at the dark skin of the Indian student and said, "Sorry, only Aryans are admitted here." Rusk was in a mood to argue and told the brown-shirt, "But this man is the purest Aryan in all Berlin." The brown-shirt, who was not as familiar as Rusk with the history of the Indian subcontinent, called his sergeant, and Rusk was arrested and taken away. For three hours the brown-shirts discussed what to do with him and finally let him go, deciding that he was just a crazy American.

Rusk witnessed the Nazi attitude toward the Jews as well. The tennis club in Neubabelsberg that he belonged to lost its lease on the court it was using, and the club members had to look around for another court. They found one that was the private tennis court of a wealthy Jewish merchant. After consulting with the authorities, the club simply confiscated it. Rusk quit the club in disgust.

Although Rusk deplored the Nazis, he thought that many of the Germans who flocked to Hitler's side were trying to "steer his policies in a reasonable direction." Business people were seeking economic recovery. The young boy in the Kemmerer family joined Hitler's S.S., not out of ideology but "because he was fascinated with riding motorcycles and wanted to be in the S.S. motorcycle corps." Later Rusk would reflect on how a tyrant or dictator "is able to dupe a lot of innocent people to support him without knowing what they are doing until it is too late." He retained a certain sympathy for the German people, despite his experiences with the Nazis. It became a tragic recollection for him that so many supported Hitler for idealistic reasons: they wanted to see the public morale of Germany restored; they wanted to see Germany respected among the nations of the world; they wanted to get away from the despair, lethargy, and economic misery. Hitler came to power "partly through the use of political pressure and the use of force on the streets, but also partly through a seductiveness that took in a lot of people until he betrayed them."

Rusk was naturally very concerned about the Nazi takeover of the German Protestant churches. He went to services each Sunday at the famous Nikolai Kirche in Potsdam, and it distressed him to see what was being done to bring the churches into line with Nazi doctrine. Christ was described as the "first great Nordic," and Teutonic mythology was substituted for the Old Testament. The "Catholics are not involved," Rusk wrote, "and remain . . . the best defense of traditional Christianity."

During his stay in Germany, Rusk continued to follow other world events as well. He was known by his fellows as somewhat of an expert on the Far East because of his study of the Manchurian crisis. In Berlin he eagerly read American magazines whenever he could get them, and constantly implored his sister to send him newspaper clippings from home. At the University of Berlin he gave a "Referat" in January 1934 on "America, England, and France in the Far East."

He was also very interested in the negotiations that led to the United States' recognition and resumption of normal diplomatic relations with the Soviet Union on November 16, 1933. He was all in favor of Roosevelt's recognition policy and thought it ridiculous to squabble about Soviet war debts. He viewed Japan as a common enemy of both the United States and the Soviet Union, and wrote his mother that the two countries "would do well to become friends, especially with the prospect of new Japanese adventures." His view was "if there are a lot of devils running loose about the world, it's a good idea to make friends with some of them! Else we'll be taken in by the devils."

Rusk was so absorbed by the events in Germany that he forgot he had intended to enter an essay contest at Oxford for the Cecil Peace Prize, a contest instituted by Lord Robert Cecil, a Conservative M.P. who had been a member of the cabinet charged with League of Nations affairs. Each year an essay was selected for the prize, which carried a monetary award of one hundred pounds. Rusk received a telegram from a friend, David French, reminding him that the deadline for submission of the essay was fast approaching. "Don't come back to Oxford if you don't submit an essay," French wrote. Rusk immediately left Neubabelsberg, took a room in a Berlin hotel, and in five days of furious work produced a "think piece" comparing the British Commonwealth and the League of Nations. The essay called for the strengthening of both these institutions and a greater role for international organizations in world affairs. He sent the completed essay to Oxford just in time to meet the deadline, and won the contest. It was one of his proudest accomplishments, and the money was very important to him at the time. He later joked that because of this he was "able to return to the United States solvent instead of spending the rest of my days in a British debtors' prison." An article about him and the winning essay appeared in *The Times* of London.

Rusk returned to Oxford in the spring of 1934 with endless stories about his stay in Germany. But time was drawing short, and there were two things on his agenda: passing his examinations and getting a job. He had several offers of employment overseas, in Turkey, China, and even Japan, but he turned them down because he wanted to return to the United States. With his instinct for being in the center of things, he felt that international relations was "where the action is," as he wrote to his father, and he concentrated his search in that area. "I'm trying to get into the State Department in Washington in a non-political job." He wrote a letter to the State Department asking for information and what kind of qualifications were necessary for a position in Western European Affairs. He received a kindly but stuffy and patronizing reply from Stanley Hornbeck, who turned him down, citing his lack of experience, and advised him to "specialize upon studies which would tend to make you an authority in some particular field of America's foreign relations or with regard to some particular problem thereof." Hornbeck became Assistant Secretary of Far Eastern Affairs just after the war—ironically, the same post that Rusk would assume in 1950.

He also thought he would like to teach politics and international relations. He wrote to Frank Aydelotte, the president of Swarthmore College, who was the American secretary to the Rhodes trustees, asking him for help in his search. The response was a cable from Mrs. Aurelia Henry Reinhardt, president of Mills College, asking if he would accept a position as assistant professor of government at Mills at a salary of $2,000 per year.

Rusk immediately sent back a cable accepting the offer, then went around Oxford to talk to the Rhodes scholars from California to ask where Mills College was located and what kind of school it was. He had never heard of the place. When he discovered it was a small women's college near San Francisco, he wrote home telling his father that "Mills is supposed to be the best college for women west of the Mississippi, and I am told the academic standards are very high." Rusk later found out that he was taking the place of Professor P. W. Buck, who was moving to Stanford, and that Mrs. Reinhardt had a practice of inviting Rhodes scholars to join her faculty. He was asked to teach four courses the first year: comparative government, international relations, municipal government, and the economic development of the United States. He was disappointed not to be assigned a course on political philosophy.

Rusk settled into what he called "a bookish sort of existence," studying for his exams. They were the first and only exams for his degree, and there was a great deal of pressure riding on them. The exams were all graded by examiners outside his own college. He first had to face ten days of written examinations and then, after a break of a little over a month, came a comprehensive oral exam. On May 20 he wrote his mother that "examinations start next week and my head is literally buzzing with the nonsense I've got to keep in it until they are over." At the end of the exam period he was exhausted, but he still had to bone up for the orals in July. He continued to study, but he took time out to attend the Wimbledon tennis tournament because several of his friends were competing, and he even refereed one of the matches.

When he went before the board of oral examiners, he was pleasantly surprised that they were very easy on him. They posed only the most perfunctory questions and were full of praise for his performance on the written examinations. Rusk was somewhat taken aback at this, because he had had difficulty, particularly with his philosophy paper, which, halfway through the exam, he had torn up and started anew. When he returned to the college and reported what had happened, the dons all congratulated him and told him he was certain to get a straight "first," the highest level of achievement. But when the results were announced, he received only a "second." The mystery was later cleared up; apparently the philosophy reader had at first mixed his paper up with another student's. When the mistake was corrected, he had to settle for a "gentleman's second," as Rusk called it. His philosophy tutor called his performance "soundness personified, his work was clear and direct. I did not think he would get a first class because he did not show the wide range of imagination which outstanding philosophy students have. But he was right at the top of our second class."

That was the official story of his performance on the exam, and although Rusk accepted it without complaint, others did not. W. C. Costin, his politics tutor, wrote to the examiners asking why they had encouraged Rusk and asked him only superficial questions in the orals. Why was he not granted the opportunity to achieve a first? They had not given him a true test. But Costin's inquiry produced only a note of apology to Rusk from the examiners.

Virtually everyone who came in contact with Rusk agreed that he had a first-class mind. But he was impatient with the academic speculation that appealed to some of the Oxford dons and repelled by theories that seemed to have no practical application. He clashed in particular with his economics tutor, who suggested that he change one of his papers to incorporate more theory. When Rusk protested, "It doesn't work that way," his tutor became quite angry and told him, "We're studying economic theory." But Rusk refused to be convinced. He regarded economic theory as merely an intellectual construct based upon certain assumptions of "economic man." He believed that "living, breathing human beings rarely make decisions based solely upon economic advantage." Rusk's turn of mind emphasized the faculty of practical reason that facilitates normative judgments. He was less at home with the faculty of pure reason and synthetic judgments which extend the bounds of thought.

On August 4, 1934, he received his Oxford diploma. He was proud and happy despite the "second" and glad to be going home. Twenty-eight years later he would receive another Oxford degree: on June 27, 1962, when he was Secretary of State, he received the university's honorary degree as a doctor of civil law. On this occasion, too, Rusk had to be content with a "second" because he shared the spotlight with Charlie Chaplin, who was awarded an honorary doctorate of letters at the same time. Even at Oxford, Chaplin drew most of the crowds, and Rusk had to settle for quiet and scattered applause. Later, at a dinner at St. John's for old members, the president of the college, his old tutor W. C. Costin, asked him to say a few words. "If I had known when I was here what was going to happen to me later on," he remarked, "I would have been frightened; but my tutors would have been terrified!"

Immediately after he received his degree at Oxford, Rusk sailed for home. He reached New York on August 15, 1934, the first time he had been back in the United States in almost three years. He wrote his mother: "Believe it or not, I'm in America again!"

In his final report to the North Carolina Selection Committee, the warden of Rhodes House summed up Dean Rusk's Oxford career:

> He has used his Oxford time very profitably, and has been alive to all his opportunities, both here and on the Continent, where by special permission, he has been allowed to spend a considerable part of his Scholarship. A man of influence in his college, and among other Rhodes Scholars. Of charming disposition, definiteness of purpose, and excellent prospects.

Excellent prospects indeed! Rusk had taken a giant step on the way that transformed a poor boy from Cherokee County to a prime mover of our nation's foreign policy. All the rest of his life the appellation "Rhodes scholar" would shine like a beacon in the night. It impressed; he could henceforth claim membership in the elite. It was a badge of accomplishment and honor like Skull and Bones at Yale for Averell Harriman and Robert Lovett, Harvard law diplomas for Dean Acheson and John J. McCloy, and for Lyndon Johnson, his appointment in 1931 as a congressional secretary (Johnson quickly discovered that he could wield power in Washington by brazenly introducing himself as a congressman). Consciously or not, Rusk had educated himself to become Secretary of State. He still lacked experience and the right connections, but these would come in time.

The Lessons of War in Asia

Colonel Dean Rusk, Deputy Chief of Staff to General "Vinegar Joe" Stilwell in the China-Burma-India Theater of Operation in World War II

AFTER spending a few joyous weeks visiting family and friends in Atlanta and Davidson, Rusk arrived at Mills College in September 1934, just in time to start the fall semester. It was his first trip West. The mountains he saw on the train coming out dazzled him, and San Francisco was one of the most beautiful cities he had ever seen.

So he would be a college professor after all. If he was disappointed at not securing his first choice in a job—the State Department or some other post that would actively involve him in fighting for the principles of international conduct in which he believed—at least he could teach. In fact, a strong professorial streak would remain in Rusk even when he later found himself the chief instrument of American foreign policy. His carefully worded pronouncements often sounded like lectures. He could always be counted on to provide a principled justification for a decision or course of action. Both President Kennedy and President Johnson became his students.

Mills, across the bay from San Francisco, was a very small college struggling to stay in existence in the midst of the Depression. Its greatest asset was its president, the large, raw-boned, acerbic woman named Aurelia Henry Reinhardt, an able administrator who seemed to keep the college running by the sheer force of her personality. A member of the Republican National Committee and a friend of Herbert Hoover, she used her political connections and commanding presence to garner the financial support necessary for the enterprise.

Rusk's arrival caused a flurry of excitement in this all-female environment. Despite his prematurely bald pate, he was attractive to women, muscular and athletic, with sharp, expressive brown eyes. From the first, he was considered the most eligible bachelor on campus; he lived in a small apartment, prominently located near the gate of the college, that was known as "the guardhouse."

Rusk's colleagues found him likable and pleasant, and were amazed that his experience at Oxford had not made him overbearing or conceited. He was reserved in manner and did not seek to impress his opinions on other people; yet he was not retiring, and quickly became involved with college affairs. President Reinhardt began to rely on him to perform various administrative duties, and, typically, leadership was thrust on him because he did everything that was asked of him so well. Within a year he was elected dean of the faculty, and he created a new program of interdisciplinary studies in philosophy, politics, and economics, based on the Oxford approach. To avoid confusion, he tried going back to his first name, David, but it was no use—everyone at Mills inevitably called him "Dean Dean."

One undergraduate that fall was not at all pleased with his arrival. Virginia Foisie, a third-year student, had just returned after spending the summer in Japan, where she had studied Japanese politics and culture. She was very interested in international relations and had signed up to take the course from Professor C. P. Buck. Now Buck had gone to teach at Stanford, and a Professor Rusk would be conducting the class. She cried when she heard the news.

Miss Foisie decided to take the course anyway, and she was pleasantly surprised by the young professor. He knew a great deal, not only about England, where he had studied, but also about the rest of the world. She thought his insights about Germany and European politics were stunning, and he knew far more than she about Japan, although he had never been there. He in turn regarded her as his best student and asked many questions about her experiences in Japan. The next year she became his research assistant. He was looking into the legal system that required appeals from British Commonwealth countries to be heard by the Privy Council and asked her to research and classify the Privy Council's decisions.

They became good friends, and Rusk began to look forward to their discussions. No matter how busy he was, he was always glad to see her when she came by his office. An attractive girl with light brown hair and blue eyes, she had been born in Boston of a family like his own that prized education and hard work. Her father had worked his way through Harvard and was a labor relations counselor; her mother had attended Wellesley. The family had lived in Washington, D.C., and in Seattle before moving to San Francisco in 1934.

In December 1935, Rusk invited Virginia to go with him to Riverside, California, to attend a conference on world affairs sponsored by the University of Southern California. He was to give a talk, and there would be discussions on a wide range of political topics and international relations. They drove down together in his secondhand Ford. It was a wonderful trip; Virginia was easy to talk to about all kinds of things, and he realized that this was more than an ordinary friendship.

On their return he courted her actively, although it was considered a bit scandalous for a professor to go out with one of his students. They went to out-of-the-way restaurants where they knew they would not run into Mills people. Often he picked her up early in the morning for a drive up into the hills to have breakfast overlooking San Francisco Bay. Despite their attempts at discretion, by all accounts it was a quite visible romance, watched with great interest in the small college community.

In the summer of 1936 Rusk came down with pneumonia. Because he was bone-tired from overwork, it hit him very hard and he was ordered to bed. The head of the political science department, Dr. Cardinal Goodwin, and his wife insisted that he stay with them. Virginia came every day to be with him and to nurse him back to health. He was in bed for two months, and the effects of the illness lingered long afterward. The crisis was a severe setback for his work and was a financial strain as well, costing $300 in medical expenses out of his annual pay of $2,000. (At this time he was still sending money back to his family in Atlanta—$25 a month.) During this time Virginia and Rusk drew even closer. Rusk opened up to her as he had with no one ever before, sharing his hopes and dreams, and Virginia felt her great admiration for him turn into love. She wrote to his mother that in spite of everything, "helping to take care of Dean was truly a joy and those two months were the happiest experience of my life." They decided to get married, and after her graduation she took a job as a laboratory assistant in the geography department to stay at Mills to be near him.

They were married on June 19, 1937, in Seattle. The Episcopal service was small and quiet, with only a few friends and family in attendance at the little ivy-covered church. There was no time (or money) for a honeymoon, and they returned immediately to Mills, where Rusk was scheduled to give a talk at a conference on international relations on June 26. They moved into a rented house high up in the Berkeley Hills overlooking San Francisco Bay. Virginia picked out the wallpaper and made curtains, but otherwise the house came fully furnished. She settled happily into her new life as wife and homemaker, and gave no further thought to the idea of an independent career. According to the standards of the time, her duty was to help her husband. It was a role she accepted without regret.

Rusk was very content with his work at Mills and was soon promoted to associate professor in addition to being dean of the faculty. He helped to organize an annual summer conference on international affairs called the Institute of International Relations. Yet his interests were developing in ways that would take him beyond Mills. His study and teaching of international relations led him to search for a standard of justice in dealings between nations; he found it in international law, and came to the conclusion that international politics without consideration of international law was empty speculation, based either on the metaphysical dynamics of a balance of power or on Machiavellian power politics of the strong against the weak. For Rusk, "purely political considerations were inadequate in resolving disputes between nations because they left out what was most essential—morality." Woodrow Wilson had made a noble effort to inject moral considerations into world politics, but had failed. Rusk saw himself as carrying on this work.

His studies at Oxford and in Germany had given him some knowledge of international law, but not enough. He wished to specialize in the subject, and for that he would need further training in law. A law degree would be a good thing to have on his résumé as well. He needed an advanced degree if he was to continue teaching. Most of the political scientists he knew had Ph.D.s, but he decided that law school would be just as good a preparation, "since lawyers and political scientists talked pretty much the same language in the international field."

In the fall of 1936 Rusk enrolled at Boalt Hall, the law school of the University of California at Berkeley. He could go to school only part-time, however, since he was holding down his full-time job at Mills. He worked at an incredible pace to keep up with his teaching duties and his law school courses. Many times he would finish teaching his own class and have only twenty minutes to drive the ten miles over to Berkeley to make a law school class. Nevertheless, he attained a high average in his first-year courses and was invited to be a member of the *Law Review,* the mark of distinction in law school.

All the while, Rusk continued to watch the international and domestic political landscape very closely. In his domestic politics he was a Democrat and a liberal, following Roosevelt's tussles with the conservatives in Congress and cheering him on. He thought that the Republican war cry of rugged individualism was empty nonsense. For him, the only real choice for the future was either more government control over economic affairs or a return to laissez-faire conservatism, which would allow big business the upper hand. He came down firmly on the side of a wider government role in order to check what he saw as "the natural greed and corruptive tendencies of business interests."

Rusk was also a firm internationalist, extremely concerned about the isolationist spirit of the country that saw intervention in World War I as a mistake and wanted simply to ignore what was happening across the oceans. His experience in Germany convinced him that Hitler was determined to carry out a plan for the conquest of Europe and wanted to establish German domination of the United States and most of the rest of the world as well. The march of events confirmed his belief. In the fall of 1935 the Italian dictator Benito Mussolini sent his troops into Ethiopia, and when Emperor Haile Selassie appealed to the League of Nations for help, neither the League nor the Western democracies could mount effective action. Thus encouraged, Hitler, on March 7, 1936, reoccupied the Rhineland in violation of both the Versailles Treaty and the Locarno Pact. The two Fascist dictators formed an alliance on October 25, 1936. Then civil war broke out in Spain, and another nationalist dictator, Francisco Franco, received open support from both Hitler and Mussolini.

Rusk was troubled by the feeble reaction of the Western powers to these alarming developments. The League was paralyzed, and the British and the French issued only weak protests. In the United States the only response was a series of neutrality acts designed to make sure the nation would not become involved in a repetition of the American intervention of 1917–18. These laws, pushed by the isolationist block in Congress and accepted reluctantly by the Roosevelt administration, mandated an embargo on arms sales to belligerents on both sides in the event of war as well as a prohibition against loans to the warring countries. Nonmilitary goods could be sold to warring countries only on a cash-and-carry basis, with shipments only on foreign vessels. American citizens were forbidden to travel on ships operated by belligerents. The isolationists, supported by pacifist and church groups, even tried to amend the U.S. Constitution to make the declaration of war subject to a popular referendum. This measure, known as the Ludlow Amendment after its principal sponsor, Congressman Louis Ludlow of Indiana, was narrowly defeated after a warning by President Roosevelt that it would "cripple any president in his conduct of foreign relations and . . . would encourage other nations to believe they could violate American rights with impunity."

Rusk thought that the arms embargo could only hurt the Western democracies while making no difference to the Germans and Italians. The neutrality acts would convince Hitler that he had nothing to fear from the United States. The open path to aggression was too tempting. So Rusk was not surprised when Hitler began to rearrange the map of Europe to his own liking. On March 12, 1938, in a master stroke of raw power, the Führer announced to the world that his native country of Austria was now absorbed into the Third Reich. He then turned his attention to the Sudetenland Germans living inside the borders of Czechoslovakia, a country allied with both France and the Soviet Union. Hitler's ultimatums, cloaked in the language of self-determination, provoked only a series of diplomatic conferences that culminated in the appeasement formula of Munich, which granted Hitler his demands in return for what amounted to only a postponement of war. Hitler's true character was revealed six weeks later when, on the infamous *Kristallnacht*, he ordered the burning of all Jewish synagogues and the temporary internment of all male Jews in revenge for the shooting of a German diplomat in Paris.

In 1939 Hitler began his campaign of aggression in earnest. He ordered his troops to occupy the rest of Czechoslovakia in mid-March under the guise of ending friction between the Czechs and the Slovaks. Then Mussolini invaded Albania on Good Friday, and on September 1, 1939, Hitler, after safeguarding his eastern flank by negotiating a nonaggression pact with the Soviets, invaded Poland. The Soviets moved into Poland from the east to complete the partition of that country. The response in the United States to these events was feeble. Congress passed a fourth neutrality act, which lifted the arms embargo, but all exports to belligerents, including weapons, still had to be sold on a cash-and-carry basis and shipped exclusively in foreign bottoms.

Rusk had thought for some time that war was inevitable. He was extremely disappointed that American and European leaders had not taken vigorous action to prevent it. Every move by Germany made the situation harder to stop. In the next year, 1940, Hitler turned to the west. He occupied Denmark and Norway, and on May 10 fell upon Holland, Belgium, and Luxembourg, then marched his troops into France. On June 22 the French government surrendered. The Germans now had reached the Atlantic Ocean and occupied the whole coast of France as far as the Spanish border.

In Asia the same pattern of unchecked aggression was in evidence. Rusk took a much greater interest in Asia than most Americans at the time because of his study at Oxford of the Manchurian crisis. In San Francisco he was a member of the Commonwealth Club, the West Coast branch of the Institute of Pacific Relations, which monitored Asian developments. In California there was much more concern about China and Japan than in other parts of the nation. Ominously for the future, Japan had linked up with Nazi Germany on November 25, 1936, by signing the Anti-Comintern Pact, by which each country promised mutual help against Soviet interference with their war aims.

Long before, during his Oxford days, Rusk had predicted continuing trouble in Asia after the Japanese seizure of Manchuria. In 1937 his fears had been realized when the uneasy truce between China and Japan came to an end after a clash of arms near the Marco Polo Bridge, eighteen miles west of Peking. The conflict soon spread, and Japan poured in reinforcements. Peking and then Shanghai fell to the invaders as Japan's armies moved into the heartland of China in an orgy of killing and torture, occupying key cities and much of the densely populated countryside. The weak Chinese government under Chiang Kai-shek was forced to move its capital deep into the interior, to Chungking in western China. In December the Japanese attacked the American gunboat U.S.S. *Panay* and three Standard Oil Company tankers in the Yangtze River.

Yet, as in Europe, the United States and other democracies were unable to agree on any firm response or coordinated policy to restrain Japanese aggression. A diplomatic conference hastily convened in Brussels by the League of Nations came to naught. Washington even allowed the Japanese to buy oil, steel, and scrap iron from the United States, though it was obviously helping them to prosecute the war in

China. The Japanese were planning a "New Order" in Asia, which involved the subjugation of China and the conquest of large portions of Southeast Asia. On September 27, 1940, Japan, Germany, and Italy concluded the Tripartite Pact, which promised mutual assistance in the event of a war with the United States. To Rusk's great relief, Roosevelt finally began to embargo sales of iron scrap, steel, and aviation fuel to Japan.

During the 1930s Rusk had kept his commission as a reserve officer in the Army, a status dating from his ROTC training at Davidson College. Congressional appropriations for the reserves were so small that he had had very little active training since leaving college. Most of the reserve training was done by correspondence—working map problems that were sent out by the area headquarters at the Presidio in San Francisco. Rusk was easily able to keep his commission with a minimum of effort and disruption of his life as a college professor at Mills and a law student at Berkeley.

But in the spring of 1940 the officers at the Presidio told him that he could expect to be called up for active duty. The Army had only about 275,000 men under arms, and a buildup was under way. Rusk was not surprised, of course; he wondered only when the summons would come. That summer he decided not to register for fall classes at Berkeley. He had completed fifty of the eighty units required for a law degree, but there was a good chance he would be called up in the middle of the semester, and he didn't want to waste the time or money. Besides, he wanted to spend more time with Virginia, especially if he was facing a long absence from home.

The letter from Uncle Sam finally arrived in December, and Rusk reported for active duty at the Presidio on December 15, 1940. He was assigned the rank of captain and was asked to take command of A Company of the 30th Infantry. It was the first time he had ever had active command of regular troops, and he felt rather green despite his extensive ROTC training.

The 30th Infantry was a part of the 3rd Division based on the West Coast, made up of the 7th, 15th, and 30th infantry regiments. It had just been mobilized, and together with the 1st Division on the East Coast, it was the only part of the U.S. Army that was rated "ready for combat." Rusk knew that was ridiculous. When he took command of A Company, he had only about 100 men instead of the 225 called for by the tables of organization. Many of the 100 men in A Company were holdovers from World War I, and obviously too old for active duty as infantrymen. There were not enough machine guns to go around, and there were no mortars at all; even the supply of ammunition was meager. On the shooting range, each man in basic training was limited to ten rounds per session. There was one jeep for the whole regiment.

Despite this, the 30th Infantry spent a great deal of time out on maneuvers, first in Marin County and later at Fort Roberts in southern California. Then the entire 3rd Division was pulled together and ordered to report to Fort Lewis in Washington State. It was the summer of 1941, and President Roosevelt had just ordered an oil embargo against Japan. Rusk and all the other men felt that war was close now; it was just a matter of time.

At Fort Lewis the 3rd Division was reorganized and given new equipment, although far less than what would be needed in combat. Meanwhile, Rusk had come to the attention of his superior officers, who considered him too valuable to be a mere company commander. He was transferred from A Company and became the assistant operations officer of the entire division. Training operations continued on the Olympic Peninsula across Puget Sound from Seattle.

In October 1941 Rusk unexpectedly received new orders directly from Washington. He was being transferred again, this time to the Pentagon to report to the War Department General Staff. He was upset because it was a desk job. His assignment would be to organize a new section of G-2—military intelligence—on British areas in Asia. It was a total mystery to him why he had been selected. He had no experience in Asia. He was deeply involved in helping to organize the 3rd Division for combat, and he tried to get his orders rescinded. The division commander protested his transfer, but the War Department insisted.

Rusk later found out why he had been ordered to Washington. A sorting machine at the Pentagon had run through a large stack of punch cards containing brief résumés of individual officers, and his card fell out because he had spent three years in England. He chuckled at the assumption that because of his experience in England he would know something about British Asia. In any case he had no choice, and he made ready to leave immediately. A benefit of the new job was that he could take Virginia with him. They now had a child, David Dean, Jr., who was less than a month old, born on October 5, 1941. The family traveled by train to Washington, where they rented a small apartment on Connecticut Avenue.

Rusk had little time to reflect upon the fact that, almost by accident, he had been propelled from company commander to the upper echelon of the United States Army. During the war his old outfit, the 3rd Division, would be sent to North Africa, later land in Sicily and fight its way up the Italian peninsula, and finally participate in the Normandy Invasion. Some of the captains in his unit were reassigned to the Philippines immediately after Pearl Harbor; those who survived were on Bataan for the infamous death march. Rusk escaped both these fates.

He reported for duty at the old Munitions Building on the Mall. The military intelligence (G-2) branch of the General Staff was just being reorganized and beefed up. It was one of five sections (G-1: personnel; G-2: intelligence; G-3: operations; G-4: logistics; and War Department planning) composing the Office of the Chief of Staff. This office, presided over by General George C. Marshall, the Chief of Staff, controlled all of the Army's activities. The General Staff secretary with immediate charge of the five sections was General Walter Bedell Smith, later Eisenhower's Chief of Staff and Ambassador to the Soviet Union. Rusk's military intelligence section was the weak sister of the lot; it had always been treated as of minor importance. A colonel, James Compton, was his immediate superior, and General Sherman Miles was Marshall's aide in charge of G-2.

When Rusk arrived, in late October 1941, he was told that his assignment would be to supply intelligence briefings to the other sections and the Chief of Staff concerning British Asia—a huge part of the world including Afghanistan, India, Burma, Malaya, Singapore, Australia, New Zealand, and the British islands in the Pacific. His only staff person was a Mrs. North, a few months short of her seventieth birthday and on the point of retirement. When he asked Mrs. North to show him the files in the Pentagon on his part of the world, she led him over to a large filing cabinet and opened a drawer marked "British Asia." He looked through it and didn't know whether to laugh or cry. It contained one copy of a tourist handbook on India and Ceylon (marked "Confidential" because it was the only copy in town and that was the only way to keep track of it); one military attaché's report from London on the British Army in Asia, dated 1925; and a clutch of newspaper articles Mrs. North had clipped from *The New York Times* during the years since World War I.

Rusk knew then he would have to start from scratch. He gathered a staff, including Robert Goheen, then a green second lieutenant just out of officer candidate school (who later became president of Princeton University), and three other officers. They went to work accumulating all the information they could from books, reports, and the like.

They contacted scholars, missionaries, sea captains—anyone with experience in the area—and interviewed them. When Rusk was asked to investigate the possibility of starting a Burmese-language program for the Army, he contacted the Census Bureau and asked for a list of people living in the United States who had been born in Burma. The search turned up about a dozen people, most with names like Jones or McConihan, obviously not natives. Only one person on the list was a genuine Burmese—a man living in a mental institution. They fished him out and made a Burmese-language instructor out of him.

Rusk was glad that in his first few days no one asked for extensive briefings. He knew that "the moment my feet went under the desk everyone would consider me an Asian expert, like it or not." When his first test came, he passed it with flying colors. A full colonel in the war plans section of the General Staff called him up and said, "Rusk, I forget; is Indochina in South China or in North China?" Rusk was able to tell him where Indochina was located, and the man thanked him and hung up very pleased. Rusk laughed and imagined him telling his staff, "Boy, do we get good support from those fellows down there!" It was his first official act relating to the area that later came to be known as Vietnam.

Rusk was amazed at the unpreparedness of the military intelligence section. And the United States was about to pay dearly for it. Rusk was in his office on December 7, 1941, when the message came in from Hawaii: AIR RAID ON PEARL HARBOR. THIS IS NOT A DRILL. The news caught everyone, including military intelligence, by surprise. The failure to find out about this attack in advance and to warn our commanders was one of the larger blunders in American history. In one stroke the Japanese destroyed the U.S. Pacific Fleet, the principal instrument of American strategic planning.

It was not that military intelligence had failed to see that the Japanese were preparing to attack. Beginning in November, Rusk recalls, everyone at G-2 knew that a Japanese move of some kind was imminent. Negotiations with Japan had broken down, and the "Magic" intercepts (the United States had broken the Japanese diplomatic code) pointed to an outbreak of hostilities. In late November, "war warning" messages were sent to General Douglas MacArthur in the Philippines and to General Walter C. Short in Hawaii. Joint military talks were held with the British and the Dutch.

In preparing for the Japanese attack, G-2 in Washington was following two large Japanese fleets in the Pacific. One of the fleets was located just off Indochina, in a position to imperil British Malaya,

Singapore, and the Dutch East Indies. Rusk's job was to follow this fleet's movements on a day-by-day basis from wireless and British naval intelligence reports. It was this fleet, he recalls, that was the focus of attention at the War Department. Everyone thought that Malaya, Singapore, or General MacArthur's forces in the Philippines were the most likely targets of the Japanese attack. The second Japanese fleet was believed to be somewhere east of Japan. The Japanese section of G-2, which was in charge of the tracking, had lost it, and its whereabouts were unknown.

On the weekend of the Pearl Harbor attack, everyone expected trouble, and Rusk went into the office on Sunday, December 7, at 6 A.M. to pore over the incoming intelligence reports. When the message came announcing the Pearl Harbor air raid, he realized that he had been following a decoy. It was the fleet that G-2 had lost that carried the planes to attack Pearl Harbor. Immediately after the news, Colonel Compton, Rusk's superior officer, showed him a memorandum that had been prepared by the Japanese section of G-2 just the week before. It listed the possible targets of the Japanese attack, and Pearl Harbor was not even on the list. "I thought I better show you this memorandum because you are never going to see it again," Compton said. "All copies are being gathered up and destroyed."

How the Japanese could catch the American fleet with its guard down became the subject of countless investigations. The accepted version at the time, the findings of a White House commission in early 1942, placed the blame squarely on the errors of judgment and dereliction of duty of the two commanders in Hawaii, Admiral Husband E. Kimmel and Army Lieutenant General Walter C. Short, and the careers of both men were severely compromised as a result. It was also speculated that President Roosevelt knew of the planned attack, but did nothing to stop it because it was the only way to assure that the United States would declare war. Rusk's account of the tragedy disputes both these theories. The failure at Pearl Harbor can be traced squarely to the "errors of military intelligence" and the high command in Washington, which promptly covered up the evidence of its mistakes.

The Japanese stroke was stunning in its boldness. In retrospect, military planners might have assumed that wiping out the U.S. Pacific Fleet was the logical thing to do before the Japanese started their war of aggression. But many thought the Japanese would not dare confront the United States directly. They would subdue the French, British, and Dutch territories in the hope that the United States would continue to stand idly by. But war had come. The public was aroused, and Congress, with but a single dissenting vote, approved President Roosevelt's request for the "legal recognition of a state of war between Japan and the United States." Four days after Pearl Harbor, Germany and Italy also declared war on the United States.

Now Rusk's job began in earnest. It was only a matter of time before the war spread to that part of the world for which he was responsible, but immediately after Pearl Harbor, Roosevelt and Marshall decided to give first priority to the defeat of Hitler. That meant the war against Japan would be a defensive one for the time being. It was a decision Rusk agreed with; he was sure the United States would win the war against both powers. In the War Department at that time was a group of three senior military men, majors and colonels who, like Rusk, had spent time in Germany. One of them, Major (later General) Albert C. Wedemeyer, had gone to the German war college in Potsdam, where he had been a student of General Alfred Jodl, who later became one of the most successful of the German generals of World War II. This group, which Rusk and the younger officers derisively referred to as the "Potsdam Club," thought Germany was invincible and advised General Marshall and Secretary of War Stimson not to get involved in a war against Germany but to concentrate on Japan. Rusk helped to counter this attitude. His views carried particular significance because of his own experience in Berlin.

Rusk's counterpart at the Office of Strategic Services was a young black officer named Ralph Bunche, who was also a specialist in British Asia. Rusk and Bunche began to work together frequently, and soon they became friends. Rusk had a very high respect for Bunche's ability. One day they were both working late, and Rusk invited him to have dinner at the War Department officers' mess. Bunche declined; there was an unwritten rule that Negroes were not allowed to eat there. "Come on," Rusk said. "We'll change that rule right now." Rusk and Bunche walked in, sat down, and tried to ignore the angry stares around them. It was crowded, and there were no incidents, but afterward Rusk received several angry notes and calls. He refused to apologize and brushed aside the complaints, appalled that discrimination against blacks existed even in official Washington.

Bunche went on to a distinguished career both in the State Department and in the Secretariat of the United Nations, and received the Nobel Peace Prize in 1950 for his work in 1948 and 1949 mediating the dispute over Palestine. When Rusk became Deputy Under Secretary of State in the Truman administration, he offered Bunche a job as

Assistant Secretary. Bunche refused, primarily because he did not want to subject his family to life in Washington. He told Rusk the story that their pet dog had died in Washington, and when they went to a pet cemetery to have it buried, they were turned away. "Of course," he laughed, "the dog was black."

Just after Pearl Harbor, Rusk met General George C. Marshall, the Chief of Staff, for the first time. Marshall was looking for a place to build an airfield close to the coast of France and hit upon the island of Guernsey as the ideal spot. Colonel Compton knew that Rusk had spent a Christmas vacation on Guernsey while he was at Oxford, and he went up to Marshall's office and said, "I've got a captain downstairs who has lived on Guernsey. He'll be able to help." Rusk went right up to see Marshall, who was sitting ramrod-straight behind a large, uncluttered desk. Rusk was immediately impressed. Marshall reminded him of a favorite teacher, intelligent, orderly, and demanding. He was firm and formal; there was no small talk.

"I hear you've been in Guernsey," Marshall said. "What kind of place is it?"

Rusk launched into a rambling description of the island as very rural with "lots of farmers and fishermen."

Marshall cut him short. "No, no," he said impatiently. "I mean what kind of *soil* do they have. Is it level? Is it rocky? We want to build an airfield there."

Rusk was taken aback and didn't know what to say. He finally admitted that he didn't know and apologized. Marshall dismissed him with a wave of the hand. "You didn't learn much, Rusk."

Upset and full of chagrin, Rusk left the room vowing never to be caught unawares again. He would not speak without being precise and adequately prepared.

In the days following Pearl Harbor, the Japanese lost no time in following up the advantage gained by their strike. They invaded Hong Kong and the Philippines and landed troops on the Kra Isthmus in northern Malaya. Rusk correctly surmised that the Japanese would attack the British base at Singapore, which guarded the strategically important Strait of Malacca. Once Singapore was in enemy hands, Burma and Australia would be imperiled. The western approach to China and the Far East would be cut off as well.

Rusk's job was to assemble intelligence reports on events in Malaya, and often General Marshall himself sat in on his daily briefings. After studying the maps and the terrain Rusk saw that, because of the dense jungle, the Japanese could not simply march their army down the peninsula. He warned that they would make a series of amphibious landings at the river mouths in order to outflank the British defenders. His prediction proved correct, and Singapore fell on February 15, 1942. Events happened too quickly to mount an effective defense, but Rusk's stock went up at G-2.

Next, Rusk turned to monitoring developments in Burma. This exotic land, up to now a remote outpost of the British Empire, suddenly took on great strategic importance. A large wedge of territory between two Asian giants, India and China, the country was mostly mountainous, but it was penetrated north to south by three great river valleys, the Salween on the east, the Sittang in the center, and the Irrawaddy-Chindwin to the west. Its major port, Rangoon, was the landing for the crucial lend-lease supplies flowing to China. From Rangoon the supplies moved north by rail to Lashio, where they were loaded on trucks and carried to China over the Burma Road, China's lifeline to the west, built by the labor of 200,000 men.

For the Japanese, the conquest of Burma had great significance. It would isolate China, where Japanese troops had been bogged down for five years, occupying large portions of territory but unable to defeat finally either the Nationalist government of Chiang Kai-shek or the Communist guerrillas under Mao Tse-tung. It would also secure the Malay barrier at the western rim of the Pacific Ocean. And once Burma fell, Japanese radio broadcasts boasted, British India would be next.

In December 1941, Burma was defended by little more than a division of British, Indian, and Burmese troops. The precarious situation of the country was compounded by the political rivalries and different priorities of everyone concerned. The Americans, above all, wanted to help China, a favored ally. Americans looked upon themselves as the special friends of the Chinese. They portrayed the ineffective, corrupt government of Chiang Kai-shek as efficient, and Chiang as a valorous, Christian, democratic leader. For the British, on the other hand, China had little importance. Churchill was interested in maintaining the empire and strengthening India both against the Japanese and the Indian nationalists. Thus Burma did not have a very high priority, and China had even less. The Chinese, in turn, had a very low regard for the British. Chiang regarded them as the colonial power that had originally violated China's sovereignty. The native Burmese, finally, hated both the British and the Chinese.

Rusk was responsible for preparing the G-2 briefings on the Burma situation. From his study of intelligence reports and the difficult terrain he concluded that the Japanese advance could not be halted. There was simply no way to get in reinforcements and supplies to the small Allied forces, especially since the British were recalcitrant. Churchill said that he could not spare troops from India because that army was responsible for the defense of the whole Middle East and was already stretched pencil thin. Rusk predicted that the British would be forced to retreat and Burma would soon fall. The major problem would be how to get the troops out in an orderly retreat. There was no road from Burma back into India.

But General Marshall and Secretary Stimson were not willing to give up in Burma so easily. Burma was crucial to China, and President Roosevelt, at the Arcadia Conference with Churchill in Washington in December, had made China paramount in U.S. Asian policy. Roosevelt thought China would become a great power and should be treated like one. Chiang was elevated to become one of the so-called Big Four world leaders, along with Churchill, Stalin, and Roosevelt himself, an unrealistic assessment that would persist during the rest of the war and afterward.

In accordance with Roosevelt's wishes, Marshall determined to mount some kind of U.S. mission to China. From discussions in the administration, the concept of a China-Burma-India theater of operations emerged, with the focus on China. Inevitably, it was referred to as the "CBI," a vast territory stretching from the Pacific Ocean on the east to Karachi on the west, an area larger than the United States with a population of over 900 million people. The man chosen to undertake the mission to China was Lieutenant General Joseph W. Stilwell, later to become famous as "Vinegar Joe." Stilwell had experience in China, spoke passable Chinese, and was one of the best field commanders in the Army. He described himself as "unreasonable, impatient, sour-balled, sullen, mad, hard, profane, and vulgar." But he was also strong-willed and determined, with an incorruptible character and strength of purpose.

Rusk had met Stilwell on one occasion in the summer of 1941. Rusk was in Seattle in the midst of maneuvers with the 3rd Division, and Stilwell was the commander of the 7th Division, headquartered in San Francisco. Stilwell was well respected as a soldier, and when it was announced he was coming to Seattle for a visit, the 3rd Division put together a program committee to host a gala dinner in his honor. Rusk was chosen to be the master of ceremonies; he was seated next to Stilwell and ran the show. Everything went well until Rusk announced that a striptease dancer was next on the program. A girl suddenly appeared and, as Rusk later recalled, "it was quite a strip and quite a tease." But Stilwell was obviously uninterested; he sat glumly through the whole thing.

After choosing Stilwell as head of the CBI, General Marshall and the War Department had to determine his orders and responsibilities, a delicate affair because Stilwell's role had to be acceptable both to the British and to the Chinese. After many discussions and conferences, his complex mission was decided. He would wear three different hats. First, he was named "Chief of Staff to the Supreme Commander of the Chinese Theater." The Supreme Commander was, of course, Chiang Kai-shek, whose position as the major American ally and head of state had to be respected. Second, Stilwell was placed in charge of the American effort to keep lend-lease supplies flowing to China. Third, he became "Commanding General of the United States Army Forces in the Chinese Theater of Operations, Burma, and India."

The problem with these fancy titles was that there were no United States forces that amounted to anything in China, Burma, or India, with the exception of the independent-minded Claire Chennault and his "American Volunteer Group," a band of about a hundred pilots known as the Flying Tigers. So Stilwell was a general without an army. It was contemplated that he would be given two divisions of Chiang's army, but any operations in Burma would be undertaken by the joint American-British-Dutch-Australian Command (ABDA) for the defense of Southeast Asia under British General Sir Archibald Wavell. Stilwell would be subordinate to Wavell and would mediate between him and Chiang Kai-shek. Not only did he not have an army, he also lacked any real command.

Stilwell reluctantly took up his duties, saying, "I'll go where I'm sent." His view of the situation was expressed in his private papers: he wrote that his mission was to "coordinate and smooth out and run the [Burma] road, and get the various factions together, and grab command and in general give 'em the works." It was an impossible task. As John Paton Davies, an erudite China expert and later a member of his staff, put it, he was "an American general without combat troops, advancing on Japan from India, about to do battle with Japanese in Burma in defense of China, and hoping to hurl an offensive from deep within the Middle Kingdom at the then dominant naval power in the world." On top of that, the CBI theater was given the lowest priority in the war by Allied and American strategists.

On March 4, 1942, Stilwell arrived in Chungking, Chiang's headquarters, just as Rangoon was falling to the Japanese. He met with the Supreme Commander, who, to Stilwell's disgust, was not interested in using his troops for offensive operations, even though he nominally had 3 million men under arms. Chiang's strategy, simply put, was to hoard his supplies, save his troops, and wait until the Americans defeated the Japanese. He thought the Allies should give first priority to defeating Japan in 1942. Then he would mop up the remaining Japanese and consolidate power in China. Chiang was particularly worried about his archrivals, the Communists, who were holed up in their mountain stronghold in Yenan, in northeast China, waiting for their chance to seize power. So he was reluctant to commit his forces to battle, arguing that the Japanese could be kept off balance through the judicious use of air power—Claire Chennault's Flying Tigers.

Nevertheless, Chiang reluctantly gave in to American pressure to use Chinese troops in Burma, at least to protect China's lifeline, the 600-mile Burma Road. He gave Stilwell the use of three Chinese armies, each only about the size of an American division. With British General William J. Slim, Stilwell tried to form a defensive line across northern Burma to prevent the Japanese from marching inland following their victory at Rangoon.

The result, as Rusk predicted, was a rout by the Japanese. Starting in Rangoon, they mounted a three-pronged offensive northward up the river valleys. The British and Indian forces fell back, and the Chinese, for the most part, failed to fight or to carry out Stilwell's orders. Chiang countermanded many of Stilwell's commands and withheld his troops from fully engaging the Japanese. When Stilwell asked a Chinese general why he wasn't using his field guns, the general replied that "the Fifth Army is our best army because it is the only one that has any field guns. If I lose them, the Fifth Army will no longer be our best." On another occasion Chiang ordered Stilwell to provide watermelons for his men: "Watermelons are good for the morale of thirsty troops."

The Japanese smashed through the Allied forces and soon reached Lashio, the terminus of the Burma Road. The only overland route to China was cut off, and with it the lend-lease pipeline. Soon the Allied armies, along with hundreds of thousands of colonial Indian civilians, were running for their lives. General Slim led the remnants of the British army on a long retreat back to India. The Chinese divisions scattered, some heading back to China, the rest into India. Stilwell collected his small command and a few refugees, a band of 114 people, and set out for India on foot, just ahead of the pursuing Japanese.

Their long march over two hundred miles of mountains, jungles, and swollen rivers captured the imagination of the people back home. By the time Stilwell reached India on May 20 the whole world knew about "Walking Joe" and his glorious strategic retreat—a feat embellished by the American press, which believed the misleading press releases Chiang Kai-shek issued in Chungking. Americans read headlines such as STILWELL'S CHINA TROOPS TRAP JAPS. At a news conference in Delhi on May 25, Stilwell told the truth: "I claim we got a hell of a beating. We got run out of Burma and it is humiliating as hell. I think we ought to find out what caused it, go back and retake it."

During the retreat from Burma, Rusk was occupied in compiling reports and briefings that contributed to the basic War Department strategy of getting as many men out as possible. Now Burma had fallen, and most of the lands Rusk watched over in G-2 were in Japanese hands. In five months of war Japan had been remarkably successful. Malaya, Burma, Singapore, the Dutch East Indies, the Philippines, and all of Southeast Asia were part of Japan's "Greater East Asia Co-Prosperity Sphere." And there was no real effort looming on the horizon to get them back. The main thrust of the war was in Europe and in the eastern Pacific. Rusk felt increasingly as if he were out of a job. His efficiency reports rated him highly, and he was promoted to major. But it was not enough to keep him from being restless and bored.

In late 1942 Rusk put in for a transfer to a post overseas. It was going to be a long war, and he wanted to have a part in it. He was sent to the elite command school for the General Staff at Leavenworth, Kansas. There he studied military operations and planning for three months, from January to April 1943, then returned to Washington to await his assignment. He thought he was headed for the European theater, but in May General Stilwell, who was home from the CBI for consultations in the War Department, picked him out of a list of names and asked him to serve on his staff. He would be chief of war plans and deputy to the chief of staff, Colonel Frank Merrill.

Rusk was happy about his new job. A friend recalls that he came home one day after shopping in preparation for his departure. He could not say where he was going, but the friend guessed it had to be Delhi because of the sunglasses and warm-weather clothing he had purchased. Rusk was looking forward to playing a more active role in the war. He admired Stilwell as a soldier and would be flying back with him to India. The only sadness was leaving Virginia and his young son, David. It was decided they would go back to San Francisco to live, where she had family and friends. Shortly before his own departure, he put them on a train for the long journey west. He would not see them again for two years.

In early June Rusk accompanied Stilwell on a circuitous flight from Washington to Delhi. The first stop was London, where they found an optimistic spirit about the war. The victory over the Germans in North Africa was fresh, and everyone believed that soon Allied troops would land on the continent of Europe and the Germans would be beaten. Stilwell and Rusk attended a lunch with Deputy Prime Minister Clement Attlee and went to a nightclub to watch a beautiful young girl sing a silly song: "We're gonna get lit when the lights come back on in London." When he saw that Stilwell was listening intently and had tears in his eyes, Rusk realized for the first time that underneath that tough, no-nonsense exterior, he had a gentle, emotional side to his character.

Rusk grew to like Stilwell immensely. Thin and wiry of build, he looked like a foot soldier rather than a general. He was also the most unselfish man Rusk had ever met; he did not care about personal glory and often disregarded his own safety. He was single-minded about winning the war. His "Vinegar Joe" image was the consequence of his impatience with obstacles to victory and with people who were less devoted to the cause than he. In private he was warm and quiet. He treated Rusk in an almost fatherly manner, telling him about his early experiences in China. He had a deep affection for the ordinary Chinese people, who suffered patiently and had accomplished so much under extremely difficult circumstances: floods, famine, and corrupt and inefficient governments. The Chinese were hardworking and had a good sense of humor. He believed that there was a natural affinity between the Chinese and American people. Stilwell wanted to win the war as much for China as he did for his own country.

After leaving London, Stilwell and Rusk flew to Cairo, where photographers took their picture as they left the plane and they were treated like celebrities. They met briefly with Allied commanders in North Africa, who were buoyed by their recent success. After several days in the desert Stilwell and Rusk again boarded their plane for the flight to Delhi.

Stilwell's mood on the long journey back to India was glum; he was discouraged and frustrated. Over a year had gone by since his retreat from Burma, he told Rusk, and there was nothing to show for it. Stilwell believed that the key to defeating the Japanese was China. Japanese armies had to be driven out of the mainland of Asia. Then

China could be used as a staging ground for air raids and, if necessary, an invasion of the home islands. The Japanese were bogged down in China, unable to subdue the country but strong enough to occupy large pieces of territory. Like the Germans in Russia, they had bitten off more than they could chew. Stilwell believed that the Chinese were capable of driving them out with American help. Chiang Kai-shek had three hundred divisions. Most of them "weren't worth a damn," Stilwell said, but with the proper training and supplies they could be molded into an efficient fighting force. To do this, Burma would have to be retaken first by a coordinated action with the British. This would open the way to China. Then offensive operations could begin in China itself with drives toward Canton, Hong Kong, and Shanghai, the three key port cities of the region.

But enormous obstacles stood in the way of Stilwell's grandiose plan. To begin with, Chiang himself refused to cooperate. He wanted to keep American war material and supplies coming, but he was reluctant to fight. Stilwell thought that Chiang might even have a kind of undeclared truce with the Japanese. Chiang found all kinds of excuses for delaying a new campaign in Burma. Stilwell had recommended to President Roosevelt that lend-lease supplies to Chiang be conditioned on Chinese cooperation, but Roosevelt had refused. The Chinese leader couldn't be served with ultimatums like a petty prince, Roosevelt said. Since the Japanese had cut the Burma Road, supplies could move into China only by air over "the Hump," the high mountains of the Himalayas. The aircraft used was the C-47 (the DC-3), a cargo plane capable of carrying only four tons. At best, it was a three- to four-hour flight from airfields in Assam to points in western China. The weather was usually very bad, and the planes were not capable of flying at altitudes as high as the mountains they had to cross. So the pilots had to weave their way through the passes, with mountains looming on both sides. It was incredibly dangerous; many planes were lost, an average of thirteen a week in 1942. Only a trickle of supplies reached their destinations.

The supply problem led to increasing friction between Stilwell and General Claire Chennault, the leader of the Flying Tigers. Chennault was fascinated by air power and believed it could win the war. His Flying Tigers achieved notable successes against the Japanese, functioning as the China Air Task Force. The pilots were known for their romantic, daredevil feats, and the Flying Tigers had captured the public imagination in the United States at a time when heartening war news was still very rare. Chennault was Stilwell's subordinate in the CBI, but that did not stop him from working against his boss.

In contrast with the dour Stilwell, Chennault was a handsome and dashing figure who carefully cultivated his image as a daredevil aviator. Rusk found him to be an insufferable egotist, vain and conceited, who cared more about his own career than the war effort. He also thought that Chennault misunderstood and despised the ordinary Chinese people, who were essential to the war, and that his own contribution was minimal.

Stilwell shared that view, and as time went on the conflict between him and Chennault deepened. Chennault believed that the Hump transports should give first priority to aviation fuel and spare parts for his fighter planes in China. Stilwell disagreed. The limited transport available should be reserved for war material necessary to equip a ground army in China to fight the Japanese. Chennault thought Stilwell was old-fashioned, incapable of understanding what air power could accomplish, and he found a ready ally in Chiang Kai-shek. If air power could win the war, Chiang would not have to commit his troops to combat and could husband his strength for later use against the Communists. Chiang and the British had already canceled the planned general offensive in Burma for the dry winter season of 1942–43. No operations were possible in summer because of the monsoon. The next chance for an offensive would be in November 1943.

With typical arrogance Chennault went over Stilwell's head and wrote President Roosevelt that with 105 fighters, 30 medium bombers, and 12 heavy bombers, he could "accomplish the downfall of Japan." And, of course, he would need full authority as the American military commander in China and total control of the airlift over the Hump. Chennault's plan got a big push when it was endorsed by Wendell Willkie, who in the fall of 1942 was making a global barnstorming tour as Roosevelt's personal representative. Willkie flew into Chungking and the Chinese plied him with food and drink. Mme. Chiang Kai-shek charmed him with her beauty and feminine wiles. Willkie promised her all the planes she wanted and invited her to visit the United States.

Mme. Chiang came to the United States for a six-month stay in November 1942. Her beauty, glamour, perfect English (she had gone to school in Macon, Georgia), and exotic Oriental charm overlaid with a veneer of American culture took the nation by storm. The press idolized her and the public adored her. Everywhere her message was the same: the United States should give priority to fighting Japan and give China more aid. She made the rounds of all the officials in Washington from Roosevelt on down, complaining about Stilwell, praising Chennault, and asking for more supplies for China.

Rusk later heard a story told by General Marshall about how he handled Mme. Chiang's visits. Marshall was a great supporter of Stilwell, and he thought Mme. Chiang was meddling where she didn't belong. She constantly pestered him about supplies for China; she wanted the most modern weapons and planes, though there were not enough even for American troops. In the bottom drawer of his desk Marshall kept a list of surplus materials that the Army no longer needed. When Mme. Chiang came to see him, he would say, "Well, that's pretty difficult but let me see what we can do." And he would pull out his list of surplus materials and gravely point out what he could supply. Mme. Chiang would leave, satisfied that she was getting what she wanted. Anything, Marshall thought, to get her out of his office.

On another occasion President Roosevelt, after a conference with Mme. Chiang, sent a note over to the War Department saying, "Madame Chiang Kai-shek has told me that she would supply an unlimited number of Chinese to provide a coolie train across the mountains— do what you can to organize it." Rusk looked at the situation, and through General Marshall a note went back to the President: "In that terrain and over the distances involved, each one of the coolies would have to eat more than three times the load he was carrying." Roosevelt didn't give up and sent back a short note saying, "Drop them food by aircraft." Marshall sent back a message saying, "Mr. President, if we had the planes to drop food to the coolies, we would have the planes to take the supplies to China to begin with."

While all this was going on in the United States, the dry season of 1942–43 came and went in Burma with no effective action against the Japanese. In February 1943 the British launched a small campaign to take the Arakan, the coastal region of Burma near India's Bengal province. But the attempt was a disaster, and General Slim again had to preside over a British retreat from Burma. The British also sent a brigade called the Chindits (named after Burmese temple lions) into the jungle to conduct commando operations behind enemy lines. The brigade commander, Brigadier General Orde C. Wingate, was an unorthodox adventurer, an advocate of what he called "long-range penetration" of enemy lines. In two groups, his men pushed across the Irrawaddy and fought some skirmishes, but they returned to India with more heroic press coverage than actual accomplishment to show for the campaign.

In late April 1943, President Roosevelt recalled both Stilwell and Chennault to Washington. There was a conference with Churchill in

Washington, code-named "Trident." Stilwell was a field commander with minimal political or diplomatic skills, and he did not effectively argue his case to Roosevelt. Chennault carried the day. He painted a vivid picture of what air power could do to the Japanese. Roosevelt thumped his fist on the desk with excitement. Chennault's point of view was supported by the British and of course the Chinese. Stilwell argued that building up China's air force was to no avail, because the Japanese would simply come in and take the airfields. That is exactly what happened in 1944. But Roosevelt had made up his mind. The airlift of supplies over the Hump would be increased, and priority would be given to supplies for the air force and building up air power. The general offensive to retake Rangoon and all of Burma—code-named "Anakim"—was shelved. In its place a limited operation in northern Burma—code-named "Saucy"—was authorized. Its purpose was to cover the air route to China and to open a new land route, a new Burma Road, to be built by Indian and Chinese laborers via Ledo and Imphal.

Marshall was furious at the President's decision. Stilwell was crushed and defeated, but in typical fashion he refused to give up. He would go on with the limited resources available and build the new road to China. It was one big contingency plan. Roosevelt thought it wouldn't be needed, but Stilwell was convinced it might yet be essential to defeating the Japanese. Once the new Burma Road was open, he could mount an offensive inside China. And he would continue to press for a big offensive to retake Burma. It would be more difficult, but he would do it.

Rusk's specialty was war plans, but Stilwell told him he would function more broadly than that. He would be based at Stilwell's rear-echelon headquarters in New Delhi, where most of his staff worked under Frank Merrill. Stilwell also had a general staff in Chungking, under Frank "Pinky" Doren.

Rusk soon became invaluable to Stilwell, and was closer to the general than anyone else save perhaps Frank Merrill. Rusk gave Stilwell his usual qualities of loyalty, dependability, and good-humored devotion. He had the energy and ability to get things done and make no enemies in the process. He mixed well with people and was a great sport at the card table and on the tennis court, the two favorite leisure-time activities in New Delhi. Even so, morale was low because much of Stilwell's staff was basically deadwood, men who were marking time, and who considered the mission a lost cause. Rusk thought that Stilwell was badly served by some of his staff, who encouraged the acerbic side of his personality. They loved it when "Vinegar Joe" was quoted in the American press with some outrageous remark. Stilwell often vented his spleen, and Rusk thought it unfortunate that his staff, instead of letting his terrible temper remain a private side of Stilwell's nature, egged him on whenever the press was around. Stilwell was becoming a folk hero, but Rusk thought it was harming the war effort. A measure of Rusk's effectiveness is the fact that once he was on the scene, the Americans began to deal effectively both with the British and with the native Indian population. Stilwell continued to have problems with Chiang that were beyond Rusk's control. But his judicious and diplomatic nature was an excellent counterpoint to Stilwell's acidity and lack of political and administrative skills.

From the time he arrived in New Delhi, Rusk found that his job was about half military and half political. On the military side, he was in charge of the basic operational planning for Stilwell's principal mission—keeping China in the war and building up Chinese forces so that they could, if needed, be used to rout the Japanese. On the political side, Rusk was in charge of relations with the British and the native Indian population. He also did most of the drafting of Stilwell's cables back to Washington, especially those having to do with his continuing squabbles with Chennault and Chiang Kai-shek.

Stilwell's style was to give Rusk a free hand; he wanted a take-charge aide, so Rusk went right to work. It was June, the hot season in India, just before the onset of the monsoon rains. Military operations were impossible until after the end of the rainy season. Thus Rusk's immediate concern was supply: how to get the ordered step-up in lend-lease goods to China in the most efficient fashion. Roosevelt wanted 10,000 tons a month to go through, an all but impossible demand. The supply system was in dreadful shape. The port of entry for American goods going to China was now Calcutta. From there they had to be moved by train up to the airfields in Assam, using an ancient, winding, narrow-gauge railway, built for the tea trade, that had been run for decades in a very casual fashion. When a train stopped to take on water, it was loaded with an ordinary garden hose, so that it took several hours for a job that should have taken only a few minutes. When the train came to a river, the tracks ended and the cars were barged across one by one, crossways, instead of pointing the barge perpendicular to the dock and loading five or six cars at a time. The Indian engineers who operated the trains often stopped off for several hours in their native villages along the way. The roadbed itself was in very poor condition as well. One of the first things that

Rusk did was to recommend that the American military take over the trains. At first the British objected, but after much discussion the Combined Chiefs of Staff accepted the idea. After several months the Americans had solved most of the problems, and tonnage to Assam steadily increased.

Next, Rusk turned his attention to the Hump flights to see if they could be made less dangerous and more efficient. He took one of the flights to see the dangers firsthand, the first of many such trips during the next two years. Many aircraft were lost on takeoff or landing, because they had to fly through some of the most dreadful weather that could possibly be imagined; when the humid monsoon came up and hit the mountains, there was a convulsion of winds and rain. Flying through mountain passes was bad enough under ideal conditions, but often visibility was limited or nil. Several peaks were said to be iron-plated with the remains of planes. Then there were the air currents. Without warning a plane would be tossed up or down several thousand feet. The saying was that flying the Hump was so bad you simultaneously thought you were going to die and were afraid you wouldn't.

More than a dozen times Rusk flew the dangerous Hump into western China on the delicate mission of persuading the Chinese to fight the Japanese. Not only was the Hump itself a dangerous ordeal, but Japanese fighter planes lurked across the Chinese border. On one flight Rusk's plane was on the ground in Chungking when an air raid siren signaled an imminent Japanese attack. It and other planes took off immediately to avoid being hit on the ground, but no sooner was Rusk's plane in the air than a Japanese Zero appeared on its tail. Then, for some reason, it went after another plane first, allowing Rusk's plane to take cover in a bank of clouds. The other plane was shot down and crashed in flames. Rusk wondered how many times he could survive a fifty-fifty brush with death.

Rusk decided to place navigational aids along the route of the Hump to make it safer, and got hold of a number of automatic direction finders in black boxes. They had to be placed on the ground in strategic locations, so he found a bowlegged Texas bush pilot and they climbed aboard one of the DC-3s with the black boxes and flew the route. When they saw an open field below suitable for a box, they buzzed it a few times to see how bad the rocks were, and then went in for a landing. After setting up the box, they took off again for the next spot. In the mountainous country of western China, their plane often attracted some of the local people, and they bargained with them to protect the black boxes. As money they used little bags of opium, the principal medium of exchange in that part of China.

Despite the improvements, fear of death was always a part of the Hump flights. The survival rate among the pilots was less than 40 percent. On one flight Eric Severeid, the newsman, and John Paton Davies, Stilwell's political officer, had to bail out over northern Burma, in an area of head-hunting hill tribes. Fortunately, they were rescued. Later Davies was on a plane that had engine trouble over the same area. It made it back to base, but during the ordeal Davies and the others on board put on their parachutes and, moving toward the door, Davies was heard to mutter, "Well, at least I know the people down there."

Corruption was rife on the Hump flights. Gold and furs, cheap in China, were favorite items for smuggling. Rusk had the sad duty of bringing court-martial charges against those who were caught. One pilot told him that anyone who didn't make a million dollars flying the Hump was crazy.

There were also troubles and misunderstandings with Washington over supplies for the CBI, which was at the end of a 12,000-mile supply line that was given the lowest priority during the war. On one occasion some small locomotives were desperately needed for the narrow-gauge railways, but the request was denied and converted jeeps were used to pull a few cars at a time. A short time later Rusk got a cable from Washington informing him that a thousand light tanks were being loaded for shipment to the CBI. Tanks were completely useless in the mountainous terrain of northern Burma, so Rusk cabled back that they were not needed. He got a message that the War Department insisted. When the tanks arrived in Calcutta, they were parked in a large field outside the city, and eventually rusted out and were sold for scrap at the end of the war. Rusk later learned that the tanks were shipped because a congressional committee making an inspection out West had noticed the tanks and asked where they were going. The Army officer conducting the tour said on the spur of the moment that they were for the CBI. So the CBI got them, like it or not.

Rusk filled his letters home with observations—often very insightful and always full of humanity—on the peoples and culture of India. He was impressed by the size of the country and its immense complexity. He took lessons in Hindi and Chinese, and became reasonably competent in Hindi. He liked the people and wrote that "even the lower classes have active minds, alert expressions, piercing eyes, and a certain agility of the body." He was appalled by the poverty and starvation he saw: "400,000,000 people are living on the edge of existence with 200,000,000 kine wandering around. Not only do they not eat these animals, but they let them compete for foodstuffs which human beings need most desperately. After many weeks I lost some money to some beggars. There are quite a few of them around with their deformities and their wails, but I decided upon arrival that I should give no alms until I had seen an Indian giving one of them something. After almost three months that happened, so I proceeded to pass out a little bakshish for conscience sake. The gifts of course made the beggars more, not less, insistent, so I'm returning to my previous state of frigidity. It's a horrible state of affairs but no one does anything about it and hasn't for 1000 years. I don't know what my own conduct should be." In 1943 the rice crop failed, adding to the general misery, especially around Calcutta. Rusk did what he could to direct food shipments to the area. "It seems to me," he wrote, "that of all the peoples of the world, these are the most wretched."

For the first time in his life Rusk came in contact with Muslim culture, and he seemed particularly fascinated by it. He visited the ruins of an old Muslim university on a hill overlooking a broad plain. He thought it "must have been a place of great beauty and charm— graceful columns and small Byzantine domes around courtyards of beautiful spreading trees." He visited the local mosque and was duly impressed by the relics of the Prophet: "one hair (red) from the Prophet's beard; one sandal worn by the Prophet, the mate of which is now in Mecca; a footprint of the Prophet miraculously impressed into a block of marble (I accept such comparatively simple miracles without question); and sheets of sacred script by the Prophet and the son of the Prophet." He celebrated the Muslim holidays, particularly since his "bearer," the boy who cleaned his room and looked after his personal needs, was a Muslim named Akbar.

He called Akbar "a fierce looking son of the Prophet" and paid him the equivalent of nine dollars a month, which upset the British, who paid only six dollars to their own bearers. Akbar gave Rusk a gift of cake on holidays, explaining that it was the custom to exchange gifts and that Rusk's present to him had to be exactly five times the value of his gift to Rusk. Akbar also increased his income at Rusk's expense by "petty frauds," submitting a bill for "soap, shine cloths, shoe laces, and a long list of trifles which he may or may not have had to buy." Rusk overlooked the matter, figuring that Akbar had more need of the money than he did.

He wrote to Virginia frequently in a humorous and easy style, telling her about small, personal happenings and complaining that most of what he was doing he could not talk about because of Army censorship rules. Their correspondence was full of concern and mutual love. Rusk lived in a Muslim neighborhood, where most of the women "prefer to keep themselves completely covered when such strange things as I walk past. Most of them cheat, however, by covering everything but one eye which they use to satisfy their curiosity about us. I've had no desire to peer under any veils, because 99% of the time you would simply find a homely creature." Occasionally, however, gloom overcame his light humor. He confessed that he was very homesick. Then he added, to reassure her, "It's nothing serious, but once in a while I feel deeply this loss of time from a life that should be concerned with other things than war."

One of his most poignant letters was written on September 5, 1943. He had been trying to catch a ride home on one of the military flights that occasionally made the trip between Delhi and Washington. He wrote Virginia, "I hate to tell you that I had a trip home depend on the toss of a coin—with the coin falling the other way! I didn't mention this to make you feel bad, but to let you know that such things do happen sometimes. At least the other fellow won this time!" A few days later, to his horror, he learned that the plane he would have taken home crashed and burned on takeoff from Karachi, killing everyone on board. Again he had survived a fifty-fifty brush with death.

Rusk had frequent contact with the press corps covering the CBI and got to know some of the journalists fairly well. One night he had dinner with Eric Severeid and Preston Glover and found their comments "quite interesting." But in the same manner that would characterize his later relations with the press, he was careful about what he disclosed to them. "It's hard to sit still under wraps without joining in such conversation," he wrote. "The tape over my lips gets awfully sticky sometimes."

Another of his concerns was the treatment accorded the black American soldiers in the CBI. In a letter home, he wrote that he often had to argue the "negro question" with "Yankee friends of mine who seem much more deeply prejudiced against the negroes than I ever thought possible." And he added, "I'm as far away from sympathizing with discrimination as I ever was. The army has many subtle and some not so subtle ways of trying to meet the problem, but it's pretty obvious that 15% of our people have no particular reason to feel a deep personal stake in the war. The remarkable thing is that they don't give us more trouble than they do under the circumstances."

There was a good deal of discomfort associated with living in India: the extreme heat, the dirt, the insects, and the "inescapable digestive disorders caused by the basic filth of this place." Malaria was a constant threat despite the fact that he was taking antimalaria pills, and he had chronic dysentery that sometimes flared into illness and fever that put him in the hospital. Air-conditioning was very rare, and he battled the heat with electric fans and matting over doors and windows. At night he was forced to bed early as the only means of escaping the "billions of bugs." He lost more than 30 pounds off his 206-pound frame in the first six months, and joked to Virginia that a "tropical tour" was the best way to lose weight. Humor was his method of coping with the problems and discomforts. He wrote that, after the heat of India, he would become "eternally attached to the zephyrs of Death Valley." He joked about keeping pet lizards to control the insect population. He vowed to go on a regimen of "less exercise and heavy eating" to protect his health. When he was hospitalized and had to take some large horse pills usually given to pregnant women, he wrote to Virginia, "What do you want, a boy or a girl?" Another method of coping was to find enjoyment in little things associated with home. He was ecstatic to be able to read a copy of Life magazine on microfilm, and a Tootsie Roll, when it was obtainable, sent him into raptures.

His letters home were also full of his thoughts about war and what it did to people. The killing of course was the worst part, the ultimate blot on the nature of mankind. He wrote, too, about the cost in "human comradeship," the disruption of civilian family and working life. "I miss these particular years because in so many ways they are irreplaceable years. It's only when I realize that the same thing is happening to at least 120,000,000 other young people that this war takes on its full picture of horror." He was proud of the Americans he met, saying that they "hate war and all that it means. They aren't excited about this one and look forward to the day they get home. But even so, they do their job quietly and steadily without flinching." That was Rusk's approach exactly. He had no illusions. He wrote to Virginia about the myth of "the sturdiness of character induced by military training." And he noted that "women at home would work their bodies and souls out to get some sort of international law working if they really understood what war does to their menfolk (not that you need to start worrying about me—I'll let you know in time for you to worry efficiently)." From his own firsthand experience of war, he increasingly looked upon international law and an international order as the keys to producing peace in the world. To his son, David, he wrote, "We have gone far when civilized men can fight to win and remain civilized at heart. Our next step is to be civilized enough to know how to live to make such wars unnecessary. And that's where you come in, David, beginning at the age of three."

Rusk avidly followed the course of the war in the European and Pacific theaters. The year 1943, which saw the invasions of Sicily and Italy, mostly by American forces, he called a "year of uninterrupted military success," and he cheered every victory because it would shorten the war. Upset when he heard criticism of Marshall and the Joint Chiefs about their prosecution of the war, he wrote Virginia not to listen to the "grandstand quarterbacks." And he was not among those who gave all the credit to the Russians for the German retreats. He always had a tendency to sympathize with those in power, the men who actually had to make the decisions. Negative talk rarely helped and only made the jobs of those in authority that much harder.

Rusk was increasingly drawn into a war of another sort, the controversies stirred up by Indian nationalists. By default he became the chief American liaison with the political and religious leaders of India. It was a delicate situation, since it was a time of growing tension between Britain and the nationalist movement. Talks on some kind of constitutional settlement had broken down, and in 1942 Gandhi had launched his "Quit India" movement. Riots ensued, and the British imprisoned more than sixty thousand, including Gandhi and Jawaharlal Nehru. Under Churchill the policy of the British was to continue British imperial power. They had created in India a first-class civil service of both Indians and Britons to run the country. And they depended on the Indian military forces, particularly the Gurkas, to help prosecute the war. But at the same time the British had maintained the Indian caste system and, in effect, imposed one of their own by creating private clubs and facilities where natives were not welcome.

Day to day, Rusk had no qualms about enjoying the special benefits of what would prove to be the waning years of the Raj. Soon after his arrival, he joined a British tennis and swimming club in New Delhi called the Gymkhana Club. Because of his Oxford background, the British considered him one of their own, and he played the part. His game of tennis improved, and he was not averse to sitting around the pool sipping drinks or engaging his British friends in a game of bridge or poker. His attentiveness to some of the pretty British nurses and secretaries earned him a mild reputation as a ladies' man, but there was never any scandal. Years later, when these reports reached President-elect John F. Kennedy while he was considering Rusk for Secretary of State, they evoked only rib-poking chuckles and the confirmation that Rusk was a "regular guy."

Yet during the war, American policy diverged fundamentally from the British. President Roosevelt strongly advocated that India, as well as the other European colonies in Asia, be given complete independence after the war, and Rusk believed in the correctness of that policy. The postwar order would not be peaceful if the European nations were allowed to preserve their colonies. Ever since Oxford, Rusk had opposed colonialism. Now one of the most difficult American problems in the CBI was how to oppose colonialism without creating frictions with the British.

At every wartime conference Churchill importuned Roosevelt to downplay his anticolonial policy. Roosevelt sent several missions to try to mediate the dispute between the British and the Indian nationalist leaders, but Indian independence was secondary to the goal of winning the war, and little progress was made. Nevertheless, when the CBI was created and it was clear that Americans would be going to India, Roosevelt wanted to demonstrate to the Indian nationalists that American troops were not to be stationed there to aid the colonial designs of the British. When he was in G-2 at the War Department, Rusk had helped create a distinctive shoulder patch to be worn by all Americans in the CBI, a brightly colored design with the red and white stripes of the United States, the sun of China, and the star of India. It was intended to separate the Americans from the British, and when British General Slim asked that it be issued to the troops under his command, Rusk had to tell him no.

The Americans (as well as the British) had to avoid trouble with the Indian nationalists, because they were entirely dependent on the Indian people for basic goods and services. There were inevitable cultural differences, some minor and quite humorous. The first time Rusk rode in a tonga, a little pony-drawn two-wheeled cart, his two hundred pounds practically lifted the small pony off the ground. From that time on, the driver, when he saw Rusk coming, would rush to get out and hold his pony down while Rusk got in. The way his clothes were washed also presented a problem. The local way of doing the laundry was to wet the clothes with cold water, lay them on some rocks, and beat them furiously with a stick. When the clothes came back, if they survived, one had to watch out for a common malady called "dhobi itch," *dhobi* being the Hindi word for launderer. The dhobi itch was a skin rash caused by contact with the laundry mark on the garment, made with the indelible juice of a poisonous plant or nut.

But there were more serious cross-cultural difficulties as well, and Rusk was often called upon to find solutions to problems with the Indian population. When the nationalists objected on religious grounds to the slaughter of cattle for food, Rusk negotiated an agreement that the slaughter would be limited to animals over twelve years old and would be carried out in screened areas. To satisfy the demand that Untouchables not be allowed to handle food, he employed a Brahman cook, because then the food could be eaten by any member of the complicated Indian caste system. The nationalists also demanded that American soldiers be given permission to marry Indian girls. Rusk's solution was that permission would be granted, but only within thirty days of the time a man was to leave for home. Under this rule marriage was rare, because a solider going home was seldom interested in marrying an Indian, but the nationalist leaders were happy that the principle had been accepted by the Army.

Rusk also had the job of coordinating war planning with the British, another touchy situation. As with the Chinese, Americans in the CBI were essentially in the position of saying to the British, "I will hold your coat; now you get in there and fight." Stilwell's relationship with the British commander, General Wavell, had been notoriously discordant.

The situation was even more complicated because Britain, in turn, depended primarily on Indian troops to fight the war. Rusk was always amazed by the relationship between the British and the Indians —that two so different peoples could be so closely tied together. He witnessed a formal military ceremony in New Delhi that exemplified this. The Viceroy of India, who stood six feet, eight inches tall, was giving the Victoria Cross, Britain's highest decoration, posthumously to a Gurka soldier. The man's widow, who came forward to receive it, was hardly four feet in height. In his dignified way, the very tall Viceroy bent down and pinned the medal on the very small woman. It was East meeting West, symbolic of the incongruity of British rule in India.

In August 1943 the Quebec Conference, code-named "Quadrant," was held, at which Churchill, Roosevelt, and their generals met to decide strategy for both Germany and Japan. The CBI was one of the main topics on the agenda. Churchill proposed, and the Americans accepted, that Lord Louis Mountbatten become the new Supreme Commander and that a new command be organized—the Southeast

Asia Command—within the CBI. Stilwell was named Deputy Supreme Commander. This didn't change much as far as the Americans were concerned. Stilwell with his small American contingent and his Chinese armies remained subordinate to the British in India, as he was subordinate to Chiang in China. But Stilwell and Rusk were enthusiastic about Mountbatten's appointment. Rusk wrote, "It has been a surprise, but a very well received one out here. His youth, experience with all services, and proved ability to get British and Americans working together are recommendations of the highest order for this job. Its full effect out here won't be known for some time probably."

Rusk's impression was based on the view that Mountbatten, at least, wanted to fight, and finally there would be some action against the Japanese. Mountbatten said his mission was "to reconquer Burma, Malaya, the Dutch East Indies, and all the places in which the British Empire's present forces received an unparalleled series of defeats on land, at sea, and in the air." This was much different from the way the Americans saw things, but at least Burma was on both countries' lists of lands to be recaptured from the Japanese.

As chief liaison with the British, Rusk saw Mountbatten frequently both in India and later in Ceylon, where the British moved their headquarters in mid-1944. Mountbatten seemed to have everything—brains, money, and good looks. Tall and regal in stature, he was always impeccably dressed with never a hair out of place. Yet he did not seem vain or overbearing. He laughed easily and related well to those around him. A small incident during one of Mountbatten's first visits to Assam confirmed Rusk's good impression of him. Just after he arrived, Mountbatten visited an American headquarters company for a snap inspection. The troops lined up, all spit and polish, and as Mountbatten approached, each one in turn advanced one step, saluted smartly, and gave his name. One of the men there had not been briefed on the expected routine. He had been working in a machine shop and was wearing his army fatigues with grease all over him. When Lord Mountbatten approached, the soldier just looked at him and said "Hi." Mountbatten did not reproach him but asked, "What is your name?" The man told him. Mountbatten then asked, "Where are you from?" The soldier said, "I am from Texas, sir." Then Mountbatten chuckled and said, "Well, I have run across a lot of Texans out here." The man smiled and said, "That's why we are doing so well." Mountbatten laughed heartily and gave the man a lusty pat on the back.

On one occasion Rusk was sitting in his office in New Delhi when a copy of a cable to Mountbatten from an American commander in Assam came across his desk. The cable was sharply worded, complaining about the condition of British hospitals and services. Rusk was surprised; the American was out of line in using such language to address the Supreme Commander. Sure enough, a short while later a cable came in from an angry Mountbatten demanding an explanation. Rusk investigated, and he was relieved to find out that the author of the original cable was none other than Mountbatten's wife, who was touring Assam. The American commander had signed it as part of the routine of sending all outgoing cables under his name. Rusk sent the explanation back to Mountbatten, and the "Supremo" gave him a good-natured apology in return.

Stilwell soon became disenchanted with Mountbatten and called him a variety of names in his diary. In January 1944 he wrote, "The Glamor Boy is just that. He doesn't wear well and I begin to wonder if he knows his stuff. Enormous staff, endless walla-walla, but damned little fighting." A little later Stilwell wrote that Mountbatten was a "fatuous ass; childish Louis; publicity crazy; a pisspot." Yet the atmosphere between Stilwell and Mountbatten was markedly harmonious, and Stilwell remained affable to the Supreme Commander, in part because of the Americans who were on Mountbatten's staff. But a great deal of the credit was also due to the diplomatic skills of Rusk, who was in charge of relations with the British on Stilwell's staff and worked very closely with J. M. "Mike" Saunders, the British liaison to Stilwell in New Delhi. Rusk was aware of Stilwell's splenetic tendencies and did his best to mute them as far as Mountbatten was concerned. He knew that despite their different objectives, harmony between the British and the Americans was essential to winning the war in Burma. That this harmony was achieved was perhaps Rusk's greatest contribution to the war effort.

During the wet season in 1943 the Americans were making preparations for the next campaign, which could only come in the winter dry season. Just as the British relied heavily on Indian troops, the Americans depended on the Chinese, and Stilwell was busy training several divisions of Chinese troops at Ramgarh (a former camp for Italian prisoners of war about two hundred miles west of Calcutta) in anticipation of the move to reconquer Burma.

The Americans were also engaged in a massive building project— the new Burma Road. Ever since the old Burma Road had been cut by the Japanese, the supply problem in China had been acute. Despite the increasing tonnage being flown over the Hump, there seemed to be no substitute for the opening of a new land route to China, which meant finding a way through the mountains, possibly bypassing Burma entirely and constructing the road through Afghanistan or Nepal. Together with the engineers, Rusk flew all over both areas, illegally and surreptitiously, to examine the terrain to see if the construction of a road was indeed feasible. They concluded it was not. The mountains were too forbidding. There was no choice but to go through northern Burma even though it was held by the Japanese, and work began on the road at Ledo in northeast India.

Rusk flew with the engineers over northern Burma to look for the best corridor through which to complete the road. In doing so he was actually violating orders; since he had worked in the General Staff in Washington, he knew about the secret plans for the invasion of Japan, and was under orders not to fly over enemy-held territory because of the danger of capture and interrogation. He felt he had no choice, but as a precaution he carried a packet of suicide pills he was prepared to take if he was captured by the Japanese.

A route was finally selected south through the Hukawng Valley. It was terrible jungle terrain, and the road had to cross rivers and snake around mountains. Bulldozers were outfitted with armored plates to deflect Japanese bullets. The work would continue over the next two years. More than six hundred miles of new construction were necessary to link up with the northern portion of the old road at Bhamo and from there into Kunming in Yunnan province. The Burma Road was a heroic effort achieved at great cost in both men and material. Ironically, by the time it was completed it was obsolete, and was never used for its original purpose.

In 1945 a larger transport, the C-54, came into general use in the CBI, a magnificent plane by the standards of the time, capable of flying above the mountains of the Hump. A fleet of C-54s could transport much more cargo to China than the overland route, which was a three-week journey by truck. Even so, Rusk would later recall, the road had to be built. It was like an insurance policy, a contingency that was there if needed. He was proud of it, and when it was finished he rode in the inaugural journey the entire length from Ledo to Kunming in a jeep. At various points along the route, thousands of people waved colored flags and banners at the convoy. There was a great celebration: the siege of China was broken. The Chinese named it the "Stilwell Road" even though by that time Stilwell had been relieved as commander in the CBI.

At Cairo in November 1943, another conference ("Sextant") was held between the Allied nations, this time including China. Roosevelt, Churchill, and Chiang Kai-shek attended. Stilwell went too, along with his aide Frank Merrill, and again one of the main topics of discussion was the CBI. After much wrangling, the incongruous coalition came up with a firm battle plan. The Burma Road justified an advance into northern Burma. That would be Stilwell's job. The British would attack farther south, in a general campaign to reconquer Burma.

Stilwell had actually begun the campaign in northern Burma before it was authorized by the Combined Command. His objective was Myitkyina, a key city on the projected route of the Burma Road. Rusk helped plan the campaign. Chinese troops from Assam (called the X Force) would push into the Hukawng Valley and seize the town of Shinbwiyang. From there they would proceed down the Mogaung Valley to Myitkyina.

When Stilwell got back from Cairo, he went immediately to the front. He was a division commander at heart, and he wanted to direct things personally. Rusk went with him for a time, and they rode around the area in a jeep visiting the troops. Stilwell was always very reckless about where he was going, and at one point they came under Japanese sniper fire. The two men climbed out of the jeep and, rifles at the ready, went looking for the perpetrators. Rusk later joked that his only combat experience came when he was teamed up with a four-star general climbing around the bush in search of Japanese snipers.

With his troops stalled in the Hukawng Valley, Stilwell, ever impatient, planned his next move. He had an ace in the hole. His constant requests for two American divisions for the CBI were denied, but in late 1943 he did receive permission to organize a small force of three thousand Americans, drawn from volunteers from other theaters. Frank Merrill, his deputy chief of staff, was given the task of organizing and commanding this force. Merrill, Rusk recalls, was an excellent soldier, devoted to Stilwell, and a regular at the poker table. Like Stilwell, he was anxious to carry the fight to the Japanese. The men he was given, however, were mostly misfits who had volunteered only to get out of the guardhouse or to rehabilitate themselves. Under Merrill's watchful eyes, they were trained in India for jungle warfare behind enemy lines. Their official name was the 5307th Composite Unit, and their operation was given the code name "Galahad." But to the press and the public they became known as Merrill's Marauders.

When Merrill was appointed to command the Marauders, the position of Stilwell's chief aide became vacant. Without hesitation Stilwell chose Rusk, who from then on had wide responsibilities as deputy chief of staff of the whole theater. He was also promoted to full colonel. He was pleased at Stilwell's confidence in him, but was not particularly excited or happy at either promotion. He wrote Virginia about his "new job," but added he was not interested in professional advancement in the Army. "I would just as soon be known as plain Mister Rusk," because it would mean the end of the war.

When the Marauders were ready for combat, in February 1944, Stilwell used them as a mobile auxiliary force and sent them into the jungle on slashing and trapping movements designed to keep the Japanese off balance and to relieve the pressure on his Chinese troops. The Marauders performed extremely well, even heroically, despite adverse conditions and months of combat without respite. Rusk admired Stilwell's genius and strength of purpose, but he thought he abused his men, expecting more out of them than they could possibly give. Nevertheless, their mission was crowned with success. On May 16 they took the Japanese by surprise at Myitkyina and captured the airstrip there. Stilwell was jubilant. "Boy will this burn up the limeys!" he wrote in his diary. Rusk was on the first transport plane into Myitkyina to bring in supplies and talk with Merrill to plan further operations.

The men at Myitkyina were in terrible shape. Most of them had not eaten for days, and many had ulcerous sores. Sleeping out in the open in fields of bamboo, they were bitten by rodents, and some were suffering from typhus. They were unable to fight effectively enough to follow up their success and capture the town of Myitkyina. The Japanese dug in and brought up reinforcements. There was no alternative but to take the town by siege. It was two and a half months later, well into the rainy season, when the Japanese commander committed suicide and his troops surrendered.

During the siege, many of the Marauders who were sick or wounded were evacuated back to Ledo. Stilwell visited them in the hospital there, and sent a message to New Delhi asking for air-conditioning. When he was told there were no air-conditioning units available, Stilwell was furious and sent a curt reply: "You and I both know where air conditioning units are. I want them up here immediately." Stilwell pushed his men unmercifully, but cared about them nevertheless.

The Myitkyina campaign buoyed everyone's spirits. It was primarily an American success and showed that American troops could fight and win against the well-trained Japanese troops. It was the first time Americans had fought a campaign on the mainland of Asia since the Boxer Rebellion in 1900. In 1944, of course, there was other good news. MacArthur and Nimitz were coming across the Pacific, and the Allies landed in Normandy to begin the reconquest of Europe.

The brunt of the rest of the campaign in Burma fell to the British. General Wingate led his Chindits deep into the jungle in a long-range-penetration foray. Rusk gave this operation the code name "Pinprick," which brought an angry reply from Winston Churchill, who ordered him to give the campaign a more suitable name: "Grapple." (Rusk later joked that "pinprick" and "grapple" were the difference between his and Churchill's places in history.) Rusk thought Wingate's mission was a waste of time and resented having to use precious aircraft to support him. But a short while later, the eccentric, hard-fighting Wingate was killed in a plane crash, a fate which, combined with his daring as a commander, made him one of the romantic legends of the war.

The British planned a general offensive for the spring of 1944, but before it could get under way Japanese forces invaded India in southern Assam in an attempt to capture Imphal and Kohima. A vigorous counteroffensive mauled the Japanese badly, and during the next dry season—the winter of 1944–45—a British general offensive in southern and central Burma finally completed the liberation of the whole of Burma.

During the Myitkyina campaign, on March 9, 1944, Rusk received a cable from Virginia telling him of the death of his father. He felt the loss keenly. He recalled his father's last letter. Rusk had written his father about his promotion and had made a sarcastic comment about carrying on the tradition of his grandfather, a colonel in the Confederate Army. His father wrote back reproving him and said that he should honor his grandfather's memory. In his grief Rusk wrote to his mother: "I still have in front of me that span of my life comparable to that part of Father's in which I knew him. My deepest prayer is that I shall spend mine with the same cleanness of heart, integrity of soul, and kindliness of spirit which marked my Father."

There was little time for mourning, however. Rusk could not even ask for emergency leave to spend a few weeks at home to comfort his mother and to deal with his father's estate. The Myitkyina campaign was just too important to leave at that crucial point.

With the campaign in Burma drawing to a successful close, attention could be turned to the original purpose of the effort in the CBI: making China an active partner in the fight against the Japanese. But in China vast new perils were developing, and Chiang's position was growing ever more precarious. Rusk thought of him as aloof, unrealistic, and ineffective as a leader, but he gave Chiang credit for having created even the appearance of a government in China. Chiang had carried the full burden of the war for almost fifteen years. Decades of turmoil had eroded Chinese institutions. The Japanese were in control of the populous areas of the country and the nascent Chinese industries. Famine had ravaged the land along with a terrible bombing campaign by the Japanese. Now Chiang was in trouble. With reports of unrest among some of his key generals, there was a real question whether he could survive. From the American point of view, if Chiang went, China might go too, with incalculable effects on the war against Japan.

On top of everything else, in April 1944 the Japanese launched an offensive in China, the first since their thrust south to Hankow in 1938. Code-named "Ichigo" (Strawberry), the offensive was supposed to force a Chinese capitulation and halt the growing harassment from Chennault's air bases in eastern China. Chennault's raids were disrupting Japanese shipping and communications, and Japan was moving to eliminate the air bases, just as Stilwell had predicted. The first phase of Ichigo was a thrust south from Hankow to link up with the Japanese troops holding Canton and Hong Kong. The second phase was a drive west to the border of French Indochina to link up with Japanese forces there.

If the Japanese campaign had succeeded, it would have complicated the war effort enormously. Despite the successes of MacArthur and Nimitz in the Pacific, the war might have been prolonged for years. In order to defeat Japan, Rusk feared, America would not only have to invade the home islands, it would have to fight a war on the mainland of Asia. This prospect was a daunting one. China was a huge, populous, complicated country. It would be folly for America to get involved in a large land war there. Rusk's urgent task was to help prevent that from happening.

Like Stilwell, Rusk respected the abilities of the Chinese. Theirs was a great civilization, a great culture. He would never forget the first time he flew into China and saw proud, intelligent people, far different from the hill tribes of northeastern Burma he had been working with to fight the Japanese. He knew that the Chinese could be effective fighters if they were well trained and properly led.

Yet Rusk had a realistic view of China; he was free of the benevolent illusions and romanticism that were popular in the American press. He often had to deal with the corruption which was an inevitable result of the unremitting years of turmoil. When he arranged for antimalaria pills for the Chinese troops in Burma, he had to assign an American officer to actually put the pills in their mouths; otherwise Chinese officers gathered them up and sold them on the black market in China. In similar fashion an American had to hand every Chinese soldier his pay to prevent the officers from skimming part of the money. The corruption even extended to dealing with the Japanese. On one occasion Rusk traveled by mule into the wilderness of northern Burma to spend a few days with a Chinese division during the Myitkyina campaign, and to his surprise General Sun Li-jen, the division commander, served shark's fin soup for supper, boasting proudly that "ten days ago that shark's fin was in Shanghai." When Rusk remarked that Shanghai was under Japanese control, Sun only smiled and said, "You Americans just don't understand us Orientals." After the Burma campaign Stilwell was careful to fly most of his Chinese army back to China. He said that the Chinese carried their boundary stones in their knapsacks, and he wasn't taking any chances.

Chinese cruelty shocked Rusk. One day while flying over the Hump, he watched a group of Chinese troops roughhousing, laughing and joking like soldiers everywhere. One man was standing near the open door of the airplane and another crawled around behind him down on all fours. As the horrified Rusk looked on, a third soldier pushed the standing man over the crouched soldier, pitching him out of the plane. All the men practically burst their sides laughing. Another time Rusk was in a taxi in Chungking when the car hit and killed a peasant walking across the road. The driver was unconcerned. The right-of-way of a taxi in Chungking was determined by the status of the passenger, he explained.

Rusk felt sorry for the ordinary Chinese soldiers, who were usually recruited from their villages by force. If the Japanese didn't burn their farms and kill them, the Kuomintang drafted them to serve in the army. In Kunming one day he saw a line of Chinese men walking single file down a road, their hands tied together with ropes. When he asked who they were, he was told that they were "volunteers" for the army.

The Chinese had an inadequate diet and almost no equipment for training. When Rusk was in China he was served two eggs for breakfast, lunch, and dinner. It was all there was to eat, and he knew that for the average soldier it was much worse. Homing pigeons were often used to deliver messages in the CBI because they were faster and more reliable than mail service. When the supply of birds was running low and Rusk asked the War Department for more, he received the reply, "It is assumed the birds themselves will furnish their own re-placements." Rusk couldn't tell Washington that the pigeons were being roasted and eaten by the Chinese troops. A few months later he was with Stilwell visiting the Chinese forces in Burma when they heard a grenade explosion. A Chinese soldier was "fishing" in the river. Stilwell was furious; he fumed at the idea that the grenade had "been brought over 12,000 miles to kill carp." In response the senior Chinese officer said a few words to his aides, and the soldier was brought in and summarily shot.

Politics, however, was the greatest obstacle that prevented the Chinese from being an effective fighting force. Stilwell's attempt to remove this obstacle would lead to his recall as the theater com-mander of the CBI and ultimately would throw into question even his patriotism and loyalty to the United States. Stilwell's recall, even more significantly, would shape the future of China and the political makeup of Asia in the postwar world. As Stilwell's deputy, Rusk was drawn into this far-reaching crisis of command.

The drama centered on three strong men and their different visions of the strategy of the war: Stilwell, Chennault, and Chiang Kai-shek. Chennault, technically Stilwell's subordinate, had bested him in per-suading President Roosevelt, over the objection of Marshall and the Joint Chiefs, to place primary emphasis on air power to win the war in China. Chennault, with missionary zeal, maintained that with a few more aircraft, spare parts, and enough ammunition, he could bring Japan to its knees. Chennault had many friends in high places and, with his aide, Lieutenant Joseph Alsop, he was adept at the games of public relations and political intrigue.

Stilwell—and Rusk, his deputy chief of staff—was not convinced. The American mission in China, for which Rusk was in charge of operational planning, was to keep China in the war and to build up Chinese ground forces to fight the Japanese. Strategically, Rusk's judgment was that the proper role of air power was to support an effective campaign on the ground. By itself air power could merely produce some spectacular incidents that made good press copy but had no fundamental or long-lasting effect. The Ichigo campaign only proved the point. As Stilwell had predicted, the Japanese were cap-turing or destroying the air bases of Chennault's 14th Air Force.

Chennault, however, blamed Japanese successes on a lack of sup-plies. The situation was desperate, and he appealed for 10,000 tons a month over the Hump. This time Marshall and the War Department turned him down. The extra tonnage could come only at the expense

of building up the B-29 air bases in west-central China that were to be
the staging ground for bombing the main islands of Japan. Chennault
was furious and blamed Stilwell. In rejoinder Stilwell said that Chennault was trying "to duck the blame for having sold the wrong bill of
goods." Fuel was added to the fire in June 1944 when Vice President
Henry A. Wallace visited Chungking as Roosevelt's personal envoy.
Chennault and Alsop convinced Wallace that Stilwell should be recalled.

Marshall and the War Department had other ideas, however. They
blocked Stilwell's recall, and Marshall, always a vigorous supporter
of Stilwell, proposed to give him command of all the Chinese forces
in China, putting him in charge in fact as well as in name. But this
required the assent of Chiang Kai-shek, the third player in the unfolding drama.

Chiang had his own agenda for the war. His tactic was basically to
refrain from fighting as much as possible, take a defensive posture,
and wait for the Americans to defeat Japan. Locked in a bitter struggle
for the control of China, Chiang was in a tenuous position. Not only
did he have to worry about his own subordinate commanders making
an attempt to gain power, he was in a life-and-death struggle with the
rebel Communist forces of Mao Tse-tung. Chiang wanted to conserve
his strength to fight the Communists after the Japanese were defeated.

Stilwell had a plan that varied with Chiang's in the extreme.
Prompted by his able political advisers, John Paton Davies and Robert
Service, both of whom spoke Chinese and knew China well, Stilwell
wanted to establish a working relationship with the Communists to
fight the Japanese. Initial contacts with Mao and Chou En-lai, his
deputy, showed that this was feasible and that the Communists were
willing to cooperate against the Japanese. To show American good
faith, Rusk personally authorized the delivery of a limited amount of
supplies to the Communists in Yenan. He also ordered that supplies
and American cigarettes be air-dropped to another Communist leader
in Indochina who would later become famous: Ho Chi Minh. He kept
in close touch with the OSS men who were maintaining friendly contact with Ho.

Rusk, who was thoroughly familiar with Stilwell's thinking, knew
that his purpose was not to intervene in China's civil war, and was in
no way disloyal to the United States. Stilwell simply was interested in
"helping anyone he could to fight the Japanese." He planned to form
a coalition army, march to the coast of China, and seize a port. Stilwell told Marshall that it would take a "stiff message" to Chiang from

Roosevelt to put him in command. On Marshall's recommendation Roosevelt sent the message. On July 6 he forcefully asked Chiang to give Stilwell "the power to coordinate all Allied military forces in China, including the Communist forces." He told Chiang that "the future of all Asia is at stake along with the tremendous effort that America has expended in that region."

Chiang's reaction was predictable, but since he was dependent on American aid, he could not turn down Roosevelt's request outright. He played for time, advancing compromise solutions. Meanwhile the military situation in China continued to deteriorate. Stilwell went ahead with preparations to assume command and to make official contact with the Communists. He expected Chiang to be forced out, raising the possibility that the crisis would produce a new democratic regime in China, one that would be acceptable even to the Communists. There was very little to build on, but he was prepared to work toward a new political solution in China.

It was not to be. Chiang Kai-shek had his way. Ironically, what prompted the final blow against Stilwell was an ultimatum sent to Chiang by Roosevelt at Marshall's prompting on September 16:

I have urged time and again in recent months that you take drastic action to resist the disaster which has been moving closer to China and to you. Now, when you have not yet placed General Stilwell in command of all forces in China, we are faced with the loss of a critical area in east China with possible catastrophic consequences. . . . The advance of our forces across the Pacific is swift. But this advance will be too late for China unless you act now and vigorously . . . to preserve the fruits of your long years of struggle and the effort we have been able to make to support you. . . .

I am certain that the only thing you can now do to prevent the Jap from achieving his objectives in China is to reinforce your Salween armies immediately and press their offensive, while at once placing General Stilwell in unrestricted command of all your forces. The action I am asking you to take will fortify us in our decision and in the continued efforts the United States proposes to take to maintain and increase our aid to you. . . . It appears plainly evident to all of us here that all your and our efforts to save China are to be lost by further delays.

The message came to Stilwell in Chungking for delivery, and true to form, he insisted on giving it in person to "Peanut," as he referred to Chiang. Rusk was in New Delhi, and no one could persuade Stilwell not to gloat in front of his enemy. "I handed this bundle of paprika to the Peanut," Stilwell later wrote, "and then sat back with a sigh. The harpoon hit the little bugger right in the solar plexus and went right through him."

But Stilwell had backed Chiang into a corner, and it was Chiang's turn to send an ultimatum to Roosevelt demanding Stilwell's recall. He was calling Roosevelt's bluff. In New Delhi, Rusk drafted Stilwell's messages back to Marshall and did his best to save him. Washington must not back down. Stilwell must be given command. A tough message to Chiang from Washington would force him to seek some compromise solution. A new leadership in China might emerge that would include the Communists, which Chiang would have to accept. It was the only way to keep China in the war. Rusk's messages convinced Marshall, who drafted a sharp rejoinder to Chiang.

Roosevelt, however, refused to take Marshall's advice. Sadly, he granted Chiang's request. Stilwell would be recalled, and on October 19 he received advance notice from Marshall. Rusk was not surprised. Too much American aid and support had been invested in Chiang Kai-shek to dump him. Politically, Roosevelt would have come in for savage attack, and militarily it would be taking an awful chance. Rusk knew in any case that Stilwell was not the right man to be the catalyst for a new democratic government in China. By temperament a commander, Stilwell was lacking in political and diplomatic skills.

Rusk saw Stilwell after his recall when he stopped in New Delhi on his way back to Washington. He was bitter, not only at Chiang but also at Roosevelt. He told Rusk that "the trouble with the Chinese is that they act too much like Americans." Stilwell was anxious that the world know the truth about his recall. He had already taken Theodore H. White of *Time* and Brooks Atkinson of *The New York Times* into his confidence. Stilwell told Rusk he was instructing Robert Service to go to Washington and give the American press the real story of what was happening in China, not merely to protect his own reputation but in order that something might be done about Chiang Kai-shek, who was leading his country down the road to catastrophe. Service distributed the story to a variety of magazines and newspapers, among them, regrettably, *Amerasia*, a newspaper with Communist sympathies. It would lead to accusations of disloyalty against Service and others during the ugly witch-hunts that followed the fall of China. Rusk considered Service, Davies, and Stilwell as wholly patriotic and loyal to the United States. He later regretted that Stilwell had not lived long enough to be able to disprove the wild accusations and hysterical charges made against him and his political aides.

Although Stilwell was relieved of his command, the American mission to establish a link with the Communists went forward. This mission, code-named "Dixie," had been suggested by the prescient John Davies as early as 1943, as a means of countering presumed postwar Soviet intentions in China. His aim was to redirect United States policies to address the real political power in China—the Communists. Mao's forces controlled large territories in North China; they were not pro-Soviet at the time, and their brand of communism was pragmatic. They were effective organizers and were willing to cooperate with the Americans and even to some extent with the Chinese Nationalist forces to fight Japan. The need for American cooperation with the Communists was seen by virtually everyone involved, even those who had no love for Joe Stilwell. Vice President Wallace and even Chennault were in favor of the plan. Rusk was in New Delhi and not directly concerned, but he was fully informed of the contacts with the Communists and presumed they would succeed. He was planning for greatly increased aid to both the Communists and the Nationalists as soon as the Burma Road could be opened.

Tragically, the Dixie mission was doomed to failure by several factors. Not the least was the person chosen to act as President Roosevelt's personal representative. Patrick J. Hurley, an Oklahoma corporation lawyer ignorant of China, was selected for the job solely on the basis that he had been a successful power broker for Roosevelt in domestic politics. He wanted to become an ambassador (which he later did), and this was a step along the way. Rusk knew Hurley and considered him a "strutting buffoon, a bull in a china shop, incapable of anything." The other major factor resulting in failure was the American policy decision made explicit by the firing of Stilwell. Roosevelt had chosen to put all his money on Chiang Kai-shek. It was a given that Chiang would not be dumped, which, in effect, gave him a veto over any American efforts in the area.

Hurley arrived in Yenan the first week of November. With a negotiating style that emphasized melodramatics, his greeting to the Chinese Communist leaders was a Western war whoop: "Yahoo!" A newly minted major general, he flaunted his status and military ribbons, and he ignored the advice of the people who could help him, the impressive group of Foreign Service officers and military men with a knowledge of China. Even so, Mao Tse-tung and Chou En-lai tried their best to cooperate. Chou went to Chungking to meet Chiang. In the end, however, Chiang refused any compromise, insisting on complete surrender by his Communist enemies. His power ebbing under the assaults of the Japanese and the conspiracies of his own commanders, Chiang was the tail that still wagged the American dog.

After Stilwell's recall, the CBI was formally divided into two theaters, India-Burma and China. General Daniel Sultan, Stilwell's deputy commander, succeed him in India, and General Albert C. Wedemeyer, the American deputy chief of staff to Mountbatten, became commander of American forces in China. There was little time to reflect on Stilwell's departure because the Japanese offensive in South China was at its height. Kweilin and Luichow fell in rapid succession, and by the end of November the Japanese had attained their goal of capturing the principal East China air bases. Japanese troops in China linked up with their forces in Indochina. Now it appeared that even Kunming and Chungking were within reach.

Rusk flew to Chungking several times to see Wedemeyer and talk over the situation. Wedemeyer was on good terms with Chiang, and on two occasions Rusk had dinner with them. He grew to like Wedemeyer, who was decisive and shrewd in command. But Chiang, Rusk thought, was a particularly tragic figure. He had to know about the corruption that was rife among his men. He had only the most tenuous control over his generals, the warlords, and the governors of the provinces. He had been forced to retreat to this wartime capital four hundred miles from the Japanese lines, to the gorges of the Yangtze River, where they hid in caves to escape Japanese bombs. He had fought alone for ten years while the Japanese invaded his country and the rest of the world did nothing to help him. A man of strong pride and moral courage, he had persisted through it all. But he was unable to come to grips with the fact that his country and its institutions were crumbling away beneath him. Rusk knew that Chiang would endure until the end; his iron will and love for China made it impossible for him to step aside voluntarily.

In order to undertake the Chinese counteroffensive, Wedemeyer's staff activated the war plans that Rusk and his group had prepared for Stilwell; they were still suitable with minimal changes because both the strategic locations and the contending parties were the same as in the summer of 1944. The plans called for the establishment of a secure base in Kunming and a drive to the coast to open a port near Canton and Hong Kong, which were to be used as stepping-stones for the planned invasion of Japan. The Stilwell-trained Chinese divisions from India were assembled to begin operations, and Rusk assisted in organizing the tactical campaign, which was called Alpha. The forces already in contact with the Japanese were ordered to slow the advance, while new forces were placed across the principal routes to Kunming. The Japanese soon found they were stretched too thin, and they abandoned their plan to march on Kunming. The Burma Road had been opened in January, and now over 45,000 tons of supplies per month were pouring into China. By late spring the Japanese had pulled out of southwestern China entirely, their ranks decimated by the need to provide replacement troops for their other divisions and to defend the main islands. The Japanese armies moved back to the north and along the coast, voluntarily giving up all of the territory won by the Ichigo offensive. As their last act of cruelty before leaving, they burned and destroyed Kweilin, Luichow, and several other cities.

There was a lull in the fighting while Wedemeyer prepared a new offensive for July or August 1945, and Rusk received a month's leave to go home to see Virginia and his young son, David. Arriving in San Francisco in June, he spent the month getting reacquainted with his family and trying to forget about the war. He later described this as "a joyous time" that helped him overcome the keen sense of loss that he felt in missing David's early growing-up years. More good news came: he was awarded the Legion of Merit along with the oak-leaf cluster in recognition of his achievements in helping to open the Burma Road and in theater operations. Before his recall, Stilwell had put him on the list to be named a brigadier general, and Rusk fully expected to receive a command during the coming campaign in the Pacific.

But just at the end of his leave he received new orders. He would not be returning to India or to China. He was being transferred to Washington to the Operations Division of the War Department General Staff. The transfer came as a total surprise, and when he inquired about the reason, he was told that the orders came on the personal instructions of General George Marshall. Rusk had drafted most of Stilwell's cables to the War Department, and Marshall had asked for the "name of the officer that has been drafting General Stilwell's messages." Impressed by the clarity and reasoning of the cables, Marshall wanted Rusk in Washington.

Rusk had clearly come a long way since the beginning of the war. He had gone from being an ROTC reserve infantry officer to being singled out by U.S. Army Chief of Staff George Marshall himself. It was heady stuff, but Rusk accepted it quietly as part of doing his job and doing it well. It was a repetition of what had happened to him at Boys' High, at Davidson, at Oxford, and at Mills College. Once again he had been singled out, not because he sought recognition, courted those in power, or had the right connections, but because he was an extraordinarily able man.

Virginia was overjoyed at the Washington assignment. The separation had been hard on her. Raising David alone was difficult. And about the time the new appointment came through, she found that she was pregnant with their second child.

With or without Rusk, there would be no more significant battles against the Japanese in China. There would be no need for Wedemeyer's planned summer offensive. The fall of Okinawa in April 1945 made China unnecessary as a base of operations for invading Japan, and the Americans had overestimated the remaining strength of the Japanese forces in China. In fact, by the summer of 1945 those forces were war weary, badly supplied, and depleted by transfers to prepare for the defense of the home islands. The dropping of the atomic bombs on Hiroshima and Nagasaki would make further resistance pointless, and the once feared Japanese army in Manchuria would simply melt away.

Observers would later point out that the entire CBI mission—to keep China in the war and to build up Chinese capability to fight Japan—was ultimately unnecessary. Rusk had a different view. The premise behind the CBI mission was entirely valid and a reasonable judgment at the time. The Japanese everywhere had fought with tenacity and ferocity. Even if Tokyo ordered the Japanese to surrender in China, American planners couldn't be sure they would do so. The whole CBI was "a giant contingency plan." MacArthur and Nimitz coming across the Pacific might have needed major supporting ground forces in China in their attempt to close in on Japan. Rusk was familiar with the plans to invade the Japanese home islands in the fall of 1945. It was predicted that such an invasion would take at least six months of hard fighting with between a half-million and a million American casualties.

Nevertheless, the wartime decisions made in the CBI had enormous political consequences in the postwar period. The decision to give unequivocal American support to Chiang Kai-shek was understandable but wrong. Chiang had refrained from fighting Japan, waiting for the Americans to come with their overwhelming power and drive the Japanese out of China. He would then be able, he thought, to crush the Communist threat with American help. But the dropping of the atomic bombs on Japan affected the future course of China as well as Japan. No American armies would come to China; Japan would leave China without direct American intervention, and Chiang would be left to fight the Communists alone. He was not up to the task. The American policy of support for Chiang was an expression of the view that his was the legitimate government of China, and the United States did not want to undermine him by giving undue support to the Communists. America had simply bet on the wrong horse. What course of events would have occurred if the Dixie mission had succeeded in establishing a relationship with the Communists remains unknowable. Mao had his own agenda, and it is difficult to believe relations between the United States and a Communist government in China would have proceeded in blissful harmony. Still, it is certain they would have been better than they turned out to be.

The prosecution of the war in the CBI also affected postwar Soviet involvement in East Asia. Because he could not get the Chinese under Chiang to fight the Japanese, Roosevelt sought and received Stalin's promise to enter the war against Japan. Stalin did so, but only at a time and in places that would further his own ends. America would have to deal with Russian expansion not only in Europe but in the Far East.

Surely the most tragic postwar political problem bequeathed by the CBI was the resurgent colonialism in the region. The Japanese, in their offensive in 1941–42, which overran the Philippines, Indochina, Malaya, Hong Kong, Singapore, and Burma and threatened India, were conquering colonies of European nations, not independent countries. Roosevelt's wartime policy was that all these areas would become independent after the war. The United States was not fighting in Asia to preserve colonialism and return these countries to their European masters. Roosevelt conducted relations with the British in the CBI on the assumption that even India would attain independence as an outcome of the war. This noble purpose, however, was frustrated by the demands of war. Churchill was utterly opposed to it. At every wartime conference he tried to dissuade Roosevelt from his anticolonial stand. He was not about to preside over the dissolution of the British Empire. The French and the Dutch, too, sought the return of their colonies.

As he became increasingly weary and ill, Roosevelt's resolve weakened. A dramatic illustration of this had occurred in 1944 when Free French special forces came to New Delhi and asked Rusk to arrange for them to be dropped by parachute into Indochina. Unsure what to do, Rusk called the War Department asking for a statement of American policy in Indochina. Months went by without an answer. Rusk sent follow-up cables, and a staff officer sent to Washington returned without an answer. Finally, in January 1945, came the reply, in the form of a Joint Chiefs of Staff position paper entitled "America's Policy Toward Indochina." On the first page it was stated that "the Joint Chiefs of Staff had asked the President for a statement of current policy in Indochina. The President's reply is contained in Annex I." When Rusk flipped the pages to Annex I, he found the words: "When asked by the Joint Chiefs of Staff for a statement of U.S. policy on Indochina, the President replied 'I don't want to hear any more about Indochina.' "

By April 1945, President Roosevelt was dead, and the new President, Harry S Truman, absorbed with myriad other matters, was even less disposed to reassert the original American purpose. The control of policy shifted to the British, and at the end of the war Lord Louis Mountbatten received the surrender of Japanese forces in Indochina. The British went back to Hong Kong, Burma, Malaya, and Singapore and remained in India. The Dutch went back to Indonesia. The French returned to Indochina. Only the Philippines was granted its independence by the Americans.

The scene was set for future tragedies and wars. The movement for independence and the dissolution of empire was inexorable. After Churchill, the government of Prime Minister Clement Attlee switched course and began the process of granting freedom to the British colonial empire in Asia. The Dutch, under pressure from the United States, granted Indonesia independence. But France, beset by weak postwar governments, fought to retain its colonies, inaugurating the Indochina wars. Ultimately, America also would be drawn into this conflict in the tragedy of the Vietnam War.

Just after the Fourth of July holiday in 1945, Rusk began his new job in the Operations Division of the War Department General Staff. It was one of the most interesting and sensitive posts in the government. As the war drew to a close, the War Department and the Joint Chiefs faced military decisions that everyone recognized would have enormous political consequences. Such was true in the case of the surrender and occupation of Germany, which was handled by the specially created European Advisory Commission made up of representatives of the Allied powers. The American delegation included representa-

tives of the State, War, and Navy Departments, but when this proved
cumbersome from the American point of view, a major new administrative body was created to handle politico-military affairs: the State-
War-Navy Coordinating Committee, known as SWNCC. The three
members of SWNCC were civilians, one from each of the departments
represented. The member from the War Department was the Assistant
Secretary, John J. McCloy. SWNCC became extraordinarily successful in bringing foreign policy formulations into military decision-
making. The secret of that success was the staff work carried out by
the Operations Division, the famous OPD of the War Department,
which also advised the Joint Chiefs of Staff, thus bringing together the
State Department and the armed forces the way the Joint Chiefs'
system coordinated the different branches of the armed forces. Rusk
found himself a member of the key committee of the OPD, the strategic policy section.

By any standard the policy section of the OPD was a remarkable
group of men who combined high intelligence and achievement with
wartime operational experience. The chief was Charles H. "Tick"
Bonesteel, a tall, genial man with a ready smile, and a Rhodes scholar
whom Rusk had known at Oxford. On the staff, besides Rusk, was
another Rhodes scholar, Colonel James McCormack, Jr., as well as
Colonel Ned Parker and Colonel Sidney Giffen, all of whom went on
to become three- or four-star generals. They reported to yet another
Rhodes scholar, General George Lincoln, predictably called "Abe"
by his men. Lincoln's section was responsible for briefing McCloy,
Secretary of War Stimson, and General Marshall.

The policy section had uniquely wide responsibilities covering all
matters that came before the Joint Chiefs and SWNCC. Its members
were called on to give quick but informed judgments on the myriad
problems of the world of 1945. They prepared "action papers" that
thoroughly analyzed problems and recommended specific decisions
and how they should be implemented, papers that usually had to be
produced in a few days or even a few hours. The group worked colle-
gially, as equals, discussing and debating problems and circulating
draft memoranda for comment by other members of the group. Their
camaraderie helped them to work out differences, and their completed
staff work represented the consensus of the group on the way a particular problem should be handled.

Rusk's role in this group was very important. He not only came up
with ideas and knew how to express them, but he was also essential
to the consensus-building process of policy formulation. His instinct

for compromise and his nonconfrontational style helped make things happen. The policy section rapidly acquired great influence and respect in the government. Tick Bonesteel's wife, Alice, thought so highly of Rusk that she bet him a case of champagne that he would end up as either President or Secretary of State.

At the time Rusk joined the policy section, it was in the midst of preparing papers for use at what would be the last of the series of wartime conferences, held at Potsdam in the ruins of Berlin in July 1945. A wide range of issues had to be briefed—such matters as American participation in the newly born United Nations, possible Soviet expansionism, the occupation of defeated Germany, and policy toward China and Indochina. The policy section was also concerned with how to find adequate food supplies to feed the people of Germany. But the most crucial set of issues faced by American planners concerned Japan. The European war had been won; V-E day was on May 8, and many of the key postwar decisions concerning Europe had already been made. By contrast, the war in the Pacific, which was primarily an American war, was still going on, with final decisions yet to be made about how to defeat Japan and the terms of surrender and occupation.

In July 1945 the policy section was studying two possible ways of forcing the unconditional surrender of Japan. Primary reliance was on the "invasion strategy," which involved landings by American troops on the southern island of Kyushu and on the main island of Honshu. The landings, scheduled for late 1945 and early 1946, were to be preceded by an air-sea blockade. Second, thought was given to the possibility of surrender before an invasion, and it was decided to issue a surrender ultimatum to Japan at the Potsdam Conference. The wording of the ultimatum was composed by General Lincoln and the policy section, and it was issued publicly to Japan on July 26, 1945.

Of course, at this time the most closely held secret in the American government was that the atomic bomb had been successfully tested and was ready for use against Japan. Only a few top OPD planners in the War Department had any knowledge of the bomb. Although General Lincoln knew in a general way what was afoot, Rusk and the other members of the policy section were not let in on the secret. Planning for the defeat of Japan by conventional methods went on as if the atomic bomb did not exist. Rusk had heard rumors of a top-secret military program named "Manhattan" involving a "big bomb," but he was aware that he was not supposed to know about it and, in true military fashion, did not make any inquiries. In fact, it was not until the Japanese Premier, Kantaro Suzuki, rejected the Potsdam surrender ultimatum on August 3 that President Truman, with the concurrence of Churchill and Stalin, decided to use the atomic bomb on Japan.

It was one of the climactic decisions of history. John J. McCloy later told Rusk that even George Marshall was frightened by the magnitude of the event. Marshall came into McCloy's office one day rubbing his hands together in nervous agitation. "McCloy," he said, "please don't let them ask me whether or not we should drop the atomic bomb on Japan. That's just not a military question." In the end, Truman alone made the decision. He told McCloy he went as far as he could to avoid it; he would have been happier had he not dropped the bombs.

Rusk was at his desk in the War Department on August 6, 1945, when a message came through that the atomic bomb had been dropped on Hiroshima. Everyone immediately recognized it as a momentous event. Rusk remembers one of his group saying, "This means war is turning on itself and is devouring its own tail. From this point forward there will be no sense in governments resolving their differences by war."

Rusk was briefed along with the other members of the policy section on the preliminary estimates of destruction and the number of people killed and injured in Hiroshima. Despite the horror of it, he never wavered in defending President Truman's decision to drop the bomb. He regarded it as a necessary alternative to the invasion of Japan, justifying it as saving more lives than it cost. It was estimated that at least half a million U.S. casualties could be expected in an invasion. Many thousands of Japanese would have died as well in defending their country and in the saturation bombing of Japanese cities that would have preceded the invasion. Many years later, when he traveled to Japan as Secretary of State, Rusk would lay a wreath on the monument to the dead of Hirosima. When the Japanese press asked him whether he had any regrets, he would tell them, "I regret every casualty of that war on *both* sides, Japanese and American, from Pearl Harbor to Tokyo Bay."

Events proceeded rapidly after the devastation of Hiroshima. On August 8 the Russians entered the war against Japan. On August 9 another atomic bomb was dropped, on Nagasaki, with equally devastating results. On August 10 the Japanese announced their intention to surrender.

Now it was time for the planners in the policy section to deal with the complicated political and military questions arising out of the surrender. A whole series of papers had been drawn up for the contingency of an early Japanese capitulation, but now these had to be reworked. Colonel Bonesteel pointed out to General Lincoln in a memo on August 9: "For your convenience a checklist indicating unfinished business re early surrender of Japan is attached. First and foremost is the fact that there is no approved surrender document, surrender proclamation, or General Order No. 1 in existence."

The policy section thereafter assumed the central role in planning for the surrender and occupation of Japan. There was little time because of the suddenness of the capitulation, and Rusk and the other colonels in the section worked practically around the clock. The decisions and documents prepared had to be approved by SWNCC and the Joint Chiefs as well as President Truman. They also had to be sent for approval to the Allies—Britain, China, and the Soviet Union. The surrender date was fixed at September 2. In the bright sunlight of hindsight, the surrender and occupation of Japan were among the most successful operations of their kind in history. That much of the work was done in a little over three weeks was remarkable. It was one of the great staff actions of World War II.

Because the drafting of documents and memoranda was a group effort, it is not possible to isolate Rusk's role in the process. He was not assigned any particular area of responsibility; rather he worked on virtually everything together with the other four staff members of the policy section. All were fully aware of the importance of the task and the fact that their work would help to determine the postwar organization of Japanese society and future U.S.-Japanese relations.

Rusk worked on the drafting of the surrender documents and MacArthur's General Order Number 1 (the occupation decree), which had to be ready and approved by all parties in time for the surrender ceremony aboard the U.S.S. *Missouri* on September 2. The preparations were extremely hectic, and a message was sent to MacArthur that there wasn't time enough to have the documents suitably embossed. They would have to fly the documents out to Japan just in time for the surrender ceremony. Rusk was given the opportunity to be one of the officers to go to Japan and witness the surrender, but he was too exhausted to make the trip. As it happened, when the colonels who went took a small boat out to the battleship *Missouri* to deliver the documents on the morning of September 2, they were met at the stairs of the ship by one of MacArthur's aides, who denied them permission to come up. "The General says it won't be necessary for you to come aboard,'' they were told. MacArthur didn't want anyone from Washington to deflect attention from himself. The disappointed officers had to turn around and fly back to Washington without witnessing the surrender. This was a side of MacArthur's character that Rusk would see more of later.

The signing ceremony aboard the *Missouri* was the exclusive prerogative of the prideful Supreme Commander, General Douglas MacArthur. With it the terrible scourge of World War II finally came to an end, exactly six years and one day after Hitler's invasion of Poland began the hostilities.

The war had greatly tempered and seasoned the idealistic young college professor Dean Rusk. Added to his education in Europe, which had allowed him to see the first faint glimmerings of the coming conflict, was his military service in the heart of the great continent of Asia, where he played an important role in military planning and intelligence. He saw the conflict of World War II as a terrible failure that must not be allowed to happen again. By both happy coincidence and his own skills and background, he was now being drawn slowly but inexorably into that establishment circle that would shape the foreign policy initiatives which he would both help formulate and later inherit. He had been an eyewitness to a world blown apart; now he would be among those charged with putting it together again.

PART TWO

THE TRUMAN YEARS

Apprenticeship at State: Cold War
Confrontations in Iran and Greece

I N 1945 the huge mass of the Eurasian continent lay virtually in ruins, physically and economically shattered by the terrible war. Japan alone had suffered the agony of nuclear attack, but other nations, from China to France, were also devastated by the long conflict. While the fighting continued, there had been little time or inclination to think about postwar political and economic reconstruction. Now, however, the Allies had to confront the urgent question of how to create a stable and peaceful world order.

Even before the end of the fighting, one dominant issue emerged for American policymakers: whether cooperation was possible with the Soviet Union and at what price. The United States had the atomic bomb and was physically untouched by the war. The Soviet Union had been ravaged, but the Red Army was occupying most of Eastern Europe, and later in 1945, Russian troops would enter Manchuria and Korea in the Far East. The looming shadow of Russian totalitarianism mocked the idealism of President Roosevelt's grand design for a postwar alliance between the Soviet Union and the United States and the Atlantic Charter agreement with Churchill, which envisioned a Wilsonian world of free trade and free, democratic nations. But America was slow to break with its wartime ally. Despite warnings from men like Ambassador Averell Harriman in Moscow about Russian adventurism, the U.S.-Soviet mésalliance endured, much like a tie that persists between two lovers who are unable to make the final break after the end of an affair.

Rusk's tour of duty on the staff of SWNCC began in July, on the eve of the Potsdam Conference, by which time the main lines of the postwar settlement in Europe were already set. The four zones of occupation in Germany and the four-power arrangements in Berlin had been agreed by Ambassador John G. Winant, the chief American delegate to the European Advisory Committee. At the Yalta Conference, in February 1945, Roosevelt had acceded to a Poland partially carved out of Germany and dominated by the Soviets. He had also granted the Russians concessions in the Far East: the southern half of Sakhalin, the Kuriles, the lease of a naval base at Port Arthur in China, the recognition of Soviet influence in Outer Mongolia and the international port of Dairen, and the control of the Chinese East Manchurian Railroad. In return, Stalin had agreed that the Soviets would enter the war against Japan within three months of the surrender of Germany. The accord was papered over with empty promises: that the Soviets would enter into a pact of friendship and cooperation with Chiang Kai-shek's Nationalist government in China and that free elections would be held in Austria, Hungary, Czechoslovakia, Bulgaria, Rumania, and Poland. Roosevelt was dealing with the power realities in Eastern Europe, where the Red Army had de facto control. "I didn't say the result was good," Roosevelt admitted. "I said it was the best I could do."

The Potsdam Conference convened in a place Rusk knew well from his student days in Berlin. President Truman even stayed in a house overlooking Griebnitz Lake in Babelsberg, which made Rusk wonder what had become of the German family he had lived with and his German friends nearby. At the conference, once again the war against Japan and the necessity to cooperate with the Russians dominated American diplomacy. Truman gave in to Stalin on the question of Polish administration of a part of Germany and agreed that it was desirable to resume normal relations with the countries of Eastern Europe, even though the Russians were obviously not going to permit free elections.

Rusk himself was acutely aware of the frictions that were developing with the Russians and was distrustful of their intentions. He knew that the Russians had not played a significant role in Asia. Not only did they decline to fight the Japanese, which was understandable given the German invasion of their country, but they refused to allow airfields in Siberia to be used to stage bombing or spy-overflight missions against Japan. Later at SWNCC he read many of Ambassador Harriman's dispatches from Moscow (some of which were undoubtedly written by George Kennan, then an unknown counselor at the Moscow embassy) about Soviet intentions and attitudes. Rusk was particularly concerned about the arrangements already agreed upon for the occupation of Germany and Eastern Europe. He believed it was a mistake to withdraw American forces from their forward positions in Czechoslovakia and eastern Germany. Another error was the failure of the United States to insist on a land corridor through eastern Germany to ensure Western access to Berlin. He did not share the view of many American officials that it was necessary to trust the Russians to preserve world peace in the postwar period. The Russians had shown their true colors at the San Francisco conference called to draft the United Nations Charter when they insisted upon Western acceptance of the puppet Communist regimes in Eastern Europe. The Soviets were out to dominate their neighbors and to prevent the fulfillment of democratic ideals in Europe.

But Rusk did not fault Roosevelt and Truman for failing to take a firmer line against the Russians. He understood the basic reasons for giving in to their demands for the present. Military concerns, he recalled many years later, dominated political considerations, and "everyone thought that the Russians would be needed to fight the Japanese." In July 1945 the general belief prevailed that it would take at least another year of heavy fighting to defeat Japan. The Japanese armies in Manchuria appeared formidable, and an invasion of the home islands would have to be mounted as well. Even those few who knew about the atomic bomb were not sure it would work, let alone produce an immediate Japanese capitulation.

As long as the war was going on, the only question was how to get it over with as quickly as possible. On a long airplane ride with General Marshall after the war, Rusk asked him why he had not taken Churchill's advice to invade Germany through the Balkan States, the "soft underbelly" of Europe. The basic reason, Marshall told him, was that such a course of action could not be justified from a military point of view. The Balkans were not "soft"; they were mountainous and difficult to fight in and hard to control. Roads were poor or nonexistent, and logistic support would have been a nightmare. Even a great army could be easily trapped and defeated. The first priority, Marshall said, was to win the war, and to do so before "our political and economic institutions melted out from under us." The quickest and best way was an attack across France and northern Europe. "I was not about to sacrifice our soldiers' lives for postwar political considerations," Marshall said.

Even so, Rusk later expressed great regret that more attention was not given to political considerations in 1945. There was a dearth of political leadership, he recalled. President Truman, whom Rusk later grew to respect and love, was still a novice, learning the ropes in the foreign policy field. And Rusk had little regard for the Secretary of State, Edward Stettinius, whom Truman had inherited from Roosevelt. Stettinius, formerly the lend-lease administrator, had been chosen by Roosevelt, who kept his own counsel, primarily because he wouldn't get in the way. In Rusk's opinion, Stettinius was "a nice man, but too dumb to be helpful." Rusk also thought Stettinius was particularly naïve when it came to dealing with the Russians. Truman finally woke up to the fact that he was being badly served, but he then appointed James Byrnes, a South Carolina politician who had been head of the Office of War Mobilization, to replace Stettinius as Secretary of State. Byrnes had little experience in foreign affairs, and the vacuum of political leadership continued at State.

After he learned of the existence of the atomic bomb, Rusk was particularly chagrined that an advisory political committee had not been established to explore the political implications of the new weapon. Policymakers thought only of the military uses of the bomb and ignored its potential political impact, especially on Stalin and the negotiations over Eastern Europe. They were also unprepared for the political effect of the bomb on Japan. Had the situation been handled adroitly, Japan perhaps could have been spared the bomb. A political committee could have at least "boxed the compass" of alternatives before the fateful decision to drop the bomb was made.

The flawed assumptions of American diplomacy became quickly apparent after the surrender of the Japanese. Because of the atomic bomb, there was no need after all for Russian help in defeating Japan. Nevertheless, the Russians entered the war in the Far East for three days in August, and the Red Army advanced in Manchuria and Korea with an eye more to political than military objectives. Now they demanded a victor's role in the postwar occupation of Japan.

Rusk, as well as the other staff members of SWNCC working on the Japanese surrender and occupation, saw clearly the implications of the new situation presented by the sudden Japanese capitulation. They were determined to keep the Soviets out and not to repeat the mistakes made in Europe. Rusk helped push for policies and decisions that, as he later put it, "gave America control of every wave of the Pacific Ocean." He initiated the idea that Pacific island territories administered by Japan under a League of Nations trusteeship should be turned over to the United States as a strategic trusteeship under the United Nations. And Russian demands for an occupation zone and joint administration of Japan were rejected. When a note was received from Stalin on August 16 asking that he be allowed to station Russian troops on the northern Japanese island of Hokkaido, Rusk and the other members of the SWNCC staff strongly opposed it, and Truman answered Stalin with a flat no. The disappointed Russian leader wired back, "I and my colleagues did not expect such an answer from you."

The surrender of Japan on September 2 was an American show; the Russians were briefed, but given no real choice over the selection of General Douglas MacArthur as Supreme Commander. The occupation of Japan would also be an American show, although Rusk argued in favor of retaining the Japanese emperor and working through him as much as possible in the postwar administration of the country. He reasoned that retention of the emperor was the best way to avoid Japanese resistance. This wise decision was a major factor in the success of the postwar reconstruction of the country and the establishment of a British-style democratic government in Japan.

On the continent of Asia, however, keeping the Russians out proved more difficult. In Indochina, it was arranged that the British would accept the Japanese surrender south of the 16th parallel. In China, a compromise was reached to allow the Russians to receive the surrender in Manchuria, while other areas were the responsibility of the Chinese under Chiang Kai-shek.

A major controversy within SWNCC erupted over whether to maintain an American presence in Korea. Byrnes advocated dispatching American troops to Korea to receive the Japanese surrender as far north as possible. McCloy at the War Department, however, feared trouble with either the Russians or the Japanese. The Army planners, who knew the difficulty of fighting in Asia, did not wish to have anything to do with an occupation on the Asian mainland.

At an all-night meeting of SWNCC heated wrangling over the issue ensued, and finally Rusk and Bonesteel were asked to propose a compromise. Wearily, they took a *National Geographic* map into an adjoining room to work out a plan while Byrnes and McCloy waited. Rusk firmly believed that the United States should maintain a "toehold" on the Asian continent, at least a symbolic presence. Korea was a relatively small peninsula, very close to Japan; it would be defensible, he thought, and a logical extension of the American position on the islands of Japan. From Korea the United States could help keep the Russians at bay and reinforce ties to the Nationalist government of China.

The question to be decided was how far north on the Korean peninsula American forces should accept the Japanese surrender. The Red Army was already in northern Korea, and there was no doubt in anyone's mind that the Russians were poised to occupy the entire peninsula. Rusk looked at the map. The line had to be identifiable and far enough north to include the capital city of Seoul. He searched for a natural boundary, such as a river or a mountain range. There was none. Only the line of latitudinal measurement—the 38th parallel— caught his eye. That would have to be it. It was a boundary that could easily be identified on any map. Bonesteel agreed, and the two men emerged to explain the proposal to the waiting committee. SWNCC accepted the idea of the 38th parallel with little discussion. Later, Rusk was somewhat surprised that the Russians also accepted it without protest.

Such a seemingly insignificant determination to select a place to receive the Japanese surrender turned out to be a momentous decision. This latitudinal line on a *National Geographic* map arbitrarily selected by tired men in the middle of the night would become the boundary between North and South Korea. Neither Rusk nor the others who made the decision were aware of the history of the 38th parallel. They did not know that in 1896 the Russians and the Japanese had signed a formal compact dividing Korea into two spheres of influence along this line. Nor did they know that the 38th parallel had been an administrative line for Japan—the boundary between two zones of occupation during World War II. Unwittingly, the Americans had selected a boundary that the Russians would look upon as a division of Korea into two geographic spheres of influence, one Russian and the other American. Tragically, another war would be fought when that boundary was violated.

After V-J day and the surrender of Japan, the vast war machine built by the United States was rapidly demobilized. The war was over, and Americans wanted to get on with peace and make up for lost time. Men shed their uniforms to return home, and machines and materials of war were quickly and quietly retired. By the summer of 1946 there was not a single division of the Army or a single group in the Air Force that was considered ready for combat. The Navy's ships were being put into mothballs as fast as berths could be found. The defense budget was scaled down by about 50 percent to a little over $11 billion a year.

Rusk felt strongly that such a complete demobilization was a mistake, but he recognized that politically no one, not even President Truman, could stop it. Nevertheless, he thought that the situation "subjected Stalin to intolerable temptations." It reminded him of an incident from his days in Berlin in 1933, when he took a canoe out on a lake and pulled it up on shore while he went into a restaurant for lunch. When he came out the canoe was gone. Rusk notified the police, and about an hour later they arrived towing the canoe. "Here is your canoe," they said. "We have the thief and he will be punished. But we're also fining *you* five marks for tempting thieves, because you did not lock up your canoe." In the same way, Rusk thought, the total demobilization after the war tempted the Russians, and he predicted as early as 1945 that great difficulties lay ahead. He did not believe that postwar cooperation with the Russians would come easily, given the Russians' character. Even during the war there had been strains. The Russians were bitter that the Allies had waited until 1944 to open up a second front in Europe. The Americans thought the Russians were late in coming in against Japan. Though the weight of the Russian effort against Hitler had been of extraordinary importance—Rusk shuddered to think what might have happened if Hitler had not made the great mistake of attacking the Soviet Union—there had been precious little cooperation between the two powers against either Germany or Japan.

After the Japanese surrender in September 1945, Rusk's work at SWNCC became less interesting and more routine. SWNCC itself, which had been at the very heart of the policy-formulating process, functioning much as the National Security Council (in many ways a SWNCC successor) would in future times, moved off center stage. In Japan most of the details of the occupation were in MacArthur's hands, and in Europe the influence of the State Department was ascendant under the new Secretary, James Byrnes. The War Department was concerned chiefly with demobilization.

The Russians tipped their hand at the London and Moscow conferences on Eastern Europe, which were held in September and December of 1945. In London, Byrnes was restrained chiefly by the presence of the Republican foreign policy spokesman, John Foster Dulles, who sided with the hard-liners in rejecting any Balkan peace agreements or recognition of the Eastern European states unless the Russians permitted the free elections they had promised. The London Conference broke up in October without agreement, and the myth of cooperation between the Soviet Union and the West was at last fully exposed.

Byrnes persisted, however, and agreed to go to Moscow to appeal directly to Stalin. The Moscow Conference was convened in December, and Byrnes, out of touch with advisers in Washington, negotiated an agreement with Stalin that promised Western recognition of the Soviet puppet governments in Bulgaria and Rumania and the establishment of a United Nations commission on atomic control.

Rusk was appalled when he read the communiqué of the conference, which he considered an appeasement document. Byrnes had been outsmarted by the Russians because of his anxiousness for an agreement. Stalin's hand had been strengthened in Bulgaria and Rumania in return for what George Kennan called "fig leaves of democratic procedure," consisting of Soviet promises to cooperate with the non-Communist opposition in those countries. Rusk was pleased, however, at the agreement to set up the United Nations Atomic Energy Commission, which listed among its goals the elimination of nuclear weapons and the establishment of controls to ensure the use of atomic energy only for peaceful purposes. He knew that the Russians were working on an atomic bomb of their own, and hoped for an international system of controls on such weapons.

For Rusk, worse than the Moscow agreement itself was the manner in which Byrnes had acted in negotiating it. He had not only cut off the channels of communication with SWNCC and the State Department, but also with President Truman himself. Byrnes told Ambassador Harriman in Moscow that he was not going to send any telegrams to Washington because "the President has given me complete authority." He had also issued the communiqué of the Moscow agreement without clearing it in advance with Truman.

This was unpardonable high-handedness on Byrnes's part. It was an open secret in the higher echelons at State and War that he regarded Truman as his inferior in knowledge and experience and thought that by all rights he should be President instead of Truman. He rankled because he had narrowly lost the fight to be Roosevelt's Vice President in 1944, in which case he would have become President. This, together with Byrnes's natural bent toward independence, caused him to act as if he were indeed the President.

Rusk thought Byrnes had overstepped his authority as Secretary of State. After all, the U.S. constitution vests the entire legal power of the executive in the office of the President. The Secretary of State has authority only through the President, and as such he does not have a policy of his own. Only the President has a policy, and it is the Secretary's duty to be his confidential foreign policy adviser and to announce and carry out the *President's* policy. The handling of the

Moscow agreement violated these basic tenets, and Rusk felt Truman had every right to be extremely displeased with his Secretary of State and would look for the right moment to fire him. Truman was in fact furious, and Byrnes submitted his resignation a few months later. He was succeeded by the austere but brilliant General Marshall.

During the last months of Rusk's time at SWNCC he became involved with several matters relating to the United Nations. The world organization, a pet project of Roosevelt and his Secretary of State Cordell Hull, was about to make its debut on the stage of international politics. Its charter had been signed on June 26, 1945; it was quickly ratified by the United States, the Soviet Union, and a majority of other states and came into force on October 24. The crucial first sessions of the important organs of the U.N., including the Security Council and the General Assembly, were scheduled for January 1946. Rusk worked on the preparations for these meetings, especially the American proposal for the provision of armed forces to the Security Council under Article 43 of the charter.

In February 1946 Rusk was discharged from the Army. For some time he had been thinking about what to do upon his return to civilian life. His first thought was to complete his law school education. He needed only one year's worth of credits to get his degree, and had almost decided to enroll in Harvard Law School. Another option was to stay in the military. He was assured that a general's stars would eventually come if he chose a military career.

In the end he chose neither, because the State Department offered him a position he could not refuse. Working for SWNCC on U.N. matters, he had come to know many of his counterparts at State, including Joseph Johnson, chief of the Division of International Security Affairs. Johnson (who later became president of the Carnegie Endowment for International Peace) asked Rusk to be the assistant chief of the division and continue to work on U.N. affairs, much as he had done at SWNCC. The appeal of the position was great, because now, after the war, the State Department was clearly dominant in the foreign policy field. Rusk liked Johnson and enjoyed working with him, so he accepted the job, at last realizing his old dream of someday working at the Department of State. Interestingly, the Division of International Security Affairs was a part of the Office of Special Political Affairs at State, whose director was a man named Alger Hiss. No storm clouds were yet visible on the horizon at State, however, and Rusk was supremely happy at his new job. His personal life, too, was serene. Virginia was content to remain in Washington, and shortly after he started at State, on March 30, 1946, his second son, Richard Geary, was born.

Rusk arrived at State already well known and liked by his peers. He had acquired the reputation of being intelligent, extremely hard-working, and an excellent colleague to boot. He was a man with the qualities of character and mind to handle the toughest assignments: a professor who was also a soldier and a man of action. He wrote clear, crisp prose, and he was not afraid of responsibility or of making decisions. But he was known as very reserved, a private man.

Rusk's education, interests, and wartime experience had coalesced into a consistent set of ideas and theories that guided his thinking in foreign affairs and international politics. His political philosophy and his analysis of international predicaments were as deeply felt and thought out as those of his famous contemporary George F. Kennan. Unlike the intellectual and eloquent Kennan, however, he never felt compelled to put them forth publicly. They were a part of his soul, the product of years at Davidson, Oxford, Mills College, and the CBI. Because he was such a private person, he never saw the necessity of revealing his fundamental tenets and beliefs, except obliquely. They would find expression in the conduct of his new job.

Rusk's philosophy was both idealistic and old-fashioned. He believed that human beings make judgments according to deeply felt beliefs and that the fundamental sources of normative criteria in international politics must be morality and international law. International law should determine the behavior of nation-states and set the criteria for making judgments about international conflict. Thus international organizations such as the United Nations have a significant role to play in relations between states because they are manifestations of the rule of law among nations. An exchange Rusk once had with Dean Acheson revealed his beliefs. As he was listening to a Rusk homily about the view of international law on a particular matter, Acheson in exasperation exclaimed, "Dammit, Dean, the survival of nations is not a matter of law." Rusk retorted, "On the contrary, in a nuclear world, the survival of nations may depend upon law."

Of course Rusk was cognizant that the League of Nations and Wilsonian principles of international law had failed to prevent World War II. That did not lead him to reject the rule of law, but rather to reaffirm it. What had led to war was the unwillingness of the democracies and other law-abiding nations to check the course of those nations that were violating the law.

By education and conviction Rusk believed that the nations charged with the greatest responsibility in maintaining the rule of law in the world were the United States and Great Britain. This position stemmed not from any superiority of the Anglo-American peoples, but from their culture and traditions. The great ideas of law and freedom had their origin in Britain and were transmitted to and developed in the United States. Thus Rusk idealized the United States as having a special mission in raising the moral standards of international society.

His faith in the Anglo-Saxon tradition of law and liberty as a beacon for the entire human race led Rusk to be, paradoxically, a convinced anticolonialist. He accurately predicted the swift and inevitable dissolution of colonial empires after the war, and thought that the United States and Britain should assist this process. Nevertheless, he was enough of a realist to leaven these views with a dose of pragmatism. He did not believe in universal American intervention to set the world right, but in the limited use of American power based on what was possible in any given situation. American conduct should be judged by the same standards of law and morality as that of other states. The litmus test should be whether an action was supportable under recognized principles of international law. Rusk rejected skepticism about the role of international law. He continued to believe that "most governments act most of the time in accordance with the law, and international law is therefore a pervasive element in relations among governments. Any nation without a reasonable legal case for its action is in for trouble in the international community."

Rusk's legalist and moralist viewpoint ran counter to the mood of the postwar period. To many people, the war had repudiated Wilson's idealistic vision of the relevance of the rule of law and international organizations. Critics and scholars such as Hans Morgenthau, Walter Lippmann, and George Kennan believed that trust in the rule of law for keeping the peace was a chimera, exposed by the carnage of World War II. These men held a skeptical view of international law: law, like ethics, justice, morality, and even ideology, was merely a weak reed in the game of geopolitical power among nations. National self-interest, not law, was the wellspring of nation-state behavior. International law, therefore, could have no instrumental significance in decision-making or in ordering the world, at least in serious disputes involving vital interests. Nation-states were restrained not by law but by the inherent limits of their own power and the constraints imposed by international political realities. The United States was merely another player in this power game, trying to shape a world congruent with its values and interests. The ambition to abolish war and power politics and to subordinate national interests to law and diplomacy in the international community was a utopian dream. George Kennan, in particular, embodied this view, and Rusk and Kennan clashed frequently in policy debates in the late 1940s when both held important State Department posts.

Kennan, an eloquent and profound thinker and writer, with a novelist's eye for phrasing and detail, had burst onto the foreign policy scene in February 1946, when his famous "Long Telegram" arrived from Moscow. In flowing, elegant prose, he sounded a tocsin against the Russians, warning that "efforts will be made to advance the official limits of Soviet power." The Soviet challenge was "the greatest task our diplomacy has ever faced": their aim was that "our traditional way of life be destroyed." Kennan elaborated on these views in the equally famous "X" article that appeared in *Foreign Affairs* in 1947. His viewpoint was personal and visionary, shaped in the cauldron of World War II and by his service at the American Embassy in Moscow.

But Kennan's impact on the change of direction that swept over American foreign policy in the period immediately after World War II has been exaggerated. A new policy of firmness toward the Soviet Union was in process long before the "X" article and even prior to the Long Telegram of 1946. The primary issue in the postwar world was "how to deal with the Russians," and the American about-face from unrealistic efforts at cooperation to direct opposition to Russian aims and actions occurred for the most part in 1945. Rusk and his colleagues at SWNCC and the prominent staffers at State were then adopting what was considered a "hard line" on relations with the Soviets. President Truman himself was a convert to the new toughness that followed the Japanese surrender.

Kennan's views had an impact, however, because of their eloquence and because they reflected the firsthand experience of an expert on intimate terms with Russian behavior. He was also preaching to the converted—telling people in Washington what they already knew or suspected to be the case: that the Soviet Union was a ruthless dictatorship whose antidemocratic and totalitarian values conflicted totally with the West, and that it was engaged in an unprincipled campaign of projecting its power to subvert the Western democracies and their values and institutions. Kennan therefore decried any attempt to make friends with the Russians by extending economic or political aid.

Rusk agreed with these views when he read the Long Telegram in 1946. He regarded it as a tour de force, a masterly and systematic exposition of Soviet behavior. He was less enthusiastic, however, about Kennan's view that Stalin, unlike Hitler, was cautious and unlikely to be adventurous in extending Soviet power. To Rusk a dictator in a totalitarian state was inherently dangerous, liable to unleash forces beyond even his own control.

Rusk also differed with Kennan on his prescription for U.S. relations with the Soviets in Europe and elsewhere. Kennan thought in terms of power realities and advocated the acceptance of a balance of power in the world between the Soviet Union and the United States. He believed that frank acceptance of spheres of influence would lead to negotiations to resolve differences and to a relaxation of tensions. Rusk was among those who opposed the balance-of-power idea. He argued that the Russians might control Eastern Europe, but the United States and other nations should not sanction it by accepting Soviet domination when it ran contrary to international law.

After Kennan came to Washington as head of the Policy Planning Staff of the State Department in 1947, Rusk became acquainted with him personally for the first time. By then Kennan was a public figure, celebrated by important journalists like Arthur Krock of *The New York Times* and lionized on the Washington cocktail party circuit. The two men disliked each other from the start. Rusk found Kennan insufferably effete and garrulous. Kennan spouted farfetched schemes that were totally useless as a practical matter, while Rusk, distrustful of "visionaries," was concerned with, as he put it, "what to do tomorrow morning at nine o'clock." As a practical man himself, Marshall ignored Kennan as much as possible, as did Rusk.

Rusk also found Kennan to be strangely inconsistent in his views. He had a dire opinion of Russian intentions and even coined the term "containment" as his prescribed American policy toward the Soviet Union. But in concrete terms he was "soft" in dealings with the Soviets. Whenever the Russians made any demand, however outrageous, Kennan always wanted to negotiate. "If the Russians wanted two provinces of Turkey," Rusk recalled many years later, "George would give them one of them." He, on the other hand, believed that when a Russian demand was contrary to international law, "we should simply have given them a flat 'no' for an answer."

The two men held opposite views about the role of the United Nations in world affairs. Rusk irritated Kennan with his tireless advocacy of the U.N. in every crisis. Kennan argued that the U.N. was not taken seriously by the Russians and could only complicate negotiations by dividing the world into pro- and anti-Soviet blocs. Rusk thought the U.N. could play a useful role because it represented the world consensus on the right or wrong of a question. As a practical matter, it was also a body in which the United States could count on an automatic majority in favor of its position on an issue. The Russians might not agree with that position and would try to undermine it, but they would not be able to ignore or keep from being influenced by the whole body. Kennan said that humanity was divided between those who placed an emphasis on order and those who placed it on justice, and he opted for order, believing human justice to be imperfect and subjective. Rusk, of course, placed the emphasis on justice. Further, he could not understand why Kennan had such a reluctance in affirming the moral superiority of American values and objectives over Soviet values. Rusk was an unabashed idealist about the American system; Kennan disliked talking of values and objectives or ends in favor of emphasizing means—good form and good manners.

Rusk and Kennan were, however, in partial agreement on the fundamental idea of containment as the postwar approach to dealing with the Soviet Union. Both men recognized that the word "containment" was just a label and rejected a simplistic view that it consisted of drawing lines on a map. Kennan, in his "X" article, called for the "adroit and vigilant application of counter-force at a series of constantly shifting geographical and political points" or at least "at every point where they [the Russians] show signs of encroaching upon the interests of a peaceful and stable world." That strategy was criticized at the time by people like Walter Lippmann as being a license for universal American military intervention. Rusk knew that Kennan never meant "containment" in that way; it was not primarily a military doctrine and it could not have universal application. But Kennan did believe containment to be a doctrine primarily designed to maintain an international power equilibrium. He also believed—despite the broad rhetoric of the "X" article—that "we must decide which areas [of the world] are key areas and which are not, which ones we must hold to with all our strength and which we may yield tactically." Rusk, in contrast, believed containment should be pragmatically based on the realities of limited American power and that diplomatic means should be its primary instrument. Further, it should be used to uphold the tenets of international law and morality in the world. Rusk also considered Kennan's view of "key areas of the world" to be too narrow. In his view, both Kennan and Acheson ignored the entire world outside the North Atlantic nations. He was opposed to such "parochialism" and saw American security interests and international law as relevant to the nations emerging from colonialism as well.

Both Rusk and Kennan held that the United States would need collective security alliances in the postwar world. But again they differed on ultimate ends. Kennan's view was that alliances were necessary only to help maintain the world power balance; Rusk saw them as an instrument for securing and maintaining the rule of law in the world. Along with Kennan, Rusk believed that in the interests of a peaceful world it was necessary for the United States to come to an accommodation with the Russians. He never tired of saying that, in a nuclear world, both nations must realize that they had to live together on the same small planet. Thus, facing down the Russians must not be the only element of U.S. policy; it must be combined with a persistent, continuing search for points of agreement. But agreements should be based on concepts of law and morality, not solely on the maintenance of a geopolitical balance of power. We had no troops in Iran; we had no guerrillas in Greece and Turkey; we were not trying to take over Berlin or set up puppet regimes in Eastern Europe. For Rusk, there was no doubt that the Soviets were the major threat to justice and peace in the world.

But he had little time for theoretical discussions in his job at State. The Office of Special Political Affairs, where he served as assistant chief of a division, was the agency within the State Department that was responsible for U.N. affairs. Rusk represented the department in the negotiations of the U.N.'s Military Staff Committee, which, under Article 43 of the U.N. Charter, was to preside over the creation of a U.N. peacekeeping force. In a memorandum on March 26, 1946, he suggested the appointment of a subcommittee to formulate the basic principles governing the organization of the U.N. forces. Once these principles had been approved, the contributions of individual nations could be specified. When the negotiations came to naught, Rusk blamed the Russians, citing their failure to cooperate with the Military Staff Committee.

Most of Rusk's time during the early months of 1946 was taken up with the first major crisis faced by the world body, the Soviet occupation of northern Iran. The presence of Soviet troops in Iran was, like so much else, a legacy of the war. Iran had been used as a backdoor route by the Allies in supplying the Soviet Union. To protect this aid pipeline and to keep Iranian oil from Hitler, Britain put troops in the south and the Russians occupied the north in 1942. At the wartime conference in Tehran in 1943, the Allies agreed that all foreign troops should be withdrawn from Iran not later than six months after the end of hostilities. In September 1945, Soviet Foreign Minister Vyacheslav Molotov agreed to a pullout by March 2, 1946. However, the Soviets used the presence of their troops in the northern province of Azerbaijan to encourage a local Communist group (the Tudeh party) to revolt against the Shah. The Soviets also blocked the Shah from reasserting control in the province.

The Iranian situation was viewed as a matter of the gravest concern by the Truman administration. The United States sent a note of protest to the Soviets suggesting that the Allied troop withdrawal date be moved up to January 1, 1946. When Molotov refused, Truman called it "another outrage." The feeling in the administration was that the Soviets were after a warm-water port on the Persian Gulf. By biting off the province of Azerbaijan they could leave their troops in Iran and in due course take control of the entire country. There was no military capability to prevent this, since both the United States and Britain were proceeding to demobilize their forces. The U.N. offered the only recourse. Dean Acheson, then Under Secretary of State, held a series of talks with the Iranian Ambassador to the United Nations, Hussein Ala, and Iran brought a formal complaint before the Security Council in January 1946.

Rusk's role in the crisis was to develop the arguments in favor of the American position, demanding that the Soviets cease their support of the Tudeh party and proceed with the withdrawal of their troops. He worked closely with Acheson and helped to write speeches for Secretary of State Byrnes, who was called in to participate personally in the Security Council debates to give credence to the importance the Americans attached to the matter. Rusk sat just behind Byrnes during the Security Council debates.

The Iran crisis did not evoke threats of military force against the Soviets. The United States simply did not have the military capability for such an action. It did not even have a credible nuclear deterrent. Rusk was told that the Nagasaki bomb was the last nuclear weapon the nation had in its stockpile, and he assumed Stalin knew this as well. So in the Security Council debates, as Rusk later recalled, "we fussed and we scolded and we criticized and we mobilized the opinion of the governments of the world and built . . . pressures on the Soviet Union."

The March 2 deadline came and went, but the Soviets made no move to withdraw from Iran. When the Security Council voted to accept jurisdiction over the dispute, the Soviet delegation, led by Andrei Gromyko, promptly walked out. The Security Council then passed a U.S.-sponsored resolution directing U.N. Secretary General Trygve Lie to ascertain Soviet intentions regarding the withdrawal of troops. In late March, after discussions with the Soviets, the Secretary General reported that they were ready to withdraw their troops within six weeks. But Acheson and Rusk were skeptical, and they arranged to bring the matter up once again before the Security Council to keep the pressure on the Soviets. When the Iranian government itself opposed a resumption of the debate, Rusk mounted a successful legal argument that the affair must remain on the Security Council's agenda because the government of Iran was under Soviet duress.

To the surprise of almost everyone in Washington, the Soviets kept their promise to withdraw their troops. And when, shortly thereafter, Iranian troops moved into Azerbaijan to end separatist rule, the crisis was successfully resolved. Only in Moscow was the real reason known for the Soviet withdrawal, but Rusk was convinced that the weight of world public opinion brought to bear in the forum of the United Nations had played a critical role. He guessed that Stalin ultimately concluded that keeping troops in Azerbaijan was not worth the price it cost in terms of adverse propaganda. The lesson for Rusk was that the Soviets could be influenced by collective world pressure. The United Nations, then safely under American control, could be an effective instrument against Soviet adventures. The Iranian episode reaffirmed Rusk's faith that the Soviets could be compelled by Western firmness to comply with international law. Rusk did not know that Truman had secretly sent Stalin an ultimatum that the United States would send in troops if the Russians did not withdraw.

In the summer of 1946 Rusk received an offer to go back to the Pentagon to work as special assistant to the Secretary of War, Robert P. Patterson. He considered the offer seriously because he was again thinking about a career in the military. Morale at State was ebbing because Byrnes had lost Truman's confidence. At least in the military, Rusk thought, he would be insulated from that kind of political infighting. Besides, he idolized General George Marshall, who was then off on a special presidential mission to China. Marshall's career made Rusk believe that he could enter the military and remain involved with international politics. He liked the idea of having a foot, like Marshall, in both camps.

So Rusk accepted the job with Patterson and shifted over to the

War Department, no longer part of the machinery of government so much as he was the personal extension of the Secretary of War. The breadth of his responsibilities was immense. He worked with Acheson on problems of Eastern Europe, particularly on policy related to Yugoslavia, where Marshal Josip Broz Tito was showing signs of independence from the Russians. Patterson was also involved in dismantling the strict racial segregation of the U.S. armed forces, and Rusk drafted some of the first military orders implementing that policy. He also followed the workings of the Far Eastern Commission, which was established by the Allies to supervise the occupation of Japan. Attending its meetings in the small Japanese Embassy building on Massachusetts Avenue, Rusk monitored the deliberations of the commission during its consideration of the draft Japanese constitution. Another matter he worked on was the procurement of food supplies for Germany and Japan to get them through the winter of 1946–47. And in the important field of government intelligence operations, both Patterson and Rusk fought hard for a centralized intelligence arrangement—the creation of what would become the CIA.

Then, in January 1947, President Truman announced that George Marshall was to be the new Secretary of State. Suddenly the State Department took on a new allure and a fresh image both publicly and for Washington insiders. Truman considered Marshall to be ''the greatest living American,'' and it was clear that State would again be at the center stage of foreign policy. Rusk was elated with the appointment and lost no time angling for a job at State. During his tenure at SWNCC he had worked closely with Marshall, and in many ways it had been the best time of his life. He did not feel it was right, however, to go to Marshall directly and ask for a job. Instead, he mentioned his availability to Ernest Gross, a young State Department lawyer, and Gross sent his name over to Dean Acheson, whom Marshall had given the task of reorganizing the department. Alger Hiss had just resigned his post at the Office of Special Political Affairs to become president of the Carnegie Endowment for International Peace, and Acheson called Rusk to ask him if he wanted the job. He accepted, turning down an offer from Patterson of a commission in the regular Army and a promise that he would become the Army's chief expert in international law.

On March 5, less than a month after his thirty-eighth birthday, Rusk began his new job at the State Department. As director of Special Political Affairs (SPA), he was now in charge of all matters of policy relating to the United Nations, functioning in fact as an Assistant

Secretary of State. Rusk had arrived. A Southerner from Cherokee County, Georgia, was now a member of the foreign policy elite, a preserve dominated by a handful of Ivy League lawyers and investment bankers. It was a very exclusive group in which everyone was on a first-name basis, and not without a certain haughtiness, a feeling of being anointed to decide questions of war and peace for the rest of the nation. Presidents might come from obscure origins in places like Independence, Missouri, but not the foreign policy establishment. Rusk would be the exception, though he was not without his own credentials. He had been a Rhodes scholar and a professor, and he had a remarkable facility for fitting in perfectly with any group, however different from his early experiences and upbringing. As head of SPA he became a charter member of Acheson's "Nine-Thirty Club," a group of high officials who met at 9:30 A.M. in Acheson's office to discuss the entire range of the foreign policy questions of the day.

The first problem for Rusk at SPA was a matter that was smoldering just under the surface in 1947 but had not yet become a public concern: possible Communist subversion of the State Department. For months rumors had been circulating that his predecessor, Alger Hiss, was a Communist sympathizer. During his earlier tour at SPA, Rusk had found Hiss to be aloof and withdrawn. He was barely civil to the "working stiffs" in the department, and Rusk considered him a "cold fish." He knew Hiss was in favor of some sort of negotiated accommodation with the Russians, but he saw no evidence that he was disloyal or had anything but the best interests of the United States at heart. Still, he took the precaution of looking at the FBI file on Hiss (the same one that John Foster Dulles saw before promoting Hiss as a candidate for president of the Carnegie Endowment for International Peace). The only thing questionable was an uncorroborated statement by Whittaker Chambers that Hiss had been a member of a Communist cell in Washington before the war. As a further precaution, Rusk ordered a security check of all the 227 people working in SPA at the time. The FBI reports came in, and every single employee passed the test. Rusk was relieved and concluded that whatever the merits of the charges against him, Hiss had made no attempt to infiltrate the State Department with Communists. He may have also thought about the letters he himself wrote home from Oxford in 1933 questioning the premises of the capitalist economic system, and the sentiment among many Americans at that time in favor of radical economic reform.

From the very beginning Rusk had excellent relations with Secretary Marshall, who had just returned from China after his disappointing mission to try to improve that country's political situation. Rusk idolized the old general and agreed with President Truman that Marshall was the greatest living American. In an uncanny way he reminded Rusk of his boyhood hero, Robert E. Lee. Marshall was from Virginia, and had the same courtly manner, aristocratic bearing, and deep devotion to duty and to his men. Rusk admired Marshall as a man but also as a teacher, and he would adopt Marshall's management style as his own when he became Secretary of State.

As the architect of victory in World War II, Marshall was an enormously popular and powerful figure, but he had no political ambitions and his health was precarious. He believed strongly in keeping President Truman informed, and Rusk thought that he showed excellent judgment in taking important questions to Truman for decision or approval. Acheson was fond of saying that "in the relationship between a President and the Secretary of State, it is of the greatest importance that both understand at all times which one of them is President." Whereas Byrnes had tended to forget this at times, Marshall never did. But Truman trusted Marshall implicitly and delegated extensively to him.

Marshall was accustomed to the command structure of the military, and he organized the State Department in the same fashion. Acheson, who served as Under Secretary, was in charge of running the department; everything to or from the Secretary of State passed through him. After Acheson resigned in June 1947, Robert Lovett took over this function. Marshall did not believe in making official decisions if he was on an extended trip away from Washington. He designated his Under Secretary as an "alter ego" to exercise this authority while he was absent. As a result, when staffers dealt with Acheson and later Lovett, it was as if they were dealing with Marshall. Often when he was away from Washington, Marshall himself would cable back asking for instructions.

This system of delegation gave enormous authority to bureau chiefs like Rusk. Marshall believed that decisions should be made at the bureau chief level as much as possible. "Don't wait for me to tell you what you ought to be doing," he would say to Rusk. "You tell me what *I* ought to be doing." He also thought that if someone was incapable of making decisions, he should be replaced by a person who could do the job. Insisting upon what he called "completed staff work," he wanted to be able to sign a piece of paper and have everything taken care of precisely as had been decided. His rule was that any memo to him could not exceed one page in length. (Rusk would often stretch this rule by using legal-size paper.) In his dealings with other countries, Marshall demanded that everything be made perfectly clear. He refused to enter into vague understandings or "agreements in principle." There could be no agreement unless all the details were spelled out in advance.

Marshall also could not abide irrelevant questions or lack of precision and accuracy. He would say, "Never send me a question without your own proposed answer. If you don't have an answer you have not thought enough about the problem." He insisted upon using just the right language in any communication, and kept an unabridged dictionary on his desk that he would thumb through frequently. But because of his health Marshall refused to work long hours. At four o'clock in the afternoon, Rusk noted, he usually put on his coat and hat and went home.

This system of delegation and discipline suited Rusk well, and he was indefatigable in adapting to it. It was a point of honor with him not to be accused of sloppy work by the "old man," as Marshall was affectionately called in the department. Rusk's slips were minor. On one occasion Marshall bawled him out for using the words "I feel" in a memo. He had a disdain for emotions in official dealings. "It is not our business to feel anything," Marshall told him. "We have to think." This seemingly minor lesson made a deep impression on Rusk. One of his first acts as Secretary of State was to send instructions to all American ambassadors abroad cautioning them to refrain from using the word "feel" in their reports back to Washington.

Marshall was totally unpretentious about himself, a trait Rusk also admired. On one occasion Marshall was called by a congressional committee to testify on U.N. matters, and since Rusk was the "expert" Marshall took him along, and they sat down together at the witness table. Marshall instructed Rusk to whisper proposed answers to the questions he would get from the senators on the committee. But he was hard of hearing and kept saying "louder, louder" when Rusk whispered the answers. To Rusk's embarrassment, he had to speak so loudly that the microphone picked up his words so they could be heard all over the room. Marshall, if he realized this, was unperturbed. He simply sat without embarrassment and repeated verbatim Rusk's answers to the committee.

Marshall believed in keeping a certain distance between himself and his staff and even between himself and President Truman. He never talked about personal matters, and no one, not even the President, called him by his first name. The story goes that one day President

Roosevelt had addressed Marshall as "George," and Marshall stopped him curtly: "It's General Marshall, Mr. President." He was addressed as "Mr. Secretary" or "General," and he preferred it that way. He believed in dealing at arm's length because he didn't want personal feelings to get in the way of policy. He, in turn, didn't "first-name" anyone either; even Robert Lovett, his closest friend in government and his alter ego as Under Secretary, was called simply "Lovett."

Rusk felt that he got along well and even had a special relationship with Marshall, but while in office there was only one instance when Marshall ever gave him a word of praise. In the fall of 1948 Marshall headed the U.S. delegation to the United Nations, which was meeting in Paris. The delegation was quartered at the Hotel Crillon, a baroque palace across from the U.S. Embassy, and there Rusk was awakened at three o'clock one morning by a call from someone in the code room at the embassy because there was a "Flash—Eyes Only" message to Marshall from President Truman. Rusk pulled on his clothes and went over to the code room and read the message, which called for an immediate answer. He spent a few minutes drafting a proposed reply and called Marshall to say he had to see him right away. He then went to Marshall's hotel suite, where he found him in his bathrobe. The old man looked strangely out of place, sitting quietly amid the ornate moldings and gilded splendor of the mirrored room. Rusk showed Marshall the message and the proposed reply. He looked it over and made a few minor changes. Rusk then got up to go back to the code room to send the reply to Truman. As he was leaving the room, Marshall smiled and said, "Rusk, there are times when I think you earn your pay." Despite his studied aloofness as Secretary of State, after Marshall left office Rusk found him very warm and full of friendly praise.

There was another distinctive characteristic to the way Marshall ran the State Department: he refused to let his own views be known in advance of deciding a problem. When he asked for an answer from staff members, he did not disclose his own thinking on the matter. He wanted them to attack the problem themselves and come to their own conclusion. Often before making a decision, he would assemble Rusk and six or seven other key aides, explain the problem, and ask each man to state his views, always starting with the most junior man. At the end of this round-robin Marshall would solemnly announce his own decision. He was like Zeus on Mount Olympus, regally consulting with the lesser gods.

Working for Marshall brought out all of Rusk's qualities of loyalty and dedication. He worked like a demon, regularly staying at his office twelve to fourteen hours a day, including weekends. The matters before the U.N. included every crisis all over the world, so Rusk was able to inject himself and his bureau (now called the Office of United Nations Affairs) into virtually every area of American foreign policy.

Considering his wide-ranging conception of his job, Rusk ruffled very few feathers and got along remarkably well with his colleagues. Much of this was due to his innate ability for teamwork. He did not hesitate to espouse an idea or make a suggestion, but if it was rejected he did not take it personally and did not hold any grudges. He could gracefully accept the majority position even when it was at variance with his own views. This characteristic was puzzling to some of the members of his staff. They doubted whether he had any deep-seated beliefs at all.

The range of policy matters Rusk took a hand in while head of U.N. Affairs was astounding. Each month it was his practice to make a list of the items on his agenda, which invariably numbered between sixty and eighty. Every month a few matters disappeared, but there were always new problems to take their place. Rusk's work inevitably cut across the regional and country-by-country State Department bureaucracy. Thus he had to keep in touch and reconcile the differences between desk officers and assistant secretaries in charge of all the geographic regions. In a department where turf was jealously guarded, it is to his credit that he carried this off with very little friction or conflict.

Rusk's approach to the United Nations was a curious mixture of unabashed idealism and a calculated use of the organization as an instrument of American policy. He often referred to the United Nations Charter—especially Articles 1 and 2, the pledge of all nations to refrain from force or the threat of force and to take collective action to maintain peace—as the "granddaddy of treaties" and the "veritable constitution of international law." He pointed out that both the United States and the Soviet Union had agreed on the charter's language. The United Nations, he would say, was "the restraining hand of the world community [in] maintaining peace, even though a troubled peace, in places where the alternative would be war." For Rusk, the U.N. Charter had a sacred character second only to the U.S. Constitution, because "the world had paid for it with 50 million lives during World War II." And, as he looked at what was happening around the world, it was the Soviet Union, by probes into the territory around its perimeter, that was guilty of violating the charter. The task of the U.N., he thought, was to build an effective world security system so that these violations could no longer occur. It was not an unrealistic view. At that time the United States could count on large majorities in both the General Assembly and the Security Council, while the Russians were ever on the defensive and had to resort to their veto in the Security Council to uphold their position.

The early months of 1947 marked the beginning of Rusk's long acquaintance with Andrei Gromyko, then the Soviet representative in the Security Council and a man with whom Rusk would cross swords for many years to come. Gromyko was a dour, laconic man, a technocrat who was obdurate and difficult in negotiation, but who had a great deal of personal charm. Despite their differences, Rusk admired Gromyko as a thoroughly competent and professional diplomat. Once when Rusk reproached him for the record of Soviet vetoes in the Security Council, Gromyko shook his finger smartly and said, "There will come a time, Mr. Rusk, when the United States will value the veto as much as we do"—an accurate prophecy of the future.

Mrs. Gromyko often accompanied her husband to the Security Council sessions, where she patiently sat listening to the debates. One day during a debate, when Warren Austin, the U.S. representative, and her husband were "going at each other hammer and tongs," Rusk went over to ask her whether she was all right. "These men are playing such childish and dangerous games," she told him. Gromyko and Rusk joked on occasion that all the problems between them could be solved by turning matters over to their wives. Another time, Rusk asked Gromyko to postpone a Security Council debate because both American delegates, Austin and Philip Jessup, were indisposed. He explained to Gromyko that these were the only two men with the authority to speak for the United States. Gromyko chided him, saying, "Oh, yes, we know. That's so they can watch each other."

When Rusk took over as chief of U.N. Affairs in March 1947, the United States was on the brink of important new departures in its dealings with the Russians. The Truman administration had decided to embark on a broad program to quell Soviet expansion in Greece and Turkey. Since the end of World War II, Soviet-backed Greek guerrillas had been fomenting civil war in the mountains of northern Greece. The Soviets also had designs on the two eastern provinces of Turkey. Both Greece and Turkey were weak, beset with economic difficulties typical of the postwar period. What prompted the American decision to intervene was the British decision to withdraw from the fray. The British could no longer afford to carry the burden of aid, and the Americans had to do something or risk Soviet domination of the entire eastern Mediterranean region.

President Truman was scheduled to deliver a major address on Greece and Turkey to Congress on March 12. Although the United States was virtually disarmed by the rapid demobilization at the close of the war, Truman's speech asked that not only economic aid be sent to both countries but also civilian and military personnel. It was sure to be a controversial proposal.

Rusk was one of those who were asked to comment on the text of Truman's speech before it was given. He thought the American case would be strengthened if a specific reference to United Nations action was included. To Rusk, the Soviet actions in Greece and Turkey were violations of the U.N. Charter. It would be remiss of the United States not to make this an issue, just as in the case of Iran. He believed the U.N. could play a useful role, but Acheson and Kennan overruled him. Acheson derisively referred to the U.N. as the "monkey house," and Kennan thought any reference to the U.N. would only complicate matters. Rusk fought hard for this point but failed; the speech only mentioned the U.N. Charter without granting the U.N. any specific role.

As it turned out, Rusk was vindicated in his judgment of the situation. After Truman's speech there was an outcry in Congress and in the press over his decision to bypass the United Nations. Senator Arthur Vandenberg, a key member of Congress, was particularly critical, and he later made a role for the U.N. a price for his support of the legislation necessary to enact the aid program. Acheson in his memoirs recalled that "I lustily cried *Peccavi!*" on the issue. He still considered the U.N. "window dressing" but consented that use of the U.N. be spelled out in the legislation. Rusk was asked to work with Vandenberg in drafting the necessary language. They met almost daily and worked out an amendment stating the aid could be withdrawn if the President found that the purpose of the aid could be accomplished by the U.N. With Vandenberg's support, Congress passed the Greek-Turkish aid bill in May.

The March 12 speech to Congress later became widely known as the "Truman Doctrine." Elevated to the status of "doctrine," it was perceived in the postwar period as having universal application—that the United States would come to the aid of all nations threatened by Soviet aggression. There is a basis for this view in the language of the speech, which declared that the "policy of the United States [is] to support free peoples who are resisting attempted subjugation by armed minorities or by outside pressures." But Rusk always believed that this was merely presidential rhetoric designed to impress Congress, not a doctrine to be applied around the world. However, Kennan and other Cold Warriors in the State Department were more worried about whether the doctrine gave the United Nations a self-appointed role as the world's policeman.

After the Greek-Turkish aid bill passed, the United States sent weapons, aircraft, and supplies to aid government forces. Even more controversial were the 250 officers headed by General James Van Fleet that were sent as advisers to the Greek Army, sometimes in front-line positions. Before the aid program was under way, however, Rusk prepared a major new initiative in the U.N. to parallel the unilateral American intervention. At a key meeting of the Secretaries of State, War, Treasury, Commerce, and Navy and a few top advisers on July 9, 1947, he helped brief Dwight P. Griswold, the chief of the American aid mission, on the eve of his departure for Greece. He made two points from the United Nations' standpoint: first, the United States must do everything feasible to permit the U.N. to observe the American activities in Greece, and, second, "the Security Council was seized with the Greek problem and we should remember that [the U.S.] case rests on the proven activities of Greece's northern neighbors in assisting the Communist movement in Greece."

Rusk was very concerned about avoiding charges of imperialism and making the United States' case before the world. In a memorandum of July 30 to Herschel Johnson, the acting U.S. representative to the U.N., he outlined the legal case:

> It is a well established doctrine of international law, incorporated in the Havana Convention of 1928 and the various treaties of 1933 between the Soviet Union and several European states, that aid given by a country to armed bands formed on its territory and dispatched across a frontier with a view to overthrowing the government of the second state is an act of aggression or threat to the peace. Surely under the U.N. Charter similar action brings into play provisions of Chapter VII.

This memorandum and the ensuing debate in the Security Council stepped up the pressure on the Soviet Union by calling for military force under Chapter VII of the U.N. Charter, instead of merely conciliation and resolution of the dispute under Chapter VI. The United States was taking the gloves off and accusing the Russians and

Greece's northern neighbors of aggression and breach of the peace. In the Security Council, of course, the Russians held a veto, and with both sides accusing each other, the council soon deadlocked.

Rusk then proposed a new tactic, one of historic significance. He would bring the controversy before the General Assembly. This shocked many, even allies of the United States, because the General Assembly was never intended to deal with cases of aggression. The advantage from the American point of view, of course, was that there was no veto in the General Assembly and decisions were by majority rule.

After several weeks of bitter debate, the effort was crowned with success. On October 21, 1947, the General Assembly voted to call on Greece's neighbors to stop furnishing aid and assistance to the guerrillas and created the U.N. Special Committee on the Balkans to observe the compliance of the parties. UNSCOB was stacked with pro-Western countries, but places were left open for Poland and the Soviet Union, which, of course, declined to participate. UNSCOB was used to bring out the facts of Communist support of the guerrillas, and based on its reports the General Assembly passed additional resolutions finding that Albania, Bulgaria, and Yugoslavia were acting contrary to the principles of the U.N. Charter. For the first time the General Assembly asserted the right to conduct on-the-spot investigations and to make a finding of aggression in an instance of a breach of international peace. The logjam in the Security Council was broken, and the pressure of world opinion was brought to bear on the Communists. It was a clever tactic that brought praise for Rusk even by men like Acheson who had little use for the U.N.

Rusk became the central figure in one more incident of the war in Greece. He was a guest for dinner on April 26, 1949, at the home of U.N. Secretary General Trygve Lie in New York, seated between Andrei Gromyko of the Soviet Union and Hector McNeil of Britain. In a memo of the conversation Rusk dictated afterward, he recalled that they were chatting about Berlin, making polite conversation. Rusk then brought up the subject of Greece and mentioned that it was high time "to do something to get the Greek problem behind us." At that, Rusk recalled, Gromyko "came up like a trout after a hook," clearly eager to have some informal discussions about Greece. Rusk did not have any instructions on the matter, and he thought it was very unusual that a high Soviet official would discuss the situation in a casual way. Nevertheless, he decided to respond to the suggestion. The three men went off by themselves for a few minutes, and Rusk and Gromyko met privately again on May 4. Gromyko was unusually flexible and conciliatory, proposing an end to the war and the holding of new parliamentary elections in Greece. Rusk reacted with caution and suspicion, knowing this was a fundamental change in policy by the Russians. Elections had been held in Greece in 1946, and at that time the Russians had denounced them. Why were they suddenly proposing new elections? What did they hope to gain? Rusk asked Gromyko whether they would respect the territorial integrity of Greece, and he answered yes; the rebel forces wanted only the opportunity to participate in new elections, which could be under international supervision.

Rusk reported the conversation to Acheson, and on May 5 President Truman was informed. Truman was described as being "deeply interested" but said Rusk should only listen to what Gromyko had to say, and that no talks on the future of Greece should be held without Greek participation. The two men met again on May 14, and soon the diplomatic wires between Athens, London, and Washington were buzzing with top-secret cables about the Rusk-Gromyko discussions.

As it turned out, Truman was right in his cautious approach to the supposed diplomatic breakthrough. Later it became clear that Gromyko, when he made the proposal, had secret information that Yugoslav leader Marshal Tito, who had broken with Moscow the year before, had decided to close the Yugoslavian border to military assistance for the Greek rebels. Gromyko knew that this would choke off the rebellion, and he was trying to salvage the situation before the Americans found out about Tito's action. Ultimately, nothing came of the Rusk-Gromyko discussions, and Rusk would later say he had "stubbed his toe" in the matter; nevertheless, these talks were the first indication the Americans had that the long effort to keep Greece out of the Communist camp was going to succeed. Gromyko's signal to Rusk showed that the tide of war had shifted. After the Yugoslavian border was closed, the Greek Army was able to pound the guerrillas into submission.

The experience of Greece and Iran convinced Rusk that the United Nations needed some "muscle," as he put it, to move against aggression and to put out small fires before they became major conflagrations. Chapter VII of the U.N. Charter authorized the use of military force under the direction of the Security Council, and Article 43 called for agreements between member states and the Security Council to make armed forces available to the U.N. Based on these provisions, Rusk advocated the creation of a large standing military force under

U.N. auspices that could be used in the service of the Western democracies. He argued, unrealistically, that such forces should be sufficient to be used against even a major power engaged in a breach of the peace, a scarcely veiled reference to the Soviet Union.

Rusk further proposed that the United States agree to make a large contribution to the U.N. force. This was apparently a way to build up the American armed forces that had been so decimated by the demobilization immediately after the end of the war. But the proposals were not well received, even by the Joint Chiefs, and Marshall had to rein Rusk in. His view was more practical—that a U.N. force could be used only against smaller states and non-U.N. members. He told Rusk through Lovett that our "present position cannot be successfully or consistently supported in negotiations." Even a small U.N. military force would not, of course, have been acceptable to the Russians. In fact, Article 43 has never been implemented, although Rusk's proposals presaged the role the U.N. would play a few years later in Korea. And later still, in the 1960s, Rusk himself changed his mind about a strong enforcement role for the U.N., believing that its military missions should be limited to peacekeeping, observation, and taking up positions between potential fighting forces.

The Greek crisis made Rusk aware of what he called "indirect aggression," the infiltration of arms and guerrilla fighters across national borders. In July 1947 he proposed a new U.S. initiative in the General Assembly to create a permanent commission to investigate threats to the integrity of states through "infiltration, Fifth Column activity, the subversive actions of minority groups, and illegal traffic in arms." He was worried about the possibility in the postwar world of aggression that is not of the classical type—organized armies crossing international frontiers—but Soviet-sponsored guerrilla activity. He wanted to establish clearly that "indirect aggression" was a violation of the U.N. Charter. But the idea was dropped after discussions with Allied governments and other members of the American delegation to the U.N., although Rusk made sure that a condemnation of indirect aggression was written into the General Assembly resolution on the Greek crisis that October.

At the same time Rusk was deeply involved in the first negotiations with the Russians on disarmament in the postwar period. The United Nations was the forum of these discussions, which were divided into two different topics: the control of atomic energy and nuclear weapons, and the limitation of conventional arms. At its first session in 1946 the General Assembly had established the U.N. Atomic Energy

Commission as agreed at the Moscow Conference in December 1945. Rusk was a strong supporter of the so-called Baruch Plan for international control of all fissionable material and the elimination of nuclear weapons. He knew that the nuclear monopoly of the United States would end because, as he put it, "nature does not play favorites among nations in the disclosure of her secrets." The Russians were bound to get the bomb sooner or later, and Rusk believed that nuclear weapons were so awful in their mass destruction of life that they must never be used.

The Baruch Plan would have entrusted an international authority with all phases of the development and use of atomic energy, starting with the mining of uranium. After the international authority was established with adequate power to inspect and verify compliance, existing nuclear weapons would be destroyed and the manufacture of such weapons would cease. In preparation for the 1947 negotiating sessions, Rusk sought assurances from the Joint Chiefs of Staff, the Secretary of War, the Secretary of the Navy, and the chairman of the U.S. Atomic Energy Commission that it was indeed firm U.S. policy that, after international controls were established, the entire U.S. stockpile of nuclear weapons would be destroyed. Rusk wanted an ironclad policy against *any* use of nuclear weapons: "The moral and political commitments to eliminate atomic weapons from national armaments apply with equal or greater force to the use of such weapons for international police action. The United States cannot afford to defend the continued existence of the bomb on the basis of any such theory."

When the negotiations with the Russians proved difficult, Rusk fought to keep the talks going, stressing the paramount importance of atomic energy control. He rejected the British position of combining nuclear disarmament with other issues. On April 2, 1948, after more fruitless negotiations with the Russians, Rusk and Under Secretary Lovett had a spirited argument over future U.S. policy on international controls. Lovett wanted to break off the negotiations and not resume them except "in the unlikely event that there should be significant new proposals or concessions" on the matter. Rusk disagreed and advocated that "[we] should leave open at this time the question of what will be done after December 1. To take the initiative now in stopping and accepting an arms race puts us under an unnecessary political handicap." In the meantime, he argued, an attempt should be made to "fill out" the Baruch proposals and examine alternative arrangements, such as a worldwide agreement without the Russians,

and controls on other means of mass destruction such as bacteriolog-
ical weapons.

Lovett, a spare, intense man of judicious temperament who had
been a Wall Street banker before his service in government, was
surprised at his young colleague's sudden impetuousness. He replied
testily that the negotiations had reached the end of the road. "The
time has come to be frank," he said, "and the time has come to stop."

Still Rusk persisted in his argument. He invoked a statement of
Secretary Marshall the previous September that the U.S. take no
initiative to terminate the discussions. "We must leave the greatest
flexibility," Rusk said. "There can be no question of dissolving the
U.N. Atomic Energy Commission or of withdrawing the United
States' offer. We never want to close and lock the door."

Lovett simply overruled him, and the negative language was inserted into the policy paper. The Russians proved equally intransigent, and there were no more meaningful discussions of international
controls on nuclear weapons.

In September 1949 the ominous news came that the Soviet Union
had successfully tested an atomic bomb. The American nuclear monopoly was at an end. Now the question was whether the United
States should develop a "superbomb"—the hydrogen bomb, which
had an explosive power many times greater than the atomic bomb—
and Acheson was charged with making a recommendation to President Truman. At State the most vociferous opponent of the hydrogen
bomb was George Kennan. In a memo to Acheson that he later said
was the most important he had ever written, he set out his argument
that development of the hydrogen bomb would propel the United
States and the Soviet Union into an arms race and preclude the possibility of future negotiations between the two countries. He believed
that if the United States refrained from developing the new weapon,
the Russians might do likewise, or at least seek a meaningful accord
on nuclear weapons.

Rusk, who by that time was Deputy Under Secretary at State, argued forcefully in favor of development of the hydrogen bomb. The
Russians, he argued, would not forgo the new weapon and would
sooner or later acquire it no matter what the United States did. He
pointed out that the American demobilization after World War II had
not been reciprocated by the Russians. Acheson was of like mind, and
on January 31, 1950, he carried a recommendation to Truman that the
hydrogen bomb research program go forward without delay.

Rusk was horrified by the thought of nuclear war, and had done all he could to "put the nuclear genie back into the bottle." But if there was to be an arms race, it was one that the United States could not afford to lose. Only American strength and resolve could keep it from "tempting thieves." In the immediate postwar years, that presumption became policy. Yet to be determined were the measures that might be used to deter the "thieves," who nevertheless could act upon their temptations in test after test of the strength and integrity of that policy.

"The United Nations Is My Client": The Birth of the State of Israel and the Berlin Blockade

U NITED Nations Affairs put Rusk in the very center of the foreign policy establishment. He became a respected insider and acquired a reputation for being a good organizer and even somewhat of an operator. "The United Nations is my client," he would say when Acheson or Lovett grumbled about his eagerness to involve the U.N. in almost every question of foreign policy. Though he was still unknown to the general public, he worked behind the scenes with many of the famous names of the time. His office in the old State Department Building on 21st Street was a command center from which he and his staff "backstopped," as he put it, the American delegation to the U.N., writing draft speeches and papers, and holding endless meetings to hammer out the American position on the issues.

The chief of the American delegation to the U.N. was Warren Austin, a former U.S. senator from Vermont, who regarded the job largely as a retirement post and believed the General Assembly had "jurisdiction over the general welfare of all the peoples of the earth." Austin's major contribution in debate, Rusk remembers, occurred during the Middle East crisis, when he earnestly called upon the Arabs and the Jews to "settle their differences in the Christian spirit."

Another member of the American delegation was Eleanor Roosevelt, who distressed Rusk somewhat because she wanted to be involved with everything and was often out of her depth. But he admired her as a great lady and an indefatigable worker, and he helped channel her activities into her main interest, human rights.

Rusk felt the delegation needed an expert on international law, so he recruited Philip Jessup, a Columbia University professor. Jessup proved to be an excellent appointment. He was an outstanding speaker whose scholarly mind was the perfect complement to Rusk's more practical intelligence, and the two became fast personal friends and close colleagues.

Out of deep conviction Rusk believed in a bipartisan approach to foreign policy, so he sought out the views of key Republicans such as Arthur Vandenberg and John Foster Dulles. He found that Vandenberg, a convert from isolationism and a power in the Senate, was willing to be helpful to the Democratic administration, but he was rather vain and insisted on being consulted and kept informed. Rusk played to this trait and became a Vandenberg favorite. Through Vandenberg he met Dulles, who was widely considered one of the chief Republican spokesmen on foreign policy.

Rusk and Dulles hit it off immediately. Dulles was known as difficult and abrasive. Honed in the rough-and-tumble of a Wall Street law practice, he was tough and uncompromising. Rusk handled him with kid gloves, ignoring his brusqueness and according him warm praise and respect. He found that Dulles's largely moral view of the struggle with communism coincided with his own. To Rusk's delight, Dulles also exhibited a lively interest in the U.N. and hinted at his availability for a post in the Democratic administration.

Rusk saw the advantage of associating a prominent Republican with the U.N. delegation and raised the matter with Marshall and Truman. There was some objection among the White House staff, but the idea was approved, and on July 30, 1947, Rusk wrote Dulles to offer him the job of .U.S. delegate to the General Assembly, promising that "as Alger Hiss's successor" he would "see that everything possible is done to permit the delegation to function with maximum effect." Dulles accepted the appointment.

During the General Assembly's session that fall, the two men did indeed function smoothly as a team, and on November 6, 1947, Rusk wrote Dulles a congratulatory note on the "remarkably effective manner in which you conducted yourself." This began a close relationship between them that would last until Dulles's death in 1959. Rusk's admiration for Dulles was reciprocated. In 1949, when Rusk was appointed Assistant Secretary for Far Eastern Affairs, one of the first messages of approval came from Dulles, who wrote Acheson: "I had hoped the Department could keep him. I consider him one of the ablest men I know in public life."

One of Rusk's major preoccupations during his years at U.N. Affairs was colonialism. He had both a deep philosophical belief in favor of self-rule for colonial peoples and a practical conviction born of his military service in Asia that colonialism was an anachronism, bound to be swept away in the postwar world. He saw colonialism as a moral issue as well, and believed that the principles for which both the United States and the United Nations stood demanded the adoption of policies in favor of independence and self-government for colonial areas.

Rusk was fully aware that American support of independence for colonial peoples would put U.S. policy in conflict, at least in certain cases, with the European allies. Nevertheless, contrary to those he called the "Europeanists" in the State Department, he argued that this must continue to be the U.S. position. America must put pressure on the European states to convince them to develop self-government for their colonies under moderate nationalist leaders. And it was through the U.N. that such pressure could be brought to bear.

The principal focal point of colonial unrest immediately after the war was South and Southeast Asia. There the pot was boiling, a portent of things to come in Africa and elsewhere. In this vast and densely populated area, three great empires were in different stages of crumbling to pieces: the British in India, Burma, and Malaya; the French in Indochina; and the Dutch in Indonesia. All three situations would develop differently and with wide-ranging and tragic consequences.

The British had changed course after Churchill's defeat in 1945, in the election which brought Clement Attlee to power. Attlee, recognizing the inevitability of the nationalist movements in Asia, embarked on a policy of negotiating the independence of India and other British colonies, hoping not to abandon the empire but to transform it and retain British influence and strategic interests. Rusk applauded Attlee's policy, which aligned the British more with U.S. interests, and he followed the British efforts and travails, particularly in India, with sympathy. But he was profoundly disappointed by the partition into India and Pakistan and the resulting disorder and slaughter. He believed that Lord Louis Mountbatten had made a serious mistake by not taking the time to settle at least the Kashmir dispute before independence was declared. The British should have attempted to "talk the fever" out of the crisis and let things settle down before pulling out, which would have enhanced the possibility of avoiding bloodshed and even partition. In Rusk's view the British "should have tried harder to seek some political formula so that India might emerge as a unified nation. It was morally wrong for them to have gone ahead with independence when they did, knowing full well that over a million people would be killed."

Once the British had left and the rioting in Hyderabad and Kashmir began, there was very little the U.N. could do except try to stop it. When the Muslim ruler of Hyderabad appealed to the Security Council, Rusk helped formulate the cautious U.S. position, which refrained from criticizing India but called for a U.N.-supervised plebiscite (which he knew India would win because Hyderabad was 80 percent Hindu) because India's "objectives would be more fully appreciated if subjected to [the] moral scrutiny of [the] world." Rusk favored U.N. action even though the embassy in New Delhi warned that it would irreparably damage American relations with India and push Prime Minister Nehru into the Russian camp. The effort came to nothing since Nehru, much to Rusk's displeasure, ignored the call for a plebiscite. The limited power of the U.N. in the situation was further demonstrated in Kashmir. In response to a Pakistani complaint, the Security Council on January 20, 1948, established the U.N. Commission on India and Pakistan to mediate the dispute, but its only real accomplishment was to arrange a cease-fire. Its plan for a U.N.-supervised plebiscite was not implemented. Nevertheless, Rusk thought the U.N. effort was worthwhile at least in averting general war between the parties.

The second European colonial empire in Asia, French Indochina, was relatively quiescent during this period, a deceptive calm masking the virulence of the troubles to come. At the end of the war the French military had returned to Indochina, as the British had to India. But the French, unlike the British, were not ready to grant independence. Rusk believed that the French would have to leave sooner or later and that they should be pushed to establish independent states in the area. This view was shared by Marshall and others at State, who were very disturbed by French intransigence in Indochina; it was a crude and repressive regime. Marshall was particularly concerned because Vietnam was proving to be a "rallying-cry for all anti-Western forces and playing in the hands [of] Communists of all areas." He gave approval to put pressure on the French to move toward independence, but this process was handicapped by the fact that postwar French governments were so weak and unable to change policy. As a result, Indochina was left to the French military, and the Communists under their leader Ho Chi Minh had seized control of the nationalist movement in Vietnam. The situation was not yet a matter of concern for the U.N., but the stage was set for the bitter civil war which would dominate the decade of the 1960s and Rusk's term of office as Secretary of State.

The situation in the third European colony, Dutch Indonesia, did elicit United Nations action, and Rusk played an important role in its resolution. Indonesia became a major preoccupation at the U.N. because of the large-scale fighting that broke out in July 1947 between the armed forces of the Netherlands and the partisans of the Republic of Indonesia, which had been proclaimed following the war by Sukarno and Mohammed Halta. A resolution adopted by the Security Council led to the appointment of the Good Offices Committee (GOC), consisting of Belgium, Australia, and the United States, and Rusk provided the necessary support for the American delegation, headed by Frank Porter Graham. One of the more peculiar problems Rusk had to solve was a dispute between the Dutch and Indonesians on where to negotiate. The Dutch asked for a conference in Indonesia, but the Indonesians wanted to meet elsewhere. As a compromise Rusk helped the GOC secure a ship from the U.S. Commander for the Western Pacific, and an agreement was negotiated aboard the U.S.S. *Renville*. The Renville Truce, as it was called, provided for an immediate cease-fire, the establishment of demilitarized zones, and supervision by the GOC.

The United States cajoled, warned, and threatened the Dutch to push them toward granting complete independence to Indonesia, and Rusk was one of the "midwives" of this process. He argued to the Dutch ambassador that the Netherlands would have more influence on the Indonesians after independence than before, and he was present at one dramatic meeting when Secretary Marshall told the Dutch Prime Minister bluntly, "You can't stay in Indonesia. If you try to do it by yourselves it would bleed you white and you still would have to get out. And there is no one prepared to help you stay in." American policy was dictated by the practical judgment that the Dutch simply didn't have the power to stay in Indonesia.

In December 1948 fighting broke out anew when the Dutch in frustration terminated the Renville Truce and began another police action, which provoked heated debate in the Security Council and a flurry of emergency meetings in Washington. Rusk argued successfully that American policy should be firm with the Dutch but that there should be no punitive action, such as a cutoff of Marshall Plan funds. His thinking was fully set out in a telegram to Philip Jessup, who was then handling the American case in the Security Council. Our policy, Rusk said, was "to promote self government and independence in so-called colonial areas." The Dutch action only encouraged the spread of communism and was a serious blow to the prospects for self-government: "We have no desire to condone or wink at Dutch action in Indonesia." Rather, it should be our policy, he went on, to act in good faith as a member of the Security Council in concert with the other members to bring about a solution. Rusk's view was that the United States should not act alone: "The United States cannot accept the role of world policeman either in a military or political sense." He also urged that we should be careful not to bring about a general break with the Dutch over Indonesia: "We must avoid putting ourselves in such a position that any wrong committed anywhere in the world and left unpunished constitutes diplomatic defeat and humiliation for the United States. . . . We must make every possible effort to obtain concerted action in such situations. . . ."

The crisis had a happy outcome. In 1949 a Round Table Conference was convened under U.N. auspices and the Dutch, with a realistic view of their own limitations of power as well as a commendable sense of justice and the ability to take difficult and decisive action, negotiated agreements of independence. On December 27, 1949, complete sovereignty was transferred to the government of the Republic of Indonesia.

Additional political difficulties would arise in later years, some of which would come to a head in the 1960s, but from the secure standpoint of hindsight the results of U.S. policy in Indonesia were as unqualified a success as it is possible to achieve in the imperfect science of international politics. Communism was forestalled, and a government eventually emerged that was friendly to the Dutch and the West, as well as interested in the well-being of its people. Such was not the case in French Indochina. There were many similarities in the two situations, yet how different were the outcomes. In Indonesia the fighting and unrest flared up immediately, and action had to be taken. In Vietnam events smoldered; there was thought to be no need for decisive action, and the opportunity to avert the looming tragedy was lost.

Rusk also battled colonialism closer to home. He applauded the American decision after the war to set up self-government in the Philippines, and he argued against the stationing of American troops in

Panama outside the Canal Zone. He was also chairman of the U.S. Working Group on the Italian Colonies in North Africa and helped to set up U.N. trusteeships in North Africa that would prepare these areas for independence. He opposed Russian participation in a multi-power trusteeship, but he also argued against a proposal for a U.S. trusteeship in Tripolitania and a British trusteeship in Cyrenaica. He was careful, however, to secure American rights to establish an air force base near Tripoli. The U.N. established trusteeships that resulted in the independence of two new states, Libya and Somalia. Less successful was the union of Eritrea with Ethiopia, for which Rusk also worked and which sparked a revolutionary struggle for independence on the part of the Eritreans that still continues.

Of all the crises that preoccupied Rusk as chief of U.N. Affairs, the one that was the most difficult and intractable was Palestine. The matchless drama of the creation of the State of Israel evoked strong feelings and emotions in Washington. The motivations and actions of President Truman, Secretary Marshall, and other high State Department officials were complex and controversial. Rusk found himself in the thick of most of the principal decisions, his performance a difficult attempt to serve the President and to follow his own judgment about reaching a solution that would be reasonably acceptable to everyone involved and prevent war. It was an attempt that failed.

Palestine, a land sacred to three religions, was ruled by the British under a mandate confirmed by the League of Nations in 1922. The terms of the mandate, which were quite general, called for "placing the country under such political, administrative and economic conditions as will secure the establishment of the Jewish national home . . . the development of self-governing institutions, and also for safeguarding the civil and religious rights of all the inhabitants . . . irrespective of race and religion." At the time the mandate entered into force, about 85,000 Jews shared Palestine with 650,000 Arabs, but Jewish immigration was encouraged, and by 1945 there were 560,000 Jews and 1,200,000 Arabs living in the region. British and American policy was ambivalent toward both the Arabs and the Jews, and King Ibn Saud of Saudi Arabia ominously warned that the United States would be compelled to choose "between an Arab land of peace and quiet or a Jewish land drenched in blood." President Roosevelt, on his return from Yalta, had pledged that he would take no action "which might prove hostile to the Arab people." That course proved to be impossible to follow. After the war the plight of Jewish refugees who had survived the Holocaust became linked to Zionism and the creation of a national Jewish homeland. The British were desirous of laying down the burden of empire, and in the background rumbled the Soviet-American rivalry of the Cold War. Arab resentment and frictions mounted. The elemental particles of crisis had converged.

The Anglo-American Committee of Inquiry was appointed in 1946 to ponder the matter. The committee's solution was a call for the immediate entry into Palestine of 100,000 Jewish victims of Nazi persecution and the creation of a state in which neither Arab nor Jew would be dominant. On April 30, 1946, President Truman announced he supported the admission of the 100,000 Jews, and later that year he appointed a cabinet-level committee to consider the problem further. Discussions with the British produced a new plan, known as the Morrison-Grady plan, which linked the admission of the 100,000 Jews to the creation of a new binational state with an Arab province, a Jewish province, a district of Jerusalem for both Arabs and Jews, and the Negev desert territory, which was largely uninhabited.

This proposal was quickly rejected by both the Jews and the Arabs, and the façade of Anglo-American unity began to crack. The British sought a unitary state where they would remain the dominant influence through friendship with the Arabs. The Americans were being pushed by domestic politics and the Zionist lobby into advocating the creation of a Jewish state. Said to be "put out" with the Jews, Truman in a fit of exasperation remarked, "Jesus Christ couldn't please them when he was here on earth, so how could anyone expect that I would have any luck?" Then, when the project for a binational state with provincial autonomy collapsed, Truman, to the dismay of the British and the delight of the Zionists, gave a speech on the eve of Yom Kippur 1946, a month before the 1946 congressional elections, calling for the "creation of a viable Jewish state." Events were moving inexorably toward a partition of Palestine.

In early 1947 the British made one more attempt to save the idea of a unitary state and called a conference in London. Prime Minister Attlee and Foreign Secretary Ernest Bevin tried to obtain agreement on a modified version of the Morrison-Grady plan, but this was again rebuffed by both the Arabs and the Jews, and Bevin announced in February that the British were "not prepared to continue indefinitely to govern Palestine themselves merely because Arabs and Jews cannot agree upon the means of sharing its government between them." On April 2 the British government turned the whole matter over to the United Nations, asking the General Assembly "to make recommendations . . . concerning the future government of Palestine."

The British referral to the U.N. was a clever move. Since they were losing the fight against partition and in the process making enemies of both sides, there was little to lose. It also seemed highly unlikely that the General Assembly would vote for partition and a Jewish state. A two-thirds vote was needed, which seemed impossible. The British move was an effort to gain time or, perhaps, U.N. approval for a unitary state with guarantees for the constitutional rights of the Jewish minority. The British announced that they would agree to any solution that was acceptable to both the Jews and the Arabs.

Events did not proceed according to plan. The General Assembly accepted the British suggestion to constitute a special body, the U.N. Special Committee on Palestine (UNSCOP), to consider the matter. Eleven nations were represented on this committee, drawn from Western and Eastern Europe, the Commonwealth, Asia, and Latin America, and on August 31, 1947, UNSCOP rendered its report. Seven members, the majority, favored a plan of partition with economic union and international trusteeship for the city of Jerusalem. The minority supported a plan for a federal state.

Among the complex reasons for the UNSCOP recommendation were, certainly, the plight of the Jewish refugees and the inept diplomacy of the Arabs. Another important factor was the attitude of the Soviets, who surprised everyone by supporting the Jews. The British had counted on a continuing stalemate, with the Russians taking the Arab side. The Soviet decision was probably a miscalculation, based on the aim of fostering maximum disruption of the British Empire.

Many in the State Department vigorously opposed the plan of partition recommended by UNSCOP. Loy Henderson of the Office of Near Eastern Affairs argued that the plan worked against the interests of the United States and that support for it would forfeit the friendship of the Arab world. The Office of European Affairs cited reports that the Soviets were using Jewish immigration for infiltration and warned of a Communist state at the eastern extremity of the Mediterranean. Marshall and Lovett also had reservations.

Privately, Rusk too had doubts about partition. He would have preferred a binational state or continuing negotiations between the Arabs and Jews to determine the question of sovereignty. He thought that Loy Henderson's arguments had merit, and he resented the Zionist attacks on a man whom he considered above reproach, and who was expressing a point of view that should be considered by the President. He was also worried about whether partition would produce war and whether the Soviets would seize the opportunity to intervene.

Despite his reservations, when the President decided to support partition Rusk loyally resolved to work for this policy. He thought of himself as a conciliator, mediating the differences between the State Department bureaus and the White House political advisers who were zealously in favor of partition. He negotiated with Henderson a document that recommended that the American delegation vote in favor of partition and against a unitary state. But they warned that this would probably lead to violence and that a decision would have to be made whether to use American forces to keep the peace. He also joined Henderson in recommending that the Jewish portion of the state be cut down in size and that part of the Negev be transferred to the Arabs. That recommendation was rejected by Truman after he was approached by the Zionist leader Chaim Weizmann.

When Truman ordered full support of the partition resolution in the General Assembly, Rusk worked hard directing the effort of the U.S. delegation to garner the necessary two-thirds vote. Intrigue was rampant at the U.N. meeting in New York, the atmosphere was tense, and the proceedings were followed with the excitement of a World Series seventh game. Crowds of demonstrators lined the sidewalks outside the General Assembly hall at Flushing Meadow. Inside, one of Rusk's jobs was to count noses so the delegation knew where things stood and when to call for a vote. He carefully kept track of the "yeas," "nays," and abstentions, and when the proceedings began, the plan for partition was far short of the necessary majority vote.

The real fear in Rusk's mind was that the Arabs would make a motion to adjourn. He knew that an adjournment motion, requiring only a simple majority since it was a matter of procedure, not substance, would pass the assembly. That might be the end of partition altogether; at the least, an entirely new effort would have to be mounted. Hoping the Arabs wouldn't think of this, Rusk watched nervously as Hussein Shamun, the Arab floor leader, mounted the podium to speak. He began by calling for adjournment, and Rusk's fears were realized. Now we've had it, he thought. Then, to Rusk's amazement, Shamun added a second paragraph to his motion, asking that a new commission be established on the matter. This turned the motion into an "important question" requiring a two-thirds majority, and it was narrowly defeated. Rusk breathed a sigh of relief; the Arabs had not recognized the importance of knowing the rules of procedure in the General Assembly. The effort to corral votes for partition continued, and on November 29, 1947, the partition resolution passed by a vote of 33 to 13 with 10 abstentions.

Even in victory, Rusk was impressed by a sight he would never forget and that evoked his sympathy. After the vote was taken, he stood transfixed as Prince Faisal of Saudi Arabia took the podium, stood there tall and erect, full of wounded pride, and spoke passionately and with great eloquence about "this great injury that has been done to the Arab people."

The partition vote produced enormous strains and antagonisms within the American government. The passionate Zionists and their allies accused many in the State Department of attempting to sabotage American policies and of being pro-British or anti-Semitic. At State, many felt that the White House was sacrificing national interests for election politics. Rusk was one of the few in the center of the fight who retained the esteem of both sides. His efforts in favor of partition had been genuine and effective, despite his doubts about the wisdom of the action. He was uniquely able to work hard in support of a policy he did not fully support. His reasoning was that he had made his views known, but the President's decision must be accepted and implemented. It was a lesson he learned from Marshall, who had always acted much the same.

The immediate result of the partition vote was that the British set a definite date for the termination of the mandate: they would withdraw their troops from Palestine on May 15, 1948. Violence in the area had been muted only because of the presence of British soldiers. Now a time bomb was ticking in Palestine, and tempers flared in the corridors of State and Defense and in the White House. Irritated and frustrated men turned from the question of "What have we done?" to "What do we do next?"

Powerful voices argued for a change in course. Loy Henderson continued his opposition to partition, arguing that the United States would be compelled to intervene militarily to enforce it and would find itself taking up arms against the Arab world. He called for a revival of the plan for a binational state and was supported by the CIA and the Department of Defense. George Kennan, who prepared a study of the situation for the Policy Planning Staff at State, was appalled at the consequences of American support of partition and worried about the effect on strategic rivalry with the Russians. He recommended a hands-off position; the United States should take "no further initiative" in implementing partition.

Rusk had still another view, and his influence and prestige were ascendant in the situation. He argued that Henderson's case was untenable because it would reverse a policy decision already made by the President. Kennan's call for neutrality was also wrong because the United States had fostered the partition and it would be morally reprehensible not to try to implement that solution. He decried the British stance of detachment as "irresponsible," and said it was due simply to the "great personal irritation of Mr. Bevin." In daily contact with the British delegation in New York, especially Creech Jones, Rusk tried to win a reversal of their position. He was also critical of the Arabs and the clandestine assistance the Arab states were giving the Palestinian Arabs.

All the same, Rusk believed that the United States should not dogmatically proceed with immediate partition if it would mean war. Searching for a practicable solution, he came up with a new idea altogether: a United Nations trusteeship for Palestine "to replace the present Mandate until such time as the Jews and Arabs could work out a modus vivendi." The United States should actively make another attempt to negotiate a solution to the problem, and the trusteeship would buy valuable time. He also argued strongly that any Security Council attempt to use armed force to enforce partition would be a grave mistake and run contrary to international law: "The purpose of the United Nations is to keep peace and not to make war."

The divisions at the State Department ran deep, and all three alternatives were debated at a meeting in February of the newly created National Security Council. In the discussions, it was Rusk's idea that carried the day. He argued persuasively for what he referred to as a "new look" at our Palestinian policy, and the creation of a trusteeship in Palestine with the U.N. Trusteeship Council as the administrative authority was formally recommended. A key aspect of this idea for Rusk was that it would allow an international peacekeeping force to be sent in to maintain order during the transitional period. The Soviets would be kept out; they would not participate in the trusteeship administration and would have no excuse for armed intervention. Nor would American or U.N. troops be used to enforce partition.

This solution, however, would have to be reconciled with White House insistence that the decision in favor of partition not be reversed. This was glossed over by the NSC recommendation (with a dissent from the military), which stated that "the U.S. should continue support for the Partition Plan in the U.N. by all measures short of the use of outside armed force to impose the Plan upon the people of Palestine." But the recommendation contained seeds of contradiction by calling for a resolution in the U.N. Security Council to ask the General Assembly to reconsider the Palestinian problem.

In Rusk's mind the apparent contradiction could be reconciled. He conceived of the two points of view as alternatives. The first effort was to support partition as the President had already decided. When that fell apart because it could not be imposed without armed force, the trusteeship idea was the fallback position. In Rusk's opinion the partition plan had already proved impossible to implement. Not everyone agreed with this estimate, however, especially many of Truman's key advisers at the White House.

Of the circle of advisers around Truman, Clark Clifford, his special counsel, emerged as the principal force. Clifford, the consummate Washington lawyer, was a bit too smooth and polished, and Rusk distrusted him. He was too much of a "political animal," too ready to sacrifice the nation's best interests for Jewish votes in the Democratic column in the next election. Clifford argued eloquently that the United States had "crossed the Rubicon" when it voted for the partition resolution and that American policy should be to take vigorous action in the Security Council to enforce it. Further, the creation of a Jewish state would prove to be a bulwark against Soviet expansion in the Middle East. Clifford spoke denigratingly of the Arabs, calling them "a few nomadic desert tribes" who would not dare go into the Soviet camp: "The Arab states have no other customer for their oil than the United States. . . . Their need for the United States is greater than our need of them." Clifford also direly predicted that failure to enforce partition "would lead ultimately to the collapse of the United Nations," which had to be protected because it "is a God-given vehicle through which the United States can build up a community of powers in Western Europe to resist Soviet aggression and maintain our historic interests. It is the best conceivable mechanism to capitalize on the Marshall Plan politically."

With such diametrically opposed positions advanced by his key advisers, it is little wonder that President Truman was confused, motivated by both sincere sympathy for the Zionist cause and a calculated need to woo the Jewish vote in the 1948 election. Rusk in his meetings with Truman noted that the Holocaust had affected the President deeply; he sympathized with the plight of the Jewish refugees and Jewish aspirations for a homeland. Nevertheless, Truman was acutely conscious of the political implications of the situation and responsive to the terrific political pressures brought to bear on him. The methods of the Zionist supporters were sometimes crude, and stories about "hardball politics" were legion. Rusk was in George Marshall's office one day for a conference with several heads of Jewish organizations when one of them began shouting and pounding the table, issuing threats to wreck the Democratic Party. Marshall pressed a button on the "squawk box" behind his desk, called the press office of the State Department, and asked that any reporters present come up right away. He then turned to the Jewish leaders and said, "Now when the reporters get here I want you to tell them exactly what you've just said to me." They calmed down and quietly left. Truman was subjected to similar threats of personal vilification and financial retaliation by many in the Jewish community who demanded nothing less than total support for their position.

Marshall was on Rusk's side, and he went to see Truman personally to obtain his approval of the NSC recommendation for the U.N. trusteeship. Truman's position was quite clear: he was in favor of partition, but he wanted to avoid war and to reconcile the opposing sides. Truman agreed to the trusteeship plan as an alternative to partition if the latter proved impossible to carry out. In the timing of the matter, however, a seed of future misunderstanding was planted. Truman told Marshall that the trusteeship could be implemented "if and when necessary," leaving the matter up in the air.

Armed with what he thought was Truman's approval, Rusk immediately prepared to announce it at the United Nations and scheduled Ambassador Austin for a speech in the Security Council on March 19. Meanwhile, over at the White House, a fortuitous incident occurred. President Truman's old friend and business associate, the Kansas City haberdasher Eddie Jacobson, came to the White House without an appointment and asked to see the President. He had been put up to this visit by Frank Goldman, the president of B'nai B'rith, who told him that the Zionists were having trouble getting through to the President. Jacobson's mission was to ask the President to see the famed Zionist leader Chaim Weizmann.

Truman welcomed Jacobson into the Oval Office as an old friend, but grew very testy when it became apparent Jacobson wanted to talk about Palestine. He had had enough of Jewish pressure and told Jacobson how "disrespectful and mean" Jewish leaders had been to him. Jacobson persisted; he begged Truman to see Weizmann, calling him "the greatest Jew who ever lived." Finally Truman consented: "You win, you bald-headed son of a bitch. I will see him."

Weizmann saw Truman on March 18, and the meeting went well. Weizmann was not heavy-handed, but charming and elegant in his demeanor and arguments. Truman was impressed and assured Weizmann he still supported partition and the Jewish cause.

Less than twenty-four hours later Ambassador Warren Austin rose to give his speech in the Security Council. His words dropped like a bombshell among the delegates:

My government believes that a temporary trusteeship for Palestine should be established under the Trusteeship of the United Nations to maintain the peace and to afford the Jews and Arabs of Palestine, who must live together, further opportunity to reach agreement regarding the future government of that country.

The State Department had done it—it had engineered a switch that, in the colorful phrasing of Robert M. McClintock, Rusk's special assistant, "knocked the plan for the partition of Palestine in the head." Jewish leaders were outraged. The Secretary General of the United Nations threatened to resign. Even Rusk was unprepared for the fury of reaction. In New York for Austin's speech, he answered questions posed by a surprised and hostile group of reporters, and then beat a hasty retreat back to Washington.

He had no sooner reached Washington when Clark Clifford called, demanding a meeting right away with Rusk and "the highest State Department officials." Rusk asked Charles Bohlen, who, as counselor at State, was the highest-ranking member of the department available, to go with him. Bohlen, a career Foreign Service officer who was one of State's leading Russian experts, was normally good-humored and full of personal charm, but on this day a dark frown overshadowed his boyish good looks. When they arrived at the White House they found Clifford in a rage. It was obvious, as Rusk later recalled, that "he was looking for someone's neck to be sliced." Clifford bluntly accused them of countermanding the President's direct instructions on Palestine. Bohlen protested and, reaching into his briefcase, took out the green original copy of the telegram of instructions to the American delegation in New York. He showed Clifford the right-hand corner of the document, with a notation in Marshall's own handwriting stating "approved by the President." Upon seeing this Clifford was placated, but hardly relieved. The President, he said, had laid down definite conditions for the trusteeship idea, and the proposal was premature. Truman had seen only the short telegram of instructions, not the text of Austin's speech, and had not known of the date of delivery in advance. His policy was now in shambles. The President would have to try to put things back together.

Truman's actual feelings on the matter have never been quite clear.

Clark Clifford and Margaret Truman have said that he was angry and outraged at Austin's speech, but that is not precise enough. Truman did, in fact, approve the trusteeship idea, and in his memoirs he describes it as "not a bad idea." Thus, a more accurate characterization of his emotions at the time is extreme embarrassment. The *timing* of the matter probably upset him more than anything else. He had just seen Weizmann and given him personal assurances of his support for partition. The very next day came the trusteeship proposal. Truman was also not prepared for the depth and fury of the adverse Jewish reaction. On his calendar for March 19 he noted: "This morning I find the State Department has reversed my Palestine policy. The first I know about it is what I see in the papers! Isn't that hell? I am now in the position of a liar and double crosser. I've never felt so bad in my life."

Undaunted by the meeting with Clifford, Rusk proceeded with the confidence that he was on the right course—trying mightily to prevent war. In a memorandum to Marshall with a copy to the White House on March 22, he set out a further analysis of the situation, underlining his main point: "Unless emergency action is taken, large scale fighting will break out in Palestine on May 16." The United Nations itself was paralyzed, and the Palestine Commission would not be able to enforce the partition resolution without armed action, a solution Rusk abjured because it would mean making war against the Arabs. The trusteeship proposal was the only chance for peace. In contrast to Henderson and Kennan—who looked on trusteeship as a reversal of partition—Rusk argued that the proposed temporary trusteeship "is [only] a means for obtaining a truce. The military truce must be accompanied by a political truce, but the political truce requires governmental machinery to take over when the British leave. The proposal is without prejudice to the eventual political settlement. It is a conservatory effort." The idea was to use the trusteeship proposal as a bridge to an eventual peaceful solution, probably but not necessarily partition.

On March 24 Rusk met with Truman at the White House together with Marshall, Henderson, and Clifford to try to reconcile Truman's support for partition with the trusteeship proposal. By this time Truman had calmed down considerably, and he fully accepted Rusk's views. Clifford harbored doubts, but he worked with Rusk and Bohlen through the night on a memorandum setting forth the new policy. At his news conference on March 25 President Truman announced that "our policy is to back up the United Nations in the trusteeship by every means necessary."

The obvious next question was whether "every means necessary" included sending American troops to Palestine. Rusk did not hesitate to propose an answer. He drafted a memo to Lovett: "Yes, if troops become necessary, along with other United Nations members." But this time he was opposed by Clifford and the White House. Clifford, who knew that Truman was reluctant to use American troops, stated that the purpose of trusteeship was "the preservation of the peace in aid of partition. Once the method which is best for this purpose is decided upon, the picture will become clearer for the decision of the kind and composition of any troops that may be useful to carry out that method."

Rusk refused to give up. In his view the trusteeship could not work without an American peacekeeping force, and on April 4 he met with the Secretary of Defense, James Forrestal, and the Joint Chiefs of Staff to discuss possible arrangements. Rusk raised a red flag: if the United States didn't go in, the Russians "could and would take definite steps toward gaining control in Palestine." The United States should be prepared to furnish troops, he argued. The Joint Chiefs were skeptical. They told him it would take a force of 104,000, larger than the British forces at their peak. But Rusk was undeterred; he argued on, obviously out on a limb. He knew the military well; it liked the idea of large bases in strategic areas. Coyly he appealed to their worst instincts, suggesting that the situation "would give us the opportunity to construct strategic bomber fields in the Middle East." Yet he also agreed with the Joint Chiefs that "the United States was not going to buy into a war between the Jews and Arabs of Palestine. . . . A war in Palestine was beyond the military possibilities of the United States." The Joint Chiefs deflected his proposal by agreeing to study the matter.

Rusk then arranged secret discussions with Jewish and Arab leaders in an attempt to bring them to an agreement. He took a suite in the Savoy Plaza Hotel in New York and met separately with Prince Faisal and the Arab delegation in one room and Moshe Shertock (Sharett) and Jewish leaders in another. Because the Arabs and Jews refused to speak directly to one another, Rusk had to shuttle up and down the hotel corridor, meeting with each in turn. The talks were kept secret because neither side was supposed to be talking with the other.

Some progress was made. Rusk tried to negotiate a political and military "standstill" to take effect when the British mandate expired. He wired Marshall that all points had been agreed upon except for the rate of Jewish immigration. Focusing on this issue, Rusk obtained agreement from the Jewish side that not more than 2,500 Jews per month would be permitted. He thought this to be a very realistic proposal, and if the Arabs would accept it the logjam would be broken. To his disappointment, Faisal refused. He distrusted the Jews too much: "We cannot accept that because they would only bring in 2,500 pregnant women and that would make 5,000," he said. The agreement fell apart.

At the same time Rusk was scolding and preaching at the British delegate Creech Jones and his staff to get them to extend the mandate or at least accept the trusteeship proposal. But the British continued to refuse, reaffirming that they were going to get out and were concentrating only on trying to localize the military conflict they regarded as inevitable. Rusk considered it a totally irresponsible position.

The trusteeship proposal finally faded into the background because of the lack of agreement, so Rusk shifted his efforts to obtaining a promise that neither side would resort to military action. On April 23 the Security Council approved the creation of the Truce Commission for Palestine, composed of the three career consular officers in Jerusalem from Belgium, France, and the United States; its mission was to prevent an outbreak of fighting.

On April 30 Rusk had a twenty-minute conversation with Truman to report on his efforts. He explained that the difficulties centered on the issue of immigration and that Jewish leaders like Moshe Shertock were being reasonable but "extremists like Dr. Silver [Rabbi Aba Silver of the Jewish Agency for Palestine] made up a formidable war party." Rusk explained his new conception of the situation: "I had indicated informally to both the Jews and the Arabs that if they had some such truce and then decided that they did not want a trusteeship but would join in working out an alternative provisional government, there would be no . . . difficulty in meeting their agreed wishes." Rusk also told Truman there was a possibility that the Arabs would accept the truce but the Jews would not. Truman replied, "If the Jews refuse to accept a truce on reasonable grounds they need not expect anything from us."

Rusk then sought assurance that American policy was firm. Truman replied, "Our policy will not change. We want a truce. Tell the Arabs that our policy is firm and that we are trying to head off fighting in Palestine. . . . Go get a truce. There is no other answer to this situation."

Rusk saw his task in arranging a truce primarily as one of convincing Jewish leaders to agree. The Arabs were already on board. He continued discussions with Moshe Shertock and Nahum Goldmann, telling them on May 6 that under no circumstances should they declare a state or a formal government in the Jewish part of Palestine. Only a provisional government was acceptable. Rusk warned darkly that if they went ahead on their own and created this obstacle to a truce, the United States would introduce a resolution in the General Assembly that would suspend the partition resolution altogether.

Even so, Rusk had doubts about the White House's resolve in staying the course. In a conversation with Philip Jessup on May 11 he made a prescient remark:

> I think what is likely to come out from down here, particularly across the way [the White House] is the idea that something has happened in fact over there [Palestine]. It is not going according to plan but nevertheless there is a community in existence over there running its own affairs. Now that community apparently is going to get an open shot at establishing itself. We have told them that if they get in trouble, don't come to us for help in a military sense. Nevertheless, I don't think the boss [Truman] will ever put himself in a position of opposing that effort when it might be that the U.S. opposition would be the only thing that would prevent it from succeeding.

One afternoon in early May an informal conversation occurred at the U.N. that had an important bearing on events. Rusk was chatting with Moshe Shertock and Creech Jones outside the delegates' lounge when Jones looked at Shertock and said, "We know you're going to have your Jewish state in Palestine." He went on to say that of course the Arab Legion (the multinational Arab force organized by the British) would move, "but only into those areas designated as the Arab state in Palestine." Rusk recalled later that "Shertock's eyes lit up like a firecracker." This was an extraordinary piece of intelligence, and immediately afterward Shertock flew to Tel Aviv to talk to David Ben-Gurion, the passionate Zionist leader who would become Israel's first Prime Minister. Rusk believed that Shertock told him what Jones had said. In any case, the Jewish attitude hardened in all respects. No doubt it was decided that it was now or never for a Jewish state.

The question remained whether Truman would stay with the State Department's policy and the truce plan. A crucial meeting was held in the Oval Office on May 12 among Truman, Marshall, Rusk, and Clifford. Clifford argued forcefully that a separate Jewish state was inevitable and that the United States should recognize it and "steal a march on the USSR.'' He told Truman that the situation presented a convenient conjunction of political interests and international statesmanship. The President could go down in history as the godfather of a new state. Marshall disagreed strongly, telling Clifford that his ''suggestions were wrong'' and were dictated only by domestic political considerations. The old general also had something to say directly to Truman. As he later reported: ''I said bluntly that if the President were to follow Mr. Clifford's advice and if in the [next] elections I were to vote, I would vote against the President.'' The meeting ended inconclusively with Truman saying only that he would look ''very carefully'' at the matter.

Marshall's remark to Truman made a deep impression on Rusk, who wondered if Marshall was close to submitting his resignation in protest. But Marshall later told him that it was not the place of the Secretary of State to resign because he disagreed with the policy of the President. ''You just don't resign when the man who has the constitutional authority to make a decision makes one,'' he said. The Secretary might disagree, he explained, but ultimately the President must decide, and ''the Secretary must explain and carry out the President's policy.'' Once again Marshall had demonstrated that loyalty was the primary function of the Secretary of State.

The fateful day of May 14 arrived. At the United Nations the American delegation had shifted to a last-ditch effort to get a resolution appointing a mediator for the situation. In the middle of the debate Rabbi Silver took the floor to announce triumphantly that the Jewish state of Israel had been proclaimed in Palestine and would go into effect at 6 P.M. A time bomb was ticking and the American delegation went about its business with even greater urgency, trying to get a vote appointing a U.N. mediator before 6 P.M.

Rusk was in Washington on May 14, following closely the progress of the debate in New York. At 5:45 P.M. he received a phone call from Clark Clifford, who said, ''The President wants you to know that a Jewish state will be declared at six o'clock and that the United States will recognize it immediately.'' Rusk was shocked and protested, ''Clark, this is going to cut right across what our delegation is working for up in New York and for which we already have about forty votes.'' Clifford was unsympathetic: ''Nevertheless, those are the President's instructions, and he wants you to get in touch immediately with our delegation and inform them.''

Upset and frustrated, Rusk called Ambassador Austin in New York. Austin was on the floor of the General Assembly, but a messenger reached him, and he came into the anteroom to take the call. Upon hearing the news Austin, incredulous and terribly angry, did not say a word to anyone. He simply "put on his hat and went home," Rusk recalled later with some amusement.

Meanwhile, two other members of the American delegation, Philip Jessup and Francis Sayre, ignorant of the news, were still seeking support for the mediation resolution. A vote was near when a staff man approached Jessup and told him of a rumor that the United States had recognized the State of Israel. Jessup thought it was a joke and shared a laugh with Sayre. How could the rumor be true when the delegation hadn't been informed? Then someone ran in with a copy of a press ticker tape and began to wave it around. The rumor was true!

Sayre felt compelled to say something. He went up to the podium, scratched his head, and solemnly announced that he had not the "faintest idea what was going on." Meanwhile, pandemonium was breaking out in the delegations. A staff man from the U.S. delegation sat in the lap of the Cuban delegate to keep him from going up to the podium and announcing that Cuba was withdrawing from the United Nations. The Polish delegate mounted the podium to announce the American action and said that he welcomed it. This prompted a delegate from Latin America to ask Jessup how it was that representatives from Poland and the Soviet Union were better informed about events in Washington than the American delegation. Ambassador El Khouri of Syria took the floor to harangue and denounce the United States.

Jessup, with remarkable presence of mind, left the confusion of the assembly hall and went outside to phone Rusk to ask what was going on. Learning the news, he issued a statement, well phrased under the circumstances, that U.S. recognition of the State of Israel did not change the basic American policy of supporting U.N. mediation efforts to prevent war. Afterward delegates from friendly governments took turns condemning the U.S. action. Even so, about eight thirty that night, the mediation resolution was adopted.

At about 6:15 P.M. in Washington, Marshall had called Rusk and told him to "get up to New York right away to keep our U.N. delegation from resigning en masse." When Rusk met with them the next day, he found things had calmed down somewhat. Austin and Sayre were particularly resentful, but felt that their honor was intact. It was the reputations of the United States and the United Nations that had been sullied. Rusk was philosophical and told them that when these kinds of things happen, "you just have to bite your tongue at the back end."

The incident was Rusk's first experience with what would become an important question in the American government: Should White House advisers usurp the role of the State Department in managing foreign policy? Rusk was a firm believer in the President's constitutional right to make decisions, but he was deeply angered by the way it had been done. In the case of the recognition of Israel, Marshall himself did not know of the decision until May 14. The State Department through its ambassadors and its U.N. delegation had been working hand in hand with a number of friendly countries to further what they thought was American policy. All the work had come to naught, and the State Department itself was discredited. Worst of all, Truman's decision meant war. On May 16 Egypt sent its armed forces into Palestine.

After the tumultuous events of May 14, Rusk and the U.N. delegation mounted an effort to get a military standstill and cease-fire. Rusk also worked to obtain help for the mission of the U.N. mediator, Count Folke Bernadotte, and his recommendation for American assistance both financially and in the form of a small contingent of U.S. Marines as observers was accepted. Still, he was fearful that at any moment the U.N. delegation's efforts would be countermanded by a telephone call from Clifford. At one point, an exasperated Rusk cabled Lovett that if telephone calls from the White House began to cut across previous instructions, Lovett should "reserve a wing at St. Elizabeth's [mental hospital in Washington] for the U.N. delegation."

After a violent week of war, both sides accepted a U.N. Security Council resolution calling for a cease-fire supervised by Bernadotte and the Truce Commission. In the summer, however, the fragile peace fell apart and intermittent fighting broke out, continuing into the fall of 1948.

In September the U.N. met in Paris, in part to escape some of the heat of the American election campaign, and Rusk was there with Marshall and the rest of the American delegation. Count Bernadotte, in an effort to settle the Palestine question, advanced a new plan which proposed a change in the partition boundaries of the State of Israel that generally favored the Arabs, specifically in the Negev. While the plan was being debated, on September 18, Bernadotte was assassinated by Jewish terrorists.

Rusk was concerned about the political pressures that would be generated by the presidential election of 1948. Foreseeing that election politics might push Truman into unwarranted support for the Jewish side, he approached John Foster Dulles, a member of the

American delegation in Paris and the man everyone expected to be Secretary of State if the Republican candidate, Thomas E. Dewey, became President. Rusk and Dulles had become friends and were in agreement that the policy on Palestine should be bipartisan. At Rusk's suggestion Dulles spoke to Dewey in early October and reported that Dewey could not give a commitment, but it was his "strong intention" not to bring up Palestine in the campaign. This was a pledge Dewey did not keep.

The State Department tried to hold the line in favor of the Bernadotte plan, and Marshall embraced it at the U.N., calling it "a fair and reasonable solution." But when Governor Dewey attacked Truman over his support of the plan, troubles began for Rusk and the American delegation in Paris. Then the Israelis mounted military operations in the Negev designed to take the area before the U.N. could act, and pressure grew for a change in the U.S. position.

In Paris Rusk was continually amazed at the thoroughness of Israeli intelligence. Late one night a "Marshall Eyes Only" message from Truman came into the code room of the American Embassy, and Rusk took it to Marshall, who sent back a reply, also in code. About six thirty in the morning, having been up all night, he went over to a small café to have breakfast. He was approached by a reporter from a Zionist newspaper who asked him about the message—it was quite evident from his questions that he was familiar with its contents. Rusk concluded that either Clifford or David Niles, the President's assistant for minority groups, was leaking information to the Zionists. "The Israelis had a direct pipeline into the White House itself," he later recalled.

Rusk continued to support the Bernadotte plan despite a growing split even among the members of the American delegation. Mrs. Roosevelt sided with the Israelis and thought Rusk was too pro-Arab, chiding Marshall for asking Rusk's advice. Rusk brought up the plight of the Arab refugees, arguing that American policy should be to resettle them in their original homes with Israeli cooperation. But American support for any compromise solution was dwindling, and following Clifford's advice, Truman issued a statement on October 25 reaffirming the boundaries of the original partition resolution of November 1947; any modifications would have to be with Israeli consent. On October 28 Truman sided openly with Israel and repudiated the Bernadotte plan.

Rusk was discouraged; he believed that that decision effectively ended any semblance of American credibility as a neutral conciliator and the chance, if there ever was any, to obtain peace in Palestine. Truman was reelected, and on November 16 the Security Council authorized the new U.N. mediator, Ralph Bunche, a black American who was a senior member of the U.N. Secretariat, to organize direct armistice negotiations between the Arabs and Israelis. Rusk was overjoyed to see his old friend, whom he regarded as skilled and brilliant, in this job; but in order to give credibility to Bunche's efforts, he scrupulously avoided giving him advice or direction. Through Bunche's patient and skillful negotiations (for which he later received the Nobel Peace Prize), a new cease-fire was agreed on January 9, 1949, and an armistice was concluded on February 24. Subsequent history has shown that the armistice came about only because neither side saw immediate hope of attaining any further objectives. War and bloodshed would soon resume in the Middle East.

The 1948 crisis over Palestine was quickly overshadowed by another confrontation that was even more dangerous: the Soviet attempt to force the West out of Berlin. Of all the postwar face-offs with the Russians, Berlin stands out as the pivotal event initiating the Cold War. More than anything else, Soviet actions in Berlin galvanized the West into action—after Berlin there was no longer any hesitancy, no turning back from a stance of unbending opposition to Soviet intentions. During the crisis Rusk, in one of his talks with Andrei Gromyko at the United Nations, offered an off-the-record opinion that it would have been better from the Russian point of view if Stalin had decided to lie low and had not pressed for advantages after the war. The United States, he told Gromyko, would have settled into its traditional posture of isolationism, and the Soviets could have had their way simply by waiting. Gromyko just gave him an enigmatic Russian smile.

The Berlin crisis began when the British and the Americans, later joined by the French, having concluded that the Russians would not permit the creation of a unified, democratic Germany, decided to begin an effort to unite the three Western zones of occupation to form a West German state. The Russian response was a blockade designed to force the Allies out of Berlin, which had separate status as a united city under the joint control of the four occupying powers. The Berlin blockade began slowly with Soviet harassment of Allied rail and highway traffic, but in June 1948 the Russians decreed a complete shutdown of all overland routes between West Germany and West Berlin; electricity in the city was also cut off.

Rusk's first involvement with the "German problem" was in June

1945, when he became staff member of SWNCC and had to draft position papers for Truman in preparation for the Potsdam Conference. In contrast to some others on the staff, he argued for a peace of reconciliation with Germany. He did not see the utility of saddling Germany with large reparation payments. His experience living in Berlin in 1933 had convinced him that the punitive peace after World War I, under which Germany was forced to pay large reparations, much of which came from the American taxpayers in the form of loans from the United States, had contributed to the bitter economic and political chaos of the Weimar Republic. The Germans had turned to Hitler for idealistic reasons; they were ashamed of the Weimar regime and wanted to restore the morale of the country. This was the chord Hitler struck, and without it he would never have been able to seize power. At the same time Rusk felt that the German people had a kind of innate "romantic adventurism" that must be curbed so that Germany, as he later put it, "would not be allowed to roll around on deck like a loose cannon." Like many, he wanted to create a unified, industrialized, demilitarized, and democratic Germany that would be economically prosperous and never again pose a threat to its neighbors.

At Potsdam the future of Germany was deferred, although Stalin accepted in principle the concept of a democratic, unified Germany. A German peace treaty was placed last on the agenda of the Allies, after all other problems were resolved. For administrative purposes the country was divided into four zones of occupation, with an Allied Control Council in Berlin. In 1946 the British and American zones were combined, but the French and Russian zones continued to function separately, both economically and administratively.

After peace treaties had been signed for Italy and the Balkan countries, the Council of Foreign Ministers of the occupying countries met in Moscow in March 1947 for the purpose of negotiating peace treaties with Germany and Austria. Secretary Marshall returned to Washington from this meeting on April 28, 1947, totally disillusioned. Europe was a mess. The Soviets were refusing to budge either on the economic or the political issues concerning the future of Germany and Austria, and to Marshall it was clear that they were trying to incorporate Germany into the Communist system. Economic and political unrest served their purpose, and they would wait until they could have their way. Something had to be done. In a radio address to the nation Marshall said, "The patient is sinking while the doctors deliberate."

The Marshall Plan for the economic recovery of Europe was the result, Rusk recalls, "of the intense discussions at the State Department that George Marshall initiated on his return from Moscow." Formally announced in Marshall's speech at Harvard University on June 5, 1947, the plan was a proposal for United States aid to begin the reconstruction of postwar Europe. It was emphasized that the plan would be developed in full consultation with European governments and would rely on their initiative. Even the Soviets would be invited to participate.

In the next four years the United States would send $13.3 billion in aid to sixteen European countries—grants and loans for food, technical assistance, raw materials, and capital construction. This program, which prevented the economic and perhaps the political collapse of Western Europe, was praised by Winston Churchill as "the most unsordid act of history." First informally called the "Truman Formula" around the White House, the program became the "Marshall Plan" at the insistence of President Truman, who believed that if General Marshall's name were attached it had a better chance in Congress, because it would be perceived as nonpolitical in character.

The development of the Marshall Plan was a group effort within the State Department under the direction of George Kennan and his Policy Planning Staff. Rusk was a peripheral player, but he sat in on many of the discussions and helped to develop some of the ideas. His principal point of view, however, was not accepted. He argued that the United Nations should be given the role of administering the plan and wanted to use the Economic Commission for Europe, a regional agency of the U.N., for that purpose. Public opinion, he said, would not tolerate bypassing the U.N., and this might jeopardize the program. Even Acheson was impressed by his arguments, but in the end the wiser view prevailed that the Economic Commission for Europe was unsuitable, since the participation of the Soviets in that body would intimidate smaller nations and block all constructive action.

After the announcement of the Marshall Plan, Rusk did some lobbying for it on Capitol Hill. He talked with Senator Vandenberg, who told him that an aid program of the magnitude of the Marshall Plan would be hard to get through Congress. "You'll have to scare the hell outta them!" he told Rusk. Ironically, it was the Russians who performed this task, as if on cue. At a conference in Paris in July, the Russians angrily rejected the American offer to participate in the Marshall Plan and stormed out of the meeting. Officials at State were secretly pleased. They knew that if there was any chance of Russian involvement, the plan would scarcely have a chance. The Russian denunciation was the very thing that was needed to ensure congressional action.

Meanwhile, talks were continuing with the French and the British to create a single economic and administrative unit out of the three Western zones in Germany. An initial step was to issue a common West German currency and to adopt currency controls aimed at the Russian zone. This further angered the Russians, who had been using captured German money presses to print large amounts of currency which they used to buy goods in the West, in effect extracting reparations from the West German economy.

The Russian response to the currency reforms was to block the Allies' access to Berlin, which lay deep within their zone of occupation. Rusk, together with Lovett, Bohlen, Kennan, and a few others, became a member of the so-called Berlin Group, whose task was to formulate the American (and ultimately the Allied) response to the Russian action.

American firmness was not a foregone conclusion; at first there was even some consideration given to abandoning Berlin. Marshall called Rusk into his office to raise the question. Berlin was militarily indefensible, and as a general his instincts were to pull back. Rusk offered to raise the question quietly at the U.N., and the first person he talked to was Lester Pearson of Canada (who later would become Prime Minister). Pearson was appalled by the suggestion and strongly opposed any retreat from Berlin. Rusk saw no need to go any further, and he reported back to Marshall the recommendation that the Allies stand firm, which was also his own view.

The resolve to stay in Berlin left the problem of what to do to preserve access to the city. The Western sector was in effect under siege, and the situation posed a very real danger of war. General Lucius Clay, the military governor of Germany, proposed sending a tank convoy through on one of the autobahns. Rusk joined with others at State in opposing this suggestion because a convoy could be easily countered by taking out the river bridges or by blocking it. In one meeting he used a homely analogy to illustrate his point: "Before you take away a fig leaf, you had better be prepared to cope with what's behind it." A convoy would force the Allies either to retreat ignominiously or to start shooting, which would probably mean a full-scale war.

A better idea, Rusk argued, was to mount an airlift to circumvent the blockade. His wartime experience in the CBI running the airlift "over the Hump" from Burma into China led him to this conclusion. A caravan of transport planes, if properly organized, could bring in enough food and supplies for the beleaguered city. The airlift idea was a master stroke; it put the onus on the Russians. They could stop it, but they would have to commit the first overt act, and they would know that shooting down Allied planes would mean war. Lovett and others at State agreed with Rusk's suggestion, and President Truman gave his approval. The Joint Chiefs were ordered to provide the necessary airplanes, and as a show of force (but only a bluff) sixty B-29 bombers were sent to Britain.

On June 25, 1948, the first "raisin bomber," as the four-engine American Dakota planes were called, landed at the Berlin-Tempelhof airport in West Berlin. For the next 322 days a caravan of these planes flew in and out of the city, braving Russian threats and bad weather, carrying a total of 1.8 million tons of food and countless supplies and other provisions. The planes were literally a lifeline; without them over 2 million people faced starvation. "Schaut auf diese Stadt!" (Behold this city!), exclaimed West Berlin's mayor as the blockade began; the United States and the world heard his plea.

Rusk argued that the United States should take the Berlin problem to the United Nations. This time his persistent recommendation that the U.N. machinery be used on every possible occasion was accepted. Acheson and Kennan, with their endemic disdain for the U.N., thought it would amount to only a propaganda battle, but Rusk set out to make the U.N. process work and convinced Marshall that it could be done.

In the fall of 1948, with a steady stream of cargo planes still flying in and out of Berlin, both the General Assembly and the Security Council met in Paris, an excellent place for putting the spotlight on the Soviets' blockade. Philip Jessup was in charge of handling the Security Council debates, and Rusk worked with him behind the scenes, striving to make an ironclad case against the Russians for acting in defiance of international law in continuing their blockade of Berlin. Every evening after dinner they met to formulate the arguments and debates for the next day. The Russians soon were on the defensive and struggled to keep the matter off the Security Council agenda. Rusk fought to keep it on, seeing the task as far more important than a propaganda exercise. He believed that if the Allies put across their case they would win, because he was convinced that "no state can ultimately persist in conduct that the rest of the world condemns as a violation of international law."

The debates droned on before packed houses in the auditorium of the Palais de Chaillot. The French had done some remodeling for the occasion, but from behind a screen leading to the adjoining Museum of Natural History, a huge dinosaur head eerily peered down at the proceedings. The auditorium had been arranged like a theater, with the delegates sitting on stage. Philip Jessup's wife went regularly to the proceedings, and one day she was knitting while listening to her husband speak. An usher approached and said sternly, "It is forbidden to knit, madame; it is rude to the speaker." Mrs. Jessup protested that the speaker was her husband and she always knitted in New York during the debates. The usher went off to consult with her supervisor and then returned to say, "It is all right, madame. If you are permitted to knit in your country, you are to knit here also."

Each day Rusk reported to George Marshall, who had set up an office in a room at the Hôtel d'Iéna, a high-ceilinged, creaky, unclean structure where on most days he worked in an overcoat because of the draft and cold. Paris was still lacking in many amenities so soon after the war and, like a highborn duchess who had gone through hard times, was trying to shake the dust of war out of her tattered skirts. Marshall's office was large, but furnished only with a small desk and a few straight wooden chairs. The only entrance led through a bathroom. The hotel had been stripped by the Germans of all furnishings; there was no rug on the floor or pictures on the walls. When Rusk remarked that he deserved more comfortable surroundings, Marshall harrumphed and told him it was better this way: "Now when some of those boys come over from the Ritz or the Georges V to ask for a billion dollar loan, they can see how I live!"

The election of 1948 was approaching, and everyone in the American delegation in Paris was glad to be out of the glare of the campaign. Marshall confided to Rusk that he intended to resign, whatever happened, so there would be a new Secretary of State at the beginning of the new presidential term. With the notable exception of Marshall, everyone in the American delegation believed that Dewey would win. In fact, a few days before the election, the Secret Service bodyguards abandoned Marshall and began protecting John Foster Dulles, who everyone assumed would be the next Secretary of State. Not only did the Americans believe Dewey would win, but all the foreign delegations at the U.N. prepared for a change in the American President as well. Dulles, a junior member of the American delegation, was courted and feted as if he were already the Secretary of State. The Philippine delegation even scheduled a party in his honor for November 3, the day after the election. When Truman won, it was too late to cancel, and Dulles and the Americans all attended, making believe nothing unusual had happened.

As Rusk had predicted, the Security Council debates, followed by large headlines in all the European papers, were effective in arousing public opinion against the Russians. They lost the battle to keep Berlin off the Security Council's agenda and were forced to resort to the veto to prevent a resolution from being passed. Afterward, they refused to participate and sat stonily through the proceedings. Berlin was also taken up by the General Assembly, where the Russians were scolded anew. Behind the scenes Secretary General Trygve Lie attempted mediation, but a peaceful resolution was nowhere in sight.

At the same time other moves directed at Soviet aggression were taking shape. On March 17, 1948, the Brussels Treaty between Belgium, France, Luxembourg, the Netherlands, and the United Kingdom had established the Western European Union to set up a joint defensive system and strengthen cultural and economic ties. Marshall and Lovett had encouraged the Brussels negotiations, and soon afterward they began discussions with Senators Arthur Vandenberg and Tom Connally about a single mutual defense system, building upon the Western European Union and including the United States and Canada. From these discussions emerged a momentous new design for a military alliance uniting the new world with the Western nations of the old world. Rusk participated in the process as well, talking with Dulles, members of Congress, and delegates from friendly countries at the U.N. The major impetus for the creation of a new Western alliance was frustration with the United Nations, which had been designed to protect human rights and foster collective self-defense. As Rusk and Dulles saw it, the fulfillment of these functions was being prevented by the Russians, and if a universal body, the U.N., could not do the job, an organization "on a less than universal basis" would have to be established to preserve world "law and order."

Rusk was charged by Marshall with the chairmanship of the group that would prepare the proposed treaty. He had had a hand in the drafting of the Inter-American Treaty of Reciprocal Assistance, concluded in Rio de Janeiro in 1947, while he was working for the War Department. At the first meeting, in April 1948, Rusk announced that he wanted to address "the question of preparing a treaty, modeled on the Rio treaty, that might be entered into by such countries all around the world as were disposed to resist the expansion of the Soviet Union." There was as yet no idea that a barrier of American ground forces would be placed against Russian expansion. The idea was primarily to give an American guarantee of the defense of Europe which, with the force of the atomic bomb behind it, would give heart to the Europeans.

On June 11, 1948, the Vandenberg Resolution passed the Senate, which recommended "the association of the United States . . . with such regional and other collective arrangements as are based on continuous and effective self-help and mutual aid, and as affect its national security." The resolution provided the authority for the United States to enter into an Atlantic alliance, and negotiations were begun that culminated in the creation of the North Atlantic Treaty Organization on April 4, 1949. The creation of NATO bound the United States to Europe as never before in history. It enmeshed the United States in a vast transatlantic security network and matched the Rio Treaty of 1947, which had established a mutual defense pact and a strong hemispheric security system for all of North and South America. Isolationism was a thing of the past, as America began to construct the postwar system of security alliances.

The Berlin blockade also accelerated the efforts already under way to form a separate government in West Germany. The Western powers saw no point in further negotiations in the Council of Foreign Ministers on the future of Germany. This too was a watershed decision. Just as the Morgenthau Plan for an agrarian, pastoral Germany had been abandoned in 1945, so too the plan for a unified, demilitarized Germany was abandoned in 1948, in the face of political realities. The unification of Germany had never been high in the priorities of the Western Allies, but the decision to establish self-government in West Germany placed that country squarely on a new path. The new Germany would be firmly bound to the West, politically, economically, and later even militarily. There was little regret in the State Department over the end of any hope for a united Germany. Rusk heard it said that even Konrad Adenauer, the leader of the Christian Democrats who became the dominant force in the new West Germany, paid lip service to unification but did not really want it because Socialist Party votes in the Eastern zone would threaten his control of a Germany centered in the Rhineland. For the Allied planners, a self-governing West German state bound securely to the West was also security against any future rise of German militarism and a bulwark against the Russians.

Rusk was an enthusiastic partisan of the "entangling" alliances and of the new concept of "collective security," both of which would ensure that the United States would never again drift into the isolationism that to him was one of the causes of World War II. He worked closely with Senator Vandenberg on the drafting of the Vandenberg Resolution; his task was to conform the resolution to the United Nations Charter and to base the concept of collective action on the principle of self-defense under Article 51. He also worked on the drafting of the NATO treaty, with particular concern for Article 5, an agreement that an armed attack against one allied nation would be considered an attack against all. He fought for the inclusion of this language and a real commitment to action by the United States, arguing that it would conform to U.S. constitutional processes because the kind of action was left to the judgment of each member state depending on the facts of the situation. Rusk was not unduly worried about preserving a congressional role in such a case, but he was concerned about a role for the United Nations, and he saw to it that the text of the treaty contained the words: "Any such armed attack and all measures taken as a result . . . shall immediately be reported to the Security Council. Such measures shall be terminated when the Security Council has taken the measures necessary to restore and maintain international peace and security." He also argued that Greece and Turkey should be included in the area covered by the treaty. This idea was rebuffed for the time being, but the two countries were later included in a protocol signed in 1951.

Among the nations of Western Europe, fascist Spain remained a troublesome question mark. Rusk participated in a high-level review of American policy toward Spain, a sensitive subject with many liberals and many close allies as well. He believed that normal relations with the United States would push the Franco regime toward liberalization and that it was "necessary to maintain a friendly atmosphere in Spain in the event of international conflict." He advocated that diplomatic relations with Spain be restored and that Spain be admitted into the U.N.; his influence was a major factor in the reversal of the American policy of ostracizing the Franco government.

Not everyone at State was in agreement with Rusk's views about present and future policy toward the Soviets. An eloquent and vigorous dissent was raised by George Kennan, who had an entirely different interpretation of events. To Kennan the Berlin blockade was a defensive move by a Soviet state that was merely trying to maintain peace and security on its own terms. Kennan did not think that the Soviet Union was capable or desirous of expanding beyond Central Europe; for him the Yugoslavian defection showed that it was unable even to maintain the present boundaries of its system. Naturally the Soviets would react to the great combinations they saw rising to threaten them. Kennan also thought it was premature to give up on German reunification. There was still time, he argued, to put forth positive proposals on this subject for a new Council of Foreign Ministers meeting and to obtain withdrawal of Allied forces from the major part of Germany. He believed the Russians would be responsive to such suggestions.

Kennan opposed NATO and the growing system of security alliances. New American commitments only complicated matters, and there was no need for a full-fledged military alliance. The Russians had no intention of using their military strength against Western Europe. Kennan had nothing but contempt for the verbalisms and legalisms that Rusk was drafting into the Vandenberg Resolution and the NATO pact. He could see no utility for such vague promises of mutual assistance based on hypothetical situations. If a future crisis presented itself, diplomatic and military action "would flow entirely of its own accord." He was against developing NATO because it "took our eye off the ball" of economic recovery. Incorporating "our" Germany into the West would just freeze the division of Europe and create grave problems in the future. Kennan was, of course, overruled on these matters.

Whatever their motives, the Soviets continued the Berlin blockade until January 1949, when Rusk astutely recognized a signal that finally led to the end of the confrontation. Stalin had agreed to answer four questions put to him by an International News Service correspondent, Kingsbury Smith, and when Rusk read Stalin's answers he noted that in his reply concerning the Russian conditions for lifting the blockade there was no mention of the currency question, the ostensible cause for the blockade in the first place. Rusk told Acheson, who had just succeeded Marshall as Secretary of State, and they had a conference with Charles Bohlen, who had also recognized the Russian signal. Acheson accepted Rusk's recommendation that inquiries be made discreetly in the United Nations, where Americans and Russians could hold "corridor conversations" out of the public eye.

A few days later, on February 15, Jessup approached Soviet delegate Yakov Malik at the U.N. and asked whether there was any significance to the fact that Stalin had left the currency question out of his reply. Malik said he did not know but would find out. A tense month went by while the Americans waited for Malik's answer. One of the reasons for the delay was that Malik, presumably upon learning that Gromyko and not he would be promoted to the job of Foreign Minister, had gone on a ten-day drunken spree, which was carefully monitored by American intelligence.

On March 15 Malik finally gave Jessup an answer: the omission of the currency question had not been accidental. Jessup was authorized to pursue the matter. The Russians still wanted the West to delay or cancel the plan for a separate West German government, but Jessup refused. Finally, the Russians agreed to lift the blockade in return for a meeting of the Council of Foreign Ministers, a face-saving gesture they knew would be accepted. The end of the blockade was considered a victory for the policymakers who believed in standing firm against the Russians. Rusk also considered it a victory for the United Nations, which had tried and convicted Stalin in the "court of public opinion" and made it counterproductive for him to continue the blockade. Propaganda perhaps, but very effective propaganda.

The end of the Berlin blockade did not produce any impetus for a thaw in relations with the Soviet Union. On the contrary, the Berlin crisis was a critical event that confirmed Rusk and most other policymakers in the view that the United States should organize a worldwide counteroffensive against Soviet-directed world communism. They did not look at this as an ideological crusade, but rather as compelled by the facts of Soviet behavior: subversion in Iran, Greece, and Turkey; broken promises concerning Eastern Europe; the 1948 Communist coup in Czechoslovakia; the occupation of Germany and the Berlin blockade; and guerrilla warfare in Asia. The Soviets were in an expansionist mode that had to be countered by effective action.

Later in 1949 Rusk participated in a systematic review of U.S. policy by the National Security Council. The effort produced a top-secret draft document known as NSC-7, which contained an analysis of Soviet intentions:

> The ultimate objective of Soviet-directed world communism is the domination of the world. To this end, Soviet-directed world communism employs against its victims in opportunistic coordination the complementary instruments of Soviet aggressive pressure from without and militant revolutionary subversion from within. Both instruments are supported by the formidable material power of the USSR and their use is facilitated by the chaotic aftermath of the war.

Rusk helped to draft this characterization of the Soviet Union. He elaborated his views in a speech on October 10, 1949, before a business group in Boston, speaking of the Soviet Union as "the cause of the deep anxiety which has marked the postwar period," not because the Soviets wish to organize their society along Communist lines, but because the "course of Russian imperialism [is] incompatible with the minimum conduct required by the international community of nations." He argued against any "overall pact" with the Soviets and said that what was needed was performance on the promises already made. His speech was so astringent that it caused Hector McNeil, the British Ambassador to the United Nations, to seek reassurance from the State Department that "it did not entirely reflect the policy of the United States."

It was, in fact, Cold War rhetoric that served notice of a new policy of toughness with the Soviets. The main issue in the world as Rusk saw it was Soviet aggression—in most cases not the direct aggression of armies across frontiers, but indirect aggression by subversion, infiltration, intimidation, and sabotage. This view was shared by those in a position of power and influence in the Truman administration. The Cold War was in full swing. America had come out of the agony of World War II with the aim of doing a better job than the previous generation of establishing a Wilsonian world order of liberal democracies and self-determination. The Soviet Union, ruled by a virulent ideology and a cruel dictator, stood in the way of that dream. The dominant thrust of American foreign policy was to counter Soviet aggression, however and wherever it might emerge.

The Far East in Ferment: The Fall of China and War in Korea

T RUE to his word, George Marshall resigned and Dean Acheson became Secretary of State in January 1949, at the beginning of President Truman's second term. He looked as if he had been born for the job. The son of an Episcopal bishop, educated at Groton, Yale, and Harvard Law School, he was witty, urbane, and somewhat of a dandy with his London-tailored double-breasted suits and sporty handlebar mustache. An Anglophile and an unlikely Democrat, Acheson had been an international lawyer with the prestigious firm of Covington and Burling in Washington before joining the government. He came to the State Department in 1941, at the beginning of Roosevelt's third term of office and at his personal invitation. Thereafter he had risen rapidly to his present post.

For all his qualifications, Rusk thought that Acheson got the job primarily because of his loyalty to the one man who counted, Harry Truman. As different as they were in both substance and style, Acheson genuinely liked and admired Truman and stood by him during the difficult 1948 campaign, when everyone else had given up. Oftentimes when Truman arrived at Union Station, back in Washington after one of his "whistle-stop" campaign trips, Acheson was the only man on the platform to greet him. Truman, Rusk recalled, was a person "who remembered that kind of thing."

Rusk liked Acheson, but did not hold him in awe as he did his beloved George Marshall. In Rusk's view no one could come close to

Marshall, and Acheson would have been the first to agree. Marshall had a special presence and charisma; Acheson, by contrast, was a mere mortal, and Rusk's relationship with him was more casual, but closer in a personal sense. He did not hesitate to debate Acheson, and on one occasion he even criticized his conduct at a press conference, urging him to be more general and evasive.

Acheson was quick and sure of himself, a pragmatist who attacked problems without regard to conceptual predispositions. A favorite saying was "We think only in action." His impatience with theory accorded with Rusk's own views, but the two men differed when it came to international law. Although Acheson was a lawyer with the canniness to rise to the top of his profession, he did not believe that law had a place in international relations. It was merely a tool to use when it suited one's purposes.

Acheson was never one, as Rusk later put it, "who suffered fools gladly." But instead of mellowing with age, he became an "old curmudgeon." He was quite outspoken and, during the period when Rusk was Secretary of State, the relationship between the two men was often strained. Rusk thought Acheson had become too conservative and impatient, too ready to shoot from the hip. When called upon by President Kennedy for advice, Acheson recommended facing down the Russians during the Berlin crisis of 1961 and invading Cuba during the Cuban missile crisis of 1962. Rusk opposed both recommendations, and Acheson spread the word that he was not tough enough with the Russians. Rusk found it ironic that when Acheson was Secretary of State some Republicans considered him to be "soft" on communism.

For Rusk, Acheson's major flaw was his European orientation. He was an "Atlantic man," Rusk recalled, one of the business-oriented Eastern elite who saw the world in terms of America and Europe and "overlooked the brown, black, and yellow peoples of the world." He cared little for Asia or Africa and had no desire to worry about them. His acceptance of President Truman's innovative Point Four initiative for technological assistance to developing nations was grudging. Truman did not consult with anyone in the State Department about this program, but merely inserted it in his Inaugural Address in 1949. Acheson had to implement it because the President had publicly announced it, but he tried to minimize it, fearing a diversion of Marshall Plan aid to Europe.

Acheson thought a great deal of Rusk and reorganized the department to give him the job of Deputy Under Secretary "for Substance," as he put it in his memoirs. He needed someone to do the work of shaping up important decisions and bringing things together into clear-cut recommendations for action. Rusk was the perfect man to bring into harmony the cacophony of views in the geographic and functional divisions of the department. Acheson defined his job as "helping the Under Secretary on policy matters and serving as chief liaison officer between State and Defense." In this capacity, Rusk was at the apex of the pyramid at State, involved in every important decision.

President Truman took up residence at Blair House (during much of his second term the White House was closed for extensive repairs), and Rusk met him there frequently. He also attended many cabinet meetings, and the more he saw of Truman the more he found to admire. He was an uncomplicated, almost ordinary man with a peppery disposition; he was quick to anger, but just as quick to smile. Despite Truman's outward lack of polish and sophistication, Rusk saw that he had the strength and flexibility of mind and spirit to grow into the job of President under circumstances that would have overwhelmed other men.

Truman called Rusk "Dean" and relied on him when Acheson was away. They worked well together. Most of the questions a President has to grapple with have no simple answers; rather, they are complex matters of judgment with dozens of secondary and tertiary considerations piled up willy-nilly, like a heap of jackstraws. Rusk admired the way Truman would "listen to a briefing from many different quarters and would pull out of the pile that jackstraw which seemed to him to be the crucial element."

Truman talked frequently about other Presidents and the choices they had made. He had a lifelong avocation of reading about Presidents, dating back to his days as a haberdasher in Kansas City, and Rusk thought that he knew more about the lives of the Presidents than anyone he had ever met. Truman told him that his favorite President was Polk, because "he had the courage to tell the Congress to go to hell on foreign policy matters." Truman was also very sensitive to protocol and the dignity of his office. He was not bothered by personal criticism, unless it was directed toward his wife, Bess, or his daughter, Margaret.

Truman was a no-nonsense kind of person, never one to beat around the bush. One day at a meeting on Korea when a tactical problem came up for discussion, General Hoyt S. Vandenberg, the Air Force Chief of Staff, said in a matter-of-fact manner, "Well, that will of course mean using nuclear weapons." At that, Truman came right up out of his chair and said, "Who says that?" Vandenberg replied, "Well, that is the basis of our war plans." Truman flashed crimson and said, "Well, you just go back and get yourself some more war plans, because you are not going to put me in the position of either doing nothing or beginning nuclear war."

On another occasion Rusk was at a cabinet meeting and everyone was uncomfortable because Vice President Alben Barkley was late. Truman started the meeting, and after a little while Barkley came in and took his place across from the President, saying, "Mr. President, I am very sorry I am late, but I was detained in the Senate. And how are you today?" With a wicked gleam in his eye Truman said, "I am sorry to tell you, Mr. Vice President, that I feel just fine."

Truman was also a bit of a cutup. One of the foreign leaders he (and Rusk) disliked the most was Jawaharlal Nehru, Prime Minister of the newly independent nation of India. Nehru was in the habit of lecturing Truman about Indochina and the folly of supporting Bao Dai, the French-backed leader in Vietnam. He also continued to resist the American attempts to force a plebiscite in Kashmir, and both Truman and Acheson considered him a poseur and a hypocrite with his holier-than-thou views. One day a letter from Nehru to Truman arrived, and Rusk took it over to the President together with his proposed reply. Truman picked up the message and made all sorts of scathing and naughty notations on it, including: "What does he want me to do, consult Mousey Dung?" Chuckling with glee, he then took Rusk's proposed reply and signed it. "Is there anything else I can do for you?" he asked as Rusk was leaving. On the spur of the moment Rusk said, "You can give me a copy of that incoming." Truman laughed and Rusk left. But a short time later he got a personal note from Truman: "Dear Dean, if you will send over that copy of Mr. Nehru's message, I will be glad to make the same notations on it that I have on mine." Rusk thought this was quite indiscreet and did not reply. Knowing it would cause a public incident if the matter ever got out, he decided to drop it. But about two weeks later another note from the President arrived: "Dammit Dean, I told you to send over a copy of Mr. Nehru's message." This time Rusk sent it, and a few days later the letter was returned with the notations scribbled on it in Truman's own handwriting. An accompanying note from Truman said that he just wanted Rusk to have it for his "memmorabilia [sic]."

In the spring of 1950 Rusk had completed almost a year as Deputy Under Secretary. He enjoyed the job, especially his close relationship with Truman and Acheson. He had also become a public spokesman for the administration and for the first time had extensive contact with the press. Rusk had his share of vanity, and he liked the publicity and the attention of the media, but he found news reporters annoying. He resented hostile questions and abhorred their practice of "prying" into the affairs of the State Department. He believed that government must be free to operate in secrecy and that knowledge about decisions should be restricted until those in authority decided to make a public announcement. At the meetings of the "Nine-Thirty Club" in Acheson's office, Rusk took the lead in cautioning others to hold information in confidence. He prided himself on being able to "play the village idiot," as he put it, to maintain silence or give a "no comment" when asked about a matter he considered to be none of the press's business.

Rusk also began to travel all over the country giving lectures on foreign policy to business groups, universities, and civic organizations. He regretted his long absences away from Virginia and his young children (his third child, Margaret Elizabeth, was born on March 14, 1949), but he regarded the sacrifice of his personal life as a necessity of his position at State. He had no hobbies or well-developed outside interests, although he enjoyed a round of golf or an evening of bridge if there was time, and when he was in New York he would try to catch a game at Yankee Stadium (he was a lifelong Yankee fan). Those who knew him best, when asked what he liked to do for fun, answered in one word: work. He did not own a house during this period; the family lived in a small rented apartment in the Park Fairfax section of Virginia. Somewhat of a loner with few close friends, he coped with the pressure of his customary seven-day weeks by going through several packs of cigarettes each day, and every evening a snifter (or two or three) of scotch.

The year 1950 was a watershed for American foreign policy and for the world. The brief dream of constructing a durable postwar peace was over. The Russians had successfuly exploded a nuclear bomb, and Americans felt threatened as never before. The United Nations was beset by disagreements, quarrels between East and West, and the threat of Communist aggression. The deep freeze of the Cold War continued unabated.

"The policymaker is constantly haunted by the error of the fatal flaw," Rusk said in 1950, in response to a reporter's question. This uncharacteristic moment of self-doubt reflected perhaps his vague sense of foreboding about the direction of policy toward Asia, which would be an unending travail for the United States in the postwar period. With respect to some problems of international relations, as he put it, "there are hundreds of major premises pulling in all directions."

American policy toward China was in particular disarray. For years there had been two goals in China: to assist the Nationalists under Chiang Kai-shek in consolidating their power and establishing a viable government, and to avoid a civil war through the reconciliation of competing political interests. Both of these purposes were swept away in the victory of the Communist forces under Mao Tsetung in 1949. The period immediately after a policy failure is particularly dangerous, often in direct proportion to the magnitude of the failure. In the case of China, the collapse was total; there were no fallback options, and the two policy alternatives available carried immense risks. On the one hand, the United States could disengage in the hope that the situation would stabilize; on the other, it could continue to support the Nationalists, who had fled to their island refuge on Taiwan. Both alternatives had their adherents, but as so often happens in such a situation, no clear choice was made, and there was drift until policy choice was again overwhelmed by events.

The "fall" of China to the Communists gave impetus to a dark side of the American character smoldering just under the surface, the political movement known as McCarthyism, after its chief proponent, the unscrupulous, opportunistic U.S. senator from Wisconsin, Joseph McCarthy. But McCarthy did not invent the movement; he merely took advantage of it and became its spokesman. Events, more than anything, stimulated the climate of hate, fear, and distrust. America had just emerged triumphant from a terrible war. Instead of basking in the glow of victory, however, the nation was under assault by the Communist menace and threatened with nuclear weapons. Half of Europe had fallen behind the "Iron Curtain," and now China was "lost" as well. It was easy to believe that this state of affairs could not have come about without the existence of a vast conspiracy that reached into the United States, and there was dark talk about "subversives" and "security risks" in government.

Those who advanced this view of the world—in political life they were concentrated in the right wing of the Republican Party—drew blood when Alger Hiss, at one time Rusk's boss and his predecessor at State, was convicted of perjury. A jury found that he had lied about giving classified documents to a self-confessed Communist agent, Whittaker Chambers. There were also grumblings about the "old

China hands'' at State: people whom Rusk was close to, Stilwell aides like John S. Service and John Paton Davies, who, it was said, had connived with the Chinese Communists to advance their cause and ensure their friendship with the United States.

In January 1950, just after Hiss's conviction, Acheson was scheduled for a press conference, and there was sure to be a question about the trial. Rusk helped brief Acheson beforehand and advised him not to make any statement about Hiss. "Just tell them the matter is for the courts and you have no comment,'' Rusk cautioned. But once he was before the newsmen Acheson got carried away, as was his wont. Rusk cringed as Acheson fanned the flames by citing a biblical injunction to charity and refusing "to turn his back'' on Alger Hiss. The old whispers about Communists and security risks in the corridors at State immediately began to grow in volume. On February 9, in Wheeling, West Virginia, Senator McCarthy launched his infamous campaign of character assassination and innuendo:

> I have here in my hand a list of 57—a list of names that were made known to the Secretary of State as being members of the Communist Party and who nevertheless are still working and shaping policy in the State Department.

McCarthy was never to prove this or any of his charges, and he was eventually censured by his colleagues in the Senate in 1954. But until his fall, both the Senate and the House engaged in an indiscriminate and destructive witch-hunt for Communists in government. Ironically, by the time McCarthy spoke out State had already quietly moved to clear up its relatively few security problems, investigations which were distorted by McCarthy and his political allies, who cited them as evidence of far-reaching Communist influence in government.

A particular target at State was the Office of Far Eastern Affairs, which was blamed for the "loss'' of China. Senators Kenneth Wherry of Nebraska and Styles Bridges of New Hampshire threatened to subpoena the chief of the division, W. Walton Butterworth, a career Foreign Service officer, to begin a full-scale investigation. Acheson bowed to the political heat and talked the chagrined Butterworth into a change of assignment. He then telephoned Senator Bridges to tell him that Butterworth was no longer in charge of Far Eastern Affairs; he had been reassigned as Ambassador to Sweden. The Republicans were temporarily placated, but everyone knew it was only a matter of time before the attack was renewed.

Acheson was visibly shaken by this sudden turn of events. He stood accused of "coddling" Communists who had "infested" the State Department, and there seemed to be little he could do to defend himself or the department. He regarded his attackers with contempt—in private he called them "the primitives"—but his credibility with the public had been damaged by his defense of Hiss.

With deep concern for Acheson's dilemma and for the Foreign Service which he had grown to love, Rusk felt compelled to act. In early March 1950 he went to Acheson with a proposal: he wanted to volunteer for the job at Far Eastern Affairs. On Rusk's part, it was a totally selfless act. "I knew [Acheson] was in trouble, and I wanted to help," he recalled many years later. Rusk's name had not come up in any of McCarthy's attacks, and he knew that he stood high with members of Congress on both sides of the aisle. He was confident he could withstand any charges McCarthy might make, and he knew no one else was going to take the controversial post, so he stepped into the breach. He was not an Asian specialist, he told Acheson, but he had served in India, Burma, and China during the war, and as Deputy Under Secretary he had kept in close touch with events in the region.

Acheson at first looked at him unbelievingly, then accepted his offer with "high respect and gratitude." The President, Acheson told him, would be "as happy and grateful as I" for this offer "above and beyond the call of duty." Acheson considered Rusk's move extraordinary—he was in effect applying for a demotion. On the organizational chart at State he would go from number three man to the third level in the bureaucracy. In seniority, the heads of the operating bureaus came after the top brass and the functional and policy staffs. Rusk's sacrifice was something the beleaguered Acheson would never forget.

On March 28 the news of Rusk's appointment broke in *The New York Times*, which interpreted it as an attempt to placate State's congressional critics. Many of his colleagues at State wondered if Rusk had suddenly lost his judgment. The post at Far Eastern Affairs was a lightning rod for critics, and he would be very lucky to escape without permanent damage to his career.

But Rusk moved quickly and brilliantly to shore up his office and fend off criticism. In the first week of April he held a conspicuous series of conferences with prominent Republicans, including Harold Stassen, then a serious presidential contender, and Robert Lovett, Marshall's now retired Under Secretary. He also contacted John Foster Dulles, by then a good friend, and, with Acheson's permission, persuaded him to serve as a consultant with the title of Special Adviser to the Secretary of State. Later he put Dulles in charge of the negotiations over a Japanese peace treaty. Some in the White House objected to Dulles's appointment, citing the "scurrilous" attacks he had made in the 1949 New York senatorial race against his Democratic opponent, Senator Herbert Lehman. But Truman backed Rusk, telling his aides, "You boys just don't understand politics. Every two years Dulles is going to take time out to be a Republican, but in between times we are going to work with him if he will work with us." Rusk also sent Philip Jessup, who was then ambassador-at-large, on a fact-finding tour of the Far East. Dulles and Jessup were a strong team that had bipartisan support on Capitol Hill.

Taking the offensive, Rusk spoke out against McCarthyism in his own low-key manner. He publicly denied Communist penetration in the State Department and said, "Charges such as [McCarthy] is making not only create disunity and bitter feeling in the country at a time when national unity is needed most, but they cause our friends abroad to wonder what kind of people we are." He also quietly came to the aid of the China experts in the department. He testified at John Service's loyalty hearing, saying that his integrity and loyalty were unquestionable, and that if Stilwell were alive, he would be able to clear up the charges, which stemmed from Service's attempts to make Stilwell's case for American support for Mao Tse-tung. Rusk genuinely admired Service and thought that he could have cleared himself by making public certain secret documents that he refused to reveal. When Acheson relieved Service from duty, Rusk heard him tell Service that he could call on him for a recommendation for any other job he wished—outside the State Department.

John Paton Davies's ordeal lasted even longer, but with the same result. Davies was investigated eight times and cleared, before a ninth loyalty board hearing found him not "disloyal" but suffering from "a definite lack of judgment, discretion, and reliability." Dulles relieved him in 1954. Rusk's testimony on his behalf was not enough to save him. Later, when Rusk was Secretary of State, he investigated the possibility of clearing Davies's name, but was told by the legal adviser of the State Department that he would have to disqualify himself because of his prior testimony for Davies. Rusk then asked Attorney General Robert Kennedy to intervene, but Kennedy refused, apparently because it might prove a political embarrassment to his brother. Rusk appointed a federal judge to conduct an impartial review of the case, and Davies was finally cleared in 1968, but the damage had already been done, not only to Davies personally but to the American government, which lost one of its few real China experts.

Even as McCarthyism rose to a fever pitch all around him, Rusk led a charmed life. McCarthy did, in fact, investigate him but abandoned the effort as unproductive. A member of McCarthy's staff later told him that they "had tried very hard to find something" on him. But none of the typical loose accusations, smears, or denunciations were leveled against him, and his name never came up in the stormy Army–McCarthy hearings. Why was Rusk spared? In part because he had excellent relations with key Republican members of Congress. But the real reason was that John Foster Dulles personally went to McCarthy and told him to "lay off Rusk."

Rusk's immunity was all the more miraculous in view of the fact that he was deeply concerned with every aspect of China policy at State, an involvement that had begun in 1945, just after the end of the war. He knew even then that the United States was faced with a dilemma. Chiang's regime was corrupt and inept. The years of war against the Japanese, including the ten years of fighting when Chiang had stood alone against them, had taken their toll. "Chinese society had lost its internal cohesiveness," Rusk later recalled; the economy, the educational system, and the administration all were in shambles. Chiang had only the most tenuous control over the provincial governors, the warlords, and even his own generals, who were always ready to go their own way. Yet he was America's ally and could not be abandoned. During his service on the General Staff, Rusk had helped draft a policy paper on China that called for continued support for Chiang Kai-shek but urged him to undertake reforms and negotiate with the Communists.

This policy had led to George Marshall's mission to China in December 1945. Truman had picked his prestigious chief of staff, the architect of victory in the war, as the only man who might be able to mediate the differences between Chiang and the Communists. But the mediation effort was complicated by the fact that the two principal Americans in China, Ambassador Hurley and General Wedemeyer, opposed the whole business. Hurley was fired by Truman in November 1945, and he went out swinging, accusing seven Foreign Service officers, including Service and Davies, of favoring the Chinese Communists, charges that presaged McCarthyism and the "who lost China" debate. Wedemeyer, Stilwell's successor in China and one of the "Potsdam colonels" trained in Germany who was sent to Asia because of his pro-German views, was now totally Chiang's man and a thorn in Marshall's side. Rusk warned Marshall about Wedemeyer and believed that his mission was doomed to fail, which is what in fact happened. Marshall came back with a "plague on both your houses" attitude, thoroughly disgusted by both the Nationalist and Communist sides. Rusk did not consider his failure a personal one; no one could have resolved the situation.

After Marshall's return the stage was set for the biggest American policy failure in the immediate postwar period: China. With incalculably tragic consequences, the United States was unable to distance itself from supporting the doomed and corrupt Nationalist regime, a fundamental mistake that reduced American influence in China to the vanishing point and contributed to the future warfare in Asia. Like most failures, the China policy was never a crisp, coherent strategy. It was rather a drift, an incremental accumulation of small steps without consideration of the larger consequences, and an unwillingness to take decisive action. No one person or circumstance was responsible. It was the result of many factors, including the lack of any alternative to Chiang in opposing communism; the Cold War conviction that there was a coordinated Russian plan to convert all of Asia to communism; the pressures of the China lobby, a pro-Chiang group backed by political payoffs and the Republican right wing; and a contagious self-delusion among high American officials.

Rusk was in a somewhat different position than most State Department officials during this period. He had extensive experience with China; he knew Chiang personally; and he remembered Chiang's perfidy in his dealings with Stilwell. He also respected the views of the China experts in the department—most of whom he had known in the CBI—who counseled against further aid to Chiang because he was simply incapable of introducing the administrative and military reforms Marshall had suggested. Chiang was also unable to use his military superiority effectively because he did not trust his generals, fearing they would act independently or revolt against him. When he sent one of his few competent generals, Sun Li-jen, to fight the Communists in northern China, he refused to let Sun's army operate as a unified force. He split it up into little pieces, rendering it totally ineffective, simply because he feared giving Sun too much power.

Even though Marshall knew the situation so well, he did not follow his instincts to disengage from the Chinese civil war. Instead, the Truman administration resumed shipments of arms in 1947, supported the China aid bill in Congress, and dispatched a fact-finding mission under General Wedemeyer. Marshall bowed to the political realities of the times. Key Republicans would not support Marshall Plan aid for Europe without assistance for Chiang in Asia, and the administration was not willing to endanger that crucial program to engage in a fight over China. American military men in China—advisers to Chiang —were also arguing that the Nationalists were strong enough militarily to hold the Yangtze River line and to control South China. One colonel who felt strongly about this committed suicide when the Communists broke through and he was proved wrong.

General Wedemeyer submitted his own report to the President in September 1947, which, predictably, called for an extensive program of economic aid to China and Russian participation in a five-power guardianship of Manchuria. He also proposed that aid be granted on the condition that Chiang request American economic and military advisers. Rusk was called in to examine the idea for a U.N. trusteeship in Manchuria, which he rejected as not feasible without a substantial commitment of American forces. He consistently argued against any American military involvement in China—he had seen what had happened in the case of the Japanese, who with millions of men could not exercise real control. Military intervention was simply beyond the realm of American capability. But like almost everyone else, Rusk did not oppose the shipment of arms and other aid to Chiang. It was unthinkable to abandon Chiang, at least while he was fighting the Communists, however badly.

By late 1948 Communist victories in the field convinced even the most sanguine supporters of Chiang at the State Department that the United States was locked into a policy that had no hope of success. Not only was a military disaster at hand, but a political one as well, as the Republican partisans of the Nationalists in Congress stepped up their attacks. At this point officials at Far Eastern Affairs decided to prepare a White Paper, a comprehensive compilation of relations with China in the postwar period that would explain and justify a shift in American policy from support of Chiang to disengagement of the United States from the Nationalist regime, as well as disclaim any American responsibility for the inability to control events in China. As Deputy Under Secretary, Rusk worked on the report and had a hand in drafting Secretary Acheson's controversial letter of transmittal.

Even as the White Paper was being prepared, Rusk was called on to meet with some of those who favored for U.S. military intervention. One of them was the archconservative Claire Chennault, who met with him on May 11, 1949. Rusk had known Chennault, of course, in the CBI, and while respecting his fighting spirit, he held his political judgment in contempt. Chennault proposed a U.S. "military mission" charged with responsibility for procuring needed supplies and training the Chinese. In his view the aid "we have given to China since August 1945 has not been used effectively because we had no such mission." Rusk's technique in talking to Chennault was not to oppose him openly, but to pose a series of questions that skillfully drew him out and exposed the complete nonsense of his plan. Rusk also had a transcript made so he could use Chennault's own words to expose his folly.

From Rusk's cross-examination, it was apparent that what Chennault wanted was a major war in China. Asked how American aid would get to Chiang if the Communists controlled all the ports in China, Chennault glibly answered that they would use Haiphong in Indochina and get the cooperation of the French. He also admitted that "full air support" by American pilots would be needed, and wanted the United States to take responsibility for food production in the area of "free China." At the end of their talk Rusk thanked Chennault for coming and said he would "study" the proposal. He judiciously told Chennault that the department would have to consider "our commitments to other areas and the necessity of reducing expenditures to the greatest extent possible."

In the fall of 1949, after the Communist victory in China, it was decided not only to withhold temporarily American recognition of the new People's Republic of China, but also to suspend further military aid to the Nationalist forces on Taiwan. Rusk even argued for the establishment of a U.N. trusteeship over Taiwan, a proposal that earned him the enmity of Chiang Kai-shek. The stage seemingly was set for a radical shift in American policy toward China. Acheson notified the National Security Council that "political and economic measures cannot prevent the communists from taking over Taiwan." On December 23, 1949, the State Department released a policy information paper to prepare officials for the fall of Taiwan. President Truman articulated the new policy in early January 1950: "The United States government will not," he emphasized, "provide military aid or advice to Chinese forces on Formosa [Taiwan]." The United States was moving toward complete disengagement in China. It was also a foregone conclusion, as *U.S. News & World Report* said in January 1950, that "soon it will be the painful duty of the United States to extend formal recognition to the communist-controlled government of China. . . . As a common sense decision in diplomacy, recognition is inevitable."

Rusk met with Oliver Franks, the British ambassador, to exchange views on British recognition and the American policy of nonrecognition. He told Franks that the United States wanted to wait and see how the new China acted. If China respected the rights of other nations, he assured Franks, American recognition would be forthcoming. Franks told him that British recognition reflected only the realities of the situation and British commercial interests in Hong Kong. Rusk expressed the hope that their two countries would eventually adopt the same policy toward China, and Franks agreed.

Rusk also maneuvered to keep the Communist government from displacing the Nationalists in the United Nations. To throw up a roadblock, he had the matter referred to a committee, and procured a vote in the General Assembly "to postpone consideration" of Chinese representation for the duration of the session, a tactic which succeeded in preventing the Communists from taking China's seat. The Russians walked out in protest. Rusk looked upon this parliamentary device as a temporary measure; he did not dream that it would continue to be used for the next twenty years.

When he took over at Far Eastern Affairs, Rusk thought China would be his main problem. He wondered whether Mao Tse-tung would be able to stay in power and asked the CIA to look for evidence of "warlordism" in the new China. He believed it would be hard for any group really to control China, but at the same time reasoned that if Mao stayed in power he should be encouraged to follow an independent path from the Russians. "Titoism" became one of Rusk's goals for China, and he looked for ways to foster a split between the two Communist giants.

He agreed with the hands-off policy toward the Nationalists, attempting to win John Foster Dulles over to the idea as a means of establishing a bipartisan China policy. But Dulles told him the Republican differences on the issue were too great. People like Congressman Walter Judd and Senator William Knowland smelled blood. China would be a major and divisive issue. America had long been involved with China and, alone among the great powers, had resisted imperialist designs and instead had fostered an "open door" policy. Americans had gone to China to build hospitals, run schools, and work as missionaries. Now China had deliberately turned its back, calling America "enemy number one," and many Americans reacted like a spurned lover.

The China issue raised elemental and bitter emotions. Acheson especially was the target of abuse by the "who lost China" faction and was terribly affected by the Republican pressures. He told Jessup and

Rusk that he would even consider recognizing Peking if it were not for the politics of the matter. As for Rusk, he thought the recriminations over placing the blame on someone for losing China were completely off the mark. "If anyone 'lost China,' " he recalled many years later, "it was Chiang Kai-shek."

But Rusk was not yet ready to agree with John Paton Davies's assessment that "the Communists are in China to stay. China's destiny is not Chiang's, but theirs." Colleagues noticed that at Far Eastern Affairs, Rusk had become overly cautious, even indecisive. Those who had worked for him at U.N. Affairs were surprised; while in charge of the U.N. desk Rusk was, if anything, sure of himself. But in that job he was not in charge of formulating policy so much as carrying it out. The issues were clearer, and there was a "right" and a "wrong" when dealing with Soviet aggression. In Asia the choices were less clear and the situation vastly more complicated. Rusk's associates complained that he had trouble making up his mind, that he "played his cards inside his shirt."

Ironically, at the very time when the Republicans were full of political bombast over Acheson's supposed dovish views on the defense of Taiwan, those who served in the higher echelons at State were occupied with the formulation of a tough new policy for dealing with communism and a justification for massive American rearmament. The embodiment of this program was a secret document known as NSC-68. Focusing on Moscow, the new policy received its impetus form Soviet possession of nuclear arms. Its main thesis was that the Soviets were out to dominate the world and that America must be prepared to fight and win a war if it came to that. Central to NSC-68 was the policy of "containment,"

> which seeks by all means short of war to (1) block further expansion of Soviet power, (2) expose the falsities of Soviet pretensions, (3) induce a retraction of the Kremlin's control and influence, and (4) in general, so foster the seeds of destruction within the Soviet system that the Kremlin is brought at last to the point of modifying its behavior to conform to generally acceptable international standards.

Rusk participated in the drafting of this document, which was primarily authored by Paul Nitze and the Policy Planning Staff. The negotiations that led to the final version of NSC-68 produced a bitter split between State and Defense and between the heads of these departments, Acheson and Louis Johnson. Acheson, an exponent of the policy of toughness, wanted an increase in military spending and armaments. Johnson, who had his eye on the presidency, wanted a balanced budget and was against any military buildup. The feud came to a head on March 22, 1950, at a meeting Rusk attended. Johnson, who was also jealous of Acheson's standing with the President, lunged forward in his chair at Acheson and began to pound the table and stomp on the floor. He then walked out, saying that he would never again participate in any meeting with Acheson. Not long afterward, a distinguished-looking military man knocked on Rusk's office door and introduced himself as General James Burns. He had just been given a new assignment, he told Rusk, by Louis Johnson: "to protect the Pentagon against that fellow Dean Rusk at State." The two men shared a good laugh. The backbiting and disagreements continued between Johnson and Acheson, and both combatants appealed to Truman. The President sided completely with Acheson. The NSC-68 policy was approved by the President in April and would become the bible of American foreign policy for the next twenty years. Shortly afterward, the emotional Johnson resigned in tears.

The new policy of toughness would soon be tested. Unknown to American officials, Communist armed forces in North Korea were preparing to attack the South. Tragically, one of the reasons for their decision to attack was the ambiguity of American policy. The Americans had remained in Korea as an occupying power after the war. But Korea was not regarded as having crucial strategic significance, and Truman had declared in April 1948 that military action by either side of that divided country would not constitute a *casus belli* for the United States. The Soviets had pulled their troops out of the North, and Truman had withdrawn American troops that summer. At the time General MacArthur, and the military generally, agreed with this course of action, saying that the American troops were "few in number and flabby." At State, Walton Butterworth of Far Eastern Affairs agreed as well. The United States should not station troops in continental Asia, he believed, because they might be easily trapped and defeated. Only one significant voice was raised against this decision. Rusk, then Deputy Under Secretary, argued that the presence of American troops deterred Communist adventurism. He lost the argument and later became convinced that if the troops had remained, North Korea would never have attacked its neighbor to the south.

There were further signals of American lack of resolve in Korea. In a speech at the National Press Club on January 12, 1950, Acheson cited "our line of defense" in the Pacific, which, he said, ran along the Aleutian Islands to Japan, down to the Ryukyus, and on to the Philippines. He pointedly failed to mention Korea or Taiwan. Rusk was in charge of the preparation of the speech, and he and Acheson met the night before to go over the marked-up drafts and settle on the final version. Rusk's view was that any speech by the Secretary of State should be carefully crafted and "flyspecked" word by word so that there would be no unwarranted statements or misunderstandings either at home or abroad. But Acheson was tired. He refused any further help and said, "Now look, we've put in enough time on this. I'm going to go home and jot down some notes and then I'll go down there and make a speech." As a result Acheson, when he gave the speech, did not have a prepared text; he was speaking almost extemporaneously.

The omission of Korea from the American defense perimeter did not go unnoticed. The Korean ambassador immediately called upon Rusk for a clarification. Senator Tom Connally publicly stated that he was afraid the United States was considering abandoning Korea. Rusk did not fault Acheson so much as the reaction in the press. He pointed out that Acheson had said in his speech that the independence of other peoples in the Pacific "would be protected under the Charter of the United Nations." He advised Acheson "to sit tight and let the matter blow over," and Acheson at a press conference in May responded to a question with only a general statement of support for Korea. Korea was having difficulty both economically and politically, and Rusk told the Korean ambassador that if the government did not do something to control inflation, the entire American aid program might be placed in jeopardy. Rusk also warned against postponing the national elections scheduled for May 30. Those elections were held, and the result severely weakened the position of South Korean President Syngman Rhee.

Years later Rusk received a report from an American businessman that he regarded as a confirmation of his view that the Korean invasion was the result of a Communist miscalculation about American intentions. The American was seated next to Soviet diplomat Andrei Vyshinsky at a dinner and asked him why the Russians pretended to think the United States was going to attack the Soviet Union. Vyshinsky replied that the Russians did not know what to think about the United States. "Look at Korea," he said. "You did everything you could to tell us you were not interested in Korea, but when the North Koreans went in, you put your troops there. We just can't trust you Americans."

Acheson's speech and the emerging new American policy toward Asia produced an effect on Taiwan as well. In early June 1950 Rusk received a secret, hand-delivered note from General Sun Li-jen, commander in chief of the Taiwan Defense Command. Rusk knew Sun well from his days in the China-Burma-India campaign during the war, when Sun had commanded one of Chiang's divisions in Burma. They had even eaten shark's fin soup together in the bush. Now Sun made a startling proposal: he would lead a military coup to oust Chiang Kaishek. The implications of this intended coup were not clear, but Sun was asking the support, or at least the acquiescence, of the United States. Sun, if he had assumed power, would have moved to end government corruption and would also have shown more flexibility than Chiang in dealing with the Communists.

The matter required a presidential decision. Rusk destroyed the message to prevent any possible leaks, aware that if Chiang found out, Sun would be killed. He then went to see Acheson, who promised to take the matter up with Truman. But before any presidential decision could be made, North Korea mounted an invasion of the South, an event which probably saved Chiang's regime, because it assured further American support.

On the evening of Saturday, June 24, 1950, Rusk and Virginia were having dinner at the Washington home of journalist Joseph Alsop, a friend since the days in the CBI. Other guests included Secretary of the Army Frank Pace, Justice Felix Frankfurter, and their wives. It was a purely social evening, and Rusk was enjoying himself. Most other top administrative officials had gone away for the weekend to escape the Washington heat. Acheson was at Harewood, his farm in Virginia. Truman was back home in Independence, Missouri.

At 9:30 P.M. the telephone rang at the Alsop home; Mrs. Alsop answered and called Rusk to the phone. The State Department code room was on the line with an important message direct from John Muccio, the American ambassador in Korea. Rusk listened intently as the message was read to him:

According to Korean army reports . . . North Korean forces invaded ROK territory at several points this morning. Action was initiated about 4 a.m. Ongjin blasted by North Korean artillery fire. About 6 a.m. North Korean infantry commenced crossing parallel in Ongjin area, Kaesong area, Chunchon area and amphibious landing was reportedly made south of Kangnung on east coast. Kaesong was reportedly captured at 9 a.m., with some 10 North Korean tanks participating in operation. North Korean forces, spearheaded by tanks, reportedly closing in on Chunchon. Details of fighting in Kangnung area unclear, although it seems North Korean forces have cut highway. Am conferring with . . . Korean officials this morning re situation.

The telegram had arrived only four minutes before; Rusk was the first official in Washington to hear the news. The North Korean attack had occurred Sunday morning, June 25 (Korea was thirteen hours ahead of Washington time).

The attack was a total surprise. Only four days before, Rusk had told a congressional committee, in response to a question about a possible North Korean invasion, "We see no present indication that the people across the border have any intention of fighting a major war for that purpose." Now he felt his heart pounding, but his first thought was that he must remain outwardly calm and composed. He hung up the receiver and quietly said to Frank Pace that they would have to go to their offices, then apologized to the Alsops for leaving. Alsop was so curious he could hardly contain himself, but Rusk did not tell anyone, not even Virginia, why they were leaving.

From the first Rusk knew that the North Korean action meant war. He and Pace discussed how it could have occurred without any advance warning. The intelligence people had blown it. MacArthur's G-2 was on leave, but there still should have been some warning of such a large-scale attack. John Foster Dulles had visited Korea on June 19, had talked to President Syngman Rhee, and had addressed the National Assembly. Rusk had read the dispatch from Dulles's party with care; the Koreans had not mentioned any possibility of attack to Dulles. Rusk also knew the military situation in Korea. The nearest American troops were in Japan, and they were far from combat ready. The South Korean army was deficient as well; reequipping and retraining had just begun to reach the battalion level of preparedness. The South Koreans were unprepared for war at the divisional level; their artillery and tanks were not sufficient. The situation was very grim.

As soon as he arrived at the State Department, Rusk called Acheson at his farm to tell him the news. He also made a recommendation: Acheson should call for an immediate emergency meeting of the U.N. Security Council. Rusk's instinct to involve the United Nations came from his experience of the usefulness of the world body during the Berlin blockade and the Soviet threats to Greece, Turkey, and Iran. He also considered it "of utmost importance that the decision to present the case . . . should appear in the morning papers simultaneously with the news of the North Korean attack.''

Acheson agreed, and telephoned Truman in Independence to inform him of the invasion and obtain his consent to petition the U.N. Then he phoned Ernest Gross, the U.S. representative on duty in New York, to get the U.N. procedures started. The Security Council was convened on Sunday in emergency session, with the Soviet delegation still absent because of its walkout in protest over the issue of Chinese representation. It was a fortunate absence from the viewpoint of the United States because, without the Soviet veto, a resolution was quickly adopted determining that the North Korean action was a breach of the peace and asking for the withdrawal of the invasion forces.

This and subsequent Security Council resolutions became the basis for both U.S. and collective U.N. action to repel the invasion. In Rusk's mind the referral to the U.N. was essential to give legal and moral credence to American military intervention. It drew resounding support around the world, although some dissenting voices were raised. Kennan was in favor of American intervention, but he saw no need for the United Nations and thought the involvement of the world body merely complicated matters. But Truman wrote Acheson afterward that the convening of the Security Council was ''the key to what followed afterwards. Had you not acted promptly in that direction we would have had to go into Korea alone.''

It was a mystery at the time why the Soviet delegate at the U.N. did not return for the June 25 meeting in order to veto the Korean resolution. Many years later Rusk asked Andrei Gromyko this question out of curiosity, and Gromyko told him that Stalin had personally telephoned the Soviet representative, Yakov Malik, and told him not to return. Stalin still believed that no American action would be taken, and the question of Chinese representation in the U.N. was of overriding importance to him. Stalin was profoundly wrong.

Sunday, June 25, was also a day of intense activity in Washington. Rusk met with officials of State and Defense that morning, and the President returned from Independence. That afternoon Rusk received a secret intelligence report that the North Korean objective was outright control over the Korean peninsula and that South Korean forces were not capable of more than limited resistance. The report left no doubt about the involvement of the Soviets: ''The North Korean Government is completely under Kremlin control and there is no possibility that the North Koreans acted without prior instruction from

Moscow. The move against South Korea must therefore be considered a Soviet move.'' The report further predicted that the defeat of South Korea would cause Japan and Europe, as well as leaders in Southeast Asia, to question the American will to combat communism. On the other hand, swift and effective U.S. intervention might cause Chinese leaders to doubt the advantage of their alliance with the Soviets and strengthen the resistance of the Nationalist Chinese. Korea, in short, was a test case that could determine the future course of the Cold War.

There was never any doubt by anyone involved in the decision that the United States would intervene to defend South Korea. Rusk was a member of the Blair House ''war cabinet'' that met each day beginning Sunday night to make the fateful decisions. The first meeting set the tone for what was to come. Without dissent President Truman made several clear-cut decisions: Americans would be evacuated under the protection of covering fighter planes; supplies and ammunition would be sent to the South Koreans; the air cover may attack North Korean tanks if necessary; and the 7th Fleet would be sent to the Formosa Strait, to take up a position between the mainland and Taiwan. The President also asked that several resolutions be drawn up to be introduced in the Security Council.

The decision to send the 7th Fleet to Taiwan was perhaps the most surprising matter to come out of this meeting. The official explanation was that it was a precaution to protect both sides against the other, but its real purpose was to prevent an invasion of Taiwan from the mainland. The Sino-Soviet Treaty of February 14, 1950, was on everyone's mind. The Korean invasion, after all, might be just the first element of a general Communist offensive in Asia. The events in Korea shocked the Truman administration into stepping up military support for Chiang. Another, less noticed decision became inevitable as well—increased aid to French Indochina.

The interposition of the 7th Fleet was something of a bluff. Military intelligence at the time counted thousands upon thousands of wooden junks up and down the coast of mainland China. The Navy used a few for target practice to see what it would take to sink them and found that shells could do very little damage short of a rare direct hit. If the Communists had sent several thousand of these junks with soldiers aboard to invade Taiwan, the 7th Fleet would not have been able to stop them. But all was quiet in the Formosa Strait.

MacArthur was in Japan when the attack came and was slow to respond, but as the week went on he became increasingly involved.

Rusk heard from Dulles, who was in Tokyo at the time, that Mac-Arthur at first considered the matter only an unimportant border incident. But in midweek the general made a well-publicized tour of the front and called for American ground troops as soon as possible; otherwise the South Koreans would suffer swift defeat. At three o'clock in the morning on Friday, June 30, Rusk along with General J. Lawton Collins, the Army Chief of Staff, and Frank Pace, the Army Secretary, held a telephone conference with MacArthur, and they unanimously agreed to recommend the use of American ground troops. At a hastily called meeting with the President at eight thirty that same morning, the decision was made.

Ironically, the main topic of discussion at the meeting was whether to accept Chiang Kai-shek's offer of 33,000 of his best Kuomintang troops. A few voices were raised in favor of the proposal, but in the end Truman and Acheson rejected it. Chiang's troops would not make that much difference and might bring Chinese intervention. Years later, Rusk had a drink with "a very high official" of the Taiwan government who told him that he was the one who had proposed the offer of KMT troops within his own government. The offer was made, he told Rusk, only on "the categorical assurance that it would be turned down by the Americans." In reality, everyone in the government opposed the idea, from Chiang Kai-shek on down. The troop offer was only a clever public relations ploy, although the Americans did not know it at the time.

Even as the decision to send in two divisions of American troops was made, the mood among Truman's advisers was grim. Many doubted whether the green Americans could stop the determined North Korean advance. When the decision to use American air power was made the Sunday before, the Air Force Chief of Staff confidently predicted that the advancing Communist tank column would be knocked out. But the planes had stopped only a few; the rest had rolled into Seoul. Would the American ground forces meet the same fate? The troops were not combat ready, but they were sent in nevertheless. "Poor bastards," Rusk called them—he knew there was no other choice. Fortunately, when the Americans arrived, the North Koreans inexplicably slowed their advance for about ten days. In Rusk's view their hesitation saved the situation from disaster. He interpreted it as a sign that the American intervention was a surprise, and that the North Koreans were waiting for further instructions from the Russians and Chinese. In any event, needed time was gained to ship in more military might to meet the threat.

Less than a month after the invasion, as American men and supplies began pouring in through the port of Pusan, the Indian government suggested a compromise based on restoration of the *status quo ante,* with the Chinese Communist government taking China's seat in the United Nations. Kennan thought the idea had some merit, especially since the Chinese had indicated an interest in the matter. Rusk opposed it, and wrote Prime Minister Nehru on behalf of Acheson that "we do not believe that the termination of the Korean aggression can be contingent in any way upon the determination of other questions which are currently before the United Nations." To Rusk, the Chinese should not be allowed to gain from their aggression. He had no doubt that China was behind the North Korean action, and he was filled with moral indignation. There was no mood to compromise within the administration. It was also inconceivable that Nehru, the butt of jokes and derision in high American policy circles, could be taken seriously as an intermediary.

In September the war took a dramatic turn for the better, when the 1st Marine Division executed a brilliant amphibious assault at Inchon, a town held by the North Koreans on the west coast of the peninsula, just below the 38th parallel. By September 27 Seoul was recaptured, and by early October MacArthur's forces were at the 38th parallel, facing only token opposition. Republic of Korea troops were allowed to cross the parallel, and they pushed up the coast close to the city of Wonsan.

Even before the Inchon landing, Rusk had been rethinking American objectives in Korea. He himself had picked the 38th parallel as the boundary between North and South, and he argued that operations in the North should not be ruled out. The 38th parallel was entirely artificial and there was no real reason to respect it. On September 9 he made a speech publicly calling for a free, democratic, and united Korea. He was the chief proponent of this idea within the administration, and it coincided with MacArthur's views as well. Between the two of them, they sold it to Acheson and Truman.

Rusk's judgment rested on several premises. First, the aggressors, especially China and Russia, were to be taught a lesson they would never forget. He cited the Japanese invasion of Manchuria in 1931 and the consequences of letting aggression go unpunished. Korea was a similar test case for aggression in all of Asia and even in Europe. If Korea was preserved, the will and capability of the Western powers could not be questioned. Second, the moral position of the United States was clear. It had not acted alone, but had received the blessing of the United Nations. Rusk immediately went about getting U.N. approval of his proposal, and on October 7 a vaguely worded resolution passed the General Assembly by a vote of 47 to 5, which he interpreted as an endorsement and which enabled him to continue to use the U.N. as a moral and legal bludgeon against the Communists.

A third basis of his reasoning was the assumption that neither the Chinese nor the Russians would enter the war. Here his thinking was confused and his judgment clouded. There were plenty of warnings from the Indians and the British, as well as reports that two Chinese divisions (composed mostly of Koreans) were moving into Korea. The Chinese Foreign Minister, Chou En-lai, himself warned the Indian ambassador, K. M. Panikkar, on October 3 that if the Americans crossed the 38th parallel China would enter the war. But Rusk chose to believe that although the Chinese were intimately involved, they would never dare to intervene militarily. He gave credence to a CIA report that the Chinese would not come in, although the CIA had been notoriously wrong during the early phases of the war and had, in fact, given no warning of the initial North Korean invasion.

Although Rusk's views coincided with MacArthur's, there was one important difference between them. Had Rusk known that the Chinese would intervene, he would not have supported an American move into the North. He wanted to avoid war with China. MacArthur, on the other hand, as Rusk later came to believe, would have welcomed a war with China. MacArthur's troops marched on Pyongyang, and soon afterward they were headed toward the Yalu River on the Manchurian border.

In the midst of the euphoria over allied victories, President Truman decided to fly to Wake Island for a meeting with MacArthur, and Rusk was asked to go along as his top expert on the Far East. Other senior officials, such as Acheson and Marshall (whom Truman had persuaded to return to his cabinet as Secretary of Defense), declined the invitation. The whole idea, Acheson said, was "distasteful" and nothing good would come of it. Rusk saw this as further evidence of Acheson's lack of interest in Asia, but he was glad to go, especially as the ranking State Department official, and flew to Wake Island with Truman in the presidential airplane, the *Independence*.

The meeting between the President and his most important general was a strange one. There was no important decision to be made, no vital question to be discussed. Critics both at the time and afterward called it basically a political trip to bolster the Democratic chances in the November elections. Rusk's view was different. Truman was a very simple man at heart. He had never met MacArthur before and, like most Americans, held him almost in awe. MacArthur was "God's right-hand man," Truman said at the time, and he just wanted to meet and talk with him. Truman and most of his party regarded the war as essentially over. Now it was time to take stock of things, and the President should confer with his brilliant and victorious general. Part of Truman's nature, according to Rusk, was his need to establish a personal rapport with the people around him. He had, as yet, little indication of MacArthur's arrogance—a characteristic he would tolerate in no man.

MacArthur was both an extraordinarily brilliant and able man and a vain and imperious one. Rusk thought that he was served badly by his staff, which functioned like the court of some Oriental potentate and encouraged the negative aspects of MacArthur's personality. The proud MacArthur did not feel he had to defer to anyone, even to Truman. There were already subtle signs of discord between the general and the President. Truman at first wanted to meet MacArthur in Hawaii, but MacArthur had told him, "I will meet you only at Wake Island," and Truman yielded.

When the *Independence* landed at six thirty in the morning on October 15, MacArthur gave the President a cordial welcome. The two men presented a study in contrasting styles. The dapper Truman was dressed in a double-breasted business suit with a dark tie, while MacArthur wore his rumpled field uniform. He stood proud and erect, eyes squinting at the President from under the visor of his general's hat, which was emblazoned with the stars of his rank and the American eagle insignia. Truman later complained that he was "wearing a greasy ham and eggs hat that evidently had been used for twenty years." Truman suggested meeting later for lunch, but MacArthur politely but firmly told him no, that they would have to complete their business quickly because he had to return to Tokyo later that morning. It was not the usual way to treat a President, but MacArthur was not a usual man.

Rusk experienced one small incident that annoyed him and confirmed his opinion of MacArthur. There was only one car on the island, a 1947 Chevrolet that belonged to the Civil Aviation Administration. Truman and MacArthur used this car, while the rest of their parties and the accompanying newsmen went around by bus. At one point Truman left the group and MacArthur and an aide walked toward the car. When Rusk went to join them, MacArthur merely looked at him coldly and said, "You will take the bus, I presume."

Rusk was reminded of an incident between Stilwell and MacArthur during the war when Stilwell was the American commander in the CBI and MacArthur had charge of the Pacific theater. One day a fighter plane from China ventured out into the Pacific to shoot some Japanese planes. MacArthur heard about the incident and sent a message to Stilwell warning him about this "intrusion" into the Pacific theater. Stilwell wired back: "Keep your shirt on, Doug."

The President's party spent only about five hours on Wake Island before taking off again to return to Hawaii. Immediately after his arrival Truman and MacArthur had gone off for a private talk. From all accounts it was a get-acquainted session and they discussed nothing of substance. Then, at about 7:45, they returned to join their advisers in the Quonset hut that served as the Civil Aviation Administration's communication center. The men sat down around a make-shift conference table consisting of five small folding tables pushed together. Besides the President and the general, there were Rusk, Jessup, General Omar Bradley, who was chairman of the Joint Chiefs of Staff, Ambassador John Muccio, Averell Harriman, and Admiral Arthur Radford, the Pacific Fleet commander. A record of the conversation exists, taken from the notes of the participants and from the shorthand notes of Vernice Anderson, Jessup's secretary, the only woman in the President's party. Miss Anderson took the notes on her own because she thought it the right thing to do. She was hidden from sight, however, listening through a slatted, closed door. Much later, when MacArthur heard that a transcript existed of the talk, he was furious. Rusk was one of those who defended Miss Anderson's action as "entirely proper."

The transcript reveals a rambling, disjointed conversation about a wide variety of subjects. MacArthur did most of the talking in answer to questions, self-assured to the point of cockiness. He never asked for advice or instructions, even from the President. He spoke as if the war was over; his mind was on the postwar reconstruction, the withdrawal of his troops, and the Korean government. He believed that "formal resistance will end throughout North and South Korea by Thanksgiving." He wanted to turn the whole matter over to the South Korean civilian government as soon as possible, because "all occupations are failures." He said he wanted to get the 8th Army back to Japan by Christmas.

Rusk brought up the idea of stationing U.N. troops—possibly Indians and Pakistanis—along the Korean and Manchurian frontiers with the Soviet Union to act as a buffer between the two Communist giants and U.S. forces. MacArthur sharply disagreed: "It would be indefensible from a military point of view." He said he was going to put South Korean troops along the borders: "They will be the buffer."

President Truman asked MacArthur, "What are the chances for Chinese or Soviet interference?" MacArthur answered, "Very little. We no longer fear their intervention." He went on to say that with American air power now in Korea, "if the Chinese tried to get down to Pyongyang, there would be the greatest slaughter." "We are the best," he declared with a seemingly unshakeable confidence in his own and his troops' abilities. The war would be over by Thanksgiving. With that assurance Truman and his party returned to Washington, well satisfied with the meeting. He gave Rusk an inscribed copy of the log, thanking him for his "efficient and able contribution to the success of this great trip."

But almost as MacArthur spoke, Chinese "volunteers" were surreptitiously crossing the Yalu River into Korea, and by late October they were engaging South Korean and American forward units. Rusk and Acheson were restive, along with the Joint Chiefs. They tried to restrict MacArthur from bombing near the Chinese border, but the President gave in to the general's entreaties and allowed him to bomb the bridges across the Yalu.

Then MacArthur took some actions that Rusk considered unbalanced. Not only was he undeterred by the appearance of Chinese troops, but he became reckless, "dividing his army into little pieces and spreading it all over the North," as Rusk later recalled. He was enough of a military man to know that in the rough terrain of North Korea the divided columns were not in a position to give each other support. But his questioning went unheeded because it was considered a military matter to be left to the judgment of the commander in the field or the Joint Chiefs. The Chiefs also had their doubts, but they were in such awe of the hero of Inchon that they were hesitant to question his deployments. Rusk's fears were realized in late November when the Chinese intervened in earnest. With no warning from U.S. intelligence, masses of bugle-blowing Chinese hurled themselves at the 8th Army and ROK units and sent them reeling. Rusk believed at the time that the Chinese acted at the behest of the Soviets, a view later confirmed by intelligence reports.

The Chinese attack shook the American government to its foundations. The war was suddenly spinning out of control. Everyone had been grievously wrong about Chinese intentions. But there was little time for recriminations. American and U.N. forces were in full retreat down the peninsula. The Chinese objective was to drive them into the sea.

Almost as much as the Chinese intervention, MacArthur's dark and ominous messages troubled Truman and his advisers. "We face an entirely new war," he reported. Reading the military reports and MacArthur's messages, Rusk and the others realized that the general was, in a not-so-subtle fashion, presenting them with a choice: either go to war against China or be driven out of Korea. MacArthur's choice was clear; he wanted to begin general war with China. He would also open up a second front by "unleashing" Chiang's troops on Taiwan. Perhaps the French could be persuaded to cooperate in Indochina as well.

Truman briefly flirted with the idea. But his military advisers told him he would have to use atomic weapons to destroy Chinese troop concentrations and ultimately Chinese cities. Truman made a few ill-considered statements to the press about considering the use of atomic weapons, which drew a negative reaction around the world and prompted British Prime Minister Clement Attlee to hastily schedule a trip to Washington. In fact, however, Truman never was close to a decision to use nuclear bombs.

Rusk counseled against any general war with China. He told Truman that, based on his experience in the CBI, war in China was unthinkable. America and its allies might mobilize several million men and at best be able to capture and hold a few coastal cities. But there was no possibility of imposing our will on the vast population of that country. It was a view that was generally accepted by the "war cabinet."

A more prevalent sentiment, especially among the Joint Chiefs, was that evacuation from the Korean peninsula was inevitable. General Collins was dispatched to Tokyo to formulate a plan for withdrawal. Rusk strongly disagreed, and at a dramatic, tension-filled meeting with Truman and Acheson on December 4 he virtually single-handedly turned this sentiment around. Invoking Churchill and the British spirit in the early days of World War II, the dark days after Pearl Harbor when the Japanese were rushing through Asia, even the example of the Russians in Leningrad holding their own against Hitler's armies, he argued that the United States must find the will to establish a strong defense line and hold firm until there was a cease-fire. Acheson was moved by Rusk's words and said, "Mr. President, we just can't let them do this to the United States." Truman accepted the advice. The

United States would stay in Korea, he decided, but the conflict was to be localized, and there should be no more talk about establishing a unified and democratic Korea. Later that month General Matthew Ridgway assumed command of the 8th Army, and with heroic effort stabilized the American and United Nations lines.

Rusk made an even more radical suggestion to the President at the meeting on December 4. "MacArthur should be relieved from command in Korea and replaced by General Collins," he told Truman. "That would allow him to concentrate on his duties in Japan." MacArthur's recent actions as a military commander were inexcusable, he argued. He had unwisely divided his army in the face of imminent attack, then sent gloomy and pessimistic messages back from the front. MacArthur had a morale problem. Rusk quoted General Marshall: "When soldiers have morale problems, it's the commanding officer's fault. But when a general has morale problems, it's the general's fault." But Truman was not yet ready to accept Rusk's advice. MacArthur would stay.

As the year 1951 began, Truman continued to prosecute a "limited war" in Korea. It was a new kind of war, dictated by military realities and increasing friction among the allies. Rusk helped to formulate the war's revised objectives. He proposed the establishment of a military position in Korea at the 38th parallel, the negotiation of a cease-fire, and finding a means for an honorable withdrawal of the majority of U.S. forces. Increasingly, the American policy aim shifted to the "liquidation of our Korean difficulties."

Limited war was unpopular in many quarters, but no more so than in the heart of Douglas MacArthur. The general continued to fret over the restrictions placed upon him. Why had the 8th Army been halted short of its mission, the unification of Korea? Why could he not bomb the power plants on the Yalu River? Why were pilots prevented from "hot pursuit" of the enemy across the Manchurian border? In his frustration, on March 24 the general directed his own ultimatum to the Chinese: either enter into negotiations to permit the unification of Korea or suffer the consequences. The statement was totally unauthorized and was bound to be counterproductive, since the Chinese now would never agree to negotiate. It was also an insult to his Commander in Chief. Senior officials in Washington wanted to relieve MacArthur immediately, but Truman was still not ready. Acheson was concerned about the political consequences and advised Truman to think the matter over.

MacArthur pressed on. Korea was the test case for the free world in how to meet Communist aggression. We were fighting Europe's war in Asia. If we won in Korea, war would be avoided in Europe as well. "There is no substitute for victory," MacArthur wrote in a letter to Joe Martin, the Speaker of the House of Representatives.

The letter to Martin spurred another round of meetings on "MacArthuritis," as Rusk began to call it. This time all of Truman's principal advisers—Acheson, Marshall, and the Joint Chiefs—agreed that MacArthur must be relieved. At last Truman was willing to act, and he asked Marshall, with Acheson's help, to draw up the necessary orders, which should be phrased simply as a change in command. Rusk was convinced of the correctness of Truman's action: a President could not permit a military commander to flaunt his disagreement on an important matter of policy. At one point Truman said, "There are a million Americans that could be President as well as I can, but goddammit, I'm President and I'm not going to turn this office over to my successor with its prerogatives impaired by an American general." Unlike Acheson, Truman did not seem worried about the political consequences. He predicted there would be a major outcry for a few weeks, but that would be all. It would soon blow over.

On Tuesday, April 10, 1951, a small incident lit a fuse under Truman and made him decide he could not afford the courtesy of a formal change in command before relieving MacArthur. General Omar Bradley and Rusk received word from the White House press secretary that the *Chicago Tribune* was reserving a space for a big story about MacArthur in the next day's paper. Knowing of the *Tribune*'s right-wing sympathies, Bradley and Rusk thought this could mean only one thing, that MacArthur had gotten wind of what was up in Washington and was going to steal a march and resign. It was about ten o'clock at night, but both men went over to the White House to see the President. When Truman heard the news he said, "That son of a bitch isn't going to resign on me! I want him fired." To make sure that he was, they drafted a statement for the press and scheduled it for release at 1:00 A.M. A few minutes later the news was out around the world. Truman didn't even wait up to see the statement released to the press; he went to bed right after the decision was made. The last thing he said to Rusk and Bradley was a generous remark entreating them not to interfere with the welcome MacArthur would get when he returned to the United States. "General MacArthur has not been home since World War II. He has not received the hero's welcome to which he is entitled and which the American people will want to give him."

Bradley went back to the Pentagon to make the arrangements to inform MacArthur. He tried to reach Secretary Pace, who was in Korea, so that he could tell the general, but he couldn't be located, and MacArthur heard the news of his dismissal on the radio like everyone else. Rusk had the job of notifying the ambassadors from the countries that had troops in Korea. In the early morning hours he called them up one by one and received reactions that ran a gamut of emotions, from the New Zealand ambassador's remark, "Well, the little man did it, didn't he?" to anger expressed by the ambassador from the Philippines.

MacArthur did indeed receive a hero's welcome from the American people, while on several college campuses Truman and Acheson were burned in effigy. Some in Congress called for Truman's impeachment and cited MacArthur's removal as further proof of the fact that the country was "in the hands of a secret inner coterie directed by the Soviet Union." When MacArthur arrived in Washington in the early morning hours of April 19 twelve thousand cheering well-wishers were at the airport to greet him, and later that day he addressed a joint session of Congress. His speech and the spectacle of his presence were unforgettable. In resonant, measured tones he defiantly stated his theme—America must not surrender to communism in Asia.

In May Congress let off steam by holding closed-door hearings on MacArthur's ouster, and the general spoke bitterly of the "political decisions" that had shackled him as a military commander. Rusk held another view. MacArthur had an aura of greatness, but his arrogance and pride made him fall short of the mark. He had forgotten that "under the Constitution the President, not a military man, is Commander in Chief." As Truman said later, "General MacArthur was insubordinate and I fired him. That's all there was to it."

No sooner had the furor over MacArthur died down than Rusk became involved in a public controversy of his own making. He was invited to speak at the twenty-fifth anniversary dinner of the China Institute in America, a friendship society militantly partisan to Chiang Kai-shek and the Nationalists on Taiwan. The banquet, held on May 18, was presided over by none other than Henry Luce, the self-appointed chairman of the China lobby. The setting was the Waldorf-Astoria Hotel in New York, in the full spotlight of the national media. It was a moment just waiting to be captured, even exploited. Rusk had received press attention before—virtually all of it extremely complimentary—but it was usually in the context of articles about the State Department or the United Nations, or local reporting about one of his speeches. But here was a chance to make a splash. He was more than up to the task.

He shared the dais not only with Henry Luce, but with two heavy-weight political figures. One was John Foster Dulles, super-hawk, super-foe of Communist China, and Rusk's friend, who was generally considered to be the Republican spokesman on foreign policy. Rusk had helped keep Dulles in the headlines by making him the chief negotiator for the Japanese Peace Treaty, while he himself worked in the background as the invisible man. The other person was Senator Paul Douglas, considered an "attractive" liberal Democrat who was going to run for President. Rusk was not known as a politician, and in such a lineup few people expected him to shine. They were wrong. He stole the show; Douglas and even Dulles were left in his shadow.

The next day he made page one of The New York Times with the headline "Rusk Hints U.S. Aid to Revolt in China." Time led off its story about the speech with Rusk's picture in the middle of the first column (Dulles took second billing). There were headlines all over the country as columnists and editorial writers puzzled over Rusk's speech. A furor erupted both within and outside the administration.

Rusk's speech was an all-out, no-holds-barred attack on the Communist government of China. His theme was that China was "driven by foreign masters" in the Soviet Union, and he alleged that the Russians were colonizing Manchuria, Sinkiang, and Inner Mongolia. The Chinese had intervened in Korea only at the wish of the Soviets, he said, and in an excess of rhetoric he even called China a "colonial Russian government—a Slavic Manchukuo on a larger scale." He then rubbed the Chinese leaders' noses in the taunt that they were not recognized by the international community: "[The government] is not entitled to speak for China in the international community of nations. It is not the Government of China. It does not pass the first test. It is not Chinese." He then added ominously, "We recognize the Nationalist Government of China. . . . That Government will continue to receive important aid and assistance from the United States." He also implied an effort to overthrow the Communist regime. "As the Chinese people move to assert their freedom and to work out their destiny in accordance with their own historical purposes, they can count upon tremendous support from free peoples in other parts of the world."

Many years later, Rusk seemed to be genuinely uneasy about this speech, dismissing it either as campaign-style oratory or as an attempt to shame the Chinese into splitting with the Soviets. There undoubtedly was some truth to both points, but neither was the whole explanation. Rusk was too judicious and careful a person not to realize his words would be taken seriously by the American public. And there is no doubt that he told his audience what they wanted to hear. Most commentators said that the speech signaled a new and tougher line and was, as *The New York Times* put it, "a virtual reversal of the policies indicated in the White Paper of 1949." Both Acheson and Truman were upset; Rusk had not cleared the speech in advance with either the White House or State's Policy Planning Staff. An angry Acheson called Rusk into his office and the two of them went over the speech line by line, Rusk arguing that the speech did not represent any change in existing policy. Acheson finally agreed.

They were right; American policy toward China had been changing, slowly and almost imperceptibly, without any systematic reappraisal or evaluation of the consequences. The wait-and-see attitude toward nonrecognition had hardened into a pillar of America's Asian policy. The arm's-length approach toward what Rusk had once called the "incompetent and corrupt" Nationalist regime of Chiang Kai-shek had turned into a warm embrace. Only seven months earlier, in response to a question about whether America should rescue its friends in China, Rusk had answered, "Let the Chinese rescue the Chinese. They know more about it." Now he repudiated that position: China was the "fatal flaw" that would taint U.S. policy in Asia for the next twenty years.

The reasons for this shift were not hard to find. The Chinese intervention in Korea had affected Rusk deeply. There must be no reward for aggression; nothing should be done to add to China's prestige. Rusk also let himself be manipulated by John Foster Dulles to the point of adopting Dulles's memoranda on China as his own and forwarding them to Acheson. Domestic politics and McCarthyism also took their toll, putting the whole administration on the defensive, and the hardened attitudes toward the Chinese were embodied in a National Security Council statement—NSC-48/4—which was signed by the President. The Republican policy toward China was adopted by the Truman administration virtually intact.

In the first few years of the postwar period the United States fought not only the Cold War with the Soviets but also a hot war with the Chinese. If the former was inevitable, the latter was not; it was brought about by tragic miscalculations on both sides. The error was compounded when, as a result of the hot war, the small window of opportunity to right our policy with China that had opened with the White Paper was slammed shut. With it, the possibility of peace in Asia also disappeared, for almost a generation.

Meanwhile, since the fateful decision in December to localize the war in Korea, the United States had been busy through diplomatic contacts trying to find a basis for disengagement from the fighting. Discussions were held among the allies, and indirect approaches were made both to the Soviets and the Chinese. Rusk looked upon the Russians as the key. At a staff meeting on April 18 he reminded everyone that "it was a little remark by Stalin which opened the way to the settlement of the Berlin blockade." He told them to be on the lookout for such an opening, and he proved to be correct. On June 23 the break came when, in an almost offhand remark to Kennan, Yakov Malik at the U.N. said that "discussions should be started between the belligerents for a cease-fire and an armistice providing for the mutual withdrawal of forces from the 38th parallel."

Rusk was cautious, but he believed the proposal called for "further clarification" and directed that Ambassador Alan Kirk approach Andrei Gromyko in Moscow. Kirk reported that Gromyko confirmed the seriousness of the proposal and added that the talks should be limited to military questions and should take place between representatives of the United Nations command and the Republic of Korea, on the one hand, and representatives of the North Korean and Chinese "volunteer" units on the other. This suited Rusk and Acheson, who were not prepared to enter into broader political discussions with the Chinese. Rusk was also bedeviled by Wellington Koo, the ambassador from Taiwan, who told him he was "greatly concerned" about the cease-fire proposal. Before the opening of the negotiations on July 3 Rusk testified before the Senate Foreign Relations Committee, where he refused to make public the American negotiating position because, he argued, "it would tip our hand in advance and create both political difficulties and problems with our allies." To be productive, the negotiations must proceed out of the public view. He also ruled out a unilateral cease-fire before a formal truce.

The truce negotiations began at long last on July 10, 1951, and were unexpectedly protracted, concluding finally in 1953, long after Rusk had left the Department of State. In his view the discussions were prolonged primarily because of two decisions made by President Truman. First, he supported the military's view that the front lines of the opposing armies, not the 38th parallel, should be the cease-fire line because he wished to retain some high ground located just above the 38th parallel. Second, Truman supported Syngman Rhee's insistence that North Korean prisoners who did not want to go back would not be returned. Rusk, somewhat reluctantly, concurred in these decisions.

At the same time that he was occupied with the war in Korea, Rusk was busy making the final peace with Japan. Since 1946 the Office of Far Eastern Affairs had been considering holding a peace conference that would formally end hostilities between Japan and the nations that had fought against it. Just as with Germany, the going proved exceedingly difficult, and many thought it was hopeless. So many problems had to be overcome and interests reconciled. The several dozen nations that had fought Japan all had their own viewpoints. The Soviets would try to disrupt any settlement that was not to their liking. China was another problem, especially after the Communist takeover. Within the U.S. government there were also competing ideas. The Pentagon wanted to station troops in Japan, and any treaty would have to be acceptable to key Republican leaders in Congress, a major difficulty considering that Truman's entire Far Eastern policy was under bitter, partisan attack. Finally, the peace settlement had to be acceptable to the Japanese people.

In August 1947 a draft treaty was circulated to the responsible officials at State and the Pentagon with the recommendation that a peace conference be held as soon as possible. The document was over one hundred pages long and full of detail, the product of endless meetings. It seemed everyone who read it saw one more "essential point" that should be included, and the draft was an unwieldy amalgamation of everyone's pet ideas. The document soon became mired down in the bureaucracy, and, as a result, when Rusk took over at Far Eastern Affairs the Japanese peace settlement was farther off than ever. The occupation was dragging on, and MacArthur counseled urgent action. It was high time to break the impasse and cut the umbilical cord to Japan. This great nation had to be prepared to take its rightful place among the world community.

Rusk decided that it would be folly to call a peace conference without quiet diplomacy in advance to ensure an acceptable settlement. He also decided that John Foster Dulles was the right man to appoint as chief negotiator in order to blunt any possible Republican opposition. He persuaded Dulles to take the job, and he convinced Truman and Acheson to accept him, in spite of Acheson's personal dislike of Dulles. A mark of Rusk's success was that journalists and historians have generally given Dulles all the credit for the Japanese Peace Treaty. Dulles was the up-front negotiator and performed admirably, but insiders at State knew that Rusk was calling most of the shots. The Japanese settlement was one of his most notable accomplishments.

One of the first things Rusk did was to see Truman about the essential terms of a settlement. Truman agreed that the hundreds of provisions and details of the prior drafts of the treaty should be junked. "Keep it simple," he said, and Rusk worked up a one-page letter for Truman to sign that contained the essential points. It would be a "peace of reconcilation." Japan would be given full sovereignty over the four main islands of Hokkaido, Honshu, Shikoku, and Kyushu. There would be no reparations or other punitive measures, and no formal limitations would be placed on Japanese rearmament or remilitarization. Japan would also agree to cooperate with the United States and its allies "for the maintenance of international peace and security in the Japan area."

Once Truman had decided the basic outlines of the settlement, the job began of selling it to the allies, the Pentagon, Japanese leaders, members of Congress, and the public. It took many months of patient diplomacy. Dulles was dispatched around the world to travel from capital to capital, his briefcase full of papers and reports. Rusk remained at home, compiling instructions for Dulles and keeping the American bureaucracy at bay, turning aside the trivia that each department thought "essential" for the treaty. The Soviets proved troublesome, and it was decided to go ahead without them. The China problem was solved by excluding both the People's Republic of China and Taiwan. To assuage Chiang and his congressional supporters, Rusk went to Tokyo and obtained Prime Minister Shigeru Yoshida's agreement that his government would establish normal relations with Taiwan and had no intention of recognizing the People's Republic. Rusk also spent five weeks in Tokyo to work out the legal and administrative terms on which American armed forces would be allowed to remain in Japan. He convinced the Pentagon to accept the conditions essential to the Japanese, pointing out, "It is short-sighted from the military point of view to think that you can maintain bases in the middle of 90 million people who are resistant to the idea."

These efforts resulted in a draft peace treaty consisting of just twenty-seven articles, two declarations, and one protocol, a remarkably short document. In July 1951 the United States invited fifty governments to attend a conference in San Francisco in early September to consider a treaty of peace with Japan "on the terms of that text." Rusk was determined to stage-manage the peace conference so that unwanted amendments could not be added, especially if proposed by the Russians. It was a foregone conclusion that they would try to disrupt the conference, and to prevent it Rusk devised some unique rules of procedure. Since the delegates were invited to San Francisco for the purpose of adopting a specific draft treaty, any amendments proposed by the Russians or anyone else would simply be ruled out of order by Acheson, who was presiding as the host Foreign Minister. "We really screwed the Russians," Rusk later recalled. "We weren't about to let them do to us in Japan what they had done in Germany."

When the Russians discovered what was happening, they promptly walked out, which did not unduly upset anyone, because no one expected the Russians to accept the treaty. The conference was a media event, one of the first to be televised live from coast to coast. Acheson's popularity rose greatly, and Dulles was very visible as the floor leader of the U.S. delegation. Rusk was less visible, but worked hard behind the scenes at persuading delegates on various points. In the end forty-nine nations signed the treaty, a great feather in Rusk's cap. He not only successfully concluded the peace treaty negotiations but also, in what many believed was an even more difficult and notable accomplishment, got two old enemies, John Foster Dulles and Dean Acheson, to work together in harmony.

On the same day the peace treaty was signed, September 8, 1951, the United States and Japan entered into another pact that sealed their future relationship: a security treaty that granted the right of the United States "to dispose . . . land, air, and sea forces around Japan . . . to [secure] Japan against attack from without," as well as against subversion from within caused by any outside power. The treaty was an important step in the new American foreign policy. Like West Germany, the defeated Japan was firmly integrated into the defense perimeter of the West against the Communist giants, the Soviet Union and China. The perimeter was further extended when a U.N. trusteeship was established for the Ryukyu Islands and Bonin with the United States as the sole administering authority. Later, when he was Secretary of State in the 1960s, Rusk bitterly opposed what he called the "attempts by the Japanese to erode our base in Okinawa on the grounds of Japanese 'sensibilities.' " In a memo to President Johnson in February 1968 he derided "Japanese whining" about Okinawa and called the reversion of Okinawa to Japan "intolerable." (Okinawa and the Ryukyus were in fact returned to Japan during the Nixon administration in 1972.) Rusk also negotiated a secret understanding with Japan in 1966 that allowed U.S. ships and planes carrying nuclear weapons to use Japanese ports and airfields. Under the accord the United States neither confirms nor denies whether its ships or planes are armed with nuclear weapons, and the government of Japan avoids asking any questions on the matter—a classic instance of the use of "creative ambiguity" in diplomacy.

The peace settlement with Japan and the accompanying security treaty helped produce other security arrangements in the Pacific as well. Australia was moving closer to the United States because of its need to obtain loans and credits to finance its immigration policy and economic development plans. In October 1950 the Australian Foreign Minister, Percy Spender, held a conference with Rusk about the possibility of Australia, New Zealand, and the Philippines entering a mutual security pact with the United States. Spender was worried about a resurgent Japan, and mentioned the fact that Australia had narrowly escaped an invasion by Japan during World War II. Rusk proposed such a pact to Acheson, and the Tripartite Security Treaty (frequently referred to as ANZUS after the signatories) was signed by Australia, New Zealand, and the United States on July 23, 1951. A similar mutual defense treaty was signed by the United States and the Philippines later that year.

These new security arrangements were concluded despite the opposition of the Department of Defense and George Marshall. Rusk and Dulles went ahead anyway, with assurances to Marshall that the Pacific nations would not participate in NATO, the Organization of American States, and other defense arrangements. Rusk also smoothed over relations with the British, who were disturbed about these pacts as well.

While some officials like Marshall felt uncomfortable with the growing U.S. security commitment in the Far East, to others it was not enough. Dulles wanted a "Pacific NATO," a multilateral pact directed against the Soviet Union and its allies that would include the countries of South and Southeast Asia: Indonesia, Malaya, Thailand, Burma, and India. Rusk asked Jessup to study the matter, and they concluded it was premature to establish this sort of alliance. Jessup reported that the governments of the area were "non-democratic; that they lacked trained personnel; that they had economic difficulties and were inefficient and corrupt; that there were military weaknesses and local communist strength; and that there was a basic distrust of the West." He "found no enthusiasm whatsoever for a Southeast Asian Union and [did] not believe that a regional pact is a very important subject." The idea was dropped. But Dulles later had his way after he became President Eisenhower's Secretary of State. The Pacific pact became the Southeast Asia Treaty Organization (SEATO), which was formed quietly on September 8, 1954.

Even without a formal security pact, the United States was becoming heavily involved in French Indochina. Tragically, the initial American policy of anticolonialism was overwhelmed by the newer, postwar policy of containment of communism. The key period of change was 1948–49. Rusk himself pointed this out in a memo written in January 1951: "The Department's policy at this time had jelled." The key events causing the shift were the success of the Communists in China under Mao Tse-tung and the Berlin blockade. The imminent takeover in China created the fear that all of Asia would go Communist, and to prevent that from happening, Indochina—which Rusk called the breadbasket of Asia—had to be denied to the Chinese. The Berlin blockade contributed to the shift in thinking because the French were now needed to play a central role in NATO and other security arrangements in Europe. The French government was notoriously weak and had to be supported both in France and in Indochina.

What was left of the American anticolonial policy was transformed into an effort called "Operation Eggshell." As the name implies, it was a delicate attempt to push the French into granting its colonies in Indochina a measure of independence. At first this new policy appeared to meet with some success. The French carved Indochina up into three "associated states"—Laos, Cambodia, and Vietnam—within the French Union. France retained power over foreign policy matters, but independent, native governments were formed in all three areas.

Vietnam was always the chief trouble spot for the French. Ho Chi Minh's guerrillas began to fight the French as soon as they returned to Indochina after the end of the war. When the French formed the associated state of Vietnam, they selected a collaborator, Bao Dai, a Paris-educated member of a prominent family, to become head of state. The United States followed the French lead and recognized the Bao Dai regime in February 1950, having announced its intention to do so some months before. There was never any American attempt to work with Ho, who was considered a Communist by the French. Ho's government, however, was recognized by both Moscow and Peking.

Thus the battle lines were already drawn when Rusk came to Far Eastern Affairs in March 1950. Even as the United States was recognizing the Bao Dai regime, top officials at State knew he had little support among his people and that his government was not viable. Yet they were willing to back Bao Dai in the hope that it would rally support to him. Rusk's predecessor at Far Eastern Affairs, Walton

Butterworth, wrote Rusk that "economic support, military items, and political moves" should be used to prop up Bao Dai. Officially the State Department extended to Bao Dai "our best wishes for prosperity and stability in Vietnam and the hope that a closer relationship will be established between Vietnam and the United States." Acheson met with French Foreign Minister Robert Schuman and agreed on a program of economic and military aid to the three associated states. In June Rusk wrote a set of further instructions to David Bruce, the U.S. Ambassador in Paris. Concerned that there was a public perception that Bao Dai was a French puppet, he urged that the French be encouraged to publicize their accomplishments "in formalizing the independence of the three states." Then came a patronizing and almost contradictory sentence: "Please assure [the French] that in presuming to make suggestions . . . concerning what the U.S. government recognizes is a family affair between France and the members of the French Union, we are giving the most sympathetic consideration to the weight of France's obligations as having primary responsibility for the area of Indochina and seek only to reduce the burden of such responsibilities."

The Korean invasion further heightened American involvement and commitment to Vietnam. Military and economic aid was increased, and it was agreed with the British that in the event of Communist Chinese attack they would "assist the French to the extent of their abilities . . . but the probability would be great that neither could provide forces for this purpose." Rusk was appointed chairman of the Southeast Asia Aid Policy Committee to coordinate U.S. military, economic, and political aid to the area. The committee worked on the assumption that "firm non-communist control of Indochina is of critical strategic importance to U.S. national interests." The area was under joint Soviet-Chinese "attack," and to repel this threat "prompt acceleration of the formation of new national armies" was needed. As the military situation for the French in Indochina deteriorated, the policy line became more strident. Rusk and other top officials told Acheson that "the military situation is so grave as to require the very highest priority treatment by the United States." On July 3, 1950, Rusk wrote to Karl Lott Rankin, the American consul general in Hong Kong, that "I have the impression that we could lose quickly in Southeast Asia but that we can win through a long, persistent, and tough effort to build the elementary institutions which are required to support the kind of society we would think worth supporting. I am convinced that we must set about the job of helping these people help themselves, perhaps in hundreds of different ways, but it will take a great deal of courage to keep picking ourselves up out of the dust of disappointment and trying again.''

A few voices were raised questioning America's deepening involvement in Vietnam. In August 1950 Charlton Ogburn, the policy information officer at Far Eastern Affairs, wrote Rusk that the "perversities of the French" were producing a "mess" in Vietnam. The French, he argued, were refusing to grant genuine independence and were pushing the United States into building up a Vietnamese army to fight for the French Union. This was, in turn, alienating the Asians, who identified us with colonialism. We were facing, he warned, a dilemma:

> . . . we have been giving the Congressional Foreign Relations Committees an impression that we are confronted with a clear case of Communist aggression in Indochina and that we are meeting it in a hard-hitting, two-fisted manner in a demonstration of positive policy. This is all right in the short run, but it is not sowing the whirlwind? — unless of course we intend when the time comes to commit American ground forces in Indochina and thus throw all Asia to the wolves along with the best chances the free world has.

Another critic was John Ohly, deputy director of the Mutual Defense Assistance Program, which administered the aid flowing to Vietnam. On November 20, 1950, he wrote a top-secret personal memorandum to Rusk saying, "I would appreciate your reading and studying it carefully—and then passing it on to the Secretary [Acheson] for his *personal* attention." Ohly called for a "thorough and realistic reexamination of our policy with respect to Indochina." He was deeply concerned about the U.S. aid program and the extent to which it would prevent effective military assistance in Western Europe and other areas:

> We have reached a point where the United States, because of limitations in resources, can no longer simultaneously pursue all of its objectives in all parts of the world and must realistically face the fact that certain objectives, even though they may be extremely valuable and important ones, may have to be abandoned if others of even greater value and importance are to be attained.

He then expressed grave concern about the wisdom of the whole undertaking in Vietnam:

As an afterthought, and by way of additional caveat, I would like to point out that the demands on the U.S. for Indochina are increasing almost daily and that, sometimes imperceptibly, by one step after another, we are gradually increasing our stake in the outcome of the struggle there. We are, moreover, slowly (and not too slowly) getting ourselves into a position where our responsibilities tend to supplant rather than complement those of the French, and where failures are attributed to us as though we were the primary party at fault and in interest. We may be on the road to being a scapegoat, and we are certainly dangerously close to the point of being so deeply committed that we may find ourselves completely committed even to direct intervention. These situations, unfortunately, have a way of snowballing.

Ohly's prophetic concerns were shared by the European bureau at State and by some in the military as well. A policy review was undertaken in the National Security Council and at the highest levels of the CIA. A grim intelligence report told of Chinese intervention in Vietnam, including advisory personnel and material. Direct intervention by Chinese "volunteers" seemed possible. Rusk personally considered the matter in a long memorandum on January 31, 1951. In his view American diplomacy and aid to the countries of Southeast Asia were having a positive effect. Those nations were "disposed to move in the direction of the United States and of the political and economic systems of which it is the principal protagonist." As he saw the situation,

the United States must decide how much it is prepared to pay in the way of military assistance to validate that success. If, upon careful consideration of all the factors involved, the United States Government decides that it can afford to supply to the countries of Southeast Asia military assistance requisite to their making a stand on their own and our behalf, well and good. If, on the other hand, it is our carefully considered conclusion that, due to the demands for military assistance from other areas of strategic importance to the United States, we cannot follow through on the military program which our political program foreshadows, then we must trim our sails accordingly. In a word, the United States has in Southeast Asia reached the point where we must decide whether we shall put up or shut up.

Rusk had no doubt that it was time to "put up," and he launched into a passionate plea for no change in course. The United States had to find a way to do what was required. The strategic, political, and

economic importance of the countries of Southeast Asia was clear. In
an optimistic country-by-country survey of the area, including Burma,
Thailand, Indochina, Malaya, Indonesia, and the Philippines, he
noted that remarkable progress was evident in each. In Indochina
"our participation in the overall operation must be greater than ever
before." The French had made important concessions and the associated states now needed "constant aid" before they would be ready
to "assume their responsibilities." There was, for Rusk, no alternative:

> Above all, we cannot afford to jeopardize the considerable measure of
> success our policy has already had in Indochina by neglecting to pro-
> vide the proper maintenance for our investment. French cooperation
> will be required at all times and can only be assured if we, ourselves,
> continue to give constant evidence of our determination to see the
> matter through. In sum, to neglect to pursue our present course to the
> utmost of our ability would be disastrous to our interests in Indochina
> and, consequently, in the rest of Southeast Asia.

Rusk saw other reasons for maintaining military aid and economic
assistance as well. Expounding what would later be known as the
domino theory, he argued that if Indochina were allowed to go Communist, Thailand and Burma would fall almost immediately and other
countries of the region would be gravely threatened. Our allies
France, Britain, and the Netherlands were counting on our aid to
Southeast Asia, and he also stressed the "strategic economic" importance of the rice, rubber, and tin produced in the area. His views
prevailed, and Acheson decided there would be no change in the
American commitment. America would continue its march to disaster
in Vietnam.

By the autumn of 1951 Rusk was coming to another turning point in
his personal life. He was forty-two years old. Between the war and
the State Department, he had spent the last eleven years in the government and he thought seriously of doing something else. He had
risen in the State Department as far as he could; many regarded him
as the number two man under Acheson. But his future was insecure.
The 1952 presidential election year was approaching, Truman was not
going to run, and the State Department would be caught up in politics
and uncertainty until a new man took over. If the Republicans won
the election, he might well be out of a job.

Dulles had talked to Rusk off and on for several months about the presidency of the Rockefeller Foundation. Chester I. Bernard, the current president, would retire on June 30, 1952, and Dulles told Rusk he could have the job if he wanted it. The pay was $40,000 a year, more than double his salary at State. It was an attractive offer to a man with three growing children.

Rusk also admitted, if only to himself and his family, that he as tired. For several years he had worked excruciatingly hard, seven days a week, on problems that were wrenching and difficult. He wanted to cast off that burden and lead a more normal family life. He decided to accept Dulles's offer.

It was a good time to leave. Rusk was just finishing up his work on the Japanese Peace Treaty, and in November he went to Japan to negotiate the last details of the status of the U.S. forces agreement with the Japanese government. On the way back, in Seattle on November 6, he gave an address, "The Underlying Principles of Far Eastern Policy," to the World Affairs Council. It was his summing up. Asia was rapidly progressing and maturing, he said, and the United States must help the Asian peoples by "broad support for their nationalist aspirations." Rusk had a vision of a broad anti-Communist coalition of Asian governments and a growing consciousness of the interdependence of the nations of the Far East in the maintenance of peace in that area. He spoke with emotion about "the reality of the principles of the United Nations Charter, the mockery of the hollow promise of communist agents, and the nature of the threat which communist imperialism poses against the newly won freedom and independence of the new nations of Asia."

On December 6, 1951, Rusk's decision to leave the State Department was announced. He would become president of the Rockefeller Foundation on June 30, 1952, and in the meantime would be a consultant to State working on the Japanese Peace Treaty. There was glowing and universal praise for Rusk and his service at State. *The New York Times* commented that he possessed "one of the keenest minds in the State Department, where in mid-1950 he undertook the difficult task of supervising our Far Eastern Affairs. His record of courageous action and willingness to tackle difficult assignments has acquired fresh luster." The *Washington Post* ran an editorial headed "Rockefeller Foundation Lucky to Get Rusk," and said that "when he was appointed, the job [at Far Eastern Affairs] had become a football of partisan strife over China; it seemed impossible that anyone could survive in it or keep his reputation intact. But . . . he has confounded the prophets. This newspaper, which has opposed the twists and turns of State Department policy toward Chiang Kai-shek, is all the more glad to take its hat off to Mr. Rusk on his new opportunity for service."

On December 6 Rusk flew down to Key West, where Truman was vacationing, to tender his resignation in person. The President was warm and kind. He wrote Rusk a two-page letter expressing genuine regret at his resignation and added, "Nothing but a clear understanding of the reasons which impel you to this action would move me to acquiesce in your wish." A year later, when Davidson College asked Truman to contribute a comment for a testimonial to Rusk, the President answered, "Dean Rusk is tops in my book."

Like a prizefighter who retires while he is still the champion, Rusk chose a propitious moment to leave the Department of State. The universal acclaim accorded him was remarkable; somehow he had risen above the partisan attacks on the administration. He had taken one of the most difficult jobs in government and not only endured but prevailed. He had the satisfaction of knowing he had played a vital role in the assertion of American supremacy around the world. He pointed with pride to his accomplishments: blunting Communist aggression in Korea, formulating the Japanese Peace Treaty, and establishing a defense perimeter of friendly nations in Asia. For the moment, at least, the Cold War confrontation seemed to be at a standstill.

Now Truman would pass into history and, under the benign leadership of the well-loved President Eisenhower, the nation would enter into a complacent decade of peace and unparalleled prosperity. When a new generation of leaders came to power in the 1960s, coinciding with the reemergence of unsolved difficulties and problems, Rusk's service at State made it natural for them to turn to him as one of the architects of the policies that would be necessary to again prevail.

PART THREE

THE ROCKEFELLER FOUNDATION

"The Man Who Wants
to Give Away Millions"

*Rusk as president of the Rockefeller Foundation,
with John D. Rockefeller III in 1952*

Rusk's life suddenly took on the aura of a Horatio Alger tale—
the poor boy from Cherokee County, Georgia, who grew up wearing
flour-sack drawers, found himself catapulted into the Eastern establishment power elite. He also began to move in the social circle of the
storied Rockefeller family. But he took it all in stride, and admonished
his children to behave properly on their visits to the various Rockefeller estates. "Now remember," he told his six-year-old son Rich on
the way to a summer gathering in Jackson Hole, Wyoming, "I don't
want you to ask them how much money they have."

His appointment as president of the Rockefeller Foundation may
have looked like a sidetrack, but the foundation was in fact a sort of
graduate school that would put the final polish on Rusk's education in
international diplomacy. In those days one could not make a career
out of high-level government service, and unlike Lovett and McCloy
(who also sat on the foundation's board), Rusk did not have law or
investment banking on Wall Street to fall back on. But the members of the foreign policy establishment—although predominantly Republican—would take care of him; he was by now one of their own.

The foundation was a place where he could continue his tutelage, have a measure of influence and visibility, be involved with the right people, and make some money, all of which would stand him in good stead in the event he was called upon for another round of government service.

Rusk was in charge of a generous slice of the Rockefeller family fortune, which had been donated to the Rockefeller Foundation through the years, beginning with the patriarch of the family, John D. Rockefeller, Sr., the ruthless visionary who had founded Standard Oil. By 1951 the foundation's capital value was $321 million and its annual income $26.7 million, which it dispensed in the form of grants to organizations and individuals all over the world. Rusk was fond of saying that he had "the best job in the country." Most people, after all, are out in the world every day trying to make money; he was trying to give it away. When asked how he decided who would benefit from the foundation's largesse, he would smile impishly and say only that the purpose of the foundation as expressed in its charter was "to further the benefit of mankind throughout the world."

Rusk was already famliar with the foundation's operation. In 1948 he had been elected a trustee, following a dinner with John D. Rockefeller III. The president at that time, Raymond Fosdick, wanted a close association with the United Nations, and Rusk provided that link. Later that year, when Fosdick retired, there was some talk of Rusk as president. But he was a shade too young, and he was not ready to leave the State Department just then anyway. But as trustee he worked with all the members of the board; their chief role was to decide on the really big grants—over $500,000—and when Dulles recommended his elevation to president, he was a known quantity to a great extent, and well liked by everyone. The only worries expressed were the obvious parallel to Alger Hiss, who had moved from State to the Carnegie Foundation, and Rusk's closeness to Dean Acheson, who was then under attack by McCarthyite forces. But Rusk assured Dulles and the trustees that there was nothing questionable in his background, and argued that it was unjust to consider service at State a disqualification from the job.

Rusk was invited to Williamsburg, Virginia, to be present for his formal election, and immediately thereafter received an invitation to have lunch with John D. Rockefeller, Jr., at his home there. He went thinking he was about to receive his marching orders, but to his surprise the soft-spoken old man told him he was not going to look over his shoulder and not to worry about what he thought. "You don't have to tell me anything,'' Rockefeller said. ''If I want to know what's going on, I can ask my son John III, who will know because he sits on the board.'' Rockefeller told Rusk that he was retired and intended to stay that way. When he had reached sixty-five, the mandatory retirement age under the rules of the foundation, one of the trustees had made a motion to waive that rule, and he had refused. ''I wrote the rules and now I'm going to have to abide by them,'' he said. Rusk liked that and respected Rockefeller, who also told him to take four to six months off and go into the wilderness to think about what he wanted to do with ''the great power you now hold to do good in the world''—a piece of advice that the sedentary Rusk did not accept.

So Rusk moved from the corridors of political power at State to the corridors of financial power in New York. He now had a suite of offices in Rockefeller Center, and he bought a comfortable home in Scarsdale, where he was one of the few Democrats in a sea of Republican suburbanites. Each day he joined the other commuters on the New York Central Railroad, studying his newspaper on the way to the office.

He was busy, but it was a dramatic change of pace and style from his frenetic seven-day weeks at State. He basked in the fact that at the foundation there were really no deadlines in the usual sense. When you were giving away money, Rusk used to say, you could wait on things as long as you wanted. He joked that much of his job consisted of writing rejection letters. ''I can reduce those down to one sentence,'' he remarked. '' 'I have nothing but praise for your ideas.' '' He might have added that he had firsthand experience at being rejected. When he was dean of the faculty at Mills, he had applied for a grant from the foundation to do a political science study and had been turned down.

In Scarsdale Rusk was active in community affairs, serving on the education board and the library committee. He was amused to find that the average salary in the Scarsdale school system was higher than the faculty salaries at Princeton University. There was a tradition in Scarsdale of volunteer help on election day, and for the 1952 contest between Stevenson and Eisenhower, Rusk sat beside one of the voting booths pulling the string to open and close the curtain as each person came to vote. His own ballot was, of course, cast for Stevenson. He also had time to devote to his children. With David and Rich, his two boys, he took part in the town's Saturday morning athletic programs. And his neighbor John Gardner, who later became Secretary of Health, Education and Welfare under President Johnson, remembers that, driving past the Rusk home in the summer, he would occasionally see the president of the Rockefeller Foundation out in the front yard digging up dandelions. Rich recalls this activity as his father's principal recreation: he would put on a bright red bandanna to shield his bald pate from the sun, tune in the Yankee game on a portable radio, and methodically work over the lawn, carefully digging out the weeds one by one.

Scarsdale had no black families, and even Jews were not welcome in certain circles. By nature Rusk was not a crusader, but he quietly made his views known on the subject of discrimination. When he was invited to join the Scarsdale Country Club, he refused because of the members' policy against allowing Jewish members. At the foundation a Jew was appointed to the New York office for the first time. And when Virginia helped to organize a dance group at the high school, she insisted that it be open to everyone, much to the displeasure of some of her white Protestant friends.

Rusk found the five Rockefeller brothers, the sons of John D. Rockefeller, Jr., to be quite different, each with his own individual abilities and interests. Nelson was the most outgoing and ambitious. David was very interested in public affairs, but wanted to remain behind the scenes. Laurance was involved in environmental and conservation activities, and was the chief business manager for the family as well. Winthrop was chairman of Colonial Williamsburg and was also establishing a cattle farm in Arkansas. Rusk got to know John D. Rockefeller III the best, since he was the chairman of the board of trustees and actively interested in affairs of the foundation.

To travel with John D. Rockefeller III was an experience in itself. On a trip to Mexico for a few days, Rusk picked up all the bills, because it was the foundation's policy to pay the expenses of trustees while traveling on official business. When they were leaving the country, the Mexican customs inspector looked at Rockefeller's passport. Part of the routine was to ask how much money each person had spent in Mexico, and Rusk could see the official hold his breath when he saw to whom he was putting the question. "Twenty-seven dollars and fifty cents," came the reply. The inspector gave him a wide-eyed look and put down $3,000 in his book. Noticing this, Rockefeller told the man he was making a mistake, that he had said $27.50. But the official waved him past, saying, "This is only for government statistics. It just won't do to say that John D. Rockefeller has spent such a small sum as twenty-seven dollars and fifty cents."

John D. III was a quiet person, but with passionate views, particularly on one subject: population control. He constantly urged Rusk to put great sums into birth control programs. Rusk shared this concern, but thought that such programs should be balanced with other funding needs. He refused to make birth control the principal focus that Rockefeller wanted. Years later, this and the taint of Vietnam apparently strained their relationship sufficiently that, after Rusk's term as Secretary of State, John D. III blocked his reappointment as a Rockefeller trustee, even though Rusk, in November 1968, had nominated him for the Nobel Peace Prize.

When John Foster Dulles was named Eisenhower's Secretary of State after the 1952 election, he discussed with Rusk the possibility of his becoming Under Secretary. It did not take long for Rusk to reject the offer. Much as he liked and admired Dulles, he felt uncomfortable with some Republican policies and the Republican right wing, whom he called "the incorrigibles." He did not want to be put in the position of being a spokesman for the Republican foreign policy.

Rusk naturally took a friendly interest in Dulles and his new job as well as the march of world events. On May 6, 1953, he sent Dulles a letter volunteering some thoughts on his first hundred days in office. Typed single-spaced on four pages, the letter contained an interesting conception of the job of Secretary of State and a gentle critique of Dulles's performance. As Rusk saw it:

> The Secretary of State flies a four-engined plane; he draws his power and support from (1) the President, (2) the Congress, particularly the Senate, (3) the professional staff of the Department and the Foreign Service, and (4) the public, with emphasis on the press. He can fly his plane on three engines and, for a considerable time, with two (as did your predecessor for a time). But at least two motors must be in good shape or there is serious trouble; it goes without saying that if all four motors are sputtering, trouble is ahead. It doesn't make life any easier to discover that sometimes the four motors don't want to move in the same direction.

Of these "four engines," Rusk regarded the first, the President, as the most important: "Leaving out personal considerations, the prestige and national interest of the U.S. require an impression of complete mutual support and confidence between the President and the Secretary of State." He advised Dulles to find an occasion, such as a joint press conference, at which he and the President could exhibit their close working relationship. Rusk also warned of the danger of meddling by presidential counselors and advisers:

I have no reason to think that you have encountered any problem of loyal cooperation from the White House advisers around the President. Men in the position of Sherman Adams and Cutler can be of great help and may be worth some special attention. The danger to watch out for is the tendency of personal advisers to be so thoroughly preoccupied with their own chief, they are tempted to consider his interests as something quite separate and distinct from those of the team as a whole. Some of Mr. Truman's advisers suffered from this affliction— to the loss of the Administration as a whole, and to the long-range detriment of their own chief.

When it came to dealing with Congress, Rusk warned against both the machinations of the Republican right wing and the risks of alienating the Democrats. He called for a bipartisan approach to the formulation of foreign policy:

You, personally, have earned a claim upon Democratic cooperation through your own bi-partisan service in the past, at some cost to your own position within the Republican Party itself. My impression is that most of the Senate Democrats would give you this cooperation . . . but that it could be lost if deeply-cutting compromises are made too readily with the Republican right wing or if strong efforts are made to make direct partisan capital on foreign policy matters. I would think that it would be good politics to take the indirect benefits of a broad, national, non-partisan, and effective foreign policy. If foreign policy is made a partisan issue, any Administration is almost bound to lose politically. The baffling complexity of foreign policy issues, the crucifying decisions which have to be made, and the certainty that there will be unfavorable as well as favorable developments in the foreign field will combine to give any opposition some issues which can be developed successfully from a partisan point of view. A public position of non-partisanship in foreign policy at least shares the responsibility for adverse developments with the opposition, and the Administration gains from favorable turns in events. The Republican success in developing the China issue was due in large part to the loss of courage and intelligence by Democratic leadership—chiefly in the National Committee and in the Senate.

Rusk admonished Dulles that the Department of State and the Foreign Service deserved his careful attention:

My impression is that this is still unsolved and that more needs to be done to obtain the complete support of your "troops." Don't misunderstand me; the problem has to some extent been inevitable with a change of Administration after twenty years. Both sides brought a degree of suspicion and uncertainty to the new situation, and I have pointed out to career people that they have a special responsibility to accept the full meaning of the decision of the electorate and to give the new team a real chance. My only suggestion is to get the "cleaning out" process over with as quickly as possible in order that those who are left can get on with their jobs with the knowledge that they are, in fact, fully trusted and that you consider them a part of your own team. The remark is gratuitous, but those career men in whom you have already placed heavy responsibility should be expected to exercise a strong personal leadership in morale matters and not allow subordinates to blame their tears on the Secretary of State. There are two pretty good rules in the Army which may apply here: (a) an enlisted man is entitled to a "morale problem" but an officer is not, and (b) if the morale of a company is low, the responsibility rests directly upon the Captain; if of a regiment, upon the Colonel, etc.

The relationship of the Secretary of State to the public also required special handling. Advising Dulles to emphasize that he was acting as Secretary of State for all the people, not a particular party or group, Rusk then offered a jaundiced view of the press:

The press is another matter. There often appear to be deep divergencies of interest between the Secretary of State and the reporters of a highly competitive press. Unless your press advisers fully understand this clash of interest and are constantly alert to it, their advice may not always be helpful. The competitive press finds it almost impossible to exercise discretion and a sense of public responsibility, with rare exceptions. If a man digs a secret out of an official or a department and takes it around to the Soviet Embassy, he is a spy; if he digs out the same secret and gives it to the Soviet Union and the rest of the world at the same time, he is a smart newspaper man. The by-line reporters and pundits ordinarily are not satisfied with the news—each wants something his rival doesn't have, and the competition exists between men on the same newspaper or wire service. Each insists upon sitting in the chair of judgment to decide what should and what should not be made public. The private citizen, therefore, finds that he cannot have his representatives (the President—not the press) decide what, in the citizen's own interest, ought to be withheld temporarily from public knowledge.

In a postscript that was revealing of Rusk's character he told Dulles, "I have not retained a copy of this letter." But it remained in

Dulles's files, and on the day Rusk took over as Secretary of State, January 20, 1961, he found a copy of the letter on his desk, delivered by Phyllis Bernau Macomber, who had been Dulles's personal secretary. Eight years later, on January 14, 1969, Rusk wrote Richard Nixon's Secretary of State–designate William Rogers, enclosing a copy of the same letter, saying, "It occurs to me that you might find this letter of some interest—and possibly even amusing."

In matters of policy the most extensive contact between Rusk and Dulles had to do with the subject of China, a problem that seems to have weighed heavily on Rusk, as if instinctively he felt that it had not been handled properly during his stewardship at State. In a letter to Dulles on June 16, 1953, he called Red China a "painful subject." Nevertheless, he sought some formula for admission of Red China to the United Nations and presumably eventual American recognition. What he advocated to Dulles was a "two China" policy, admitting Red China as a member of the U.N. General Assembly but allowing Taiwan to retain its seat as well. He told Dulles, however, that "it seems inconceivable that we or our allies should agree to Peiping's admission without getting something important for it." As minimum conditions for Chinese admission, Rusk unrealistically suggested: (1) agreement that Taiwan be treated as an independent nation, (2) liquidation of Chinese assistance to Ho Chi Minh, (3) the substitution of India for China as a permanent member of the U.N. Security Council, and (4) the admission of Japan to U.N. membership.

Dulles was impressed, and after the Korean War was settled, he called on Rusk to explore the possibilities for a change in American policy. Rusk agreed to undertake very discreet, private conversations with Senator Walter F. George of Georgia, chairman of the Senate Foreign Relations Committee. George was resistant, but Rusk eventually persuaded him that something should be done. Before concrete steps could be taken, however, politics intervened. When Governor Herman Talmadge of Georgia announced that he would run for George's Senate seat in 1956, George took a close look at the political situation in Georgia and decided he would not run again. Regrettably, that ended the attempts to resolve the problem; Dulles concluded that even the Republicans could not risk a fight on China without a strong ally on the Senate Foreign Relations Committee.

Rusk soon discovered that even the venerable Rockefeller Foundation was under siege by the forces of McCarthyism, and much of his time during the first three years of his tenure was taken up defending the foundation against charges of subversion in investigations conducted by two separate congressional committees. Staff members of the committees went through virtually every grant the foundation had made throughout its long history seeking to uncover specific cases of abuse. The "incorrigibles" in Congress painted a picture of the foundation as abusing its tax-exempt status and giving away money to support frivolous and subversive activities. They alleged that the private charitable foundations of the country were a channel through which funds were given to left-wing organizations. Some in Congress wanted to end their tax-exempt status or to assert government control over their grant policies.

To refute these charges Rusk had to immerse himself in all the details of past grants and foundation policies. He met with legal counsel to plan the defense strategy and had to prepare countless documents for submission to the congressional committees. The highlight of the investigations came with personal appearances by Rusk himself, first before the Cox Committee in 1952 and then before the Reece Committee in 1954. In both instances he handled the hostile McCarthy-like questioning of some of the committee members with ease and aplomb. He was thoroughly prepared and had total mastery over the facts of every grant or incident the commmittee could bring up. His manner was judicious and respectful, he never lost his perfect composure, and his answers were full, complete, and disarmingly simple. His virtuoso performance succeeded in tearing the carefully built case against the foundation to shreds.

In one exchange before the Cox Committee on December 9, 1952, Rusk was confronted with charges that the Rockefeller Foundation had made substantial grants to support Russian-area studies at Cornell and Columbia Universities. In response he explained the purpose of the grants in detail and defended them with a quote from General Eisenhower, who in his inaugural address as president of Columbia University had said, "The facts of communism shall be taught here— its ideological development, its political methods, its economic effects, its probable course in the future." His questioner, taken aback, said, "Do you suppose he meant 'study' instead of 'taught'?" Rusk, knowing he had his opponent in a hammerlock, eased up the pressure in gentlemanly fashion: "I have no doubt whatever, Mr. Counsel, that when General Eisenhower used that expression, he meant that we should study about communism, not that we should teach communism."

A mark of Rusk's skill in handling the hostile questioning was that he never aimed to crush his opponents. He would try to satisfy their basic concerns where possible, without compromising his essential points that the foundation should be totally free of government interference and that its tax-exempt status should be preserved. Despite his private revulsion against McCarthyism, he never denounced the investigating committees or attacked the intelligence or integrity of its members. He merely attacked the charges themselves and added, "It is hard to believe that the committee has taken them seriously." Questioned as to specific organizations, such as the Institute of Pacific Relations, which stood accused by the McCarthyite committees, he defended them and the purpose of the grants based on "the information available to the Foundation at the time." Yet Rusk agreed with his questioners in vigorously denouncing communism and said that he would not allow money to be given to any organization on the Attorney General's list. On some grants, he added, information subsequently revealed "would have raised questions which, if not satisfactorily answered, would have led the Foundation to withhold further support." Defending a grant to the distinguished chemist Linus Pauling—whom Rusk would later tangle with on the issue of the Vietnam War—he made the point that the foundation was glad to support Pauling's scientific work, even though he "is capable of being a little frivolous in other fields." Rusk never lost sight of the fact that his purpose was to defend and assert the independence of the great foundations of the country, and he did not use the committee hearings as a soapbox to make a political statement about the evils of McCarthyism or anti-Communist witch-hunts. He carefully limited his criticisms to the committee's staff and did not criticize the members themselves. It was an eminently successful strategy, but one that did not endear him to liberals, who would have liked him to make a more sweeping and general attack on McCarthyism.

Rusk administered the Rockefeller Foundation with a light touch that some people found confusing. He refused to get too involved with details; he saw his role as dealing with external relations and policy issues, and he wanted the officers who worked for him to exercise broad responsibility. Delegating day-to-day operations to a secretary, he didn't call his people in unless he had something important to discuss with them. His style left some of the officers with a sense of drift, a feeling that they didn't know what he was thinking. Rusk was, in fact, purposefully indirect in his approach. "You can't knock people down except once or twice a year," he said later. "Otherwise they won't function for you." When he disagreed with one of his staff, he would simply make a humorous reference instead of saying, "You're totally wrong." To initiate a new direction or a new idea, he would say to his staff, "This is something we might think about. See if you can come up with something." He did not readily lower the boom on those who might have deserved it. He communicated with people by asking questions and making suggestions, all the while testing their ideas.

Occasionally Rusk puzzled his staff by raising a ruckus over petty financial matters. When he found a closet at the foundation filled with toilet paper, he made inquiries and ordered the practice ended. It was wasteful to store so much toilet paper instead of buying it periodically from a supplier. He also examined the telephone connections at the foundation and ordered a reduction after determining that no one ever had to wait to use a line. Yet he told staff members that when they traveled to Europe, they should take more time and go by ship rather than by air, so they would arrive rested and ready to do business.

If he was distant with his staff, Rusk made it a point to keep in close touch with the foundation's board of trustees. He believed in working trustees, not figureheads. He had full board meetings twice a year and between meetings met with the trustees individually to gather their ideas and to inform them about foundation affairs. He spent much of his time searching out and visiting with "the best people in all sorts of fields who might provide ideas." "It is easy to give away money," he said. "What's hard is finding an idea that is worth a nickel." He had a nose for forging personal connections with the people who might provide those ideas, and he traveled far and wide, talking with politicians, scientists, artists, educators, administrators, and business people all over the world.

On his first trip to London he was greeted at the airport by a group of reporters who questioned him closely about what he was doing and how many checks he had brought with him. The next day *The Times* of London ran a story about his visit under the headline "Man Who Wants to Give Away Millions." The article told of a "golden cascade" pouring down "ceaselessly from the nice fat block of the world's best investments. The flood of money gets wider and deeper with each passing year." Also included was the fact that Rusk was staying at Claridge's. Soon after his arrival he went off to Oxford for a few days and, returning to Claridge's, asked if there was any mail. The clerk gave him a funny look and said, "Yes, your mail is in your room." When he entered he found the bathtub filled with letters from all over England. He solemnly had it all boxed up and sent home to be answered by his staff.

Occasionally there were humorous happenings. One day a young man came into the reception room at the foundation's offices and insisted on seeing the president. Asked what he wanted, the man said that Mr. Rockefeller had left his entire fortune to him on his twenty-fifth birthday and "today is my twenty-fifth birthday, so I want to see the president of the foundation about turning the funds over to me."

The foundation divided its affairs, and by implication those of mankind, into four great divisions: medicine and public health, natural science and agriculture, social science, and humanities. Of these, public health long had been the principal concern. Early in the century the foundation had funded a campaign against hookworm, particularly in the South. Rusk remembered that when he went into the sixth grade his teacher told him that he had to wear shoes to school because of hookworm. When he reported that to his mother, she didn't believe him, and he was embarrassed when, the next day at school, he was the only one without shoes. People in some towns drove out the hookworm teams with sticks and stones; the Yankees were coming down to get rid of the South's "lazy worm."

Under Rusk's leadership the foundation took a new turn, reorienting its priorities from an almost exclusive concern with domestic programs to international programs, particularly the needs of the underdeveloped countries of the world. In 1955 he sent a memorandum to the trustees justifying this new direction and explaining his purpose: "The underdeveloped countries of today are borrowing ideas and aspirations and have examples of more 'advanced' countries before their eyes; but they lack capital, trained leadership, an educated people, political stability, and an understanding of how change is to be digested and used by their own cultures." To remedy this he set about organizing and funding a variety of programs to benefit developing countries in Latin America, Africa, and Asia. He even obtained the trustees' approval to dip into the capital of the foundation for a period of time in order to finance ambitious new technical assistance programs, concentrating on improvements that would have maximum impact and lasting value: upgrading universities, instituting training programs for leaders and scientists, funding libraries for the foreign offices of developing countries, and developing improved varieties of foodstuffs such as blight-resistant potatoes and superior breeds of rice, corn, and wheat. Rusk drew on his early life in Cherokee County for ideas on how to transform the developing world. He was convinced the answers lay in education, food production, population control, and public health. During his term the Rockefeller

Foundation was particularly successful in funding agricultural research, what became known as the "Green Revolution" in countries like the Philippines, India, and Mexico.

In planning and administering these programs, Rusk tried to maintain an arm's-length distance between the foundation and the U.S. government. He resisted "suggestions" from Washington and warned the officers of the foundation not to be captured by the government. The scale of funding for government needs was so vast that even the Rockefeller money would hardly make a difference. And Rusk said no to CIA Director Allen Dulles's request to give to the CIA memoranda of conversations between foundation officers and the leaders of foreign countries.

Rusk also began new programs of funding education and the arts. The foundation contributed a wide range of projects, from Lincoln Center in New York to performances or exhibitions of the works of young artists. Private universities, particularly in the South, received support, and black education was singled out for special attention. On one occasion the trustees wanted to make a large gift to an organization for black scholarships, but the foundation's lawyer brought up the point that the grant was probably illegal because it was limited to blacks. Rusk broke the impasse by raising the question: "Who is going to complain? Will the Attorney General of New York file suit against us?" The grant was approved.

Rusk also visited with many of the leaders of the black colleges in the South, and one conversation with Benjamin Mays, the president of Morehouse College, touched him deeply. The Rockefeller trustees were thinking about liquidating the General Education Fund, and Rusk asked Mays whether the money should all go to support black education. Mays said no, that it would be wrong, because whites need education as much as blacks.

Rusk cast a skeptical eye on some of the foundation's funding efforts. Behavioral psychology and progressive education were areas that he cut severely. Early in his term as president he met with a group of behavioral scientists at Averell Harriman's home in New York and, after they talked for a while, he said bluntly, "Unless you people can tell me what you are doing in terms I can understand, I am not going to be sure you understand what it is you are doing." The Rockefeller Foundation did support the work of Dr. Kinsey on the sexual behavior of the American male, but Rusk cut off funds for the companion work on the American female. He argued that Kinsey's research methods were flawed, but he was also motivated by his instinct that the foundation should avoid controversy whenever possible.

Sometimes Rusk approved a grant against his better judgment and it came back later to haunt him. One of his science officers approached him with a proposal to study why particular insects have a strong preference for certain types of plants but leave others alone. Rusk's initial reaction was, "That's easy—it's because some plants taste better than others." The officer gave him a pained look and said that that was not a scientific way to go about finding an answer. So the foundation funded a two-year study, in which, at the end, it was determined that "gustatory sensation plays the dominant role" in insect eating behavior.

One interesting dilemma Rusk faced was whether or not to answer the pleas for money from his various alma maters who now realized their good fortune in having an alumnus as the head of the world's richest foundation. For the most part he resisted the temptation and deflected not-so-subtle hints from Davidson and Mills. Oxford proved to be another matter, however, and he approved a major grant for a legal collection at the Bodleian Library.

Rusk was never accused of letting personal friendships play a role in deciding the foundation's beneficiaries. His staff saw him as scrupulously fair and impartial. There was one touching occasion, however, where friendship made a difference. On a trip to visit Duke University and the University of North Carolina, he met with Preston Epps, his old high school teacher of Greek, who was a faculty member in the classics department at North Carolina. They spent the evening together with Rusk's old Davidson classmate Spec Caldwell, now a history professor at the university, and during the course of their talk it became evident that Epps had never visited Greece, though he had spent his whole life studying Greek history, language, and culture.

A few weeks later Epps received an invitation to go to Athens as a representative of the Rockefeller Foundation to inspect the archeological digs in the agora in order to determine whether a grant for a major reconstruction project was warranted. He accepted the invitation, and for the first time visited the ancient sites and ruins that were his life; the trip was the highlight of his professional career. He submitted a detailed report, which recommended that the agora site be left alone because extensive reconstruction work would mar its beauty. On his return, Rusk recalls, Epps thanked him with tears in his eyes. Even much later Rusk would never admit that friendship had anything to do with his selection of Epps. He simply said that Epps was the best-qualified man for the job, which was probably correct.

Rusk made an exception to his rule of keeping the government at arm's length when Dulles asked if the foundation could get involved in Eastern Europe. Rusk believed that Dulles felt responsibility for the upheavals in Eastern Europe because his talk of rolling back communism had encouraged false hopes, and the foundation could extend private aid whereas U.S. government grants might be rejected for political reasons. He set up aid programs for Hungarian refugees and exchange programs for Polish scientists and professors (an instance, Rusk would wryly point out, of Rockefeller grants to known Communists). While out at the airport to meet a group of Polish scientists, he watched with satisfaction as one of them got off the airplane and kissed the ground in a tribute to the United States.

Rusk also went to Budapest to discuss several grant projects just after the abortive Hungarian uprising. Meeting with Communist officials of the Kádár government, he was asked to consider donating expensive medical equipment for the main hospital in Budapest. Rusk asked them what guarantee they could provide that the Russians wouldn't load it on a train for shipment to Moscow. An official looked at him and said quietly, "Well, I can't guarantee that won't happen, but if it does, it would be the most valuable money the Rockefeller Foundation ever spent, because every Hungarian would know about it within twenty-four hours." Several times on this trip Rusk found that a small cross of St. Stephen, symbol of the Hungarian resistance movement, had been slipped into his pocket. When he asked to visit the Lenin Institute of Public Health in Budapest because it had received considerable past support from the foundation, he was surprised that no one seemed to know where it was or what he was talking about. Finally, an official said to him, "Oh, you mean the *Rockefeller* Institute?" which was the name the Hungarians called it among themselves.

Throughout his years at the Rockefeller Foundation, Rusk kept in contact with foreign policy matters. He was constantly in touch with officials in Washington and spoke frequently all around the country on foreign policy themes. He also traveled extensively abroad, making a point to visit with foreign office officials in other countries. He became the chairman of the influential Council on Foreign Relations, which brought him into frequent contact not only with officials in Eisenhower's State Department but with old cronies from the Roosevelt and Truman administrations as well.

While not abandoning his policy of toughness and preparedness in dealing with the Russians and the Chinese Communists, Rusk put new emphasis on finding a basis for cooperation and better understanding to find solutions for common problems. He regarded the death of Stalin in 1953 as an excellent opportunity for the West to end the Cold War confrontation through negotiations. With John J. McCloy, Harriman, Bowles, Arthur Dean, and Henry Wriston, he participated in a study of Soviet-American relations that was published as a book, *Russia and America: Dangers and Prospects,* by Henry L. Roberts. He advocated new approaches to the Russians: cultural exchanges, economic ties, arms limitation talks—a never-ending search for meaningful negotiations, what Rusk called "little threads" of cooperation between East and West.

In an effort to establish an international, nongovernmental forum to discuss matters of common concern to the Western alliance, he helped organize a committee of private citizens called the Bilderberg Group, headed by Prince Bernhard of the Netherlands. Invited participants included about ninety prominent Americans and Europeans, who at yearly conferences in the 1950s discussed better coordination in dealing with common problems such as the unification of Germany, improvement of the chances for peace in the Middle East, and how to foster a greater measure of freedom in Eastern Europe.

The most tragic event of the decade for Rusk was the 1956 Suez crisis. After Egypt seized control of the Suez Canal and excluded Israeli ships, the Israelis struck against the Arab armies, which provoked intervention by Great Britain and France. The United States, acting under the Uniting for Peace Resolution of the U.N. General Assembly, demanded that Britain and France cease their intervention and required the fighting parties to disengage. For Rusk the tragedy of Suez was that the American action split the NATO alliance. The invasion by Britain and France had caught Eisenhower and Dulles by surprise. Rusk believed that had the British and the French consulted with the United States in advance and worked out a reasonable case for intervention, the break between the allies could have been avoided. Instead, Eisenhower became angry and Dulles was unable to prevent a sharp American response.

Long after the events took place, Rusk visited Dulles in the hospital. Dulles was dying of cancer, and he wanted to talk about his papers and the disposition of his effects after his death. It was a sad conversation between two friends. At one point Dulles said, "You know, Dean, I would not have made certain decisions that I made about Suez had I not been sick at the time." He did not elaborate, and Rusk let it go at that. He did not deem it appropriate to inquire further of a dying man. But Rusk returned to the foundation and gave some thought to a study of the problem of ill health among top government officials and how it might affect policy judgments.

Rusk did not know to what extent Dulles's ill health produced the American misunderstanding with the British and French over Suez, but he did remember an awkward incident during the time of the Japanese Peace Treaty negotiations. Part of Dulles's job at that time was to keep the British Foreign Minister, Anthony Eden, fully informed. But Dulles neglected to tell Eden about the promise the Americans had extracted from the Japanese that Japan would recognize Chiang Kai-shek as the legitimate ruler of China. Eden did not know of this agreement until he read about it in the newspapers after the Japanese had acted to recognize Taiwan. He was furious, and Rusk thought that the incident produced a lack of trust between Eden and Dulles that continued during the Eisenhower administration. He believed that this lack of trust was at least in part responsible for the great misapprehensions that developed at the time of the Suez crisis.

Another pet project on which Rusk worked together with Dulles was the idea of holding a conference of former colonial states under the leadership of the United States. The objective was to bring together leaders of nations of diverse racial and ethnic makeup to show that they shared the same ideas and aspirations of human freedom, economic development, and world peace. Rusk believed that the emancipation of colonies in the post–World War II period was "a great chapter in human history." He spoke often about the magnitude of the task and took pride in the fact that it had been accomplished largely without bloodshed. A conference to commemorate this achievement and to plan future cooperation would be appropriate. The idea never took concrete form, however, and was dropped with Dulles's declining health.

During his years with the Rockefeller Foundation, Rusk gave a good deal of thought to how the United Nations could best be used for its main purposes: the preservation of the peace and the avoidance of international conflict. He developed a theory of the functioning of the United Nations that he called "parliamentary diplomacy" and that was the subject of many of his speeches around the world. He believed that the U.N. was an indispensable international institution that had done a remarkable job in settling disputes and in circumscribing the impact of those it had not settled. The U.N. provided a forum in which a genuine world community was emerging, where the structure of peace "is built by thousands of small bricks, [and] where U.S.

policy is at home because the purposes of the Charter are congenial to the long range policies and purposes of the American people.''

Rusk also affirmed the importance of debate in the United Nations:

> The continual pressure of the Charter upon debate in the presence of a world community is a powerful political fact not to be disregarded. Opinion is also power, and what people think about conduct has a lot to do with what kind of conduct they will support or oppose. It is particularly important where the problem is to lead a great democracy such as ours to take action, burdensome and costly action at times, to try to make the world somewhat more decent in which to live.

After analyzing the nature of such debate, he then attempted to define its utility:

> Nevertheless, debate is a substitute for *more* violent means and not a substitute for *less* dangerous techniques. It is a substitute, or the last clear chance if you like, before self-help or organized sanctions. Risks in debate are to be measured against more violent means, and on that basis the risks may be well worth taking.

He then elaborated a theory of the reasons for submitting issues to parliamentary debate in the U.N.:

> Does debate act as a poultice for extracting inflammation out of conflict, or does it result in the spreading of infection? It does both. There are times when United Nations debate—prolonged, boring, discouraging—is, in fact, a sophisticated, useful, and often planned device for finding time in which the fever can subside.

But Rusk did not believe that the United Nations could solve all the world's problems. He cautioned that ''we can support and strengthen the United Nations without smothering it with affection.'' And he expressed his belief that ''no question should be tossed into the world body without knowing what we are going to say or do in the United Nations.'' If we fail to consider this in advance, we create confusion and surrender the respect of our diplomatic colleagues.

Rusk also warned against what he called ''the dividends of obstinacy.'' His point was that the Soviet Union, by simply being obstinate, could put pressure on the United States and other Western countries to close the gap between two positions by unilateral action.

Rusk believed this was dangerous and should be avoided when undertaking open debate.

Rusk's view of the United Nations was in the end a very realistic one. The debate process could not close wide gaps between differing points of view, and the multiparty debate format was not always conducive to finding a solution. What the U.N. debate process could do was to delay or avoid violent action by producing a search for an alternative. It could also mobilize world opinion and buy valuable time to produce a climate for meaningful negotiations. Rusk pointed out that the beginnings of a settlement both of the Berlin blockade crisis and the Korean War occurred in the quiet corridors of the United Nations, which provided a natural meeting place for informal contact among adversaries.

During the last years of his term at the Rockefeller Foundation, Rusk was involved with the preparation of an extensive study and review of American foreign policy sponsored by the Rockefeller Brothers Fund: *The Mid-Century Challenge to U.S. Foreign Policy.* He presided over the fashioning of this report as chairman of the fund, although it was written by eminent scholars and officials from the nation's universities and the Council on Foreign Relations. Rusk thought it was appropriate to undertake a fundamental reexamination of American foreign policy in light of the changed conditions in the 1950s. There had been a great revolution in the world; scores of new nations had emerged. Nuclear arms now threatened mankind as never before. The Cold War and the standoff between the Soviet Union and the United States were facts of life, a frustrating stalemate that had produced American self-doubt and loss of purpose. The theme of the report was that the United States should not remain passive in the world but should develop and sustain a creative, active foreign policy that shaped the world according to American ideals and purposes.

Late in 1959 Rusk gave the Elihu Root lectures at the Council on Foreign Relations, in which he drew heavily from the ideas expressed in the report. His first lecture, entitled "The President," was printed in the prestigious journal *Foreign Affairs.* The first paragraph of that lecture was indicative of his views:

The United States, in this second half of the twentieth century, is not a raft tossed by the winds and waves of historical forces over which it has little control. Its dynamic power, physical and ideological, generates historical forces; what it does or does not do makes a great deal of difference to the history of man in this epoch. If realism requires us to avoid illusions of omnipotence, it is just as important that we do not underestimate the opportunity and the responsibility which flow from our capacity to act and to influence and shape the course of events. Involved is not merely a benign concern for the well-being of others but the shape of the world in which we ourselves must live. The range within which the nation can make deliberate choices is wide; if we do not make them deliberately, we shall make them by negligence or yield the decisions to others, who will not be mindful of our interests. When the emphasis of discussion falls too heavily for my taste upon the limitations on policy, I recall from early childhood the admonition of the circuit preacher: "Pray as if it were up to God; work as if it were up to you."

Rusk was upbeat, optimistic, and activist in his view of American foreign policy. He believed that in our conduct of foreign policy we must have two strings to our bow. On the one hand, we should be tough and prepared to do battle. On the other hand, we should always look for possibilities of negotiation, cooperation, and compromise. Presidential authority was an article of faith to him. The President had a special role to play in the American democracy because he alone was elected by all the people. In Rusk's view a strong and activist presidency, especially in foreign affairs, was a necessity.

It was an appealing vision, especially for a young man named John Fitzgerald Kennedy who believed himself to be the harbinger of a new political generation in the United States. Elected to the presidency in 1960, Kennedy sought to reinvigorate the country, both domestically and in the field of foreign affairs. He wanted a clear break with the passive and conservative policies of Eisenhower and Dulles, and in his search for a Secretary of State he solicited the advice of the members of the foreign policy establishment of the Roosevelt and Truman years, including their heir apparent, Dean Rusk.

When Rusk's name began to appear in press speculation about who would be joining the Kennedy administration, several of the Rockefeller Foundation trustees called and told him that he should not consider taking a job in government. They did not want to lose him, and they tried to convince him that he would not function well in the Kennedy bureaucracy. But they added one qualification: "There is one post you cannot turn down, and that is Secretary of State." And key figures, Lovett and Acheson among them, were recommending him for the job.

There is no doubt that Rusk wanted the post, that consciously or unconsciously he had been preparing himself and had even schemed for it by writing "The President" piece in *Foreign Affairs*. But he did not campaign for the job. He did not have to make the customary phone calls to inject his name into the process, and throughout he was suitably modest and unpretentious. At the lunch table at the foundation offices, when people mentioned the speculation about his becoming Secretary of State, he would say, "The only reason they might be thinking of me at all is that I have been away long enough that they have forgotten I've got feet of clay."

When in the end Kennedy called to offer him the post, everyone was happy for him. He was still unknown to the world at large, but considering his education and career, he was uniquely qualified to be Secretary of State. No man of his generation had better credentials for the job or more experience in the field of foreign policy. He was, in fact, far more experienced than the President he would serve. And now all of his qualifications, his temperament, his ideals, and his diplomatic and political skills would be put to the supreme test.

A Visual Chronology of Dean Rusk in the Truman, Kennedy, and Johnson Years

The Truman Years: 1945–1952

THE nuclear devastation that ended World War II also signaled the beginning of an entirely new kind of global conflict: the Cold War between the two great world powers, the United States and the Soviet Union. Dean Rusk, a Rhodes scholar trained in international law, fought on the front lines of the Cold War from its inception. He joined the State Department in 1946 at the personal invitation of Secretary of State George C. Marshall. There, under Marshall's successor, Dean Acheson, he rose quickly through the ranks to become an important member of the Democratic foreign policy establishment and an adviser to President Harry S Truman.

SECRETARY OF STATE GEORGE C.
MARSHALL

MARSHALL'S SUCCESSOR, DEAN
ACHESON

Rusk believed deeply in the newly created United Nations as an instrument of world peace, but he was also a leading advocate of the Cold War policies of "containment" to deter, by force if necessary, Soviet military aggression and Communist subversion. During the Berlin Blockade in 1948 it was Rusk's idea to get supplies into the beleaguered city by military airlift, a recommendation that stemmed from his wartime experience of supplying Nationalist China by flying goods over the Himalayas from Burma.

The Cold War took an ominous turn in 1949 when the atomic bomb was added to the Soviet arsenal and China fell under Communist control. Rusk volunteered for the politically sensitive post of Assistant Secretary of State for Far Eastern Affairs. He almost alone among high State Department officials escaped unscathed from the Communist witch-hunts led by Senator Joseph R. McCarthy—but only because his friend, top Republican John Foster Dulles, warned McCarthy to "lay off Rusk."

BREAKING THE BERLIN BLOCKADE

SENATOR JOSEPH R. MCCARTHY

RUSK WITH JOHN FOSTER DULLES

WAR IN KOREA

War in Korea shattered the uneasy equilibrium between East and West in 1950, and Rusk approved of Truman's "police action" to drive the invading North Korean Communists back across the 38th parallel, the line of demarcation between the two warring countries that Rusk himself had arbitrarily selected during the closing days of World War II. In October 1950, as Deputy Under Secretary of State, Rusk accompanied Truman to Wake Island to confer with General Douglas MacArthur about his conduct of the war. Unimpressed by MacArthur's vanity, promises of quick victory, and determination to widen the war, Truman dismissed the general, a decision in which Rusk played an influential part. Although peace and restoration of the status quo did not come until the Eisenhower Administration, Rusk counted the "limited" war fought in Korea a success. This belief would profoundly affect his counsel and conduct as Secretary of State during the war in Vietnam.

TRUMAN AND MACARTHUR ON WAKE ISLAND

WITH PRESIDENT KENNEDY IN THE OVAL OFFICE

The Kennedy Years: 1961–1963

NEWLY elected President John F. Kennedy surprised the world with his choice of Dean Rusk as Secretary of State. Although virtually unknown to the general public, Rusk had become an influential member of the Eastern power elite during his term as president of the Rockefeller Foundation in the 1950s. In the first of a series of explosive Cold War confrontations, the Kennedy Administration immediately suffered a staggering setback in Cuba at the Bay of Pigs. Rusk had opposed the invasion and at the last moment persuaded the President not to expand direct American military involvement, but later he loyally defended Kennedy's actions. His was always the voice of reason and caution in the free-for-all meetings of the President's advisers, and after a tentative start, the two men grew to trust and admire each other.

DEFEAT AND CAPTURE FOR ANTI-CASTRO FORCES AT THE BAY OF PIGS

WITH HIS SOVIET COUNTERPART, FOREIGN MINISTER ANDREI GROMYKO

Kennedy and Rusk were confronted by still another crisis when Soviet Premier Nikita Khrushchev demanded the withdrawal of Western powers from Berlin in 1961, an ultimatum that resulted in the construction of the infamous Berlin Wall. Rusk helped diffuse that crisis by "talking the problem to death" in patient negotiations with Soviet Foreign Minister Andrei Gromyko.

The gravest crisis of all came with Khrushchev's covert attempt to arm Cuba with Soviet nuclear missiles in 1962. Kennedy demanded their withdrawal, and his decisive stand, counseled by Rusk and falling just short of war, ultimately induced the Soviets to comply.

A'N AMERICAN DESTROYER HALTING A SOVIET FREIGHTER DURING THE CUBAN MISSILE CRISIS

CONFRONTATION WITH KHRUSHCHEV ACROSS THE CONFERENCE TABLE AND IN AN INFORMAL GAME OF BADMINTON

The world drew back from the brink of nuclear disaster, and only a year later Rusk traveled to Moscow to sign the historic accord that banned the testing of nuclear weapons in the atmosphere. His final confrontation with Khrushchev was in a friendly game of badminton (without a net), which Rusk diplomatically permitted the Soviet premier to win.

The Johnson Years: 1963–1968

Wɪᴛʜ the tragic assassination of Kennedy, Lyndon B. Johnson succeeded to the presidency and persuaded Rusk to remain as his Secretary of State. The cool, detached Rusk and the impetuous, emotional Johnson seemed to have little in common. But both shared rural Southern backgrounds and both had risen to great power through the sheer force of their wills. The two men achieved an intimacy, and Rusk attained a level of influence with Johnson that he had not enjoyed with Kennedy.

© White House Photo

WITH PRESIDENT JOHNSON IN THE OVAL OFFICE

WAR IN VIETNAM

ANTIWAR PROTEST AT CORNELL

Although Rusk traveled extensively and worked endless hours on the conduct of State, his chief preoccupation became the war in Vietnam. The long-simmering conflict between North and South Vietnam gradually escalated in violence, and with the lesson of Korea in mind, Johnson and Rusk met the Communist challenge with ever-increasing military force, including the bombing of North Vietnam. As casualties mounted and with victory nowhere in sight, voices of protest were raised, first on university campuses and finally from every segment of the American population. Because he was the administration's chief spokesman, the conflict became known as ''Dean Rusk's War,'' and his own son, a student at Cornell, begged him to end the bombing of the North.

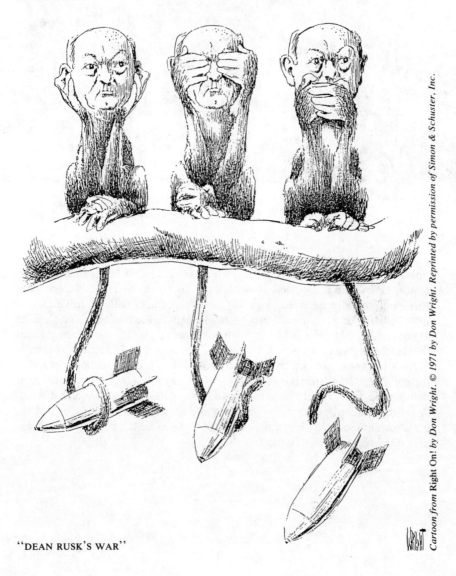

"DEAN RUSK'S WAR"

STALEMATE

Every military effort to compel the Communists to come to terms failed until, as a final inducement, a frustrated and saddened Johnson, subtly encouraged by Rusk, decided to withdraw from the 1968 presidential race. Rusk's diplomatic skills led to a major arms agreement with the Soviet Union in the closing days of the Johnson Administration: the Nuclear Non-Proliferation Treaty. But the conflict in Vietnam dragged on into the Nixon Administration, ultimately becoming known as "the only war America ever lost."

Rusk left the State Department and public life in broken health, rejected by former friends and unable to find a job. A man with a profound belief in democratic values and the principles of international law, he had directed American foreign policy with loyalty and distinction throughout one of the most tumultuous decades in history, only to become trapped in the paradox of waging war to preserve peace.

PART FOUR

THE KENNEDY YEARS

"It's Our Turn Now and We Will Do Better": Inside the State Department

---

Iɴ January 1961 Rusk assumed the post for which it seemed he had been predestined, moving into his new office on the seventh floor of the Department of State amid a swirl of high praise. Editorial writers called attention to his competence, energy, and intelligence. His practical experience in diplomacy and foreign policy was universally acclaimed. His portrait graced the cover of *Time,* which regarded him as the key appointment of the new administration. But the news media clearly had a hard time getting a "fix" on the man; *The New York Times* praised his liberal orientation, while *Business Week* called him conservative.

Rusk too was caught up in the euphoria of the moment. The glamour of President Kennedy and his wife was infectious. There was a sense that the torch had passed and that all things were possible for a new generation of leadership in America. "It's our turn now and we will do better," Rusk later said, recalling his mood. At fifty-one, he was older than the President but still felt very much a part of the same generation. Both of them had fought as young men in World War II, and although they had since traveled along very different roads, they now had succeeded to the mantle of ultimate power.

Kennedy and Rusk were, in fact, an oddly mismatched couple. Their heritages were diametrically opposed—Kennedy's roots were in the Catholic south of Ireland, Rusk's in the Scotch-Irish, Protestant north. Kennedy was the product of the benevolent Catholicism of his native Boston, with its tolerance of frailty and the human condition. Rusk's Presbyterianism was cold, austere, unbending. Kennedy's mind was restless, inquisitive, wide-ranging, and irreverent; he liked nothing better than to chew over ideas in sharp debate. Rusk's intellect was penetrating, but orderly and hierarchical; his more limited stock of ideas flowed from deeply held first principles. Even their senses of humor were opposites: Kennedy's wit was mordant and sarcastic, Rusk's wry understatement. Given their enormous differences in style and temperament, Rusk had reason to be apprehensive about how well he could work with Kennedy.

Still, he sensed that it was an extraordinary time to be Secretary of State. In his first press conference Rusk spoke of "revolutionary" change and "a world in turmoil, reshaping itself in a way which is at least as significant as the breakdown of the Concert of Europe" in the nineteenth century. He contrasted the situation to that in 1952, when a member of the incoming Eisenhower administration could say that few major changes in foreign policy were necessary because the world situation was expected to remain pretty much the same as during the previous administration. What was new in the 1960s was the economic and political change sweeping over the "Third World"—the vast assemblage of peoples outside the orbits of influence of both the Soviet Union and the United States. Rusk saw himself as the first Secretary of State who would be called upon to deal with these peoples as citizens of independent nations, and he believed that the United States should be in the vanguard of this "revolution of rising expectations." His altruistic goal was that the United States should "take the lead in building a world in which men can be free under law and in which the human spirit will not be subdued by hunger, disease, and despair."

Despite such high-flown thoughts, Rusk had a deep appreciation for the routine and unspectacular aspects of foreign policy making. He often made reference to the fact that at any given time the United States was participating in ten or more obscure international meetings somewhere in the world. Several thousand cables flowed in and out of the State Department on a daily basis. It humbled him to realize how little of this he could even keep up with as Secretary. Yet he emphasized the importance and utility of the routine of the department. "A great deal of our work in the Department of State," he would say with a certain pride, "is perhaps on the boring side." Rusk's patience with the slow march of the bureaucracy at State set him apart from many of Kennedy's advisers with a more glamorous view of foreign policy making. Arthur Schlesinger, Jr., the noted Harvard historian who functioned as a freelance adviser to the President, accused Rusk of rejoicing in the "tedium" of diplomacy.

Many of Rusk's critics saw him as a somewhat smoother version of his close associate and predecessor John Foster Dulles. Both men were staunch anti-Communists, and containment of the Soviet Union and China was the hallmark of their policy. Yet there were differences between them, of substance as well as style. Rusk and Dulles had different starting points. For Dulles, anti-Communism was a moral imperative. Rusk was much more of an idealist, whose article of faith was the American system and who saw an abiding coincidence between American self-interest and his altruistic goals for other nations of the world. Further, Rusk thought that Dulles had stressed the negative aspects of foreign policy, and he was uncomfortable with slogans like "brinkmanship" and "massive retaliation." He wanted to devise instead a more positive strategy for a stable world order. His was a grandiose, ambitious, America-centered vision of using our power to lead what he called a "revolution of freedom" and a "revolution of economic and social progress" in the world.

The foremost element of this strategy was to maintain American strength and determination. By this he meant not only military strength but also American productivity and social progress. Rusk had an innate populist faith in human progress, which was rooted in his Georgia boyhood in an underdeveloped part of the world that was being transformed by the combined strength of private initiative and wise government programs. A second pillar of Rusk's concern was to strengthen the worldwide system of defense alliances and "collective security." This meant not only increasing military assistance and vigilance along the "frontiers of freedom" but also strengthening ties with industrialized nations and encouraging regional groupings of friendly nations.

Third, Rusk wanted to forge a long-term partnership with developing nations to carry forward their economic and social progress. Foreign aid was therefore essential, not just to tie Third World nations into the Western system, but to better the lives of their people. Rusk disagreed with Dulles's insistence that those who are not with us are against us and that developing nations should align themselves with the United States. He saw nothing wrong with "genuine neutralism" as long as a government was trying to better the lot of its people. He thought Dulles's worst mistake had been to cancel American aid for Egypt's Aswân Dam project in a fit of pique with Egyptian President Gamal Abdel Nasser, which led the volatile Nasser to nationalize the

Suez Canal. The subsequent military intervention by Britain, France, and Israel, which the United States had to oppose, caused a disastrous split with our principal allies.

Rusk also had subtle but important differences with Dulles over policy toward the Soviet Union and Communist-dominated nations. He thought Dulles's calls for a "rollback" of the Iron Curtain got him in trouble because it gave false hope that the United States would intervene militarily in Eastern Europe. Rusk believed that Soviet domination of Eastern Europe "could not be an issue of war and peace in an age of nuclear weapons." His policy was to stand firm, and to inject Western ideas of freedom through increased contacts and trade with the nations of Eastern Europe. At the same time he sought to open negotiations with the Soviet Union wherever possible. "When we are able to find common interests which the free world and the communist bloc share, we must be prepared to talk and negotiate about ways of acting together to fulfill those interests—even if they are narrow," he said. Especially in the area of arms control, it was necessary to search for common ground with the Soviets.

Judged from the vantage point of history, these propositions stand up well. Rusk can also be credited with initiating or emphasizing several new themes of American foreign policy whose importance has grown over the years. He saw the nature of the rivalry between the superpowers not merely as a competition between the Soviet Union and the United States, or as a confrontation between the ideologies of communism and capitalism, but rather as a contest between those who believe in freedom and human rights and those who would deny them. He was among the first to assert that the United States should promote respect for human rights and fundamental freedoms. "On the one hand," he said, "are those who believe in change through persuasion and consent—through means which . . . respect the individual. On the other are those who advocate change through the subjugation of the individual and who see in the turbulence of change the opportunity for power." To be credible, however, this concern for human rights must carry over into the domestic sphere of U.S. policy. He pointed out that the "problems of discrimination here in our own country are the largest single burden we bear in the conduct of our own foreign relations."

Rusk was an advocate of military strength and commitment to a system of alliances, not for their own sake but as a deterrent to war. "One must be prepared to make war in order to avoid war," he said. But strength and commitment alone were not sufficient to avoid war.

He was the first Secretary of State to initiate means of ending Cold War confrontations through a persistent search for possible areas of agreement between East and West. He did not regard it as contradictory to couple a policy of firmness with continuing contacts, negotiation, and even cooperation with the Soviet Union. Rusk's long-range goal and the touchstone of his thought and action remained the establishment of a world order based on Articles 1 and 2 of the United Nations Charter: a free community of nations; resolution of disputes by peaceful means through principles of justice and international law; and international cooperation to ensure respect for human rights and economic and social progress. Many who heard him speak of these goals accused him of being trite or of being a naïve Wilsonian idealist. But he really believed in these ideals with a conviction that approached religious faith. His was a remarkably consistent vision developed over the years, the product of his early experience, his education at Davidson and Oxford, his service in World War II, and his prior tour at the Department of State.

The State Department which Rusk presided over in 1961 was much different from the one he had left only nine years before. He was in charge of 23,455 employees—more than twice the number in the Truman administration—including over 6,000 Foreign Service officers serving in other nations. The United States had diplomatic relations with ninety-eight countries, and this number was increasing rapidly as more new nations emerged from colonialism each year. But Rusk was denied the opportunity to organize the State Department to his liking; most of the key appointments were chosen by the Kennedy staff. Chester Bowles was named Under Secretary. Adlai Stevenson was chosen Ambassador to the United Nations and given cabinet rank. G. Mennen "Soapy" Williams, a former governor of Michigan, was appointed Assistant Secretary for African Affairs. George Ball, associated with Stevenson, was given the post of Under Secretary for Economic Affairs. Averell Harriman became a roving ambassador-at-large. Stevenson, Bowles, and Harriman scarcely hid their disappointment at not being named Secretary of State and their view that they would do a better job than Rusk.

The only man Rusk was allowed to bring to State was George McGhee, a personable Texan and an old friend from the Truman administration, whom he later named Under Secretary for Political Affairs. Even to fill this post, Rusk had to resist Kennedy's desire to appoint Walt Rostow. He had nothing against Rostow, he explained, but merely preferred his longtime associate McGhee for the job. (Iron-

ically, insiders at State would blame McGhee as well as Bowles for
the administrative difficulties that developed in the department and
for which Rusk took much of the heat.) In marked contrast to the
situation at State, Robert McNamara, Kennedy's Secretary of Defense, was allowed to choose virtually all of his top assistants.

Rusk immediately experienced the first of many difficulties with
Robert Kennedy, the President's younger brother, just appointed Attorney General. Robert Kennedy seized control of the appointment of
new ambassadors at State in an effort to find posts for a number of
key Kennedy political supporters. Rusk believed that experienced
Foreign Service officers should be appointed to ambassadorships, except for those which were clearly ceremonial. He won a few rounds
by going directly to the President, but in general Robert Kennedy had
his way. Rusk later remarked that the Prime Minister of Ireland had
asked him, "Mr. Secretary, when are you going to send us an ambassador with whom we can talk foreign policy?"

Rusk admired Robert Kennedy's energy, but he considered him
erratic and unprincipled. Two more different personalities can
scarcely be imagined. Kennedy—especially during these early years
—was dynamic, impatient, and impetuous. Rusk was staid, quiet,
orderly, and cautious. Kennedy was steadfastly devoted to his
brother; Rusk was loyal, not to a man, but to the office of the presidency. Kennedy was young and athletic, Rusk was not. Kennedy, in
a campaign to make public officials more physically fit, once asked
Rusk to go for a hike on the Washington towpath. Rusk politely declined, saying that he had been an infantry commander in the war and
had done all the walking he was going to do in his life.

As Attorney General, Robert Kennedy was the government's top
lawyer, and on one occasion Rusk called him for legal advice. President Kennedy had asked him to make a certain expenditure and, after
searching the relevant congressional appropriations, Rusk could find
no authority to spend the money; he asked Robert what to do. Robert
reacted impatiently, and told Rusk to go ahead: "Don't worry about
it," he said. "If you go to prison, we'll make sure that your salary will
continue."

Robert Kennedy was very interested in foreign policy, and Rusk
thought he performed creditably on many occasions, especially during
the Cuban missile crisis. Much of the time, however, Rusk thought he
was meddling. He usually suffered Robert's exuberant intrusions in
silence, but when Robert pressed him to allow American businesses
abroad to organize lobbying efforts and even demonstrations in favor

of U.S. foreign policy, Rusk decided to complain directly to President Kennedy. The President, to Rusk's relief, sided with him. "Let Bobby have his say in some of these matters," the President said, "because he is very much interested in them. But if he ever gets in your way, I want you to speak to me about it." That seems to have established an uneasy, if temporary, truce between the two men, and Rusk never felt that he had to take orders from Robert Kennedy. Ironically, John Kennedy had consulted with Rusk and asked his opinion before naming his brother Attorney General. Rusk had told him to be relaxed about the appointment, and, if he really wanted him, to go ahead. Being President is a lonely job, Rusk said, and every President needs someone in his official family he really knows and trusts. Most of the members of the cabinet were not cronies or long-time Kennedy associates.

As Rusk settled into his new job, he soon discovered there was a great disparity between his preconceptions of the office of Secretary of State and the reality. He began by adopting the management style of his model and teacher, George Marshall, and to a lesser extent, Dean Acheson. Just as Marshall had made Robert Lovett his alter ego, Rusk told Bowles that their relationship would be central to the management of the department. Bowles would be his alter ego to the extent that when people talked with him, they should feel that he spoke with the authority of the Secretary himself. Bowles was also to take responsibility for the day-to-day flow of business, and if Rusk was absent he was to act on his own.

Rusk also believed in delegating heavily to the assistant secretaries and desk officers in the department and lectured them on not being afraid to make decisions. He reiterated the Marshallian statement: "Don't ask me what you should be doing—you tell me what *I* should be doing." Urging his desk officers to give "what my father used to call prayerful Presbyterian consideration" to their jobs, he told them to "ask yourselves every day how have I committed the United States by not acting—by inattention or inadvertence?" Only important decisions should come to the Secretary's desk, and then preferably in the form of a one-page memo clearly outlining the alternatives and recommendations. Many of his subordinates at State found this management style a puzzle. They expected a more "take charge" Secretary who would concentrate on getting the big mass of the bureaucracy moving.

Rusk conceived of his own function as twofold: he was the President's counselor on foreign policy concerns, and he was a diplomat—

the chief public spokesman for American foreign policy other than the President himself. There were many other tasks, of course, which ranged from working with Congress to ceremonial functions, but he hoped to keep these at a minimum; they were secondary to his more important duties. Rusk was very much in the tradition of a British civil servant, and he kept by his desk a dog-eared copy of Sir Harold Nicolson's book *Diplomacy*—the bible of the British Foreign Office.

In fact, the job of Secretary of State was the most difficult in the government, even more demanding (except for the burden of ultimate responsibility) than the presidency itself. Rusk's day began at 7:45 A.M., when he would be picked up at his house for a working ride to the office, and he typically would not return home until after 10:30 at night. On Saturdays and Sundays he would vary this routine only by wearing casual clothes to the office. For eight years he averaged only one evening at home with his family per month. *U.S. News & World Report,* at the end of Rusk's first year in office, called him "Washington's busiest man."

About 25 percent of Rusk's time was taken up in relations with the Congress, talking to individual senators and congressmen and testifying before committees. Although he was given high marks for keeping in touch with Congress and was on cordial terms with key congressional leaders, he was often exposed to the rough-and-tumble of congressional logrolling. On one occasion Senator Robert Kerr of Oklahoma came to him and offered a deal. "I am interested in the price of oil and the price of beef," he said. "If you will help me, I will give you some help on foreign aid." Rusk refused; he knew that Kerr was speaking of his personal interest in oil and beef, not just the interest of his constituents.

To foster friendly relations with Arab countries Rusk lobbied members of Congress to lift the restrictions on imported oil, but he was soundly defeated by Kerr and domestic oil interests. Afterward, explaining the matter to King Saud of Saudi Arabia, he asked the King: "How come the Arab world has so much oil?" "Because God gave you infidels all of the water," came the reply.

A blizzard of paperwork came through the State Department each day in the form of cables and dispatches from American embassies and installations around the world. Rusk carefully husbanded his time, and only a few each day received his personal attention. In a wry comment on the situation, he told the story that Thomas Jefferson, when he was Secretary of State, had reportedly said to a friend, "You know, I haven't heard from our Minister in Spain this year. If I don't hear from him next year I will write a letter."

Rusk had badly misjudged the amount of travel he would have to undertake as Secretary of State. On taking office, he had told Kennedy that he would stay in Washington and leave the travel to others. But in the first few months of 1961 he attended a NATO conference in Oslo, a SEATO conference in Bangkok, a CENTO meeting in Ankara, and a peace conference in Geneva. After his first two years Rusk found that he had outdone even John Foster Dulles and was the most traveled Secretary of State in history.

Ceremonial functions also took up much of his time. Ambassadors were constantly coming and going, and visiting foreign ministers and prime ministers had to be entertained and feted. At least outwardly, every nation, large or small, had to be treated equally by the American Secretary of State. Rusk kept getting trapped on the Washington party circuit, until one day Averell Harriman told him what to do. "You proceed once down the receiving line, greeting and talking to everyone. Make sure you spend a special time with any ambassador, so that everyone in the room will wonder what you are talking about. Once you arrive at the end of the line, simply keep going out the back door." Rusk adopted this practice, and it worked wonders for his schedule—except, he recalled, at the Dutch Embassy, which had no back door.

Inevitably, Virginia had a new role to play as the wife of the Secretary of State, and she did it well; one account called her "a unique asset to U.S. foreign policy." Her life was much changed by her husband's appointment. She left her spacious home in Scarsdale reluctantly and went house-hunting in Washington by herself, since her husband had no time to accompany her. (For the first six months of 1961 the Rusks lived in a suite in the Sheraton Park Hotel.) The house she found—on Quebec Street in northwest Washington—was much smaller than the one in New York, but it was all they felt they could afford. It was also encumbered with a restrictive covenant prohibiting resale to blacks, which the Rusks refused to sign.

Rusk made Virginia his personal representative at parties and social affairs. She attended all the national-day celebrations at foreign embassies and invited the wives of foreign and U.S. ambassadors to her house for coffee and conversation. Stories of her kindnesses abounded. In 1965 Pat Johnson, the wife of U. Alexis Johnson, U.S. Ambassador in South Vietnam, fell and broke her elbow. Because she was living alone in an apartment on Connecticut Avenue and had no one to care for her, Virginia promptly moved in for several days and attended to her needs.

David Halberstam, in *The Best and the Brightest,* characterized

Virginia Rusk as "dowdy," implying that she (as well as her husband) did not quite fit into the glittering Washington scene. Newspaper accounts of the time belie this. Although she was by nature rather quiet, absorbed in her family, Virginia became "one of Washington's most incessant party-goers," and she made "a terrific impression on the Washington diplomatic corps." She spoke frankly about the loneliness of her life, with her children off to college and her husband working long hours. It was not a very happy time for her, but she bore up well. In public, as one writer observed, "her serene smile and unfailing poise gave her great dignity and charm." Another called her "a diplomat with a deft touch. Mrs. Rusk comes in for more frank praise than almost any other figure on the Washington diplomatic scene. From the newest . . . third secretary to the suave and knowing veteran of many posts, to each this unassuming cabinet wife communicates instinctively that behind her outstretched hand there is meaning."

Upon taking office in 1961 Rusk (as well as the whole new administration) was faced with fundamental problems: How to make the foreign policy process of the government work effectively? How to mold the machinery of government into a smooth and consistent operation to serve the interests of the President and the country?

These questions have taken on new urgency in the years since the 1960s, particularly during the administrations of Nixon, Ford, Carter, and Reagan, in which bitter feuds between government agencies, presidential advisers, and policymakers became what has been called a "national blood sport" that has harmed the formulation and implementation of American foreign policy. Before the Kennedy administration, although there were intimations of the conflicts to come, it was taken for granted that the Secretary of State would play the chief role in carrying out the President's foreign policy, and that it would even be—at least in its essentials—bipartisan in character. In the 1960s those assumptions began to break down.

The situation Rusk faced was unique. He was serving a President inexperienced in foreign policy matters but who, it was widely announced at the time, wanted to be his own Secretary of State. The President's brother, the Attorney General, wanted to become expert in foreign affairs. The Secretary of Defense, Robert McNamara, brilliant and effective, held strong views and obviously would be very influential in the new administration. Adlai Stevenson, who had dearly wanted the job of Secretary of State, was a member of the cabinet and held a position of influence through his post as U.N. Ambassador. The CIA was also working to assert its will, often with little supervision or control. Moreover, President Kennedy appointed a strong team of experts on foreign affairs to his White House staff, headed by a longtime Kennedy associate, McGeorge Bundy, Assistant to the President for National Security Affairs, and Walt Rostow, his deputy. To make matters worse for Rusk, he was the administrator of a staid and stodgy State Department bureaucracy that had changed little—except for a vast increase in numbers—since before World War II. Rusk had no political or personal ties to the new President and his close advisers. And this diverse assemblage was not used to working together and did not even know one another very well.

The odds against making a strong team out of such a group of players were very long indeed. That they succeeded amazingly well—although not without some missteps along the way—can be credited in large measure to Rusk. Although his noncombativeness and courtly ways were often misjudged as weaknesses, his unassuming manner, combined with intelligence, integrity, wit, and dogged persistence, was just what was needed. But credit is also due to Bundy, Mc-Namara, Ball, and the rest—and especially to President Kennedy, who performed with skill and magnanimity to get people working together effectively.

Before things came together, however, there were many frustrations and difficulties. The Marshallian scheme Rusk used to organize the State Department simply did not work. The men who took up their jobs at State in 1961 were new to each other and to Rusk. They had little idea how to interact effectively or how to establish decision-making channels. They looked to Rusk for strong leadership, both in formulating policy and promoting the primacy of the department. But Rusk disappointed; he had quite another idea. His model of delegation of responsibility called for most decisions to be made at lower levels. He wanted his colleagues to "fill up the horizons of their responsibility." For Rusk the great problem in a bureaucracy was drift, the avoidance of decisions. He wanted his staff to take action, to make decisions. He would disturb them only if they were going off in the wrong direction.

By the summer of 1961 a consensus had developed that Rusk was a very difficult man to work for. He refused to take charge. No one ever knew what he was thinking. When his assistant secretaries asked him for guidance, he would merely ask probing questions and end by saying, "I want you to be Secretary of State for a while. You just do what you think is right." His aides complained that Rusk was reticent, shy, and uncommunicative. They said that he saw all the facets of a problem but that he had trouble coming to a decision. A story making the rounds at the State Department was that the White House had called to ask whether anyone had ever discovered what Dean Rusk thought about anything.

White House staffers began to complain that they had trouble getting anything worthwhile out of the State Department bureaucracy. A paper on Cuban policy prepared by the Bureau of Inter-American Affairs emerged as a complex thirty-page laundry list of all possible moves, and Kennedy at a meeting of the National Security Council cast it aside in disgust. The department took forty-three days to draft a response to Nikita Khrushchev's demand on Berlin, finally coming up with a meandering product that, the French newspaper *Le Monde* caustically commented, seemed "modeled on a Soviet note." The process at State failed to rise above the tiresome and conventional; bottlenecks developed in the system as key personnel refused to act. Directionless and adrift, people at State fretted while their power was increasingly usurped by more vital centers of the government.

The grumbling soon became a major public issue, and news reports told of "disarray, confusion, and uncertainty." Safely in retirement, the increasingly outspoken Acheson remarked that the department was getting to be like a feudal monarchy, composed of individual dukedoms competing for power and influence. He referred to Soapy Williams as the Duke of Michigan and Stevenson as the Grand Seigneur of New York. The U.N. was the Department of Public Emotion. Neither Rusk nor President Kennedy was amused.

Kennedy reacted in characteristic fashion. When he was worried about something, he frequently placed a call directly to the country desk officer concerned, which rarely achieved its purpose and only injected further chaos into an already disjointed decision-making process. Rusk complained that Kennedy succeeded only in "scaring the hell out of the desk officer and disrupting my system of delegation." Then Kennedy increasingly bypassed State altogether when it came to major problems. He named Paul Nitze, Assistant Secretary of Defense for National Security Affairs, to head up a task force on Cuba. He chose Roswell Gilpatrick, Deputy Secretary of Defense, for a task force on Vietnam. Adolf Berle, Jr., was brought in as a special White House aide to take charge of Latin American affairs. Kennedy also looked more and more to the men around him at the White House for advice, working papers he could use, and policy formulation. McGeorge Bundy became his principal adviser and confidant in foreign affairs. A class split was developing, much as it would in later administrations, between the White House and the State Department. State was described as a "pool" into which the administration dipped or did not dip, as it chose, to formulate policy.

To many observers, Rusk seemed not to notice or to care about what was happening. He was characterized as "mysterious," "faceless," "a Buddha." But if he was neglecting the internal affairs of the department, it was because he was busy working on the more important substantive problems that arose during the first year of the Kennedy administration, chiefly Cuba, Laos, and Berlin. He was resisting Nikita Khrushchev's demand to replace Secretary General Dag Hammarskjöld with a three-person "troika" at the United Nations. He attended the SEATO conference in Bangkok in March to rally the allies to stand firm on Laos. He met frequently with McNamara to reformulate defense policy to place new reliance on conventional weapons. With Kennedy, he met with President Kwame Nkrumah of Ghana to try to convince him to support U.S. policy in the Congo. He met with Soviet Foreign Minister Andrei Gromyko over Laos, as well as with a procession of foreign leaders like Adenauer of Germany and Macmillan of Britain. He worked with Congress on Kennedy's "grand new plan" for foreign aid. In April came the disaster of the Bay of Pigs, and immediately afterward he attended the Geneva Conference on Laos and the NATO foreign ministers' conference in Oslo. Then came the June summit conference between Kennedy and Khrushchev and a Russian ultimatum on Berlin.

For all the activity, Rusk disclosed little about his own thoughts and desires. He was judicious in the extreme, adhering to his belief that public diplomacy was usually harmful. In his press conferences he even carefully controlled his facial expressions when answering a question. "There are times," he would tell his associates, "when a Secretary of State must learn to say nothing at considerable length." Finally, Rusk's ways produced exasperation in official Washington. As James Reston wrote in July 1961, it was "just that, somehow, the Secretary of State has not quite managed to organize his department effectively, serve as principal adviser to the President, shine in the presence of all the other foreign policy experts . . . act as chief negotiator abroad, educate the public, console the Foreign Service, attend five state dinners a week, satisfy the curiosity of 2,500 Washington correspondents, testify brilliantly on Capitol Hill, tame Khrushchev, develop the underdeveloped, deflate the overdeveloped, and stamp out Castro." Reston's tone was bemused, but the concern was real.

Ironically, as more questions were being raised in the summer of 1961 about Rusk's stewardship of the State Department, he was quietly gaining stature in the eyes of the man who counted most: President Kennedy. Few were aware of it, but Rusk's personal access to the President was steadily increasing. In the early months of 1961 he saw Kennedy relatively little. But by August the two men were meeting several times a week, often three or four times a day. It appears that Kennedy took some time to become accustomed to Rusk and to value his counsel.

The rise in Rusk's stock with Kennedy began in April with the Bay of Pigs, the botched CIA-sponsored invasion of Cuba. Rusk met alone with Kennedy several times to try to talk him out of approving the invasion plan. He lost the argument. But after the invasion proved an embarrassing and costly failure, Rusk closed ranks. He did not mention his opposition even to his close associates in the State Department.

From that time on, Kennedy knew that Rusk was someone he could trust. In 1962, on a trip to Britain to meet with Prime Minister Macmillan, Kennedy and Rusk went to dinner at Chequers, the Prime Minister's country estate, just before departing for home. After dinner they rode to Heathrow Airport, Rusk in one car with Lord Home, the British Foreign Secretary, and Macmillan and Kennedy in another, and when they arrived at the airport Macmillan was three sheets to the wind from drinking highballs. He came up to Rusk and put his arm around him. "Rusk," he said, "I've got to get to know you better. Jack has been telling me that you were opposed to the Bay of Pigs, but that after it happened you acted as if you had done it yourself."

Rusk also advised Kennedy not to agree to a summit meeting with Khrushchev in Vienna. Kennedy went anyway, and was shocked by Khrushchev's ultimatum over Berlin. Upon his return he put the Berlin problem largely in Rusk's hands.

Kennedy's new confidence in Rusk went largely unnoticed, even by some White House insiders, because of Rusk's insistence on speaking frankly only when alone with the President or in a very small group—generally with Bundy and McNamara. At National Security Council meetings Rusk would sit impassively or would ask probing questions without revealing his own thoughts. His reserve came from his Marshallian view that a Secretary of State should reserve judgment until all had had their say. He also did not want to appear to argue with the President in front of other people, for fear it would be leaked to the press. "There should be no blue sky showing between a President and his Secretary of State," he would say.

By the summer of 1961 Rusk was discussing with Kennedy a thoroughgoing overhaul of the machinery of the State Department. Kennedy now realized that he could not possibly be his own Secretary of State. And both men knew that something had to be done so that State could once again become an effective policy arm of the government. Even with the confidence of the President, Rusk could work on only two or three major problems at a time. The day-to-day competence and efficiency of the department had to be strengthened.

A major difficulty in the department was the personality and style of the Under Secretary, Chester Bowles. Rusk's hectic schedule and his preference for extensive delegation made it absolutely essential to have a good manager in the number two position in the department. Bowles, by all accounts, was ill-suited to the task. He talked in windy abstractions about policy and had no conception of his job as an organizer and manager. When a cable came into the State Department from a head of state, it would often lie on his desk unanswered. He was uninterested in detail and wanted to make policy instead.

Neither Rusk nor Kennedy got along well with Bowles, and they looked for a way to remove him as Under Secretary. It was easier said than done. Before he became Secretary of State, Rusk considered Bowles a good friend. He generally agreed with Bowles's liberal views on foreign policy, and they had frequently talked politics when Rusk was president of the Rockefeller Foundation and Bowles was a member of the board of trustees. Bowles had a distinguished business and political career before coming to State. He had been a successful advertising executive, governor of Connecticut, and a congressman from that state. He had resigned from Congress to help Kennedy in his campaign, and when Kennedy was elected Bowles had fully expected to be named Secretary of State. Rusk, who had not actively sought the appointment, was almost apologetic to Bowles after he was named, and was at first happy to see Bowles appointed Under Secretary. Now he gave Bowles assignments out of the country and tried to shift the day-to-day work of the department to George Ball.

Kennedy found Bowles tiresome and unhelpful as well. The President was an impatient man who liked people to come to the point, and Bowles had a rambling style, often thinking out loud, saying outrageous or imprecise things and refining his thoughts while he was speaking. But he had a strong liberal following, and Kennedy knew it would be difficult politically to get rid of him.

It was Bowles's conduct during the Bay of Pigs that sealed his fate with Kennedy. Bowles was against the operation, and he wrote Kennedy a memorandum giving his reasons. Afterward, Bowles made a cardinal mistake: he leaked the story that he had opposed the invasion plan. Kennedy was furious; one of his principal aides was trying to show him up. Robert Kennedy went to Bowles with some tough talk: "You might have been against it [the Bay of Pigs] before, Chet," he said, "but you are for it from now on." Then Bowles compounded his problems by writing Kennedy a letter denying he had leaked the story to the press. Both Kennedy and Rusk knew the denial was false.

By mid-July speculation was rife that Bowles would be asked to resign. Some of the more liberal press raised a ruckus, saying it was ironic that the first head to roll at State would be that of Bowles, who had opposed the Bay of Pigs. Kennedy announced that Bowles would be retained—for the time being. Meanwhile, Rusk intensified his efforts to induce Bowles to accept a roving ambassadorship of some kind—to get him out of the country and out of the line of decision. But Bowles refused to take the hint.

The ax finally fell on November 26. A sweeping shake-up—dubbed the "Thanksgiving Day Massacre"—was announced at State that had quietly been worked out between Rusk and the White House. Bowles was named a "special representative and adviser on African, Asian, and Latin American affairs." Several months later he was appointed Ambassador to India. George Ball took Bowles's spot as Under Secretary, George McGhee became Under Secretary for Political Affairs, the number three job in the department, and Averell Harriman was named Assistant Secretary for Far Eastern Affairs. Kennedy insisted that Rusk name Walt Rostow as chairman of policy planning. Rusk resisted only because he did not know Rostow well, but the two of them quickly established a harmonious working relationship. Rusk successfully opposed Richard Goodwin, Kennedy's candidate for Latin American Affairs, on grounds of youth and inexperience. Robert F. Woodward stayed in that job, and Goodwin was named his deputy.

George Ball emerged the key man in this shuffle. A man of intelligence, wit, and charm, Ball was from the Midwest, a lawyer by profession, and had divided his time between government service in the Roosevelt and Truman administrations and law practice in Chicago and Washington. A close friend and confidant of Adlai Stevenson, Ball joined the Kennedy administration at the behest of Stevenson and Senator William Fulbright. Tall and craggily handsome, distinguished-looking if slightly rumpled, Ball became a force at State by dint of his forthright manner, quiet competence, and excellent judgment. He was a problem solver who could analyze a situation and prescribe a solution. He also had the negotiating skills to see matters through to a final resolution.

Although Ball's initial appointment at State was to handle economic matters, Rusk soon began to give him broader responsibilities, especially because of Bowles's unreliability. Like everyone else, Ball had a difficult time relating to Rusk. The Secretary's apparent indifference to his activities and decisions bothered him. Unlike many others, however, Ball was finally able to penetrate Rusk's reserve. When he expressed his concern about the need for a closer dialogue with Rusk to Lucius Battle, Rusk's executive secretary, to Ball's surprise Battle burst out laughing and said, "Only the other day Dean told me, 'I wish I knew what Ball's doing; he goes his own way and never talks to me.' " Ball later wrote, "That colloquy cleared the air; thereafter, the Secretary and I established regular and thoroughly satisfactory communications." This often took the form of sharing drinks in Rusk's seventh-floor office. Almost every evening about six o'clock Rusk called Ball, Rostow, Battle, and occasionally a few other insiders into his office for an informal gathering. Known as the "bottle club," it was a break for Rusk before he continued with his evening appointments or activities.

Ball was the ideal Under Secretary. He not only managed the creaky bureaucracy well but also became Rusk's true alter ego on matters of policy. Ball took over principal responsibility for handling many crises—rebellion in the Congo, the dispute between Greece and Turkey over Cyprus—as well as relations with Europe and economic concerns. He was fully capable of assuming the role of Secretary of State himself, but he remained loyal to Rusk. With a clear idea of both Rusk's strengths and weaknesses, he tried to enhance the first and compensate for the second.

The two men saw eye to eye on most problems, but Ball did not hesitate to express his differences with Rusk on important issues, such as American intervention in the Dominican Republic in 1965 and the escalation in Vietnam. Ball's opposition did not bother Rusk because he knew it was honest and deeply felt. In his disagreements with Rusk, Ball never attacked his motives or impugned his character. Nor did he resort to sneak attacks through leaks to the press. When Ball lost the argument, as he did on Vietnam, his disagreement did not turn into bitterness and he continued to work effectively on other problems. Ultimately Ball did resign, in 1966, when "the Vietnam nightmare had passed the point where I could significantly influence policy," but the Rusk-Ball relationship remained cordial. In 1967 Rusk watched Ball on a television interview and afterward wrote him a teasing note: "Warm congratulations on your performance in Sunday's international Meet the Press. What a hawk you turned out to be on Vietnam!"

With the reorganization of the State Department, Kennedy began to eliminate some of the special task forces and committees and gave their tasks to the regular channels at State, Defense, and the White House. Rusk simplified the levels of command at State to three: the Secretary or Under Secretary, the Assistant Secretary, and the country desk officers. He instituted an operations center so that, for the first time, the State Department would be open twenty-four hours a day. "An unavoidable consequence of the world being round," Rusk commented wryly, "is that, at any given moment, only a third of the world is asleep. The other two-thirds is awake and up to something."

Rusk made a few other changes in the department that cast light on his personality, but make it hard on historians. ("There are some things," he says, "that history does not deserve to know.") It was customary for the executive secretary to listen in on phone conversations between the Secretary of State and the President and prepare a memo concerning significant points for action. Rusk, obsessed with confidentiality, ended this practice. He had direct access to Kennedy by phone, and the two men talked several times a week, but no records were kept of their conversations. Rusk was also horrified that cables marked "Secretary Eyes Only" were routinely copied and sent off to several levels at State, Defense, and the White House. He instituted a new communications channel—called Cherokee after the obscure Georgia county where he was born—and ordered that no one else was to have access to incoming or outgoing cables. Rusk had a constant fear of being "bugged," and several times called security men to check on suspicious crackling sounds in the telephone lines. His worries were directed not so much at the Russians as at the FBI chief, J. Edgar Hoover. He made a point of telling Hoover in Kennedy's presence that if he ever found a tap on his telephone or a bug in his office, he would immediately resign and go public with the evidence.

Rusk also persuaded Kennedy to issue an order to all Foreign Service personnel designating them the "primary representatives of American foreign policy abroad." On his trips to other countries he never failed to include the U.S. ambassador when he conferred with foreign leaders (in marked contrast to Henry Kissinger in the 1970s, when the U.S. ambassador would have to be briefed after Kissinger's visit by the foreign government's officials). Morale improved both at State and in the Foreign Service, and by December 1961 reporters were writing about the "comeback of the State Department" and "new strength" for Dean Rusk. There were still problems, and no longer was State the only foreign policy show in town, but it was back in the center of policy formulation.

Although he became what many said was President Kennedy's principal adviser on foreign relations, there was always a sense that Rusk did not quite fit into the New Frontier. Rusk and the President came from very different backgrounds, and in the pictures of the two men together, especially at Palm Beach or Hyannis Port, there was a noticeable contrast between the youthful-looking, often casually dressed President and the moon-faced, bald, serious, suit-clad Secretary of State. Their relations were closer than anyone guessed, but they were official, not personal. Rusk was never a member of the inner circle; he did not play touch football and was never thrown into the swimming pool at Robert Kennedy's house, Hickory Hill. He was, by his own admission, a bit of a "square."

Rusk was the only member of the cabinet Kennedy never called by his first name. He always referred to Rusk as "Mr. Secretary." Some thought it a mark of Kennedy's displeasure with Rusk, but it was in reality the mark of a subtle understanding between the two men. Rusk harked back to George Marshall, who believed in arm's-length relationships between people with high public responsibility, and Kennedy, who was very perceptive of other people, had an intuitive appreciation of this. Rusk often sat next to Jacqueline Kennedy at White House dinners, and she once remarked, "You know it is very significant that my husband always calls you Mr. Secretary." Rusk took it as a compliment and a sign of respect.

Rusk's relationship with the President was cordial but professional. He grew to like Kennedy very much and thought him to be both intelligent and courageous. He was fond of ideas and liked to surround himself with a wide variety of people with different points of view. Kennedy and Rusk met frequently in the Oval Office or upstairs in the President's bedroom after Kennedy arose from his customary afternoon nap. Following his press conferences, which were held at the State Department, Kennedy usually visited Rusk's office for a talk. They were also in frequent touch by telephone; Rusk was free to call the President directly without going through any of the White House aides. Some of these conversations were less than satisfactory; Kennedy assumed he could say anything over the telephone, but Rusk was guarded, assuming the Russians were listening.

In private conversation President Kennedy was a very practical, skeptically minded person, impatient with fuzzy thinking and people who did not quickly come to the point. Often when a visitor in the Oval Office went on too long, he would rock quickly back and forth in his rocking chair and tap his teeth with his fingernails. His wit and penchant for practical jokes were always close to the surface. On one occasion Rusk had to see Kennedy on urgent business and flew down to Palm Beach. When he arrived, the President was dressing and finishing breakfast, and he was asked to wait. After a little while Caroline Kennedy, then about five years old, came out to greet him. "Hello, Mr. Secretary," she said. "I am very worried about the war in the Yemen. Please tell me what is happening in the Yemen today." Rusk was amazed at the child's precocity, but before he had a chance to answer he heard a snicker coming from behind a screen at the end of the room. The President came out laughing happily. He had put her up to it.

Kennedy normally kept his personal life to himself or to a small circle of friends. On a July 1963 trip to Italy, however, he asked Rusk to arrange a night in a beautiful spot somewhere so he could relax. Rusk called his friends at the Rockefeller Foundation and obtained permission to use the foundation's Villa Serbelloni on the shores of Lake Como in the Italian Alps. Kennedy liked the idea, and insisted on being dropped off by helicopter and left entirely by himself. Even the servants were asked to leave, and Kennedy dismissed his security men. When Rusk arrived the next day to pick him up, Kennedy was aglow. He had never spent such a wonderful time, he said. "It was strongly suspected," Rusk later recalled, "that Kennedy had not spent the night alone."

Jacqueline Kennedy seemed to Rusk to be a beautiful and glamorous but melancholy figure, burdened by her role as First Lady and trying desperately to carve out a normal life for her two children. Her chief interest was art, which her husband did not appear to share. Rusk arrived at the White House one day to see Kennedy, who came down to his office from the upstairs living quarters. "I'm glad you called," he said. "I was up to my neck in art with Jackie."

If Rusk was self-effacing and unassuming as Secretary of State, it was because he knew that Kennedy wanted him to play that role. He sought neither power nor publicity. Kennedy told him early in their relationship that if anything good happened, he wanted it announced at the White House, and Rusk scrupulously complied. To a large degree he held his own eloquence, wit, and ability to spellbind an audience in check.

At times, however, Rusk's skill at capturing a moment flashed through, usually when he was free to be himself and did not have to play Secretary of State. One of these moments came at a special dinner held in New York in May 1963 to celebrate forty years of publication of *Time* magazine. The invited guests included the famous and the elite from across the nation—film stars, writers, politicians, sports figures, business leaders—all those who had made the cover of *Time* through the years. In this glittering and disparate assemblage, Rusk emerged as the star. Just back from an exhausting trip to India, he was the only man present in a white dinner jacket—because that was what he had on when he left Delhi. He stepped to the podium and, without a word on paper, stirred the gathering with an impromptu address about the purposes of American foreign policy. It was in essence an eloquent reiteration of his principal concerns: the rule of law and the importance of freedom and human rights. *Time* thought enough of the speech to reprint it in its entirety.

Rusk was never considered a politician, and he never sought to become one. Those who knew him best were well aware that he had both the ability and personality if not the desire. In late 1961 he came up as a possible candidate for governor of New York. His refusal: "I am not interested, not eligible, not qualified, and not about to do it." He felt a political career would mean "having to give up a certain sovereignty of soul."

Rusk was also secure enough to feel comfortable with the fact that he was not President Kennedy's only adviser on foreign affairs. He recognized that the foreign relations of a great power are too complex, too varied to be dominated by any one man. It was necessary to choose special envoys from time to time, like Harriman and Robert Kennedy. McGeorge Bundy and his staff were essential in the White House. Others, like McNamara and Stevenson, also had jobs that made them essential members of Kennedy's foreign affairs team.

If Rusk had problems with the White House, they were not generally caused by McGeorge Bundy, the President's National Security Adviser. And Bundy remembers that his diffficulties with State were more with the department's bureaucracy than with Rusk. Both men agree that their personal relationship during the Kennedy years started out well and got better, although they had not known each other before serving together in the administration.

McGeorge Bundy was in many ways Rusk's foil. A member of one of Boston's old families—his mother was a Lowell—Bundy was used to privilege and rank. At Groton, Yale, and as a junior fellow at Harvard he had excelled, and, at home in the world of ideas, he became a professor of government at Harvard. There his reputation grew, and he was named dean of the college at the age of thirty-four. Although a Republican who had even worked for a time as a speechwriter for John Foster Dulles, Bundy became a Kennedy favorite in the 1950s and thus had the advantage over Rusk of being a member of the President's inner circle.

Despite the differences between them, Rusk and Bundy in many ways possessed virtues that were complementary. Bundy, though exasperated at times by Rusk's secretive ways, respected his long government experience, diplomatic skills, and ability to deal with Congress. Bundy, in turn, was more creative and incisive than Rusk; he had total access to Kennedy and was unencumbered by any responsibility other than to serve the President's interests. Rusk was not resentful of Bundy's important influence; he considered Bundy indispensable to the policy formulation process. Bundy, knowing what Kennedy wanted and needed, could shape the bureaucratic product of the State Department to suit the President's wishes. He could keep track of the implementation of important actions so as to be ready to inform the President of their status at any moment. But by Bundy's own account, he "never sent a message on anything more important than Mrs. Kennedy's schedule in New Delhi without clearing it first with the Secretary of State."

The Rusk-Bundy relationship proved that the National Security Adviser and the Secretary of State can work together in relative harmony. Both men were team players; neither tried to undermine or steal a march on the other. Each knew his proper role. The National Security Adviser did not have cabinet status; Bundy was merely a member of Kennedy's staff, in protocol on a level with a deputy under secretary. Rusk considered Bundy capable of being Secretary of State, however, and fully expected that Kennedy would appoint him to the job if he were reelected to a second term. At one point Rusk tried to get him appointed as his deputy under secretary, but Kennedy wanted him to stay at the White House. After Kennedy's death, however, Bundy's influence and drive soon waned. Johnson's effusive and disorderly style upset him, and he had severe doubts about the nation's course in Vietnam. In early 1966 he left to become president of the Ford Foundation, though his loyalty and friendship for those who remained in the government made him refrain from public criticism of the war.

Rusk was also at pains to establish an excellent working relationship with the Secretary of Defense, Robert S. McNamara. His memories of the destructive feud between Louis Johnson and Dean Acheson in the Truman administration had convinced him that harmony between State and Defense was absolutely essential to the functioning of an administration. McNamara, whom Rusk had never met before they were both named to Kennedy's cabinet, was an intense man, as tightly wound and self-controlled as Rusk but, if anything, more hard-minded. He had risen to the top in the world of big business, at the Ford Motor Company, where success was measured in terms of the bottom line. Unlike Rusk, he was used to making a big bureaucracy work. There were no complaints of drift or indecision at Defense; McNamara was clearly in charge.

Rusk established regular meetings with McNamara, usually on Saturday mornings, when they could talk at length. Rusk thought it was important that they resolve their differences by themselves, in order to present a common viewpoint to the President. The two of them had quite different approaches to problems: McNamara looked at everything in terms of numbers, charts, and graphs; Rusk tended to rely on instinct and judgment, picking out the key factor from among many confusing considerations. But although their reasoning was different, each found that they usually came out with similar positions in the end. George Ball thought their relationship was a little too harmonious —that the President would sometimes benefit from differing opinions on the issues. Rusk tended to defer to McNamara's judgment on military matters. On the other hand, he resisted McNamara when it came to diplomatic policy. He recaptured control over the Vietnam task force—which had been lodged in Defense under Roswell Gilpatrick—by saying to McNamara, "If you want to direct our embassy in Vietnam, then give me the marines."

Rusk worked less well with Adlai Stevenson at the United Nations. He found Stevenson to be personally charming and effective as U.N. Ambassador, but in Rusk's opinion he had two weaknesses: he had trouble making up his mind, and he was a poor negotiator. For both the remedy was strong guidance from the White House and from State, which Bundy and Rusk provided in the form of instructions, speeches, and position papers. In any negotiation in which Stevenson was involved, Rusk learned not to provide him with a fallback position until the very end. If Stevenson knew the government's fallback position, Rusk recalled later, "he would reach that point in about the first five minutes of the negotiation."

Stevenson, for his part, had growing doubts about his usefulness as

U.N. Ambassador, especially after Lyndon Johnson became President. He frequently complained to Rusk that he was simply executing instructions and that his views were not taken into account. By the summer of 1965, when he died suddenly in London as he was leaving the U.S. Embassy, he was telling friends of his "complete dissatisfaction with the policies of the Secretary of State and the President," especially with respect to China, Vietnam, and the Dominican Republic.

Particularly frosty relations existed between Rusk and Arthur M. Schlesinger, Jr., the distinguished Harvard professor and historian who was a White House counselor and the unofficial chronicler of the Kennedy administration. Rusk distrusted Schlesinger from the start; Schlesinger was too much of an academic and inexperienced. He talked too much, a quality that always disturbed Rusk. Schlesinger was also soft, too willing to deal with the Chinese and the Soviets, and unimpressed with the analogies dear to Rusk and his generation about the lessons of World War II and the paramount necessity of standing up to aggression in any form.

Rusk believed that it was demeaning for the Secretary of State to argue with a mere White House counselor—he told associates of his disdain for those "without operational duties" and scornfully pointed out that "Arthur is over in the East Wing with the social secretaries" —so his response to Schlesinger was to stonewall, to say nothing at all when he was around, which often affected the conduct of business. One morning, a Rusk aide remembers, a high-level group from State accompanied the Secretary to confer with Kennedy about Berlin. But Schlesinger was there, and Rusk pointedly neglected to tell the President what State's position was. Afterward, he told the aide that "Schlesinger is the biggest gossip in town," and he was afraid of a leak to the press.

Schlesinger, for his part, saw Rusk as the chief obstacle to needed adjustments, both in style and substance, in the conduct of foreign policy. Rusk's appointment had been a mistake; Kennedy had not done his homework, and did not know he was getting someone little different from John Foster Dulles. Rusk lacked the flexibility of mind to be Secretary of State. Schlesinger would have preferred Harriman, Stevenson, or Fulbright for the job. Rusk was too tied to the policies of the past; Schlesinger was more liberal than Rusk and, probably, Kennedy as well. He wanted new departures with respect to Latin America, China, Cuba, and, most of all, Vietnam. And for Schlesinger the cardinal sin was that Rusk was a poor administrator; he blamed Rusk for the fact that the State Department bureaucracy moved with glacial slowness.

Schlesinger continually irritated Rusk by sending him memos containing gratuitous advice, often patronizing in tone: "In connection with instructions to embassies concerning Cuba, you may want to consider the following points . . ." Rusk considered Schlesinger importunate and his expertise at the "gee whiz" state of development. He did his best to ignore him. But Schlesinger had his revenge. In the summer of 1965 excerpts from his book *A Thousand Days* began to appear in *Life*. He attacked Rusk as "Buddha-like" and "irrevocably conventional" and said that Kennedy had intended to allow Rusk to leave after the 1964 election and seek a new Secretary of State. Headlines appeared around the country: "Rusk Annoyed JFK" and "How the State Department Baffled Him [Rusk]." Although books by Theodore Sorensen and others somewhat contradicted Schlesinger's account, the notion has persisted that Kennedy and Rusk did not get along.

Rusk considered Schlesinger's slur unfair, because only Kennedy had known the understanding under which he was serving as Secretary of State—that for financial reasons he would remain for only one term. In September 1963 Rusk had in fact gone to see Kennedy and told him that he was ready to quit his post early if Kennedy wanted to reorganize his administration in advance of the 1964 election. But Kennedy declined to accept Rusk's resignation, saying, "No, I want you to stay. Don't bring that up again. I like your guts, and I don't have many people around here with any guts." Rusk's plans to resign in 1964 were changed only by the assassination and President Johnson's insistence that he stay on.

After the articles in *Life*, Rusk called Schlesinger and told him about his one-term understanding with Kennedy. Schlesinger said that he would have presented a different picture had he known, but made no public correction. Rusk suspected that Schlesinger's accusations were motivated by his disagreement over Vietnam and were part of a campaign on behalf of Robert Kennedy to discredit him and, through him, Lyndon Johnson. That suspicion seemed confirmed when Johnson, in late 1965, called Rusk over to the upstairs sitting room at the White House and told him, amid gales of presidential laughter, that Bobby Kennedy had just offered him a deal: "If you fire Dean Rusk and replace him with Bill Moyers, I won't run for President in 1968." No such deal was made. Rusk remained in office and emerged in the eyes both of his detractors and supporters as the major architect of American foreign policy in the 1960s.

At the beginning of the decade, however, none of this could be foreseen. Despite turbulent crises abroad, it was a quiet time at home.

The certainties of the postwar world, both pleasant and unpleasant, had not changed much since the 1940s. Americans were interested in economic prosperity; almost every year was confidently seen to be better than the year before, and children expected to live better than their parents. When the new-model cars came out, there was little change except for more horsepower. In football it was the Green Bay Packers, in baseball the Yankees, and Roger Maris hit sixty-one home runs. Television was hot (*The Medium Is the Message* was the title of a best-selling book of the time), and the most popular show of 1962 was an inanity called "The Beverly Hillbillies." American youth gathered around jukeboxes, and the lyrics they heard reflected their concerns: "I've waited so long for school to be through, / Paula, I can't wait no more for you."

The Cold War and nuclear weapons were on everyone's mind; a whole new generation was growing up that could not even remember a time when these perils did not exist, but everyone tried not to think about it. Young boys faced military service, and their girlfriends would wait for them. But American was at peace, its rivalry with the Soviet Union channeled into a space race to see who would be the first to land a man on the moon.

In the distance, however, new voices were beginning to be heard. Martin Luther King, Jr., an eloquent black preacher, talked about first-class citizenship for Negroes and nonviolent protest. "We feel that we are the conscience of America. We are its troubled soul." At the movies the "New Wave" was sweeping in from France and Italy; films like *Last Year at Marienbad* and *The 400 Blows* challenged Hollywood's banality. Folk singing, guitars, and banjos swept the country. Joan Baez and her songs of protest captured a growing mood of nonconformity and social concern. Pete Seeger, Theodore Bikel, and Bob Dylan went down to Mississippi singing a song about black civil rights:

Oh deep in my heart,
I do believe
We shall overcome—some day.

In 1960 Barry Goldwater, then a little-known U.S. senator from Arizona, wrote *The Conscience of a Conservative,* which was avidly read by initiates and passed from hand to hand like a treasured possession. In 1963 Betty Friedan's powerful book *The Feminine Mystique* called for the liberation of women from traditional roles. Sexual mores were beginning to loosen and found expression in an undulating dance called the twist and in the popularity of magazines with nude centerfolds such as *Playboy*.

Quite simply, a new generation was coming of age and America was moving away from the postwar consensus built by the generation that had fought World War II. Political and social values were losing their stability. Eisenhower, the man who had presided over the placid 1950s, had said, "America today is just as strong as it needs to be. America is the strongest nation in the world, and she will never be damaged seriously by anyone from the outside." In the turbulent 1960s, the upheaval would come from within.

"We Have to Save This Man":
The Bay of Pigs

IT is one of the ironies of history that the Eisenhower administration, having ringed the Soviet Union and China with a comprehensive series of alliances, found itself troubled by a small island scarcely ninety miles from the Florida coast. On January 1, 1959, Fidel Castro at the head of a mere handful of ragged troops entered Havana and overthrew the unpopular and corrupt regime of the Cuban dictator Fulgencio Batista.

Castro at first promised to restore constitutional government and civil liberties, but his schemes for radical reform of property rights, his nationalization of American and native business operations, and his increasingly anti-American rhetoric led to deteriorating relations with the United States. The Eisenhower administration made no attempt to test Castro's early apparent good intentions—Dulles was critically ill at the time, and died in May 1959. The Russians, however, sent Deputy Prime Minister Anastas Mikoyan to Havana in February 1960 to conclude a loan and trade agreement. Washington in turn reacted by cutting the import quota on Cuban sugar and placing an embargo on the sale of oil to Cuba. One of Eisenhower's last acts before leaving office in January 1961 was to break off diplomatic relations with Cuba. Thus a policy of implacable enmity was bequeathed to the Kennedy administration that would lead to the Bay of Pigs and the Cuban missile crisis.

On his second day as Secretary of State, Sunday, January 22, 1961, at ten o'clock in the morning, Rusk, along with other top members of the Kennedy administration, received a briefing on Cuba. Allen Dulles, the Director of the CIA, and General David Gray, the liaison officer between the CIA and the Joint Chiefs, told the grim-faced group that the CIA was training and equipping several hundred Cuban refugees for possible military use against Castro's Cuba. The meeting was not long, and there was little comment because none was called for. It was only a contingency plan, something President Eisenhower had initiated the year before. The objective was to overthrow Castro, and the Cubans were being trained in assault tactics. The whole project was top secret and must remain so. The Cubans were being trained at camps deep in the jungles of Guatemala. In Florida a government in exile was being formed. It was not mentioned that among the organizers of the Cubans were Howard Hunt and Bernard L. Barker, later of Watergate fame. Nor was it mentioned that the chief proponent of this project in the Eisenhower administration had been Vice President Richard Nixon.

Rusk did not pay particularly close attention to the plan, assuming there would be plenty of time for discussion later. But he did wonder vaguely why he had not been told about it during the transition (President Kennedy had known the details since November). It was Rusk's first substantive meeting with Kennedy as well as with Robert McNamara. They were all still relative strangers to one another. He knew Allen Dulles slightly, as a man devoted to his late brother, and as a shadowy figure who was content to serve as "Mr. Inside" to John Foster Dulles's "Mr. Outside." Later Rusk reflected that the CIA established its tradition of "bad habits" when that agency and the State Department were run by the two Dulleses and Allen had to answer only to his brother.

On January 28 the Cuba project was again considered, at a meeting of the National Security Council. Dulles and Richard Bissell, the CIA's Director for Operations, explained the need for going ahead with a plan to overthrow Castro. He was about to receive MiG airplanes and arms from the Soviet Union, and time was growing short. Questions were raised, and it was decided to refer the CIA plan to the Joint Chiefs of Staff for evaluation. Rusk was asked to have the State Department prepare an action plan to isolate Cuba diplomatically in the Organization of American States. Because he regarded the CIA and the military aspects of an anti-Communist coup as outside his responsibilities, he did not reveal anything about the plan to his colleagues at State.

Although Rusk was among the inner circle of those who knew about the Cuban operation, he felt cut out of the decision-making process. Without consulting him, Kennedy had offered the job of Assistant Secretary for Latin American Affairs to Adolf Berle, Jr., an elder statesman from Roosevelt's New Deal administration. Berle had refused, saying that the post of Assistant Secretary was not prestigious enough; Kennedy then named him the head of a special task force at Latin American Affairs, also without consulting Rusk. As a result Latin American Affairs remained in the hands of Thomas Mann, a holdover from the Eisenhower administration. Mann, who knew about the CIA plan all along, never briefed Rusk during the transition. Kennedy chose to work on the Cuban venture primarily through Berle, Mann, and their aides in the White House, Richard Goodwin and Arthur Schlesinger, Jr.

So Rusk was in an awkward position. He was nominally in charge, but Latin American policy was clearly being run from the White House. Berle and Schlesinger went off on a tour of Latin American capitals to drum up support against Castro. Again no one consulted Rusk, and his pride would not let him, the Secretary of State, go hat in hand, knocking on doors, asking if there was anything he could do. Not until the summer of 1961 did Rusk succeed in recapturing Latin American Affairs and getting his own choice, Robert F. Woodward, a career Foreign Service officer then serving as Ambassador to Chile, appointed as Assistant Secretary.

The Cuban plan was discussed again in February. After a presidential press conference held in the auditorium of the State Department, Kennedy came up to Rusk's seventh-floor office with Berle, Mann, and several of their aides. They went into his conference room, and Kennedy asked everyone in turn to state his views. Rusk was the only one to express any reservations, and he felt mortified. Kennedy was treating him as an outsider, on a par with his most junior advisers. He seemed to pay more respect to Assistant Secretary Mann than he did to the Secretary of State. The whole experience offended Rusk's profound sense of hierarchy and order. He thought of his days in the Truman administration, when Harry Truman would have turned the matter over to the Secretary of State and the Secretary of Defense and asked for an opinion. "Well, I did not let that kind of thing happen again," Rusk said later. "I would not take part in that kind of session."

Rusk was next called to a meeting in the Cabinet Room at the White House on March 11. Richard Bissell, tall, erect, and articulate, presented the plan, pointer in hand. The brigade of Cubans training in Guatemala would make an amphibious landing on the beaches near Trinidad with tactical air support. It would be a surprise assault that would catch Castro off guard. Trinidad, on the southern shore of central Cuba, was chosen because it was near the Escambray Mountains, where untold numbers of anti-Communist guerrilla fighters were holding out in the hills against Castro's militia. Bissell was confident that the landing would trigger uprisings and armed rebellion against Castro's forces. Once a beachhead was secured, a provisional government could be landed.

The Joint Chiefs' evaluation of the CIA plan was favorable: the conclusion, prepared by General Gray, was that "this plan has a fair chance of ultimate success and, even if it does not achieve immediately the full results desired, could contribute to the eventual overthrow of the Castro regime." General Gray omitted the military meaning of "fair," which he knew to be 30 percent in favor of success and 70 percent against. The Joint Chiefs also glossed over the fact that their favorable recommendation depended on political factors—a sizable popular uprising and follow-up forces.

Rusk was increasingly skeptical of the plan, but at the meeting he confined himself to making observations and posing questions which he hoped would cause second thoughts. How could this be done while keeping American involvement secret? What would happen if the brigade did not succeed? He proposed an alternative plan: the brigade should land on the eastern end of the island just adjacent to the American base at Guantanamo Bay. Then, if the attack was unsuccessful, they could retreat to Guantanamo. If they were successful and established a bridgehead, they could be supplied from the base. But the Joint Chiefs argued strongly against Rusk's idea. They wanted Guantanamo kept out of the invasion altogether.

Allen Dulles, arguing for the invasion plan, darkly pointed out that if it was called off there would be a "disposal problem" of what to do with the brigade of Cubans, who would be angry and would expose the role of the CIA in covert operations. There would also be a political problem; the story would spread that the United States (meaning Kennedy) had "lost its nerve and turned chicken" at the last minute. Castro would then be stronger and could never be overthrown except by an all-out invasion.

Kennedy reluctantly agreed that the Cubans should be allowed to return to Cuba, but with a minimum of political risk. The Trinidad plan was too spectacular; the "noise level" of the operation had to be reduced, and he asked for a new plan to conceal United States involvement. In case the predicted popular uprisings failed to emerge or other difficulties were encountered, it would be better if the invaders were able to "melt away" into the Escambray Mountains.

After this meeting Rusk left Washington for two weeks to attend a SEATO conference in Bangkok. In his absence Under Secretary Chester Bowles went to the White House briefings, learned of the invasion plan, and became an opponent of the whole idea. Meanwhile, the CIA planning for the invasion continued. Bissell came up with a new landing site, a remote area of the Zapata swamps near the Bay of Pigs, fifty miles west of Trinidad. One of the reasons this site was chosen was that there was an airfield near the shore. (By coincidence, Castro knew this area very well—it was one of his favorite fishing spots.) Kennedy also authorized the preparation of a White Paper on Cuba to make a political case for the invasion. Released publicly on April 3, this document accused Castro of betraying the revolution, establishing a totalitarian Communist state, a satellite of the Soviet Union, and engaging in an "assault on the hemisphere" by fomenting revolution and disturbances in other countries. His regime was a "clear and present danger" to the Americas. On April 5 James Reston of *The New York Times* called the tone of this statement "sharp and even ominous," in marked contrast to the administration's conciliatory line on Laos. The principal author of the White Paper was none other than Arthur Schlesinger, Jr., who was privately writing memos to the President opposing the invasion.

On Friday, March 31, the day Rusk got back in the office from his trip to Bangkok, Bowles, deeply concerned, handed him a two-page memo outlining his reasons for opposing the invasion plan. He said that if the White House seemed determined to go ahead with it, he wanted to take his objections directly to Kennedy. Strangely, Rusk listened without comment, although Bowles's objections, based on the nonintervention pledges the United States had agreed to in the Bogotá Pact establishing the Organization of American States, closely paralleled his own thoughts. Rusk's relations with his Under Secretary were ebbing, and making common cause with the voluble Bowles was out of the question. He merely promised to deliver the memo to the President.

President Kennedy was in Palm Beach. Rusk went to see him to report on the SEATO conference and the situation in Laos, and they talked about Cuba as well. Alone with Kennedy, he told the President frankly that he opposed the invasion altogether. Although he was uneasy about the military aspects, he argued against it primarily on other grounds. First, the invasion would be difficult to handle politically. The operation could not be conducted on a covert basis; the hand of the United States was bound to show, and it might undercut the efforts for a cease-fire in Laos or encourage the Russians to try something in Berlin. Acting unilaterally also bothered Rusk. He predicted an uproar in the United Nations and in the Organization of American States. The invasion was contrary to international law: the United States was not under attack, and it could not be justified as self-defense. He was also skeptical about whether there would be a popular revolt in Cuba and whether the forces Castro had organized for controlling the country could be so easily overwhelmed.

But Kennedy brushed these considerations aside. Unrealistically, he believed that American involvement could be kept secret. He told Rusk that the plan had been scaled down to nothing more than an infiltration of Cubans back to their homeland. No men or planes would depart from American soil, and the landing would be an all-Cuban operation. If Castro could be overthrown, it would make a dramatic difference in the hemisphere. And what, he asked, would he do with the Cuban freedom fighters if he canceled the landing? Rusk advised him at least to announce unequivocally in advance that there would be no intervention by U.S. military forces in the case of any Cuban effort to overthrow Castro. Kennedy agreed.

Since Kennedy had made his decision, Rusk did not even bother to give him the Bowles memorandum. The day before, Senator William Fulbright, who had traveled to Florida with the President aboard Air Force One, had argued against the plan and had given him a comprehensive memorandum. Kennedy was not interested in any more argument on the question.

On his return to Washington, Rusk told Bowles that the plan had been greatly modified and that it was not necessary for him to see Kennedy. Bowles then asked whether the revised plan would make page one of *The New York Times*. Rusk replied he did not think so— a conclusion that was, of course, profoundly wrong. But Rusk did not level with Bowles because he believed that he would leak the operation to the press. Above all else, Rusk was not going to be a party to sabotaging the plan.

On April 4 was what some have called the "climactic" meeting on the Bay of Pigs—certainly an exaggeration, because by then Kennedy had already made up his mind. The meeting, held in the State Department in the conference room next to Rusk's office, began with an impassioned plea by Senator Fulbright opposing the landing. The President then called for a vote. Berle said, "Let 'er rip." Mann said that he had reservations about the new landing site, but gave his assent. The Pentagon, represented by Secretary McNamara and Paul Nitze, also voted yes. Rusk was strangely silent, and when he was asked, he equivocated; he later explained that this was because the President already knew his position.

After the meeting Schlesinger and Goodwin mounted an effort to get Kennedy to reverse his decision. They received a sympathetic hearing from Rusk, but little else. "Maybe we've been oversold on the fact we can't say no to this," he said mournfully. He told Schlesinger that he would draw up a "balance sheet" on the project and try to see the President. "It is interesting to observe the Pentagon people," he said. "They are perfectly willing to put the President's head on the block, but they recoil from the idea of doing anything which might risk the virginity of Guantanamo." Rusk suggested to Schlesinger that someone other than the President make the final decision and do so in his absence—someone who could be sacrificed if things went wrong. Schlesinger later called this idea "curious"; he did not realize that Rusk almost certainly was suggesting himself and invoking the doctrine of "plausible deniability."

Rusk met again with the President on April 11, 12, 13, and 15, and saw no indication that he was going to change his mind. Kennedy was troubled, but firm in his decision. Rusk had the impression it was a "razor's edge" type of decision for Kennedy, but he had made it and would live with the consequences.

In the early morning hours of Saturday, April 15, the operation began with a preliminary air strike against Cuba carried out by Cuban exile pilots taking off from Puerto Cabezas in Nicaragua. The objective was to secure air superiority for the invasion by destroying Castro's planes on the ground, but they succeeded in damaging only five of the approximately thirty planes. The CIA cover story for the attack was that the air strike was the work of defectors from Castro's own air force. To lend credence to the story, one of the pilots shot up his own plane, a B-26, and flew from Nicaragua directly to Miami, where he was whisked away by U.S. officials. But unexpectedly, one of the real attackers got in trouble and had to make an emergency landing in Key West.

That morning at the United Nations, Raúl Roa, the Cuban Foreign Minister, took the floor to denounce the air raid and accuse the United States of aggression against Cuba. Adlai Stevenson, the American ambassador, was caught unawares. He had not been told of the Bay of Pigs operation until April 8, when Schlesinger had given him a quick and very vague briefing.

Rusk was in his office when a frantic message came in from Stevenson asking how to respond to Roa's accusations. Rusk was also confused. All the briefings on the invasion plan had been oral, and he remembered nothing about any preliminary air strike. In fact, an air strike was not in the original Trinidad plan but had been added for the Bay of Pigs landing while Rusk was in Bangkok. Incredibly, Rusk believed the CIA cover story, and Stevenson was so informed. Reassured, Stevenson denied Roa's accusations and read a speech blithely repeating the CIA cover story. Almost immediately the story began to come apart, as astute reporters noted differences between the markings of the exile planes and Cuban Air Force B-26s. Stevenson, caught in a lie, was furious and sent Rusk an angry note. He told aides that he had been deliberately tricked by his own government.

The air strike had the effect of letting Castro know that an invasion was imminent—the only thing he did not know was where. The invasion force had embarked on Friday and was already at sea; D day was Monday, April 17. Meanwhile, Kennedy kept to his routine and left Washington early Saturday afternoon for his weekend retreat at Glen Ora, Virginia. It was a studied attempt at normalcy; if he had stayed in Washington, the press would have been alerted that something was up.

As the CIA cover story on the preliminary air strike fell apart, Rusk became increasingly concerned about the second air strike, which he knew was scheduled for the day of the landing. Now that the CIA fig leaf had fallen, he feared that a second strike from Nicaragua would "raise the international noise level" to an intolerable degree and give Stevenson more trouble at the U.N. There would be no plausible way to deny the American role in the invasion. Rusk thus decided that further air strikes from Nicaragua should be canceled. The brigade would have to establish a beachhead and secure the airfield at the Bay of Pigs so that the planes could be brought to Cuba before they were allowed to carry out further air strikes. On Sunday, April 16, Rusk talked the matter over with McGeorge Bundy, who agreed. Then Rusk called Kennedy at Glen Ora.

Confused about the details of the second air strike, Kennedy had not realized that the sorties were to be flown from Central America. In a long talk about strategy, Rusk put on his former military hat and advised the President that the operation could not possibly succeed unless the Cuban armed forces themselves revolted against Castro. The second air strike was not going to make any difference. The lumbering B-26s flown in from Nicaragua could not possibly search out and destroy all of Castro's planes, most of which would be hidden in hangars.

Kennedy was finally convinced, and canceled the second air strike. After he put down the phone he sat quietly and shook his head, then got up and paced the room. Those with him at Glen Ora said that they had never seen him so gloomy. Meanwhile, Bundy called Richard Bissell. "The B-26s are to stand down," he said. "That's an order from the President."

Bissell and General Charles Cabell, Deputy Director of the CIA, were extremely upset by the order. Cabell, who felt that the air strike was vital, said it was like being hit by "a falling bomb." Bissell and Cabell went over to the State Department to talk with Rusk, arriving at his office about 7 P.M. Countering their argument that the air strike was necessary to protect the landing ships as well as the men, Rusk said that an air strike would not be effective: the ships were supposed to discharge the men before dawn, and from his experience in World War II he knew that air operations had to be intensive and applied over a long period of time if they were to knock out an opposing air force. The three men then discussed whether to call off the landing. Bissell said that was impossible. "The landing is committed and it is too late to call it off."

Reluctantly, Rusk said he would again call the President. He got Kennedy on the line and explained Cabell and Bissell's argument. "But I am still recommending in view of what's going on in New York," he said, "that we cancel." Kennedy once again grimly agreed. Rusk turned to the men and said, "The President agrees with me. Would you, General Cabell, like to speak with the President?" Cabell declined. "There's no point in my talking with the President," he said. Rusk had the impression that the general "did not want to argue with his commander-in-chief."

Later that evening Rusk went over to the Sheraton Park Hotel to get some sleep. Bissell and Cabell maintained a vigil at the CIA operations center, Quarters Eye. Gloom and anger were pervasive, both at the CIA and at Puerto Cabezas in Nicaragua. Men swore and pounded their desks. When General Gray informed the chairman of the Joint Chiefs, General Lyman Lemnitzer, who was spending a quiet evening at home, of the cancellation of the air strike, Lemnitzer "couldn't believe it."

At four in the morning on Monday, April 17, Cabell could stand it no longer. The landing was a few hours away, and without air superiority the brigade was doomed. He went to the Sheraton Park Hotel and woke up Rusk. The situation was desperate, he argued. It was now too late to bring in the exiles' planes from Nicaragua—only American air power could save the day. The aircraft carrier *Essex* was steaming offshore near the invasion site, and he asked for U.S. jets. Rusk told him that was out of the question: the President had already announced at his press conference a few days before that under no circumstances would U.S. forces be involved in any effort to overthrow Castro. To use American air power would make a liar of the President.

Rusk again got Kennedy on the telephone at Glen Ora, waking him up. He then handed the phone to Cabell, who made the request and went through a number of air support options. Kennedy made no reply but asked to talk with Rusk. The conversation was brief. Rusk hung up and told Cabell that all the requested options were disapproved. The *Essex* would not be involved in the invasion and would stay at least thirty miles out to sea.

The invasion force reached the beaches of Cuba and landed as scheduled in the early morning hours of April 17: a brigade of 1,500 men against the whole Cuban military. (The first man to land on the beach was actually an American, Gray Lynch, a CIA agent, who fired the first shots of the invasion.) Several C-46s dropped an additional 177 paratroopers northeast of the beachhead. It was up to the brigade's few B-26s to give whatever air cover they could to the landing. Against Kennedy's orders, several Americans under contract to the CIA also flew missions in relief of the Cubans, either on their own or authorized by Bissell. A radio on Swan Island, off the Honduran coast, called on the Cuban armed forces to revolt. A clandestine radio transmitter sent cryptic messages, supposedly to a Cuban underground, whose size had been dramatically exaggerated by the CIA: "Alert. Alert. Look well at the rainbow. The first will rise very soon. Chico is in the house. Visit him. The sky is blue. The fish is red." The head of the Cuban exiles' revolutionary council, José Miró Cardona, and his associates were flown from New York to a secret rendezvous in Florida, whence they would be taken to the first available piece of "free Cuba" to proclaim a new government.

Fragmentary reports of the landing began reaching the outside world. Rusk held a press conference at ten thirty that morning and gave an incomplete account of what was happening: "The American people are entitled to know whether we are intervening in Cuba or intend to do so in the future. The answer to that question is no. What happens in Cuba is for the Cuban people themselves to decide." He then opened the floor to questions. At this early time, the press was surprisingly docile and Rusk was able to shunt their questions aside ("That is a question for the future. . . . I must stand on the statement I have just made"). The next morning *The New York Times* carried the headline:

ANTI-CASTRO UNITS LAND IN CUBA;
REPORT FIGHTING AT BEACHHEAD;
RUSK SAYS U.S. WON'T INTERVENE

Rusk was also busy trying to limit the damage in the U.N., where Soviet Deputy Foreign Minister Valerian Zorin was calling for collective action to halt the invasion. Under instructions from Rusk, Stevenson issued a technical denial: "No offensive has been launched from Florida or any other part of the United States."

By Tuesday morning, April 18, reports coming into the Cabinet Room, now a makeshift command center, made it clear that the operation was a debacle. There had been trouble from the first. The landing craft had run aground on coral reefs (another CIA failure: the agency's photo interpreters had assured the men that the dark areas offshore were only seaweed). The paratroopers were easily overwhelmed by Castro's forces. An invasion ship carrying extra ammunition was sunk. Castro's air force—creaky T-33s and B-26s—wreaked havoc on the men on the ground and outfought the brigade's B-26 bombers. American pilots from the *Essex,* who were authorized to overfly the area on reconnaissance, chafed at the restrictions placed upon them. Forbidden to attack ground targets or to seek air combat, they could only watch Castro's planes and tanks chase the brigade back to the sea. An American A-4D jet with a lock on a Castro T-33 going after a brigade B-26 was forbidden to fire. There was no popular uprising, and the vaunted rebellion of Castro's army failed to occur. As a precaution Castro had arrested thousands of suspected sympathizers the weekend before.

Rusk went over to the White House that afternoon for a meeting with Kennedy and the invasion group in the Cabinet Room. An angry note had arrived from Khrushchev denouncing the invasion and promising "all necessary assistance" to Cuba. With Soviet experts Charles Bohlen and Foy Kohler taking the lead, a tough reply from Kennedy was drafted, saying that in the event of "military intervention by outside force, we will immediately honor our obligations under the Inter-American system to protect this hemisphere from external aggression." At Rusk's suggestion this sentence was added: "I trust that this does not mean that the Soviet government, using Cuba as a pretext, is planning to inflame other areas of the world."

That evening Rusk entertained Greek Premier Constantine Karamanlis at a formal dinner at the State Department. Kennedy was busy with a congressional reception. At midnight the President and his tired advisers assembled once more in the Cabinet Room. Everyone was dressed in white-tie formality except for the Joint Chiefs, who wore their dress uniforms, their medals dangling from their chests. The splendor of the gathering was a counterpoint to the gloomy mood. Bissell, grim and ashen, gave yet another briefing, pleading once again for American jets from the *Essex* and a destroyer to knock out Castro's tanks. Kennedy and Rusk both said no. "I don't want the United States to get involved in this," Kennedy said.

Rusk brought up the idea that the brigade could melt away into the hills. That was the plan, he argued. Bissell shook his head. It was impossible. The Escambray Mountains were fifty miles away, and none of the men of the brigade had any guerrilla training. Rusk was amazed. He felt deceived. No one, not General Lemnitzer, not Kennedy, had realized the guerrilla option had in fact become impossible once the landing site was changed to the Bay of Pigs.

The discussion turned to the possibility of rescuing the surviving members of the brigade. It would still take American air power and a destroyer to perform such a mission, and Kennedy was inclined to do something. Jets from the *Essex* with their markings painted out could fly cover for another brigade B-26 bomber run. Rusk opposed even this, saying that the mission meant a deeper commitment. But Kennedy cut him off. "We are already involved up to here," he said, raising his hand up to his nose.

It was too little too late. The men aboard the *Essex* thought the restrictions imposed upon the rescue mission were onerous and ridiculous. Painted-out markings would not disguise the distinctive silhouette of the American planes, and if the deception did work, they were more likely to be shot at, since many of Castro's gunners would not shoot at American planes. The next morning when they took off, they found that the brigade's B-26s had arrived early and two were shot down. The rescue mission was aborted, and the remaining men of the brigade surrendered or fled into the swamps.

On Wednesday Kennedy's advisers came together in the Cabinet Room once more. Everyone was exhausted; they had been up all night. The failed invasion was on their conscience. The purpose of the meeting was not clear. They knew only that they had to go on. Kennedy had been in office only ninety days. How could the defeat be handled so it would not indelibly taint the whole new administration?

Kennedy was everyone's chief concern. How would the new President react? There were rumors that he had taken it very hard and had been close to tears. (Schlesinger said later that, in the bedroom with his wife, tears filled Kennedy's eyes and ran down his cheeks.) To Rusk's relief, when the President came in he looked tired but composed. The Cuban exile leaders in Miami were coming to Washington, he said. They were distraught and upset. The Cubans had suffered more than anyone. Kennedy clearly had the men from the brigade on his mind.

Then Kennedy was called out of the room for a few minutes, and while he was gone Robert Kennedy began to speak in a voice filled with emotion. He had not taken part in any of the invasion planning, but he was more upset than anyone. He spoke bitterly: "All you bright fellows have gotten the President into this, and if you don't do something now, my brother will be regarded as a paper tiger by the Russians." Glaring angrily around the room, he wanted action. No one quite knew what to say. They stared at him numbly.

It was Rusk who broke the awkward silence. Some of those present could hardly believe their ears as the quiet, mild-mannered Secretary of State exploded into words. Rusk was afraid everyone would try to distance himself from what had happened, leaving the President holding the bag. Seated next to Kennedy's empty chair, he made an impassioned plea to close ranks around the President. A grievous mistake had been made. They all shared in the blame. He pounded the arm of the President's chair with his left hand over and over again. "What matters now is this man. We have to save this man!"

The Bay of Pigs was a major foreign policy setback for the Kennedy administration. Khrushchev could crow that the United States had been deterred by Soviet power. The confidence of America's allies in the new administration was shaken. Serious deficiencies in the decisions and judgment of the government were exposed. Nevertheless, the defeat did not permanently cripple the new administration. The President and those around him were able to bounce back in an amazingly short time.

Kennedy handled the defeat with grace and valor. He did not take a partisan stance, blaming the Eisenhower administration whose plan he inherited. Nor did he attempt to cast public blame on those in his own administration. Although he began quietly to make changes, he thought that everyone was to blame; the management process itself was flawed. He launched a quiet investigation headed by General Maxwell Taylor, but the emphasis was on *what* went wrong, not *who* was to blame. He refused to be cowed or diverted from his essential objectives. "We do not intend to be lectured on intervention by those whose character was stamped for all time on the bloody streets of Budapest," he declared in a nationally televised speech on April 20. "It is not the first time that Communist tanks have rolled over gallant men and women fighting to redeem the independence of their homeland." He announced that he intended "to profit by this lesson" and reaffirmed his resolve in the struggle against totalitarianism. Above all, Kennedy refused to shift the blame. "There is an old saying," he remarked in a press conference, "that victory has a hundred fathers and defeat is an orphan. . . . I am the responsible officer of this government and that is quite obvious."

Rusk took no satisfaction from the fact that he had opposed the landings. It grieved him to see the President wounded. When rumors cropped up that he had not been in favor of the operation, he went out of his way to squelch them. But he reproached himself for not having argued more forcefully against the invasion. He also blamed the debacle on the fact that he and the men around Kennedy were new to one another and were still trying to work out their relationships. There had been a tendency for everyone to sit in his own area of responsibility and ignore the larger context of the decision. The operation had been too closely held, all intelligence coming from the CIA, which also had operational control of the plan. The CIA could hardly be objective in the matter. Rusk had not been permitted to discuss the plan with the Bureau of Intelligence and Research at State, which might have supplied information on the situation in Cuba different from what the CIA was providing. In a meeting with staff members Rusk apologized and told them the reason for the debacle was his own failure to involve the people who should have been involved.

Rusk also thought he had served the President badly in not insisting on a hard look at the military aspects of the landing. He felt he should have suggested that Kennedy ask the Joint Chiefs of Staff what they would require if the U.S. were conducting the invasion. He had no doubt the Joint Chiefs' plan would have involved sustained preliminary bombing of Cuba and the landing of at least two full divisions of combat troops backed up with full Army, Marine, Navy, and Air Force support. It would then have been obvious that an invasion by an inexperienced brigade of 1,500 men had no chance of success. Rusk did not regret his decisions to cancel the second air strike and to withhold American air cover. Even with this support the brigade would not have been strong enough militarily to have a chance against Castro's forces. He believed those in the CIA knew this all along and were scheming to put the President in the position of having to order a full-scale American attack.

He kept his thoughts to himself. But a week after the landing, *The New York Times* published a story that Rusk was "almost alone in having pointed out in advance that the venture might fail." And when it did fail, "he was one of the few who was not saying 'I told you so.' " Unlike Chester Bowles, who leaked his opposition to the invasion to the press—and whose days at State, because of his "I told you so," would be numbered—Rusk had demonstrated the quality he believed to be the sine qua non in a Secretary of State: loyalty. That same quality earned him Kennedy's increasing confidence and trust. The fledgling President had learned an important lesson, and Rusk took charge of a new Cuba policy that barred armed intervention but involved an extensive diplomatic and economic offensive.

In May Rusk went before the Senate Foreign Relations Committee to give closed-door testimony on the botched invasion and to defend Kennedy's Cuba policy. It was a potentially acrimonious session that he handled flawlessly. And at its conclusion—less than three weeks after what came to be known as the Bay of Pigs—the chairman of the panel's Subcommittee on Latin American Affairs, Wayne Morse, said that he felt he could "speak for all the Senators present in placing complete confidence and support in the able leadership" of Mr. Rusk and President Kennedy.

The Bay of Pigs was an American blunder, but it did not destroy the new administration. It did end, however, the feeling of brash self-confidence, the naïve idea that Kennedy and his team of bright advisers could do no wrong. Hubert Humphrey reported to Rusk a meeting with British Prime Minister Harold Macmillan shortly after the Bay of Pigs at which Macmillan said that the crisis "had seasoned JFK a great deal." The same could be said for Rusk.

"You and I Are Still Alive": The Cuban Missile Crisis

I N a secret hearing before the Senate Foreign Relations Committee on May 1, 1961—just after the Bay of Pigs—Rusk was asked to assess the implications of a Cuba allied with the Soviet Union. His response: "I think jet fighter bombers and *missiles in Cuba* could impose a degree of blackmail upon the United States in our dealing with our problems in all parts of the world, which would be extremely serious for us."

Less than eighteen months later this fearful hypothesis came to pass: the Soviet Union began to place medium-range ballistic missiles in Cuba in defiance of an express warning by President Kennedy that such an action would raise "the gravest issues." In so doing the Soviet Union was attempting, in one master stroke, to change the strategic balance between the United States and the Soviet Union and with it the political balance as well. Khrushchev was no doubt emboldened to make the radical move of putting offensive missiles in Cuba by the bungled American action at the Bay of Pigs. Largely the same group of men were called upon to handle this second crisis. Happily, they had learned much, both about themselves and the process of government.

The Cuban missile crisis brought the world to the brink of nuclear disaster. Certainly nothing like it has happened before or since. The superpowers confronted each other boldly, with the threat of nuclear war hanging in the balance. Rusk played a key role in this life-and-death drama, although, characteristically, he attempted to mask much of his participation and has never written about it since.

As Rusk's statement to the Senate Foreign Relations Committee showed, the Kennedy administration was acutely aware of the possibility of a Soviet attempt to use Cuba as a missile base, and the intelligence services were watching the situation closely. But it was not until the late summer and fall of 1962, when the United States was in the middle of an election campaign, that allegations were raised, particularly by Senator Kenneth Keating, Republican of New York, that the Soviets did indeed have missiles in Cuba.

Soviet arms shipments had been moving into Cuba since at least July 1962. Surveillance was stepped up: there were more frequent U-2 flights over Cuba and increased activity by CIA agents. The administration became aware of the arrival of surface-to-air missiles (SAMs), bombers, and a variety of other equipment. The line was drawn, however, at offensive (surface-to-surface) missiles. The administration was willing to accept the SAM sites and the coastal defense system, convinced that the Soviets would not try to introduce offensive missile systems into Cuba. Administration spokesmen charged that Senator Keating was repeating rumors for political purposes.

Nevertheless, the possibility of offensive missiles was not excluded, and surveillance was continued. But when the SAM sites became operational there was increased danger that one of the high-flying U-2s would be shot down. To lessen this risk, at Rusk's suggestion the Committee on Overhead Reconnaissance (COMOR) changed the overflight pattern from end-to-end flights over Cuba to a peripheral pattern that dipped in and out of Cuban air space. This was a mistake because it meant that parts of Cuba could not be photographed from the air. The decision was made, however, when CIA Director John McCone (who had replaced Allen Dulles earlier in the year) was honeymooning on the French Riviera; after he returned, it was decided at a meeting on October 4 to resume the end-to-end flights.

The actual discovery of offensive missile sites occurred on Monday, October 15, 1962, when CIA photo analysts had the opportunity to interpret pictures taken the day before by two U-2 aircraft. This was the first time since September 5 that the whole of Cuba had been systematically photographed, but Rusk was convinced that the sites were new and that the Soviets had waited until the very end of the buildup period to bring in the offensive missiles. They were also brought in very quickly. Everything appeared to be prefabricated in the Soviet Union, down to the concrete covers for the cables running from the radar sites to the missile launchers. Rusk thought the operation was "a superb logistical job" by the Soviets, although they made the mistake of using the same configuration for the Cuban sites as for similar sites in the Soviet Union, which made them relatively easy to discover.

Rusk learned of the missile sites on Monday evening, October 15, during a State Department dinner for visiting German Foreign Minister Gerhardt Schroeder, when he was called to the telephone and told by Roger Hilsman, director of the State Department's Bureau of Intelligence and Research. Other high government officials were informed at the same time, except for President Kennedy. McGeorge Bundy took it upon himself, in a controversial judgment, not to bother the President until the next morning, after a full report could be assembled.

Like everyone else, Rusk regarded the news as grave. Missiles in Cuba would dramatically enhance Soviet first-strike capability. "What concerned me," Rusk recalls, "is that the Russians would be able to knock out our SAC [Strategic Air Command] bases with almost no warning." The missiles would also change the political balance in Latin America and even in Europe. Later, a high Soviet official (probably Anatoly Dobrynin—Rusk refuses to say) told him that what the Russians had in mind was to get the missiles in quickly and secretly and then issue an ultimatum on Berlin just after the American elections in November.

On Tuesday morning, October 16, the President, after being informed by McGeorge Bundy, convened a high-level executive committee—which immediately became known as Excom—to deal with the crisis. Excom was an ad hoc group of officials from the departments immediately concerned as well as trusted advisers of the President: Vice President Lyndon Johnson, Rusk, McNamara, Robert Kennedy, General Maxwell Taylor (chairman of the Joint Chiefs of Staff), General Charles Carter (acting head of the CIA while McCone was again temporarily out of town), George Ball, U. Alexis Johnson, Edwin Martin (Assistant Secretary of State for Inter-American Affairs), Theodore Sorensen (special counsel to the President), Douglas Dillon (Secretary of the Treasury), McGeorge Bundy, Roswell Gilpatrick (Deputy Secretary of Defense), Llewellyn Thompson (former U.S. Ambassador to the Soviet Union), and Paul Nitze (Assistant Secretary of Defense). Charles Bohlen (just named Ambassador to France), Adlai Stevenson, Dean Acheson, and Robert Lovett were

also called in and consulted. The next twelve days would test the
expertise of even this remarkable assembly of men.

This first meeting began with a discussion of the photographic evidence, then Rusk was called on by the President to present his views.
Although he went down some dead ends, the ideas he suggested set
the tone for the debate that raged during that momentous week.

Rusk called for action "to set in motion a chain of events that will
eliminate this base." He then laid out the options. A "quick strike"
could be undertaken—an air strike, which he thought could be done
without an invasion of Cuba. But "if we have a few days," he strongly
urged diplomatic action: consultation with allies in the Organization
of American States and direct contact with Castro to tell him that
Khrushchev planned to trade Cuba for Berlin and to give him an
ultimatum to break with the Soviets.

In the subsequent freewheeling discussion, everyone accepted
Rusk's statement of the objective of the American response: the removal of the missiles rather than the broader purpose of eliminating
Castro. They rejected, however, Rusk's idea of acting in conjunction
with the allies. It would simply take too much time to organize a
response by the OAS and NATO. It would also alert the Russians and
enable them to respond, further complicating the effort to remove the
missiles.

At this time McNamara and Taylor were in favor of a hawkish
response: an air attack not only against the missile sites but also
Castro's airfields and potential nuclear storage sites. Vice President
Johnson weighed in with an even more hawkish tirade, ridiculing the
idea of even informing the allies or Congress before mounting a massive air strike. "We are not going to get much help from them," he
said. Johnson wanted to "stop the planes, stop the ships, stop the
submarines and everything else . . . from coming in." At the conclusion of the meeting Kennedy seemed to be leaning toward an air strike
and called for further consideration of the alternatives, which he described as (1) a strike limited to the missile bases, (2) a larger air strike,
and (3) an invasion.

Excom reconvened on Tuesday evening at six thirty, and this discussion, too, was inconclusive. Everyone recognized the need to explore the options—as well as Russian reaction to any action they
might decide—before making a final decision. They also concluded
that the issues were more complex than originally thought. Mc-
Namara advanced a new military option: "a blockade against
offensive weapons entering Cuba" and "open surveillance reconnais-

sance." Rusk emphasized that "any course of action involves heavy political involvement. . . . [W]e have to consider what political preparation . . . is to occur before an air strike or in connection with any military action."

On Wednesday President Kennedy flew to Connecticut for a speech at New Haven to fulfill a campaign commitment to Abraham Rubicoff (it had been decided that cancellation of this visit would have aroused suspicions of a crisis in the White House). But Excom, minus the President, held intensive meetings all that day at the State Department in George Ball's conference room. Rusk attended these meetings only sporadically, and he was later criticized for not being more forceful and for relinquishing his natural role as chairman of the committee. But Rusk, like President Kennedy, was a prisoner of his prearranged schedule. Although preoccupied with the missile crisis, he had to meet other commitments to avoid arousing suspicion. On his schedule for that day were numerous activities, arranged months in advance, including coffee with labor leader George Meany; a luncheon in honor of the Crown Prince of Libya; meetings with ambassadors from Libya, Japan, and Jordan; and a dinner in honor of German Foreign Minister Gerhardt Schroeder. In between these activities he squeezed in meetings with Dean Acheson for over an hour and with Charles Bohlen briefly to talk about Cuba. He dropped in on the Excom meetings for less than an hour in the morning and again in the afternoon, but said relatively little, contenting himself with listening to the discussions and asking questions.

At this stage Rusk was genuinely puzzled about what to do. In this he was not alone—almost everyone else was undecided too. In retrospect that was a very good thing. The luxury of several days of indecision allowed careful examination of the problems and options in an atmosphere of freewheeling give-and-take without the egotism of men who have already made up their minds and are interested only in defending their own positions. Rusk's greatest concern was to "box the compass," as he put it—to explore all the alternatives by putting them out on the table and examining them from every angle.

At ten o'clock that evening, after the dinner for Schroeder, Rusk again joined the Excom meeting, and he surprised several of his colleagues by reading from a paper he had prepared on the air strike option. He asked them to think about the following scenario: On Wednesday, October 24, after informing Macmillan, de Gaulle, Adenauer, and possibly Turkey and a few Latin American countries, suppose the United States were to carry out a limited air strike against the missile bases in Cuba. This would be accompanied by a simultaneous presidential announcement to the world and a formal appeal to the U.N. and the OAS. What would the Russians do? He expected a Russian response in the form of an attack on Berlin, Korea, or the American missile bases in Turkey. "What would happen then?" he asked. NATO armed forces would certainly go into action. So the United States, he concluded, faced a dilemma. "But if we don't do this we go down with a whimper. Maybe it's better to go down with a bang," he said sarcastically.

Some of those present were appalled and thought he had suddenly become a super-hawk. In fact he was only trying to stimulate discussion. Acheson, who had been called in that day for consultation, was a proponent of the air strike, reinforcing the views of the Joint Chiefs, and Rusk was trying to force everyone to think that action through. It had the desired effect, and his statement provoked a sharp debate. Robert Kennedy and George Ball argued forcefully against a surprise air strike as an irreversible step contrary to American traditions. The analogy of the surprise air strike on Pearl Harbor came to everyone's minds. As Robert Kennedy dramatically put it, "My brother is not going to be the Tojo of the 1960s."

The next day, Thursday, October 18, Rusk had more time to devote to Cuba, and attended an eleven o'clock White House meeting with the President and Excom. McCone began the session with an intelligence briefing: work on the missile sites was continuing, and the first Soviet medium-range missile in Cuba would be ready for launching in eighteen hours. Time was running short. Although the CIA could not confirm if the Soviet missiles were armed with warheads, Rusk recalls, "if we had waited until they had nuclear weapons, it would have been too late." The men were also cognizant of the fact that the American press could not be kept in the dark forever. Already there were questions and rumors. A decision had to be made by the weekend at the latest.

At this meeting a clear division began to emerge between a group headed by McNamara, Robert Kennedy, and Ball that favored a blockade of Cuba, and a faction composed of McCone, the Joint Chiefs, Acheson, and Bundy that favored the air strike. Rusk said little, but sounded a note of caution; he was against any surprise attack. Without prior consultation with the United Nations, the OAS, and even Khrushchev, they would forfeit all hope of international political support for American actions. It was obvious that both of the principal alternatives had to be refined and developed before a presidential decision, and Excom formed working groups for this purpose. Ball was chosen the head of the blockaders, and Bundy was made the leader of the air strikers.

That afternoon Rusk visited both working groups without identifying with either one. He reasoned that as Secretary of State it was his job "to stand above the working groups and reserve judgment on a final choice until the alternatives had been fully developed and it was time to make a recommendation to the President."

For Rusk a decisive turn came during the meeting with the blockade group. Llewellyn Thompson was there as the Soviet expert, and Rusk asked him about Soviet reactions to the two options. Thompson replied that the Soviets had a very legalistic view of international relations, and that their reaction might be affected by the legality of whatever American action was decided. Struck by this, Rusk immediately left the meeting to see Leonard Meeker, the State Department's deputy legal adviser (the legal adviser, Abram Chayes, was in Paris attending a meeting). He asked Meeker to prepare a thorough analysis of the legal situation. Meanwhile, Robert Kennedy asked his deputy at Justice, Nicholas Katzenbach, for a similar review.

At four thirty Rusk and Thompson went to the White House to brief President Kennedy, who was scheduled to meet shortly with Soviet Foreign Minister Andrei Gromyko. They advised Kennedy to be very guarded if Gromyko brought up Cuba and not to disclose the fact that the United States had evidence the Soviets were putting offensive weapons into Cuba. Rusk strongly believed we should not tip our hand before deciding what to do. He did not want to give the Russians an opportunity to issue an ultimatum, which would make matters much more difficult to resolve. Kennedy agreed.

When Gromyko met with the President, he was almost jovial and full of assurances of goodwill. He complained, however, of the anti-Cuba campaign in the United States and repeated the Soviet line that the missiles in Cuba were only antiaircraft weapons incapable of reaching targets in the United States. Kennedy replied that the United States had no intention of invading Cuba, but that the American people were very concerned over the Soviet arms buildup. He read aloud his September 4 statement that the United States would not tolerate offensive weapons in Cuba. Gromyko merely listened with his usual poker face, but Rusk and Thompson noticed that his interpreter jumped in his chair "as though he had been given an electric shock." Both concluded that Gromyko knew about the missile bases and that his assurances to Kennedy were lies.

In the evening Rusk hosted a formal dinner in Gromyko's honor on the eighth floor of the State Department. He deliberately steered clear of any discussion with Gromyko about Cuba, and the two of them became engaged in a desultory conversation about Berlin and whether the Soviet Union or the United States was responsible for beginning the Cold War. Just one floor below, the Excom task forces were continuing their deliberations.

At ten o'clock the Excom members (minus Rusk and Thompson, who were still with Gromyko) went to the White House for another meeting with the President. Nine of them piled into a single limousine for the trip to avoid the suspicion that would have been aroused by a cavalcade of cars arriving at the White House. Alexis Johnson recalls that Robert Kennedy sat on his lap during the ride, and someone quipped that it would be a hell of a story if the limousine were involved in an accident along the way. After midnight Ball, Johnson, and Martin returned to the State Department to brief Rusk and Thompson about the meeting. They reported that Kennedy was leaning toward a blockade, but that a final decision had not been made. There would be yet another day of Excom meetings.

On Friday the President left for still another campaign trip, to Cleveland and Chicago. At eleven that morning Rusk met with the Excom blockade task force in Ball's conference room and called on Leonard Meeker to give his report on the legal case for United States action against Cuba. At this point Robert Kennedy interrupted and insisted that his deputy, Katzenbach, be allowed to speak first. Katzenbach said that according to international law, U.S. military action would be fully justified under the principle of self-defense and that no prior declaration of war was necessary.

Meeker then followed with a more sophisticated legal analysis. He disputed Katzenbach's claim that military action could be justified under the principle of self-defense, because no shot had yet been fired and there was no sign of an imminent attack on the United States. Instead, he suggested a limited blockade or "defensive quarantine"— the first use of this term—of Cuba that could be justified under international law. The quarantine, which could be carried out by American ships and planes, would prevent any ships from going to Cuba if they were carrying offensive weapons. He further argued that the defensive quarantine could also be justified by OAS approval, under the Rio Treaty, as regional action for the maintenance of peace and security.

Rusk wholly approved. All the pieces of the puzzle had suddenly fallen into place. He deeply believed that the best chance for success lay in choosing a course of action that was in accordance with international law. The term "quarantine"—a *limited* blockade—also had a legal meaning and avoided the characterization of American action as an act of war, which was not the case with a blockade. A defensive quarantine would be fully defensible in the eyes of the rest of the world, and the idea of OAS approval as the justification of U.S. action appealed to Rusk's commitment to collective security. The United States would not be acting alone but would be joining with its allies in what was essentially a peacekeeping action. Going to the OAS had the further advantage of marrying the military option to his original emphasis on a diplomatic solution to the problem.

Having firmly decided in favor of the quarantine option, Rusk spent the rest of the day meeting with individual members of Excom, trying to build a consensus recommendation for the President. He held discussions with Robert Kennedy, McNamara, Ball, Johnson, Martin, and Thompson. In the White House, too, the limited blockade was emerging as the clear first choice. By Saturday morning Sorensen had produced a working draft of a speech in which the President would announce his decision. Sorensen's masterly prose embraced the quarantine concept but left open the possibility of armed action—including an air strike—if the missiles were not removed.

If the quarantine was now the favored policy, no one was under any illusion that it assured success. In truth both of the two principal options had weaknesses. The air strike might take out the missiles (although this was highly doubtful—the chief of the Tactical Air Command said that an air strike could not guarantee the destruction of all missiles and nuclear weapons in Cuba), but it would kill thousands of Cubans and Russians. And no one could predict how the volatile Khrushchev would react. The quarantine, on the other hand, offered no assurance that the missiles already in Cuba would be removed. Nevertheless, Robert Kennedy called the President in Chicago with the news that Excom was ready with its recommendations. President Kennedy, feigning illness, cut short his campaign trip to return to Washington.

At two thirty on Saturday afternoon Excom met with the President. In accordance with cabinet protocol, Rusk was the first person asked for his views. He handed the President a short memo in his own handwriting. Kennedy handed it back and said he wanted to hear his opinion orally. Rusk recommended the quarantine: it was the least violent course and would preserve other options, including more drastic action later. But most important of all, it would give Khrushchev the time to sort out his own alternative courses; he could reflect on the situation and, it was hoped, decide on a responsible course of action. Rusk thought it imperative to look at the crisis from Khrushchev's standpoint. "When two nuclear superpowers are at each other's jugular vein, it is very important that one side not drive the other into a corner from which there is no escape." Recalling his service with Chinese forces in the China-Burma-India theater in World War II, he said that he was sometimes frustrated when the Chinese refused to surround a Japanese unit, citing an ancient Chinese military doctrine that you must never completely surround your enemy because, "if you do, he will fight too hard. You must always leave him a route to escape." He concluded his remarks by reading from his prepared memo: "We should not suppose that [the quarantine] will be an inconsequential action. It will produce a crisis of the gravest importance."

McNamara and Robert Kennedy also argued in favor of the quarantine. Lyndon Johnson, asked his opinion by the President, said, "You have the recommendation of your Secretary of State and your Secretary of Defense, and I would take it." But the meeting soon turned into a full-scale debate as the strengths and weaknesses of the air strike and quarantine positions were probed. Adlai Stevenson brought up additional considerations, saying that the President should consider withdrawing from Guantanamo and pulling American missiles out of Turkey in return for a plan to demilitarize and neutralize Cuba. In the end the President chose the quarantine alternative as the way to begin, reserving the air strike and other options for later. Like everyone else, he knew it was a shot in the dark. "The ones whose plans we're not taking are the lucky ones," he said.

The decision having been made, President Kennedy scheduled his speech to the nation for 7 P.M., Monday, October 22. In the meantime the State Department had to implement the diplomatic component of the course decreed by the President. Preparations were made for emergency sessions of the U.N. and the OAS. Coded messages were sent out to U.S. embassies around the world advising of the President's decision and telling them to be prepared for riots and demonstrations. Special presidential letters were prepared for transmittal to forty-three heads of government, including Macmillan, de Gaulle, Nehru, Fanfani of Italy, and Diefenbaker of Canada. The State Department's task force on Berlin was charged with developing a plan of response if Khrushchev retaliated on that front. The President's speech was also sent, in code, to the American Embassy in Moscow, with instructions to deliver it to Khrushchev one hour before the scheduled nationwide broadcast.

On Sunday morning, as Rusk was shuttling back and forth through the streets of Washington from meeting to meeting, he looked out his car window and saw people on the streets quietly enjoying the brilliant autumn weather, oblivious to the vast and dangerous crisis about to engulf them. As he watched them, his mind went back to the time when he was a small boy, growing up and attending the Presbyterian church. He remembered the Westminster Catechism and thought about the first question he had memorized: "What is the chief end of man?" The answer: "To glorify God and to enjoy Him forever." Now, in this crisis, "this first of all questions had become an operational question before the governments of the world. It raised the ultimate question: What is life all about?"

That Sunday, Rusk also called Dean Acheson at his farm in Sandy Spring, Maryland, and asked him to hand-carry the President's message on the crisis to the principal NATO allies, with special attention to the prickly Charles de Gaulle. Acheson reluctantly agreed, and when he arrived in Paris he called on de Gaulle at the Elysée Palace. After explaining the situation and President Kennedy's decision to invoke the quarantine, Acheson offered to show de Gaulle the photographic evidence of Russian missiles in Cuba. De Gaulle declined with a sweep of his hand, saying, "No, Mr. Acheson, your government would not deceive me on a matter of such great importance." De Gaulle then asked Acheson whether the purpose of his visit was to consult or to inform him. Acheson replied that he was merely informing him; the decision had already been made. De Gaulle replied that that was fine. "Tell President Kennedy that France will be with the U.S. It is exactly what I would have done." The other NATO allies followed suit.

The rest of Rusk's day was consumed with feverish meetings and preparations. His calendar for Sunday, October 21, records thirty-five separate meetings he attended. Finally, late that evening, he reviewed the work with his staff, sighed audibly, and told everyone to go home and get some sleep. "By this time tomorrow," he said, "we are going to be in flaming crisis."

Monday was a day of building tension. Rusk worked to implement the diplomatic scenario, which had been prepared by Alexis Johnson. At six o'clock, while Ball was briefing the ambassadors from allied countries in the International Conference Room at State, Rusk met with Russian Ambassador Anatoly Dobrynin. Dobrynin had arrived smiling pleasantly and chatted affably with reporters before going into the State Department. In his office, Rusk simply informed Dobrynin of the discovery of Soviet missiles in Cuba, gave him a copy of President Kennedy's speech, and went over with him in detail what the United States intended to do. Dobrynin became visibly upset. "I could see Dobrynin age at least ten years right before my eyes," Rusk said later. "He reacted as a man in physical shock." Rusk concluded that Dobrynin had not been informed by his own government of even the existence of the missiles, let alone the fact that the United States might find out about them. When Dobrynin emerged from the twenty-five-minute meeting, the reporters outside found him "grim and shaken." Asked whether there was a crisis, he merely snapped, "You judge for yourself."

Rusk then went to the White House, where President Kennedy was meeting with congressional leaders in advance of his speech. Robert Kennedy later called this encounter "the most stressful of all meetings." Everyone in the room was shocked. One senior Republican senator, a member of the Senate Foreign Relations Committee, groaned and fell forward onto the table with his head in his hands. Senators Russell of Georgia and Fulbright of Arkansas argued passionately for an air strike. Kennedy, his emotions already strained to the limit, looked irritated, but left the room calm and composed. One of the senators turned to Rusk and said, "Thank God *I* am not the President of the United States."

At seven that evening Rusk joined Thompson to watch Kennedy's speech on television. It was a powerful statement, the most important speech of Kennedy's life. To an anxious and horrified nation, he announced the presence of offensive Soviet missiles in Cuba and the American response of a defensive quarantine to guard against any further buildup. He called upon Khrushchev to "halt and eliminate this clandestine, reckless, and provocative threat to world peace." Rusk marveled at Kennedy's behavior as the crisis came to a head. At no time did he appear fearful or out of control. "He's acting like a real President," he thought, full of sympathy and admiration.

Immediately after the President's address Rusk met with sixty-five ambassadors of the nonaligned group of nations in the International Conference Room of the State Department. He showed them the photographic evidence of the missiles and asked for their understanding and support:

It is inconceivable to us how the Soviet leaders could have made so gross an error of judgment, with respect to our necessities, our strength or our will. If we seem to be pointing the finger at the Soviet Union rather more than at Cuba, it is because we consider Cuba to be the victim of this situation. Our information is that on these sites . . . Cubans are not permitted to be present. Soviet guards bar this area not only from Cuban civilians but from the Cuban military. . . .

We do hope that the Soviet leaders, who made a great error of judgment, will find some way to pull back and to get on the track of the peaceful settlement of issues and disputes. But I would not be candid and I would not be fair with you if I did not say that we are in as grave a crisis as mankind has been in, and this deeply affects the lives and fortunes . . . of all of you represented in this room.

It was a "very grave, very sober" session, Rusk recalls. After his speech about forty of the ambassadors lined up to shake his hand and wish the United States well. Rusk was touched to the core by their expressions of support.

Rusk stayed at the State Department until after 1 A.M., meeting with foreign ambassadors and preparing his presentation to the OAS, scheduled for the morning. It was after two when he finally arrived home and crawled into bed for a few hours of troubled sleep. Khrushchev's response to the American action was on his mind. What would the Russian leader do? "A nuclear strike was a definite possibility," he later recalled. Two Secret Service men were in Rusk's basement with orders to maintain communications and, in the event of a nuclear exchange, to evacuate Rusk and his family to a secret location. Rusk placed little store in such plans. He could not imagine that the security men would abandon their own families to save his in the event of war. And, he thought, "if the President and Secretary of State remained alive, the first band of shivering survivors who got hold of them would probably hang them from the nearest tree."

When Rusk awoke the next morning his first thought was, "I'm still here—this is very interesting." At least Khrushchev had not responded with an immediate nuclear strike. He got dressed and went immediately to the State Department, where he found Ball in his office still asleep on a couch. "George," he said, smiling broadly, "we've won a great victory: you and I are still alive!"

Overnight Rusk's prediction of a flaming crisis had come true. *The New York Times* carried the story in inch-high headlines: U.S. IMPOSES ARMS BLOCKADE ON CUBA. KENNEDY READY FOR SOVIET SHOWDOWN. A huge armada of ships and planes was assembling in the Caribbean to implement the limited blockade. And already Soviet countermoves had begun. Civilian traffic from West Germany into

Berlin was slowed by intensive border checks. The Soviet news agency TASS issued a government statement accusing President Kennedy of piracy, unheard-of violations of international law, and provocative acts that might lead to thermonuclear war.

At 8:50 A.M. Rusk entered the all-important meeting with the OAS. Under the OAS Charter a two-thirds vote was necessary for collective action. Rusk and his deputy Ed Martin had judged that this would be forthcoming, and now it was time to see if they had called it right. In his speech to the delegates Rusk stressed the Soviet "partnership in deceit with Cuba" and pointed out that the new offensive capability in Cuba was not only directed against the United States but also "will be able to carry mass destruction to most of the major cities in the western hemisphere. In the face of this buildup, no country of this hemisphere can feel secure, either from direct attack or from persistent blackmail." He called on the OAS to act without waiting for simultaneous consideration by the U.N., since "we have the primary responsibility and duty."

The OAS session lasted all day. Delegate after delegate rose to endorse the action against Cuba. They paraded to the telephones, asking for instructions from their governments. Rusk offered a resolution calling for the immediate dismantling and withdrawal of all offensive weapons in Cuba and authorizing the use of force "individually or collectively" in a limited blockade. At 4:45 P.M. the members finally voted. Nineteen votes were cast in favor and none opposed. Uruguay abstained, but the next day cast an affirmative vote, making approval of the resolution unanimous. One of the delegates, Bolivia's Ambassador Sarmiento, actually voted yes without waiting for instructions from his government (he could not get through by phone), taking his political life in his hands, gambling that he would be upheld. He turned out to be correct, and Rusk singled him out for special thanks.

The unanimous OAS support for the blockade appeared to have a major effect on the Russians. Rusk's personal diplomacy and long-standing rapport with the organization bore rich fruit. Robert Kennedy, one of those who had bitterly opposed any resort to the OAS, later attested to the significance of the OAS vote: "It . . . changed our position from that of an outlaw acting in violation of international law into a country acting in accordance with twenty allies legally protecting their position."

That same day Adlai Stevenson, with help from Rusk, Harlan Cleveland (Assistant Secretary of State for International Organization

Affairs), John McCloy, and Arthur Schlesinger, began to argue the American case at the United Nations. Although there was no hope for the passage of a legally binding resolution because of the Soviet veto in the Security Council, Stevenson's speeches attracted widespread support and praise, including unanimous backing by the NATO allies, justifying Rusk's faith in the United Nations as an arena for parliamentary diplomacy.

But despite the success on the diplomatic front, the Russians, at least publicly, appeared unmoved. At the Soviet Embassy a spokesman said that Soviet ship captains were under orders to defy the quarantine. U-2 photographs analyzed at the Pentagon showed twenty-five ships on their way to Cuba, their courses unchanged in the past twenty-four hours. The President asked Robert Kennedy to call on Ambassador Dobrynin, to convince him of American resolve. Kennedy saw Dobrynin that evening and told him that time was running out, with devastating implications for the peace of the world.

Wednesday and Thursday, the first days of the quarantine, were filled with tension. What would happen when the first Russian ships reached the American vessels on station? There was great danger of war if the Navy had to sink a Russian ship. Rusk was in the Cabinet Room seated next to President Kennedy when the report came in that a dozen of the Soviet ships had changed course or stopped. The welcome news inspired no rejoicing or shouting, only profound relief. Rusk turned to Bundy and whispered, "We were eyeball to eyeball, and the other fellow just blinked." His offhand remark was soon flashed around the world by the press and has become a part of the folklore of the crisis. Rusk was referring to a childhood game he had played in Georgia, in which he and a playmate would stare at each other at close range until the first one blinked. But, he says, "I was in no sense minimizing the seriousness of the crisis or claiming victory; rather the profound seriousness of the matter reduced sophisticated men to the most elemental forms of their being."

Once it was confirmed that the most suspect Russian ships had turned back, Rusk supported Kennedy's decision to allow other Russian ships, primarily oil tankers, to pass through the blockade without being boarded after identifying themselves. Like Kennedy, he believed it was necessary above all not to do anything to humiliate Khrushchev. Everyone knew, however, that at least one ship had to be stopped to make the blockade credible. They carefully chose the *Marucla,* a Panamanian-owned vessel registered in Liberia under Soviet charter, which they knew would not be a direct affront to Khrushchev. The search went without incident, and the vessel was allowed to proceed to Cuba.

Despite the avoidance of conflict at sea, new tensions came to the fore because of CIA reports that work on the missile sites inside Cuba had speeded up. The medium-range missiles would be operational in a few days, and no one knew whether they were armed with nuclear warheads. With that information the original dilemma now reemerged: the blockade could not affect missiles already inside Cuba. Pressure mounted on Kennedy to order an air strike or an invasion. Time was short and preparations had to be made. D day was set for the following Tuesday in a race to take action before the missiles became operational. American troops massed in Florida, and more troopships steamed east through the Panama Canal. The President ordered a program for setting up a civilian government in Cuba after the invasion. No one knew how the Russians would react, and the world once again teetered on the nuclear brink.

On Friday, October 26, Rusk was holding a meeting in his office with Robert Kennedy and McGeorge Bundy when word came that John Scali, a television reporter (later Ambassador to the U.N.), urgently wished to see him. Rusk stepped outside for a few minutes. Scali had important news. He had been approached by Alexander Fomin, a known KGB operative in the Russian Embassy, who told him there might be a basis for settlement of the crisis: the removal of the missiles under U.N. supervision in return for a pledge by the United States not to invade Cuba. Rusk quickly scrawled a note for Scali to give to Fomin:

I have reason to believe that the USG [United States Government] sees real possibilities in this and supposes that representatives of the two governments could work this matter out with U Thant and each other. My impression is, however, that time is very urgent.

At almost the same time, word came that a letter was being transmitted over the teletype linking the State Department with the American Embassy in Moscow. It was a letter from Khrushchev to President Kennedy. Rusk called in Thompson and Ball and took the letter to Kennedy at the White House. The letter was long and rambling; the men thought it came directly from Khrushchev without alteration by the Soviet Foreign Ministry. In a forthright tone, Khrushchev talked of the "knot of war" and said, "Let us not only relax the forces pulling on the ends of the rope, let us take measures to untie that knot." In another sentence Khrushchev stated: "If assurances were given by the President and the government of the United States that the USA would not participate in an attack on Cuba . . . if you would recall your fleet, this would immediately change everything." No decision was reached, but the President and Rusk were optimistic that the letter might contain the seeds of a compromise. They turned it over to State Department experts for analysis and scheduled an Excom meeting for the next morning.

When Excom assembled at ten o'clock Saturday morning in the White House, the optimism of the night before turned to dust. A new message from Khrushchev was being broadcast by Radio Moscow. Unlike the previous letter, it was recognized as official and business-like in tone, the product of the Soviet Foreign Ministry. The letter contained an important new condition for settlement of the Cuban crisis: removal of the American Jupiter missiles in Turkey.

While the meeting was in progress, another lightning bolt arrived. Rusk was called out of the room to take a phone call. It was a report from the Pentagon that a Soviet SAM had shot down one of the American U-2 reconnaissance planes over Cuba. Later it was reliably reported that the Cubans, not the Soviets, had pulled the trigger. But blood had now been spilled, and Rusk knew that the hawks in Excom would raise the cry for immediate retaliation, even invasion. There were an estimated 35,000 Russian troops in Cuba, and that would mean war. For the first time during the crisis, Rusk lost his composure and tears welled up in his eyes. Acheson, who had follwed him into the room, said sharply, "Pull yourself together, Dean, you're the only Secretary of State we have."

These two developments were so discouraging that many of those present at the meeting thought the situation was already out of control —that the Russians wanted war. The more hawkish members of Excom demanded action. President Kennedy, however, refused to be panicked into any irrevocable act. He decided that an answering message had to be drafted and sent to Khrushchev to try once more to avoid escalation.

There was general agreement that the United States could not accede to the Soviet demand to pull the Jupiter missiles out of Turkey. These were part of the NATO commitment, and removing them as part of a deal with the Soviets would be unacceptable to the alliance. Later it was reported that President Kennedy did not know about the missiles in Turkey, or that he was angry because they had not been removed. Some even stated that Kennedy had ordered them removed previously but that the State Department had been dilatory. In truth, Kennedy knew about the missiles and had not ordered them removed. He never expressed any displeasure to Rusk over the issue of the Turkish missiles. It was generally known that the missiles were obsolete and unnecessary, and in the spring of 1961 Rusk had talked over their removal with Selim Sarper, the Turkish Foreign Minister. The Turkish government expressed great concern at that time because removing the missiles would be a political embarrassment, since the parliament had just passed a belated appropriation bill to pay for them. Rusk reported this conversation to President Kennedy, who decided the missiles should remain for a reasonable time, until the newer fleet of Polaris submarines was fully operational in the Mediterranean.

Excom debated and labored throughout the day to draft a message to Khrushchev. In the end, at Llewellyn Thompson's suggestion, taken up by Robert Kennedy, it was decided simply to ignore the second letter concerning the missiles in Turkey and respond to that part of the first Khrushchev letter that called for a pledge not to invade Cuba. A deal was offered: You remove your missiles and forces from Cuba under the supervision of the U.N.; we will then give assurances there will be no invasion of Cuba. The President also promised to end the quarantine and to negotiate a settlement along the lines of Khrushchev's October 26 letter.

That left the matter of the missiles in Turkey. If nothing was said, Khrushchev would almost surely reject Kennedy's proposal. He could not publicly back down from his demand. But the United States could not publicly offer to remove them. It was Rusk who solved this dilemma. At a meeting in the Oval Office he suggested that Khrushchev be given the oral message that, while there could be no deal over the Turkish missiles, the President was determined to get them out and would reliably do so after the crisis was resolved. The proposal was quickly accepted by Excom and approved by the President. It was simple but brilliant advice. Bundy, who was present, described Rusk as

deeply, indeed passionately, committed to the proposition that the central task of the Secretary of State was to try to help the President—*the President,* not his staff or his relatives. He had been listening all day to the President's very own insistent unwillingness to let an intransigent position on these unwanted weapons stand between his country and the safe removal of the Soviet missiles from Cuba. Rusk shared this sentiment, but even if he had not his mind would have turned to the ways and means of meeting the President's concern. Characteristically, with a reticence both natural and self-enforced, he had kept his counsel during the larger meeting. Now in the Oval Office, though he probably would have preferred a still smaller group, he spoke out. It was the right voice at the right time, with the right advance preparation and the right advice.

At Rusk's suggestion, Robert Kennedy was chosen to deliver the President's letter and the oral message to Ambassador Dobrynin. Kennedy also gave Dobrynin a sharp warning: Khrushchev should fully understand that if the missiles were not removed immediately, they would be taken out by military action. When Dobrynin asked about the Jupiter missiles, Kennedy told him that the President had long been anxious to remove them and that within a short time they would be gone. He demanded an answer from Khrushchev by the next day.

After Robert Kennedy had been dispatched to see Dobrynin, there was little to do but wait and hope. Tired men went home to get some rest. Rusk, however, lingered on at his State Department office, sensing instinctively that there might be some new development or that the President might need him.

That evening a call came from the White House that Kennedy wanted to see him, and when he arrived, the President looked troubled. The two men, meeting alone, focused on one overriding question: What would they do if Khrushchev refused to accept the deal Robert Kennedy had proposed to Dobrynin? Kennedy was disturbed because his options were narrowing. Preparations for air strikes and the invasion of Cuba were going forward. Tuesday, October 30, was D day, when full-scale war would break out in the Caribbean unless the Soviets came to terms. It was only about twenty-four hours before the necessary orders had to be given; then there would be no turning back. Kennedy was fully prepared to issue the orders, but he wanted to avoid war. Wasn't there something else that could be done if Khrushchev gave a negative response? Was there a last chance for peace?

Kennedy and Rusk again turned their attention to the missiles in Turkey. What a red herring those missiles were, they agreed. They joked about the fact that the Jupiters were both obsolete and vulnerable. Rusk laughingly said he had heard that a tourist driving down the highway could shoot holes in their skins with a .22-caliber rifle. It was anyone's guess, he added, which way the missiles would fly if they were ever fired; they were as likely to take off backward as toward their targets in the Soviet Union. Yet they might still be used as a bargaining chip in this deadly game.

Kennedy and Rusk then formulated a secret fallback plan to avoid war if the Soviets rejected the overture delivered by Robert Kennedy. According to this plan, which Rusk revealed only in 1987, "Kennedy instructed me to telephone . . . Andrew Cordier, then at Columbia University, and dictate to him a statement which would be made by U Thant, the Secretary General of the United Nations, proposing the removal of both the Jupiters and the missiles in Cuba."

Although this option never had to be used, it was a brilliant proposal that would have avoided war and allowed both sides, through the intermediary of the United Nations, to come to an agreement without seeming to make humiliating concessions. The United States would remove the obsolete missiles from Turkey, not at the demand of the Russians, but at the request of the Secretary General of the United Nations, in an effort to avoid war. The Russians, in removing the missiles in Cuba, could make the same claim.

In revealing this secret plan Rusk characteristically portrayed the idea as President Kennedy's. In fact, the proposal was vintage Rusk. "I had known Andrew Cordier for many years in New York," he recalls, "and I trusted him. During his years at the U.N. he was known as an expert parliamentarian. He sat next to the president of the Security Council during all the debates. He also had ready access to U Thant. I suggested to Kennedy that he let me, through Cordier, transmit a new proposal to U Thant. Kennedy readily agreed because he would not let the Jupiters in Turkey become an obstacle to the removal of the missile sites in Cuba, because the Jupiters were coming out in any event. A temporary disruption of the alliance or our relations with Turkey was preferable to war. And Mr. Cordier was to put the statement in the hands of U Thant only after a further signal from us." It was typical of Rusk that he came up with an option to avoid war that would be acceptable to the adversary. It was also typical that in this supreme hour of peril, when world peace hung in the balance, he looked for a solution that involved the United Nations, which could play a useful role in getting an agreement that the superpowers might be unable to reach if left to themselves. Kennedy clearly was relieved by the new plan. A stark choice between war and peace was a decision he hoped he would never have to make. Both of them slept easier that fateful night.

In the Kremlin, Soviet leaders too faced a grim decision: how to react to Kennedy's ultimatum to Dobrynin. No doubt they were also aware that the American preparations for air strikes, an invasion, and a stepped-up blockade were going forward. On Sunday morning, October 28, just after nine o'clock, Radio Moscow transmitted Khrushchev's reply: he agreed to remove the missiles from Cuba under United Nations supervision.

Rusk, like everyone else, was immensely relieved, but again there was no wild rejoicing, no gloating. Emotions were too high and nerves too taut. The matter was simply too serious for claims of victory. What was important was that peace would be preserved and that nuclear war would not blight the progress of mankind.

Rusk immediately met with the Washington press corps and warned them against jubilation; he did not want any crowing in Washington to inspire Russian second thoughts. "I think we will still have a Cuba problem on our hands," he cautioned. Nevertheless, the worst of the crisis was over, and the world had stepped back from the brink. Rusk went home early that day from the office—at eight o'clock in the evening.

Ironically, after the accord had been reached by the two superpowers, it was the Russians' turn to experience difficulties with Cuba. Castro was furious at the decision, and he angrily refused to allow U.N. supervision of the removal of the missiles. Khrushchev even sent Deputy Premier Anastas Mikoyan to placate him, but it did no good. The CIA reported that Mikoyan was spending an extraordinarily long time in Cuba and that even though his wife died in Moscow while he was away, he did not return for the funeral.

Mikoyan stopped in Washington before returning home. His reports on Castro were far from complimentary. "That man is crazy," he said. Castro had kept him waiting for ten days, refusing to see him, until he finally said, "If you don't see me tomorrow morning, I am going home and you will be sorry." "But you Americans," Mikoyan said, "must understand what Cuba means to us old Bolsheviks. We have been waiting all our lives for a country to go communist without the Red Army, and it happened in Cuba. It makes us feel like boys again." The Russians never could persuade Castro to accept U.N. supervision, but, as promised, they dismantled their missile sites and pulled out their bombers, closely monitored by American ships and planes. Nevertheless, the Kennedy administration never explicitly reaffirmed its no-invasion pledge. (Ironically, that pledge was given later, during the Nixon administration.)

The Cuban missile crisis was an awesome reminder of how the existence of nuclear weapons had rendered obsolete the traditional rules of strategic confrontation and warfare. The crisis began because of Soviet misapprehension of American interests and intentions. It was resolved without war because there was time for careful deliberations, accurate information, effective communication, and unremitting control on both sides. American firmness was important, but also flexibility and forbearance, which left the door open to a peaceful solution. Above all, both sides had an overriding interest in avoiding the precipice of nuclear disaster.

Nevertheless, the crisis did not ease the confrontation between the superpowers. On the contrary, Rusk believes, it "led to the downfall of Khrushchev," who was removed from office in 1964, and "the arms race accelerated as the Russians were determined never to be humiliated again." And just after the missile crisis, Rusk heard an ominous report that a Soviet diplomat in New York had said, "You got the better of us this time, but we will never let it happen again."

"It Will Be a Cold Winter":
Confrontation in Berlin

C UBA was by no means the only battlefield in the Cold War. In 1961, when Kennedy assumed the presidency, that war was entering its most dangerous phase. In the Kremlin, Nikita Khrushchev, ebullient, volatile, and impulsive, was at the height of his power. A few years before, during Eisenhower's second term, he had begun to deploy intercontinental ballistic missiles, and now, for the first time, American cities were within range of Soviet nuclear power. Eyeing the young new President, Khrushchev saw an unparalleled opportunity for the Soviet Union. Kennedy and his administration were inexperienced, possibly even weak. Khrushchev, on the other hand, had consolidated his power and was ready to act.

As a result, in the first several months of 1961 the Kennedy administration was confronted with Soviet-initiated crises wherever they were in a position to stir up trouble, including Laos, the Congo, and Berlin. The Soviet challenge was an elaborate strategic struggle, a chess game with deadly stakes between East and West, with the Soviets prepared to employ any means short of all-out war. When he first took office Kennedy could not possibly have known the difficulties he would face. But he had no illusions and seemed even prescient about the future. In his first State of the Union speech he surprised Congress with a gloomy prediction: "No man entering upon this office . . . could fail to be staggered upon learning . . . the harsh enormities of the trials through which we must pass in the next four years. . . . Each day we draw nearer the hour of maximum danger."

Kennedy's somber mood had been stimulated by reading a State Department "Crisis Book," a review of Cold War issues prepared under Rusk's direction. From the moment he became Secretary of State, Rusk was preoccupied with the Soviet challenge and how to mobilize the nation and its allies to meet it. His first speeches as well as his first talks with President Kennedy sounded the theme of a world caught up in revolutionary changes, and "reaching out for domination in the midst of these changes is a communist world which is bringing large resources and renewed energy to the extension of its controls in Latin America, Africa, the Middle East, and Asia. It would be a mistake for us to underestimate the formidable contest in which we shall be engaged in the decade of the sixties."

Rusk recognized the gravity of the Soviet challenge, but he called for a new approach on how to deal with it. He advocated "dignified diplomacy" instead of Cold War rhetoric and saber-rattling:

> The issues called the cold war are real and cannot be merely wished away. They must be faced and met. . . . They will not be scolded away by invective nor frightened away by bluster. They must be met with determination, confidence, and sophistication.

Elaborating on this idea, he stated that the goal of his diplomacy would be to remove unnecessary or pointless irritations and to keep channels of communication open. "Our discussion, public or private, should be marked by civility; our manners should conform to our own dignity and power and to our good repute throughout the world." Rusk thereby set himself apart from the "brinkmanship" employed by his predecessor, John Foster Dulles, and signaled a willingness to use diplomatic channels to defuse global tensions.

Rusk's first important initiative in the new administration was to advocate a fundamental change in American defense policy. After the Korean War the Eisenhower administration had embarked upon a strategy of reducing conventional military forces and relying instead on nuclear striking power to deter Soviet aggression. With the decline of conventional forces, the defense posture of the United States was that Soviet adventurism would be met by, in John Foster Dulles's ominous phrase, "massive retaliation"—the all-out use of nuclear weapons in response to attack.

Rusk, like many strategists of the time, considered this doctrine outdated and unrealistic. The major Soviet threat was against weak but independent nations, not a direct attack on the United States. Now that the Soviet Union itself had intercontinental ballistic missiles, it was simply not credible that the United States would use nuclear weapons as a first line of defense. Rusk believed that conventional weapons and manpower should be increased to give the United States the capacity to fight local and limited wars to combat the Soviet threat. He regarded nuclear arms as weapons that must not be used; their only function was deterrence: to prevent other nations from using them against the United States or its allies. He wanted at least to "lift the threshold of provocation" at which the President might feel constrained to bring nuclear weapons into action.

In February 1961 Rusk initiated discussions on defense issues with Robert McNamara, and he found a receptive ear. The two men agreed that there was no way to draw a sharp distinction between foreign policy and national defense policy and that it was necessary for them to work together in harmony. McNamara told Rusk he deeply believed that military policy should be the "servant of foreign policy," and they planned to have frequent private talks and to encourage contacts at all levels between Defense and State. Rusk instructed his aides to give the Defense Department access to all foreign policy information and planning documents. Cooperation between State and Defense became the cornerstone of policy formulation, and it is a tribute to both men that there was never a hint of rivalry between them or their two bureaucracies.

McNamara was enthusiastic about the idea of reforming military doctrine and asked Rusk to outline the proposal in a memorandum. Rusk did so with the help of his old comrade in arms Charles H. "Tick" Bonesteel III, a friend from his Rhodes scholar days at Oxford and the SWNCC who was now a major general and special assistant to the chairman of the Joint Chiefs of Staff. With Rusk's memo in hand, McNamara started a high-level inquiry; the military services were asked to review their forces in light of the assumption that the United States might have to fight small wars without resorting to nuclear weapons.

Following a pattern that was to become familiar, Rusk and McNamara then took the idea to President Kennedy, and at a meeting in the Cabinet Room with Kennedy and other national security officials they heard a briefing by Pentagon experts on the disastrous effects of a nuclear exchange—the wholesale killing that would be caused by the initial explosion and the subsequent fallout. Kennedy was clearly shaken. When the meeting was over he got up quietly and returned to the Oval Office. Rusk followed, and when they were alone Kennedy simply turned to him and said grimly, "And we call ourselves the human race."

In the ensuing discussion Rusk found the normally lighthearted President surprisingly sober-minded. They talked about how it was necessary to do everything possible to ensure that Kennedy would never be faced with making the fateful decision of using—or of not using—nuclear weapons. The briefing and the President's reaction made an indelible impression in Rusk's memory. Years later he would say that such a briefing on the awesome effect of nuclear weapons should be a mandatory exercise for every American President and every Soviet leader.

Kennedy gave the green light for the plan, and a major reorientation of American defense policy was under way. In a message to Congress drafted largely by McNamara and Rusk, Kennedy announced the new doctrine and called for an increase in conventional forces to defend against "forces of subversion, infiltration . . . guerrilla warfare or a series of limited wars." The administration then embarked on the military buildup. The defense budget rose from $43 billion to $56 billion from 1960 to 1962, and the armed forces increased by 300,000 men in 1961 alone. Characteristically, Rusk, once the changes in military policy were set in motion, receded into the background and was perfectly content to have McNamara and Kennedy get the political credit. *Time* was one of the few news sources to recognize that the new doctrine had come about "largely at the urging of Secretary of State Dean Rusk."

Rusk's role was not lost, however, on certain Air Force generals and planners who feared (correctly) that the conventional arms buildup would mean elimination of some of their obsolescent missiles and experimental nuclear airplanes. They leaked Rusk's memo to sympathetic reporters, who accused him of "abandoning nuclear strike power" and said that he "favored sharp restrictions on the use of nuclear weapons in war and diplomacy." McNamara moved to quell the Air Force campaign, which he knew was inspired by interservice rivalry; the same impetus had created the so-called missile gap, also exposed as false, which held that the Soviet Union would have a superiority in intercontinental ballistic missiles by the early 1960s.

Rusk made sure that the change in policy would not be misinterpreted in Moscow by issuing a statement clarifying that he "favored strengthening the conventional forces of the [West] while maintaining its nuclear power." Furthermore, "there should be no doubt that in case of a massive assault by the communists, the West would use the force and weapons it found necessary to halt the attack. These forces would include nuclear power if that was the only alternative to defeat." His statement did not stop the John Birch Society from denouncing Rusk as a Communist, and the next day he greeted his staff with a deadpan "Well, comrades . . .''

It was a crisis-filled year, and none was so serious as the Soviet-Western conflict over the status of Berlin. Khrushchev once told Rusk, in his homely peasant way, that Berlin was the "testicles of the West," which he could grab and squeeze whenever it suited him. The divided city, under four-power control since 1945, was militarily indefensible from the Western point of view. The United States had a token force of eleven thousand men to deter Soviet aggression, but West Berlin, located over a hundred kilometers inside East Germany, could be taken at any time. Only political pressures and the threat of all-out war had so far protected the city.

The Berlin problem, of course, was not new. Rusk had been involved in the first crisis, in 1948–49, when the Russians had imposed a blockade to force the Allies out of Berlin. A new phase in the struggle began in 1958, when Khrushchev demanded that a German peace treaty be signed to terminate the four-power administration of the city. This spurred a round of negotiations during the Eisenhower administration, which continued until Khrushchev, with great fanfare, aborted the four-power summit meeting in Paris in May 1960 after an American U-2 spy plane was shot down over the Soviet Union.

Now, in January 1961, Khrushchev renewed the pressure. He again demanded an end to Allied occupation and a new status for Berlin as a demilitarized "free city." He threatened that if the West refused his demand, the Soviet Union would sign a separate peace agreement with the East German state and that the East Germans would take over from Soviet authorities control of air, rail, and highway supply routes between West Germany and Berlin. The West would then have to negotiate with East German authorities to secure new terms of access to the city. This strategy cleverly sought to consolidate Soviet control through its East German puppet state.

Berlin was one of the first problems on which Rusk briefed President Kennedy. On January 28 he sent the President a full chronology of the situation and the text of the Soviet demands. Stating his views on the problem at a press conference on March 9, Rusk emphasized the Western commitment to the freedom of West Berlin and said that any Soviet peace treaty with East Germany would be a violation of the status of Berlin under international law. Averell Harriman, the President's roving ambassador, pointedly renounced the concessions that had been discussed during the 1959 negotiations. "All discussions on Berlin," he said, "must begin from the start."

At the NATO Council of Foreign Ministers meeting in Oslo in May, Berlin was high on the agenda. The European allies were apprehensive, both about the strength of American commitment to the defense of Europe and about the new administration and Secretary of State. Coming on the heels of the Bay of Pigs debacle the month before, the meeting was a crucial test of American leadership.

Rusk passed the test with flying colors. When the five-day session was over, there was unanimous feeling that he had dominated the meeting, impressing the delegates with his grasp of the allies' individual problems as well as with his "frank and intelligent appraisal" of the harsh facts of Soviet policy. With McNamara, Rusk led the delegates through a "brutally frank exposition and a reasoned political argument" for a conventional buildup of NATO forces. He described the French and British nuclear deterrents as only a marginal and expensive addition to U.S. power. He pledged that the United States would commit Polaris nuclear missile submarines to NATO, although he was vague about who would control them. He argued that NATO should broaden its role to meet the Soviet challenge in areas outside Europe, including Southeast Asia, Cuba, and the Congo. He won approval of a strong NATO statement pledging to maintain the freedom of West Berlin and opposing a separate Soviet peace treaty.

When the meeting adjourned, delegates cited the favorable personal impression Rusk had made as reason for the conference's ringing affirmation of American leadership. "For the first time in ten years," said a Scandinavian diplomat, "I know where America wants to go and I am content to follow." This show of allied unity and confidence in the United States was, however, a fragile consensus. It would not be long before the strains in the alliance would begin to show.

Shortly after Rusk's return from Europe came news that Khrushchev had invited Kennedy to a meeting in Vienna in early June. Rusk counseled against the meeting: there was no time for adequate preparation, and summit meetings were inherently dangerous. The "Big Four" summit in 1955 at Geneva had merely served to lull the West to sleep while Moscow made inroads in the Middle East, the 1959 summit between Khrushchev and Eisenhower at Camp

David had masked a basic misunderstanding about progress toward a Berlin settlement, and the 1960 summit in Paris had been wrecked by Khrushchev's denunciation of the United States after the shooting down of the U-2 spy plane over Soviet territory. But Kennedy took the advice of his Soviet experts and agreed to meet Khrushchev in Vienna on June 3 and 4.

Leading up to the Vienna summit, Kennedy journeyed to Canada to see Prime Minister John Diefenbaker, a meeting that produced a memorable minor incident. The opportunistic Diefenbaker was not John Kennedy's favorite person—the White House considered him unreliable and resented his playing off the United States for political advantage at home. To prepare Kennedy for the meeting Walt Rostow wrote a memo listing "talking points," very terse and blunt phrases to remind Kennedy of the topics for discussion. At the conclusion of the meeting Kennedy inadvertently left the paper behind, and Diefenbaker found it. Rusk became involved when the American ambassador in Ottawa reported that Diefenbaker was threatening to make the memo public to embarrass the President—at one point the memo referred to Diefenbaker as a "son of a bitch." Rusk took the matter to Kennedy, and the President just laughed. When informed of the reference to Diefenbaker, Kennedy joked, "It can't be true—I don't know him well enough for that." And he added, "You can tell him if that had happened to us, we would have Xeroxed a copy and sent it back right away."

The approaching Vienna summit produced an atmosphere of optimism and hope for a breakthrough to eliminate some of the tensions of the Cold War. On the way to Vienna the President and his party would stop in Paris to talk with Charles de Gaulle. Rusk flew to Paris with Kennedy aboard Air Force One, and from beginning to end the visiting Americans were bathed in Gallic magnificence and splendor. Rusk had never seen so many flags as lined the presidential motorcade route and the Place de la Concorde. Half a million people turned out to greet them. Jacqueline Kennedy was at her prettiest; she so charmed the French that President Kennedy was moved to remark, "I am the man who accompanied Jacqueline Kennedy to Paris, and I have enjoyed it." They were treated to a candlelit dinner in the Hall of Mirrors at Versailles and a ballet performance in the Louis XIV Theater.

The talks with de Gaulle matched the formality of his reception of his American guests. Rusk thought him a pompous stuffed shirt. With Kennedy he was polite and dignified, but there was no personal warmth. Rusk had the impression that de Gaulle, the last of the major figures of World War II, "thought of the younger generation of leaders as mere boys." He noted with amusement that when Foreign Minister Couve de Murville entered the room to greet de Gaulle he clicked his heels and bowed low like a schoolboy greeting his teacher.

De Gaulle told Kennedy that Europe (which for de Gaulle meant France) must organize its own defense, independently but in cooperation with the United States. The proposal to transfer Polaris submarines to NATO could not qualify as a European defense, because the United States would retain ultimate control. He doubted American willingness to act to defend purely European interests. He told Kennedy that France would prefer a three-power *directoire* to organize the defense of the West: the United States representing the new world, Britain representing the Commonwealth, and France speaking for Europe. Kennedy disagreed, saying that such a directorate would disregard the independence of other nations and that only the United States had the power and the will to defend Europe.

De Gaulle also told Kennedy to stand firm on the Berlin issue when he met with Khrushchev. There was no point in even discussing Berlin with the Russians, he said. But if they attempted to move on Berlin, it would mean general war.

After the glamour of Paris it was on to Vienna, but the departure of Air Force One from the airport was marred by a moment of high comedy. Jacqueline Kennedy fretted because her maid, who was in charge of bringing her luggage, was late. As the smiling President and his wife walked up the ramp to the plane to wave good-bye, a foppishly dressed courtier ran out from the crowd yelling, "Stop that plane!" Just then a station wagon careened around a corner on two wheels and lurched to a halt. It was the unfortunate maid, with Mrs. Kennedy's trunks and valises piled high in the car.

In Vienna Rusk briefed Kennedy along with the Soviet experts Harriman, Bohlen, and Thompson. He advised Kennedy to limit his talks with Khrushchev to a *tour d'horizon* of world problems. It should be a get-acquainted meeting to explore each other's views to see whether there could be some constructive actions later. Rusk cautioned against entering into point-by-point negotiations with Khrushchev. That should come later, through regular diplomatic channels. Once the meeting got under way, this tactic seemed to work on the question of Laos—there would be apparent agreement between Kennedy and Khrushchev to get out of Laos and leave the Laotians alone. But on Berlin, Kennedy would be presented with a surprise ultimatum. The existing German borders must be legalized: East Berlin should be under the complete control of East Germany and West Berlin designated an international city.

The public welcome for Kennedy in Vienna was every bit as tumultuous as in Paris. People turned out by the hundreds of thousands for a glimpse of the young President and his elegant wife. At one point Rusk found himself riding through the city in the presidential limousine with Kennedy between meetings. He experienced what it was like for the President to be the object of such wild adulation. Crowds thronged about, and a smiling Kennedy turned to him and said, "Rusk, you make a hell of a substitute for Jackie." By contrast, when Khrushchev rode through the streets of Vienna there was only a stony silence. Rusk felt somewhat embarrassed by this implicit insult. Khrushchev also seemed to envy Kennedy's youth and vitality. Noticeably affected by the situation, Khrushchev's mood became gloomy and somber.

During the meetings between the two men, Rusk thought that Khrushchev was particularly brutal with Kennedy. He began each session with an ideological harangue, which Kennedy refused to return in kind. At one point Kennedy said, "Look, Mr. Chairman, you aren't going to make a communist out of me and I don't expect to make a capitalist out of you, so let's get down to business."

A more humane side of Khrushchev appeared only when Rusk, quite by chance, brought up the topic of Soviet agriculture. Khrushchev was immediately interested, and Rusk was amazed at how quickly he switched from stale ideology to a lively discussion of the problem of improving agricultural productivity. Rusk told Khrushchev about his years at the Rockefeller Foundation and its sponsorship of scientific efforts to develop genetically improved strains of grain and other food plants, including a variety of corn developed in the United States with a vegetation period of only sixty days. Khrushchev was so impressed that he referred to the incident later, in his October 1961 speech to the Twenty-second Congress of the Communist Party. Khrushchev also spoke to Kennedy about a new model of tractor he had heard was being manufactured in the United States. "Will you sell me one?" the wily Khrushchev asked. Kennedy smiled and said, "I won't sell you one, Mr. Chairman, but I will think seriously about selling you 1000!"

When the conversation turned to Berlin, Rusk thought Khrushchev clearly tried to intimidate Kennedy. In blustering terms he said that the Berlin situation was intolerable and would have to be changed.

Kennedy replied that the Western powers were present in Berlin and would not be driven out—that Berlin was a matter of vital interest to the West. Khrushchev then said that in December 1961 the Soviet Union would sign a peace treaty with East Germany, and at that time East Germany would become totally responsible for its territory, including access rights to West Berlin. "And if there is any attempt to interfere with these plans," he added, "there will be war."

Rusk was taken aback by the word "war." In diplomacy "war" is never used, and Khrushchev was obviously trying to bully the United States. But Kennedy did not flinch. He looked Khrushchev straight in the eye and said, "Then, Mr. Chairman, there will be war. It will be a cold winter."

Kennedy was upset by the meeting. Khrushchev, he later told British Prime Minister Macmillan, was "much more of a barbarian" than he had expected. He was shaken not only by the ultimatum, but also by the idea that Khrushchev thought he could intimidate the President of the United States. He was uncertain how to respond to such blunt talk, and in press conferences and communiqués Kennedy spokesmen said only that differences concerning Berlin were unresolved. But Rusk and others who knew of the ultimatum did not underestimate the gravity of the matter. To those involved, Berlin was the most serious crisis since the end of World War II, because it involved a direct face-off between the United States and the Soviet Union in a situation where both sides (and especially the West) were committed to the possible use of nuclear weapons. Rusk was sent to Paris to brief de Gaulle, and Foy Kohler went to Germany to see Adenauer. Only on June 10 did the full extent of the crisis become public knowledge, when the East German press agency published the Soviet aide-mémoire given the Americans at Vienna.

Whatever the motives for the Soviet ultimatum on Berlin, the timing, at least, had to do with the Bay of Pigs. At Vienna Khrushchev had taunted Kennedy over the bungled invasion, and he intended to capitalize on it. It was not lost on the Soviets that Kennedy, having undertaken the invasion of Cuba, had failed to carry it through; he had shown himself to be indecisive and weak. Soviet strategy over Berlin now sought to test him again by raising the tension to the point where the West would yield to Soviet demands rather than accept the alternative of war. The Soviets were further motivated by the increasing flow of refugees out of East Germany and by the belief that there were people in the Kennedy White House who might be amenable to a new approach—and perhaps concessions—on Berlin. There was also evidence that Khrushchev was under pressure from militarists and opponents of peaceful coexistence in the Soviet Politburo.

As Khrushchev kept up the pressure immediately after Vienna, Kennedy and his advisers were faced with the task of framing a Berlin policy and drafting an appropriate reply to the Soviet aide-mémoire. As the crisis deepened Kennedy became increasingly preoccupied with it, to the point where his aides knew he was thinking of virtually nothing else. Rusk played a key role in giving advice, coordinating with the Allies, and carrying out policy, and the crisis had the effect of increasing their mutual respect, their knowledge of each other, and their ability to work together. Kennedy later would be highly pleased by Rusk's performance, but at the outset there were several difficulties.

Just after Vienna Rusk formed a Berlin task force in the State Department headed by Foy Kohler, Assistant Secretary for European Affairs, and his deputy, Martin Hillenbrand. At Kennedy's request Rusk also called on Dean Acheson to prepare a report on the situation. In late June Acheson's recommendations provided a starting point for the real debate over Berlin policy. Regarding the situation as a test of wills, a pretext to make the United States back down, Acheson advocated a tough, militaristic response to the Russians. There was no point in negotiations, and even a willingness to go to the conference table would be fatal, since the Soviets would regard it as a sign of weakness. Acheson proposed to meet the crisis through a buildup of nuclear and conventional forces. If there was any interruption of access, there should be a sizable Allied ground probe into Berlin over the autobahns. Above all, it was necessary to persuade Khrushchev that the United States had the resolve, if necessary, to go on to nuclear war. (Interestingly, Acheson's position was very similar to de Gaulle's.)

Acheson's report polarized positions, especially at the White House, and produced debate within the administration. A White House group, led by Schlesinger and Carl Kaysen (a staff member of the National Security Council), as well as some in the State Department, such as Abram Chayes, the legal adviser; Ambassador Llewellyn Thompson; and George McGhee, director of Policy Planning, thought Acheson's proposal was too stark and posed the danger of going quickly down the trail to nuclear war. Advocating a policy that would emphasize negotiations and political moves to defuse the crisis, they wanted to develop negotiating alternatives leading to a possible compromise.

At a meeting with this group Acheson was at his imperious best. He regarded them as fools, and he did not suffer fools gladly. He entered the room "with a scowl on his face, as if he smelled a dead dog," Rusk later remembered. When the task force decided that Chayes should begin work on some negotiating alternatives, Acheson was contemptuous. "You'll see," he said. "You will try, but you will find that it just won't write."

Rusk, as was his wont, did not take a strong position either for or against Acheson's report, which disappointed the more activist members of the "negotiation" camp. Schlesinger called him "circumspect" and complained that "no one quite knew where he stood." Chayes went into a "great funk" and talked "in great despair" to Schlesinger and to Henry Kissinger. But Rusk was biding his time and was firmly in control. Working with Kohler and Hillenbrand, chewing over ideas about what to do, he saw a danger in a rush to judgment on Berlin policy. First, nothing could be finally decided until after consultations with the Allies. Second, he was aware that the Russians were watching the situation closely. The least indication of a change of policy from a high American official would be seized upon as weakness or a concession, and the Russians would only intensify their demands. Third, the United States was basically content with the status quo; it was the Russians who were trying to force changes. As far as Rusk was concerned, America already had a Berlin policy— there was no need to hurry to draw up a new one.

The Berlin problem was especially tricky because the Soviets were not threatening force or war. Indeed, they were only threatening peace—the conclusion of a peace treaty with East Germany. The first belligerent act, if it came, would come from the West. Thus the Russians had put the Allies in a dilemma: they could either threaten force or risk being "niggled to death," as Rusk put it, on their access rights to West Berlin.

Although Rusk was noncommital in the debate between the "Achesonians" and the "negotiators" within the administration, he was far from silent. From the first he became the administration's point man as far as public statements were concerned. In news conferences and public statements that were page-one news all over the nation, he argued the American case on Berlin. There were two thrusts to his campaign: he pounded home the Allies' legal rights, claims, and commitment to Berlin, and he skillfully maneuvered to put the Soviets on the defensive by making it clear that they were the perpetrators of the crisis. He accused the Soviets of "heightening world tension" by "militant" speeches on Berlin. He also ridiculed the Soviet analogy that a peace treaty with Germany was like the peace treaty with Japan, saying that the Japanese treaty was concluded with a representative Japanese government and that the United States had given the Soviets an opportunity for full consultations. (He neglected to mention, however, his strategy at the Japanese Peace Conference of procedurally ruling every Soviet suggestion out of order.)

Meanwhile, President Kennedy became more and more impatient. At a meeting at Hyannis Port on July 8 he made it clear he wanted action; he was tired of bureaucratic foot-dragging. Why was it taking so long? He asked McNamara for a report on the military options, and Rusk was ordered to prepare a reply to Khrushchev's Vienna aide-mémoire as soon as possible. It had been over a month since Vienna, and the State Department still had not come up with a response to Khrushchev's ultimatum. Sources at the White House leaked to the press that it was one more example of State Department incompetence.

In fact, the White House critics and their allies in the press were off the mark. Kohler and Hillenbrand had actually completed their draft note in reply to the Soviet aide-mémoire within a week of the Vienna summit—record time considering that the response had to be coordinated with both the British and the French. The delay decried by President Kennedy was the result of sloppy review procedures in the *White House,* not the State Department. The draft note had not reached the President because Ralph Dungan, a White House staffer, had locked it in his office safe—to which only he had the combination —and, without telling anyone, had gone off on a two-week holiday. And when Hillenbrand, after a few days, asked what had happened to the draft, he received only evasive replies. Finally the White House admitted that the draft could not be found, and Hillenbrand sent over a copy, which, incredibly, was also lost for several days. None of this comedy of errors was told to President Kennedy by his staff. State took the blame, and it was soon all over Washington that Kennedy was "disgusted and upset" with the performance of his State Department.

The draft note disappointed Kennedy and his White House advisers. Instead of outlining a "clear negotiating position," it was a legal brief detailing the history and substance of Allied rights in Berlin, full of international law and negative in tone, and replete with quotations from Potsdam and various Geneva conferences. Kennedy promptly called in Sorensen, who produced a shorter version in more flowery prose.

White House dissatisfaction with the note reflected a basic differ-

ence in view between the Kennedy advisers (and the President himself) and the Berlin task force—Kohler, Hillenbrand, and Rusk. The
note bears Rusk's fingerprints—understated and unassuming in tone,
with citations from the U.N. Charter and references to Soviet perfidy
concerning Berlin in the postwar period. It was not without elegance,
however, as the following passage shows:

> Peace does not come automatically from a "peace treaty." There is
> peace in Germany today even though the situation is "abnormal." A
> "peace treaty" that adversely affects the lives and rights of millions
> will not bring peace with it. A "peace treaty" that attempts to affect
> adversely the solemn commitments of three great powers does not
> bring peace with it.
>
> There is no reason for a crisis over Berlin. If one develops it is
> because the Soviet Union is attempting to invade the basic rights of
> others. All the world will plainly see that the misuse of such words as
> "peace" and "freedom" cannot conceal a threat to raise tension to the
> point of danger and suppress the freedom of those who now enjoy it.

Even though the note disappointed those who were looking for
ideas for a negotiating breakthrough that would lead to a whole new
policy for Central Europe, Rusk and Kohler did not go down that
road, because they believed, simply put, that a good negotiating position for the Allies did not exist. And desirable as it might be to have
some normalization of the situation in Central Europe, this was not
the time to try for it, in the face of a Soviet ultimatum. Kohler and
Hillenbrand were career Foreign Service officers who had dealt with
Berlin since 1958. They were convinced that the White House people,
who had come late to the problem, were simply trying to reinvent the
wheel. They had won Rusk over to their side and now were trying to
"educate" the President. But their views were perilously close to the
Acheson position, which was unpopular in the White House.

Kohler and Hillenbrand also disagreed with the White House insistence on rewriting their submission. They regarded the Sorensen draft
as "essentially a political speech" that was "impossible to use in a
diplomatic exchange." Hillenbrand added that "we would have become a laughingstock had the White House persisted in using it for
anything more than a presidential gloss."

Rusk knew that from the standpoint of dealing with the crisis in a
practical manner something more was needed. There was no basis for
negotiations, but talking was always preferable to nuclear war. He

thought of a way around the dilemma, and at a meeting with Kennedy on July 23 he suggested a new approach. We could not accede to the Soviet demand for full-scale negotiations, but we could agree to hold "exploratory talks" to see if there was a *basis* for negotiations. It was a delicate and subtle distinction typical of Rusk's mind. Kennedy and the Berlin task force readily agreed. They were ready to seize on anything that might defuse the crisis. At the same meeting possible military measures were discussed, but Rusk successfully opposed the idea of declaring a national emergency and argued for a quiet military buildup.

On July 25, 1961, President Kennedy delivered a nationally televised speech on the crisis. It was a tough speech in which he outlined three vital interests that were not negotiable: the American military presence in Berlin, access to the city, and the security and freedom of the city. Beyond this the United States was willing to talk about "actual irritants" in West Berlin if there were "proposals, not demands . . . not concessions of our rights." He went on to say: "We cannot negotiate with those who say, 'What's mine is mine and what's yours is negotiable.' But we are willing to consider any arrangement or treaty in Germany consistent with the maintenance of peace and freedom with legitimate security interests of all nations." As a counterbalance to American willingness to talk, Kennedy announced a military buildup. There would be a partial mobilization of reserves and an increase in the draft.

Now it was necessary to gain the support of the Allies, and Rusk went to Europe in early August. The East Germans had heightened the crisis on August 1 by announcing that foreign aircraft had to register with their air safety center before using the air corridors to Berlin. The East German leader, Walter Ulbricht, ominously hinted that he would move to shut down the Allied Air Safety Center and turn over flight control to East German authorities.

In Paris Rusk met with the NATO Council of Foreign Ministers. Although the headlines at the conclusion of the conference proclaimed "Agreement on Berlin," in fact the foreign ministers were badly split. France's Couve de Murville adamantly refused to allow the word "negotiation" to appear anywhere in the final communiqué. Rusk spent an exasperating entire day of the conference arguing over this one word and, losing his patience, angrily told his colleagues that if they ever again spent more than fifteen minutes on a communiqué he would absent himself. At one point he collared Couve de Murville in the corridor and urged him to telephone de Gaulle to get permission to end the impasse. Couve de Murville only looked at him strangely and said, "One does not telephone President de Gaulle." The Germans were also nervous about negotiations, but Foreign Minister Heinrich von Brentano was willing to go along with the "exploratory talks" idea. Rusk made common cause with his good friend Alec Douglas-Home, the British Foreign Secretary. Agreeing that, whatever the French attitude, they would stand together, Rusk and Lord Home formulated a strategy of "talking the problem to death." They would be prepared to talk on and on, just as repetitively as the Russians. "Exploratory talks" did not necessarily imply any obligation to come to an agreement.

Rusk also went to see de Gaulle at the Elysée Palace, but the French leader remained unmoved. He would have nothing to do with any talks on Berlin, even of an exploratory nature. When Rusk brought up the question of the French base at Bizerte, Tunisia, which was at the center of an international crisis likely to be the focus of the fall session of the United Nations, de Gaulle became visibly angry and spoke to him icily. "Bizerte is a totally French affair," he said. De Gaulle was also in political difficulty over Algeria, and there were even rumors of a coup d'état. Rusk said the United States wanted to be helpful in any way possible, but de Gaulle brushed the suggestion aside, as if it were beneath him to ask for American help.

Next, Rusk went to see Adenauer at his vacation villa in Cadenabbia, Italy, on the shores of Lake Como. Adenauer was showing his age and getting rather grumpy. In the first half-hour with Rusk he rambled on about his friend John Foster Dulles and how he was such a good Secretary of State. This was interesting because on several occasions, Rusk remembered, Dulles had spoken to him about his problems with Chancellor Adenauer. Apropos of the Soviet menace, Adenauer also lectured him about the great historical confrontation between the Teutons and the Slavs, referring to the latter as the "hordes from the East."

Once they got down to business, however, Rusk found the old Chancellor quite flexible and agreeable. He did not oppose negotiations that did not compromise basic rights. Rusk told Adenauer that the Americans, French, and British were prepared to accept Germany as a full partner in the consideration of Berlin and German questions. The best hope, Rusk said, was for an inconclusive negotiation. "My greatest ambition," he said, "is to pass the Berlin question on to my successor."

Rusk returned to Paris on his way home and announced to the press that "the world can expect negotiations" on the looming Berlin crisis. "Exactly where and how will be decided by our governments," he said. A major diplomatic offensive would be launched "in the near future." The American military buildup would also continue, and economic countermoves against the Soviet bloc would be readied for action if the crisis reached the acute stage. Contacts with the Soviets would be maintained at multiple diplomatic levels—at the U.N., in Moscow, and at various Eastern, Western, and neutral capitals. It was all a masterly bluff.

Meanwhile, the numbers of refugees fleeing into West Berlin from East Germany had reached staggering levels. Over four thousand people a day were "voting with their feet," as Rusk put it, until August 13 when, without any warning, the East Germans began to erect barbed wire barriers to seal the border separating the divided city. This action—the Berlin Wall—caught Rusk and other administration officials completely by surprise. Rusk called Kennedy at Hyannis Port, and they quickly dismissed the idea of taking military action. There was no practical military option apart from going in with massive force. And if the wall at the border was knocked down, there was nothing to stop the East Germans from building another one fifty yards farther back. Although the wall violated the four-power postwar Berlin agreement, which specified free access between sectors of the city, that had never been an issue of war and peace. (East Berlin had in fact been separated from West Berlin administratively since 1948.) The announced American "vital interests" remained intact, so Rusk and Kennedy contented themselves with a vigorous protest to Moscow against the illegal East German action. Rusk denounced the wall as a confession of Communist failure. Kennedy ordered a U.S. battle group of fifteen hundred men to West Berlin over the autobahn through East Germany and sent Vice President Johnson to Berlin.

Moscow rejected the protest, and the East Germans set new travel restrictions to East Berlin, but they were careful to add that "as regards the traveling of West Berlin citizens abroad along the communications lines in the German Democratic Republic, former decisions remain valid." Kennedy and Rusk took up this point in rejecting military action, as if a tacit understanding had been reached with the Soviets: "Available information," Rusk said, "indicates that measures taken [by the Communists] thus far are aimed at residents of East Berlin and East Germany and not at the Allied position in West Berlin or access thereto." The Berlin Wall was a Soviet gamble that succeeded.

American acceptance of the wall, however, did not resolve the larger crisis. President Kennedy was pleased with Rusk's diplomatic initiatives but was still worried that no concrete political position had been decided. On August 21 he wrote an impatient three-page memo to Rusk saying, "I want to take a stronger lead on the Berlin negotiations. . . . Both the calendar of negotiation and the substance of the Western position remain unsettled, and I no longer believe that satisfactory progress can be made by Four Power discussion alone." Kennedy went on to say he liked Rusk's idea of issuing an invitation to the Soviets for negotiations, but he needed a "clear paper" on "an agreed position." And to prevent Rusk from stalling, he added, "by Friday of this week—August twenty-fifth." He then stated some guidelines for the position he wanted to take:

—Do *not* insist on the maintenance of occupation rights if other strong guarantees can be designed.
—Consider well the option of proposing parallel peace treaties.
—Do not put too much distance between our initial proposals and our fallback position. Our first presentation should be, in itself, as persuasive and reasonable as possible.
—Make the framework of our proposals as fresh as possible—they should *not* look like warmed over stuff from 1959.

Rusk received this communication with a heavy heart. He thought Kennedy was on the wrong track. Bringing concessions to the bargaining table—such as a willingness to end occupation rights—and being persuasive and reasonable were just not the proper tactics to use with the Russians. He made no response to the memo, but went to see Kennedy personally. As gently as possible he told the President he understood his need for action but that it was impossible to formulate a negotiating position that would not amount to concessions. The Russians would simply take any Allied negotiating position and cut it in half. "It is not always a mistake to do nothing," he told Kennedy, "if you have a reason for doing nothing." He must have been persuasive, because Kennedy allowed him to proceed, to try things his way. In reflecting upon this episode, Rusk said later, "When arguing a position, it helps to know the difference between rape and seduction."

Before talks could get going on Berlin there was another significant development. Beginning in 1958, under the Eisenhower administration, the United States, the Soviet Union, and Britain had been engaged in negotiations at Geneva seeking to reach an agreement on banning nuclear weapons tests. All three nations were observing a de facto test ban during the talks. When he came into office Rusk made the negotiation a priority and handpicked the American chief negotiator, Arthur H. Dean. Rusk was in favor of continuing the nuclear test moratorium, and he believed the United States should not be the first to resume testing. To emphasize the importance of the negotiations, he attended the conference in March, the first to be held after the Kennedy administration took office, and he found the talks hopelessly deadlocked over a Russian demand that any inspection system to verify compliance with a test ban be under the supervision of a three-member directorate composed of a Communist, a neutralist, and a Western representative. This would effectively give the Soviet Union a veto on verification, which was unacceptable to the United States.

During the summer of 1961 the United States put new pressures on the Soviets to bargain realistically on arms control. Congress approved the creation of the Arms Control and Disarmament Agency, proposed by Kennedy and backed by Rusk, which would develop, in Rusk's words, "a workable disarmament plan." Rusk and Stevenson prepared an initiative for the fall session of the United Nations to put pressure on the Soviets to achieve a test ban treaty.

On Monday, August 28, 1961, the 337th session of the test ban talks resumed in Geneva. The Soviet delegate Senyon Tsarapkin (the Americans referred to him as "Scratchy") snubbed the U.S.-British proposal and refrained even from saying it would be "studied." "It is useless," he said, spouting the Soviet line, "to talk of a test ban accord except as part of an agreement on general and complete disarmament." This signaled a new hardening of the Soviet position, and on August 30 the Soviets announced that they would resume nuclear weapons testing. From his vacation retreat on the Black Sea, Khrushchev gave an interview to two British MPs in which he said he intended to resume nuclear testing "in order to shock the Western powers into negotiations over Germany and disarmament." Rusk found out later, however, that the decision to resume testing, and a related decision to extend the tour of duty for servicemen in the armed forces, made in Moscow while Khrushchev was on vacation, were forced on him by his political opponents bent on securing gains for the military and preventing him from entering into negotiations with the West over Berlin.

When Kennedy received the news that the Soviets were resuming nuclear testing, he was angry and concerned. He recalled Arthur Dean from Geneva and met with his advisers and members of Congress to ponder what to do. On August 31 came word of the first Soviet test, exploded in the atmosphere over Central Asia. Atmospheric tests were particularly disturbing to the President because of the large impact from nuclear fallout. Rusk was aware of this danger as well; in 1955 and 1956, as president of the Rockefeller Foundation, he had approved research by the National Academy of Sciences to study the global impact of nuclear testing in the atmosphere. He spent long hours with the President, and there was broad agreement that the Soviet Union had lost the war of nerves over testing and had suffered a propaganda defeat. They knew that if the Russians persisted, the United States would have to resume testing as well, but Kennedy decided to hold off, to make one more attempt to halt the tests.

Rusk huddled with Arthur Dean, John McCloy, and Glenn Seaborg, the chairman of the Atomic Energy Commission, and they came up with a new idea. Rusk favored a total halt to nuclear testing as long as there could be verification against possible Russian cheating. The Russians opposed on-site verification, so it was impossible to get a total ban on nuclear weapons tests. But nuclear testing in the atmosphere posed no verification problem. The current series of Russian tests showed that the United States had the technical means to determine whether the Russians were testing in the atmosphere. Why not, Rusk suggested, propose a ban of nuclear tests in the *atmosphere?* Rusk worked out the proposal with President Kennedy and the British, and it emerged as a joint appeal by Kennedy and Prime Minister Macmillan directly to Khrushchev for an immediate agreement "not to conduct nuclear tests which take place in the atmosphere and produce radioactive fallout." The proposal stated that "the United States and the United Kingdom are prepared to rely upon existing means of detection, which they believe to be adequate, and are not suggesting additional controls." It was proposed that the agreement be concluded immediately by representatives of the three nations in Geneva.

Rusk did not hold out much hope for success, since the Russians were in the midst of their round of testing. He fully expected the appeal to be rejected, but at the very least it would be a propaganda victory for the Western side. Nevertheless, it injected into the disarmament debate the idea that would ultimately become the Limited Test Ban Treaty in 1963. But the time had not yet come. The Soviets rejected the appeal, and on September 6 the United States announced it would resume underground nuclear testing, reserving a decision on atmospheric tests.

Kennedy was now readily accepting Rusk's advice, and there was new confidence between the two men. The improved relationship was the product of many subtle things, but most of all it was the result of their getting to know one another and becoming familiar with each other's manner. The President gradually grew accustomed to Rusk's understated style and became more comfortable with his advice. And Rusk accepted Kennedy's activism and determination to run his own foreign policy. But both knew that Kennedy could not possibly be his own Secretary of State, maintaining a constant, informed, and detailed watch over all of foreign policy. Kennedy was also happy that Rusk never objected when he called in outside experts to consult with on foreign policy, such as Acheson and McCloy. The more he heard the advice of these outside experts, the more Kennedy realized the value of Rusk. Although the President always remained in charge of foreign policy, more and more he saw the wisdom of operating through his Secretary of State.

Rusk's public image remained somewhat of a puzzle. He looked, as one reporter described him, like "a combination of your friendly bartender and Socrates." He kept his counsel and spoke very guardedly about his relations with the President. The Washington press corps simply could not get used to a man who appeared to be not only humorless but also remarkably free from the usual human foibles. In a town filled with personalities who were larger than life and who sought to attract attention to themselves, Rusk was strangely reticent and retiring. He avoided bold, quotable pronouncements on foreign policy and spoke carefully and unassumingly about major issues. The press kept waiting for him to emerge from his cocoon and criticized him for a lack of flair. But Rusk did not try to change his image; it was "something of an advantage to have a lack of flair," he told intimates, and he deliberately "ran from anything that smelled of hamminess."

At his press conferences, which were at first held in the large State Department auditorium, Rusk was clearly uncomfortable in front of the TV cameras. He soon shifted his press conferences to the smaller International Conference Room at State, where he could sit down and talk with reporters in a more conversational tone. His public speeches were also far from memorable. He avoided sweeping general statements and colorful phrases in favor of cold, rational analysis that did not quote very well. Yet the press acknowledged his growing influence. *U.S. News & World Report* in September 1961 called him "next to President Kennedy and his brother Robert, actually the most important official in Washington," and pointed out that "all final presentations on major foreign policy recommendations are now being made by Rusk.''

By September 1961 the Soviet Union was clearly on the defensive because of worldwide concern about its resumption of nuclear testing and its inflexible attitude on Berlin. Negotiations on Berlin between Rusk and Gromyko finally got under way on September 21 in New York City. Both men were in New York for the fall session of the General Assembly, and they agreed to periodic meetings on the Berlin crisis. Thus began a studied minuet between Rusk and Gromyko. In many ways their talks were an elaborate charade, skillfully prepared and carried out by Rusk to "take the fever out of the Berlin crisis." As he later recalled, "We talked and talked at great length about nothing." Gromyko began their first session by repeating Khrushchev's ultimatum at Vienna, that the peace treaty with East Germany would be signed and that any interference from the West would mean war. Rusk answered him by saying, "Wait a minute, if you want war, you can have war in five minutes. But if you don't want war, then we better sit down and talk about it."

The meetings were quite formal, with Gromyko insisting on speaking in Russian though he knew English well. Rusk was just as glad, because this tended to drag the meetings out and obscured communication between the two sides. Gromyko would endlessly repeat the contents of the Soviet note over Berlin and state the Soviet threat to sign a peace treaty with East Germany by the end of the year. Rusk was just as repetitious as Gromyko, asserting in formal terms U.S. rights in Berlin and the inability of the Soviets to bargain those rights away in any treaty with the East Germans. Rusk would also warn Gromyko against Soviet coercion or interference with Allied access rights to Berlin. Then each side would spell out its vital interests in Berlin. But just to even up the discussion, Rusk would dangle some suggestions about what might be done to ameliorate the situation. These included an agreement between the Soviet Union and the East Germans to guarantee Allied rights to Berlin; Allied recognition of the Oder-Neisse line as the border between Germany and Poland; a marginal reduction of Allied forces in Berlin; and an Allied agreement not to give nuclear weapons to West Germany.

Ultimately the talks broke down into discussions of fine points. Rusk asked Gromyko the meaning of the word "guarantee." Gromyko probed how far the United States would go on recognition of East Germany. Doing all he could to stall, Rusk repeated diplomatic formulas and warned that the United States would negotiate only on a reasonable basis. He also harped on the theme that the deadline for the conclusion of the peace treaty would have to be extended; there was no possibility that agreements could be reached by the end of the year. Any tentative conclusions resulting from the exploratory talks would have to be further negotiated and cleared with the Allies as well. The United States could not speak for the Allies, and consultations would take time.

The Rusk-Gromyko talks continued in October with both sides taking a hard line. News reports described them as "inconclusive" or "deadlocked." In Berlin there were more border incidents and shootings of fleeing refugees by East German guards. The wall dividing the city was fortified, and police exchanged shots across the border. Nevertheless, to keep things going, the White House put an optimistic face on the negotiations. On October 1 Kennedy said he was "encouraged" and announced that he was asking the Allies for advice to find a formula for a Berlin accord. He said that a reasonable formula could be discussed with the Soviets if accommodation, not humiliation, was their purpose. Alec Douglas-Home in London termed the talks "constructive."

The negotiations with Gromyko were tailor-made for Rusk's personality. He was perhaps the only American negotiator who could be just as repetitive, intransigent, and noncommittal as Gromyko. His task was simply to try to wait him out. He stated over and over again that the Allied presence in West Berlin was not owing to the Soviets, and what the Russians did not have they could not take away. Occasionally he employed more colorful language ("You're asking us to buy the same horse twice").

There were a few amiable moments in the exchanges between the two men. Despite their roles, it was evident that they respected and even liked each other personally. Before and after the talks there were opportunities for repartee, such as teasing each other about the similar color of their suits (dark blue). On one occasion Rusk asked Gromyko if he could give him an Accutron watch as a present, explaining that it was based on a new principle of timekeeping, the tuning fork, and that it had come out of the U.S. space program. Gromyko, mindful of the Americans' view that the Russians were out to steal Western technology, teasingly asked, "Would you mind if I show it to our engineers?" "I've already taken care of that," Rusk said, and gave him the watch, which had an open face with the works inside exposed for all to see.

The two men even played games with each other in deciding where and when to meet. Once when Rusk wanted to set up a meeting, he waited to talk to Gromyko in the General Assembly president's chamber, expecting that he would come by. When he did not, Rusk went out into the corridor and caught sight of Gromyko surrounded by reporters. He made no attempt to walk up to him because he did not want it to appear to the newsmen that he was chasing the Soviet Foreign Minister. Instead, he sent Bohlen to the assembly floor to talk to Gromyko and invite him for lunch at the Waldorf-Astoria Hotel.

The lunch, held two days later, turned out to be another marathon encounter, in which both sides stated and restated their arguments while the hors d'oeuvres grew cold. After the substantive talks they stayed on and fell into an easy banter until five thirty in the afternoon. An amazed U.S. aide found them "as friendly and as chatty as could be."

On October 6 President Kennedy invited Gromyko for a talk at the White House. Kennedy had been receiving back-channel reports through newsmen and diplomats of a more flexible Soviet tone, and he wanted to see if Gromyko would signal any break in the negotiations. Disappointed that he held to his hard line, Kennedy told Gromyko, "What you want is to trade an apple for an orchard. We don't do that in this country." Afterward, Rusk described the talk as "interesting." Gromyko termed it "useful."

The exploratory talks were going nowhere, but the United States made it clear that they should continue, and a new Kennedy-Rusk strategy sought to shift them to a lower level. Ambassador Llewellyn Thompson was called home from Moscow and briefed on the crisis. It was decided to ask the Russians to move the talks to Moscow, where they would be conducted by Ambassador Thompson. If the talks could be transferred to Moscow and handled at the ambassadorial level, they could be conducted out of the limelight, and this would defuse the crisis.

Then, on October 17, Premier Khrushchev, addressing the Twenty-second Congress of the Communist Party, abruptly withdrew his deadline for a German peace treaty. He said that war was not inevitable between the Communist and Western world. Referring to the Rusk-Gromyko talks on Berlin he said, "We have the impression that the Western powers are displaying a certain understanding of the situation and that they are inclined to seek a solution for the German problem and for the West Berlin issue on a mutually acceptable basis." He added that the main thing to do was to settle the Berlin question and that the deadline of December 31, 1961, was no longer important. He was content to rely on the talks between the two countries.

The administration breathed a quiet sigh of relief. The situation in Berlin remained serious, but the crisis was no longer an imminent threat to world peace. The removal of the ultimatum was the core of the U.S. position, and that had been achieved. It appeared that Khrushchev was ready for a respite from crisis. The Soviets had attained some minimum objectives. The construction of the Berlin Wall had stemmed the refugee flow and stabilized the East German state. The resumption of nuclear testing had been a propaganda loss, but the Soviet military had been able to conduct thirty-one nuclear weapons tests. Now able to take a softer line, Khrushchev not only removed the ultimatum on Berlin but also called for an end to nuclear testing and an agreement on complete disarmament. And, apparently, the American military buildup and firm negotiating stance had convinced Khrushchev that his campaign to intimidate the new American administration had failed. At the same time, the fact of the negotiations gave Khrushchev the argument he needed to placate the hard-liners in the Politburo—why not get into those exploratory negotiations with the Americans and see what would come out of them?

The lifting of the Soviet deadline was the occasion for both Washington and Moscow to call a brief hiatus and to plan future strategies. Gromyko conferred with Khrushchev in Moscow, and Rusk reported somberly at a press conference: "The talks which we had with Mr. Gromyko did not give us immediate hope that this matter would be easily settled. . . . On the substance, we are not in sight of land." On the ABC television program "Issues and Answers," Rusk said there was no prospect for immediate negotiations and there were no new approaches by the West to the Berlin crisis. He was still playing a waiting game, watching for the next Soviet move. His aim was to achieve what he called a modus vivendi—a live-and-let-live arrangement with the Soviets on Berlin which would leave the situation unchanged and be enforced primarily by a desire on both sides to avoid armed conflict.

Potentially dangerous border incidents continued to occur. When the East Germans demanded passport identification of Allied civilians going into East Berlin, the Americans brought up ten forty-ton Patton tanks and trained their guns on the "Checkpoint Charlie" border crossing. The Soviets reacted by bringing in their own tanks, which produced an ominous Soviet-American military confrontation. After a day the Soviet tanks withdrew, apparently on direct orders from Khrushchev. At Rusk's urging the American tanks were also withdrawn, and the face-off was ended. Like his recommendation not to take action to remove the Berlin Wall, Rusk's strategy was to stand

firm, but to refrain from pushing the Soviets into military confrontations over matters that did not involve the announced American vital
interests in West Berlin. Toward the same end he argued successfully
for placing restrictions on the freedom of action of the U.S. commander in Berlin, General Albert Watson, which brought an angry
denunciation from General Lucius Clay, whom Kennedy had sent to
Berlin at the height of the crisis to be his personal ambassador.

New talks on Berlin began in January 1962 in Moscow between
Ambassador Thompson and Gromyko. They were a continuation of
the Rusk strategy of "exploratory talks," and Rusk and the Berlin
task force maintained a tight control. Thompson's instructions for
each meeting were drafted by the task force and approved by Kennedy and Rusk. Thompson sent back detailed accounts of each talk,
which were analyzed in Washington and used for the preparation of
the next round. These talks were, in fact, designed to fail. Thompson
was allowed to present one new idea—international control of the
land, water, and air routes to West Berlin—and it was rejected by
Gromyko.

During the Thompson-Gromyko talks the Soviets launched a new
program of harassment—disrupting the Allied air corridors to West
Berlin by dropping metal chaff (which interfered with navigation in-
struments) and preempting designated Allied air space. The United
States responded by sending in demonstration flights of military aircraft. Both military and civilian Allied aircraft continued operations,
defying Communist pressures. In the event of an incident the United
States had contingency plans to provide fighter escorts for flights into
the city.

In March, in the midst of the new crisis, Rusk led the American
delegation to the Eighteen-Nation Disarmament Conference in Geneva. He presented the Western plan for a nuclear test ban and a step-
by-step cut in arms and troop levels, but his main purpose was to
open new discussions with Gromyko on the Berlin crisis. Rusk and
Lord Home angrily protested to Gromyko over the air corridor
harassment and told him there could be no movement in the talks
while it continued. In early April, when the air corridor disruption
ceased, it was widely attributed to Rusk's patience and firmness with
Gromyko.

By now Rusk's marathon negotiations with Gromyko were getting
to be a source of black comedy among the Foreign Service officers on
his staff. The phrase "nothing gained, nothing lost" was applicable to
their every encounter. During the Geneva Disarmament Conference

it was announced that Rusk's return to Washington would be delayed because the special Boeing 707 jet that was to bring him back was "not available." The announcement sounded peculiar, and two of his aides started a rumor that Rusk had lost the 707 to Gromyko in a card game and would have to keep on playing until he won it back. (Rusk was known for his habit on long airplane rides of playing bridge from lift-off to touchdown.) In fact, Rusk had continued his talks with Gromyko for three and a half hours longer than expected, and when he emerged he announced that he would return to Washington that night. The aides winked at one another. "Good old ace-in-the-hole Rusk," one of them said over a toast as the 707 took off. "He won it back after all. As usual, nothing gained and nothing lost."

With the situation quieter in Berlin, Rusk agreed to new talks in Washington with Soviet Ambassador Anatoly Dobrynin. With the President's approval he formulated a new package to submit to the Soviets: (1) a U.S.-Soviet undertaking to prevent the spread of nuclear weapons; (2) an exchange of nonaggression declarations; (3) the establishment of a number of East-West committees to handle technical contacts between the two Germanys; (4) the formulation of an international authority to supervise travel between West Berlin and West Germany; and (5) a permanent conference of deputies of the Allied and Soviet foreign ministers to meet regularly on Berlin.

Rusk attempted to clear the new proposal with the West Germans, but underestimated the hostility of Adenauer and the Foreign Ministry. On April 13, three days before Rusk's first meeting with Dobrynin, the Germans leaked the proposal to the press in an obvious attempt to sabotage the negotiations. Adenauer was particularly displeased with the idea of an international authority, and he predicted failure of the talks. Rusk was extremely upset and protested the "breach of confidence" to the German ambassador in Washington, which raised Adenauer's hackles, and he accused Rusk of a personal affront.

This unfortunate breach with Bonn occurred because of a fundamental misunderstanding of the nature of Rusk's proposals. Although he could not say so publicly, Rusk looked on the proposals as merely a probe, a continuation of the "exploratory talks" agenda designed to talk the problem to death. In putting out the idea of an international authority Rusk was in no way giving up on the essential Western position—the continued presence of American, British, and French troops and free access to West Berlin. Any international supervision would be only "window dressing," and Rusk felt that West German interests were fully safeguarded. He thought the Germans did not appreciate the fact that he was attempting an exceedingly difficult and delicate diplomatic operation, in a highly explosive situation in which the United States, as the major Western nuclear power, had the heaviest burden and responsibility.

Despite the embarrassment Rusk and Dobrynin commenced their talks, and Rusk continued his strategy of holding out what Gromyko called "glimmers of hope" while remaining firm on essential issues. Rusk said that the Soviets were handling the Berlin dispute "responsibly" but reported no progress on the central questions. German opposition provided an excuse for him to abandon the five-point American proposal, and the talks were suspended while Rusk went to Europe to consult with the Allies. President Kennedy supported his diplomacy with a speech insisting that the West must continue the talks. On his return from Europe Rusk held one last talk with Dobrynin, on May 30, and with unusual frankness a State Department official said Dobrynin and Rusk "just kept going around in circles." Rusk announced their mutual desire to "keep on talking," however, and cited the uncertainty of America's relations with its NATO partners and differences with West Germany as reasons forcing him to stay with generalities in the talks. His remarks were disingenuous, designed to mask his policy of outwaiting the Russians. On July 25, at the Disarmament Conference in Geneva, Rusk again conferred with Gromyko about Berlin with the same result: no progress. The Russians now reverted to a harsher line; they resumed harassment in the Berlin air corridors and threatened once again to sign the peace treaty with East Germany.

In the summer of 1962 Khrushchev seemed to have come to the realization that he had underestimated American firmness on Berlin. Negotiations had failed to achieve his objective. It was time for a new strategy, and he chose a daring and ingenious course. He was unwilling to risk all-out war by moving the Red Army into West Berlin or by shooting down Allied military aircraft in the corridors, but he could immensely increase the pressure on the United States by putting offensive missiles in Cuba. Sometime in the summer of 1962, probably in July, when Raúl Castro, the Cuban Minister of Armed Forces, visited Moscow, Khrushchev struck a deal for the installation of Soviet missiles on Cuban soil. In a diplomatic note on September 5 Moscow bluntly stated its newly militant strategy: "The question is not one of discussing incidents and consultations. It is necessary, at long last, to liquidate the occupation regime in West Berlin on the basis of signing a German Peace Treaty, to liquidate the NATO military base, and to withdraw the troops of the three powers from West Berlin.'' Western diplomats thought that the Soviets would not propose new Berlin negotiations until after the U.S. congressional elections in November. Khrushchev believed that he could take advantage of American preoccupation with the elections to install the missiles in Cuba. Then, in November, he planned to return to the Berlin question with the United States facing this new threat.

But the Soviet plan backfired when high-flying U-2 planes discovered the missile sites in Cuba on October 14, before they were operational. The premature discovery of the sites, the calculated American response of a selective blockade, and the threat of an invasion of Cuba caught Khrushchev unawares, and he was forced to back down.

During the Cuban missile crisis Rusk and other officials were aware of its probable linkage with Berlin, and the Berlin task force was charged with anticipating possible Soviet moves and preparing appropriate American responses. It was a surprise to Rusk that Berlin remained quiet during the crisis. That Khrushchev did not move into Berlin was testimony to the fact that during the long months of the crisis American firmness had convinced him that the defense commitment to West Berlin was credible. In Cuba, Khrushchev retreated because of the very real threat of an American invasion. He was not willing to risk all-out war.

The Cuban missile crisis was a watershed event in Soviet-American relations. The Cold War was far from over, but the Soviet Union became much more prudent and circumspect about putting direct pressure on U.S. vital interests in Berlin and elsewhere. Kennedy and Rusk, in a sense, had proved themselves; Khrushchev knew that the Americans could not be intimidated. As a result the Soviets gradually put the Berlin crisis on the back burner and were content to call for a mutually acceptable agreement on Berlin in the indefinite future. This in effect returned Berlin to the status quo before the crisis, with the important exception of the Berlin Wall and the attendant Allied acceptance of partition of the city.

Inevitable by-products of the Berlin crisis and of the Kennedy-Rusk policy of ambiguous negotiations with the Soviets were strains and fissures in the NATO alliance. The United States in the negotiations over Berlin was following its own interest in achieving a relaxation of tension and stabilization in Central Europe. Kennedy and Rusk saw an overwhelming mutual interest of the Soviet Union and the United States in preventing nuclear war. Kennedy was moving to achieve détente with the Soviets through local settlements and arms limitation. The French, on the other hand, were confident that Khrushchev did not want war, and opposed any move to negotiate with the Russians as naïve. The Germans were also nervous about negotiations that would increase international acceptance of East Germany and make the German dream of unification ever more remote.

The rift in the NATO alliance over Berlin, however, was merely symptomatic of larger disputes between the United States and its European allies. By the 1960s these countries had emerged economically and politically from the ravages of World War II. They were in a mood to assert their independence, and their perceived interests were in some respects different from those of the United States. Many of the policies of the Kennedy administration exacerbated these differences. The desire of the United States to champion the independence of developing countries from their colonial masters produced conflict with Portugal in the case of Angola, with Belgium in the case of the Congo, and with the Netherlands in the case of Indonesia. The emphasis of the United States on a buildup of conventional forces caused doubt in Europe about the depth of the U.S. commitment to defend Western Europe with nuclear weapons. The American preoccupation with conflicts in Laos, Vietnam, Africa, and Cuba raised the fear that European countries as NATO allies would be drawn into far-flung regional conflicts. American concern over the spread of nuclear weapons made policymakers in Washington unenthusiastic about the independent nuclear deterrents in Britain and France.

Rusk was one of the architects and chief proponents of the so-called grand design for an Atlantic partnership between the United States and a strong and independent Europe. The grand design was a comprehensive vision of new political, strategic, military, and economic goals for NATO under the leadership of the United States. Politically it depended upon the formation of a "United States of Europe," a Europe united under the aegis of the European Community, the Common Market, a process that had already begun with the formation of the European Coal and Steel Community in 1952 and the European Atomic Energy and Economic Communities in 1958. Six nations— France, Germany, Italy, and the Benelux countries—were forming an economic union and taking tentative steps to coordinate political policies as well. American policy saw the preferred course of evolution of the Common Market as embracing other NATO allies as well, especially Britain. With the inclusion of Britain, a true European political union could be achieved.

The Kennedy administration envisioned a new strategic role for the United States and a united Europe. Together these two blocs would form an Atlantic community, an overwhelming counterweight to the Sino-Soviet bloc. The Atlantic community would have the power to meet Communist expansion anywhere in the world, especially in Asia, Africa, and South America. The prosperity of the Atlantic community would also prove to be an irresistible draw for Eastern Europe, possibly even succeeding in prying the Soviet satellites away from the Communist bloc. Militarily, the NATO allies would be expected to join the United States in building up conventional forces. The Kennedy administration suggested an interim target of thirty divisions under NATO command. These forces could be used to deter Soviet aggression in Europe and put down Communist-sponsored local uprisings in other areas of the world. The grand design left no role for independent nuclear forces except those of the United States. France and Britain would be required to give up their independent nuclear forces or to integrate them as multilateral nuclear deterrents under the control of the NATO alliance.

To satisfy the aspirations of non-nuclear NATO nations to have a voice in nuclear planning, the Kennedy administration put forth the idea of a multilateral force of ships and submarines manned by crews drawn from all of the NATO countries. In a politically united Europe, this multilateral force could become the nuclear arsenal for Europe.

The Atlantic community would also have an important economic component. Rusk supported a new round of tariff cuts between the United States and its trading partners, especially Europe, and proposed expanded trade legislation that would implement free trade and end protectionism. Some of the Kennedy's advisers expressed reservations about getting trade legislation, but Rusk was adamant. Free trade was essential both with Western Europe and the developing countries of the world. In the end Kennedy agreed to go for a strong bill. "If we're going to have a fight," he told Rusk, "let's have a fight about *something*," and the Trade Expansion Act became the basis for the "Kennedy Round" of international trade negotiations, the most far-reaching trade legislation of the postwar period.

In hindsight the grand design was overoptimistic and overambitious. It failed to recognize the truculence of European disunity and the very real differences in interests between the United States and Europe. The military aspects of the grand design were left to McNamara, George Ball was in charge of economics and trade, and Rusk himself took the lead in selling the political and strategic value of the grand design to the Europeans. He went to the NATO ministers' conferences and regularly made the rounds of European capitals to create a sense of unity in the alliance. He was given high marks for his diplomacy and established particularly close relationships with European leaders such as Macmillan and Lord Home in Britain, Spaak in Belgium, and Fanfani in Italy. Rusk believed that the United States should play a strong role in leading the Europeans. By force of diplomacy alone, he attempted to mold Europe in conformity with the grand design. It was perhaps too active a role, producing dissension and resentment among some European leaders. Even friendly diplomats such as Lord Home advised that he should not continue to speak up so much about European unity and the role of the NATO alliance. Home recalled to him the advice an elderly colonel gave to his young officers: "If you want to lead, then you must say 'come' rather than 'go.'"

Rusk, however, persisted in his campaign for strong U.S. leadership in the NATO alliance. His resentment and frustration in failing to achieve his goal began to center especially on France. De Gaulle was difficult to deal with at best, and Rusk's temperament and his training, firmly in the tradition of a British diplomat's, exacerbated his relations with de Gaulle and the differences between the United States and France.

De Gaulle was perhaps the only world leader with whom Rusk was unable to establish any kind of rapport or understanding. A major reason was the personalities of the two men. Rusk's cultural values were very much rooted in the Anglo-Saxon traditions of the American South. With British diplomats he was immediately at home, launching into conversation about Oxford or his dealings with Mountbatten in India during World War II. He traced the political landmarks that ruled his life, the U.N. Charter and the U.S. Constitution, to the Magna Carta, English common law, and British political philosophy. He had far less understanding or appreciation of French culture and history. In his school days he had chosen to concentrate on German rather than French.

De Gaulle, Rusk thought, was "living in an anachronistic dream world of the France of Joan of Arc and Louis XIV." Instinctively Rusk saw Britain as the natural leader of the European side of the Atlantic partnership. He could not comprehend that de Gaulle, regarding France as the equal of Britain, refused to accept this. From de Gaulle's viewpoint, the Americans were discriminating between Britain and France as members of the alliance. They had refused the idea of a *directoire* composed of France, Britain, and the United States to guide the affairs of the free world, but insisted upon maintaining the "special relationship" with Britain. "I have told you," de Gaulle said to Rusk, referring to the *directoire* proposal, "how you could have the cooperation of France, and you refused." On the issue of nuclear weapons, Rusk in the councils of the administration defended the right of the British to possess an independent nuclear deterrent and advocated increased sharing of American nuclear secrets with the British. Yet he argued against helping France achieve nuclear weapons capability or ballistic missile technology.

Each time Rusk saw de Gaulle he became more discouraged and suspicious of the French leader's motives. De Gaulle brought out a closely guarded aspect of Rusk's personality: his anger. C. L. Sulzberger of *The New York Times* reported seeing Rusk after a NATO meeting. "You have found me in a bad mood," he said. "I'm so goddamned sore at de Gaulle."

Rusk's meetings with de Gaulle were always icily formal and correct, without the slightest hint of personal warmth. De Gaulle would begin by asking Rusk to transmit his greetings and respects to President Kennedy, then he would pause and say, "Monsieur le Secrétaire, je vous écoute." (Mr. Secretary, I am listening.) Rusk was compelled to lecture to the French President, there was rarely any give or take, and de Gaulle never volunteered a subject for their discussion. He restricted himself to blunt and sometimes angry comments on Rusk's speeches.

De Gaulle adamantly refused to budge on the issue of the French nuclear force. He said that France could not be sure of the nuclear commitment of the United States. When Rusk lectured de Gaulle on European unity and the necessity for Europe to speak with one voice on international affairs, de Gaulle commented, "Well, what is Europe?" Pointing with his finger as if at an imaginary map, he said, "Here are the Benelux countries." And he brushed them aside with a wave of his hand. "In the south, there is Italy," and he scoffed, "Psshhh. Then, there is Germany," he continued, "and Germany must be kept in its place. And there are the British. But the British are not Europeans, they are Anglo-Saxons." Then he smiled benignly. "And here is France at the heart of Europe, the soul of European culture." To de Gaulle, France *was* Europe.

Rusk increasingly blamed de Gaulle for discord in the NATO alliance. "The only reason for any disarray," he told Sulzberger, "is de Gaulle. The military strength of NATO and economic progress are much better now than ever. There is intensive consultation on all questions and everything is moving—except de Gaulle.'' In his pique over de Gaulle, Rusk began to exclude France from consultation on matters concerning the alliance. He made it clear that on questions such as the multilateral nuclear force and NATO conventional warfare planning the United States would go ahead regardless of French opposition. Rusk believed de Gaulle's tactics frustrated his own "Olympian" purpose. He found irony in the fact that had de Gaulle thrown himself into the leadership of the "grand design," he would have become the real spokesman of Europe.

The Kennedy administration's policy of heavy-handed American leadership of the alliance and exclusion of the French was ultimately unsuccessful. Failing to listen to the NATO allies and demanding adherence to American policies did more harm than good; collective security meant little if the United States insisted on going forward alone with no more than lip-service support from its allies. Too much direction in an alliance was as dangerous as too little, as the United States was later to find in the case of Vietnam.

European exasperation and lack of confidence in American leadership of the alliance were vividly brought out in the December 1962 Skybolt missile affair. In 1960 President Eisenhower had agreed to sell the Skybolt—a modern air-to-ground missile—to the British as the future delivery system for their nuclear weapons. The British had relied on Skybolt and placed substantial orders for it. In the summer of 1962, however, McNamara told British Defense Minister Peter Thorneycroft that the administration was considering the cancellation of Skybolt because of serious technical flaws and excessive cost. In McNamara's view new missiles such as Minuteman and Polaris made Skybolt redundant. The British, however, were counting on Skybolt. They hoped to convince the Americans to go ahead with development of the weapon at a meeting between Prime Minister Macmillan and President Kennedy at Nassau scheduled for December 18. Rusk talked the matter over with McNamara in advance of the conference. He tried to persuade McNamara that the political consequences of the decision would be disastrous and that the British would interpret the cancellation as an American attempt to force them out of the nuclear "club." McNamara was undeterred, and Rusk deferred to his judgment. Perhaps because he saw what was coming, Rusk chose not to attend the conference. At Nassau, Kennedy informed Macmillan what he already knew, that Skybolt had been canceled. Macmillan skillfully played upon Kennedy's sympathy; he told him the cancellation of

Skybolt would be a political bombshell at home. He spoke also of the special relationship between Britain and the United States. If he could not have Skybolt, he wanted Polaris, which would preserve Britain's independent nuclear force.

In the end Kennedy relented and offered Polaris to Britain. To keep up the appearance that U.S. policy was to discourage independent national nuclear forces, language was added to their agreement that the British Polaris system would be a part of the NATO nuclear force unless preempted by Britain's "supreme national interest." To placate de Gaulle it was decided to offer Polaris to France on the same basis. It was not a good-faith offer, because they knew de Gaulle would turn it down.

The Polaris decision satisfied no one. In Britain it was accepted with misgivings because it raised British defense costs. For de Gaulle the decision seems to have been the final blow which demonstrated U.S. favoritism toward Britain and the necessity for France to take an independent course. The U.S. unilateral decision to cancel Skybolt showed how the Americans could not be trusted to protect anyone's interest but their own. The Polaris decision was proof of the special relationship between Britain and the United States. De Gaulle easily saw through the language of the agreement labeling the British Polaris a multilateral force, and he knew the offer to France was not seriously meant.

The next month, January 1963, de Gaulle let fly two political thunderbolts: he vetoed British membership in the European Common Market—Britain was too different from the other members and not ready for entry into the club of Europe—and he signed a treaty with Adenauer for Franco-German cooperation. The two historical enemies agreed to develop common strategic and tactical military doctrines and to consult on political and economic policy.

These events caused consternation in Washington. Rusk was less concerned than Under Secretary George Ball. Rusk viewed the Franco-German treaty as a positive development because it confirmed beyond all question the definitive rapprochement of two nations that had fought in two world wars against each other. Rusk preferred to take the long view; he predicted changes in French policy after de Gaulle. He was only partially right. The Franco-German treaty was primarily of symbolic importance; it was overshadowed by the broader movement of European cooperation, and Britain eventually entered the Common Market, in 1971. But Gaullist-style independent action and differences in the NATO alliance persisted. The "grand design" failed or faded into the far distant future. It was, however, a noble vision and one that, had it come about, would have made the world a safer place.

If 1963 was the year when the severe strains in NATO showed themselves, it was also a year of significant progress in relations with the Soviet Union. A new round of talks on the deadlocked test ban negotiations opened in New York in January, and for the first time the Russians accepted the principle of on-site inspections on Soviet territory—they proposed to allow three per year. At the next round of negotiations, in Geneva, the U.S. side proposed seven per year, but this was too many for the Russians and the talks once again stalled.

In May Rusk opened discussions with Anatoly Dobrynin in Washington. He found Dobrynin shrewd and intelligent, a man who would transmit U.S. views accurately back to Moscow and was willing to work at finding possible areas of agreement. Their relationship was almost cordial, and they were on a first-name basis. Rusk resurrected the proposal for a limited treaty banning nuclear tests in the atmosphere, in outer space, and underwater. Dobrynin was receptive but noncommittal. Rusk told Dobrynin that the main issue for the United States was verification. He wanted a treaty that did not depend solely on trust. Only the limited test ban was verifiable without on-site inspection.

In June President Kennedy delivered a speech at American University in Washington proposing a "strategy of peace" and an end to the "vicious and dangerous cycle" of the Cold War. He announced a new effort to achieve a test ban treaty in Moscow in July and said that the United States would refrain from nuclear testing in the atmosphere in advance of the conference. Kennedy accepted Rusk's suggestion that Averell Harriman represent the United States at the Moscow conference. There was indication of a Soviet change in attitude when Kennedy's speech was reprinted in full by *Izvestia,* the major afternoon Moscow newspaper. On June 20 the Soviets also agreed to establish a "hot line" emergency communications link between the White House and the Kremlin to reduce the risk of accidental war.

Rusk was in Washington when news came of a "breakthrough" in the Moscow negotiations. Khrushchev had decided to accept a test ban limited to the atmosphere, outer space, and underwater. On July 18 Rusk met with Kennedy to discuss the news. He had never seen the President in a happier mood. After so many difficult and dangerous times, there was new hope. One problem remained: Khrushchev wanted to couple the limited test ban treaty with a nonaggression pact between NATO and the Warsaw Pact.

Rusk saw this as a scheme to get the West to recognize East Germany, which he knew would be unacceptable to Bonn, and it was decided to promise Khrushchev only "substantive discussions" for an East-West nonaggression pact. Rusk suspected additional Russian motives. "They know NATO will not attack and that we will not give Germany nuclear weapons. The Russians have twenty-two divisions in East Germany, but they are there primarily to keep things under control and to frighten the Poles and the Czechs." He saw Khrushchev as worried about the stability of the Eastern frontier. "If there were a stabilized agreement on the situation in central Europe, we could work out what Khrushchev seems to want." Another reason for Khrushchev's acceptance of the limited test ban was the Sino-Soviet split and rising tensions on the Soviet Union's border with China.

Rusk led the administration's efforts to gain approval of the Test Ban Treaty by a skeptical U.S. Senate. Significant voices were raised against it, including Barry Goldwater of Arizona. Acheson denounced the sudden "flirtation" with the Russians. At hearings before the Senate Foreign Relations Committee, Rusk gave what Senator Everett Dirksen called "an excellent presentation—a good many things were clarified." Rusk stressed that the treaty would end the growing and dangerous problem of nuclear fallout in the atmosphere: "We have an obligation to safeguard the genetic integrity of the human race." He also said that "there is nothing in this treaty that is inconsistent with vigilance. The treaty itself," he pointed out, "does not rely on trust."

Rusk cautioned against euphoria and warned against expecting détente with the Russians. He said that the treaty was a first step and that he did not expect any general settlement of Cold War issues. There would be a step-by-step approach in future negotiations. Problems should not be linked together; they must be worked out carefully, one at a time. He held out hope for progress: "The most important thing about the treaty is, therefore, what it may symbolize and what new paths it may open."

The Senate approved the treaty in August by a vote of 80 to 19. Rusk then took on the job of selling the treaty to the Germans. On August 10, after a seven-hour talk with Chancellor Adenauer and Foreign Minister Gerhardt Schroeder in Bonn, he won their approval, assuring them that any future nonaggression pact would be linked to effective guarantees on the security of West Berlin.

Rusk led the American delegation to Moscow for the formal signing of the treaty. It was his first visit to the Soviet Union. Gromyko met him at the airport, and there were broad smiles all around. Rusk declared that the United States was resolved to make the test ban treaty "a turning point in the affairs of mankind." The treaty itself, he said, "can do no more than prevent the world from becoming even more dangerous than it has been in the past. But it can be regarded as a first step to be followed by others that can accumulate into a genuine effort to make this a less dangerous and, eventually, a peaceful planet."

At the signing ceremony, in the vaulted, white marble Catherine Hall in the Kremlin's Great Palace, Rusk initialed the treaty for the United States, followed by Lord Home for Britain and Andrei Gromyko for the Soviet Union. More than one hundred other nations would follow them in accepting the treaty. Rusk clinked champagne glasses with Khrushchev in a toast to "peace and friendship." Khrushchev took credit for the idea of the limited test ban treaty, saying it was a Russian proposal agreed to by the two Western powers. Rusk diplomatically agreed. A band played George Gershwin's "Love Walked In," and the reception after the treaty-signing was filled with warm smiles, firm handshakes, and friendly jokes. Khrushchev posed for pictures with the elders of the Russian Orthodox Church.

Khrushchev invited Rusk to his office for a private visit. Warm and friendly, he spoke to Rusk about the bravery of the Russian people. Rusk said, "Mr. Chairman, you don't have to persuade me of that. We know the Russian people are brave." And he recalled the defense of Leningrad by the men, women, and children of the city under the most terrible circumstances over a period of three years, describing it as "one of the great epics in the history of warfare." He saw Khrushchev's eyes fill with tears. Turning to a lighter subject he asked Khrushchev how it was that he, as an old Bolshevik, quoted the Bible so much. Khrushchev launched into a ten-minute talk about his childhood and the old priest who had been his first teacher. He had great affection for the priest; he told Rusk that "he had learned Russian largely through reading the Bible."

Khrushchev was leaving the next day for a vacation at his villa in Gagra, on the Black Sea, and he asked Rusk to join him for "friendly discussions." In Gagra Rusk found the Soviet Premier relaxed and informal, dressed in an embroidered Ukrainian peasant shirt. They sat at a conference table which had been set up on a verandah overlooking the rocky, sun-drenched coast. Rusk was impressed with the beauty of the site and the luxury of the villa, filled with Oriental rugs and fine furniture. Khrushchev suggested a swim in his pool, and

Rusk, taking no chances on offending his host, agreed, even though he did not know how to swim. He donned a set of water wings and paddled around in the pool.

Afterward, Khrushchev challenged him to a game of badminton. In stocking feet on an Oriental rug, they played a few points without a net. The official Soviet news agency TASS reported that Rusk started out fast but Khrushchev pulled ahead and won. "You play well," Rusk told Khrushchev. "Practice," Khrushchev replied. American reporters were left to wonder how the fifty-four-year-old Secretary of State, a former tennis player at Oxford, could lose to the portly sixty-nine-year-old Soviet Premier. Rusk was noncommittal as usual, but hinted that the win was another triumph for Russian diplomacy.

The discussions between the two men were friendly but inconclusive. Rusk was amazed that during the several hours he spent at Khrushchev's villa not once was the Premier interrupted by a note or a phone call. Khrushchev was obviously still preoccupied with Berlin. At one point Rusk was taken aback by the blunt question "Are you really prepared to use nuclear weapons to defend Berlin?" Then Khrushchev looked him coldly in the eye and said, "Macmillan has told me he will not use nuclear weapons to defend Berlin. De Gaulle has told me the French will not use nuclear weapons either. What makes you think the Americans will use nuclear weapons if we move into Berlin?"

Rusk tried not to show his surprise at the question as he formulated a response. "Well, Mr. Chairman," he said, carefully choosing his words, "you had better believe that we Americans are just damn fool enough to do it." Khrushchev became very subdued.

On his return to Washington Rusk found a kind note on his desk from President Kennedy: "I understand that you are planning to take a little vacation next week, and if your plans have not been finalized I would like to again suggest that you spend some time at Camp David. I hear that it is beautiful right now and it is unoccupied." He took advantage of the offer, and on August 19 went to Camp David with his family for four days of relaxation. It was the first respite from his seven-day-week, sixteen-hour-day schedule since taking office.

The test ban treaty and the "good feeling" of Moscow did not, of course, lead to a general settlement or a solution to Cold War issues. It did, however, demonstrate the ability of the superpowers to cooperate to remove a dangerous threat to human life and to retard the spread of nuclear weapons. It was significant psychologically as well, showing that the United States and the Soviet Union could take an important step in arms control. If it was not a new era in relations between the superpowers, there was at least a new mutual willingness to enter into discussions to defuse world tensions.

Rusk's statement in 1961 to Chancellor Adenauer that his greatest ambition was to be able to pass the Berlin problem on to his successor turned out to be prophetic. Although his own further negotiations on Berlin and Central Europe foundered, an accord between the Soviet Union and West Germany on Central Europe's frontiers in 1970 opened the way for a new four-power agreement in 1971 guaranteeing Western rights to Berlin. Since that time Berlin has happily been removed as a flashpoint of tension between East and West. Rusk, however, could claim credit for one remarkable achievement. In the space of only three short years he had skillfully maneuvered Khrushchev's impulses toward direct confrontation away from Cuba and Berlin to a friendly game of badminton.

"The Battleground of Freedom":
Crises in the Third World

THE process of decolonization was irresistible, the source of sweeping change throughout the world. By 1961 forty new nations had sprung into existence since World War II, nineteen since the beginning of 1960, and many more would follow. Rusk came into office seeking to establish a new American policy toward these developing countries and the "nonaligned" nations of the world. He rejected John Foster Dulles's view that neutralism was "immoral" and thought it was wrong to suppose that every nation not for the United States was against it. He spoke of a world in turmoil, in the midst of a revolution of rising expectations, and he believed that the United States could capture the moral leadership of this movement because of its history and values. The United States, he pointed out, had been one of the first nations in the history of the world to throw off the yoke of colonialism, and it had demonstrated the power of a free, democratic society to build a nation and fuel economic and social progress.

Rusk had a unique insight into the developing world because of his childhood in Cherokee County and his work at the Rockefeller Foundation. In his speeches to African and Latin American leaders he would tell them that he had been born in an area, rural Georgia, which in many ways was a developing country, without adequate roads, housing, or education. He pointed to the fact that, in his lifetime, it had been changed through private initiative and wise and humane government policies. During his years at the Rockefeller Foundation he had visited many Third World countries. He was familiar with their problems and knew something about how to help solve them.

Rusk saw the United States' role to be the establishment of a far-reaching program of foreign aid and the encouragement of private investment and trade with developing countries. He took the lead in selling the Alliance for Progress and various other foreign aid programs to Congress. His emphasis at first was on economic and social progress rather than military assistance: foreign aid had "more solemn purposes" than merely meeting the threat of communism. In Latin America, he said, there was a need to reduce the gap between the rich and the poor. "This is the real issue, not to be confused with Sino-Soviet penetration."

In May 1961 he unveiled an innovative four-year, $26 billion foreign aid program to assist developing countries, which he called the "battleground of freedom," to reach the stage of self-sustaining long-term growth. He called for a new type of aid program under a unified administration, the Agency for International Development, which should have borrowing authority to finance long-term commitments. Not only capital projects but also social facilities—low-cost housing, model farms, schools, sanitation projects—should be financed. Technical assistance and food aid should be provided. There would be a country-wide plan for each nation to coordinate aid funds with money from local sources and loans from international agencies and foreign banks.

The bright promise of this "new day" for neutralism and the campaign to "make the world safe for diversity" was too ambitious and idealistic to last. Congress not only refused to grant long-term development authority, but each year slashed both the amount of money and the number of countries eligible for aid. The plans for social reform drew opposition in recipient countries from the entrenched power elites. Many of the problems proved too overwhelming to resolve. Most of all, however, the realities of the Cold War intruded. Looming East-West conflicts commanded attention, draining resources and the energies of the Kennedy administration. Economic development and social progress in the Third World became secondary to keeping countries out of the Communist camp. At a National Security Council meeting on January 22, 1963, President Kennedy said he wanted to make it clear that aid was to serve the security of the United States and was not primarily for humanitarian purposes.

With the rapidly growing number of newly independent nations in the world, primarily in Africa and Asia, Rusk was faced with the problem of how to devote even a small part of his precious time to the foreign ministers and ambassadors of each. To get to know them he spent two weeks every September in New York at the United Nations, meeting all the foreign ministers and delegates and discussing their needs and problems, armed with thick black briefing books on each nation. In his office, on the slide-out tray of his desk, he kept a map of Africa so he could check the exact location of each African country before talking to an ambassador. Rusk was the first Secretary of State who dealt with a world that was not predominantly European in character and orientation.

In Latin America, Cuba dominated his personal diplomacy. Castro was seeking to export his revolution, sometimes by violent means, to other countries of the hemisphere, and Kennedy was determined to prevent any additional Communist beachheads in Latin America. In January 1962 Rusk led the American delegation at the conference of the Organization of American States in Punta del Este, Uruguay. Kennedy wanted the OAS to invoke economic and diplomatic sanctions against Cuba. The mission, Rusk's first appearance before the OAS, turned out to be a substantial success. As Arthur Schlesinger, who accompanied him, wrote, "[H]e strove coolly to work out the best possible combination of condemnation and consensus." In one speech he evoked his own background to argue why the way of the United States was superior to that of Cuba:

Perhaps you'll forgive me for a personal recollection. Like millions of present day North Americans I spent my earliest years in what people would now call underdeveloped circumstances. We were pre-scientific and pre-technical; we were without public health or medical care; typhoid, pellagra, hookworm, and malaria were a part of the environment in which providence had placed us. Our schools were primitive. Our fathers and mothers earned a meager living with backbreaking toil.

Neighbor helped neighbor to build a house, a barn, or to pass along news about new projects and new methods. They joined together to build roads until public funds could take over the burden. They pooled their limited resources to hire a school teacher or a doctor. Bits of capital began to accumulate and this was reinvested in growth and development. More and more young people managed to get to the university and more and more of these brought their learning back to the benefit of their own people.

These changes did not take place without struggle. Years of thought and work and debate were required to prepare America for the necessary steps of self-help and social reform. . . . But a succession of progressive leaders, determined to bring about social change within a framework of political consent, carried through an "alliance for progress" within the United States.

In personal meetings with delegates Rusk patiently worked on getting the strongest resolution possible against Cuban subversion. When the conference deadlocked he won a postponement of the vote to gain time. In the end he achieved a two-thirds majority—fourteen votes—to expel Cuba from the OAS. Only Cuba voted against the resolution; six other members abstained. Rusk received high praise for his performance. When he returned to Washington he was given an emotional welcome on the White House lawn by President Kennedy, Vice President Johnson, and leading members of Congress. "Rusk," declared Kennedy, "did himself great credit and he did his country credit." At Kennedy's insistence Rusk gave a fifteen-minute nationwide radio and television report on the conference. Castroism, he said, was officially labeled as incompatible with the American system and would remain isolated both economically and politically.

Some years later, in November 1965, during another visit to Uruguay, Rusk was the target of the only physical attack he experienced during his eight years in office. While he was laying a wreath on a ceremonial occasion in downtown Montevideo, a short, slight man described by the press as "semi-youthful" darted out of the crowd toward him, followed immediately by a burly Uruguayan security guard. Rusk's six-foot-three American bodyguard went into action and promptly tackled the wrong man—the security guard—thinking that he was the greater threat. The young man reached Rusk before anyone could stop him, but when they were face to face, Rusk recalls, he became rather frightened and looked uncertain about what to do. Then, throwing back his head, he pursed his lips and tried to spit at Rusk, but nothing came out. As a startled Rusk looked on, the man simply shouted, "This is in the name of my people." He then fled and was quickly seized by police.

The photographers on the scene made no attempt to intervene, but instead backed up to focus their cameras. At least one caught the incident on film, including the precise moment the man was trying to spit at Rusk. He jumped up and down shouting, "I got it, I got it!" There was only a minor problem—there was no spit in the picture. But the next day the photo appeared on page one of *The New York Times* showing the man's head tilted back, a big wad of spit hanging from his lips, and another blob, as large as a golf ball, heading ominously toward the unflinching Rusk. Someone clearly had dubbed in the spit. In the accompanying story Rusk was quoted as saying, "With the exception of one young individual whose welcome seemed to be a little unconventional," he found Uruguay "extremely hospitable."

Communist subversion was also a matter of concern in the Dominican Republic in 1961. The Kennedy administration, like the Eisenhower administration, was opposed to the ruling dictator of that country, Rafael Trujillo, a corrupt and repressive tyrant, fearing the Dominican Republic could become another Cuba. The policy of the Bureau of Inter-American Affairs at State, which Rusk inherited, was to force Trujillo out, but Rusk was worried about the consequences of an American-led campaign to oust him. Just after taking office, on February 15, 1961, he wrote a memo to President Kennedy warning of a Communist takeover if the elimination of the windfall sugar quota for the Dominican Republic resulted in Trujillo's downfall. But American officials in Santo Domingo, primarily from the CIA, continued to put out feelers to non-Communist dissidents.

On May 30, 1961, Trujillo was assassinated by a clique of rebellious military officers. The news of the assassination was withheld in the Dominican Republic, but the CIA notified Washington, and Rusk was the first high official to learn of Trujillo's death. The President was in Paris at the time to see de Gaulle (Rusk was preparing to join him), and on the morning of June 1 he telephoned Kennedy with the news. Later that day Pierre Salinger, the President's press secretary, made the first public announcement of the assassination, by a slip of the tongue to reporters. Rusk immediately gave Salinger "unshirted hell" because Trujillo's son Ramfis happened to be in Paris, and Rusk was afraid he (and the rest of the world) would think that the United States had something to do with the murder and would make a statement to mar the President's visit. (Kennedy also reproached Salinger, saying, "We now have later intelligence that Trujillo may not be dead." And Salinger replied, "Mr. President, if he's not, I am.")

In fact, allegations of American complicity were close to the mark; the CIA station chief in the Dominican Republic had known of the plot against Trujillo and had even supplied machine guns (which apparently were not used) to the conspirators. The CIA, it seemed, had acted on its own, and Rusk later testified to Congress that he had not known of the CIA role or the intentions of Dominican dissidents to kill Trujillo.

Rusk and Kennedy moved quietly to keep Ramfis from coming to power and threw U.S. support behind Joaquín Balaguer, the nominal President under Trujillo. Later, they were bitterly disappointed when, in an election on December 19, 1962, Balaguer was defeated by Juan Bosch, a visionary writer and intellectual who was thought to be incapable of stable leadership. Bosch's election set the stage for more unrest, which would erupt into crisis in 1965, during the Johnson administration.

An area of the world that was relatively quiet in the early 1960s was the Middle East, where U.N. forces stationed on the frontier between Israel and Egypt maintained an uneasy truce. President Gamal Abdel Nasser of Egypt was one of the neutralist leaders of the world with whom the Kennedy administration wished to establish good relations. Rusk went along with this effort, but he considered Nasser unstable and resented his anti-American tirades. In private conversation Nasser was agreeable and pleasant, but speaking before a large crowd he could not resist the temptation to launch into bitter attacks against the United States.

In September 1962, after the death of the Imam of Yemen, Nasser intervened in a civil war over the succession, backing republican forces against the royalists. When Saudi Arabia began to aid the royalist side, there was fear of a wider conflict. Rusk tried to persuade the Egyptians and the Saudis to disengage, but there was nothing he could accomplish because the United States had little influence in the region. After the outbreak of the Yemen war, all further efforts to better relations with Nasser proved futile.

Rusk took an active role in the affairs of the Central Treaty Organization (CENTO), a strange alliance initially including Turkey, Iraq, Iran, and Pakistan, which was created by John Foster Dulles to protect what he called the "northern tier" against the Soviet Union. Both the United States and Britain were "associated members" committed to cooperation in security and defense arrangements. Originally called the Baghdad Pact, the organization officially changed its name to CENTO in 1958 after Iraq withdrew as a member.

By the 1960s the leaders of the CENTO countries were using the organization primarily as a means to build up their own military establishments and as a source of foreign aid. Nevertheless, the organization was an American defense commitment, and Rusk faithfully attended all the CENTO meetings, emphasizing the solemn promise of the United States to defend the area against possible Soviet aggression. He became acquainted with the Shah of Iran, whom he regarded as an "earnest man who was hardworking and knowledgeable about world affairs." He clashed with the Shah, however, over the buildup of Iran's armed forces. Rusk believed that the Shah was diverting resources away from the economic and social development of his country, and he did his best to restrain the leader's appetite for arms.

Rusk's talks with Mohammed Ayub Khan, the President of Pakistan, were dominated by Ayub Khan's hatred of India and the problem of Kashmir. In Rusk's view Pakistan was interested in building up its army primarily to threaten India. He tried to get negotiations started between Pakistan and India over Kashmir and to work out their problems so that they could form a common front for the defense of their northern frontier.

Rusk felt little warmth or affection for Prime Minister Nehru of India, who treated him as if he were a member of a lower Indian caste. He also deeply resented the strident anti-Americanism of Nehru's Foreign Minister, Krishna Menon. When Rusk talked with Nehru, who had a deep feeling for the Vale of Kashmir because of his family ties to the area, Nehru would stare out the window and seem not to hear, making replies that were uncommunicative and in the nature of a brush-off. All Rusk's efforts to resolve the problem of Kashmir met with frustration. After a 1965 meeting during hostilities between India and Pakistan he wrote, "Neither has taken our advice seriously for the past 17 years—it is not up to the United States to settle this affair. The U.N. and the British should be out in front."

When India took over the Portuguese colony of Goa by force in December 1962, Rusk believed the action exposed the hypocrisy of Nehru's and Menon's sanctimonious embrace of nonviolence. He incurred the wrath of the American ambassador in New Delhi, John Kenneth Galbraith, as well as the resentment of some in the White House, for his failure to put pressure on the Portuguese to withdraw voluntarily from Goa before the Indian invasion. After the takeover, Rusk sided with the Portuguese and condemned the Indian action. He could not condone military force, despite its purpose of ending colonial rule.

On the way home from a CENTO meeting in 1961 Rusk stopped in Belgrade to pay a call on Marshal Tito. He was well disposed toward Tito because Yugoslavia's defection from the Warsaw Pact in the 1940s had opened the way for a solution to the guerrilla problem in Greece. Tito saw himself, Nehru, and Nasser as the leaders of the nonaligned group of nations. Rusk was proud of the fact that he was the first Secretary of State to visit Yugoslavia and happy that the warmth of his reception would give the Russians cause for worry. Tito impressed him as "thoughtful, articulate, and well informed." Deploring congressional restrictions on foreign aid to Yugoslavia, he believed that past aid had been essential in keeping that country independent of the Soviet bloc.

Regional disarmament was a constant theme Rusk raised in his talks with Third World leaders. He saw no need for large military establishments in the nations of the Third World and argued that instead of spending money on arms they should give priority to economic and social development. He worked unsuccessfully to get an arms limitation agreement between India and Pakistan, and in the opening speech at the Geneva Disarmament Conference in March 1962 he called on the Third World representatives to open negotiations among themselves on ways to limit their own military forces. This suggestion, he later noted, was met with "colossal indifference." The Foreign Minister of Nigeria came to him and boldly denounced the whole idea. "In fact," he chided, "if we can get you and the Soviet Union to disarm, my country will be able to buy arms more cheaply." Rusk believed that at least he had exposed the hypocrisy of Third World leaders who applauded arms control for the superpowers but had very little interest in it for themselves.

The Kennedy administration was the first in American history to be faced with the task of devising a foreign policy toward Africa. As the one continent not tied by alliances to the United States, Africa was not vital to U.S. security, but there was determination to prevent penetration by the Communist bloc. Russian and Chinese Communist agents were active in Ghana, Guinea, and Mali, and were seeking to establish a Central African base in the chaotic Congo. Rusk and Mennen Williams, the head of the Bureau of African Affairs at State, agreed that the United States should identify with the movement for decolonization and should offer development aid to the newly emerging states. At the same time Rusk believed that the United States should deliberately downplay its role in Africa and be content to serve as a "junior partner" to the British and the French. He cautioned U.S. ambassadors in Africa against trying to become what he called "Mr. Big" in African capitals. He thought it unwise to try to supplant the British and the French, who had vastly more experience, as the chief Western influence.

Rusk believed that Africans were basically resistant to Communist ideological penetration and thought development aid and the wooing of key leaders would cause the new African states to identify with the West. He reported to Kennedy that even Gromyko had remarked that

"Africans don't make very good communists." The major problem in the region was how to mold the newly independent African nations, whose frontiers were accidents of European colonization, into viable political and economic units. Rusk sought to encourage the emergence of regional economic groupings, such as an East Africa Federation and a West Africa Federation.

In Africa personal diplomacy was important, and Rusk advised Kennedy to organize warm White House receptions for visiting African leaders, especially Sékou Touré of Guinea and Kwame Nkrumah of Ghana. At the State Department's urging Kennedy wrote President Nkrumah on June 29, 1961, and promised American aid to construct a $25 million hydroelectric project on the Volta River. That summer, however, the mercurial Nkrumah denounced the United States at a meeting of nonaligned nations in Belgrade and warmed up to the Soviets, signing an aid agreement for the training of Ghanian cadets in Moscow. The Russians seemed to encourage a messianic streak in Nkrumah, who believed that he was divinely ordained to become the leader of all Africa. Kennedy became disturbed and in September 1961 held up the final decision to finance the Volta dam.

On December 5 the Volta project was again considered at a meeting of the National Security Council. Kennedy asked, "How can we justify a decision to help Nkrumah in the light of his leftward and authoritarian course?" Robert Kennedy strongly opposed the dam and advised his brother to cancel it. Douglas Dillon agreed, calling Nkrumah another Castro. But Rusk argued forcefully in favor of the project. "We have made a commitment," he said; a refusal to go forward would be misunderstood all over Africa. For Rusk the issue involved the integrity of the President; other nations must be able to rely on the word of the United States. The matter had been fully reviewed in June, and the President had committed himself. The United States must honor its commitments—this was one of Rusk's deepest beliefs. Reluctantly the President agreed and allowed the project to proceed, although, he said, "I can feel the cold wind of [Robert's] disapproval on the back of my neck." The Volta dam was a success, and later even Robert Kennedy admitted this was the correct decision.

The Kennedy administration had a chance to demonstrate its commitment to anticolonialism in March 1961, when it supported an Afro-Asian resolution in the U.N. Security Council that called for self-determination in the Portuguese colony of Angola. Portugal was a NATO ally and the custodian of an important NATO air and naval base in the Azores, so the vote carried risks for American defense policy. The State Department was split on the issue, and it was Rusk who made the recommendation, accepted by Kennedy, to vote in favor of the resolution. It was essential to convince the Africans and Asians that the United States meant what it said about colonialism.

That month Rusk went to Lisbon to see Antonio Salazar, the Portuguese dictator and Prime Minister, a visit he later called an "eerie experience." They met in a room in Salazar's palace in which the curtains were drawn and the lights very dim. The Portuguese strongman sat behind a large desk, looking "like a ghost" and saying very little. Rusk explained the reasons for the U.S. vote and asked him to grant independence to Portugal's African colonies, but it was evident that decolonization would not take place as long as Salazar was in power. At one point he said, "I cannot give in Africa what I cannot grant to my own people. You Americans go around talking about freedom, but you succeed only in implementing communism."

The major African crisis the Kennedy administration confronted was the civil war in the Republic of the Congo. The former Belgian Congo, now called Zaire, became independent on June 30, 1960. The Belgians had pulled out precipitously in the face of rioting in the capital city of Léopoldville, leaving a government woefully inadequate even to keep order. In the summer of 1960 a United Nations peacekeeping force intervened to prevent civil war. By the time Kennedy became President the weak and inept central government in Léopoldville headed by Joseph Kasavubu faced major rebellion, and the Congo was threatened with disintegration. In the south, in Elisabethville, the capital of Katanga province, the wily Moise Tshombe had announced the creation of an independent state. Katanga was the richest area of the Congo, endowed with important mineral resources, notably diamond and copper mines. In the north, in Stanleyville, the pro-Communist Antoine Gizenga, with help from Nasser's Egypt and the Soviet Union, announced the formation of a rebel government that claimed sovereignty over the whole Congo. Another Congolese leader, the charismatic Patrice Lumumba, who was pro-Communist and antiwhite, had been imprisoned by Kasavubu.

Reviewing Congo policy with Kennedy on February 1, 1961, Rusk made three recommendations: that the U.N. peacekeeping force be granted a broader mandate to control all principal military elements in the Congo; that Kasavubu be encouraged to establish a broad-based coalition government that would include "Lumumba elements" but not Lumumba himself; and that the U.N. be given a greater administrative role in the country. His underlying aims were to blunt Communist penetration in the Congo and to prevent its disintegration into many different tribal-based units.

A crisis began, however, when on February 13, 1961, Lumumba was killed under suspicious circumstances—just after Kasavubu had turned him over to Tshombe for safekeeping. The Soviet Union blamed the U.N. force created by Secretary General Dag Hammarskjöld and angrily called for Hammarskjöld's dismissal and the election of a "troika"—representatives from the Western, Communist, and neutralist camps—to replace him. In the Congo Lumumba's death spurred new unrest, and Kennedy in a stern warning to the Soviets pledged that the United States would oppose any government that tried to intervene unilaterally.

After the warning to the Soviets, Rusk placed more confidence than ever in the U.N.'s ability to manage the situation. The U.N. force was controlled by Hammarskjöld's deputy, Rusk's old friend Ralph Bunche, and they exchanged views often during the crisis. The U.N.'s main task was to arrange for the Congolese parliament to form a government of national unity, and in July the intelligent but bland Cyrille Adoula was named Prime Minister and Defense Minister. There were two main dangers to the fledgling Adoula government, Gizenga's insurrection in Stanleyville and the continued armed secession in Katanga. The first was handled easily: the Congolese parliament voted to censure Gizenga, and U.N. troops moved unopposed into Stanleyville to restore law and order.

The problem of Katanga proved more difficult. Tshombe's rump regime in Katanga had important backing in Belgian financial circles interested in the profits of the diamond and copper mines. Tshombe was also aided by a white mercenary army—Belgians, South Africans, and Rhodesians—and there was political support in both Europe and the United States for a "free Katanga."

Rusk feared that military action to end Katanga's secession might precipitate full-scale civil war, giving the Russians an excuse to intervene. The U.N. troops, the "casques bleus," as they were called, maintained an uneasy vigil, adhering to their peacekeeping duties. In September, however, fighting broke out with the Katanga rebels, and Rusk had a brief spat with Hammarskjöld. He called Hammarskjöld to tell him that the President was "extremely upset" that the U.N. troops were engaging in military operations. Hammarskjöld became "infuriated" and accused him of taking the part of the Katanga rebels. A few days later, on September 17, 1961, Hammarskjöld was killed in an airplane crash in the Congo, where he was trying to arrange a cease-fire. When he learned the news Rusk was visibly shaken and saddened; he especially regretted their last, acrimonious exchange, for he genuinely admired Hammarskjöld because of his inner strength and, most of all, his passionate belief in the principles of the U.N. Charter.

After the death of Hammarskjöld the Soviets stepped up their campaign in the United Nations for a rotating troika as Secretary General. The Russian proposal was an obvious attempt to dilute the power of the Secretary General and ultimately the United Nations itself. Rusk spent much of his time in diplomatic efforts to kill the troika idea, and by October the Soviets knew that their campaign was a lost cause. Rusk threatened a veto in the Security Council, and a majority of the nonaligned nations opposed the suggestion as well. After the Soviets finally dropped their demand, U Thant of Burma was elected as Secretary General. Most observers gave Rusk the major credit for preserving the office of Secretary General and his authority to manage peacekeeping operations.

After the resolution of the troika controversy, Rusk maintained his opposition to the use of force by U.N. troops to end the Katanga secession. On November 11, 1961, he wrote a memorandum to the President arguing against "a solution by force to the problem of Congolese unity. . . . Pressures from the government of the Congo, the Soviet Union, and the more extreme Africans and Asians will be directed toward adoption of a new United Nations mandate requiring the U.N. task force to support the Congolese army in a military operation designed to bring about the reintegration of Katanga. We will make every effort to resist these pressures. The United Nations and the government of the Congo could only win a pyrrhic victory if it were to abandon the course of conciliation and persuasion." Despite Rusk's views the United States accepted a strong resolution in the Security Council on November 24 giving the Secretary General a mandate to use "a requisite measure of force, if necessary" for the apprehension of mercenaries in Katanga.

Rusk feared that the fighting could lead to a split in the NATO alliance. He also had doubts whether the U.N. forces had enough military power to succeed against Tshombe's army. By early December, however, there was no choice but to use military force, and Rusk, working closely with Bunche, reevaluated his position. Fighting once again broke out between Katanga mercenaries and U.N. troops, and Rusk reluctantly approved a limited U.N. military action designed to "quickly achieve control of the key points in Elisabethville, communications centers, power stations, small airfields, and industrial centers.'' He asked McNamara for the Defense Department view on what it would take for the U.N. force to succeed in its mission, worked out the details of a military plan with Bunche, and was instrumental in providing U.S. air transport to reinforce the U.N. troops in Elisabethville.

Rusk undertook diplomatic efforts to reassure the British, Belgians, and French of U.N. intentions in order to try to obtain their cooperation. He argued that there was no satisfactory alternative to limited military force: ''We cannot urge the U.N. to cease its military activities in Katanga. To try to force the U.N. to let Katangan military opposition again prevent it from implementing its mandate would destroy for good the image of the U.S. as a supporter of the U.N.'s collective efforts and would open the door to communism in central Africa by destroying all possibility for continued moderate control in the government in Léopoldville.'' Rusk believed that if the U.N. effort in Katanga failed there either would be a left-wing extremist takeover in Léopoldville or the Congo would disintegrate into three or more splinter states. ''In either case, the extremists, with the help of the Soviet bloc, would continue warfare until Katanga was brought under their control. Their efforts would eventually result in a direct military confrontation of East and West in the Congo.''

Rusk still argued against allowing the U.N. to apply ''its entire military means'' to occupy Katanga and destroy the Tshombe regime. This, he said, ''could result in serious damage to the industrial potential of the province, greatly risk the lives of European and African populations, and might require considerable time and troop reinforcement on the U.N. side. The U.K., France, and Belgium would certainly oppose such action.'' Rusk called for negotiations with Tshombe to parallel the U.N. military action. That policy seemed to be succeeding when, on December 14, Tshombe agreed to negotiate with Adoula. A cease-fire was called on December 18, and three days later Tshombe and Adoula met in Kitona, a town in the southwestern Congo. There, in the presence of Bunche and the U.S. Ambassador, Edmund Gullion, they signed an agreement in which Tshombe accepted the authority of the central government.

It appeared that the crisis in the Congo had been resolved, but that hope was premature. In 1962 Tshombe went back to his old ways, operating independently of the central government: he refused to transmit tax revenues to Léopoldville and denounced the Kitona agreement with Adoula. Tshombe's defiance was supported by the

Belgian copper-mining company Union Minière du Haut Katanga, as well as conservative opinion in Belgium, the United States, France, and Britain.

Rusk, preoccupied with other matters, left the situation to George Ball, who worked out economic and financial pressures on the Katanga government in coordination with the Belgians. But Tshombe continued to play the game of agreeing to American and U.N. conciliation efforts and then not carrying through his commitments. On September 29, 1962, Ball wrote a memo to the President pessimistically stating that "barring some new major effort, our plans for the Congo are slowly sinking in the African ooze." Only after another round of fighting between U.N. troops and Katangan gendarmes in December 1962 was Tshombe defeated. Katanga finally was reintegrated into the central government in January 1963.

Rusk thought that the outcome in the Congo was the best that could be expected under the circumstances. The unity of the central government was preserved, possible Soviet penetration of Central Africa was blunted, and the Congo had a chance to evolve as a united, pro-Western country. The United States had also gained a measure of respect in Africa by its firm support of decolonization and its opposition to European interests that would have maintained Katanga and its rich resources as a neocolonialist reserve. The damage to the NATO alliance was not long-lasting; Belgium, France, and Britain, although they opposed the U.N. military efforts for domestic political reasons, fully understood the aims of American policy and in the end cooperated to defeat the Katanga secession.

The end of the Katanga secession did not, however, end the crisis. In 1964, after Lyndon Johnson became President, there were new troubles. So-called Simba rebels stepped up guerrilla warfare in the northeast, near Stanleyville, and with Chinese Communist help declared a war of national liberation against the central government. By a bizarre turn of events, Tshombe returned from exile in Spain in June 1964 and was named Prime Minister by President Joseph Kasavubu early in July. Tshombe immediately hired another white mercenary army to combat the Simba rebels, which alienated other African governments. American officials were embarrassed at having to work with Tshombe, but they too were interested in quelling the rebellion.

The new crisis came to a head in November 1964 when Simba rebels in control of Stanleyville rounded up over three thousand whites from nineteen countries and held them hostage. Tshombe's army drove toward Stanleyville, but this only increased the danger that the hos-

tages would be massacred. Reluctantly, American and Belgian officials decided they would have to act. George Ball convinced President
Johnson to allow the use of American C-130 transport planes to mount
a rescue operation.

The Belgian cabinet met on the crisis, and Paul-Henri Spaak, the
Foreign Minister, called Rusk from Brussels: "I am here at a cabinet
meeting and would like to know the American view on this matter."
Rusk told him, "We are prepared to do whatever you want to do. If
you wish to commit your paratrooper battalion, we will make our
planes available and do everything possible to make the operation a
success. If you decide you do not wish to do so, we will understand."
Spaak was amazed: "Do you mean to say that the great United States
of America is leaving this decision to Belgium?" Rusk said, "Yes,
that is exactly our position." "That's incredible!" Spaak replied. "No
decision affecting Belgium has ever been made in Belgium before,"
he remarked, only half in jest. Spaak was elated and the cabinet made
its decision. The Belgian paratroopers would go in to save the
hostages.

At dawn on November 24, 1964, twelve U.S. C-130s dropped 545
Belgian paratroopers over Stanleyville. The rescue operation was a
great success, and the hostages were freed with minimal loss of life.
Two days later the Americans and Belgians cooperated in another
rescue operation 240 miles from Stanleyville, near Paulis, to rescue
several hundred additional hostages.

After the hostage rescue missions the Chinese-inspired Simba rebellion faded, but upheaval in the Congo continued. In October 1965
President Kasavubu dismissed Tshombe, and in November General
Joseph Mobutu deposed Kasavubu in a coup d'état. The United
States and its European allies wearily and reluctantly recognized the
new military government. Working with this military dictatorship was
now the only alternative in the Congo. The reality of American policy
in Africa fell short of its ideals.

In his efforts to improve relations with black Africa, Rusk soon
found that one of the greatest obstacles was racial discrimination at
home. In the 1960s, numbers of black diplomats from African nations
came for the first time to live and work in Washington, and Rusk
found that they were systematically excluded from many hotels, restaurants, and clubs, not only in Virginia and Maryland but in the
capital itself. He also had to deal with widespread discrimination prac-
ticed against African students in the United States. On one occasion
a group of African diplomats came to his office and discussed their

biggest problem of the moment: where to get a haircut in Washington. An exasperated Rusk finally told them, "You can get a haircut the same place I get my hair cut, and that is the little room next door. Any time you come by, a barber will be here in thirty seconds."

Rusk sought the advancement of black employees at the State Department and the appointment of black Foreign Service officers. When he realized that a longtime messenger at the State Department had reached the top of his pay scale and was no longer eligible for annual raises, he appointed him Assistant to the Secretary. He also asked for a review of the Foreign Service test to determine whether there was any bias against black applicants. Among the blacks he promoted within the department was Carl Rowan, who served as Assistant Secretary for Public Affairs and later as Ambassador to Finland. One day Rowan told him an amusing story. He lived in a neighborhood not far from Rusk and happened to be outside mowing his lawn without a shirt when a big Cadillac drove by and a dignified lady rolled her window down, put her head out, and called to him: "Boy! Oh, boy. What are they paying you to mow this grass?" Rowan turned to her and said, "Well, as a matter of fact, the lady of the house lets me sleep with her." Suitably shocked, the woman drove off in a huff.

Rusk was a critic not only of racial segregation that affected foreign diplomats, but also discrimination against and segregation of American blacks. He was outspoken in defense of the Justice Department's regulations against interstate bus segregation. When he was requested to speak in Atlanta before the Georgia State Bar Association, he asked the president, Robert Troutman, whether the Georgia bar had any black members. "It doesn't now," Troutman replied, taking the hint, "but it will by the time you get here." Rusk later boasted that he single-handedly integrated the Georgia bar.

Rusk was also the first administration witness to testify in favor of President Kennedy's civil rights bill in 1963, which banned racial discrimination by all businesses serving the public. When Rusk entered the white-columned caucus room to give his testimony before the Senate Commerce Committee, many of the senators present settled in for a slow day. Few fireworks were expected from the mild-mannered, judicious Secretary of State. But his testimony surprised. In soft tones, with an accent still reminiscent of his Georgia country boyhood, Rusk spoke out eloquently against racial discrimination as a moral liability for the United States and a propaganda asset for the Communists:

Racial discrimination here at home has important effects on our foreign relations. This is not because such discrimination is unique to the United States. Discrimination on account of race, color, religion, national or tribal origin may be found in other countries. But the United States is widely regarded as the home of democracy and the leader of the struggle for freedom, for human rights, for human dignity. We are expected to be the model—no higher compliment could be paid to us. So our failures to live up to our proclaimed ideals are noted—and magnified and distorted.

After completing his statement Rusk gave the committee several examples of discrimination against foreign ambassadors and diplomatic personnel in the United States, terming the situation "intolerable." He was immediately attacked by Strom Thurmond, then a Democrat, from South Carolina. "Mr. Secretary," Thurmond snapped at him, "aren't you lending support to the communist line?"

Rusk stiffened noticeably but answered politely: "Why, of course not, Senator," he said icily. "I am here as Secretary of State of the United States to advise the committee of my views." Then Thurmond said, "Mr. Secretary, I'm not sure that you understood my question. I am from South Carolina." Laughter rippled through the spectators when Rusk retorted, "Senator, I understood your question. I am from Georgia."

But Thurmond was not yet through; he pressed Rusk further, asking if he "favored Negro demonstrations." Rusk replied, "Well, Senator, there are various types of demonstrations. I would not wish to make a blanket statement, but I would say this, sir, that if I were denied what our Negro citizens are denied, I would demonstrate."

As the noon bell ended the hearing, Republican Senator Norris Cotton whispered something to the acting committee chairman, John Pastori. Pastori relayed the message aloud: "Mr. Secretary, you have been one of the most effective witnesses that has ever appeared before this Commerce committee." At that the gallery burst into applause, and Senator Thurmond shouted into his microphone, "The audience here is packed with civil righters and left-wingers."

Actually, an account in *Time* later reported, the hearing room was "packed with tourists come to see Washington's prime attraction of the day—a Georgian telling a South Carolinian why racial discrimination is 'incompatible with the great ideals to which our democratic society is dedicated.'"

"We'll Have to Do It in Vietnam": Southeast Asian Turmoil

T HIS is the worst mess the Eisenhower administration left me," John Kennedy grumbled to Rusk after a meeting with the outgoing President just before his inauguration. Eisenhower had taken Kennedy and Rusk aside for a talk about decisions they would face right away, and he had advised them to put troops into Laos, "with other nations if possible, alone if necessary." Laos, he said, was the front line in the defense of Asia against Communist domination.

If the idea of Laos being the linchpin of Asia seems ludicrous in hindsight, it was conventional wisdom in 1961. Laos, bordering on four non-Communist nations—Cambodia, Burma, Thailand, and South Vietnam—"dangled like a rich plum from Asia's heartland," according to *Time*. It was Laos, not South Vietnam, that gave birth to the domino theory, invented by Eisenhower and stated over and over again by politicians and the press. Communism in Laos would spread to its four neighbors and, as *Time* put it, "with those countries under the Red Flag, India would be outflanked . . . Indonesia . . . would be easy plucking." Malaya and Singapore would become "easy stepping-stones for Communist expansion to the ultimate peril of Australia and New Zealand."

The entire range of U.S. policy toward Asia in 1961 was beset with an air of unreality. First, there were the alliances. The outbreak of the Korean War had stimulated the initial round of collective security arrangements, pacts that Rusk helped negotiate while he was head of

Far Eastern Affairs at State. In August 1951 there was a mutual defense treaty with the Philippines, which for that country was aimed more at the Japanese than anyone else, and was the price America had to pay for the Philippines to go along with the plan for a peace of reconciliation with Japan. This was followed by the security treaty with Japan itself, in September 1951, which the Eisenhower administration replaced in January 1960 with a new and stronger treaty of mutual cooperation and security. Then came a tripartite pact with Australia and New Zealand, commonly known as ANZUS, which, like the Philippine treaty, was aimed at containing any future Japanese expansion, at least from the point of view of the two governments "down under." Treaties were also concluded with South Korea in 1953 and the Republic of China in 1954.

Most important of all was the alliance known as SEATO, the Southeast Asia Treaty Organization. That the name echoed NATO was no accident; SEATO was intended by its principal author and proponent, John Foster Dulles, to be for Asia what NATO was for Western Europe, a "bulwark against communist aggression." SEATO was deemed necessary because of the French defeat by the Communist Viet Minh at Dien Bien Phu in 1954. Because the French refused to grant true independence to their colonies in Indochina after World War II, Laos, Vietnam, and Cambodia had not participated in the great wave of decolonization that swept over Asia as Pakistan, India, Burma, Indonesia, Malaya, and the Philippines gained their independence. When the French were finally expelled, in 1954, it was the Communists who could claim the credit, and the movement for independence was tragically transformed into a Communist cause. The initial mistake of U.S. policy in Southeast Asia in the 1940s was not to pressure the French, as the Truman administration pressed the British and the Dutch in Asia, to let their colonies go. The concern was that if the United States pushed the weak French governments of the time too hard, France would not be able to play its role in NATO as a bulwark against the Soviets. By 1950 it was too late. The "fall" of China in 1949 and the Korean War had made Southeast Asia into a new battleground against communism, and the Cold War took precedence over independence and decolonization.

After Dien Bien Phu and the Geneva Conference of 1954, which partitioned Vietnam into North and South and confirmed the independence of Laos and Cambodia under international auspices, Dulles created SEATO at a conference in Manila in September 1954. Its members were an oddly assorted lot: Australia, France, New Zealand, Pakistan, the Philippines, Thailand, the United Kingdom, and the United States. The majority of the SEATO members were non-Asian, and Pakistan joined only under the impression that the alliance might be directed against its enemy, India. There was even some question about whether its scope of protection extended to Laos, Cambodia, and South Vietnam. Although these states were not members, Dulles had pushed through a protocol including them. William Bundy, at the time the CIA staff assistant on the National Security Council, believed the Dulles effort contained an element of bluff.

One of those who was not comfortable with the SEATO treaty in 1954 was private citizen Dean Rusk. He worried about the vast new obligations it imposed, and the way it was accepted in Congress with virtually no debate. As Secretary of State, however, Rusk considered SEATO to be "a solemn treaty commitment binding upon the United States to act to meet the common danger." In later years he would point out that SEATO had been approved by the Senate by a vote of 82 to 1.

Another problem, with tragicomic overtones, was the U.S. relationship with Achmed Sukarno, the President of Indonesia. Since his nation was the most populous and one of the most important in Southeast Asia, Kennedy was anxious to establish good relations with Sukarno, who was also a leader of the neutralist bloc of nations in the U.N. When Sukarno visited Washington in the spring of 1961 Kennedy and Rusk met him at the airport, and Rusk arranged an elaborate diplomatic welcome. Sukarno offended from the first, and both Kennedy and Rusk were soon seething with rage, although they maintained an outward calm. Sukarno took his warm welcome merely as his due, saying, "It is wise of President Kennedy to invite one of Asia's leaders at the start of his term." He also asked his State Department hosts to arrange call girls for himself and his party (the request was politely rejected). In his private conversations with Kennedy, Sukarno seemed most interested in talking about the sexual attributes of his favorite movie stars, especially Marilyn Monroe and Gina Lollobrigida. And after he returned home he sent back an invitation, which landed on Rusk's desk, for Jacqueline Kennedy to visit Indonesia—without her husband. Rusk cabled back a rejection and told the President that he was not going to have Mrs. Kennedy visit that "international lecher." Later he heard a story that Sukarno's fourth wife had commented about his reputation as a ladies' man. "Well, I can tell you there's nothing to it," she said. "It's all a bluff. On that I am an expert."

It was not long before Sukarno caused real trouble. In 1962 he threatened war with the Dutch over West New Guinea (Irian Barat to the Indonesians). His claim was not based upon ethnic or cultural affinity so much as the idea that since West New Guinea had been a part of the Dutch East Indies it should be a part of Indonesia. Once again Rusk was put in the middle between a NATO ally and the anticolonialists' automatic support for Sukarno. He tried to mediate the dispute, but Joseph Luns, the Foreign Minister of the Netherlands, stubbornly refused. When military action seemed imminent, Luns telephoned Rusk and asked for American military aid. "We are going to put eight thousand men in," he said. "The rest is up to you." Rusk declined to help, telling Luns, "We are not going to mobilize the farm boys out of Kansas and the steelworkers from Pittsburgh to do a job that the burghers of Amsterdam are not prepared to do for themselves." Later that year the Dutch bowed to the inevitable, and Irian Barat was brought under United Nations control; it became a part of Indonesia in 1969.

At about the same time Sukarno embarked on another adventure, attempting to prevent the formation of the Malaysia Federation, a union of the former British territories in the region. After the independent federation was established in 1963, Indonesia declared a state of "confrontation" and organized a series of guerrilla raids from Indonesian Borneo. Rusk declined British and Malaysian appeals for American help. In a note to the British in September 1964 he said that "the United States will not feel itself responsible for Malaysian escalation unless there has been a previous agreement on our side. What steps," he asked, "are Malaysia and its Commonwealth allies taking to reinforce their own military capabilities?" Happily, the Malaysian confrontation eased after General Kemusu Suharto deposed Sukarno in 1966.

By far the greatest anomaly in U.S. policy in Asia in the 1960s was the attitude toward China. Eisenhower had continued the rigid opposition to opening bilateral relations and admitting the People's Republic of China to the United Nations. Just before the inauguration, he said to Kennedy, in Rusk's presence, "I'm going to try to support you every way I can on foreign policy, but there is one point on which I would oppose you strongly—the seating of Communist China in the U.N. and bilateral recognition."

Rusk felt that it was high time to open a dialogue with the People's Republic of China and, if possible, find some formula that would permit a two-China policy—diplomatic relations with both Taiwan and the People's Republic. He also thought it was inevitable that Communist China would be admitted to the United Nations. In his confirmation hearings he opposed recognition of the People's Republic only on the grounds that Peking demanded abandonment of Taiwan as a precondition.

Realizing the sensitive nature of the question, Rusk broached the subject of a change in China policy in May 1961 at a moment when he and Kennedy were alone together in the Oval Office. He found Kennedy unreceptive to his arguments. The politics of the matter, Kennedy explained, made it impossible to contemplate any change for the time being. He felt keenly the thin margin of his victory in 1960. Since Congress had passed a resolution opposing recognition of Communist China, he was also afraid that if he opened the question he would suffer a double defeat: outspoken rage in Congress as well as a rebuff in the end by the Chinese. It was a question to be deferred to his second term, if he received a greater mandate in the 1964 election.

Rusk got up to leave, and Kennedy called him back. "What's more, Mr. Secretary," he said, "I don't want to read in the *Washington Post* and *The New York Times* that the State Department is thinking about a change in China policy." Rusk nodded his assent, and thereafter resisted his colleagues, particularly Stevenson and Bowles, who wanted to begin a campaign for a two-China policy at the U.N. Many in the State Department thought Rusk was unduly rigid on China, but in reality the rigidity was Kennedy's.

In his public statements Rusk continued to take an unwavering hard line against Communist China. When the split between Moscow and Peking became apparent, in 1961, he saw little benefit for the United States; if anything, the Chinese brand of communism was more virulent, militant, and hostile to U.S interests. He also believed that the Chinese and Soviets would find a way to patch up their quarrel. When China attacked India in October 1962, in a dispute over the China-India border in the Himalayas delimited at a conference in Simla in 1914 by British diplomat Sir Arthur McMahon, Rusk twitted Nehru for his nonalignment policy and sent a mission under Averell Harriman to confer with India about defense needs. (Ironically, Rusk knew the specious circumstances under which the McMahon Line had been drawn; at Oxford he had met one of the negotiators, who told him that every evening during the conference the British received a full intelligence report on the Chinese negotiating position.)

On one occasion Rusk was himself twitted by Gromyko over China. When Kennedy first took office two Americans were being held prisoner in China, and Rusk tried several ways of freeing them without success. Finally he asked Gromyko if he could put a word in at Peking. "Why don't you do that yourself?" Gromyko replied. Rusk patiently explained, "As you know, we don't have diplomatic relations with Peking." Whereupon Gromyko grinned and said, "Then take it up with Chiang Kai-shek."

During the first months of 1961 the Kennedy administration watched the situation in Laos closely and kept its powder dry. The Russians were in Laos; their Ilyushin-14 planes brought in forty-five tons of equipment a day from Hanoi. Just before Kennedy's inauguration Khrushchev had given a speech advocating wars of liberation, and Laos seemed to be the test case. Ironically, most of the weapons being flown in were found to be U.S. made, captured by the Viet Minh at Dien Bien Phu.

It was hard to tell the chief players in the drama without a program. On the Communist side was the Pathet Lao, a Viet Minh–directed guerrilla group whose leader was the mustachioed, burly Prince Souphanouvong. The Western-backed leader, recognized as Premier by the United States, was Prince Boun Oum, a man so inept that the CIA described him as "a sort of Buddhist Falstaff." The real power was a man dredged up by CIA Director Allen Dulles, General Phoumi Nosavan. Just before the advent of the Kennedy administration, General Phoumi had forced the former Premier, Prince Souvanna Phouma, a neutralist (he called his doctrine "neutrality in neutralism"), into exile in Cambodia. To vote Boun Oum into office, the CIA had flown National Assembly members into the capital, Vientiane, to cast their ballots. All forty-one of the legislators voted their approval, and it was then announced that the rest of the fifty-nine-member assembly could not be found. To make things even more interesting (or complicated), Souvanna Phouma and Souphanouvong were half-brothers. And presiding over all three Laotian factions was King Savang Vatthana, whom everyone recognized as chief of state.

Laos in 1961 resembled nothing so much as a comic-opera satire of Cold War politics. It was an Asian *The Mouse That Roared,* a film popular at the time, about a small fictitious country that contrives to lose a war to the United States in order to receive foreign aid. For in Laos, the U.S.-Soviet confrontation was the major industry. The United States poured money into the country—$310 million in six years, $26 for each Laotian each year, about one-half the per capita income (no one knows what the Russians spent—perhaps they supplied the other half). The country became so prosperous under the

onslaught of aid that in Sayaboury province the governor decreed that
every elephant had to wear a license plate. Of the 2 million people in
the country, 90 percent, by one estimate, thought the world was flat
—and populated only by Laotians. Soldiers who had never seen tanks
built fortifications out of sharpened bamboo poles (usually topped
with phallic symbols). In the last week of January 1961, Premier Boun
Oum called a press conference—and never said a word. His Education Minister, who was also poet laureate, announced that he had
asked the help of SEATO to quell the Communist threat, then later
denied it, explaining he was only trying to reassure the poor foreigners
in Vientiane. Asked whether the government wanted SEATO to intervene or not, he said, "Of course not. If SEATO intervenes there
would be a world war, and nobody wants that."

The battles between the Communist Pathet Lao rebels and government forces were usually quite gentle affairs. There were stories of
great clashes, but very few casualties. In February Rusk received a
report that both sides had declared a truce so they could celebrate
together at an annual water festival at the crumbling temple of Wat
Phou in the Mekong Valley. Another time, King Savang called off the
war to cremate the body of his father, the old king Sisavang Vong,
who had died eighteen months before and had been preserved in for-
maldehyde. Rusk cabled King Savang warning him to take precau-
tions against attack, and the king replied, "There won't be an attack,
because I am cremating my father." He explained the Laotian way:
"My people only know how to sing and make love."

Some in the administration, especially Walt Rostow, wanted to put
twenty-five thousand American troops into the Mekong Valley to bolster the government forces, but Rusk opposed it. He saw no purpose
in committing American troops in a landlocked country with difficult
terrain whose people lacked any spirit for the fighting. Then, in early
1961, he proposed a diplomatic solution. His plan, set forth in a memorandum to the President, called for King Savang to declare the neu-
tralization of the country and the establishment of a neutral nations
regional organization including Burma and Cambodia. Moreover, the
government of Laos must be broadened, Rusk argued, to include
Souvanna Phouma. President Kennedy finally agreed, saying, "If we
have to make a fight for Southeast Asia, we'll have to do it in Vietnam."

Thus in March 1961 Rusk approached Gromyko with a new American proposal on Laos: the United States would accept a genuinely
neutral Laos, and a Geneva conference should be called to arrange a

cease-fire and negotiations for the withdrawal of all foreign troops. Rusk went to Geneva in May to open the negotiations. The Foreign Minister of the People's Republic of China, Chen Yi, was also there, and Rusk, remembering John Foster Dulles's pointed refusal at the Geneva Conference in 1954 to shake Chou En-lai's hand or even acknowledge his existence, went up to Chen Yi and put out his hand in greeting. Chen Yi was startled and at first he backed away, but then he took Rusk's hand and chatted with him for a few moments.

The negotiations led to the Laos accords of July 1962. Laos was to become neutral, and a new coalition government was formed with Prince Souvanna Phouma as Premier. General Phoumi and Prince Souphanouvong became deputy premiers. All foreign troops were to withdraw within seventy-five days, and the territory of Laos was not to be used as an avenue for infiltration or subversion of neighboring countries. The government of Laos was to make a declaration that it would no longer recognize any military alliance, a reference to SEATO.

The Laos accords were an attempt to seek a formalistic solution to the problem of Southeast Asia, but it did not work. The Communists refused to allow the coalition government to operate in that part of Laos under control of the Pathet Lao. The International Control Commission was not permitted to administer or enforce the accords. And Laos continued to be used as an infiltration route by the North Vietnamese. Complaining to Gromyko about the lack of enforcement of the agreements, Rusk received the impression that the Soviets resisted putting pressure on Hanoi for fear of pushing North Vietnam into the arms of China.

The failure of the Laos accords was strikingly similar to the fate of the Vietnam peace agreement of 1973. But in 1962 the accords had special meaning. The Kennedy administration had real hope for the agreements, and there was bitter disappointment when they were not enforced. It had been a good-faith attempt to solve the problem of Southeast Asia by negotiation, and now the administration was being accused of having "written off" Laos. It was an experience that would later influence the course of the war in Vietnam. Rusk had placed his trust in negotiations once and it had not worked; he was not going to let the same thing happen again in Vietnam.

The Kennedy administration inherited a civil war in Vietnam being conducted by guerrilla units directed from the North. The United States had long since replaced the French as the chief supplier of military and economic aid, and there were about 750 U.S. military advisers in Vietnam, most of them working for the CIA. The government in the South was in the hands of President Ngo Dinh Diem, who from the first received American support.

Certain assumptions went unquestioned by Rusk and most other Kennedy men at the time they took office. Vietnam was yet another crisis point of the Cold War, an arena of aggression stirred up by both the Soviet Union and China. Because South Vietnam was within the perimeter of U.S. collective defense arrangements under SEATO, there was a clear commitment to its security. The frontier between North and South Vietnam was accepted as an international border, although it had been drawn as a provisional line at the Geneva Conference of 1954. And since the free elections envisaged for 1956 had not been possible, Vietnam was regarded by policymakers as a permanently divided country, much like Germany and Korea. There was no serious consideration of the option of withdrawal, although there were those who doubted the wisdom of the American commitment, such as George Ball, Chester Bowles, and John Kenneth Galbraith, Ambassador to India.

The first decision Kennedy faced on Vietnam was whether to approve the new Counterinsurgency Plan which had been developed by the outgoing administration. The plan called for financing an increase in the Vietnamese Army from 150,000 to 170,000 men as well as an increase in the Civil Guard. At a meeting in the White House on January 28, 1961, that was primarily devoted to Cuba, the Counterinsurgency Plan was discussed. Rusk raised no objections, but commented on the plight of U.S. diplomats in Vietnam. He was aware of the corruption and repression by the Diem government; there was widespread dissatisfaction with Diem, and he was holding thousands of political prisoners. "Diem is extremely sensitive to criticism," Rusk remarked. Our diplomats are "caught between pressing Diem to do things he does not wish to do and the need to convey to him American support." He was also worried about the freewheeling nature of the CIA role in Vietnam, and he vetoed the appointment as ambassador of General Edward G. Lansdale, a famed CIA agent who had played a leading role in Vietnam and the Philippines, in favor of career diplomat Frederick E. "Fritz" Nolting. The Counterinsurgency Plan was routinely approved by Kennedy on January 30.

For most of the rest of 1961 Rusk stayed away from involvement in the Vietnam morass. He was busy with more pressing matters concerning Berlin, NATO, and Laos, and it seemed to him primarily a military problem for the Department of Defense. He was noncommittal on prospects for assigning more U.S. troops to South Vietnam, saying it was a "question for the future." He remained in favor of increased economic and military aid for Diem and rejected the idea that Vietnam represented excessive concern for the periphery of the Cold War. "If you don't pay attention to the periphery," he argued, "the periphery changes, and the first thing you know the periphery is the center."

In Vietnam, meanwhile, the war continued to go badly and dissent against Diem's rule increased. Kennedy received a gloomy report from General Lionel McGarr, head of the Military Assistance Advisory Group, that Diem controlled only about 40 percent of South Vietnam and that the Vietcong guerrillas were effectively immobilizing 85 percent of the South's military forces. Diem asked for more American aid, including a bilateral defense treaty and American combat troops.

In October Kennedy sent a mission of officials from State, Defense, the military, and the CIA under the leadership of General Maxwell Taylor and Walt Rostow to look over the situation. The report of the Taylor-Rostow fact-finding mission was to be the last word in producing a decision on how to save South Vietnam. After a week's tour of the war zone Taylor and Rostow sent their report to the President, recommending the immediate introduction of eight thousand American combat troops (which would be disguised as flood-relief workers) to begin a "massive joint effort to halt Viet Cong aggression." The report made it clear that more troops would probably be necessary as well.

Rusk was on a trip to Japan when he read the Taylor-Rostow report in the first week of November. He was in accord with most of the conclusions reached, but balked at the introduction of American combat troops. The negotiations over Laos were continuing, the Berlin crisis had not yet been resolved, and he was worried about the impact of the use of American military forces in Vietnam on these and other Cold War confrontations in the world. He cabled Kennedy arguing against the recommendations, adding that the United States could still walk away from Vietnam at this early stage, but if the Taylor-Rostow proposals were carried out a guerrilla struggle would become a full-scale war.

When he returned to Washington Rusk was disappointed to learn that McNamara was ready to give his qualified approval to the Taylor-Rostow report. He looked upon it as a final commitment to send as many troops as necessary to convince Hanoi that "we mean business," although he believed the maximum number required "will not exceed 205,000 men." Rusk persuaded McNamara to soften his position, and the two men worked out a joint recommendation for the President. The Rusk-McNamara memorandum strongly affirmed the American commitment to South Vietnam, but the introduction of combat troops was reduced to a contingency plan. Instead, the memorandum argued for the immediate introduction of additional U.S. advisory and technical forces.

Rusk also wanted an intensive diplomatic effort: consultations with other SEATO nations, diplomatic approaches to the Soviet Union and Britain as cochairmen of the Geneva conference, as well as to the other signatories to the 1954 Geneva Accords. He emphasized "our intent to return to full compliance with the Geneva Accords as soon as" North Vietnam did so. He was hoping that diplomatic pressure would lead the Soviets to restrain North Vietnam and bring about a settlement. Kennedy, who was not disposed to commit combat troops, took the recommendation. Promising additional advisory and technical aid, he asked Diem to "galvanize" the Vietnamese effort, for which "no amount of extra aid can substitute."

Although Kennedy had rejected the option of sending American combat troops to Vietnam, the decisions made after the Taylor-Rostow mission dramatically increased American involvement in the war. By October 1962 there were 10,700 American military personnel in South Vietnam. Most were involved in training Vietnamese units and in helping with communications and supplies, but American GIs were also accompanying the Vietnamese into combat and piloting helicopters to ferry the Vietnamese troops into action. There were official denials that Americans were engaged in combat in Vietnam, but increasing numbers of Americans were being killed and wounded. There was escalation on both sides. South Vietnamese troops at least nominally committed to the war reached a quarter-million men. And the number of Vietcong guerrillas was estimated to be about 25,000 at the end of 1962. The cost to the United States of supporting the war mounted as well, $400 million a year by late 1962.

The principal South Vietnamese government plan to win the war was the "strategic-hamlet" program. In order to pacify the countryside, where the Vietcong in many areas were operating at will, the rural population in those areas was herded into several thousand strategic hamlets, behind bamboo fences and barbed wire, with armed militiamen standing guard. By 1963, according to government statistics, 8 million villagers, 59 percent of South Vietnam's population, were living in the six thousand strategic hamlets. A second element of the government's strategy was to defeat the Vietcong in the countryside through what were called "clear-and-hold" missions. Scores of helicopters, often piloted by Americans, carried troops into battle on these missions, and by May 1963 the number of Americans killed in Vietnam had reached seventy-three.

During 1962 and 1963 Rusk was not involved in the operational details of Vietnam. He did, of course, keep in close touch with what was happening and, as the chief foreign policy spokesman for the administration, helped to guide the evolution of American involvement with his public statements. He was careful to reiterate the U.S. commitment to see the Vietnam matter through and was lavish in his promises of increased American aid to the Diem regime. But, chastened by his experience in the peace negotiations over Laos, he became increasingly reticent and cautious about entering into negotiations on Vietnam. "There can be peace overnight in Vietnam if those responsible for the aggression wish peace," he declared. The situation was just as simple as that. He saw no need for complicated or prolonged talks. For Rusk it was a question of making the Communists decide to leave Vietnam alone. He saw little to talk about in the situation, and the possibility of peace negotiations was further complicated by the fact that Moscow and Peking were competing for influence in Hanoi.

Rusk also firmly denied reports that surfaced from interviews with returning American advisers and correspondents in Vietnam that the war was going badly. He cited improvements in supply and intelligence operations and in the Vietnam command structure as evidence that, in fact, the Vietnamese were winning the war. He pointed to the growing effectiveness of operations now being conducted by the Vietnamese military. By the end of 1962 there was a burst of optimism in the administration about prospects for an end to the fighting in Vietnam. The strategic-hamlet program seemed to be succeeding, and the number of casualties among the Vietcong seemed to prove the effectiveness of the clear-and-hold operations. In fact, the optimism was misplaced. The United States in its evaluation of the war was almost totally dependent on data supplied by the Diem regime. The strategic-hamlet program was far less successful than supposed and was stirring up resentment among the peasants forcibly resettled in fortified villages, especially in the Mekong Valley. Rusk would later admit that he and the rest of the government were "misled" by Diem's optimistic reports.

Rusk tried without success to gain tangible support from the allies for the effort in South Vietnam. Britain gave lip service to the U.S. position but refused to help. It was withdrawing from its historic responsibility east of Suez and, preoccupied with the troubles in Malaysia, was unwilling to take on additional burdens. France was adamant in its opposition to involvement in Vietnam. Rusk went to de Gaulle asking for help and was brushed off. "There will never be another French soldier in southeast Asia," de Gaulle told him. Vietnam was a "dirty country," and the Americans should leave it alone.

De Gaulle's attitude enraged Rusk and added further to his distrust of the French leader. He saw no comparison between the inability of the French to win in Southeast Asia and the capability and correctness of the American effort. France, a moribund power, had simply been defending its colonial interests. The United States was a superpower fighting for freedom, its motives altruistic. With more than a touch of hubris, he did not take de Gaulle's warning seriously that the Americans would get bogged down in an unending struggle in Vietnam.

Rusk's efforts to gain support from other NATO allies also failed. He complained that they were interested only in Europe and refused to undertake the wider responsibilities of the alliance. Petulantly, he reminded them that the NATO alliance stretched to the Bering Strait. The SEATO allies other than Britain and France shied away as well. New Zealand and Australia cited political difficulties as an excuse for giving only token help. Pakistan refused all support and was interested only in pursuing its conflict with India. Although Rusk deeply believed in collective security, he was faced with the realization that the United States would have to do the job alone. With renewed fighting in Laos there was further concern about the danger to Thailand, a SEATO ally, and in talks in Washington with the Thai Foreign Minister, Thanat Kohman, Rusk worked out a communiqué announcing that the United States considered Thailand's independence and integrity vital to its national interests and would honor its pledge to defend Thailand under the SEATO treaty even if no other SEATO nation was willing to act.

In 1963 there was a great increase in unrest in South Vietnam caused by the repressive practices of the Diem government. The crisis was caused by the government campaign against the Buddhists, 80 percent of South Vietnam's population. Diem, a Catholic, consistently favored the Catholic minority in government and military service, causing resentment among the Buddhists. Mme. Nhu, the sharp-tongued wife of Ngo Dinh Nhu, the brother of President Diem, launched a morality campaign outlawing adultery, abortion, polygamy, concubinage, divorce, and dancing. Buddhists in the historic city of Hue were not allowed to unfurl their religious flags for the birthday celebration of Gautama Buddha. Many Buddhists believed that Diem and the Nhus were trying to crush Buddhism and make Catholicism the state religion. Buddhist demonstrations were cruelly suppressed by government forces, which only increased the unrest, and in a spectacular ritual suicide a seventy-three-year-old monk set himself on fire in protest against Diem. A young girl of eighteen tried to cut off her left hand "as a humble offering to Buddha while our religion is in danger." The climax of the campaign against the Buddhists occurred on August 21, when government forces sacked and desecrated the Buddhist pagodas in Saigon and Hue and imprisoned over a thousand people as suspected Communist sympathizers.

The attacks were traced by American intelligence to Nhu's secret police, and Rusk watched the repression against the Buddhists with increasing dismay. It haunted him that the United States might be tied to a "losing horse" in Vietnam. American pressure on Diem for reforms fell on deaf ears; he ruled in the style of a French governor, listening to no one. In addition, the American ambassador, Fritz Nolting, was too closely tied to the Diem regime. Rusk wanted an ambassador who would be strong enough to force Diem to change his ways. President Kennedy proposed Edmund Gullion, a career diplomat, but Rusk saw the need for a stronger figure.

Henry Cabot Lodge and Rusk had known each other quite well when Lodge was in the Senate, and they became friends when Rusk was serving at the Rockefeller Foundation. In a talk just after Kennedy took office, Lodge told Rusk that he thought he had one more tour of public service in his system. He did not want to waste his time on an easy job, he said, but if something really challenging came along he would be glad to take it on. Rusk remembered the conversation and concluded that Lodge would be the ideal Ambassador to South Vietnam. He was a Republican and strongly independent, a respected figure who had been Richard Nixon's running mate in the 1960 presidential race. If anyone could, Lodge would handle Diem. Kennedy agreed, and Lodge was appointed ambassador in the summer of 1963. In Lodge's final visit to Rusk before leaving for Saigon, Rusk told him that he was deeply distressed over the Buddhist crisis and wanted him to take a strong lead to bring about a greater degree of peace and security in the country.

On August 22, 1963, only a day after the assault on the pagodas,

Lodge arrived in Saigon to take up his post. Martial law was in effect, and his motorcade sped from the airport through deserted streets guarded at every intersection by armed soldiers. The enforced calm disguised an intrigue-filled city and persistent rumors that Washington was losing confidence in the Diem regime.

Rusk was not in daily touch with events in South Vietnam during this period. He had spent the first two weeks of August in Moscow, Leningrad, Gagra, and Bonn at the test ban treaty signing ceremony and its aftermath. During the tumultuous week of unrest in Saigon he was on vacation at Camp David, and afterward went to New York to see some old friends at the Rockefeller Foundation. On Saturday, August 24, in a rare moment of relaxation, he went to Yankee Stadium to watch the Chicago White Sox beat the Yankees 3 to 0. When he got back to his hotel he was unexpectedly confronted with a fateful decision. Averell Harriman (then Under Secretary for Political Affairs) and Roger Hilsman (Assistant Secretary for Far Eastern Affairs) were working on a cable instructing Ambassador Lodge on how to handle the latest rumors and intrigues in Saigon.

The principal theme of the cable was how to deal with the Nhus, whom everyone believed to be behind the repression of the Buddhists. Lodge was authorized to give Diem what amounted to an ultimatum: that the U.S. government could no longer tolerate a "situation in which power lies in Nhu's hands." Lodge was also authorized to tell key Vietnamese military leaders that "the U.S. would find it impossible to continue to support" the government of South Vietnam unless the Buddhist grievances were met and the Nhus were removed from power. It was, in essence, a call for a coup.

Ball phoned Rusk and read him the text of the cable. In an apparent misunderstanding between the two men, Rusk was under the impression that President Kennedy, who was relaxing at Hyannis Port, had already decided the matter, and so gave it little thought. From what he knew of the situation, he agreed the Nhus should be removed. Reluctant to enter into a prolonged discussion over an open telephone line, he voiced cautious approval of the cable. In fact, Kennedy had not given his assent; when Ball had reached him before talking to Rusk, he had said only, "If Rusk and Gilpatrick agree, George, then go ahead." (Gilpatrick was handling the matter for Defense in McNamara's absence.) By this casual process of decision, a coup for the removal of Diem was set in motion.

There followed a period of indecision and doubts both in Washington and Saigon. In a series of meetings beginning Monday, August 26,

McNamara, Taylor, and McCone voiced strong misgivings about supporting a coup. The President also had doubts. Lodge, however, was already acting on the instructions in the August 24 cable and vigorously supported the coup idea. Rusk said it was important to make it clear that Washington was not changing its "existing directive"—the August 24 cable—but at the same time, reflecting the President's doubts, he changed course perceptibly, cabling Lodge that he wanted details in advance about the coup plans and the composition of a new government and asking him to make another approach to Diem to get rid of the Nhus. Faced with American indecision and new doubts about the forces at their disposal, the Vietnamese generals hesitated. Rusk was relieved; he had cabled Lodge on August 30 warning of the danger of an abortive attempt and the absence of "bone and muscle" among the Vietnamese generals.

But the week of indecision, as the *Pentagon Papers* state, left the United States "without a policy and with most of its bridges burned." Rusk chaired a meeting on August 31 with the purpose of deciding "Where do we go from here?" Hilsman continued to argue against support of any Nhu-dominated regime, and Paul Kattenburg of the Vietnam task force said that the United States would be thrown out in six months if the regime remained in power. He added that the meeting should consider "a decision to get out honorably." Brushing his views off as "largely speculative," Rusk said that policy should be guided by two factors: "That we will not pull out of Vietnam until the war is won and that we will not run a coup." The only conclusion reached by the meeting was to cable Lodge for his advice.

As policymakers in Washington tried to regroup, it was apparent that they were caught on the horns of a dilemma: How could pressure be brought to bear on Diem without endangering the war effort? On September 12 the National Security Council accepted a plan, drafted by Rusk, for instructions to Lodge to give Diem a chance to act on reforms. In the subsequent cable to Lodge, Rusk reiterated that the American objective was "a secure and independent South Vietnam [although] at some future date, it may be possible to consider a free, independent and non-communist unified country." The "key question," he told Lodge, was the loss of political confidence, which was largely due to the "two Nhus." He instructed Lodge to "concentrate on Diem himself to make him see that everything he had been working for in the past ten years is threatened with collapse." He left to Lodge's judgment the specific pressures necessary to get Diem to act. But he added, "We should not threaten what we will not or cannot deliver and . . . we are not yet ready to cut off assistance which affects the war effort."

In late September a mission headed by McNamara and Taylor went to South Vietnam to talk to Diem and survey the situation. Their assessment was heavily influenced by what they expected to find, and they saw what they wanted to see. Deceived by faulty figures and reports from the South Vietnamese government, they judged that the military program had made "progress" and was "sound." They recommended withdrawal of 1,000 of the more than 16,000 U.S. military personnel by the end of the year, and predicted that the major part of the war effort would be completed by the end of 1965. They found fault only with the political situation and the Diem regime.

At an October 5 meeting of key members of the National Security Council, including Rusk, the President approved the conclusions of the McNamara-Taylor mission. In fact, the troop withdrawal plans were intended primarily to pressure Diem for reforms; the President directed that no formal announcement be made of the implementation of the troop withdrawal. A cutoff of selected aid programs was also approved, but not announced to the press.

While excluding active initiation of a coup against Diem, instructions cabled to Lodge on October 6 made it clear that it was the U.S. purpose "not to thwart a change of government." Lodge was told to maintain close touch with the Vietnamese plotters, headed by General Duong Van Minh, but not to be drawn into advising on operational plans. The United States was attempting a balancing act between not doing anything for which it might be held responsible and preparing for a change in the government. This policy was self-contradictory, and as William Colby, the Director of the CIA, said later, the cables between Washington and Saigon maintained an air of unreality, suggesting "that it's really the generals who are going to decide, and not [the United States], about the removal of Diem."

Once this policy was set, Rusk seems to have maintained a discreet distance from involvement in the details. He took several trips, and was in Germany when a final "green light" cable for the coup was sent to Lodge on October 27. Rusk was uncomfortable with the situation but saw no alternative. After he returned from Germany he attended the National Security Council meetings on October 29 and 30. By that time the chief concern was whether the coup was going to succeed. There was fear that the generals would fail and inconclusive fighting and political chaos would result. Rusk was also worried about the fate of Diem and Nhu and cabled Lodge to take whatever steps he could to ensure their safety.

The coup came on November 1. The generals were victorious, but, unexpectedly, both Diem and Nhu were assassinated. Rusk was upset and disturbed by the assassinations but, like everyone else, accepted the event as an unfortunate outcome of the situation beyond American control. He cabled Lodge a personal note of praise for his "superb handling of a very complex and difficult series of events." And in a cable to all diplomatic posts he expressed optimism about prospects for the new government: the coup was a "first step forward to representative government," and democratic freedoms were expected to be implemented. The Military Revolutionary Council appointed Vice President Nguyen Ngo Tho as head of a provisional government. That seemed to satisfy Washington, but "cause for concern" was expressed at the appointment of General Mai huu Xuan as director general of police, because he was the person whom intelligence reports pointed to as the assassin of Diem and Nhu.

The coup resulting in the new government for South Vietnam and the assassinations of Diem and Nhu was the last crisis of the Kennedy administration. In one of the fateful ironies of our time, President Kennedy himself was assassinated in Dallas on November 22, only three weeks later.

What Kennedy would have done in Vietnam had he lived has been a rich subject of speculation. There is evidence that just before his death he had great doubts about the American course in Southeast Asia. He told Senator Mike Mansfield that he was thinking about a complete military withdrawal from Vietnam, but "I can't do it until 1965—until after I'm reelected." Kennedy remarked to his friend Kenneth O'Donnell that "if I tried to pull out completely now, we would have another Joe McCarthy scare on our hands." And on November 20, 1963, Kennedy asked his young aide Michael Forrestal to "organize an in-depth study of every possible option we've got in Vietnam, including how to get out of there."

But Kennedy never mentioned any of his doubts to Rusk or said that he was thinking of withdrawing from Vietnam. If he had told Rusk that he had decided to withdraw but was delaying his decision until after the 1964 election, Rusk would have advised him not to wait but to find a political solution—perhaps modeled on the Laos accords— to implement a withdrawal right away. Rusk strongly believed that no President should leave American troops in a combat situation for political purposes, and he would have carried out the Laos option had Kennedy advised him to do so. In the last analysis, however, all speculation as to what Kennedy would have done in Vietnam is futile. At the same time, it is false to assume that the Kennedy administration's policies led inexorably to the fateful decisions of the Johnson years. At the end of the Kennedy administration, Vietnam was not yet an American war.

On November 22, 1963, Rusk, together with five other cabinet members, had just finished a meeting in Honolulu on Vietnam and were in an airplane over the Pacific on their way to political and economic talks in Tokyo. As the ranking cabinet officer Rusk received the first message that the President had been shot in Dallas: KENNEDY WOUNDED PERHAPS FATALLY BY ASSASSIN'S BULLET. His initial reaction was disbelief, and he ordered the communications men aboard to get in touch with the White House and Admiral Harry D. Felt at CINCPAC (Commander in Chief Pacific) in Honolulu. He also told the pilot to return immediately to Hawaii.

On the two-hour flight back, fragmentary reports of the tragedy continued to filter in. An AP bulletin said that the President had been shot in the head. Admiral Felt had arranged for a jet to take Rusk to Dallas. Then Pierre Salinger, the White House press secretary, who was aboard the plane, told Rusk that a message under the code name "Stranger" had arrived from the White House ordering the plane to return to Washington. Who was "Stranger"? It went through Rusk's mind that there might be a national or international conspiracy against the government of the United States. They searched the plane for five minutes frantically trying to find a code that would reveal the identity of "Stranger." Finding none, Rusk told Salinger to find out who "Stranger" was: "We don't know what is happening in Dallas. Who is the government now?" Salinger broke code to ask the White House. There was relief when the answer came that "Stranger" was Major Harold R. Patterson, a trusted White House communications officer.

Only seconds later a message arrived that the President was dead. Rusk walked to a microphone in the front of the plane to announce the terrible news:

> Ladies and gentlemen, this is the Secretary of State speaking. We have received official confirmation that President Kennedy is dead. I am saddened to tell you this grievous news. We have a new President. God bless our new President and our nation.

After a collective cry of anguish, there followed several minutes of stunned silence, grief, and tears. No one talked for several minutes; each person was alone with his thoughts. For Rusk the grief was too deep to be expressed. He made an effort to hold himself together, realizing that it was his duty to provide an example of strength in that hour of tragedy. But at one point his security man noticed tears rolling down his cheek.

After about twenty minutes Rusk quietly asked each of the accompanying cabinet officials—Treasury's Douglas Dillon, Interior's Stewart Udall, Agriculture's Orville Freeman, Commerce's Luther Hodges, and Labor's Willard Wirtz—to come with him into the rear cabin of the plane to talk about the problems the country would face and what each of them could do in the circumstances. It was a somber colloquy. Rusk exhibited a quiet leadership. "There was absolutely no doubt of who was in charge at that tragic moment," said one official who was there.

Rusk took the time in the midst of the confusion to pen a personal note of condolence to Jacqueline Kennedy: "May God give you and your children strength and comfort." He also ordered Ball to carry out an immediate study, country by country, of what foreign policy problems would arise from the assassination of the President. When the news reached the plane that Lee Harvey Oswald had been arrested by police and that he had lived in the Soviet Union and was a member of the Fair Play for Cuba Committee, Rusk was surprised. Like everyone else, he had believed that the President's assassin must be a member of the right-wing lunatic fringe. "If this is true," he said of the news, "it is going to have repercussions around the world for years to come."

Rusk's most important task when he arrived in Washington was "to ensure that there would be an orderly succession of authority and that this would be apparent to the rest of the world." He immersed himself in the details of the funeral and the planning of the arrival and care of the numbers of foreign heads of state and other guests, chief among them President de Gaulle of France. Rusk met de Gaulle at the airport and thanked him for coming. "Don't thank me," de Gaulle said. "The little people of France demanded that I come." Rusk was particularly worried about an attempt to assassinate de Gaulle and offered him the use of a bullet-proof car in his travels around Washington and on the trip to the church for the funeral mass. De Gaulle brusquely declined and said it was his wish to walk with the others behind Mrs. Kennedy.

At the time Rusk discounted any possibility that a foreign government could be implicated in Kennedy's death. Later, in 1975 during the Church Committee hearings, he heard for the first time the evidence of extensive CIA plots to assassinate Castro in the early 1960s.

He testified before the committee that he had no knowledge of any of these CIA plots. At one meeting he recalled that Ambassador Llewellyn Thompson had once told him of a rumor that the CIA was planning to assassinate Castro. Rusk and Thompson had both laughed, thinking it was a cruel joke. When he learned of the CIA plots against Castro, Rusk was incensed. He had testified before the Warren Commission investigating the Kennedy assassination that he knew of no motive or reason why a foreign government would be involved in a plot against Kennedy, while Alan Dulles, who was sitting in the room as a member of the commission, made no attempt to correct him, although Dulles certainly knew of the assassination plots.

Rusk was aware that the CIA was preoccupied with Castro, especially during the period following the Bay of Pigs. The CIA was attempting to harass Castro by all sorts of dirty tricks, such as spoiling shipments of sugar out of Cuba destined for Western Europe. Rusk opposed such petty harassments and vetoed those he knew about as being foolish and unproductive. He was in the dark, however, about the extent of the CIA's involvement against Castro.

Over a year after President Kennedy's death, in May 1965, Rusk journeyed to England as President Johnson's representative to speak at the dedication of a British memorial to President Kennedy and to accept an acre of land—part of the field of Runnymede, where the Magna Carta was signed—given by the British people to the United States. Under a bright British sky on a beautiful spring day, looking out on the emerald green countryside, in the company of Queen Elizabeth II and Jacqueline Kennedy, Rusk gave perhaps his most eloquent address:

> On behalf of President Johnson and the American people, I thank Your Majesty, your Government, and your people. We shall cherish this memorial to a President who shall be forever young. "At the going down of the sun and in the morning" we shall remember him. And we draw strength and confidence from the knowledge that all who pass this way shall be reminded of the common dedication of the British and American peoples to the cause of human liberty—a reminder which has its roots here in seven and a half centuries and its promise through all time to come.

President Kennedy's death marked the end of a unique relationship in Rusk's life and of a special chapter in the history of the nation. In the space of only three short years all of Rusk's doubts about Kennedy's youth and inexperience had been dispelled. Kennedy had grown into the job of being President and he, as well as those around him, had learned to exercise the great powers and responsibilities of the office with temperance and wisdom. For Rusk, his premature death was a deep personal tragedy. The tragedy for the nation, he believed, was that Kennedy had stood on the threshold of a greatness that might have been his legacy to the nation had he lived to carry out his programs to achieve international peace and domestic harmony. As it was, he would be remembered chiefly for "facing one crisis after another." He had indeed made good on his commitment to "assure the survival and the success of liberty." But Kennedy "was confronted by so many crises during his Presidency," Rusk remarked with sadness, "that he was not the kind of President he would really have preferred to be."

PART FIVE

THE JOHNSON YEARS

"Peace in Vietnam Rests with Hanoi": Escalation in Vietnam

Meeting with Lyndon Johnson immediately after President Kennedy's assassination, Rusk stressed a single theme: the necessity for continuity in foreign policy in the transition to a new administration. President Johnson took the advice. "This nation will keep its commitments," he vowed in his first speech to the nation, "from South Vietnam to West Berlin."

Not incidentally, the embodiment and symbol of continuity in those first difficult weeks at the end of 1963 was Rusk himself. Johnson made sure that he was at his elbow when he met with the multitude of foreign leaders and dignitaries during and after Kennedy's funeral. But Rusk thought that the new President should have the opportunity to build his own cabinet and circle of advisers. On November 27, 1963, he wrote to Johnson: "I wish to place the office of the Secretary of State at your disposal, and I therefore tender you my resignation to be effective at any time." Johnson called immediately to ask him to remain in his post. Rusk agreed and was suddenly thrust into new prominence. *Time* featured him on its cover on December 6, 1963, as "a promise of continuity and action."

Johnson, of course, was totally different from President Kennedy as a leader, both in substance and style. He had grown up in poverty, had received a mediocre education, and had achieved political success through an extraordinary urge for power and an uncanny ability to manipulate and mesmerize those around him. Rusk had never felt personally close to Kennedy, but in Johnson he found someone whose instincts and emotions, if not his intellect, were close to his own. Both were Southern boys made good. Johnson was born in a three-room clapboard farmhouse in Texas just six months before Rusk was born in similar circumstances in Cherokee County, Georgia. They had followed very different paths to prominence, but each shared secret feelings that they didn't quite belong, especially in the lustrous world of the Kennedy administration. Both knew that some of Kennedy's men made fun of them, cracking jokes about their inability to keep pace with the brilliance of the Eastern elite who surrounded Kennedy. Each had suffered in silence, but they shared the pain of wounded pride.

The personalities of both Rusk and Johnson had metamorphosed to some degree to compensate for their being "rural Southern" and to help them get along with and even dominate their peers. Johnson's style was volcanic and elemental; he was earthy and crude. He overwhelmed people with a combination of flattery, cajolery, and threats made real by the fact that he understood implicitly what he was up against and what it would take to get someone to carry out his wishes. Rusk, on the other hand, was enigmatic; he was self-contained, unflappable, and indefatigable. He learned very early to get what he wanted by careful preparation, total command of the facts of any situation, and complete mastery over himself and his own emotions. In motivating others, he disclosed as little of himself as possible.

There was no need for such caution with Johnson, however, and when they were together he and Rusk chatted like boys, arguing facetiously about who had grown up poorer and recalling the shared details of their early years—old-fashioned telephone systems, life without electricity, the Southern food they both liked. At times they seemed to talk in a kind of shorthand punctuated by winks, laughs, and gestures. Rusk was a frequent visitor at the LBJ Ranch, and on one occasion the President took him on a tour of his boyhood home. "I don't have to tell you what that is," Johnson said, pointing out an old-fashioned metal potty under the bed, and the two men shared a hearty laugh.

The relationship between Johnson and Rusk had begun while Johnson was serving as Kennedy's somewhat neglected and maligned Vice President. Rusk was too busy to see much of Johnson, but he did not overlook or deride him. He carefully listened to Johnson's views and assigned a Foreign Service officer to the Vice President's staff so that he would get current information about every foreign policy matter of importance. Johnson expressed great affection for Rusk from the start. "Some of the people around [Kennedy] are bastards," he told his brother shortly after the election, "but I think [Kennedy] has treated me all right. He's had me briefed by Rusk and some of the other Cabinet members, and I especially like Dean Rusk. He's a damned good man. Hard-working, bright, and loyal as a beagle. You'll never catch him working at cross purposes with his President. He's just the kind of man I'd want in my Cabinet if I were President."

Johnson had an innate distrust of people he considered intellectuals or "eggheads," but Rusk was different—an unquestioned intellectual but one who was practical and down to earth. As a result he quickly became a Johnson intimate and saw the new President even more often than he had consulted with President Kennedy. Yet even Johnson learned to respect Rusk's famed icy detachment. In public, at least, they called each other Mr. President and Mr. Secretary. And Rusk's brusque telephone manner was a running joke. On several occasions Johnson burst into Walt Rostow's office in the White House decrying in mock anger, "He's done it again! Will you please tell the Secretary of State not to hang up on the President of the United States!"

Rusk had little trouble transferring his loyalties from Kennedy to Johnson. He had never thought of himself as serving Kennedy personally; he was in the service of the presidency. Johnson was rather inexperienced and insecure about foreign policy, but Rusk never patronized him or made him feel he was incapable of really understanding a complex foreign policy question. On the contrary, Rusk bolstered his confidence, constantly reminding Johnson that as Vice President he had traveled widely and had kept in touch with major foreign policy issues. He endeared himself further when he told an interviewer that he had been absolutely amazed at Johnson's instant recognition of scores of foreign dignitaries at the Kennedy funeral and his personal knowledge of the problems they faced in their respective countries.

Rusk also overlooked or forgave Johnson's vaunted crudeness and exuberance in dealing with foreign officials. As Vice President traveling in India, Johnson had caused a stir when he ordered the pilot of his plane to take a different course, causing Indian Air Force jets to scramble to meet him as an intruder. Later, in the Taj Mahal, he tested the acoustics of the magnificent dome by shouting a Texas rebel yell. On a visit to the Vatican he had his helicopter land right in the middle of Pope Paul VI's private garden. And when the startled pontiff came out to meet him, Johnson presented him with a gift—a package containing a life-size bust of himself, which he proudly opened with a jackknife he drew from his pocket, much to the shock of his host.

Even after he assumed the presidency Johnson's gaffes continued. He met with de Gaulle briefly in Rusk's office at the State Department during a reception for the visiting foreign dignitaries who had come to Kennedy's funeral and invited him to come again to the United States as a sequel to President Kennedy's visit to Paris. De Gaulle told him to take the matter up through normal diplomatic channels. Later that day Johnson met with the governors of several states and in a characteristically expansive mood told them that de Gaulle had agreed to visit Washington. When de Gaulle heard this he was furious. He later flatly refused a formal invitation because of the incident, taking the position that his visit to Kennedy's funeral was the return of Kennedy's visit to France.

Rusk never complained about Johnson's antics; he either quietly tried to control them or smoothed over the damage. On a state visit to Malaysia, Johnson suddenly became upset when his hosts kept playing "The Star-Spangled Banner" over and over again. "Will you tell these damned people to stop playing the National Anthem," he said to Rusk. "Mr. President, there are just some things you have to tolerate," Rusk replied. On many occasions Rusk was sympathetic toward Johnson's excesses and even defended them. When after his gallbladder operation Johnson lifted up his shirt to show the world his scar, Rusk blamed it on the Washington press corps: "Those SOBs were clamoring to see into every aperture of his body," he told his aides. "Now they complain when he gives them their wish."

President Johnson conceived the role of the Department of State in far different terms than President Kennedy. In his first meeting with the National Security Council, on December 5, 1963, he announced that the State Department "would be the central force in the framing and execution of the foreign policy of this country under the President." And Rusk found that Johnson meant what he said. In contrast to Kennedy, he believed in a more orderly, bureaucratic style of government that placed cabinet officers in charge of their particular policy domain. This was especially true with respect to foreign policy.

As Rusk got to know the new President better he found that Johnson was "a man in a hurry." He often spoke about his massive heart attack in 1955, when his blood pressure had dropped to zero and he was not expected to live. Very conscious of his mortality, he talked about the few years that might be left to him and what he wished to accomplish. At first, foreign policy was not high on his agenda. He saw his presidency rather as an opportunity to work for the abiding domestic goals he wanted for the nation: eliminating poverty, giving all people, black and white, an equal chance in life, and providing everyone with a good education and productive, meaningful work. His was the classic vision of the Democratic Party since the time of Franklin D. Roosevelt, and he was consumed by it, utterly convinced that he could bring it about. Johnson intended to leave foreign policy to the professionals, the "fancy pants boys," as he called them. Unlike Kennedy, he had no conception of being his own Secretary of State. He would rely on the State Department to run the diplomatic side of foreign policy.

Johnson did change the foreign policy-making process itself. He found the wide-open, freewheeling National Security Council meetings favored by President Kennedy cumbersome and unproductive. Early in 1964 he began the custom of the "Tuesday lunches" in the White House, and they continued throughout his presidency. At these lunches the President met with a core group of his advisers to discuss pressing foreign policy questions. Over a low-calorie meal of fish or small cuts of meat served in the family dining room, which featured colorful wallpaper depicting the great battles of the American Revolution, they decided questions of peace and war. Consequently, the Tuesday lunch became the most important high-level meeting on national security affairs in the American government. At the outset there were only three "charter members" besides the President, obviously those advisers Johnson felt most comfortable with—Rusk, McNamara, who remained Secretary of Defense, and McGeorge Bundy, the National Security Adviser. Around Washington these three men, together with the President, became known as the "awesome foursome."

This was heady wine, even for someone as influential as Rusk. Unlike Kennedy, Johnson never tried to bypass Rusk and work with lower-echelon State Department officials without his knowledge. He did not assign matters to McGeorge Bundy or create special task forces without Rusk's approval. Ben Read, Rusk's executive secretary, immediately noticed the difference: Johnson "had great faith and trust in Secretary Rusk and . . . expected the Department to carry more of the load than it had been."

Rusk was quite content with this new state of affairs. It suited his conception of the office of Secretary of State—to be the President's chief foreign policy adviser. In the relaxed, intimate surroundings of the Tuesday lunches he could voice his opinions directly to the President without having to endure a rough-and-tumble debate with peripheral staff people, which he thought demeaning. There was no danger of leaks; the press would not hear of any disagreements between Johnson's advisers or between the President and his Secretary of State. Rusk believed no blue sky should ever show publicly between him and the President.

All this was very different from the management style President Kennedy had used to make decisions. Kennedy liked to chew over a whole range of ideas with people of different points of view. He wanted to see the issue dissected by people holding strong views in order to sort out the strands of a decision and to see how well various arguments held up when they were tested. Meetings of the National Security Council or Excom were symposia of freewheeling debate. Kennedy had listened to anyone whose opinion he respected without regard to whether he was a cabinet member or a very junior staff person. Once in the meeting everyone was equal—only ideas and judgment mattered.

Rusk continued to get along well with McNamara and Bundy, and they often met together before seeing the President to work out a common position. Johnson, unlike Kennedy, did not like disagreement among his advisers. He did not want to referee between competing points of view. Consensus and harmony were his trademark, and the four men, especially at first, held very similar views. They did not worry about a dangerous aspect of this closed, concentrated decision-making process: that they would become increasingly insulated from real debate about the wisdom of their course. Although Rusk and others did not stifle dissent in their departments, it seldom reached the President's ears. Johnson also did not like questions raised about a decision once it was made. After taking an action, one lived with the consequences; there was no turning back. It was an approach that generated little intellectual ferment. When the "awesome foursome" got together, everything seemed so clear, so easy to understand. They were confident; it was impossible that all four of them could be wrong.

As time went on, the Tuesday lunches were broadened somewhat to include other officials and the military, but the same basic, closed format prevailed. William Bundy and Ben Read, whose job it was to draw operational conclusions from the lunch-table discussion, were increasingly appalled and frustrated by the unsystematic and narrow nature of the inquiry. There was great danger of misunderstanding too. Read wryly commented that sometimes after talking to Rusk and

Walt Rostow (who succeeded McGeorge Bundy as National Security Adviser) about conclusions reached, he wondered whether they had indeed been at the same lunch.

Outside of his "Tuesday cabinet," his aides, and a few members of Congress, Johnson regularly solicited the views of close friends, especially two Washington lawyers, Abe Fortas and Clark Clifford. This made Rusk uncomfortable, especially when the practice continued after Abe Fortas was named a Justice of the Supreme Court. Rusk thought Fortas and, to a lesser extent, Clifford were ill-informed and that their advice, given without responsibility for the consequences, was of little value.

With his new status and the State Department's new prominence, Rusk put aside all thoughts of resigning after the 1964 election, as he had originally planned. He turned down several opportunities for jobs outside the government, including an offer to become chancellor of the University of Georgia. The President wanted and needed him; he felt valued as never before. Johnson showered him with praise. In a birthday note to Rusk he wrote: "I thank the Lord for that winter day in Georgia when you came along, my wise counselor and friend."

Another sentiment shared by Johnson and Rusk was their antipathy toward Robert Kennedy, who remained in the post of Attorney General. Each had tolerated his snubs and taunts in silence while President Kennedy was alive, but now he was the odd man out. On Saturday mornings Kennedy continued to visit Rusk at his office and talk over foreign policy matters, bringing his large dog along with him. On one occasion the dog jumped all over the staid Rusk, an annoying experience made particularly so because Kennedy split his sides laughing. Kennedy also made the rounds of people in the department, and aides at State believed he was trying to build a case against Rusk.

Johnson soon moved to decrease Kennedy's influence and to cut off the back channels of communication between the White House and the State Department. One falling ax that was particularly gratifying to Rusk was the resignation of Roger Hilsman as Assistant Secretary for Far Eastern Affairs. Rusk had long been annoyed with Hilsman, a man with close connections to the Kennedys, who he felt was undermining him, leaking to the press, and acting independently in conjunction with sympathetic White House staff. He blamed Hilsman, who was overly fascinated with counterintelligence, for his part in masterminding the American role in the coup in Vietnam against Diem. It was Hilsman who had been responsible for the coup cable in August, which had been initiated without the knowledge of either

Rusk or Under Secretary George Ball. Johnson, even more strongly than Rusk, felt the coup against Diem had been a mistake and fatalistically mused whether Kennedy's assassination had somehow been a mystical retribution for the murders of Diem and Nhu. Johnson gave the green light to remove Hilsman, and Ball fired him. Later, Hilsman became a vocal critic of the Vietnam War, and Rusk felt he unfairly disavowed his own role in the deepening involvement of the United States in the war.

Most at the State Department welcomed these changes and Rusk's growing power. His subordinates, particularly those who worked directly with him, commented that he was "a wonderful man to work for," kind and considerate. They respected his incisiveness in thought and action and his ability to absorb and retain information. But they also worried about him, thought he was pushing himself too hard, spreading himself too thin. "His idea of relaxation," recalled one aide, "was to wear a Hawaiian shirt to the office on Sunday."

But there was another view as well. Some of the assistant secretaries and desk officers, although they respected Rusk, still thought he was playing things too close to the vest, that it was his nature to be uncommunicative, and they could not adequately do their jobs unless they knew more about what he was thinking. There was a feeling of drift and caution that hindered progress.

Johnson's reorganization also heightened the frustration of the liberals, both in and outside the administration, who wanted bold policy moves and a streamlining of the Department of State. Largely identified with the Kennedy wing of the Democratic Party, they saw State under Rusk as conservative, stuffy, cautious, and inept. John Kenneth Galbraith, back at Harvard after his stint as Ambassador to India, brought these concerns to Johnson's personal attention in a letter of February 21, 1964, calling for Rusk's replacement as Secretary of State:

Dear Mr. President:
Let me put the basic problem before you. I am not an admirer of the State Department but I approach it without any ax to grind and I approach it with a serious concern for the problems it presents to you. This Department, to be blunt about it, stands between you and a potentially magnificent performance as President.

Kennedy spent most of his time running foreign policy and delegated domestic policy and the Congress to the Cabinet and his staff. Given your background on domestic policy, your political ability on the Hill, you will do just the reverse and should. Although Kennedy delegated domestic policy to strong leadership, it suffered at times from lack of White House attention. You will be delegating foreign policy to weak leadership. The cost will be even greater.

The proof of this is now in. . . . The Department acts out of domestic political innocence and fear of the American Right. As a result, it regularly takes a position that it cannot bring off or defend. It tries to prevent Chinese recognition by the French and fails; Security Council intervention in Cyprus and fails; block trade with Cuba and fails; and outlaw negotiations on the [Panama] Canal and fails. Also by trying to take these positions, it leads the opposition to believe it is right. Then having failed, it chalks up a defeat. This the press blames not on the Department but on the Administration. . . . It is a pattern endlessly, endlessly repeated.

It is my distinct impression that the Department is susceptible and indeed welcomes strong *political* leadership—that given such leadership, it will do a passably good job. I have never talked with you about Bill Fulbright. It has always been my feeling that Kennedy's most serious mistake was not in following his first instincts and making Bill Secretary of State. Harriman also has the kind of political experience which would qualify him. But here I get into an area where your knowledge of men is far ahead of mine. But of this I am sure: American foreign policy is successful when it is in the hands of men of liberal political stature who have a clear knowledge of how to lead both the Department and American political opinion. It is aimless and weak when it passes to experts who do not have the power to carry through on their convictions and who act out of fear of the American conservatives whom you handle so brilliantly on the domestic scene.

Johnson, of course, dismissed this request out of hand. He believed Galbraith's views were part of Robert Kennedy's efforts to recapture a measure of control over foreign policy. Far from accepting Galbraith's advice, Johnson moved to distance himself from Kennedy and the liberal wing. In an elaborate charade he blunted the pressure to make Kennedy his running mate in 1964 by pretending to find a "boomlet" in Georgia for Rusk as Vice President and for Secretary of Agriculture Orville Freeman in Minnesota. Then Johnson solemnly declared he was excluding any member of his cabinet from consideration, thereby eliminating Kennedy without the political damage of a direct attack. With Kennedy himself he was even more blunt. When, in the Oval Office, Kennedy suggested with regard to some matter that President Kennedy would never have made that decision, Johnson looked at him coldly and said, "President Kennedy isn't the President anymore. I am."

Despite the foreign policy reorganization, new ideas and initiatives were distinctly lacking in the first years of the Johnson presidency. Most of the creative energy of the new administration went into domestic affairs, civil rights, and the beginnings of what Johnson called his vision of the Great Society. In foreign affairs, optimism and vigor ebbed. Much of the reason for this lay in the fact that the world was becoming far more dangerous and complex; the era of unquestioned American preeminence and dominance over most of what happened on the globe was ending. American interests were threatened in ways that were difficult or impossible to control.

The men in charge were also bone-tired. They had already been through crises of extraordinary magnitude and danger. Their natural reaction was to hunker down and revert to safeguarding elemental American interests around the world, holding together the alliances and fighting Communist inroads and subversion in traditional ways. This approach was also a product of the fact that 1964 was an election year. The conservative wing of the Republican Party, led by Barry Goldwater, who would win the Republican presidential nomination later that year, was raising questions about American resolve against Soviet aggression. It was no time for new foreign policy initiatives that might provide ammunition against Johnson in the forthcoming presidential campaign. The grand initiatives of the Kennedy administration—such policies as the Alliance for Progress in Latin America, closer relations with neutralist countries and the newly emerging nations in Africa and Asia, and an era of negotiations with the Soviets— were either put in cold storage or were overwhelmed by events. American foreign policy became essentially reactive, concentrating on what Rusk called "centers of infection" around the world.

Fortunately, the crises and trouble spots in 1964, although serious, did not engage the superpowers directly or involve the threat of nuclear war. In Latin America the administration was concerned with Cuban attempts to export its revolution. The discovery of a Cuban arms cache in Venezuela and other subversive activities brought on a Rusk-led effort, crowned with success, to wring yet another resolution of condemnation and economic boycott against Cuba out of the Organization of American States. Rusk steadfastly rejected proposals by Fulbright and other liberal senators to seek accommodation with Cuba. When Cuba cut off the water supply to the American base at Guantanamo, he reaffirmed that the United States would retain the base for the "indefinite future" and helped arrange for an independent source of supply. The American policy toward Cuba would continue to be that "Castro communism must be isolated politically, economically, militarily, socially, and spiritually." Rusk tried without success to convince Britain and other allies to stop trading with Cuba. One day in 1964 Alec Douglas-Home, then the British Prime Minister, raised Johnson's ire by announcing, just after a meeting with the President at the White House, that Britain would sell buses to Cuba. "He should have said that in the House of Commons," Johnson fumed, "not on my front steps." Rusk had to calm the President down.

In other trouble spots around the world Rusk similarly was motivated to use American influence or covert aid to contain Communist subversion. When fighting broke out between the Greeks and the Turks on Cyprus, he publicly warned the Russians to stay out and sent George Ball to forestall a Turkish invasion of the island and a Greco-Turkish war.

In the face of a Turkish threat to intervene militarily, Rusk personally drafted a letter to Prime Minister Ismet Inonu of Turkey, sent under President Johnson's signature, warning that if Turkey went to war and the Soviet Union intervened, the United States would consider its obligations under NATO as not binding and would not come to Turkey's defense. It was an extraordinary measure, taken as a last-ditch effort to prevent war between two allies, and all the more meaningful because Rusk had sympathy for the Turks as the aggrieved party in the dispute, largely caused by the scheming Archbishop Makarios III, who wanted to force union of Cyprus and Greece. The letter, which Ball called "the most brutal diplomatic note I have ever seen" and "the diplomatic equivalent of an atomic bomb," was an essential element in preventing war.

By skillful diplomacy Rusk and Ball succeeded in quieting things down and establishing a U.N. peacekeeping force. Cyprus was a textbook example of how crisis diplomacy attained virtually every aim: forestalling Soviet intervention, maintaining the peace between two bitter antagonists, and preserving relatively good relations with all the contending parties.

In Africa, Rusk helped manage covert aid to combat Communist support of rebel activity in the Congo and in Zanzibar. Although he approved of CIA activities in the Congo, he was embarrassed by the disclosure that CIA-sponsored Cuban exiles were flying sorties against the rebels; he had been told their activities would be confined to training missions.

Indonesia was yet another problem in 1964 because of President Sukarno's policy of confrontation and subversion of the British-supported state of Malaysia. Lacking other means of influence, Johnson and Rusk abandoned the Kennedy administration's efforts to work with Sukarno and cut off all aid, reverting to the policy of isolating Sukarno and cooperating with the British. Rusk was gratified when in 1965 and 1966 anti-Communist generals in Indonesia seized power from Sukarno.

In Panama, trouble erupted in January 1964 with one of America's traditional allies over American control of the Panama Canal. When American troops opened fire to quell an angry riot, Panama broke diplomatic relations with the United States and the controversy simmered, for political reasons in both countries, until after the American presidential election of 1964. Rusk, who had long believed that American occupation of the Canal Zone was indefensible in light of the United States' espousal of a policy of anticolonialism around the world, quietly helped convince Johnson to enter into negotiations with Panama for a new treaty on the canal. But because it looked as if the canal would be inadequate to accommodate future needs of the military and of world commerce, the President also proposed that a new sea-level canal be constructed. Planners in the Department of Defense even advocated that the new canal be dug with the use of nuclear weapons. Rusk, who always was chary of any use of nuclear weapons, was adamant in his opposition, and the idea was quietly shelved.

Much of Rusk's time was taken up by the problems of the NATO alliance. Once again France was the major irritant. De Gaulle plotted an independent course, extending recognition to Communist China and opposing the American proposal for a multilateral force (MLF)—mixed national crews aboard NATO submarines carrying nuclear weapons. De Gaulle saw the MLF as an unnecessary provocation to the Soviets and a method of pressuring France into renouncing its independent nuclear deterrent. Rusk advocated the MLF as part of collective security and denounced de Gaulle's "unrealistic nationalism," adding in an excess of rhetoric that "absolute national sovereignty was outmoded in the modern world."

In reality Rusk's support of MLF was lukewarm at best, and he never threw his full weight behind it. In the 1960s there were European demands for a larger voice in nuclear planning, and MLF was advanced by the United States as a way of satisfying them. But Rusk knew that no U.S. President was going to surrender final control over firing nuclear weapons, and that the idea of a German finger on the nuclear trigger would upset the French and the British as much as the Russians. Although Rusk was satisfied with the status quo, he ad-

vanced MLF as a compromise position that would allow allied participation but American final control in nuclear matters. MLF really
foundered because the British and the Germans could not come to an
agreement on the issue, and with French opposition as well, the proposal was dropped.

As usual when he crossed swords with de Gaulle, Rusk had difficulty. De Gaulle took the further step in 1967 of pulling France entirely out of the military arm of NATO, and when he told Rusk to his
face that he wanted "every American soldier out of France," Rusk's
anger and impatience boiled over. "Does that include the dead Americans in the military cemeteries as well?" he asked. De Gaulle fell
silent, and Rusk felt a measure of satisfaction that he had at last gotten
in one good lick at de Gaulle. He was also angered when de Gaulle
announced, in defending his nuclear "force de frappe," that France's
missiles could be fired "in all azimuths," implying against the West
as well as the East. On seeing Couve de Murville, Rusk bluntly twitted
him, asking, "Should we take this into consideration in our own tar-
geting?" In Rusk's view de Gaulle's conception of the defense of
Europe was old-fashioned; he envisioned, first of all, a battle for Germany, and only after Germany fell, a battle for France. In vain Rusk
tried to convince him that in a nuclear war France would be a front-
line state from the start.

In relations with the two principal Communist antagonists, the Soviet Union and China, there was little movement. Rusk had not abandoned his aim of cautious probing for prudent agreements on specific
issues with the Soviets, and he continued regular contacts with Andrei
Gromyko, but there was no progress. Not ony did American domestic
politics during the election year get in the way, but the Soviet Union
was going through a leadership crisis of its own, which became evident when Nikita Khrushchev was suddenly ousted in the fall of
1964.

Rusk searched briefly for ways to begin a more normal relationship
with Communist China. In December 1963 he had approved a Roger
Hilsman speech in San Francisco testing the waters for a possible
two-China policy. In April 1964, on an official visit to Taiwan, he
pointedly avoided any statement that Nationalist China was the sole
rightful representative of the Chinese people, intending a signal of
flexibility to Peking as well as to the American public. But the efforts
were in vain, blunted by domestic politics and, later, by the worsening
war in Vietnam.

All the while, Rusk kept up his killing schedule, working seven days a week, keeping twenty to thirty appointments a day. The constant travel and endless rounds of meetings with foreign leaders and attendance at conferences were taking their toll on his mental and physical well-being. Insiders at State and the White House worried about his health. McGeorge Bundy appealed directly to Johnson to get Rusk to slow down:

> Your Secretary of State very much needs a rest. Twice in the last week he has spoken to me about nightmares, and once about his doctor telling him that he must have time off soon. Last night I sat next to Virginia Rusk, and she is deeply worried about him. . . . I think you should send him away for a solid ten days somewhere. . . . The only way in the world to make him go is to give him an order from the President of the United States. I have no travel plans and George Ball seems physically very tough right now. Between us, we can mind the store.
>
>   I put this matter urgently because it is almost unheard of for Dean or Virginia to give any sign of weakness, so that when I hear from both of them my ears go up like a beagle's.

But Rusk continued to drive himself. His inner strength was great, and few outsiders noticed his fatigue. His vision, however, seemed to narrow, and he reverted increasingly to the old, tested themes of his experience: the absolute necessity of collective security to keep the peace in a nuclear age, and the deterrence of aggression by Communist states preaching subversion against the free world.

By far the greatest challenge the Communist world posed to the Johnson administration was, of course, Vietnam. Only two days after Johnson assumed the presidency, on November 24, 1963, Rusk attended the first meeting he held on Vietnam. They discussed the recommendations of top-level officials following the Honolulu meeting of November 20–22, which Rusk had just departed when he heard the news of President Kennedy's death. There was no wide-ranging reassessment of policy. After a gloomy report of increased Communist activity from CIA Director John McCone, Johnson reaffirmed the American commitment: "[I am] not going to be the President who saw Southeast Asia go the way China did." President Kennedy's October 2 withdrawal order of one thousand troops was not rescinded publicly, but it was fudged; troop rotations were juggled so that the thousand men returned home without decreasing the total number of Americans in Vietnam. At this time Rusk joined others in opposing a proposal by the military to begin a bombing campaign in Vietnam. However, in January 1964 the situation worsened: secret intelligence reports showed that increasing numbers of North Vietnamese troops were coming south along the Ho Chi Minh Trail.

Few questions were raised concerning the American commitment in Vietnam in 1964. After all, the determination to help a friend in need was an American ideal going back at least to the time of Woodrow Wilson. Rusk in his public statements articulated that ideal. Vietnam had no important strategic or commercial value to the United States; the American interest was simply to safeguard freedom. That was considered sufficient:

> We have no desire for any bases or permanent military presence in that area. We are interested in the independence of states. That is why we have more than forty allies. That is why we are interested in the independence and security of the non-aligned countries. Because, to us, the general system of states represented in the United Nations Charter is our view of the world that is consistent with American interests.

Rusk constantly invoked the SEATO treaty in defending the American commitment to Vietnam. Although he had doubted the wisdom of SEATO when it was concluded during the Eisenhower administration, the treaty pledge was now an article of faith: "I do not believe that we can be honorable in Europe and dishonorable in Asia. I do believe that the United States must keep its pledged word." In less eloquent terms he expressed the same thought to a NATO Council of Ministers meeting in 1965, saying that "they must not expect the United States to be a virgin in the Atlantic and a whore in the Pacific." The sanctity of commitment was basic to Rusk. He told an interviewer:

> The idea in the minds of leaders in Moscow and in Peking that they had better be careful because those fool Americans just might do something about it is one of the principal pillars of peace in the world. . . .
> It has to do with the maintenance of peace in a system in which the United States has security treaties with more than forty nations.

Also fundamental in Rusk's view was the necessity for the United States to deter aggression. Harking back to his experience just after World War II, he drew parallels with the past:

Try and imagine a map of the world if it were redrawn as it would have been had we and others not been interested and concerned in what happened in Iran, Turkey, and Greece, and Berlin and Korea . . . the Philippines . . . Malaya and in Southeast Asia, or how the map would look if the missiles had successfully been established in Cuba.

Rusk's determination not to accept the French solution for a neutralist South Vietnam was reinforced by the experience with the Laos accords of 1962. From the beginning of that settlement North Vietnamese forces violated Laos's neutrality, and in the spring of 1964 the Pathet Lao, backed by Chinese Communists, drove government forces out of the key Plaine des Jarres. Rusk urgently conferred with Soviet Ambassador Dobrynin, but the Russians either could not or would not restrain Communist forces in Laos, because they were caught up with the Chinese in a competition for influence. Rusk saw this and counseled firmness in Vietnam. He had helped arrange the Laos accords in all good faith; if they could not work, how could a similar approach work in South Vietnam?

In his thinking about Vietnam, Rusk always had in mind the parallel with Korea, and he often invoked this similarity in his private and public statements: "In Korea the international community proved that overt aggression was unprofitable. In Vietnam we must prove— once again . . . that semi-covert aggression across international boundaries cannot succeed." The objective in Vietnam was also the same as in Korea:

We fought the Korean War, which like the struggle in Vietnam, occurred in a remote area, miles away, to sustain a principle vital to the freedom and security of America—the principle that the communist world should not be permitted to expand by overrunning one after another of the arrangements built during and since the war to mark the outer limits of communist expansion by force.

In his approach to the prosecution of the Vietnam War as well, Rusk always drew on his Korean War experience. He was cautious and did not want an invasion or extension of the war to the North. He had made the mistake in Korea of assuming the Chinese would not intervene, and he was not going to see it made again. He believed Chinese intervention would be disastrous because it would bring great pressure to bear for the use of nuclear weapons. Similarly, provoking the Russians would create a face-off between the superpowers and the danger of a nuclear exchange. Rusk strongly believed in staying as far away as possible from the brink of nuclear war. He therefore espoused the idea of a *limited* war:

> I do believe that when we reflect upon the consequences of the alternatives, primarily the alternative of abandoning Vietnam or of translating this into a larger war, the overwhelming majority of the American people would prefer to see us attempt to bring this to a peaceful conclusion without abandoning Southeast Asia and without a general war. . . . We have been in this situation before.

The war would also have a limited objective. There was no territory to be conquered or positive gain sought. Strategically, all Rusk was trying to do in Vietnam was to prevent something, although sometimes it was tactically necessary to go on the offense:

> When we speak of "winning" we do not have in mind the destruction of North Vietnam or a change in the character of its regime. . . . Our objective is simple—to assure those to whom we are committed by treaty they will not be overrun by external forces. . . . In the larger sense, "winning" means that it will be demonstrated that a course of aggression that could lead to general war will be stopped.

Rusk envisioned the desired end of the Vietnam war as a negotiation which, as in Korea, would reaffirm the approximate *status quo ante*. The problem was how to maneuver the North Vietnamese into accepting this:

> These men in Hanoi are not men from Mars; they are not different from other human beings. Every crisis that has been resolved since 1945 has been resolved by discreet and private contacts in which both sides agree that it is in the interest of both sides to resolve the problem peacefully.

The method Rusk thought best to convince Hanoi to enter into such negotiations was the policy of gradualism—measured military actions and responses to make clear American resolve to stay the course. Once it was clear to Hanoi that America was not going to abandon its commitment, Rusk reasoned, the Communist side would be pushed into negotiations. Rusk looked constantly for a signal similar to those which ended the Berlin blockade in 1949 and the Korean War in 1953, an informal invitation to come to the bargaining table, which led him to reassert on every occasion the firmness of American resolve and to declare that "peace in Vietnam rests with Hanoi."

In 1964 the situation in Vietnam was spinning more and more out of control. Both militarily and politically there was deep trouble. The strategic-hamlet program was not working, and more of South Vietnam's provinces were effectively under Vietcong control. The National Liberation Front, the political arm of the insurgency, expanded its operations and called for negotiations between various interested groups in South Vietnam "as a solution to the great problems in the country." The number of Vietcong attacks increased as they seized the initiative militarily. Hanoi was supplying leadership, direction, and crucial material to the NLF, but the substantial part of the Vietcong effort was indigenous to the South.

In the face of this, Johnson assembled his principal advisers at a meeting, and it was determined to send McNamara on another fact-finding trip to Saigon. Rusk took what the summary record calls "a sober view, even a pessimistic view" of events in Vietnam, but he called for action—whatever was required—"to overcome these weaknesses."

The McNamara trip in March 1964 deepened American involvement and laid the groundwork for future escalation. McNamara, Maxwell Taylor, and John McCone barnstormed the country in a show of support for the South Vietnam government. Key recommendations growing out of the trip were not only additional support for the South Vietnam government but also plans to bomb targets in North Vietnam. A policy called "graduated overt military pressure" against North Vietnam was routinely approved.

Rusk himself went to Vietnam at the President's suggestion on April 19. He met with Ambassador Lodge; Paul Harkins, the U.S. Commander of Forces; and General Nguyen Khanh, who had taken power in South Vietnam in a coup the previous January. The visit was intended to provide political support for Khanh, and Rusk was concerned with the inadequacy of funds for military aid. "As compared to the cost of a war or our withdrawal," he said, "the amount of money we are spending in Vietnam is small."

A short time afterward, on May 30, Rusk again went to Saigon, after attending the funeral of Indian Prime Minister Jawaharlal Nehru in Delhi. This time Lodge took him on a tour of some of the battle areas. They left from Bien Hoa airport near Saigon, which was jammed with fifteen long, sleek U-2 aircraft being used for reconnaissance over Laos, Cambodia, and North and South Vietnam. Rusk gritted his teeth and hoped the "newsies," as his staff called the press, would not recognize them.

He and Lodge and their staff boarded an old DC-3 and took off, ostensibly headed south to the area of the Mekong Delta, but after several minutes one of Rusk's aides remarked that "something is wrong." The sun was coming in the plane windows from the wrong direction; they were headed north. Rusk's security men grew apprehensive, but Lodge explained that they were going to Da Nang—he had put out the story that they were going to the delta as a safety precaution.

At Da Nang the group boarded a helicopter gunship for a flight to a government strategic hamlet. On the way Lodge leaned over and grabbed the chopper's machine gun, playfully wheeling the gun barrel across everyone's face. The gunner blanched and grabbed it away, crying, "No, no, no!" When it was under control, he explained that the gun was armed and ready to go. "Man, all you've got to do is touch that thing and it's going to go off."

On the flight Rusk mused about how many men it took to complete the security arrangements for his visit out into the countryside. He could see choppers all around him, and below two choppers were skimming low, just over the trees. Lodge explained that "those guys are there to draw fire if we come across the enemy." Hearing that, Rusk decided not to make any more trips into the field during the war; he did not wish other people to endanger their lives for the sake of his security.

On the way home from Saigon in early June, Rusk attended the next high-level meeting on Vietnam, in Honolulu. There was more discussion of bombing targets in North Vietnam and Laos and agreement for increased military pressure in the South. A hamlet-by-hamlet program for clearing and holding the countryside was approved, and American personnel would be added at all levels, as military province and district advisers and battalion advisers. Rusk brought up the necessity of preparing American public opinion for a wider war. It was agreed that the passage of a congressional resolution would be a deterrent to both North Vietnam and China. In June work began on a draft resolution to put Congress on record supporting the administration's Southeast Asia policy.

During this period Rusk began to spend most of his time on Vietnam, leaving other State Department matters largely to Under Secretary George Ball. His major concern was the instability of the government of South Vietnam, which was racked with factionalism

and strife. In January General Duong Van Minh had been deposed in
a swift, bloodless coup d'état led by General Khanh. It was administration policy to back Khanh, even though he was unpopular outside
of his base of support in the army. Khanh's coup did not end the
bickering in Saigon, however, and Rusk could not understand why
the South Vietnamese did not put their quarrels aside and fight the
Vietcong. He cabled Lodge: "Is there any way [to] shake the main
body of leadership by the scruff of the neck . . . ?" Invoking his experience in China, Burma, and India during World War II, he suggested to Lodge that stability could be achieved only "with a
pervasive intrusion of Americans into their affairs."

When Ambassador Lodge resigned in June, Rusk, as well as Mc-
Namara and Robert Kennedy, offered to take his post. President
Johnson insisted he needed Rusk and McNamara in Washington.
Rusk, in turn, vetoed the appointment of Kennedy, suggesting the
ambassadorship would be too dangerous and would raise the specter
of another tragedy for the Kennedy family. The President decided
instead to appoint Maxwell Taylor, and a career Foreign Service officer, U. Alexis Johnson, was named deputy ambassador. This completed the assignment of a new American team in Vietnam; a few
months before, General William Westmoreland had replaced Paul
Harkins as the U.S. Commander of Forces.

Rusk's diplomatic efforts and the new high-level American attempts
to produce unity in Saigon were unsuccessful. In August came Buddhist rioting in protest of emergency powers promulgated by the government, and a cycle of coups and countercoups began, as the
generals and power brokers in Saigon played musical chairs for control of the government. Despite the deteriorating situation, Ambassador Taylor publicly claimed "steady progress" in the Vietnam War.
In fact, he was receiving reports that the Saigon government controlled only 30 percent of the country's territory; 20 percent was in
the hands of the Vietcong and the balance was a dangerous no-man's-
land.

In the summer of 1964 the frustrated men who were in charge of the
American conduct of the war were looking for some dramatic way of
demonstrating American resolve in Vietnam. There was a growing
belief in the military that bombing North Vietnam—hitherto inviolate
—was the only means of persuading Hanoi to give up its campaign of
subversion in the South. The South Vietnamese generals were also
arguing for military action directly against the North. Clearly, an incident that would provide an excuse for bombing would serve many

purposes. It would provide support for the war in the United States as well, both in Congress and among the American people.

The hoped-for incident occurred in early August when the *Maddox,* an American destroyer, was attacked by North Vietnamese torpedo boats in the Gulf of Tonkin. At the time of the attack the *Maddox* was on an intelligence-gathering mission, part of a covert operation known as "De Soto" patrol. The *Maddox*'s venture into the Gulf of Tonkin beginning on July 31 coincided with a second secret operation, "Oplan 34-A," a program to send South Vietnamese commando patrols based in Da Nang on raiding forays along the North Vietnamese coast. On the night of July 30, 1964, a 34-A patrol led by American advisers raided two small islands in the Gulf of Tonkin. Early on Sunday morning, August 2, the *Maddox* came under attack by three North Vietnamese torpedo boats, which were easily repelled by the *Maddox,* assisted by planes from the aircraft carrier *Ticonderoga.*

Rusk and other advisers met with Johnson immediately after word of the attack reached Washington. The President was calm and willing to believe the attack had been a mistake. He ordered an augmented patrol: the *Maddox* would be accompanied by the destroyer *C. Turner Joy.* He later would have ordered a third destroyer into the gulf as well, but was dissuaded by Ball, who believed the De Soto operations were a provocation.

On the night of August 3 another 34-A raid was conducted on the coast of North Vietnam, and Commander John J. Herrick on the *Maddox* sent a message early on August 4 that electronic monitoring of North Vietnamese communications showed that they considered the *Maddox* patrol a support element of the raiding parties. Then at 7:40 P.M. Saigon time (7:40 A.M. in Washington), Herrick sent a message, based on the radio intercepts, that the North Vietnamese were preparing to attack the *Maddox* and the *C. Turner Joy.* Later that morning McNamara and officials at the Pentagon received a series of messages relayed from CINCPAC (Commander in Chief Pacific, then Admiral Ulysses S. Grant Sharp, Jr.) in Honolulu that the two destroyers were under continuous torpedo attack.

Later investigation has cast doubt on whether the second attack in the Gulf of Tonkin ever occurred. Neither destroyer was hit, and no torpedoes exploded. The attack orders in the radio intercepts could have been directed against the 34-A raids. The two destroyers took evasive action immediately after the news of a possible attack, and sonar readings from the *Maddox* interpreted as torpedoes could have been the echo of the vessel's own sonar beam hitting the rudders.

Subsequent interviews with crew members of the destroyers were inconclusive.

Upon learning of the radio intercepts on August 4, Rusk went over to the Pentagon, arriving at about 11:30 A.M. He urged retaliation this time, and other senior advisers—McNamara, McGeorge Bundy, and McCone—were of like mind. Rusk was not surprised by the reported attack. He had cabled Taylor the day before: "We believe that present OPLAN 34-A activities are beginning to rattle Hanoi, and the *Maddox* incident is directly related to their efforts to resist these activities. . . . We have no intention yielding to pressure." Rusk called the attack "unprovoked and unjustified"; he rejected the view that the 34-A activities were a provocation, arguing that South Vietnam was merely exercising its right of self-defense.

Conveniently, August 4 fell on a Tuesday, and Rusk joined the President, Bundy, McNamara, McCone, and Cyrus Vance (McNamara's deputy at Defense) for the regular Tuesday lunch. Johnson had already made up his mind to retaliate, and the discussion concerned only how many and what kinds of targets to hit. It was Rusk who persuaded the President to limit the retaliation to bases in North Vietnam and not to attack Haiphong, Hanoi, or more general targets. So the President ordered that preparations for the air strike begin. He also decided to seize on the opportunity to exact a resolution of support from Congress. He ordered Rusk to provide a draft, and that afternoon the Tonkin Gulf resolution was hastily prepared by Abram Chayes, the legal adviser at State, working from a draft prepared months before by McGeorge Bundy. Meetings with the congressional leadership were scheduled for later in the afternoon.

In the middle of these excited preparations, at 1:59 P.M., a message from Herrick on the *Maddox* reached Washington: "Review of action makes many reported contacts and torpedoes fired appear doubtful. Freak weather effects on radar and overeager sonarmen may have accounted for many reports. No actual visual sightings by *Maddox*. Suggest complete evaluation before any further action taken." This message was discounted, however, by men who had already decided to act. At 2:08 P.M. Admiral Sharp, talking with a McNamara aide in the Pentagon by telephone, gave his assurance that, despite Herrick's message, an attack had taken place. There was no disposition to wait for further confirmation in Washington. Johnson must not appear to be vacillating, and preparations were already going forward with a momentum of their own. It was left to McNamara to pull together the evidence. Rusk was willing to rely on the intercepts alone as the basis for retaliation.

Rusk strongly urged Johnson to ask Congress for passage of the Tonkin Gulf resolution. He believed that one of Truman's errors in the Korean War had been not to put Congress on record in unequivocal support of the administration's intervention. Rusk believed that constitutionally the President did not need a congressional resolution to prosecute the war, but it would prevent later political backbiting. At his insistence the Tonkin Gulf resolution was drafted very broadly, authorizing the "United States, as the President determines, to take all necessary steps, including the use of armed force, to assist any member or protocol state of the Southeast Asia Collective Defense Treaty requesting assistance in defense of its freedom." Rusk and Johnson took these words very literally; the resolution was a blueprint for later escalation. After it passed Congress with only two dissenting votes in the Senate, Rusk believed that the war in Vietnam had legal sanction under both domestic and international law. The resolution would also serve as a powerful warning to Hanoi.

Johnson later came to doubt that the second attack in the Tonkin Gulf had ever taken place. He told Carl Rowan, the head of the U.S. Information Agency, that "I'll go to my grave believing the military pulled a fast one on me there. I just can't fully trust the sons of bitches." He told Ball the same thing: "Hell, those dumb, stupid sailors were just shooting at flying fish." On the evening of August 4, however, President Johnson was not greatly concerned with ferreting out the truth of the matter; the greatest urgency was placed on mounting the air strikes in time for the President to go on television that evening and announce the retaliation to the American people.

Just after the Gulf of Tonkin incident, a powerful but carefully guarded voice of dissent appeared in the inner circle of presidential advisers. George Ball found himself in complete disagreement on the question of American involvement in Vietnam. In his judgment the military situation as well as the political instability of successive governments in South Vietnam were hopeless. Continuation of the war would entail unacceptable costs for the United States, both in lives and treasure. He emphasized the risks of escalation and urged a settlement and withdrawal that would be in effect a disguised capitulation. (Basically the same denouement that would occur in the Nixon administration almost ten years and 50,000 American lives later.) Ball, who was spending only a small fraction of his time on Vietnam (Rusk was preoccupied with Vietnam and Ball was doing almost everything else at State), raised his concerns informally with Rusk, evening after evening, frequently over a drink in the privacy of Rusk's office.

Ball and Rusk were usually on similar wavelengths both personally and professionally. Rusk, a man of guarded but deep emotions, loved Ball as a brother and had enormous respect for his competence and judgment. In later years he would say that Ball was the closest associate he ever had in government and that he was fully qualified to be Secretary of State. Ball was Rusk's alter ego in the sense that when Rusk was away from Washington, Ball acted with the full powers of the Secretary of State. There was never any doubt among subordinates at State that Ball was the last word on policy in the areas of his responsibility; Rusk always backed him up.

On Vietnam, however, Rusk was immovable. Hanoi simply could not be allowed to take over its neighbor by force. When Ball told him the war in Vietnam was not winnable, Rusk invoked the experience of World War II and Korea. He recalled for Ball the events of March 1942, when Hitler's armies were "smashing at the gates of Leningrad, Moscow, and Stalingrad; France was overrun; Rommel was rushing through North Africa toward Cairo." American intelligence was telling Roosevelt that the Soviet Union would be out of the war against Hitler in six to eight weeks. The Japanese had just destroyed the American fleet at Pearl Harbor and were rushing through the Pacific with seemingly no way to stop them. "What," he asked Ball, "if President Roosevelt had gone on nationwide radio and said, 'My fellow Americans, the jig is up'?" In Korea, too, Rusk recalled that "the allied forces were pinned down in that very small perimeter around Pusan at the tip of the peninsula. But we stuck it out and prevailed."

His fundamental disagreement with Ball on Vietnam did not affect their excellent working and personal relationship. Rusk trusted Ball completely, knew that he was sincere and was not trying to undermine him or the President. He urged Ball to take his views to President Johnson, McNamara, and other key advisers. "The President is entitled to hear your views as well as mine," he told Ball. Rusk's magnanimity surprised Ball as much as his narrow inflexibility exasperated him. Rusk was a complex character, with the intelligence and generosity of spirit to respect views other than his own, especially if they were sincerely held. In the end he was trapped by his adherence to his own deeply held principles; he was unable to judge their limitations or to determine when his assumptions no longer applied.

When Ball presented his arguments to McNamara, he found even less understanding than with Rusk. McNamara approached everything in purely quantitative terms. He saw the war as a numbers game of how many troops, how many air strikes, how much effort would be required to win. There was no question that the United States, with its superior resources, planes, and men, could raise the stakes to a level that would be unacceptable to the North Vietnamese. When Ball approached Johnson with his arguments, the President gave him a sympathetic hearing but remained unmoved. Ball thought Johnson had doubts but was in awe of, even to the point of feeling inferior to, his two brilliant advisers McNamara and Rusk. Johnson was also captivated by the story of the Alamo; the United States just couldn't walk away from a fight.

After the Gulf of Tonkin incident, the American election of 1964 was soon in full swing. The Republican standard-bearer, Senator Barry Goldwater, attacked the Johnson war policy from his vantage point on the right, arguing in favor of a "final push for victory" and bombing of the North. Rusk campaigned discreetly for Johnson's re-election, speaking out on Vietnam and painting Goldwater as an extremist whose views would lead to a dangerous escalation of the war. Rusk, as well as other administration officials who spoke out on the war, was caught up in a balancing act—condemning Goldwater-style escalation while carefully leaving the door open for postelection decisions to widen the war. There was a policy hiatus as any decisions to change existing policy were suspended until after the election, but contingency planning went ahead for the bombing and American troop increases.

Under these circumstances Rusk's press conferences and speeches were very guarded and carefully phrased. Misleading and vague, he spoke in generalities and half-truths. He was unequivocal about the commitment to South Vietnam, but echoed the Johnson campaign theme that the United States sought no wider war and did not intend to substitute Americans for Asians in the conflict. Disingenuously, Rusk vehemently denied that any major turn in Vietnam policy was being postponed until after the election, saying that "we are not concealing anything or . . . marking time or refusing to make the decisions that are required." To leave the door open, however, he said that he could not predict what would happen in the future because "the communist forces are writing the scenario." He defended his part in the campaign by telling reporters that when the foreign policy of the United States is discussed, "the Secretary of State should not be the only person to remain silent."

All the while, Rusk was making quiet diplomatic probes to try to end the conflict—but on American terms. He met frequently with Soviet Foreign Minister Gromyko, and at Nehru's funeral he held discussions with Soviet Deputy Premier Aleksei Kosygin on Vietnam. He asked J. Blair Seaborn, the Canadian member of the International Control Commission (set up to deal with infractions of the 1954 Geneva Accords), to serve as an intermediary with Hanoi. Everywhere his message was the same: the United States would leave Vietnam if North Vietnam agreed to an independent South Vietnam and gave up its aggression. He rejected an overture by U.N. Secretary General U Thant to hold talks with Hanoi; he did not trust Thant and suspected that the talks, if held, would focus only on American capitulation.

Johnson was returned to office, and immediately after the November election the administration's Vietnam policy underwent a high-level review. There was an air of desperation to the discussions, which the participants tried their best to keep out of the press. Although various policy options were considered, the only serious talk was of escalation. Rusk was in favor of escalation, but preferred to leave the details to McNamara and the military (much to Ball's discomfort). Rusk did sound warnings, however, about provoking the Russians or the Chinese. From his experience in Asia during World War II, he had a healthy skepticism about the effectiveness of any bombing campaign and its ability to change the course of Communist leaders. He advocated bombing of infiltration routes and supply depots, rather than large-scale operations in the North.

By early 1965 the pace of policy formulation was outrun by events. In January there was another military coup in Saigon, and in early February McGeorge Bundy went on yet another fact-finding mission. Vietcong attackers bloodied the American military installations at Pleiku and Qui Nhon. In response American and South Vietnamese jets hit military bases in North Vietnam, and a program of sustained bombing, code-named "Rolling Thunder," was approved. Rusk was in Florida recuperating from a severe case of the flu, but he concurred in these decisions.

On February 25, 1965, he set out his thinking in a rare personal memorandum to the President. "Everything possible," he argued, should be done "to throw back the Hanoi Vietnam aggression without a major war if possible." He called for an increased effort by the South Vietnamese but also the "immediate stationing in Da Nang of a Marine Battalion combat team to be reinforced promptly if the security situation calls for it." He also advocated "air strikes into North Vietnam—directly linked to specific events in South Vietnam." But he also reiterated his contention that the United States should not seek any "national military presence" in Southeast Asia or the "destruction by military means of the regimes in North Vietnam or mainland China.''

Thus, by March 1965 a new reality had emerged. America was now committed to bombing the North and using air power in support of troops in the South. The rules of engagement for U.S. ground troops also were changed: they were no longer simply advisers; their mission now was to "advise and assist" the South Vietnamese in combat operations. Most ominously of all, on March 9 two battalions of U.S. Marines were deployed at Da Nang. Their arrival came at the end of several days of persistent denials by the Defense Department that any American units were being sent to Vietnam.

Rusk said that the troop landings represented no change in American policy in Vietnam. This was the administration line, put out by order of the President, who did not want to cast a shadow over his Great Society program then pending in Congress. The reality was that a sea change in policy had occurred. American troops were now in Vietnam as self-contained, operational combat units. No longer could the United States claim to have only a support role. Its prestige and fighting men were committed; America was at war.

"I Have Become a Symbol of the War": Stalemate in Vietnam and the Six-Day War

T HE Americanization of the Vietnam War, and the incessant bombing campaigns after 1965 in particular, were the triggers of a new and strident social force in American life: the radicalization of the generation born during and after World War II. To this generation the experiences of Rusk and his contemporaries (the leadership of the country was largely in the hands of men who had served as line officers during the war) were dim historical memories. The youth of the 1960s were shaped by new realities and experiences. From childhood they had been bombarded with the venomous rhetoric of the Cold War. They had lived their whole lives with the threat of nuclear destruction hanging over them like the sword of Damocles. Many came from affluent middle-class families and had greater access to education than any generation before them, and they began to question the standards and values of their elders.

The civil rights movement was the first of the upheavals of the 1960s, and the youth of America embraced it, many against the wishes of their more traditional or prejudiced parents. They also embraced the sexual revolution, and young women were liberated, psychologically by the feminist movement and sexually by the pill. Rebellion was everywhere. Pop music gave way to rock and songs of social protest. Girls burned their bras and boys burned their draft cards. Hemlines rose to the point of indecency, culminating in the micro-miniskirt, and both sexes discovered hair, the more the better, as a symbol of their liberation. In their search for new forms of "meaning," increasing numbers discovered drugs—first marijuana, then more dangerous hallucinogenic, "mind-expanding" drugs like LSD. Some actively sought meaningful social change; others simply "dropped out."

Protest against the war in Vietnam from American youth first attracted widespread public attention in 1965, coinciding with the vast American escalation. It was begun by small but vocal groups of students who saw no reason for a policy of global containment of communism and objected to war in principle, except for the clearest kind of self-defense. Unlike the radical left of the '30s, '40s, and '50s, the student protesters eschewed Marx and Lenin in favor of Thoreau, Emerson, and Whitman as their spiritual ancestors. As the war grew, the radical leaders commanded more and more attention, among them Mario Savio and other student radicals at the University of California at Berkeley; Staughton Lynd, a professor of history at Yale; and Tom Hayden, who in 1962, while student editor of the *Michigan Daily,* helped found Students for a Democratic Society.

The protesters called for a unilateral withdrawal of the United States from Vietnam. Arguing from their own concept of a higher morality, they condemned the United States but overlooked or minimized Communist treachery and atrocities. They extolled or excused the policies of such leaders as Mao and Castro. "We refuse to be anti-Communist," declared Lynd and Hayden, "to justify a foreign policy that is no more sophisticated than rape." The tactics of the so-called New Left were borrowed from the civil rights movement, with which its adherents also sympathized. They began a series of "teach-ins" on university campuses, as well as demonstrations, sit-ins, lie-ins, and protest marches, staged to gain media attention. The protests and demonstrations were broadly aimed at the universities, government, and business, which they considered the "establishment," part of the "system" of oppression.

The war in Vietnam, however, was their primary target. Demonstrators created havoc at the Pentagon, which they called the "house of death." Recruiters from Dow Chemical, the manufacturer of napalm, attracted demonstrations on several college campuses. A Catholic priest poured vials of blood over records at a Selective Service office in Baltimore. A Navy recruiter was trapped in his auto by demonstrators at Oberlin College. And war protesters began to dog Rusk at all his public appearances, shouting him down and carrying signs:

RUSK KILLS CHILDREN FOR PROFIT and DEAN RUSK—LBJ'S SECRETARY
OF HATE.

The student radicals did not reflect the views of the majority of the
American people or even of most students at that time, but they had
an undeniable impact on the mood of the country. Young and old alike
were increasingly troubled and confused by the war, even if they saw
no alternative to American policy. After 1965 Vietnam became a war
of attrition. American casualties increased dramatically, and by early
1966 the flag-draped coffins started coming home by the score each
week. Winning was not gaining ground or conquering territory; it was
killing and maiming, vividly displayed day after day on the evening
news.

Many Americans began to wonder if it was worth it. Anxiety grew,
especially among college students who were subject to the draft. They
were the ones who were most affected by the war, who faced interruptions in their lives, and who were forced into personal decisions about
life and death, peace and war, self and country. By 1966 the universities, formerly quiescent, were in ferment, hotbeds of political and
social debate. The young—the baby-boom generation—were suddenly discovered as a potent social force. They had demographics on
their side. In 1966 there were 24 million people—one-eighth of the
population—between the ages of thirteen and nineteen. The number
of students enrolled in colleges and universities surged to over 7 million. And by 1967, on most of the nation's campuses, protest and
dissent were part of the air one breathed.

America soon became a country pulled apart along generational
lines. There was an abundance of exuberant youthful idealism, but
plenty of arrogant pride as well, the determined convictions of those
who believed they had a monopoly on truth and morality. But amid
the rash of songs and symbols of rebellion, one slogan stood out and
gradually began to cross the gap between the generations: "Make
Love Not War." In one of the memorable photographs of the time, a
student is shown stuffing a carnation down the barrel of the raised
rifle of a national guardsman.

At first the unrest on the campuses and the rebellious culture of the
mid-sixties made little impact on Rusk or most of the members of the
Johnson administration. Rusk was reminded of his Oxford days before
World War II, when the students in their folly overwhelmingly voted
against taking up arms for king and country. He mistakenly interpreted the student revolt as a return to the isolationism that he had
railed against in the 1930s. The students were at best misguided, and

at worst subversive, and he brushed them aside as of little consequence despite the attention they received. Most Americans, the polls
showed, supported the President on the war. Dissent, he believed,
served Hanoi, because it gave the impression that American resolve
was weak. Thus he redoubled his efforts to demonstrate the strength
of that resolve. He also lashed out at the critics of the war. In response
to a protest advertisement in *The New York Times* signed by almost
five hundred university faculty members who opposed the war, Rusk
said they were ''talking nonsense'': ''I sometimes wonder at the gul-
libility of educated men and the stubborn disregard of plain facts by
men who are supposed to be helping our young to learn.''

Meanwhile, in the fateful watershed months of the summer of 1965,
the military and political situation in South Vietnam was becoming
desperate, much more so than the administration was willing to acknowledge publicly. Despite the American bombing campaign in the
North and the presence of 70,000 American troops, the war was being
lost. Provincial capitals were being overrun by Vietcong and North
Vietnamese troops; South Vietnam was in danger of being cut in two
by the enemy. Intelligence reports from the U.S. Embassy in Saigon
described many of the South Vietnamese army units as ''useless'' and
said there was danger of imminent collapse of the war effort. In June
there was another upheaval in the military junta holding effective
power. Phan Huy Quat, the Prime Minister, was forced to resign and
was replaced by Nguyen Cao Ky, an air force pilot and a member of
the junta. Another ''young Turk'' of the Armed Forces Council, Nguyen Van Thieu, became chief of state and head of the armed forces.
The changes did not quell the unrest in the country, and agitation
continued, especially among the Buddhists. Ky reminded most Americans of the ''Red Baron'' character in the ''Peanuts'' cartoon or of a
refugee from some grade-B World War I movie. With his pomaded
black hair, thin mustache, natty clothes, and ever-present dark
glasses, he hardly looked like a statesman. While publicly expressing
satisfaction and approval of the Thieu-Ky government, privately administration officials were saying they had reached ''the bottom of the
barrel.''

In the face of these new setbacks in June and July 1965, President
Johnson made the most important decision of the war—one that put
the country on a course of escalation that was to last until the ago-
nized reappraisal of March 1968: to commit the United States to an
open-ended ground war in South Vietnam, conducted primarily with
American combat troops. The immediate occasion for this decision

was a request on June 7 by General Westmoreland for forty-four battalions—almost 200,000 men—from the U.S. and its allies. "No more niceties about defensive posture and reaction," said Westmoreland. "We [have] to . . . take the war to the enemy." America was going to take over the war.

Rusk was not yet convinced of the need for such a large commitment. With McGeorge Bundy, he argued at a meeting with the President on June 8 that the line should be held at 100,000, to see what progress could be made with that many troops. He was also uncomfortable with the idea of using American troops for search-and-destroy operations; he did not want to give up the option of describing their mission as essentially defensive in character. Later that day the State Department's press spokesman, Robert McCloskey, in a remarkable display of candor, revealed that Westmoreland had been given authority to use American troops in offensive combat operations. Johnson was furious about this "leak" until Rusk went over and calmed him down. "He'll be giving his future briefings somewhere in Africa," Johnson fumed. "A press secretary has a rough job," Rusk remonstrated. "He has 100 times a day to stub his toe, and mistakes will happen. He's doing a good job." So McCloskey stayed on at State.

The troop increase decision was debated at length by the President and his small circle of advisers—Rusk, McNamara, Bundy, Taylor, Ball, and a few others—who were fully aware of its momentous nature. It was the last opportunity, everyone knew, to hold the line on troop increases in Vietnam. There was already talk of the need for a huge force of over 600,000 men. In the end, at a meeting on July 21 the President decided, in his favorite phrase, to "put in his stack." The only significant voice of dissent was Ball, who spoke in favor of what was regarded as a "high-risk" strategy of peace and compromise. The meetings were not stormy, and most senior advisers concurred.

"We will stand in Vietnam," announced Johnson at his press conference on July 28. But he did not explain the full extent of his decision, saying only that the number of U.S. forces would be increased from 75,000 to 125,000 and that he would not call up the reserves. Almost as an afterthought, he added that "additional forces will be needed later, and they will be sent as requested."

In reaching this decision Johnson consulted not only with his staff but also with members of Congress, Senators Richard Russell and Mike Mansfield, and the "wise men"—Dean Acheson, Robert Lovett, and other former officials. According to Ball, Johnson harbored more doubts than either of his two principal advisers, McNamara and Rusk. Of the views and arguments he studied, one—Rusk's—seemed to be of "greater weight," according to William Bundy, Assistant Secretary for Far Eastern Affairs. It was presented in a rare memorandum prepared by Rusk—an exception to his policy of never putting anything on the record—no doubt inspired by the importance he placed on the decision. The memorandum was short and to the point and contained only one principal argument:

> The central objective of the United States in South Vietnam must be to insure that North Vietnam not succeed in taking over or determining the future of South Vietnam by force. We must accomplish this objective without a general war if possible.
>
> The integrity of the U.S. commitment is the principal pillar of peace throughout the world. If that commitment becomes unreliable, the communist world would draw conclusions that would lead to our ruin and almost certainly to a catastrophic war.

Rusk's conclusion was reinforced by frequent personal conversations with the President, and it paralleled McNamara's views. William Bundy was struck by the evolution of Rusk's thinking on the war:

> So Dean Rusk, skeptical in the fall of 1961 and uncertain in January of 1965 that South Vietnam had the political cohesion to be worth going all out for, had now concluded that to walk away from an American commitment, to temporize in our actions to meet it, to do anything short of all we possibly could, would pose the gravest possible danger to world peace. General war must be, if necessary, risked, for such a risk would be less than the risk of general war that might arise if the communist world concluded the U.S. would not carry through on an undertaking once it became difficult.

Johnson was convinced as well, although at the July 21 meeting he worried whether "Westerners can ever win in Asia." Yet he rejected pulling out: "Wouldn't all these countries say Uncle Sam is a paper tiger—wouldn't we lose credibility breaking the word of three Presidents?"

Rusk's thinking, which he pressed upon the President, was based largely on his experience during the Korean War. The North Vietnamese were using the tactics of guerrilla warfare rather than invasion, but they had the same objective as the North Koreans in 1950: to take over their neighbor by force. The United States had to demonstrate its resolve, which, as in Korea, meant the commitment of American troops, and to create a stalemate, which would show Hanoi that it could not succeed. At this point logic would dictate that Hanoi, like North Korea, would enter into realistic peace negotiations. Rusk thought this could be accomplished without general war if the United States made it clear it was not threatening the separate existence of North Vietnam and thereby provoking the Russians or the Chinese. He accordingly opposed any invasion of the North and any bombing that would constitute a threat to China. The war for Rusk was a contest of wills, and he was confident the American will would prevail. He embraced the concept of an open-ended but limited war without any realistic assessment of capabilities and costs on the American side. Sadly, it was a strategy that would work only if the North Vietnamese were playing by the same rules.

If Rusk's conception of the war was rooted in the past, so was the way he thought the decisions about the war were to be made and disclosed. Although he respected the power of Congress and got along well with individual members, he believed that only the President could properly make decisions committing American troops. The President was, after all, the Commander in Chief, a status Rusk took very literally. Under instructions from Johnson—who also thought of Congress as basically a body to be manipulated—Rusk told its members only what was absolutely necessary. Testifying before the Senate Foreign Relations Committee on April 30, 1965, he withheld the information that the President had approved troop increases in Vietnam up to 81,700, with another 41,000 being considered. He blandly informed the committee, "We have there now about 34,000 troops. It is very much under contemplation that it might be necessary to add to those forces."

He also rejected the entreaties of the Foreign Relations Committee to seek congressional approval before any further troop increases. The prosecution of the war demanded that such decisions be made by the President independently, Rusk believed. Afterward, in nothing more than a gimmick, the Johnson administration strategy was to seek congressional approval of a "supplemental budget request" to pay for them. In that guise any member of Congress voting against the bill could be accused of not supporting U.S. troops in the field. By contrast, the administration knew, seeking *prior* approval of a troop increase would only have engendered debate and division that would have harmed the war effort.

The American public was treated in much the same manner. Low-visibility decisions and a step-by-step process of troop commitment would allow a buildup without arousing the ire of—or fully informing —the American people. Rusk argued that the war should be fought "in cold blood": a limited war with limited aims could be conducted as dispassionately as possible, without disruption to most Americans' daily lives. He convinced Johnson not to call up the reserves to fight the war because it would impart too great a sense of urgency to the nation. The American people must become accustomed to fighting limited wars, Rusk believed, because this was the challenge of communism. The President had his own motives for keeping everything low-key: he did not want to endanger the passage by Congress of his Great Society domestic program.

Rusk also profoundly distrusted the press. It was part of his personality to be reserved, to stay out of the spotlight. Now, as the administration's chief spokesman on foreign policy, he was called upon to face often hostile reporters. He regarded the press as having motives fundamentally different from his own. They were not patriots and did not have the best interests of the country at heart. Their business was to make headlines, to get a story. "No blood, no news, is their creed," he often said. They harmed the war effort by negative reporting, distortion, and falsehoods; they never saw the full picture. Worst of all, some members of the press regarded themselves as self-appointed experts. Rusk was outraged when both Walter Lippmann and Arthur Krock sent him messages saying that if he would like to call on them, they would be glad to see him. He was upset when they invaded his privacy. The day after he took his fifteen-year-old daughter Peggy, dressed in an evening gown, out to a Washington hotel to see the singing group Peter, Paul, and Mary, he complained that all the reporters at the department were asking, "Who was that chick the Secretary was out with last night?"

Before every press conference Rusk, who was at ease and eloquent in informal settings, was nervous and taut. The cameras and hostile reporters unnerved him. It became his habit to down two scotches before every meeting with the press, which his staff called his "medicine." In response to questions he was often vague and evasive. He never disclosed options under consideration, and although he denies having lied to the press, his half-truths and incomplete answers were frequently misleading, as when, in June 1965, he told reporters that U.S. troops had only a defensive role in Vietnam, when in fact he knew that offensive operations were shortly going to be approved. This angered reporters, who often knew the full story through leaks anyway.

Rusk took some time to adjust to the glare of publicity. "Eighty percent of the questions I get are about the future," he complained to his staff. "People don't want to know what happened last week or last month, they want to know what's going to happen next week or next month, and I'm not going to speculate on that. But I just can't stand there before 600 reporters and a battery of television cameras and answer 80 percent of the questions by saying, 'Damned if I know.' " On occasion, with individual reporters, Rusk would lose his composure completely and lash out in anger. In a fury about a minor story by Tom Wicker claiming, during one of the periods of domestic unrest in Vietnam, that the Buddhists had taken control of a radio station in Hue, Rusk approached him at an embassy dinner and, red-faced, finger jabbing, said, "Why does *The New York Times* always get things incorrect?" (Wicker turned out to be correct.) On one occasion Rusk exploded at a reporter over a negative story about Vietnam, asking, "Whose side are you on?" In response to another critical article he acidly commented, "None of your papers or your broadcasting apparatus are worth a damn unless the United States succeeds. They are trivial compared to that question."

Rusk exasperated Lawrence Spivak, the host of "Meet the Press," by objecting to Spivak's introductory statement that the reporters' questions are designed only to elicit news and "they are not responsible for their questions." "Now look, Larry," Rusk said, "you say this every time, but dammit, these reporters can be as responsible for their questions as I am for my answers. So if you say that this time, I am going to say that I am not responsible for my answers." "You wouldn't do that," Spivak said. Rusk smiled. "Try me and see." Spivak left out the statement.

Rusk's half-truths, McNamara's false optimism, and Johnson's manipulations, conspiracies, exaggerations, and distortions caused what was loosely known as the "credibility gap" between administration policy in Vietnam and its public articulation. As the number of troops in Vietnam reached 200,000 in late 1965, many Americans recalled with bitterness Johnson's oft-repeated campaign statement, "We seek no wider war." A sick joke circulating at the time went: "People told me that if I voted for Goldwater in 1964, we would have 200,000 men fighting a war in Vietnam within a year, and by God, they were right!" Rusk pointed out that the "no wider war" theme of the 1964 campaign had always been qualified by words like "seek" and "hope." But many thought it a cruel delusion just the same—campaign rhetoric, after all, is not something to be parsed, like a lawyer's brief. Rusk's defense of Johnson was the equivalent of saying "You didn't read the fine print."

Yet, despite rancorous incidents, there was an undercurrent of respect between Rusk and the press. The "working stiffs" of the Washington press corps liked him because he did not play favorites; he gave them the same information he gave to the *Times*'s James Reston and the *Washington Post*'s Walter Lippmann. Reporters also marveled at how Rusk loosened up at informal gatherings. He started a "bottle club"—a weekly meeting over drinks—with the regular State Department correspondents. "To have a drink with Dean Rusk," one of the bottle-club men said, "is to like Dean Rusk." There was also a glimpse of the "real" Rusk on long plane rides, when he was away from the pressures of his duties and there was nothing much to do. Staff members would say the only time they saw Rusk relax was when he was trapped in the sealed tube of an airplane at 35,000 feet. Then he cast off his office and became again just an affable Southerner, playing bridge or poker and laughing easily. Carl Rowan remembers that one day, on the way back from a conference in Geneva with Gromyko, Rusk joined a group of newsmen who were in the middle of a poker game. "Hey, fellahs," he called, "am I eligible to get in this game?" Everyone nodded and two of them jumped up to give Rusk a seat. He waved them off. "Hell no, I don't want your seat." And he went back to the ice cooler, dragged it about twenty feet down the aisle, threw a blanket over it, and sat down to play. Even those who got to know Rusk informally, however, did not feel they understood him. He was agreeable, soft-spoken, and even-tempered, with a facility for lucid explanations of difficult issues. But he was a mystery, an enigma; they kept waiting for him to emerge, to become outraged or passionate about some cause or event, but he disappointed them. All were struck by his reticence and reserve; reporters were astonished to find that they could find no one—whether secretary, aide, or colleague—who felt really close to him.

When in the summer of 1965 *Life* magazine published excerpts from Arthur Schlesinger, Jr.'s book *A Thousand Days* disclosing that President Kennedy was baffled and disappointed by the "Buddha-like" Dean Rusk and intended to fire him after the 1964 election, the press largely came to Rusk's defense. Most editorial and news commentary regarded Schlesinger's attack as a mischievous attempt to discredit Rusk to the advantage of the liberal Kennedy wing of the Democratic Party, which opposed the war in Vietnam and other aspects of Johnson's foreign policy. It was called an irresponsible use of "the idle chitchat of a dead man" and condemned as "kicking a man when he is unable to answer because of his office." With columnists coming to his defense, the "Rusk must go" movement withered on the vine. In fact the attack had the opposite effect, eliciting sympathy and buoyant praise for Rusk's performance. William S. White wrote in the *Washington Post* that "no Secretary of State in three decades has been more influential, more warmly liked in Congress." And John Hightower of the Associated Press wrote that "Rusk's persistence in sticking to the middle of the road, plus his reputation for intelligence, integrity, and industry, have combined to make him a political asset to both President John F. Kennedy and President Johnson in ways the politicians in the first year did not foresee."

Rusk was personally hurt by Schlesinger's blast, but he handled it well. Rather than try to meet the attack, when asked about it he simply smiled and said, "Washington is a very wicked city." In a snide reference to Schlesinger, he also commented that he did not intend to write his memoirs, because he wished to protect the confidences of his colleagues in government. Privately, he was more cutting, telling a few associates that one day he was with President Kennedy when Schlesinger made some "off-the-wall statement" about foreign policy. After Schlesinger left the room Kennedy chuckled and said, "Arthur is sometimes very amusing in the Rose Garden."

Schlesinger's attack had the effect of even further cementing Rusk's relationship with Johnson, who was also derided in the book: Schlesinger quoted Robert Kennedy as saying in dismay when Johnson accepted the offer to become John Kennedy's running mate in 1960, "My God, this wouldn't have happened except that we were all too tired last night." Johnson pointedly went out of his way to praise Rusk, saying at a news conference that he was not only first in the cabinet, but he's "number one with me" as well. "He's got judgment and courage," Johnson told all who would listen. "He has the compassion of a preacher and the courage of a Georgia cracker. If you're going in with the marines, he's the kind you want at your side." At a National Press Club luncheon in Washington shortly after the book was published, Rusk was introduced and received a standing ovation from all, with the notable exception of Arthur Schlesinger, who was seated just in front of the head table and conspicuously did not rise. Johnson, who was also there, was seen to go quietly over to where Schlesinger was seated. "What's the matter, Arthur," he asked, "is something wrong with your legs?"

In the midst of the protracted debate on Vietnam in the crucial year of 1965, the Johnson administration had to deal with another difficult crisis: the Dominican Republic. There had been unrest in that Caribbean country since the death of Trujillo in 1961. Coups and counter-coups racked the Dominican Republic until, in December 1962, constitutional government was ostensibly restored with the election of Juan Bosch, an intellectual who believed in social reform. President Kennedy, along with Rusk, had hailed Bosch's victory and feted him when he came to Washington early in 1962 on an official visit. Despite the public enthusiasm for Bosch, however, Rusk was warned by other Latin leaders—Rómulo Betancourt of Venezuela, José Figueres Ferrer of Costa Rica, and Luis Muñoz Marín of Puerto Rico—that Bosch was a poet and dreamer; he would not be able to organize and administer a government and would not last a year in office.

The prediction proved correct when, on September 25, 1963, Bosch was ousted by the military and other groups in a bloodless coup and sent into exile. Power was now in the hands of the military, headed by the staid Colonel (later General) Elias Wessin y Wessin and a former automobile dealer, Donald Reid Cabral. The new regime promised elections by the fall of 1965, but because of economic factors (there was a terrible drought that spring, and the price of sugar, the key Dominican export, had dipped below three cents per pound on the world market) and the factionalism left over from Trujillo, it was evident that the country was a tinderbox ready to explode. The regime in power was not hated, but it had little popular support. Several Army officers planned a coup to take place in June, but a measure of the unrest was that even the rebel leaders could not control events, and the rebellion began early in April 1965.

On the morning of Saturday, April 24, fighting broke out at two army bases. At first there was confidence that the government forces of General Wessin would easily prevail, but by Monday, April 26, there was widespread anarchy, especially in the capital, Santo Domingo. Army officers loyal to Juan Bosch were fighting to take over the government, but there were also army units who favored a Trujillo-style dictatorship, and members of three different Communist parties were active in the city, as well as armed civilians. During the next three days the situation continued to deteriorate. Neither General Wessin nor any other power was able to restore a semblance of order. Youths called "Tigres," armed with machetes, roamed the streets, killing and looting. Public services—power, light, and water —were unavailable in many areas. Civil authority broke down completely, and police were special targets of the mobs. At least 2,500 people were killed between April 25 and 29. Snipers were active at the wall surrounding the U.S. Embassy in Santo Domingo, and Americans in the city were told by the embassy to go to the Embajador Hotel on the outskirts of the city to await evacuation.

After a new government junta was formed on Wednesday, April 28, there was a lull in the fighting. Ambassador W. Tapley Bennett advised George Ball by telephone that no help was needed, but Bennett changed his mind abruptly when a rebel mob broke into the offices of the Agency for International Development, snipers began firing at the evacuation areas around the embassy, and an armed gang lined up the evacuees at the Embajador Hotel and began firing submachine guns over their heads. At 5:16 P.M. a "critic"—highest priority—message from Bennett arrived at the White House. "American lives are in danger," it read, and requested U.S. Marines to establish a beachhead around the Embajador Hotel to assist in the evacuation of Americans and other foreigners. When the message arrived President Johnson was huddled with Rusk, Ball, McNamara, McGeorge Bundy, and White House press secretary Bill Moyers, discussing Vietnam. With no dissent, the decision was made to respond, and within hours four hundred Marines landed on the island to secure the embassy and evacuation areas around the Embajador Hotel. It was the first time since 1921 that U.S. Marines had gone ashore on business in the Caribbean, and the first time since the Nicaragua intervention of 1927 that they had been used in all of Latin America.

There is no question that the first American intervention on April 28 was motivated primarily by the desire to protect endangered American citizens. Critics have claimed that the danger was overblown, but it would have been foolhardy in the extreme to wait until blood had been spilled. What has remained controversial, however, is the second phase of the Dominican operation, the landing of additional American troops in massive numbers—14,400 by May 2, and eventually a total of 22,000 men. Juan Bosch, who remained in Puerto Rico, and many of his supporters accused the United States of sabotaging the return to constitutional government of the Dominican Republic. Many in the United States agreed, and the intervention was criticized widely in Latin America and in Europe, especially by the French.

The President's decision to intervene massively—supported publicly by Rusk, though in private he was arguing for a greater role for the OAS—was motivated by the fear of a bloodbath in the country (an OAS call for a cease-fire on April 30 had been ignored) and by the fear of another Castro-style dictatorship in the Caribbean. Critics have disputed both reasons, and they were given ammunition by exaggerated statements both in Washington and from the embassy in Santo Domingo. When Johnson in a speech talked about "headless corpses" in the streets, Rusk hurriedly called Bennett and told him, "For God's sake, see if you can get some pictures right away." The White House also released a list of known Communists operating in the Dominican Republic, and some of the information turned out to be false. Yet there is no doubt the basic facts claimed by the administration were correct: although Bosch was not a Communist, several Communist groups were trying to use him to take over the country. Rusk had little respect for Bosch, who had had his chance and failed. He was also revolted by what he considered Bosch's lack of courage and his double-talk. Bosch was reluctant to return to Santo Domingo without protection, and he asked for an American military escort even as he was denouncing the landing of American troops. Ambassador Bennett regarded Bosch as "half crazy" and a troublemaker. Rusk was also enraged by *The New York Times* reporting, particularly because he believed that their chief correspondent in the Dominican Republic was acting as a political adviser to Bosch.

There was also a great deal of hypocrisy behind the objections to American intervention. Bennett was approached by many Dominicans, including the secretary general of Bosch's own party, who asked for secret meetings, at which they told him they wanted the Marines but would have to denounce the U.S. action publicly. The papal nuncio and the ambassadors of Argentina, Colombia, and Ecuador all privately told Bennett that Marine intervention was essential. In Washington the Mexican ambassador to the OAS told Rusk privately that the United States should go in, but that, of course, Mexico would have to object. Rusk also received a message from de Gaulle, asking that the American protection zone be moved over five blocks to take in the French Embassy—even as France was severely criticizing the American intervention.

The American action was also criticized because it was unilateral and in violation of the OAS Charter. Johnson had a poor opinion of the OAS, saying at one point that "they couldn't pour warm piss out of a leather boot." He insisted on running the show himself, acting both as Commander in Chief and the State Department's desk officer for the Dominican Republic. Rusk, however, recognized the need for OAS participation from the beginning, and even before the initial decision to commit the Marines he had formally asked the OAS Council to discuss the Dominican situation. The OAS eventually did take action, calling for a cease-fire on April 30 and on May 6 establishing an inter-American peacekeeping force, but this came on the heels of the American intervention. Rusk also believed that sending in the Marines to cope with the emergency was in accordance with international law. The chief of the Dominican governing junta, Pedro Bartolmé Benoit, had requested help (Ambassador Bennett tried to get this in writing, but in the confusion did not), the situation had degenerated into a state of anarchy, and Americans were in danger. Under the circumstances it would have been irresponsible to stand idly by, waiting for the OAS to act.

The U.S. intervention in the Dominican Republic was both justified and successful. It opened the door to relative stability and democracy for that country, and through the patient efforts of an American team led by OAS Ambassador Ellsworth Bunker, a provisional government was created to prepare for free elections. The American vital interest in the Dominican Republic was clear and unequivocal: situated five hundred miles from Miami and next door to Puerto Rico, a Communist Dominican Republic would be unthinkable. The cost of the intervention was not disproportionately high, and the military involvement was overt and in sufficient force so that there could be no effective challenge to the mission. The troops were also speedily withdrawn. The OAS, moreover, largely because of Rusk, was not ignored and played a significant role. Lingering doubts were caused primarily by President Johnson's bluster and the fact that the reasons for the landings were not effectively explained at the time.

The Dominican affair quickly receded from public view, but Vietnam was always there, growing like a cancer and becoming all-consuming. And as the war expanded Rusk became more and more deferential to McNamara and the Joint Chiefs on matters of strategy and tactics. Ball thought he was too willing to go along with whatever McNamara and the military wanted. But Rusk did not think it was his role to challenge the military, and he did not want any hint of dissension in the administration to come out in public because it would only encourage Hanoi. Rusk usually quickly agreed with McNamara's decisions. "In for a penny, in for a pound," an aide heard him tell McNamara, talking about a decision to base bombers in South Vietnam.

Yet he did not hesitate to give McNamara advice, again drawing on his experience in Korea and in Burma during World War II. He deplored the fact that there was no joint allied command—the Americans and South Vietnamese ran separate operations, not to mention the Koreans, Australians, New Zealanders, and other forces. It would be better to have an integrated command structure, as in Korea, he told McNamara; this would allow better use of the South Vietnamese, who could be molded into an effective fighting force, as Stilwell had done with Chinese troops in Burma. The Koreans were effective, and could also be given a larger role. But an integrated command was resisted by Westmoreland and the Joint Chiefs, who had little regard for non-American troops.

Rusk also did not like the fact that the air war was under the operational control of CINCPAC in Hawaii; in effect this meant there were two wars, the air war in the North and the ground war in the South. Admiral Sharp and his cohorts, Rusk thought, were making the same mistake as Claire Chennault in China, thinking that air power alone could win the war. He believed the air strikes could be effective only if closely coordinated with the war in the South.

Rusk worried because the U.S. military seemed to have no good strategy for dealing with guerrilla warfare and hit-and-run insurgency operations. The only way Westmoreland knew how to deal with the situation was to request more men. Rusk thought that Johnson too readily acceded to Army recommendations, and believed that the American forces had too great a ''tail,'' soldiers who never saw combat and spent their time in the bars and officers' clubs in Saigon. Television also had a pernicious effect on the war effort. Every evening the American people saw the carnage of war on the news. What would have happened, he wondered, if Guadalcanal, the Anzio beachhead, or the Battle of the Bulge had been carried on television every day? Rusk came to believe that some form of censorship should have been imposed at the beginning of the war.

The U.S. Army never developed a consistent strategy for stopping the infiltration of regular North Vietnamese units into the South. This infiltration was the key new element of the war, beginning in 1965, comparable to the more dramatic entry of Chinese troops into the Korean War. Rusk thought that American troops should have formed a line across South Vietnam and Laos to stop the infiltration; the Army believed, however, that it was better to concentrate on holding all the provincial capitals and principal cities in the South. Rusk, however, opposed any idea of invading North Vietnam. When Walt Rostow, who succeeded McGeorge Bundy as National Security Adviser, put forward a plan for a MacArthur-style amphibious landing of troops around Vinh, in the narrow neck of North Vietnam, Rusk voiced his fear of riling up the Chinese. Rostow thought he was a captive of his bad experience with the Chinese during the Korean War.

Rusk was directly involved with the bombing of North Vietnam. At each Tuesday luncheon Johnson, Rusk, and a small circle of advisers went over the list of targets submitted by the Pentagon and made determinations. Much of the time Rusk exerted a moderating influence on the often extreme demands of the military to bomb civilian targets and areas around the cities. From his knowledge of bombing in World War II, he had little faith in the efficacy of the bombing campaign to force Hanoi to yield. He opposed bombing Hanoi, Haiphong, and other population centers because it would bring about needless civilian casualties and, if anything, would increase North Vietnam's will to fight. He argued that Haiphong should be left alone because if the port city were destroyed, the Russians, who brought supplies in largely by water, would lose their influence in Hanoi, leaving the field to the more dangerous Chinese. When it came to airfields, supply depots, bridges, infiltration routes, and other military targets, however, Rusk thought the bombing was effective and necessary to increase the length of time it took to bring men, weapons, and supplies into the South. The bombing also demonstrated the American will to continue the fight, but it could not win the war.

Johnson looked primarily to Rusk to get peace negotiations started. After a long period of temporizing on whether he would hold peace talks with the Communists, in April 1965 the President made headlines with a speech at Johns Hopkins University, offering to begin diplomatic discussions with North Vietnam "without prior conditions." Hanoi immediately denounced the proposal as a "fraud" and put forth its own plan for talks on the basis of peaceful reunification of Vietnam in accordance with the program of the National Liberation Front. Nor did Hanoi make any response to a five-day bombing pause in May.

In looking for an opening to negotiations with Hanoi, Rusk was not willing to compromise the basic American demand that North Vietnam must end its aggression. He advised Johnson to rebuff an effort by U Thant to set up a meeting with Hanoi because Thant wanted to include talks with the National Liberation Front, and Rusk thought he was simply interested in finding a face-saving solution for an American withdrawal. In November 1965 McNamara proposed a Christmas bombing pause based on a recommendation from Llewellyn Thompson that "the Russians thought something good might come of it." Rusk was skeptical and wanted assurances that Hanoi would reciprocate in some way. He thought a bombing halt was a card that could be played only once, and still looked for a quiet signal such as those which had resulted in the ending of the Berlin blockade and the Korean War. When, on December 4, McGeorge Bundy reported that

Dobrynin had also said that the Russians would be able to help if there was a bombing pause, Rusk's hopes rose, and he joined in approving a long pause that lasted thirty-seven days, accompanied by a major peace initiative, as Johnson sent Harriman, U.N. Ambassador Arthur Goldberg, and Mennen Williams to confer with every Eastern European and neutralist leader who would talk to them. Rusk himself conferred with Hungarian Foreign Minister Janos Peter. When nothing came of this Rusk, in a meeting on January 26, urged a resumption of the bombing, adding that a report on the pause should be made to the U.N. Security Council in order to "mute" Senator Wayne Morse, a noted dove who was advocating repeal of the Tonkin Gulf resolution. Johnson agreed, saying, "I was against the first pause, and the second pause. It has created a situation of doubt. . . . I've played out my pause—not from 115 countries have I gotten anything." But he added, "I want you men to evolve for me political moves and peace moves—initiatives of my own . . . because I guarantee that the Fulbrights and the Morses will be under the table and the hard liners will take over—unless we get [peace] initiatives."

Rusk believed that the Russians were the key to getting peace talks going. He had long private discussions with both Gromyko and Dobrynin, and from these talks he became convinced that the Russians were trying to help and had little interest in seeing the United States bogged down in Vietnam. Gromyko and Dobrynin blamed the Chinese for the failure of Hanoi to come to the bargaining table. They explained to Rusk that their hands were tied, at least temporarily; the Soviet Union had to help Hanoi to avoid pushing North Vietnam totally into the Chinese camp.

Rusk was willing to accept this explanation because of his fundamental belief that the Soviets, while they were adversaries, were interested in avoiding confrontation with the United States. Moreover, he had been through so many crises with Gromyko and Dobrynin that he regarded them almost as friends. He liked both of them personally, and in their meetings there was genuine warmth and pleasantries about the health of their wives and children. He trusted them perhaps a little too much. In contrast, he considered China the primary adversary in the Vietnam War. China was a renegade state that had to be tamed and taught a lesson. China was also in an expansionist phase, Rusk feared; it was looking to dominate Southeast Asia as well as other Third World countries in Africa—the Congo, Mali, Ghana, and Tanzania. In 1966 the terror of the Cultural Revolution began, confirming his convictions.

Rusk made an overture to China, but his plan was ill-conceived and ineffective. In April 1966 he gave a statement on China to the House Foreign Affairs Committee, which was billed as "the first major exposition of U.S. policy on Communist China since 1958." He held out a hand of friendship, predicting that China would someday become a great power that "would be expected to have close relations—political, economic, and cultural—with the United States." At the same time, however, he listed the unchanged lines of American policy with respect to China: support for the government on Taiwan and opposition to U.N. membership for the People's Republic of China except under stringent conditions. Not surprisingly, the initiative was ignored by the Chinese.

After this failure Rusk again switched to a hard line, calling the Chinese "blatant advocates of violence." Then, at a news conference in October 1967, he caused a great stir by referring to the dangers of "a billion Chinese armed with nuclear weapons." His statement caused several reporters to accuse him of racism, of raising the cry of a "yellow peril" loose in the world, and Senator Eugene McCarthy called for his resignation. Rusk was bitterly angry at the racist interpretation of his speech, but he stood by his remarks.

About this time Chiang Kai-shek came to Washington for a state visit, and Rusk and Chiang had a frank discussion about Vietnam and the chances of Chinese entry into the war. Chiang was bitter and bellicose, railing against what was happening on the Chinese mainland and the madness of the Communist leaders. No one could know what they would do if they felt provoked. But as he was about to leave, the wizened old warrior, who had fought the Communists all his life, turned and shook his finger at Rusk: "But don't you *ever*, Mr. Secretary, even *think* of using nuclear weapons against China!" Blood, after all, Rusk reflected, was thicker than water, especially in the case of the Chinese.

After 1966 China became increasingly enclosed within itself, caught up in the whirlwind of the Cultural Revolution. The Soviet Union could not or would not be of much help in Vietnam, and the war dragged on, a terrible growing monster. The numbers of casualties on all sides—American, South and North Vietnamese—grew staggeringly large. Outrages inevitably were also perpetrated against civilians: villages were burned or destroyed, crops were ruined; there were beatings, torture, and death. The massive American intervention was matched by North Vietnam in will, if not numbers of men and matériel. The situation became steadily worse; the government in the South was weak, ineffectual, and corrupt, and the American troops, if they were not losing, were making no progress in winning the war.

In mid-1966 McNamara, from his statistical analysis of the Communist forces, the degree of pacification of the countryside, and the rate of infiltration, came to a startling conclusion: the war was not winnable militarily. Despite the introduction of large numbers of American troops, the ratio of friendly to enemy strength had only increased from 3.5:1 to 4:1 since the end of 1965. The United States would be unable to "achieve decisive attrition" by introducing more troops; North Vietnam was clearly capable of adjusting to American strategy, and the result was only a "higher level of military standoff." Nor had the air war effectively prevented supply or infiltration into the South. McNamara's grim assessment was disputed by the military and by advisers such as Walt Rostow, who continued to believe the United States was winning the war. Rusk took a middle course, arguing that we had "established a militarily impregnable position in Vietnam" and that negotiations would come if only we were patient.

But McNamara's assessment, which was kept secret, produced a greater willingness on the American side to negotiate, and Rusk and Arthur Goldberg launched a peace offensive that fall in the United Nations. Again they searched for a formula to bring Hanoi to the bargaining table, proposing to stop air attacks and withdraw American forces if North Vietnam made similar concessions. Hanoi in return insisted on four preconditions for peace: unconditional cessation of the bombing; withdrawal of all American and allied forces; removal of foreign armaments; and an opportunity for the Vietnamese to settle their "internal differences" among themselves. To Rusk this was only an unacceptable demand for an American surrender.

Nevertheless, he pressed on with the theme of mutual disengagement and withdrawal. In a speech on October 12 he asked North Vietnam for private discussions to "clarify" the peace proposals. "The objective," he said, "is to achieve an organized peace, enlisting the cooperation of many nations." He also cautioned against "those who want to go all out—apply maximum power and get it over with." At a conference on the war with allied leaders in Manila at the end of October, the offer was strengthened, and the communiqué promised an allied withdrawal six months after the North Vietnamese pullout and a reduction of violence in the South. The initiative came to nothing—there was no response from North Vietnam, and it was attacked by Richard Nixon and Republican leaders as a disguised "abandonment of South Vietnam."

In early 1967 there was a glimmer of hope. Hanoi seemed to drop its four conditions to peace talks and hinted that negotiations could begin if the United States unconditionally stopped the air raids in the

North. Rusk was cautious and let it be known that the Johnson administration "must know what the reaction would be before it was prepared to halt raids in the North." In a concession, however, he announced that the United States was prepared to discuss acceptance of the National Liberation Front as a "full negotiating party" if peace talks were convened.

In February, during the Tet holiday truce, it was decided, over the strenuous objections of the military, to test the reaction of the North Vietnamese by a day-to-day bombing pause. Soviet Premier Kosygin was in London at the time, and President Johnson authorized the British to open discussions that might lead to peace negotiations with Hanoi. "We are prepared," Johnson wrote Prime Minister Harold Wilson, ". . . to inform Hanoi that if they will agree to an assured stoppage of infiltration into South Vietnam, we will stop the bombing of North Vietnam and stop further augmentation of U.S. forces." This proposal became known as the "Phase A–Phase B" formula: the United States would stop the bombing (Phase A) in return for some immediate steps (Phase B) by Hanoi to stop infiltration. In negotiating with Kosygin, the British worked closely with U.S. Ambassador David Bruce and Chester Cooper, a CIA veteran who was then deputy to Ambassador-at-Large Averell Harriman. Rusk was very optimistic; he told congressional leaders on February 8 that he was "convinced that the Soviet Union would be prepared to see this matter settled on the basis of the 17th parallel and the *status quo ante*."

While the British were talking with Kosygin in London, President Johnson unadvisedly decided to open another channel to Hanoi. He wanted to make a personal appeal to North Vietnamese President Ho Chi Minh so there would be no misunderstanding. He called in Rusk and Rostow, and the three of them worked on a letter to Ho that would contain the Phase A–Phase B formula. The heart of the letter, sent on February 8, proposed a deal to Ho in order to get peace talks under way: "I am prepared to order a cessation of bombing against your country and the stopping of further augmentation of U.S. forces in South Vietnam as soon as I am assured that infiltration into South Vietnam by land and by sea *has stopped*."

Meanwhile in London the British negotiators, in hand with Bruce and Cooper, who had not been informed of the letter to Ho, had drafted their own version of Phase A–Phase B, which called for cessation of North Vietnamese "augmentation of forces" rather than cessation of infiltration. On October 9 William Bundy, in a cable approved by Rusk, told Cooper that this formulation was unacceptable because it would allow North Vietnam to send equipment without restriction and forces in the guise of rotation. On February 10 Cooper and the British worked out new language with Kosygin. The key phrase in the proposal—consistent with Bundy's October 9 cable—was that the United States would stop the bombing "as soon as they are assured that infiltration from North Vietnam *will stop.*"

When this formulation was received from Cooper in Washington, Rusk immediately noticed the change of tense—from "has stopped" in the President's letter to "will stop" in Cooper's draft (incredibly, Cooper still did not know about the President's letter). After discussions with the President, Rostow called Cooper in London and told him that the agreement with Kosygin would have to be made consistent with the President's letter to Ho. Bundy also cabled Cooper on February 11 to say that the President's formulation was necessary because "we face immediate specific problems of three [North Vietnamese] divisions poised just north of the DMZ. We must be in position to insist that these cannot be moved into SVN just before [the] undertaking [to stop infiltration] takes effect."

Both Cooper and Prime Minister Wilson were shocked by these instructions. Rusk was also disappointed, but he loyally stood by the President's decision to insist on his original phrasing. There should be no doubt of the President's toughness and credibility when it came to dealing with North Vietnam. A cable arrived from Wilson complaining that the "change of tense" had created "a hell of a situation" for his talks with Kosygin.

The next day, February 12, Wilson, Cooper, and Bruce made one last attempt to get agreement between Washington and Kosygin. They proposed that North Vietnamese forces remain in place north of the 17th parallel in return for a U.S. extension of the Tet bombing pause. They cabled Washington for approval, and all day and into the evening they waited for a response from the White House, while Kosygin became increasingly restive. The reason for the delay was that a bitter argument was raging in Washington: Rostow and the military were against extending the pause; Rusk and McNamara were in favor. Later in the evening Wilson received the President's decision: he agreed to the proposal, but set a deadline of 10 A.M. London time, February 13, for North Vietnam to accept. After talking with Kosygin at his hotel in the early hours of February 13, Wilson cabled Johnson for an extension, and a new deadline of 4 P.M. was set. This was still considered utterly ridiculous by both the American and British negotiators; they needed several days. Bruce called Rusk and pleaded for a further extension. Rusk was brusque, reflecting his own disappointment; the British had been given all the time they were going to get, he told Bruce, and he should not call again.

There was no response from Hanoi, and U.S. bombing of North Vietnam resumed promptly at 4 P.M. London time on Monday, February 13, 1967. A disappointed Wilson later wrote that "a historic opportunity had been missed." But Johnson, for all his willingness to negotiate, and despite McNamara's increasing pessimism, had not fundamentally changed his mind about the war. He was still not ready to give up his basic aim of victory in Vietnam.

"Everyone wants to negotiate," Johnson said in frustration. "I just wish someone would produce a North Vietnamese willing to talk." He told a story about a reluctant football player in his native Texas. "Give the ball to Brown," said the coach to his right guard as he sent in a play. The play was run, and Brown didn't get the ball. So the coach sent in another player, saying, "Tell the quarterback to give the ball to Brown." Again nothing happened. A third time the coach sent in the play, repeating, "Give the ball to Brown." Still the play was not run. When the quarterback came out, the coach said, "I thought I told you to give the ball to Brown." "You did," said the quarterback, "but Brown, he say he don't want the ball!" Ho Chi Minh, like Brown, didn't want the ball.

Vietnam was becoming Rusk's personal agony. He increasingly felt caught between the President, who was under the influence of the hawkish Rostow and the military—Sharp, who thought the war could be won with bombing, and Westmoreland, who thought search-and-destroy missions were the answer—and the doves—Fulbright, Frank Church, and the rest in Congress who wanted to pull out, echoing the demonstrators in the streets. The only way to end the war was to negotiate, but negotiations on terms the President was willing to accept seemed to be out of reach, and withdrawal was unthinkable. Rusk also worried that, with the rising tide of American dissent against the war, Hanoi would lose any incentive for negotiations.

On February 4, 1967, for the third time, Rusk's round, bartender-like face had graced the cover of *Time*. The article called him "the President's busiest foreign policy adviser, articulator, and lightning rod." For months Rusk had tried to stake out a middle ground on the war. With increasing frequency he was summoned to Capitol Hill to testify before the now hostile Senate Foreign Relations Committee. After these grueling sessions Rusk came out looking haggard and upset. "The poor guy," said Senator Joseph Clark, "had a pretty hard time between the hawks and the doves. I don't know who gave him the hardest time. The hawks were unhappy, the doves were unhappy, and Rusk was unhappy.''

About this time Rusk developed a peculiar pain in his stomach. At first he thought he was getting ulcers, but when the doctors checked him out they found nothing. He was relieved, but the pain continued unabated and increased. Refusing to slow down or even admit he needed a rest, he kept going with a stoic strength of will and a steady diet of aspirin.

After the failure of the British peace initiative and the Phase A–Phase B formula, attention focused on the North Vietnamese demand for unconditional cessation of the bombing as a prerequisite for negotiations. Many influential Americans, such as Senators Robert Kennedy and Jacob Javits, added to the pressure on the administration by publicly calling for a bombing halt. But Johnson adhered to his demand for reciprocal actions by Hanoi as the price for stopping the air war, and Rusk defended administration policy by pointing out that the North Vietnamese had taken advantage of past bombing pauses to move men and arms into the South.

Still, the search went on for a way to get peace talks started. Rusk was primarily responsible for the "San Antonio formula," which was announced by the President in that city on September 29, 1967. The United States will stop the bombing, the President declared, "when this will lead promptly to productive discussions" with the other side. And "the United States would assume that while discussions proceed, North Vietnam will not take advantage of the bombing cessation." This statement was about as far as the President was willing to go, but it brought no response from North Vietnam.

By the fall of 1967 dissent on the war was mounting everywhere. The antiwar movement, which had begun on the nation's campuses, was spreading to the mainstream of American life. Now the polls showed that fully 50 percent of the people were against the war. Demonstrators were abroad all over the land; at the White House, the Pentagon, and in every major city, thousands marched for peace.

Rusk became their special target. His every appearance was marked by war protesters, and, much to the distress of his wife, Virginia, pickets marched in front of his home. Everywhere he went there were signs and shouts of "Murderer!" and "Stop the bombing!" Through it all he remained cool and unflappable, at least on the surface. But he was increasingly concerned about the effects of the protests on Hanoi. "If I were Ho Chi Minh," he told colleagues, "and I saw 100,000 people marching against the war in Washington, I would not negotiate either, in spite of all my military losses.''

So Rusk redoubled his efforts to show both Hanoi and the American people that the United States would stick it out in Vietnam. At a speech on December 6, 1967, to the National Association of Manufacturers at the Waldorf-Astoria Hotel, he stressed the improvements in the non-Communist areas of Asia, such as the economic growth of Japan and the "long strides" forward of Indonesia; South Vietnam, too, must be given its chance to prosper as a free nation. He also counseled against escalation as well as against withdrawal, seeking to assure Hanoi that protest demonstrations would not affect policy. His icy imperturbability about the demonstrations extended even to his wife. "If he is bothered by them," Virginia told an interviewer, "he wouldn't tell me about it." But deep inside, the protests were gnawing at Rusk. "I have always tried to be a man of peace," he told a colleague in an unguarded moment. "I have worked for peace all my life, but now I have become a symbol of the war."

Just when the protest demonstrations were at their height, and the youthful generation marching in the streets was concentrating its fury on Rusk for being hopelessly out of touch, there came sensational news: Dean Rusk's only daughter, Peggy, was to be married to a black man, Guy Smith. To protect the privacy of the couple the Rusks tried to hush up the news, and most of the nation learned about it only when a photograph of Peggy and Guy, emerging from the church just after the wedding, appeared on the cover of *Time* (September 29, 1967), as well as on front pages of newspapers all across the country.

Rusk, who did not oppose the marriage and escorted his daughter down the aisle of Stanford University's Memorial Church, pronounced himself "very pleased" and tried to downplay any significance to the matter. As usual, he deplored the publicity; he tried but failed to kill the *Time* cover story. Peggy and Guy, he told friends, "did not consider themselves symbols of anything and deserved to be let alone." The exposure would only increase the burden on the couple.

In fact, most of the nation handled the story well—a measure of how much progress had been made on civil rights. Rusk received some hate letters, and there were some frosty editorials, especially in the South, but other than the initial blast of publicity, reaction was muted and even favorable. Student protesters against the war were surprised and fascinated; the editor of the student newspaper at Columbia University pointed out that "they had all these negative feelings toward Rusk, but now they have this charming story to contend with.'' A black-power proponent in New York said, only half in jest, ''I wonder to what lengths Dean Rusk has to go in order to gain support for his and Johnson's war in Vietnam.''

Privately, Rusk was concerned about the effect the news of the marriage would have on Johnson. He knew that the President himself would find no fault. His commitment to equality and civil rights was deep and genuine, rooted in his emotions, Rusk found—rather different from President Kennedy's commitment, which had been primarily intellectual. Rusk was worried that the news would increase the already intense political pressures on Johnson and subject him to more attacks, particularly from the Southern bloc in Congress.

When he saw Johnson he made it clear that he would resign if the marriage caused difficulty for him. ''If you think that this wedding will make it more difficult for me to maintain my relations with the Senate or the Congress, I will take that into account,'' he said. Johnson merely shrugged him off. ''Forget it,'' he said. ''I've already spoken to Senator Russell [of Georgia] about it and he said it wouldn't make any difference at all.'' And he added, ''I want you to be Secretary of State as long as I am President.''

Vietnam was not the only insoluble problem Rusk faced in the waning years of the Johnson presidency. A dangerous crisis was brewing in the Middle East, where the Arabs and Israelis were becoming embroiled in a new and dangerous confrontation that would culminate in the Six-Day War of 1967. The outbreak of war was preceded by American policy drift that allowed an unhealthy polarization of superpower interests in the region, as the Americans and Soviets chose up sides. The Kennedy administration's experiment to gain influence with President Nasser of Egypt had foundered when Congress, over Rusk's opposition, ended aid to Egypt. American influence was restricted to the conservative Arab oil states and, of course, Israel, to which aid, including arms, was dramatically increased. The Soviets in turn sought client states in Egypt, Iraq, and Syria and shipped them accelerating numbers of weapons and other aid.

The crisis, which came to a head in May 1967, was precipitated by what was in all probability a miscalculation: the Soviets, seeking to increase their influence as Syria's and Egypt's protector, fomented rumors that Israel was mobilizing against Syria. Rusk had this information checked and found that it was false, but the Arabs became excited. President Nasser, always eager to pose as the leader of the Arab world, ordered a mobilization of the Egyptian Army on May 14,

1967, and on May 16 he demanded a limited withdrawal of the U.N. emergency force that had been stationed on the Egyptian-Israeli border since the Suez crisis of 1957. The Israelis also began an immediate mobilization.

Then unexpectedly, on May 19, Secretary General U Thant announced that the U.N. would more than comply with Egypt's demands by withdrawing the entire U.N. emergency force. Rusk and other U.S. officials were shocked. They, as well as the Soviets and probably Nasser too, had expected Thant to delay, as well he could have under the elaborate 1957 agreement constituting the U.N. forces. Thant's move was a major blunder that thrust the region into immediate crisis, with the attendant danger of a superpower confrontation. Nasser responded with yet another foolish move: he announced a blockade of Israeli access to the Strait of Tiran, guarding the entrance of the vital Gulf of Aqaba, which all knew to be a *casus belli* for Israel.

Rusk and other members of the administration quickly began a desperate attempt to prevent the outbreak of war. President Johnson announced that the Egyptian blockade of an international waterway was illegal and called for its removal. Rusk and McNamara conferred with congressional leaders, and they found only one unanimous viewpoint—that the United States should not intervene. Senator Kennedy told Rusk that "my Jewish friends in New York tell me we should stay out."

Rusk was not seriously advocating intervention, but he wanted to put together a multilateral force of ships to open the straits. He tried to arrange such a force, conferring with the British, and at the same time contacted Russian, Arab, and Israeli diplomats to get agreement for restraint. President Johnson and Rusk met with Israeli Foreign Minister Aba Eban, and they believed they had a commitment that Israel would not attack first. The Soviets told Rusk that they would restrain the Egyptians, not surprisingly, since both Soviet and American intelligence agreed that the Israelis would win any conflict in less than ten days. The effort to create a multilateral force foundered, however, when only the British, Dutch, and Australians agreed to participate.

When the Israeli attack came, on June 5, Rusk and other officials were taken by surprise. The Russians apparently were surprised as well, for they activated the hot line, the first use of the direct line between the Kremlin and Washington. Rusk and other advisers hurriedly gathered with Johnson in the White House Situation Room to try to convince Soviet Premier Kosygin that the Americans had nothing to do with the attack and would join in an effort to get a cease-fire. Rusk sent an apologetic message to Gromyko: "We are astonished by preliminary reports of heavy fighting between Israeli and Egyptian forces. We have been making a maximum effort to prevent this situation." He also implied that the Israelis had acted in bad faith: "We had assurances from the Israelis that they would not initiate hostilities pending diplomatic efforts."

By the time a cease-fire resolution could be arranged at the U.N., the Israelis had conquered the entire Sinai Peninsula, the Gaza Strip, and the West Bank. There were tense moments in the Situation Room just before the cease-fire went into effect, when the Israelis were marching on Damascus and Kosygin over the hot line was threatening "necessary actions including military." Johnson ordered the 6th Fleet to maintain its readiness, but also took action to finalize the cease-fire, which confirmed the Israeli victory.

Rusk was less sanguine than some other American officials about the stunning Israeli triumph. While he thought that the initial Israeli attack might have been justified on the grounds of self-defense, he was disappointed that a cease-fire had not been arranged in the first days of the fighting, before Jordan entered the war and the Israelis conquered Egyptian and Jordanian territories. He also did not accept the Israeli explanation that their attack on an American intelligence ship, the *Liberty*, during the conflict was merely accidental. He sent off an angry note to Eban that the attack was "incomprehensible."

When next he saw Aba Eban after the 1967 war, the two men had a testy exchange. Rusk called on Eban to formulate a plan for the return of occupied Arab territories. When Eban demurred, Rusk reminded him that for twenty years the United States had assured the Arabs that Israel had no territorial ambitions and that, on the first day of the Six-Day War, Israeli Prime Minister Levi Eshkol had announced in a radio address that Israel had no expansionist designs. Eban merely shrugged his shoulders and said simply, "We have changed our minds." As Eban went out the door of his office Rusk called after him, "And don't you be the first power to introduce nuclear weapons into the Middle East." "No," Eban replied, and then he smiled thinly. "But we won't be the second."

The finest contribution of the Johnson administration to Middle East peace, and a landmark of diplomacy, was U.N. Security Council Resolution 242, approved on November 22, 1967, which Rusk personally worked on, although the negotiations were left to U.N. Ambassador Arthur Goldberg. The resolution, which both Egypt and Israel accepted, provided the outlines of the peace settlement Rusk favored: an end to the state of belligerency in the Middle East and the right of every nation, including Israel, to "live in peace within secure and recognized boundaries"; guaranteed freedom of navigation through international waterways; a just solution to the refugee problem; and Israeli withdrawal "from territories occupied in the recent conflict." The fact that the resolution specified withdrawal "from territories" and not "all" or "the" territories was a "constructive ambiguity" which, Rusk believed, would allow for some adjustment of boundaries if agreed by both sides, and for the demilitarization of certain areas, such as the Golan Heights and Gaza.

Resolution 242 and the attempt to remit the Middle Eastern blood feuds to diplomacy were the initial steps in a new American policy to make the United States an active catalyst of a peace process in the region. The approach to the Russians was the first attempt to enlist them in a joint approach to finding a solution. Rusk wanted, in fact, to create a new, evenhanded American posture toward the Arabs and Israelis, building on his experiences with the recognition of the State of Israel in 1948. As in Vietnam, however, peace in the Middle East was elusive.

"I Almost Floated Like a Balloon": SALT and the Paris Peace Talks

I N 1968, as both the war in Vietnam and the controversy surrounding it reached a crescendo, Rusk, loyal to the President and to his beliefs, deliberately took on the mantle which so many had avoided: protagonist in the Vietnam debate. He was constantly in the limelight now, quoted daily in the press and on television. He became more than ever the official spokesman, and scapegoat, for the most controversial war in the nation's history—"Dean Rusk's war."

His performance won praise, especially for his courage and composure, but also great criticism, and in making public appearances he was forced to come and go like a thief in the night. The President could barricade himself in the White House, but Rusk had no place to hide. Demonstrators dogged him with their taunts. "Wanted for Murder" leaflets carried his picture. The press was more and more hostile, tired of his homilies about the 1930s and appeasement bringing on World War II. His reticent manner and repeated Cold War clichés rankled. A favorite press joke had Rusk whispering to a reporter, "Off the record and strictly between us, not for publication, I will say that the war will be over if the other side stops fighting."

Rusk was a "survivor," as he himself said, "in for the duration." One by one the powerful men around the President had slipped away, disenchanted, used up, or burned out by the war. George Ball, McGeorge Bundy, John McCone, and even Robert McNamara stepped aside. McNamara's defection particularly distressed Rusk. He felt as if he had "lost a brother" and regretted that McNamara had given up too soon.

Unlike Rusk, McNamara had put his faith in numbers—of men, of air strikes, of firepower. When they did not add up to the result he expected, it undercut his whole philosophy of life, and he almost cracked under the strain. In his inner turmoil he became both a dove and a hawk, saying one thing to his liberal friends, another to Johnson and Rusk. The peace movement tormented him, especially the sight of a Quaker man outside the Pentagon who, with a baby in his arms, was preparing to set himself on fire, putting the baby safely aside only just before lighting his own funeral pyre. Before resigning, McNamara began the study of the Vietnam War that would come to be known as the Pentagon Papers. He did not tell Rusk his plans, but Rusk later became convinced the study was intended to help Robert Kennedy in his political campaign against the President.

With McNamara gone, Rusk more than ever felt it his duty to defend the President, to stand as a bulwark against the forces that threatened to overwhelm them. Although outwardly calm, he was under extreme stress, not only from the rising tide of criticism but also from the weight of the increasing number of casualties in the war—hundreds were now dying each week on the American side alone. The mysterious pain in his stomach became worse, and when he went home late at night he lay stretched out on the living room floor, groaning in agony. His staff became worried; one remarked that he seemed to live on cigarettes, scotch, and aspirin, although he never appeared to be under the influence of alcohol. Rusk was worried, too, about the future of his family. He had two children in college and his savings were almost exhausted. Virginia was going through the agony with him, but could be of little help since he was so seldom home. His family faced the prospect that when he left office he would be broke and unemployed.

The personal attacks on his credibility and his integrity particularly upset Rusk. He resented charges that he was an interventionist and wanted the United States to be the world's policeman. Vietnam, he later recalled, "obscured all the positive things that were happening" and "all the crises where the United States did not get involved, such as the 1965 dispute between India and Pakistan and the confrontation between Malaysia and Indonesia." He wrote to Congressman John A. Blatnik, one of his ever present critics, that "we did not bomb North Vietnam until the 325th Division of the North Vietnam regular army moved into South Vietnam."

In January 1968 Rusk sent a plaintive but determined note to the U.S. Embassy in New Delhi asking that the Indian government—one of the most strident in its criticism of the American action in Vietnam —be informed that "it will do no good . . . to try to negotiate us down from the San Antonio formula without having something solid from Hanoi that moves tangibly in the direction of peace." He pointed out that the United States withheld its military power: "We have not mined Haiphong and we have not attacked international shipping into that port. There are no U.S. forces operating in Cambodia. We have held our hand under very severe provocations. We have tried for years to obtain . . . compliance with the Accords on Laos. There would be no violence in Laos today if Hanoi would join with all of the other signatories and comply with those accords." But Hanoi was "pouring its forces in and through the demilitarized zone" between North and South Vietnam, and so the issue came down to "when a North Vietnamese battalion is marching down the road, we must decide whether to get out of its way or stop it. We have decided to stop it."

Two shocks punctuated the opening months of 1968. In January the U.S.S. *Pueblo,* an intelligence vessel, was seized by North Korea and held in the North Korean port of Wonsan with its eighty-three-man crew. As best the administration could determine, the vessel had been operating in international waters off the North Korean coast, so the seizure was in violation of international law. Rusk counseled against any military reaction to the incident; he did not want to risk the outbreak of another Korean War, and he was concerned for the safety of the crew. He also argued against Rostow's idea of seizing a Russian vessel in retaliation. (There were no North Korean vessels to grab.) That would, he said, only compound the outrage and would make impossible any constructive Russian influence on the North Koreans. Patient negotiation at Panmunjom resulted in freedom for the crew in December, after a farcical charade in which the United States signed a confession of espionage in North Korean territorial waters and immediately repudiated it as totally false.

The second, even more serious event was the Tet offensive in South Vietnam in February 1968. Beginning at Khe Sanh, an American stronghold in the highlands near the DMZ, the North Vietnamese attack spread over the length and breadth of South Vietnam. More than a hundred towns and cities simultaneously came under fire, including Saigon, where the grounds of the American Embassy were penetrated, and Hue, the ancient capital near the coast, which was held for several weeks. During the assault on Saigon, General West-moreland was forced to take refuge in a windowless command center, and Ambassador Bunker fled to a secret hideout. The fighting lasted a month, and there were bloody battles in the streets before the Viet-cong and North Vietnamese were repulsed.

Although the American and South Vietnamese counterattack suc-ceeded, the Tet offensive had an electric effect on a nation lulled by optimistic statements from the military that the war was being won. That the Vietcong could mount such an offensive with over half a million American troops stationed in the country seemed incredible. As *Time* commented, the combination of the *Pueblo* and the Tet offen-sive made the United States look as impotent as a "beached whale." After Tet, a clear majority of middle America turned against the war. The credibility of Westmoreland was as decisively shattered as his confident assessments of progress. Johnson's general approval rating in a Gallup poll in March 1968 reached a nadir of 36 percent. The Tet offensive was a military defeat but a psychological victory for North Vietnam, a dramatic reminder that the attainment of American objec-tives in Vietnam was nowhere in sight.

The military, however, seemed oblivious to the domestic situation in the United States. General Westmoreland, with incredible aplomb, saw Tet as an occasion for yet another change in strategy, similar to the shift that had occurred in 1965. He wanted to "take the war to the enemy" by conducting major offensive operations and attacking the "sanctuaries" in Laos, Cambodia, and North Vietnam. This com-bined with increased bombing, especially around Hanoi and Hai-phong, would be a "two-fisted policy" to win the war. Supported by the Joint Chiefs, Westmoreland submitted a request to the President for 206,000 additional troops, which would have involved billions of dollars more added to the defense budget and a call-up of the National Guard and reserves—in effect, the declaration of a national emer-gency. The President, Rusk, and other advisers went over this new request at a briefing by the chairman of the Joint Chiefs, General Earle Wheeler, at the White House on February 28. Wheeler's presentation was a bizarre mixture of gloom and optimism that the new strategy and more troops would win the war.

Johnson's old friend Clark Clifford took office on March 1 as Sec-retary of Defense, succeeding McNamara, and as his first task he was charged by the President to consider Westmoreland's troop increase request. Clifford, silver-haired and ruggedly handsome, was now an almost legendary figure. For years he had operated behind the scenes, combining a silk-stocking law practice with private advice to a succession of Presidents. Now he held a major cabinet post, and his assignment could hardly have been more important or far-reaching. Events were propelling the United States to make grave decisions with respect to Vietnam. Clifford had previously expressed hawkish views in his informal advice to the President, and at first he assumed that the question was not whether but how Westmoreland's request would be implemented. But in considering the troop increase, he began his own private process of reexamining the premises of the war, which would transform him into a force for moderation. Very soon he realized that the real question he had to examine was: Should the United States continue to follow its present course in Vietnam?

With his total involvement in the war, Rusk was ahead of Clifford's thinking. From the first, he knew that Westmoreland's proposal for a 206,000-man troop increase had almost no chance of approval. The United States had reached a watershed on Vietnam. Tet had changed the situation drastically in two ways: the Vietcong insurgency had been defeated militarily, and American public opinion at the grassroots level had swung against the war. It was time to move on to a new chapter in Vietnam, and these developments opened up fresh possibilities for peace negotiations. In any case Rusk was convinced that American policy had to change—to aim for either a negotiated solution or a de facto reduction of the American effort. He attended the initial meeting of Clark Clifford's task force on March 1, but did not go back for subsequent meetings, sending his deputy, Nicholas Katzenbach, in his stead. Even at the initial meeting Rusk merely listened, choosing to remain silent. He was not going to be a contributor to Clark Clifford's reeducation on the war. He saved his advice for the only man who really counted, Lyndon Johnson.

Johnson and Rusk had developed an extremely close bond of understanding and trust because, as Rusk later put it, "We spent so much time in the same foxhole together." Each of them instinctively knew what the other was thinking. When Johnson went into one of his frequent tirades, Rusk knew exactly which words to take seriously, and what's more, Johnson knew that Rusk knew how to handle him. After Johnson had calmed down Rusk would go and see him privately and say, "Wait a minute, Mr. President . . ." or "Did I understand you to say that . . . ?" In March 1968 Rusk saw the President daily and was in frequent telephone contact. He was the adviser who carried the most weight with Johnson. As White House news secretary George Christian put it, "It was Rusk's judgment he wanted

in the end, and Rusk's judgment he followed." On another occasion
he told the journalist Arthur Krock that "Rusk is kind. . . . I never
heard him say an ugly word about anyone. He's got sense and heart."
Years later Johnson would tell his biographer Doris Kearns, "I love
that Dean."

On the evening of March 4 the report of Clifford's task force was
discussed in a meeting at the White House. Although it called for the
deployment of 22,000 new troops to Vietnam and a call-up of 245,000
reservists, it was phrased in such cautionary terms that the President
did not make a final decision. The most important outcome of the
meeting for Johnson, if not for the other participants, was a proposal
by Rusk. As an alternative to additional forces he suggested a partial
bombing halt—restricted to north of the 20th parallel—as a device to
try to get peace talks going with Hanoi. Rusk knew that Johnson
would not be well disposed to such a proposal. Ever since the failure
of the thirty-seven-day pause in 1966 Johnson had opposed, even
ridiculed, suggestions to stop the bombing. But Rusk had thought the
matter over carefully and taken steps to prepare the President. That
morning he had sent over a memo given him by the British ambassador, Sir Patrick Dean, that told of a tactic—"fighting *and* negotiating"
—used by the Communists, but one that America could profitably
adopt. The President had paid particular attention to this because it
was from Rusk. So now, listening to the bombing halt proposal, Johnson thought for a moment and said, "Get on your horses—let's get
something ready on that."

The next day, March 5, Johnson and his advisers assembled for the
regular Tuesday lunch. Rusk pressed the bombing halt idea further.
Reading from a memo he had prepared in advance, he said that a
partial bombing halt would not make any real difference on the battlefield since the monsoon season in North Vietnam would make bombing the far north difficult in any case. Furthermore, the partial halt
would allow areas of the North immediately adjacent to the battlefield
to be bombed to fully protect American men in the field. If the halt
was to have any chance to spur negotiations, Rusk said, it would have
to be unconditional, not merely a pause. He had been in contact with
Rumania's Deputy Foreign Minister, Gheorghe Macovescu, who had
said the time might be ripe for arranging peace talks if the bombing
could be stopped. Rusk pointed out that if there was no response, the
bombing could be resumed.

Rusk also argued strongly against Westmoreland's troop increase
proposal. There were enough men in Vietnam to prevent any danger

of military defeat. Although he admired Westmoreland's patriotism and devotion to duty, Rusk faulted him for not developing a successful strategy for combating the insurgency in the North. All he knew to do was ask for more men and matériel. Rusk, through Ambassador Bunker in Saigon, had been negotiating with President Thieu and had obtained an agreement for 65,000 additional South Vietnamese forces. There was no need for more American troops.

Johnson was impressed with Rusk's case, which was strongly opposed by the Joint Chiefs and Rostow as well as some at the Pentagon. It was the only peace suggestion on the table, and it had been made by Rusk, who Johnson knew had given it a great deal of thought. But for the President the time was not right. He was not going to make his speech on Vietnam until the end of the month, and if the bombing halt was approved and became public knowledge, it would not have a fair chance. Johnson abhorred leaks; he had almost a pathological need to surprise. He was also aware that Rusk was scheduled to testify on March 11 before the Senate Foreign Relations Committee. Refraining from a decision would allow Rusk to deny that a bombing halt was in the works.

Rusk began to work on the President in private, and he knew what approach to use. Tet had been a great military victory, he told Johnson, but "many Americans at the grass roots, quite apart from these college demonstrators and people like that, have come to the conclusion that if we cannot give them some idea when this struggle is going to be over, we might as well chuck it." He also argued that "we have taken 600,000 casualties in dead and wounded since the end of World War II in support of collective security. We put up 90 percent of the non-Korean forces in Korea, 80 percent of the non-Vietnamese forces in Vietnam. And that's not very collective. So if my Cherokee County cousins were to say to me, 'Look, if collective security means 50,000 dead Americans every ten years, and it is not even collective, maybe it's not a very good idea.' " He was not arguing for a withdrawal, only a scaling back of the fighting and a greater role by the South Vietnamese. Johnson was still not convinced and told Rusk that he looked tired. "Your courage keeps me going," Rusk replied. "These days are an exercise of sheer spirit."

Meanwhile, *The New York Times* had obtained information about Westmoreland's troop increase recommendation, and a furor of protest arose in the nation. On world financial markets traders rushed to buy gold, precipitating a monetary crisis. In the New Hampshire presidential primary on March 12 the peace candidate, Senator Eugene

McCarthy, won 42 percent of the vote, very nearly defeating the President. The political challenge to Johnson escalated further when, a few days later, Robert Kennedy declared his candidacy.

The depth of the dissent and protest over the war was brought home to Rusk in a personal sense as well. His son Rich, a student at Cornell University, telephoned him in tears when he heard about the troop increase proposal and begged him not to approve it. A sensitive young man who had served in the Marines, although not in Vietnam, Rich felt strongly that the war was wrong, and that the killing and death were, at least in part, his father's fault. For Rusk it was a devastating blow.

On March 11 and 12 he testified on the war situation before Fulbright's Senate Foreign Relations Committee and gave a vintage performance that won high marks from Johnson. Hawkish and unyielding, Rusk gave no indication of a change in policy, except to say that Vietnam was "under review from A to Z." Curiously, he even told the committee that Hanoi "will not accept a partial cessation of the bombing as a step toward peace in any way, shape, or form." He was loyally preserving the role of peacemaker for the President.

Additional pressures to change course were brought to bear upon the President. On March 15, U.N. Ambassador Arthur Goldberg, who did not know about Rusk's partial bombing halt proposal, sent Johnson a lengthy memorandum advocating a total bombing halt down to the 17th parallel. On the same day, during a lunch with the President, none other than Dean Acheson told him that the war could not be won, and that he was being "led down the garden path" by the military. Johnson was unhappy and frustrated, and he went into one of his tirades. "Let's get one thing clear," he shouted at his advisers at a meeting on March 16, ". . . I am not going to stop the bombing." But Rusk knew this was just bombast, Johnson's way of coming to a decision.

Afterward, Rusk quietly met with the President to argue that both bombing halt proposals deserved a fair hearing, and received his permission to cable Bunker to get his opinion on what would be acceptable to the Thieu government. Rusk was confident his plan was the better of the two. The partial bombing halt would look all the better to Saigon when compared with the Goldberg alternative. "The response was predictable," Rusk later recalled. As Johnson stated in his memoirs: "Rusk had the best understanding of the way I wished to move." And Bunker soon replied, as expected, that the limited bombing pause would be best, especially if it was accompanied by increased military support for the Saigon government.

Still unwilling to come to a decision, President Johnson delivered a tough and fiery speech in Minneapolis on March 18, declaring, "We must meet our commitments in the world and in Vietnam. We shall and we are going to win!" But even as he spoke, news came that the previous week 509 Americans had been killed in Vietnam. And that same day Senator Robert Kennedy, before a wildly cheering crowd at the University of Kansas, attacked the President's war policy as "bankrupt." Kennedy's entry into the presidential race was having a seismic impact on the political landscape all over the country. Meanwhile, U.S. war planes ranged north in their biggest raid of the month, attacking targets near Hanoi and Haiphong as well as in the panhandle south of the 20th parallel. News reports said that the Tet offensive had caught General Westmoreland completely by surprise, calling the episode a "massive failure of intelligence."

The President's political advisers reported that his Minneapolis speech had hurt him badly, and it became increasingly clear that Johnson might lose the Wisconsin primary, scheduled for April 2. Pressures were building, and something had to give. At the Tuesday luncheon on March 19, Rusk told General Wheeler, "We need some good news from Vietnam, Bus." The next morning Johnson telephoned Clifford in a desperate state. "I've got to get me a peace proposal," he said. The State Department sent over Rusk's bombing halt proposal as background material for a proposed presidential speech on Vietnam. Johnson also met with Goldberg to discuss his proposal for a complete bombing halt. The President was drawing closer to his decision.

On March 20 and again on March 22, Johnson held meetings to discuss his speech on Vietnam with his inner circle, including Rusk, Clifford, Goldberg, and McGeorge Bundy. Harry McPherson, one of Johnson's "kitchen cabinet," had the job of drafting the speech. He had come to hate the war, but had dutifully prepared what was called a "we shall overcome" speech, an uncompromising line with no bombing halt without reciprocity and no peace initiative—in short, nothing new. Almost no one was satisfied with the draft speech. Goldberg, joined by Harriman and Hubert Humphrey, argued for a complete cessation of the bombing. Rusk continued to argue for a partial halt without conditions, "to see what will happen."

Clifford became exasperated with Rusk and suspicious of his motives. The relationship between the two of them went back to the days of the Truman administration when they had crossed swords over recognition of Israel. Clifford saw Rusk as insincere, playing his old hawkish games. The partial bombing halt was a ploy that Rusk knew would have no effect; it was only cosmetic. After it did not work, Johnson could announce grandly that he had tried, and had no choice but to return to the same old policies. By now Clifford's transformation on Vietnam was complete, and he was utterly convinced of the need for negotiations and disengagement. He suggested a series of steps for peace, beginning with the partial bombing halt, and offering to go further, based on reciprocal actions by the North Vietnamese. Rusk and Clifford became the central protagonists in the long meetings, and their exchanges grew bitter and sharp. "Our ideas were completely different," Clifford later recalled, "and we wanted a bombing pause for completely different reasons. What I was urging was a real effort to start negotiations . . . a change in policy."

Rusk had his own suspicions about Clifford. He was an operator, a political animal, with his eye on the Wisconsin primary and the domestic political scene. Rusk was afraid things were moving too fast. He had not lost sight of the basic objectives in Vietnam and knew that Johnson had not either. Clifford's proposal was also only a new version of what had been tried before—a pause based on reciprocity which would impose conditions on Hanoi that Rusk knew they would not accept. "I felt we should just stop the bombing without imposing conditions, and therefore keep our options open," he said later.

The meetings ended in an impasse. Even Rusk, when asked pointblank, had to admit the chances that a partial bombing halt would buy negotiations were next to none. Everyone in the room faced a dilemma, and at the end of the meeting it was Rusk who summed things up:

Mr. President, I believe it is the consensus of your advisers that a partial reduction in the bombing would be insufficient to produce talks. The North Vietnamese have always insisted that the bombing be stopped completely, and without conditions, before talking. On the other hand, we cannot stop the bombing altogether without risking the security of our troops. The North Vietnamese have given no sign that they would not use a total cessation to attack our bases and the cities. Unfortunately that is the situation.

"Okay," the President said, "that looks like the way it is," and directed that the peace proposals be taken out of his speech and studied separately. Gloom pervaded the room. Clifford was profoundly discouraged and assumed it was the end, that there would be no steps toward peace. McPherson's heart was heavy. "The signal was being given," he thought, "that we are not going to do it. I never had any instructions to put a bombing pause in the speech, or to seriously consider it."

Rusk was the only one of Johnson's advisers who knew better. It was clear to him that two factors were motivating the President. First, he did not want to tip his hand quite yet. He wanted to preserve his freedom of action and, even more important to the President, his freedom to surprise. He did not like "putting these things on paper and then later reading about them in the newspapers," Rusk later recalled.

But that was not all. Rusk was privy to the biggest secret of all, a political bombshell: Johnson was seriously considering not running for reelection in 1968. He had spoken to Rusk privately about this for over a year. Johnson was tired and worried about his health and the strain of another term. He did not want to end up incapacitated like Woodrow Wilson, and Mrs. Johnson was urging him not to run. During the month of March, Johnson talked about it often. "I do not think I can unite this country any more," he said. He did not disclose, even to Rusk, that he had made the decision not to run. But Rusk knew the President's mind and was all but certain what he would do.

Rusk also believed that Johnson's decision not to run could be the critical factor necessary to get peace talks going. The partial bombing halt was not enough. But if it was coupled with the President's decision not to run for reelection, Hanoi just might be willing to begin negotiations. Rusk, in stating to the President the dilemma they faced in Vietnam, was pushing him to make this final decision. It was, perhaps, the only chance. He dared not broach the subject with Johnson directly; in typical Rusk fashion, he worked on the President subtly, through suggestion and innuendo, prodding him in the direction he believed he wished to go. Furthermore, time was growing short if Johnson was going to announce that he would not run. Johnson had told him how he admired Truman because he had announced his intention not to run early enough to allow his man, Adlai Stevenson, to be nominated. Humphrey would be Johnson's choice, and a decision now would give Humphrey time to mobilize his forces and take the nomination away from Kennedy or McCarthy. It was now or never. Rusk was confident that the President would act.

On the same day, March 22, Johnson further signaled his thinking by announcing at a press conference that he was relieving General William Westmoreland of his command in Vietnam. The move was widely interpreted as an indication of tactical changes in the war. Westmoreland was associated with the costly search-and-destroy strategy which had taken so many American lives. In a less publicized action Johnson also dismissed Admiral Ulysses Sharp, U.S. Commander in the Pacific, the proponent and architect of the ineffective air war in the North. Belatedly, he was cleaning house, sweeping away those primarily responsible for the military strategies that had failed to win the war.

In the days that followed, McPherson and Clifford undertook further attempts to make the President embrace a peace initiative. McPherson submitted a draft speech that announced a partial bombing halt north of the 20th parallel and suggested that representatives be sent both to Rangoon and Geneva to await the North Vietnamese. Johnson immediately showed it to Rusk, who said he would "take care of it," meaning that he knew the President's mind and would make sure he got what he wanted. Clifford, who believed the President needed some "stiff medicine," decided to convene the "wise men," the group of distinguished elder statesmen, who he knew now opposed the war.

They assembled at the White House on March 25, the grizzled old lions who had largely created American foreign policy in the postwar period—Dean Acheson, Omar Bradley, Matthew Ridgway, John McCloy, Averell Harriman, Robert Murphy, and Arthur Dean—and some of the younger generation—Cyrus Vance, George Ball, McGeorge Bundy, Henry Cabot Lodge, Maxwell Taylor, and Abe Fortas. There was some dissent, but surprisingly, and in contrast to an earlier meeting of the same group the previous November, a clear majority now opposed the war. Johnson, listening to their remarks, scribbled on a notepad in front of him: "Can no longer do the job we set out to do"; "Adjust our course"; and "Move to disengage."

The next morning Johnson invited them to return, and at lunch in the White House General Creighton Abrams, who had flown in from Vietnam and would shortly be appointed the new American commander there, gave what Rusk thought was an impressive presentation. He told them how much more could be done to build up South Vietnamese forces so that they could take over greater responsibility for the defense of their own country. It was now clear to all that there would not be any important increase in American troops in Vietnam.

On Thursday, March 28, Clifford, McPherson, William Bundy, and

Rostow met in Rusk's office for what was ostensibly a session to "polish" the final draft of the President's speech on Vietnam, which was scheduled for the following Sunday. The draft was McPherson's eighth, and it still reflected the "we shall overcome" tenor of previous attempts. Johnson continued to play his cards close to his chest, and no one but Rusk knew his thinking.

Clifford had read the draft and was loaded for bear, ready for a knockdown fight with Rusk. He had prepared like the brilliant lawyer he was, as if going to court to argue his case. But incredibly he had almost completely misread the situation. He was still caught up in a "them against us" mentality, viewing himself as the head of a lonely group of conspirators trying to turn the President around. He would talk guardedly over the phone, asking about people, "Is he one of us?" He had a vision of the President saying, "We are going to stay with it until I nail the coonskin on the wall."

Clifford still viewed Rusk as his principal antagonist. He began by attacking the speech; it was entirely too hawkish. The beginning phrases, "My fellow Americans, tonight I want to talk to you about the war in Vietnam," marked it as a war speech. "The President," Clifford said, "cannot give that speech. It would be a disaster." He suggested a change in the first line to read, "My fellow Americans, tonight I want to speak to you of *peace* in Vietnam." Clifford wanted a *peace* speech and spoke eloquently of how all the major elements of the American community—businessmen, the press, professionals, students, the intellectuals—had turned against the war. All the while he was watching Rusk intently, awaiting the expected clash.

To Clifford's surprise, it never came. Rusk was no longer in opposition; he was even agreeable. Clifford went on with his argument for more than an hour. Rusk remained silent; he never said, as he might have, "There is no need for all that, the President agrees." Rusk protected his confidences to the bitter end.

When Clifford had finished his discourse the group got down to business and began redrafting the speech to emphasize peace. They also included language embodying Rusk's original proposal for a partial bombing halt. Clifford was elated. He, as well as almost everyone else, thought that this meeting had turned everything around. The President could not reject the unanimous advice of both his Secretary of State and his Secretary of Defense. Clifford reflected later:

In that morning the whole tone of that speech was changed. It was not changed over the opposition of [Dean Rusk]. I don't understand what

was going on that day. I felt only a deep sense of gratification that the
changes were being made. I didn't explore. I didn't say, "Dean, old
friend, what's happened?" or anything like that. When two men are
friends, as we were, and yet they are disagreeing on the principal policy
question of the day, it does interfere with your personal relationship to
some extent. . . . I think I probably assumed that he had had enough
of me. He probably assumed I had had enough of him.

Clifford could not have known that Johnson's Vietnam policy had
not shifted on March 28, but several days before. Rusk's shift in
attitude only paralleled the President's. In newspaper comment at the
time Clifford got the major credit for the President's change of heart.
But in reality Rusk had played the decisive role.

At six thirty in the evening Rusk, Clifford, and the others met with
the President in the Cabinet Room with the revised draft in hand.
Johnson read it and was pleased, especially about the peace offer.
Still, he refused to tip his hand for fear of a press leak. He "indicated
he did not want to comment further at that time."

After the meeting Johnson met alone with Rusk and told him to
move at once to obtain South Vietnamese approval of the plan, including the partial bombing halt and a smaller-than-anticipated American
troop increase of 13,500 men. The message was sent that evening. On
Saturday, March 30, cables containing the announcement went out to
U.S. embassies around the world. Rusk left Washington later that day
to attend a SEATO meeting in Wellington, New Zealand.

On Sunday, March 31, the President gave the speech on national
television, and the American people learned for the first time that a
turning point had been reached in the Vietnam War. Johnson announced a unilateral deescalation of the war:

> Tonight I have ordered our aircraft and our naval vessels to make no
> attacks on North Vietnam, except in the area north of the demilitarized
> zone where the continued enemy buildup directly threatens Allied for-
> ward positions. . . .

Then came the surprise ending, his stunning withdrawal from the
presidential race of 1968:

> I shall not seek, and I will not accept, the nomination of my party for
> another term as your President.

Rusk did not hear the speech. He was in an airplane over the South
Pacific, on his way to New Zealand. Just after the speech was deliv-

ered, however, he received a call from the White House. "The President wants you to know," the caller said, "that there was an additional paragraph in the speech he gave tonight." The caller did not tell him what the paragraph said, and Rusk did not have to ask. He knew the President had withdrawn, the gesture that had the best chance to get peace talks going. He felt relieved and hopeful.

Three days later Radio Hanoi broadcast a message that North Vietnam "declares its readiness to appoint a representative to contact the United States representative . . ." to discuss "the unconditional cessation of United States bombing raids and other acts of war . . . so that talks may start." At last Hanoi was willing to begin negotiations; Johnson's speech had had the desired effect. Rusk later learned through the Rumanian connection that it was Johnson's withdrawal statement that convinced Hanoi to respond.

Thus, by April 1968 the Johnson administration was fully committed to a political settlement and withdrawal of American troops from Vietnam. Peace talks would get under way at last. Johnson, Rusk, and Clifford dearly wanted to complete the process, or at least put the settlement in place, before Johnson left office the following January. But questions abounded. What kind of political settlement would be acceptable? Would there be time to do the job?

There was delay in getting the talks started with Hanoi, an indication of things to come. Both sides jockeyed for a suitable site for their meeting. Hanoi suggested Warsaw or Phnom Penh, both unacceptable to Washington. Rusk proposed a list of five cities in neutral countries: Geneva, New Delhi, Rangoon, Jakarta, and Vientiane. Paris was also in his mind, but he deliberately left it off the list, hoping the leaders in Hanoi would propose it on their own; he knew they would not accept it if they appeared to be agreeing with the United States. The ploy worked; Hanoi suggested Paris, and Rusk then had to convince Johnson, who was nervous about de Gaulle's influence if the talks were held in the French capital. The President, after consulting with Rusk, named Averell Harriman and Cyrus Vance the chief American negotiators to meet with Xuan Thuy, the head of the North Vietnamese negotiating team.

The maneuvering over the site was costly both in time lost and the attitudes of the participants. In April and early May Hanoi built up its forces in the South and launched new raids on cities and towns in South Vietnam. U.S. warplanes responded with their largest strikes of the year, although restricted to south of the 20th parallel. This caused Johnson a credibility problem because the 20th parallel was 225 miles north of the border of South Vietnam. His March 31 speech had referred only to bombing "areas north of the demilitarized zone," not the 20th parallel line. (In fact, the bombing was restricted to the 19th parallel.)

The talks finally opened in Paris amid great fanfare on May 13, in the Majestic Hotel on the Avenue Kléber. At first Hanoi appeared to be willing to enter into full discussions about the political future of Vietnam, but when the talks got under way they restricted them to "preliminary conversations" about stopping the American bombing and "other acts of war." In these circumstances the negotiations soon degenerated into a bitter exchange of charges and countercharges. Even after the initial invective, the two sides were not able to enter into substantive discussions. Harriman opened up a new channel for secret talks, which were held in a house in the suburbs of Paris, but it did no good. The Americans wanted to talk about infiltration and political issues; the North Vietnamese would talk only about the bombing. Tragically, the whole summer was wasted in futile negotiations; there was no movement at all.

Now time was growing short, but there was no new attempt by the Johnson administration to break the impasse. The President, supported by his hawkish National Security Adviser, Walt Rostow, reverted to a tough stance and even considered resumption of the bombing, until Rusk and Clifford talked him out of it. Rusk himself was cautious and somewhat equivocal. Harriman and Vance had been disappointed when they met with Rusk at the State Department just before leaving for Paris. Rusk had warned against leaks and told them he did not want the peace talks to become a pressure point on Lyndon Johnson. Their instructions were to find out what Hanoi was willing to do in return for a complete bombing halt. They were not to make any proposal or even to discuss any fallback positions. There had to be a quid pro quo, he emphasized, for the next American move.

Harriman repeatedly told Rusk, both before and after going to Paris, that if there was to be quick progress the bombing of the North had to be stopped completely. But Rusk was not yet willing to recommend this step. He was also vague about an acceptable political settlement. He talked in general about withdrawal of American and North Vietnamese forces and internationally supervised elections in the South, but the broken Laos accords of 1962 were continually on his mind. He rejected any formal role for the Vietcong in a new South Vietnamese government because he was not willing to gamble on another Laos-type Communist deception.

Thus Rusk, probably the only person who could have influenced

Johnson on the matter, held back. His native caution, which had served him so well on other occasions, now trapped the country in a prolonged war. It was not a time for caution but for action. When the peace talks began, the election was less than six months away. And the nation was in extraordinary straits. Not only the unpopular and costly war but other terrible events signaled a deep malaise in American society. On April 4 Martin Luther King, Jr., was murdered in Memphis, causing a paroxysm of burning and violence in cities across the land. A few weeks later, on June 6, Robert Kennedy was killed by an assassin's bullet, terribly disrupting and blighting the 1968 electoral process. Afterward, the fringes of the antiwar movement turned ugly and violent, venting a destructive rage. On June 19 fifty thousand people marched in Washington in support of the poor, frustrated by the unfulfilled promises of the administration's Great Society programs. The war was causing economic woes as well—a dramatic rise in inflation and a crisis of confidence in the dollar.

Besides ending the war in Vietnam, Rusk had one other great task he wanted to finish before he left office: the completion of significant agreements with the Soviet Union. He did not believe in allowing Soviet support of North Vietnam to interfere with his policy of constantly probing for better relations between the superpowers. He was acutely aware that he was the first Secretary of State to serve during a time when a full exchange of nuclear weapons was an operational possibility. His greatest task was to prevent nuclear war. It was "too late in the day," he contended, for the United States not to try to find areas of common agreement with the Soviet Union. He had established a close rapport with Foreign Minister Andrei Gromyko and Ambassador Anatoly Dobrynin, and though he had a realistic view of Soviet intentions, he became convinced that they too wished to work out ways to move away from confrontation.

Rusk believed in a policy of being completely honest—if not completely open—with the Soviets about U.S. intentions and interests. Each side must know where the other stood to avoid miscalculations that, in a nuclear world, might prove fatal. Just as the United States had vital interests, so did the Soviet Union. It was unrealistic to believe the Soviets would "roll over and play dead" if they were threatened. Each side would stubbornly protect its vital interests, so conflicts must be approached with care and persistence in finding ways to live together. Rusk had an unspoken agreement with Gromyko and Dobrynin not to mislead and to report accurately each other's statements and views.

This policy had helped defuse small incidents before they grew into large crises and had made possible new areas of Soviet-American cooperation. When the Soviets shot down an American reconnaissance plane that wandered off course and crossed into East Germany, Rusk, through discussions with Dobrynin, was able to win quick release of the crew. When Khrushchev was ousted in the fall of 1964, Rusk, relying on information from Gromyko, announced that the change held no danger for the West and signaled no important shift in Soviet policies. Narrow but significant agreements had been concluded by the two sides: a treaty banning nuclear weapons from outer space in 1966; a consular convention in 1967; a civil aviation agreement establishing passenger service between Moscow and New York; and an agreement for cultural exchanges. Rusk also helped start negotiations under the auspices of NATO for a mutual reduction of conventional forces in Europe. A new word, "détente," began to be used to describe Soviet-American relations; Rusk preferred to call it a "new prudence" between the superpowers.

In the summer of 1968 Rusk was dreaming of capping his efforts with even more important accords. He was working on a treaty with the Russians to prevent the spread of nuclear weapons and wanted to enter into talks to limit and reduce strategic missiles. Halting the spread of nuclear weapons had been important to Rusk since the 1950s, and its urgency increased after China developed "the bomb" in 1964. He was intensely worried about what would happen in the future when smaller states—India, Pakistan, Brazil, Israel—had access to nuclear weapons. In the United States and the Soviet Union, he believed, there were no "itchy fingers" on the nuclear trigger, and Britain and France would never start a nuclear war. But in more unstable, smaller countries with bitter hatreds of their neighbors, anything could happen.

Rusk worked unsuccessfully to get India and Pakistan to renounce nuclear weapons. And he sought Russian cooperation so that neither the Soviet Union nor the United States would transfer nuclear weapons to other states or assist them in acquiring nuclear technology, except for peaceful purposes. As early as 1962, in informal conversation with Gromyko, the two men had agreed that "our two countries share a common interest in preventing the further diffusion of nuclear weapons." When the time was ripe, they would move to implement the understanding.

The breakthrough came in July 1968 with the conclusion of the Nuclear Nonproliferation Treaty, which Rusk helped to draft after playing the major role in developing and negotiating the terms. In addition to restraining the nuclear states from transferring their weapons to others, the treaty prohibited non-nuclear states that became signatories from manufacturing or acquiring nuclear weapons. Most of the nations of the world have since adhered to this treaty, and a measure of its success has been the fact that, although a few countries such as India, Israel, and South Africa have developed nuclear weapons capability, no nation has publicly claimed membership in the nuclear "club" since the treaty was signed.

The successful negotiation of the Nuclear Nonproliferation Treaty produced an atmosphere conducive to further U.S.-Soviet discussions on arms limitation. New technologies were on the horizon that both sides knew would engender a costly arms race. The Soviets were developing an antiballistic missile (ABM) defense system, and the United States was working on its own Safeguard ABM system. By 1967 McNamara and Rusk had concluded that any ABM system developed would be obsolete by the time it was deployed, since the other side would inevitably move to counter it. Unless agreement was reached to limit ABM development, each side would spend billions on these systems and gain nothing.

In 1967 Rusk had arranged the meeting in Glassboro, New Jersey, between President Johnson and Premier Kosygin, who happened to be in New York visiting the United Nations. Glassboro was chosen as the site because it was equidistant between New York and Washington and neither leader wished to appear anxious to call on the other. Many subjects were discussed at this mini-summit, but the Americans made a special point of bringing up the need for both sides to limit ABM systems. It was evident that Kosygin did not agree, and there was blunt talk between him and McNamara. "You don't understand," McNamara told Kosygin. "Whatever you do, we will maintain our deterrent and build more missiles." Kosygin became upset and pounded the table, saying, "Defense is moral; offense is immoral." Nevertheless, after Kosygin returned to Moscow, Soviet planners studied the issue and came to the same conclusion as McNamara. Following the Nuclear Nonproliferation Treaty in 1968, the Soviets agreed to open discussions that would lead to the signing (in 1972) of the ABM Treaty, an agreement to limit development of defensive missile systems.

Rusk believed that a treaty on defensive systems should set the stage for a mutual reduction of offensive systems as well. In 1968 the United States had a large lead on the Soviets, both in land-based and sea-based missiles, but Rusk knew it was merely a matter of time before they achieved parity. Moreover, a new technology was on the horizon that would, if it was not controlled, multiply tenfold or more the number of nuclear warheads on both sides. The United States was working on a new generation of offensive missiles called MIRVs— multiple independently targeted reentry vehicles. A MIRV missile carries its warheads on a "bus" equipped with its own inertial guidance system, so that one missile can transport ten or more nuclear warheads, each of which can be independently targeted. The Soviets were beginning their own MIRV program, and Rusk thought it essential to work out an agreement to limit this technology before it got out of hand on both sides and produced another costly arms race.

On Wednesday, August 21, 1968, Rusk planned an important announcement: he and Dobrynin had completed secret negotiations, and President Johnson would go to Leningrad in September to meet with Soviet leaders to open new Strategic Arms Limitation Talks, nicknamed SALT. Both defensive and offensive weapons would be on the agenda, and Rusk optimistically thought that there was even a chance for some agreement before the end of the year, during Johnson's term in office. Rusk had high hopes of winding up his eight years in office with a historic arms control breakthrough with the Russians.

Regrettably, it was not to be. A few hours before the announcement of the Leningrad summit, on Tuesday, August 20, Warsaw Pact tanks rolled into Czechoslovakia. Rusk was on Capitol Hill testifying in Congress when an aide handed him a note concerning the Soviet action. After he had confirmed it, he telephoned Dobrynin to tell him the planned summit was canceled. Going to Leningrad now would make it appear the President minimized the seriousness of the invasion of Czechoslovakia.

Rusk had no advance warning of the invasion. As recently as three weeks before, he had asked Dobrynin point-blank whether the Soviets were going in, and he had said no. Rusk believed Dobrynin was telling the truth, and he later discovered that the invasion was decided upon only three days before it occurred. There was disappointment in Dobrynin's voice when Rusk telephoned him. They both felt a historic opportunity had been lost. How could the Soviets think they could go ahead with the SALT talks and at the same time move into Czechoslovakia? The normally jolly, voluble Dobrynin had no answer.

Rusk was dismayed by the Soviet invasion, but there was no safe way to counter it. Events in Eastern Europe simply were not issues of war and peace between the United States and the Soviet Union. At the same time, however, Rusk warned the Soviets against moving into Rumania or Yugoslavia, which also had exhibited independent tendencies, though under the firm control of their Communist parties. Dobrynin assured him there would be no such move, but Rusk watched the situation carefully and conferred with NATO leaders. There was little else to be done. The stillborn Prague Spring was an indigenous movement unaided by the United States. Rusk believed that the Soviets were willing to tolerate a certain independence on the part of their more peripheral satellites like Rumania and Yugoslavia, but could not accept the erosion of Communist Party control in Czechoslovakia.

His hopes for a summit and arms talks dashed, Rusk concentrated on the one problem that was always with him: Vietnam. For five months the fighting had continued while the meetings in Paris dragged on, each side, as Rusk put it, "talking past each other." Then, in October, on the eve of the American election, came a new chance for peace. There was an uneasy lull on the battlefields. Infiltration was down, and shelling of the cities had almost stopped. Perhaps the other side was getting tired too. Rusk dined with Gromyko on Sunday, October 6, and began to suspect something was up. When he explained the American position in the negotiations—that the bombing could be stopped, but only with some reciprocal action by Hanoi— Gromyko listened with unusual interest. He was "particularly non-combative," Rusk told his colleagues at State.

A few days later word arrived both from Paris and the Russians that Hanoi might be willing to accept, as "understandings," the American conditions for complete cessation of the bombing: an end to shelling the cities in the South, security of the DMZ, and expanded talks including the South Vietnamese. The sudden breakthrough was perhaps the result of Russian pressure, applied to influence the election in favor of Hubert Humphrey, and reflecting the long-standing distaste of the Soviet leadership for Richard Nixon.

A series of intense meetings began at the White House on October 14 to consider the new development. Rusk was all in favor of going forward, but stressed the need to make sure things rested on solid ground. America could not invest 28,000 dead and throw everything away for a dishonorable peace. "It's the beginning of a new chapter which will be very difficult," he warned. Spirits rose when Ambassador Bunker reported from Saigon that President Thieu concurred in the peace initiative.

Then complications set in. President Johnson, acutely conscious of the election campaign and unwilling to stop the bombing without a clear guarantee of when the expanded peace talks would begin, told Harriman to demand peace talks within twenty-four hours of the bombing halt. This was rejected by the North Vietnamese, who wanted a two-week delay. They also upped the ante, saying the bombing halt had to be "unconditional," a term the Americans were not willing to accept. Then the South Vietnamese balked as well. It looked as if everything was coming undone.

Johnson was perturbed and unsure which way to move. Rusk, at the President's bidding, took charge of the October peace initiative. Although the President's two chief advisers, Rusk and Clifford, were of the same mind on the bombing halt, there were subtle differences between them. Clifford wanted to force things; Rusk did not. Clifford was in a hurry to "winch down" the war. Rusk was willing to take reasonable risks, but it was unthinkable to throw away military and political success in Vietnam because of war weariness. They had come so far. He was convinced they had won the war on the battlefield. Now they had to win the peace. He had grander plans: not only a settlement in Vietnam but a restoration of peace in all of Southeast Asia. Rusk was tough-minded and patient, working to coordinate the various players as the struggle for peace was played out on a vast canvas: in Paris with Harriman, Vance, and the North Vietnamese; in Saigon with Bunker, Thieu, and his generals; in the various capitals of countries with troops in Vietnam; and in Washington, where the most important player of all, Lyndon Johnson, still doubted whether he should end the bombing.

The stakes were high. Not only did peace hang in the balance, but in all probability the election of the next President as well. Humphrey and Nixon were informed of the peace initiative, and their respective camps nervously awaited developments, knowing that a bombing halt on favorable terms might make the difference, as the polls showed Humphrey rapidly closing on Nixon's lead.

In Paris, Harriman and Vance were working feverishly for agreement with the North Vietnamese. Harriman held virtual round-the-clock secret sessions with Thieu and Le Duc Tho, North Vietnam's *éminence grise*. Soviet diplomats were playing a major role now, meeting with Vance and the North Vietnamese negotiating team. The Russians pushed hard, from their own motives, trying to get North Vietnam to accept the American position.

Harriman was almost in despair. He despised Johnson and viewed Rusk with considerable suspicion, doubting their will to act. He particularly bridled at a Rusk message sent on October 16: "MUST have day certain for the beginning of talks in which *the Government of South Vietnam is present.*" Rusk was adamant about South Vietnamese participation: "This . . . is the only, repeat only, immediate and visible sign that Hanoi has moved [to make concessions] at any point."

Harriman believed that it was too much to condition a cessation of the bombing on the North's accepting South Vietnamese participation, and he was not optimistic. He considered Johnson to be a Texas cowboy, and Rusk's mind to be frozen in the 1950s. His differences with Rusk were subtle but real. He respected Rusk but thought him too rigid, unfit for the number one job at State. It was demeaning to serve under a man like Rusk. Harriman was older, the only man in the administration with direct links to Roosevelt's time. He had been at the center of things when Rusk was an obscure staff man. Later, when he was governor of New York, Harriman had wanted to be President. Rusk, as president of the Rockefeller Foundation, had supported Stevenson. Rusk had no guts, Harriman thought. He remembered talking something over, agreeing on something with Rusk, just before a meeting with Johnson. But when they got into the meeting and it was clear Johnson had a different view, Rusk clammed up, refusing to disagree with the President. Nevertheless, Harriman never let up; he kept pressing the North Vietnamese to come to an agreement. He wanted the bombing halt before the election—Humphrey *had* to win. He could not abide Richard Nixon. Harriman was repulsed by the idea of a Nixon presidency.

On October 27 the North Vietnamese finally caved in to the pressure and accepted the American formula. Now Johnson's doubts had to be removed. General Creighton Abrams was summoned all the way from Saigon to allay the President's fears. He arrived at the White House in the middle of the night on October 29 and met with Johnson, with Rusk seated on the President's right, puffing on his Lark cigarettes. When asked whether the bombing could be stopped without causing additional allied casualties, Abrams answered with an unhesitating yes. Johnson turned immediately to Rusk, and as he looked into the President's eyes Rusk could see that that was it—Johnson was won over. To make sure, Johnson polled everyone in the room. All agreed—the bombing should stop. Rusk said he had no reluctance at all, "as long as we recognize this isn't moving us into Paradise."

Plans were laid to stop the bombing that same day, October 29, at 7 P.M. Washington time, a full week before the election. The new peace talks could get under way on November 2, and work began on a nationwide presidential address. Now that he had made his decision, the President was eager to get it done.

Then, once again, hopes were dashed. Rusk received a message from Thieu: he couldn't possibly begin negotiations in Paris in three days—Ky had to choose a delegation, and he wanted assurances from North Vietnam that the National Liberation Front would not be recognized as a separate delegation at the widened talks.

The bombing halt was put off. The President was exasperated. Tempers flared in Paris, Washington, and Saigon. Harriman in Paris had blunt words with Pham Dang Lam, the South Vietnamese observer, who promptly cabled Thieu saying he suspected a "trick" in the negotiations. On October 31 a Vietcong rocket slammed into a Catholic church in Saigon, killing nineteen people. Thieu hardened his resistance to participating in the talks.

Rusk felt caught in the middle, between Harriman, who was desperate for the bombing halt to begin, and Thieu, who was trying to delay. He acceded to the delay, hoping that Bunker could bring Thieu around, and reiterated his view that South Vietnam had to be given a chance to survive as a nation; we could not allow our own impatience to flush down the drain everything we had worked so hard for. Clifford vehemently disagreed; whether the Thieu regime survived was not important, and it probably did not deserve to survive. But Bunker was pressing for a delay, and at Rusk's urging Johnson agreed.

Harriman was furious at both Rusk and Bunker. In his opinion Bunker was not accurately reporting to Thieu and was taking his side. Rusk had had an opportunity to choose between him and Bunker and chose Bunker's position. Harriman never forgave either of them.

A crucial two days went by as Washington waited for Bunker in Saigon to convince Thieu. Bunker assured Thieu that the National Liberation Front would not be anything more than a part of Hanoi's delegation, but this was not enough. Thieu would not be convinced. By Thursday, October 31, it was clear that Bunker had not succeeded in mollifying Thieu. Johnson, at the urging of his political advisers, reluctantly decided to go ahead—he would give his speech and stop the bombing; perhaps then Thieu would come around. To everyone's regret, Thieu did not.

At eight o'clock that evening a fatigued and worn-looking President faced the nation on television to make the announcement: "I have now ordered that all air, naval, and artillery bombardment of North Vietnam cease as of 8 A.M. Washington time, Friday morning." Peace talks would begin on Wednesday, November 6, in Paris, the President continued, and South Vietnam was "free to attend."

Even then, Thieu was recalcitrant. On November 2 he announced publicly that South Vietnam would not participate in the Paris peace talks. He demanded that North Vietnam appear alone at the bargaining table and not "bring along representatives of the National Liberation Front as a separate delegation." Xuan Thuy in Paris now also entered the fray, saying that four delegations—the two Vietnams, the National Liberation Front, and the United States—all had a right to be represented at the talks. The sad feud with Thieu poisoned the widened peace talks and probably cost Hubert Humphrey the election. Many Americans suspected a trick, and unnamed Republican spokesmen fueled the fire, saying that the situation cast doubt on President Johnson's "credibility in stopping the bombing."

After Nixon was elected on November 5, Thieu continued to drag his feet. Four weeks went by before Saigon sent a delegation to Paris, and then the talks hung suspended over a parody of diplomacy—discussions about the shape of the negotiating table. The differences between Rusk and Clifford grew sharper, but it did not matter now, as the Johnson administration drew to a close.

Was Thieu's determined resistance and delay a trick? At the end of October, Rusk remembers, American intelligence had reported an extraordinary effort by noted Republicans to influence Thieu and hold up the announcement of the bombing halt until after the presidential election. Anna Chennault, the Chinese-born widow of General Claire Chennault, was the central figure involved, but reports also named high-level Nixon campaign officials, vice-presidential candidate Spiro Agnew, and two Republican senators. They were in contact with representatives of South Vietnam, urging, "Nixon is going to win; a Nixon administration will be more friendly to Saigon than the Democrats will be; stick with us and we will stick with you."

Both Johnson and Humphrey pondered whether to go public with the information. But to charge the Republicans with trying to sabotage the peace talks was a serious matter that would further shake an already divided and disturbed nation. They had no evidence that Richard Nixon was personally involved. Rusk and Clifford both counseled against public disclosure. Humphrey decided not to bring it up.

In the light of subsequent perfidy by some members of the Nixon administration, one wonders if this was another "dirty trick," and if it was in fact the decisive element for Thieu. If so, the Watergate scandal pales in comparison. Harriman predicted that if Nixon was elected the war in Vietnam would go on for another four years, and he was correct. The bombing would resume, 27,000 more Americans would lose their lives, and tragically, a wider war would continue before the final withdrawal of American troops under cover of the one-sided Paris accords of 1973, whose terms could have been obtained in 1968, and the ultimate humiliating fall of Saigon in 1975.

After almost eight years on the world's stage, at the center of power, Rusk, like other members of the administration and the President himself, prepared to leave office. "Like any GI in a foxhole," he told a reporter, "I will welcome my replacement with open arms." He did not mind the idea of obscurity. In his last month as Secretary of State he was at a reception, and a long line of people filed past to shake hands. One of them, a little old lady, looked at him closely and said, "I didn't get your name." He told her, and she asked, "What do you do?" He said, "I work for the State Department." "Oh, how nice," she said, moving on. He was amused, and rather pleased to realize that not everyone in the world knew who he was.

He spent some time worrying about what he would do after leaving office. He had no business or profession to fall back on, and he had not sought nor did he receive the lucrative offers customary for famous men. Finally his friends at the Rockefeller Foundation awarded him a special grant for a year so that he could rest and unwind.

He did have one better offer. After Chief Justice Earl Warren resigned from the Supreme Court, Johnson told Rusk that he wanted Abe Fortas to move up to Chief Justice and then he would nominate him for Fortas's seat. Rusk refused, saying he was not a lawyer, but Johnson said, "I've checked that, and you don't have to be a lawyer to go on the Supreme Court." When Rusk protested he would never be confirmed by the Senate, Johnson said, "I've talked to Senator Russell, and he said you will be confirmed very easily." But Rusk still declined the offer, and Johnson probably knew that he would.

Johnson was unstinting in his praise of Rusk as his administration ebbed. On December 9, 1968, a message arrived for Mrs. Rusk from the President. "The man who has served me most intelligently, faithfully, and nobly," it read, "is Dean Rusk." He sent a generous check to the State Department to help buy a going-away present: a copy of a portrait of Benjamin Franklin hanging at the American Embassy in Paris that Rusk had admired.

On January 17 a party honoring Rusk was held in the lobby of the State Department. President Johnson presented him with the Presidential Medal of Freedom and announced the establishment of a scholarship in his name at the Lyndon B. Johnson School of Public Affairs at the University of Texas. He called Rusk "this decade's man of the ages," and said, "History will rank him high above those who deserve to be called statesmen." The applause reverberated through the cavernous lobby, and Rusk's eyes became misty in a rare display of emotion. He smiled when he was presented with a silver plate engraved with a *New Yorker* cartoon, a picture of a doe and a stag in the forest. The stag was saying to the doe, "Remember dear, if we get through today, we'll be out of season."

His last days in office were uneventful; he passed the time saying good-bye. Andrei Gromyko, his Cold War adversary for over twenty years, came by with warm words of praise. Ambassador Dobrynin also dropped in and joked about how Rusk had taught him to drink American bourbon. One of Rusk's aides, who had never seen the Secretary drink anything but scotch, promptly branded this another Russian lie.

On January 20, the day of Richard Nixon's inauguration, Rusk was at home watching on television. The moment that the new President finished taking the oath of office was one of exhilaration—"I almost floated like a balloon," he said later, knowing that his responsibilities had ended at last. Afterward, he mentioned this to Lady Bird Johnson, who smiled and said, "That's very interesting, because I was sitting next to Lyndon on the platform that day, and at that same moment, he let out a great groan of relief."

From Pariah to "Professor Rusk"

Dean Rusk, Sibley Professor of International Law at the University of Georgia

"DEAN Rusk is quite frankly out of a job," a former Johnson cabinet officer told *The New York Times* almost a year after the end of the Johnson administration. Of all the high officials who had served with Johnson, Rusk had the hardest time settling into private life. He felt ill both mentally and physically. His stomach pains persisted. The toll of working sixteen-hour days, seven days a week for the past eight years had finally caught up with him. He paid the price in emotional exhaustion and deep depression. His family seriously doubted he would ever come out of it. For weeks on end he could do very little, and he adamantly refused to seek help or even admit that he had a problem.

Not only did he have difficulty finding work, but many people, including many former friends, despised him. Vietnam, heating up again under Nixon, hung heavily over him. His part in that unhappy conflict seemed to be the only thing people remembered or talked about. He was a former college professor and dean, but now he was unwelcome on most campuses. When the Johns Hopkins School of International Studies quietly gave him the use of a small office in a

building whose construction he had funded as president of the Rockefeller Foundation, some students objected and threatened to burn it
down. The prestigious Eastern universities and organizations that had
once courted and feted him when he was president of the Rockefeller
Foundation and chairman of the Council on Foreign Relations now
would have nothing to do with him. Never a party-goer, and retiring
by nature, he became something of a recluse, spending long hours
reading and watching television, occasionally going to sports events.
The few invitations he received to speak he declined: all anyone
wanted him to talk about was Vietnam. It pained him to speak of his
role in the war; he wanted to turn to other things.

Out of place in Washington, he began to look again to his native
region, the South. He still had friends at Davidson College, and his
old friend "Spec" Caldwell was a respected history professor at the
University of North Carolina at Chapel Hill. He made a few unpubli-
cized visits to speak at classes and seminars. He enjoyed teaching
again, and the polite Southerners received him with respect even if
they did not agree with his views. His friends tried to win him a
permanent appointment to the faculty at North Carolina, but he was
turned down by the administration, which feared trouble with radical
student elements. "He did have something to do with Vietnam, didn't
he?" the chancellor sarcastically remarked.

However, the University of Georgia, where he had once been offered the chancellorship, quietly courted Rusk. It was somehow fitting, a chance to teach a few miles from the farm where he was born.
He told Georgia officials that he would respond favorably to a faculty
appointment, the chance "to pull up stakes in Washington and go
home."

But even this was controversial. Several members of the State
Board of Regents, supported by Governor Lester Maddox, opposed
Rusk on the grounds he was "too liberal" and his daughter was married to a Negro. The outspoken Governor Maddox said Rusk's appointment would "further the objectives of the international
communist conspiracy." And a board member, Roy V. Harris, a high-
ranking officer in the White Citizens Councils of America, said of his
daughter's marriage: "He didn't have to let him court her for ten
years, and he didn't have to march down the aisle and give her to
him."

His friends quietly lobbied on his behalf. Lyndon Johnson telephoned around the state to garner support. The university president,
Fred Davison, threatened to resign if the appointment was rejected.

At last the regents approved his appointment by a vote of nine to four, and Rusk immediately accepted. When he arrived on campus in the spring of 1970, in the midst of more campus unrest because of Nixon's decision to send American troops into Cambodia, he did not know what to expect. To his great relief, the president of the local SDS came up to him and stuck out his hand in greeting. "I don't agree with you," the young man said, "but welcome home, Mr. Secretary."

His appointment as Sibley Professor of International Law at the University of Georgia began yet another fruitful chapter in Rusk's life, and his family credits this as saving him from a total nervous and emotional collapse. Still, there were those who objected that he did not have a law degree and was not qualified to teach international law. He answered his critics by quoting Harry Truman, who went to Harvard to give a lecture on international law. When a smug Harvard student asked, "Mr. President, what do you know about international law?" Truman answered, "I've had the opportunity to make plenty of it."

Rusk gradually overcame the doubters by refusing to live off his past accomplishments and digging into his teaching duties like a newly appointed assistant professor. His classes were popular, and he became the faculty adviser to the Black Students Association. He was accessible to students, and his self-deprecating humor and lack of pomposity was disarming. When people addressed him as "Mr. Secretary," he waved them off, saying it made him feel as if he were out on parole. He was just plain "Professor Rusk." "When I studied law at Berkeley before World War II, I wanted to be a teacher of international law," he said frequently. "Now, after some interruptions, I have finally made it."

He remained intensely interested in international affairs, and succeeding Secretaries of State quietly sought his counsel. He commiserated with William Rogers and Cyrus Vance over their troubles with White House aides, and when Henry Kissinger called to ask whether he should resign during the Watergate scandal, Rusk advised against it. Worried about President Nixon's mental stability during Watergate, he told Kissinger that a temporary bar should be interposed between the President and the nuclear weapons trigger. Kissinger assured him this had already been done.

As the war in Vietnam receded from the nation's consciousness, Rusk became more in demand as a speaker. He accepted the invitations of all kinds of groups, from local garden clubs to national television. Everywhere, he sounded familiar themes of the sanctity of

American democracy and the necessity to organize a durable peace, not only by reconciling disputes between nations but also by resolving the problems of the environment, population, and social justice. He saw a danger in an America that was turning increasingly inward and isolationist after the experience of Vietnam:

> I can understand those who say, "If [Vietnam] is what collective security means, maybe it is not a very good idea." I am concerned, however, that there is not enough public discussion on how to organize a durable peace, if not through collective security. To this question, each generation must find its own answer. I myself do not attempt to advise today's young people on how to answer the question. They must find out for themselves.

With time there came a "new respect for the old Dino," as Hugh Sidey commented in a retrospective article in *Life*. On Rusk's seventy-fifth birthday in 1984, Secretary of State George Shultz threw a party for him in Washington, and all his old friends were there. A former adversary, the *Washington Post*, even congratulated him and complimented his integrity. The University of California at Berkeley, which had been at the center of the antiwar movement, decided to award him the law degree that he had to forgo when his studies were interrupted by World War II. "It is an earned degree," he remarked proudly one day, "not an honorary one."

Unlike many of the men who participated in the decisions of the war in Vietnam, Rusk did not greatly modify his views with the passage of time. His mistake was, he said, "to underestimate the persistence of North Vietnam and to overestimate the patience of the American people." Yet the American people put up with the war for the better part of eight years—twice as long as either the Civil War or World War II—before they turned against it.

He has consistently "refused the opportunity to say mea culpa" about his role in the war. "I concurred in all the major decisions," he says, "and I would not do anything different based on the information we had at the time." He remains convinced that "the machinations of the press," the "foolish protests," and all the demonstrations in the streets made the peace movement an unwitting ally of the North Vietnamese and stiffened their resolve to fight. He believes the North Vietnamese could not have taken the tremendous casualties inflicted upon them without suing for peace had they not become convinced by press accounts of the protests that politically the United States could not stay the course.

Rusk also defends the policy of limiting the war, and he is critical of Nixon's use of greater force against North Vietnam and the "hard-and-fast" bombing campaign and invasion of Cambodia and Laos. Under Johnson, he remembers, the bombing of Laos was carefully worked out in consultation with Prince Souvanna Phouma and the government of Laos, and a similar secret agreement existed with Prince Sihanouk of Cambodia. Nixon's subsequent unrestrained military actions in these two countries upset their fragile balance, helping to set the stage for the genocide and unspeakable horrors of the 1970s.

Rusk remains unmoved by the argument on the right that the United States was "not allowed to win" the war in Vietnam because of constraints placed upon it by the civilian leadership. The policy of a wider war, he says, would have engendered "unacceptable risks."

"What we wanted to do," he explains, "was to achieve our mission in Vietnam—to keep the North from overrunning the South—without bringing Chinese conventional forces into the war. Our military took the view—and from a military point of view it makes sense—that a war against Chinese forces would necessarily become a *nuclear war*. When you look at the potential consequences [of that], it becomes a very different matter for the President of the United States. We did not want to act in such a way as to guarantee that the Chinese would enter with large numbers of ground forces. We could not have handled that with conventional forces alone," he adds ominously. "We simply did not want a much larger war, which Chinese entry would have involved."

Rusk rejects his critics who say that the United States lost the Vietnam War. "In terms of our objective the war was won from a military point of view. The failure at the end was a political one in terms of support by the American people and the reactions in Congress." Yet he concedes that "our military has not yet worked out a doctrine for handling armed insurgencies." In hindsight, it would have been better to "build a line across South Vietnam in the far north to create a zone that would be a block against infiltration." Rusk also concedes that the policy of step-by-step escalation was ill considered. "When President Kennedy decided to increase the number of American troops in Vietnam, he should have put in a stack of blue chips at the very beginning—say a hundred thousand men—to make it very clear to Hanoi that we were going to take this [war] very seriously." The biggest tactical failure of the war, he says, was not to have formed a joint military command: "If we ever—God forbid—have to do anything like this again, I would hope that we would have a unified command for the entire effort."

Thus Rusk, virtually alone among those who were involved in the key decisions on Vietnam, remains unbowed. Almost all of his contemporaries—McNamara, McGeorge Bundy, Clifford, and the rest—repented of their initial hawkishness even before they left office. Rusk's persistence can be explained by two factors: his loyalty to President Johnson, who even more than Rusk did not want to preside over an American defeat, and his view of the Soviets.

From long experience Rusk was convinced that toughness was the only way to deal with the Soviets, that they would endlessly probe and push at the perimeters of their regions of influence and expand wherever they found American weakness. But it was also Rusk's experience that the Soviets backed off in the face of American firmness. This had happened twice in Berlin, in Korea, in Cuba, in Iran, and in Greece and Turkey. Accustomed to a bipolar world in which the United States and the Soviet Union largely controlled events, Rusk believed that American firmness would pay off in Vietnam. He kept looking for the diplomatic signal or clandestine contact that would indicate the Soviets and their North Vietnamese clients had decided to give in. But it never came.

Ironically, Rusk, who spent his entire public life confronting the Russians and thought he knew them well, may have been taken in by a clever Soviet strategy. He believed that his two closest Soviet contacts, Gromyko and Dobrynin, shared his view that "the United States and the Soviet Union have a special responsibility for peace in the world." Gromyko and Dobrynin led him to think that the Soviets were doing their best to restrain the North Vietnamese and that it was the Chinese Communists who would not agree to terms. In 1968, while briefing presidential candidate George Wallace, Rusk told him that the problem in Vietnam was that "the Russians can't deliver Hanoi." Rusk also relied on Dobrynin to check out reports of "peace feelers" by North Vietnam through Poland, Hungary, and even the United Nations. Dobrynin invariably reported back that there was nothing to them. In telling Johnson about Dobrynin's supposed peace efforts Rusk wrote, "We must protect Dobrynin on this." In reality, it was more likely that the Soviets *would not* (rather than could not) "deliver" Hanoi; there was no reason for them to help the United States pull its chestnuts out of the Vietnam fire.

The tragedy of Vietnam was the result of the fact that those who led the country into war lacked a sense of proportion. The national interest in Vietnam was always ambiguous and, as subsequent events have shown, was in actuality minimal. Rusk always glossed over this point: when asked to define the national security interest in Vietnam, he invariably stated only that "Congress has recognized the national interest in Vietnam by passing the Gulf of Tonkin resolution." In fact, Rusk was wont to point out that the United States had no real interest in Vietnam: it desired no military bases, oil, or natural resources in the region. For Rusk the American intervention had only one aim: to stop Communist expansion.

Rusk also exaggerated the American commitment to South Vietnam. The SEATO treaty, which he relied upon, was a flimsy legal basis. A bluff from the start, SEATO did not mandate a military response, especially when other SEATO members were unwilling to supply more than token aid. Rusk was genuinely fearful that if the United States did not "answer the bell" in Vietnam, the Europeans would lose faith in NATO. But virtually all the NATO allies, schooled in realpolitik, derided the American action in Vietnam as a waste of effort and a distraction from the defense of Europe.

Yet there is regret if not shame in the American failure in Vietnam. If the commitment was exaggerated, if the dominoes did not fall as predicted in Southeast Asia, the American withdrawal opened the way for the terrible campaign of aggression and genocide in Cambodia and Laos that gave the final lie to North Vietnamese claims of moral superiority. No one can deny, after the brutal tyranny, cruelty, and inhumanity of the victors, that Indochina would today be far better off had America prevailed.

For the war in Vietnam was not fought by bad men for evil motives; it was fought by good men, like Rusk, who had an exaggerated vision of the capabilities of American leadership and rectitude in the world. Vietnam was not an aberration, but an enactment of the central values that have dominated American foreign policy since the time of Woodrow Wilson. Those who prosecuted the war acted not out of arrogance —the thesis of David Halberstam's book *The Best and the Brightest* —but out of faith and pride in America.

That, more than anything, has made the experience of Vietnam so unsettling. An important part of our national mythology was tested in that war and found wanting. After this rebuff Americans could no longer think of themselves and their role in the world as they had before. There was a new feeling of helplessness and an inability to control events and shape the world as they would like. Rusk believes that the chief danger after Vietnam is isolationism. A greater danger perhaps is disillusionment, a move away from the traditional idealism of America to a new cynicism holding that ideals, principles, and morality in our national and international affairs do not really matter.

Dean Rusk dominated his times as have few Secretaries of State before or since. Inevitably, the stigma of Vietnam will forever be attached to his name, but he deserves to be remembered for more than that. For almost a generation he was a significant influence over decisions of war and peace for our nation and the world. He was well prepared by training and experience for the role of Secretary of State, but by a terrible irony his experience, while at times an asset, weighed him down as well. His career shows the extent to which policymakers are tied, not only to their own premises and values, but also to past policies, prevailing political winds, and the circumstances of crisis. Through it all Rusk tried to steer a principled course, emphasizing international law and the utility of international organizations in a world committed to power politics. And he stood his ground to the end, fighting for the values that dominated his life.

ACKNOWLEDGMENTS

WHEN Dean Rusk left the Department of State on January 20, 1968, he took with him only copies of his own tax returns, leaving all official documents and papers in the custody of the U.S. government. This was an act of principle on his part, reflecting his strong belief that all such papers belong not to individuals but to the people of the United States. This was his practice in prior tours working for the government as well. Thus there are no "Rusk papers," except for the post-1968 period. I have had access to these, as well as to personal memorabilia, with Rusk's kind permission. I have also been allowed to read the personal correspondence that is in the family's possession, with the generous permission of Richard Rusk.

Although Rusk was not given to writing memos and took care to see that his telephone and other conversations were not recorded, the documents and papers he generated during the Kennedy and Johnson administrations are, of course, essential as primary sources. These are found at the Department of State, the John F. Kennedy Library, and the Lyndon B. Johnson Library. Both presidential libraries have extensive collections of oral histories, including a history dictated by Dean Rusk in 1969 and 1970. Many of the pertinent documents are still classified or accessible only in "sanitized" form. A selection of the available documents relevant to the decisions in which Rusk participated has been assembled as part of the Dean Rusk Research Collection in the University of Georgia library. For the Vietnam War period, the *Pentagon Papers* were an essential source.

Throughout his life, Parks Rusk collected newspaper articles and other materials pertaining to his brother. These can be found in the Dean Rusk Research Collection.

For Rusk's public career before he became Secretary of State, the volumes of the Department of State's *Foreign Relations of the United States* series (hereinafter cited as *FRUS*) are invaluable. I have also consulted documents in the National Archives.

I have found very useful a complete calendar of Rusk's appointments and phone calls during the time he was Secretary of State, generously provided by the Lyndon B. Johnson Library.

Rusk's speeches, transcripts of television appearances, and press conferences are available in the volumes of the *Department of State Bulletin* (hereinafter cited as *DSB*). His early speeches as Secretary of State are reprinted in the book *The Winds of Freedom,* edited by E. K. Lindley (1963).

William P. Bundy has generously permitted me to read his excellent unpublished memoir and penetrating account of the decisions of the Vietnam War.

The most indispensable source was Dean Rusk himself. I have interviewed him at great length, usually in collaboration with his son Richard Rusk. Several hundred hours of these interviews are on tape and preserved in the Dean Rusk Research Collection. I have also benefited from Dean Rusk's kind cooperation in this project, in hundreds of informal conversations and almost daily association during a period of about four years. Richard Rusk has been most kind and cooperative in calling to my attention specific items of interest. Quotations from Rusk not otherwise attributed are from my conversations with him; most are on tape in the Dean Rusk Research Collection.

I have also had the benefit of tape-recorded interviews with the following persons, conducted by Richard Rusk and myself, which are available in the Dean Rusk Research Collection:

Martin Hillenbrand
Richard Holbrooke
Ben Read
Clark Clifford
Harlan Cleveland
Nicholas Katzenbach
McGeorge Bundy
Alexis Johnson
Alexander Haig
Lucius Battle
Douglas Dillon
John J. McCloy
Walt Rostow
William Bundy
Ken Thompson
Ted Sorensen
Arthur Goldberg
Carl Rowan
Tapley Bennett
John Candler
George McGhee
Willard Wirtz
Edwin M. Martin
Andy Steigman

Harry Schlandeman
Coby Swank
Virginia Wallace
Eugene Rostow
George Ball
William Schaufele
Jim Greenfield
Gus Peleuses
Jane Mossellem
Ruth Gillard
Kappy Sherman
Mary Bennett
Arthur Schlesinger, Jr.
Robert McNamara
John Mabbott
John Slade
Orville Freeman
James R. "Spec" Caldwell
Louise Martin
Dr. Frontis Johnston
David French
Katherine Q. (Kitty) Branch
Eric Stein

I am especially grateful to Savanna Jackson Mapelli, who collected and organized much of the research material. Without her energy, intelligence, diligence, and skill, this project could not have been completed.

Another person whose skill has been critical to this project is Nelda Parker, word processor *non pareil,* who endured without complaint the typing of innumerable drafts and revisions.

N O T E S

PROLOGUE
page

12 "I would be glad . . .": The original source of this story, which is entirely fictitious, is McGeorge Bundy.

13 quintessential representative of the "establishment": See Richard Rovere, "Notes on the Establishment in America," *American Scholar,* vol. 30, no. 4 (1961), pp. 489–95.

13 final decision over the whole of our foreign policy: See George Ball, *The Past Has Another Pattern* (W. W. Norton, 1982), p. 360.

18 an article Rusk had written: Dean Rusk, "The President," *Foreign Affairs,* April 1960, p. 366.

18 Robert Kennedy later said: Arthur M. Schlesinger, Jr., *Robert Kennedy and His Times* (Ballantine, 1978), p. 240.

22 For the exchange between Dean Rusk and Senator George Aiken, see U.S. Congress, Senate, Committee on Foreign Relations, *On the Nomination of Dean Rusk, Secretary of State Designate,* 87th Cong., 1st sess. (1961), p. 17.

25 Sorensen's sister: Ted Sorensen interview, Feb. 10, 1985.

CHAPTER 1
page

29 The Rusk family: The name Rusk comes from an old Scandinavian word meaning a small piece or crust of bread that is refried to become crisp. A family joke is that this shows that at

page

least the Rusks are not half-baked.

30 Thomas Jefferson Rusk: There are two biographies: Cleburne Huston, *Towering Texan: A Biography of Thomas J. Rusk* (1971), and Mary Whatley Clarke, *Thomas J. Rusk, Soldier, Statesman, and Jurist* (1971).

31 Louisville Presbyterian Theological Seminary: An account of this institution may be found in Louis Weeks, *Kentucky Presbyterians* (1983).

33 excellent basic education: Kitty Branch interview, May 26, 1985.

33 "superior brain" and description of Rusk: Ibid.

36 most popular boy: John C. Candler interview, June 13, 1985.

CHAPTER 2

page

39 Rusk's classmates remember him: James R. Caldwell interview, June 6, 1985; Dr. Frontis Johnston interview, June 6, 1985.

40 gawking at all the tall buildings: James R. Caldwell interview.

41 his roommate remembers: Ibid.

41 headed for a career in business: Chalmers Davidson interview, June 5, 1985.

43 two ardent suitors in her life: Louise Martin interview, June 5, 1985; James R. Caldwell interview.

page

43 The night was dark and cloudy: Letter from Dean Rusk to his mother, Oct. 13, 1931.

43 "butcher your Negroes": Letter from Dean Rusk to his mother, Oct. 30, 1931.

48 "isolationism": On the isolationist mood of the country, see generally Selig Adler, *The Uncertain Giant: 1921–41 American Foreign Policy Between the Wars* (Macmillan, 1965).

49 His friends at Oxford: Letter from Van Lochhead, July 1, 1985.

63 "soundness personified . . .": Letter from John Mabbott, Dec. 20, 1984.

65 Lyndon Johnson, his appointment: See Robert A. Carow, *The Path to Power* (Knopf, 1982), pp. 255–256.

CHAPTER 3

page

82 "I'll go where I'm sent": Barbara Tuchman, *Stilwell and the American Experience in China, 1911–45* (Bantam, 1971), pp. 293–327.

82 "an American general . . .": John P. Davies, *Dragon by the Tail* (W. W. Norton, 1972), p. 225.

99 "to reconquer Burma . . .": Philip Ziegler, *Mountbatten: A Biography* (Knopf, 1985), p. 223.

100 Stilwell soon became disenchanted: Ibid., p. 247.

page

109 "I have urged . . .":
Tuchman, *Stilwell*, pp. 629–
630.

111 code-named "Dixie": See
David Dean Barnett, *Dixie
Mission* (Berkeley, 1970).

112 they were still suitable:
Charles Romanus and Riley
Sunderland, *United States
Army in World War II: Time
Runs Out in the CBI*
(Department of the Army,
1958), p. 57.

114 CBI mission . . . ultimately
unnecessary: See Davies,
Dragon by the Tail,
pp. 340–41.

116 European Advisory
Commission: Ray S. Cline,
*The United States Army in
World War II* (War
Department, Operations
Division, 1951), p. 323.

118 acquired great influence and
respect: Ibid., p. 331.

118 other members of the policy
section were not let in: Ray
S. Cline, *Case Study:
Planning the End of the War
Against Japan* (War
Department, Operations
Division, 1951), p. 347.

119 "please don't let them . . .":
John J. McCloy interview,
Jan. 11, 1985.

120 Bonesteel's memo on August
9: Cline, *Case Study*, p. 350.

120 The decisions and documents:
The SWNCC and other
documents are reproduced in
*Foreign Relations of the
United States* (hereinafter
FRUS) 1945, vol. 6.

120 one of the great staff actions:
Cline, *Case Study*, pp. 350–
351.

CHAPTER 4

page

126 "I didn't say . . .": Beatrice
Berle and Travis Jacobs,
eds., *Navigating the Rapids,
1918–1971: From the Papers
of Adolf Berle* (Harcourt,
1973), p. 477.

126 At the conference, once
again: Charles Bohlen,
Witness to History (W. W.
Norton, 1973), pp. 225–40.

128 demanded a victor's role:
message from Stalin to
Truman, Aug. 22, 1945,
FRUS 1945, vol. 6,
pp. 687–88.

129 "I and my colleagues . . .":
Ibid., p. 687.

129 the Russians were briefed:
See Joseph Goulden, *Korea:
The Untold Story of the War*
(Times Books, 1982), p. 4.

132 "fig leaves . . .": See Walter
Isaacson and Evan Thomas,
The Wise Men (Simon and
Schuster, 1986), p. 345.

132 "the President has given
me . . .": Robert Donovan,
Conflict and Crisis (W. W.
Norton, 1977), p. 157.

133 Byrnes submitted his
resignation: Byrnes
resigned in April 1946. The
resignation was the result of
the friction between Truman
and Byrnes and Truman's
desire to run his own foreign
policy. Byrnes hung on as
Secretary until General
George Marshall could take
over after his mission to
China, in early 1947. Byrnes
and Truman never did
establish a satisfactory
working relationship. See

page

Dean Acheson's account in *Present at the Creation: My Years in the State Department* (W. W. Norton, 1969), pp. 190–93, 210–11. Upon his return from Moscow, President Truman demanded to see Byrnes and met with him aboard the presidential yacht *Williamsburg*. There are conflicting accounts of this meeting, but it is quite certain that Byrnes got a dressing-down by the President or his advisers. See Donovan, *Conflict and Crisis,* pp. 159–60. Byrnes's view is supported by Robert L. Messer in *The End of an Alliance* (University of North Carolina Press, 1982). Messer's account is unconvincing and is clearly colored by a pro-Byrnes bias. In the end it is probably irrelevant whether Truman read or sent the letter to Byrnes. The letter clearly reflects what Truman was thinking at the time, and it is certain Byrnes incurred the President's displeasure. The Messer account (p. 149) incredibly blames Truman for Byrnes's independence, saying that Truman was not interested and did not ask him what was happening in Moscow. This criticism is unfair to Truman and shows profound ignorance of the way government should and does function: the President should not be required to ask the Secretary of State when

page

he wants to find out what is going on. Another error in Messer's account is the statement (p. 164) that at Potsdam both Truman and Byrnes wanted to keep the Soviet Union out of the war with Japan, presumably because of the successful test of the atomic bomb. This goes against Truman's own express statement of his motivations at Potsdam and Dean Rusk's recollections as well. Despite the successful test of the atomic bomb, which came in the middle of the Potsdam Conference in July, too late to influence policy, no one, not even Truman, knew whether the bomb could be successfully exploded over Japan or what effect that would have on the Japanese. The change in policy toward the Russians on Japan came after, not before, Hiroshima. See also Bohlen, *Witness to History.*

135 Critics and scholars: Hans J. Morgenthau, *Politics Among Nations,* 5th ed. (Princeton University Press, 1973), pp. 4–15; Walter Lippmann, *U.S. Foreign Policy* (Little, Brown, 1943); George F. Kennan, *American Diplomacy 1900–1950* (University of Chicago Press, 1951), and *Realities of American Foreign Policy* (Princeton University Press, 1954).

136 "X" article: Kennan, "The Sources of Soviet Conduct" (title he gave to his "X"

page

article), *Foreign Affairs,* July 1947, pp. 566–82.

136 His viewpoint was personal and visionary: See Kennan, *Memoirs 1925–1950* (Little, Brown, 1967).

138 Kennan disliked talking of values: Barton Gellman, *Contending with Kennan* (Praeger, 1984), pp. 30–32.

138 Kennan, in his "X" article: Kennan, "The Sources of Soviet Conduct," pp. 576, 581.

138 Kennan's view: See Ronald Steel, *Walter Lippmann and the American Century* (Little, Brown, 1980), pp. 443–44; see also Kennan's National War College Lecture, Dec. 18, 1947, quoted in Gellman, *Contending with Kennan,* p. 39.

139 Rusk represented the department: Alger Hiss to Secretary of State, *FRUS* 1946, vol. 1, p. 20.

139 In a memorandum on March 26, 1946: Memorandum by the Assistant Chief of the Division of ISA, March 22, 1946, ibid., p. 766.

139 Rusk blamed the Russians: Memorandum by the Assistant Chief of the Division of ISA, May 3, 1946, ibid., p. 785.

140 "another outrage": Truman, *Year of Decisions* (Doubleday, 1955), p. 551.

140 Security Council debates: See *FRUS* 1946, vol. 7, p. 317.

141 Only in Moscow: Rusk did not know that President

page

Truman had sent Stalin an ultimatum on the issue of Soviet troops in Iran. See Seyom Brown, *The Faces of Power* (Columbia University Press, 1983), p. 37.

143 the same one that John Foster Dulles saw: Bohlen, *Witness to History,* p. 192.

145 "Never send me a question . . .": *Department of State Bulletin,* Oct. 31, 1949, p. 656.

149 He believed the U.N. could play: *FRUS* 1947, vol. 5, pp. 124–25.

149 Acheson and Kennan overruled him: Ibid., p. 127.

149 "I lustily cried Peccavi!": Acheson, *Present at the Creation,* p. 224.

150 However, Kennan and other Cold Warriors: Kennan, *Memoirs;* Steel, *Walter Lippmann.*

150 He made two points: *FRUS* 1947, vol. 5, p. 216.

150 In a memorandum of July 30: Ibid., pp. 876–77.

151 On October 21, 1947: GAOR, II, Resolutions (A/519), pp. 12–14. Resolution 109 (II) of the General Assembly.

151 UNSCOB was stacked: Resolution 193 (III); GAOR, III.1, Resolutions (A/810), pp. 18–21; Resolution 288-A (IV); GAOR, IV, Resolution (A/1251), pp. 9–10.

151 He was a guest: *FRUS* 1949, vol. 6, pp. 301–3.

152 President Truman was informed: Ibid., p. 303*n.*

153 He argued, unrealistically:

page

FRUS 1947, vol. 1, pp. 676–677.

153 "present position cannot": Ibid., p. 662.

153 In July 1947: Ibid., pp. 446, 567–70.

154 In preparation for: Ibid., 572–73.

154 "The moral and political . . .": Ibid., p. 573.

154 He rejected the British position: *FRUS* 1948, vol. 1, p. 403.

154 On April 2, 1948: Ibid., pp. 318–21.

155 "We must leave . . .": Ibid., pp. 318–24.

155 In September 1949: Acheson, *Present at the Creation,* pp. 345–49.

CHAPTER 5

page

158 "I had hoped . . .": Dulles to Acheson, February 1949. National Archives.

160 "objectives would be . . .": *FRUS* 1948, vol. 5, p. 387.

160 Rusk favored U.N. action: Ibid., p. 395.

160 In response to a Pakistani complaint: Security Council Resolution 39, Jan. 20, 1948.

160 "rallying-cry for all . . .": *FRUS* 1947, vol. 6, p. 97.

161 A resolution adopted: 5/514; SCOR, II, No. 82, p. 2179.

161 The United States cajoled: See the very complete account by Philip Jessup, *The Birth of Nations* (Columbia University Press, 1974), pp. 42–92.

162 His thinking was fully set

page

out: *FRUS* 1948, vol. 6, pp. 597–99.

163 Tripolitania: *FRUS* 1949, vol. 4, p. 533.

163 Cyrenaica: *FRUS* 1948, vol. 3, p. 954.

163 Palestine: See generally William Roger Louis and Robert W. Stookey, eds., *The End of the Palestine Mandate* (University of Texas Press, 1985).

163 The matchless drama: There are many fine accounts; see in particular William Roger Louis, *The British Empire in the Middle East, 1945–1951* (Oxford University Press, 1984), and Michael Cohen, *Palestine and the Great Powers, 1945–1948* (Princeton University Press, 1982).

163 Rusk found himself: Dan Kurzman, *Genesis 1948* (World Press, 1970), p. 559, writes that "Israelis who dealt with Rusk regard him as having opposed the creation of the Jewish State with possibly more zeal than any other top State Department official." For a defense of Rusk see Jessup, *Birth of Nations,* p. 255.

163 "between an Arab land . . .": *FRUS* 1945, vol. 8, p. 687.

164 "Jesus Christ couldn't . . .": Donovan, *Conflict and Crisis,* p. 319.

165 Seven members, the majority: *New York Times,* Sept. 1, 1947, p. 1.

165 Loy Henderson: Donovan, *Conflict and Crisis,* p. 324.

page

166 But they warned: *FRUS* 1947, vol. 5, pp. 1264–66.

166 That recommendation was rejected: Cohen, *Palestine,* p. 289.

166 Intrigue was rampant: Donovan, *Conflict and Crisis,* pp. 330–31.

167 He called for a revival: Cohen, *Palestine,* p. 347.

167 George Kennan, who prepared: *FRUS* 1948, vol. 5, pp. 545–54.

167 Rusk had still another view: Ibid., pp. 556–62.

168 All the same: Ibid., pp. 587–589, 617–18.

168 "The purpose of the United Nations . . .": Ibid., p. 618.

168 the creation of a trusteeship: Ibid., p. 632.

168 "The U.S. should continue support . . .": Ibid.

169 Clifford argued eloquently: Ibid., pp. 690–95.

169 Truman was acutely conscious: See Clark Clifford, "Factors Influencing President Truman's Decision to Support Partition and Recognize the State of Israel," *American Heritage,* April 1977. But Clifford attempts to refute the "revisionist" historians who state that Truman's motives were purely political.

170 Marshall was on Rusk's side: *FRUS* 1948, vol. 5, pp. 749–750.

172 he was angry and outraged: Margaret Truman, *Harry S Truman* (William Morrow, 1973), p. 387.

172 "not a bad idea": Harry S

page

Truman, *Years of Trial and Hope* (Doubleday, 1956), ch. 12.

172 "This morning I find . . .": Margaret Truman, *Truman,* p. 388.

172 In a memorandum to Marshall: *FRUS* 1948, vol. 5, pp. 750–51.

172 he worked with Rusk: Ibid., p. 760n.

172 At his news conference on March 25: Ibid.

173 Rusk did not hesitate: Ibid.

173 "the preservation of the peace . . .": Ibid.

173 on April 4 he met: Walter Millis, ed., *The Forrestal Diaries* (Viking, 1951). See also Warren I. Cohen, *Dean Rusk* (Cooper Square, 1980), p. 24.

173 "the United States was not . . .": *FRUS* 1948, vol. 5, p. 833n.

174 On April 30: Ibid., pp. 877–79.

175 He continued discussions: Cohen, *Palestine,* p. 374.

175 "I think what is likely . . .": *FRUS* 1948, vol. 5, p. 967.

175 Clifford argued forcefully: Ibid., p. 976.

176 Marshall disagreed strongly: Ibid., p. 975.

176 At the United Nations: Jessup, *Birth of Nations,* pp. 277–79.

178 "reserve a wing . . .": *FRUS* 1948, vol. 5, p. 1630.

178 he approached John Foster Dulles: Ibid., pp. 1439–40, 1448–49, 1463.

179 plight of the Arab refugees: Ibid., pp. 1331–32.

179 Truman issued a statement: Ibid., p. 1513.

page

182   "Truman Formula": *New York Times,* June 5, 1987, p. 13.

182   The development of the Marshall Plan: Kennan, *Memoirs,* pp. 325–53; Acheson, *Present at the Creation;* Harry Bayard Price, *The Marshall Plan and Its Memory* (Cornell University Press, 1955); Joseph M. Jones, *The Fifteen Weeks* (Viking, 1955).

182   He argued that the United Nations: *FRUS* 1947, vol. 3, p. 236.

183   "Before you take away a fig leaf": Eric Stein interview, Feb. 13, 1986.

184   and convinced Marshall: Marshall's doubts are given in Avi Shlaim, *The United States and the Berlin Blockade, 1948–1949* (University of California Press, 1983), pp. 353–54.

186   "on a less than universal basis": Dulles to Rusk, March 24, 1948. John Foster Dulles Papers, Princeton University Library.

186   At the first meeting: Louis J. Halle, *The Cold War as History* (Chatto & Windus, 1967), pp. 183–84.

187   He worked closely with Senator Vandenberg: *FRUS* 1948, vol. 3, pp. 92–96.

188   He also worked on: *FRUS* 1949, vol. 4, pp. 113–15.

188   "necessary to maintain a friendly . . .": Ibid., p. 731.

189   Kennan had nothing but contempt: Kennan, *Memoirs,* pp. 402–9.

189   no mention of the currency question: *FRUS* 1949, vol. 3, pp. 694–95.

189   Jessup approached Soviet delegate: Bohlen, *Witness to History,* p. 284.

189   On March 15: *FRUS* 1949, vol. 3, pp. 695–97.

190   He elaborated his views: *Department of State Bulletin,* Oct. 24, 1949, p. 630.

CHAPTER 6

page

192   Dean Acheson became Secretary of State: Acheson, *Present at the Creation,* p. 249.

193   he even criticized his conduct: Rusk to Acheson, April 11, 1949. 501.BB., Balkan/4–1149, National Archives.

194   shaping up important decisions: Acheson, *Present at the Creation,* pp. 255–56.

196   "The policymaker is constantly . . .": *Time,* Jan. 8, 1951, p. 13.

197   On Joseph McCarthy, see generally John G. Adams, *Without Precedent* (W. W. Norton, 1983), and William Buckley, *McCarthy and His Enemies* (Regnery, 1954).

198   State had already quietly moved: Barry Rubin, *Secrets of State* (Oxford University Press, 1985), pp. 55–56.

198   reassigned as Ambassador to Sweden: Acheson, *Present at the Creation,* p. 431.

199   applying for a demotion: Ibid., pp. 431–32.

200   "Charges such as . . .":

page

Atlanta Constitution, April 8, 1950, p. 5.

201 Why was Rusk spared?: See David Halberstam, *The Best and the Brightest* (Penguin Books, 1972), pp. 323–25.

203 U.N. trusteeship in Manchuria: *FRUS* 1947, vol. 7, pp. 320–24.

204 U.S. "military mission": *FRUS* 1949, vol. 9, pp. 520–523.

204 Rusk even argued: *FRUS* 1949, vol. 2, pp. 149–51.

204 "political and economic measures cannot prevent . . .": Roger Hilsman, *To Move a Nation* (Doubleday, 1967), p. 293; U.S. Congress, Senate, Hearings Before the Committee on Armed Services and the Committee on Foreign Relations, *Military Situation in the Far East,* 82d Cong., 1st sess. (1951), p. 1667.

204 President Truman articulated the new policy: Ibid. See also Robert Blum, *The United States and China in World Affairs* (McGraw-Hill, 1966), p. 108.

204 "soon it will be . . .": *U.S. News & World Report,* Jan. 18, 1950, p. 10.

206 John Paton Davies's assessment: Foster Rhea Dulles, *American Policy Toward Communist China 1949–1969* (T. Y. Crowell, 1972), p. 27; Acheson, *Present at the Creation,* p. 135.

207 The feud came to a head: *FRUS* 1950, vol. 1, pp. 203–6.

207 not regarded as having crucial strategic significance: John Spanier, *The Truman–MacArthur Controversy and the Korean War* (Belknap Press, 1959), pp. 17–19.

208 The Korean ambassador immediately called upon: *FRUS* 1950, vol. 7, pp. 40–43.

208 Senator Connally publicly stated: Ibid., pp. 64–68.

208 do something to control inflation: Ibid., p. 41.

209 he would lead a military coup: According to Dean Rusk, Chiang Kai-shek never found out about the proposed coup. General Sun was cashiered and placed under house arrest in 1955 for "culpable negligence" in allowing young Formosan officers to petition and complain to U.S. General Maxwell Taylor at a military review ceremony.

211 secret intelligence report: *FRUS* 1950, vol. 7, pp. 148–54.

213 "a very high official": Rusk refuses to name the official involved.

214 "we do not believe . . .": *FRUS* 1950, vol. 7, p. 406.

214 he was filled with moral indignation: Kennan, *Memoirs,* p. 495.

214 On September 9 he made a speech: *Department of State Bulletin,* Sept. 18, 1950, p. 23.

215 He gave credence to a CIA report: *FRUS* 1950, vol. 7, p. 933.

page

218 masses of bugle-blowing
     Chinese: Ibid., p. 1264.

220 the war's revised objectives:
     Ibid., pp. 1588–89.

224 adopting Dulles's
     memoranda on China: *FRUS*
     1950, vol. 6, p. 349, and
     vol. 1, p. 314.

225 "it was a little remark . . .":
     FRUS 1951, vol. 7,
     p. 354.

225 called for "further
     clarification": Ibid., pp. 558–
     559.

226 In August 1947 a draft
     treaty: *FRUS* 1947, vol. 6.
     p. 478.

227 "It is short-sighted . . .":
     Cohen, *Dean Rusk,*
     p. 71.

228 "attempts by the Japanese
     . . .": State Department file,
     Box 927.

228 negotiated a secret
     understanding: See *New
     York Times,* April 7, 1987,
     p. 1.

229 In October 1950 the
     Australian: *FRUS* 1950, vol.
     6, p. 147.

229 despite the opposition of:
     FRUS 1951, vol. 6, pp. 201–
     202.

229 Rusk also smoothed over:
     Ibid., pp. 204–6.

229 Jessup reported that the
     governments: *FRUS* 1950,
     vol. 6, pp. 69–76.

230 "The Department's policy
     . . .": *FRUS* 1951, vol. 6,
     pp. 16–19.

231 "economic support, military
     items . . .": *FRUS* 1950,
     vol. 6, p. 690.

231 "our best wishes . . .":
     Ibid., p. 711.

page

231 Acheson met with . . .
     Schuman: Ibid., p. 812.

231 "in formalizing the
     independence . . .": Ibid.,
     p. 828.

231 "assist the French . . .":
     Ibid., p. 836.

231 "firm non-communist control
     . . .": Ibid., pp. 887–89.

231 "the military situation is so
     grave . . .": Ibid., p. 900.

231 Rusk wrote to Karl Lott
     Rankin: Karl Lott Rankin
     Papers, Princeton University
     Library.

232 ". . . we have been giving
     . . .": *FRUS* 1950, vol. 6, p.
     864.

232 "I would appreciate . . .":
     Ibid., pp. 924–29.

233 A grim intelligence report:
     Ibid., p. 958.

233 "disposed to move . . .":
     FRUS 1951, vol. 6,
     pp. 16–26.

234 Dulles had talked to Rusk:
     See the correspondence
     between Dulles and Rusk
     during this period, Rusk file,
     John Foster Dulles Papers,
     Princeton University
     Library.

235 On the way back:
     *Department of State
     Bulletin,* Nov. 19, 1951,
     pp. 818–21.

235 "the reality of the principles
     . . .": Ibid., p. 823.

236 "Dean Rusk is tops . . .":
     Cohen, *Dean Rusk,* p. 76.

CHAPTER 7

page

240 But Rusk assured Dulles:
     Rusk to Dulles, Nov. 11,

page

1951. John Foster Dulles Papers, Rusk file, Princeton University Library.

247 and his answers were full: Rusk's testimony can be found in U.S. Congress, House of Representatives, Select Committee to Investigate Tax Exempt Foundations, 82d Cong., 2d sess., on House Res. 561 (November and December 1952).

247 In one exchange: Ibid. (Dec. 9, 1952), pp. 507–10.

248 "You can't knock people down . . .": Interview of Kenneth Thompson, who was then Rusk's executive assistant, by Richard Rusk, Jan. 20, 1985.

252 The Epps story is from James R. Caldwell interview.

255 "parliamentary diplomacy": See Rusk, "Parliamentary Diplomacy—Debate vs. Negotiation," *World Affairs Interpreter*, vol. 26, no. 2 (University of Southern California, July 1955), p. 121.

257 "The United States . . .": Rusk, "The President," *Foreign Affairs*, April 1960, p. 366.

CHAPTER 8
page

263 But the news media: E.g., *Business Week*, Dec. 17, 1960, p. 23.

264 "a world in turmoil . . .": *Department of State Bulletin*, March 20, 1961, p. 395.

264 "take the lead . . .": *Department of State Bulletin*, April 10, 1961, p. 516.

265 "tedium" of diplomacy: Arthur M. Schlesinger, Jr., *A Thousand Days* (Riverside Press, 1965), p. 434.

266 "When we are able . . .": Rusk, "Our Positive Strategy," in *The Winds of Freedom* (Beacon Press, 1963), p. 57.

266 "On the one hand": Rusk, "The Tragedy of Cuba," *Vital Speeches* 28, Feb. 15, 1962, p. 259.

266 "One must be prepared . . .": *Department of State Bulletin*, Dec. 17, 1962, p. 913.

267 accused him of being trite: Walter Lippmann, "The Secretary Misunderstood," *Newsweek*, Nov. 6, 1967, p. 23.

267 He had nothing against Rostow: I.M. Destler, Leslie H. Gelb, and Anthony Lake, *Our Own Worst Enemy?* (Simon and Schuster, 1984), p. 184. It is asserted that Rusk "vetoed" Rostow. This is too strong. Rusk merely preferred McGhee.

270 "Washington's busiest man": *U.S. News & World Report*, Sept. 11, 1962, p. 52.

270 keeping in touch with Congress: See William Shannon, "Dean Rusk and the President," *Commonweal*, March 29, 1963, p. 6.

271 "a unique asset . . .": Dorothy McCardle, "Distaff

page

Side Practices Tea Cup Diplomacy," *The Virginian Pilot and the Portsmouth Star,* April 1, 1962, p. E3.

272   "one of Washington's . . .": Donnie Radcliffe, "Mrs. Dean Rusk," *Washington Star,* Feb. 18, 1962, p. E1.

272   "a terrific impression . . .": McCardle, "Distaff Side."

272   "her serene smile . . .": Frances Lewine, "Mrs. Rusk Makes Small Talk Count," *Washington Post,* March 17, 1963.

272   "a diplomat with . . .": Patricia Saltonstall, "Rusk Reception Sparkles," *Washington Evening Star,* Dec. 20, 1962, p. B8.

272   "national blood sport": Destler, Gelb, and Lake, *Our Own Worst Enemy?,* p. 48.

273   They had little idea: Abram Chayes oral history, JFK Library Oral History Collection, p. 128.

273   "fill up the horizons . . .": Dean Rusk oral history, JFK Library Oral History Collection, p. 81.

274   "I want you to be . . .": Roger Hilsman oral history, JFK Library Oral History Collection, pp. 5–6.

274   His aides complained: Hilsman, *To Move a Nation,* pp. 35, 40–43.

274   "disarray, confusion, and uncertainty": Murray Marder, "Process of Adjustment Disarrays State Department," *Washington Post,* July 15, 1961, p. A1.

275   State was described as a "pool": Ibid., p. A9.

275   As James Reston wrote: *New York Times,* July 19, 1961, p. 28.

276   Kennedy's new confidence in Rusk: Comments on the relationship did appear in the press, however.

277   Chester Bowles: Hilsman, *To Move a Nation,* p. 36.

278   he wrote Kennedy a memorandum: Chester Bowles, *Promises to Keep* (Harper & Row, 1971), pp. 327–28.

278   "You might have been against it . . .": Schlesinger, *Robert Kennedy,* p. 508.

278   Then Bowles compounded: Bowles to JFK, April 28, 1961. Kennedy Papers, Presidential Office Files (POF), Box 114A, JFK Library.

278   it was ironic that: James Reston, *New York Times,* July 19, 1961, p. 28.

278   "Thanksgiving Day Massacre": For an account of this incident see Theodore C. Sorensen, *Kennedy* (Harper & Row, 1965), p. 270, and Walt Rostow, *The Diffusion of Power* (Macmillan, 1972), p. 163.

279   Ball was finally able to penetrate: Ball, *The Past Has Another Pattern,* p. 169.

280   "Warm congratulations . . .": State Department file, Box 927.

281   had an intuitive appreciation: Walt Rostow interview.

282   He sought neither: Theodore C. Sorensen, *The Kennedy Legacy* (Macmillan, 1969), p. 83.

page

284 He could keep track: Bundy to Rusk, Feb. 3, 1961. Kennedy Papers, POF, Box 87, JFK Library.

284 "never sent a message . . .": McGeorge Bundy interview, Nov. 11, 1985.

287 "In connection with instructions . . .": Schlesinger to Rusk, April 24, 1961. Kennedy Papers, POF, Box 115, JFK Library.

287 Although books by Theodore Sorensen: Sorensen, *Kennedy,* pp. 270–71.

287 the notion has persisted: Halberstam, *The Best and the Brightest,* p. 344.

289 Eisenhower, the man: *New York Times,* May 2, 1962, p. 1.

CHAPTER 9
page

291 among the organizers of the Cubans: Peter Wyden, *Bay of Pigs* (Simon and Schuster, 1979), pp. 29–33.

291 Allen Dulles, arguing for: Schlesinger, *A Thousand Days,* p. 242.

293 Kennedy reluctantly agreed: Ibid., pp. 242–43.

294 "clear and present danger": *New York Times,* Aug. 4, 1961, p. 14.

294 "sharp and even ominous": *New York Times,* April 5, 1961, p. 36.

294 privately writing memos: Schlesinger, *A Thousand Days,* pp. 240–41, 252–56.

295 Bowles then asked: Bowles, *Promises to Keep,* p. 329.

page

295 "climactic" meeting: Schlesinger, *A Thousand Days,* p. 251.

296 called this idea "curious": Ibid., p. 255.

296 was suggesting himself: John B. Henry and William Epinosa, "The Tragedy of Dean Rusk," *Foreign Policy,* Fall 1972, p. 166.

298 Lemnitzer "couldn't believe it": Wyden, *Bay of Pigs,* p. 205.

299 At four in the morning: Ibid., pp. 204–6.

301 The men aboard the *Essex:* Haynes Johnson, *The Bay of Pigs* (W. W. Norton, 1964), pp. 140–72.

302 (Schlesinger said later that . . .) Arthur M. Schlesinger, Jr., "The Bay of Pigs—A Horribly Expensive Lesson," *Life,* July 23, 1965, p. 75.

302 He spoke bitterly: Walt Rostow interview.

302 exploded into words: Ibid., and Rostow, *Diffusion of Power,* p. 163.

303 headed by General Maxwell Taylor: Sorensen, *Kennedy,* p. 308.

304 "almost alone in . . .": *New York Times,* April 24, 1961, p. 1.

304 "speak for all . . .": *New York Times,* May 2, 1961, p. 3.

CHAPTER 10
page

305 "I think jet fighter bombers . . .": U.S. Congress, Executive Session of the

page

Senate Foreign Relations
Committee, 87th Cong., 1st
sess. (1961), vol. 13, part 1,
p. 349.

305   "the gravest issues": *New
York Times,* Sept. 5, 1962,
p. 1.

305   The Cuban missile crisis:
Among the many fine
accounts of this crisis see
Elie Abel, *The Missile Crisis*
(J. B. Lippincott, 1966);
Robert F. Kennedy, *Thirteen
Days* (W. W. Norton, 1969);
Abram Chayes, *The Cuban
Missile Crisis* (Oxford
University Press, 1974);
Graham Allison, *Essence of
Decision* (Little, Brown,
1971).

306   allegations were raised:
Congressional Record, 88th
Cong., 2d sess., vol. 108, pp.
18359–61.

306   convinced that the Soviets:
Chayes, *Cuban Missile
Crisis,* p. 11.

306   But when the SAM sites:
Ibid., p. 12*n.*

307   McGeorge Bundy took it
upon himself: Bundy to JFK,
March 4, 1963. Kennedy
Papers, POF, Box 115, JFK
Library.

308   then Rusk was called on:
Cuban Missile Crisis
Meetings, transcript No. 28,
Item 1, pp. 8–10. Papers of
John F. Kennedy, JFK
Library.

308   McNamara and Taylor were
in favor: Ibid., pp. 11–13.

308   Vice President Johnson
weighed in: Ibid., p. 20.

308   At the conclusion: Ibid.,
p. 27.

page

308   "a blockade against . . .":
Ibid., Item 2, p. 9.

309   "any course of action . . .":
Ibid., p.10.

309   he was later criticized: Abel,
Missile Crisis, p. 58.

309   On his schedule: Dean
Rusk's appointment books,
October 1962, LBJ Library.

309   On Wednesday, October 24:
Sorensen, *Kennedy,*
p. 686.

310   "But if we don't do this
. . .": Abel, *Missile Crisis,*
pp. 69–70, says it was
Thursday afternoon.
Sorensen's account appears
to be accurate. By Thursday,
according to George Ball in
*The Past Has Another
Pattern,* p. 292, Rusk was
against a surprise air strike.

310   "My brother is not . . .":
Sorensen, *Kennedy,* p. 686;
Ball, *The Past Has Another
Pattern,* p. 291.

310   McCone began the session:
Abel, *Missile Crisis,* p. 71.

311   " . . . given an electric
shock": statement by Dean
Rusk, SEATO council
meeting, April 8–10, 1963,
National Security Files, Box
248, JFK Library.

312   Just one floor below: Ball,
*The Past Has Another
Pattern,* p. 292.

312   Meeker then followed:
Chayes, *Cuban Missile
Crisis,* pp. 15–16.

313   The term "quarantine":
Ibid., p. 15*n.*

313   a short memo in his own
handwriting: This memo,
which is still classified, is in
the Secretary of State's file

page

on Vietnam, State
Department file, Box 924.

314 "The ones whose plans
. . .": Abel, *Missile Crisis*,
p. 94.

315 De Gaulle then asked: De
Gaulle later was persuaded
to examine the photographs
and was duly impressed by
their clarity and scope. Ibid.,
pp. 112–13.

316 When Dobrynin emerged:
New York Times, Nov. 3,
1962, p. 7.

316 "It is inconceivable . . .":
Abel, *Missile Crisis,* p. 125.

317 inch-high headlines: *New
York Times,* Oct. 23, 1962,
p. 1.

318 "partnership in deceit . . .":
*Department of State
Bulletin,* Nov. 12, 1962, pp.
720–23.

318 "It . . . changed our position
. . .": Kennedy, *Thirteen
Days,* p. 121.

319 began to argue the American
case: Ibid., ch. 13.

321 "Pull yourself together . . .":
Eugene Rostow
interview, June 1986.

321 refused to be panicked:
Khrushchev showed similar
restraint. On that same
Saturday an American
weather plane incredibly
wandered off course on a
transpolar flight and ended
up in Siberia. MiG fighters
were scrambled, but the
Soviets did not order the
plane shot down. It returned
to base unharmed.

321 Some even stated:
Schlesinger, *Robert Kennedy
and His Times,* p. 519; Abel,

page

Missile Crisis, pp. 190–91;
Allison, *Essence of Decision,*
pp. 141–42.

322 In truth, Kennedy knew: See
Ball, *The Past Has Another
Pattern,* p. 306n.

322 Excom debated and labored:
Cuban Missile Crisis
Meetings, transcript, Oct.
27, 1962. Papers of John F.
Kennedy, JFK Library.

322 "deeply, indeed passionately
. . .": McGeorge Bundy,
"The Cuban Missile
Crisis," unpublished paper,
p. 67.

323 When Dobrynin asked:
Kennedy, *Thirteen Days,*
pp. 108–9.

323 Preparations for air strikes:
McGeorge Bundy doubts
that Kennedy would have
ordered an air strike or
invasion even if Khrushchev
had rejected the Saturday
Kennedy letter. He believes
the President would have
simply stepped up the
blockade because no one
could be sure an air strike
would not produce a nuclear
strike from Cuba on
American cities, and
Kennedy was not going to
risk this. Bundy, "Cuban
Missile Crisis," pp. 57–59.

CHAPTER 11
page

328 "Crisis Book": *Time,*
Feb. 10, 1961, p. 9.

328 "reaching out for . . .":
*Department of State
Bulletin,* April 10, 1961,
p. 516.

page

328 "the issues called . . .":
     Ibid., p. 517.
328 "Our discussion . . .": Ibid.
329 With Rusk's memo: Charles
     J. V. Murphy, "Grand
     Strategy: Is a Shift in the
     Making?" *Fortune,* April
     1961, p. 116.
330 "largely at the urging . . .":
     Time, April 7, 1961,
     p. 21.
330 "favored strengthening . . .":
     William J. Jorden, "Rusk
     Backs Use of Nuclear
     Arms," *New York Times,*
     Feb. 21, 1961, pp. 1, 6.
331 a full chronology: Rusk to
     JFK, Jan. 28, 1961.
     Germany–Berlin General
     folder, National Security
     Files, Box 75–81, JFK
     Library.
331 press conference on March 9:
     New York Times, March 10,
     1961, p. 6.
332 "brutally frank exposition
     . . .": *New York Times,*
     May 11, 1961, p. 4.
334 "Stop that plane!": Abram
     Chayes oral history, JFK
     Library Oral History
     Collection, pp. 236–37.
335 Rusk told Khrushchev:
     Robert M. Slusser, *The
     Berlin Crisis of 1961* (Johns
     Hopkins University Press,
     1973), p. 328.
336 "much more of a barbarian":
     State Department file, Box
     924.
336 become public knowledge:
     New York Times, June 11,
     1961, p. 1. For the text of the
     aide-mémoire, see
     *Documents on Germany
     1944–1985,* 4th ed. (1986),

page

     Department of State
     Publication No. 9446.
336 Soviet strategy over Berlin:
     Slusser, *Berlin Crisis,* p. 8.
336 The Soviets were further
     motivated: Martin
     Hillenbrand interview,
     Feb. 2, 1986.
336 There was also evidence: See
     generally Slusser, *Berlin
     Crisis.*
337 Kennedy became
     increasingly preoccupied:
     Schlesinger, *A Thousand
     Days,* ch. 15.
337 Rusk played a key role:
     Martin Hillenbrand
     interview.
338 "circumspect": Schlesinger,
     A Thousand Days, p. 383.
338 "great funk": Abram Chayes
     oral history, JFK Library
     Oral History Collection,
     pp. 247–48.
338 "heightening world tension":
     Washington Post, June 23,
     1961, p. A1.
339 Kohler and Hillenbrand:
     Martin Hillenbrand
     interview.
339 legal brief: See Note from
     the United States to the
     Soviet Union on the
     Question of Germany and
     Berlin, July 17, 1961,
     *Documents on Germany
     1944–1985,* Department of
     State Publication No. 9446.
339 shorter version: Statement by
     President Kennedy on a
     German Peace Settlement
     and the Status of Berlin, July
     19, 1961, ibid.
340 Kohler and Hillenbrand also
     disagreed: Martin
     Hillenbrand interview.

page

342   Next, Rusk went to see
      Adenauer: Memorandum of
      conversation, Aug. 10, 1961
      (Germany–Berlin General
      folder), National Security
      Files, Box 82, JFK
      Library.
343   "the world can expect . . .":
      Washington Post, Aug. 11,
      1961, p. A11.
343   confession of Communist
      failure: *New York Times,*
      Aug. 16, 1961, pp.1, 10.
343   set new travel restrictions:
      New York Times, Aug. 23,
      1961, p. 3.
344   three-page memo: JFK to
      Rusk, Aug. 21, 1961.
      National Security Files, Box
      82, JFK Library.
345   "in order to shock . . .":
      New York Times, Sept. 2,
      1961, p. 1.
345   were forced on him: Slusser,
      Berlin Crisis, p. 169.
345   When Kennedy received the
      news: Sorensen, *Kennedy,*
      p. 619.
346   propose a ban of nuclear
      tests in the atmosphere?:
      This is Dean Rusk's
      recollection. It is
      corroborated by Harold K.
      Jacobsen and Eric Stein,
      *Diplomats, Scientists, and
      Politicians: The United
      States and the Nuclear Test
      Ban Negotiations*
      (University of Michigan
      Press, 1966), pp. 282-83.
347   Yet the press acknowledged:
      U.S. News & World Report,
      Sept. 11, 1961, p. 52; E. W.
      Kenworthy, "Evolution of
      Our Number One
      Diplomat," *New York Times*

page

      Magazine, March 18, 1962,
      p. 31.
351   the argument he needed:
      Martin Hillenbrand
      interview.
351   "The talks . . .":
      *Department of State
      Bulletin,* Nov. 6, 1961,
      p. 746.
351   The Soviets reacted: Slusser,
      Berlin Crisis, p. 180.
352   sent back detailed accounts:
      Martin Hillenbrand oral
      history, JFK Library Oral
      History Collection, p. 23.
352   Rusk's patience and
      firmness: *New York Times,*
      April 5, 1962, p. 1; and
      Martin Hillenbrand
      interview.
354   In the summer of 1962: Jack
      M. Schick, *The Berlin Crisis,
      1958–1962* (University of
      Pennsylvania Press, 1971),
      p. 211.
354   In a diplomatic note:
      *Department of State
      Bulletin,* Oct. 15, 1962,
      p. 559; *New York Times,*
      Sept. 6, 1962, p. 2.
355   after the U.S. congressional
      elections: *New York Times,*
      Sept. 17, 1962, p. 1.
355   Khrushchev believed: Rusk
      asserted this theory on the
      basis of conversations with a
      "high Russian official"
      whom he refused to identify.
      During the Cuban missile
      crisis Gromyko brought up a
      linkage of Cuba and Berlin in
      his talk with President
      Kennedy on Oct. 17, 1962,
      but both Kennedy and Rusk
      refused to discuss the matter.
355   the Soviets gradually:

page

Address by Chairman Khrushchev in East Berlin, Jan. 16, 1963, *Documents on Germany 1944–1985,* Department of State Publication No. 9446.

359 argued against helping France: Rusk memorandum, May 5, 1961, Doc. No. 4770, National Security Files, Box 70–71, JFK Library.

359 "You have found me . . .": C. L. Sulzberger, *The Last of the Giants* (Macmillan, 1970), p. 826.

359 "The only reason . . .": Ibid.

360 The British had relied: Harold Macmillan, *At the End of the Day, 1961–1963* (Harper & Row, 1973), p. 347.

362 resurrected the proposal: *Department of State Bulletin,* June 17, 1963, p. 931.

363 "The most important thing . . .": *New York Times,* Aug. 18, 1963, p. E1.

366 an accord: Quadripartite Agreement on Berlin, Signed at Berlin, Sept. 3, 1971, *Documents on Germany 1944–1985,* Department of State Publication No. 9446, pp. 1135–43.

CHAPTER 12

page

368 "more solemn purposes": *Department of State Bulletin,* May 22, 1961, pp. 247–48.

368 "This is the real issue . . .": Tad Szulc, "Rusk Calls

page

Latin Poverty 'Real Issue' in Hemisphere," *New York Times,* May 5, 1961, p. 10.

368 "battleground of freedom": U.S. Congress, Senate, Committee on Foreign Relations, *International Development and Security,* part 1, 87th Cong., 1st sess. (May 31, 1961), p. 12.

368 National Security Council meeting: Remarks of President Kennedy to the National Security Council Meeting of January 22, 1963, National Security Files, Box 314, JFK Library.

369 "[H]e strove coolly . . .": Schlesinger, *A Thousand Days,* p. 782.

370 Rusk received high praise: Tad Szulc, "Rusk Team Wins Latins' Respect," *New York Times,* Jan. 30, 1962, p. 5.

370 "Rusk," declared Kennedy: Chalmers Roberts, "Rusk Is Congratulated by Kennedy, Legislators," *Washington Post,* Feb. 2, 1962, p. 1.

370 page one of *The New York Times: New York Times,* Jan. 17, 1965, p. 1.

371 he wrote a memo: Rusk to JFK, Feb. 15, 1961. National Security Files, Box 66, JFK Library.

371 CIA station chief: Interview with Tapley Bennett, former Ambassador to the Dominican Republic, June 10, 1985.

371 intentions of Dominican: U.S. Senate Committee on Foreign Relations, *Alleged Assassination Plots*

page

Involving Foreign Leaders
(W. W. Norton, 1976), pp.
203–4.

371 Rusk and Kennedy moved
quietly: Rusk to JFK,
undated. Dominican
Republic General folders
7/61–8/61, National
Security Files, Box 66, JFK
Library.

372 Rusk went along: Cohen,
Dean Rusk, p. 211.

375 National Security Council:
Notes for Record, NSC
Meeting on Volta Dam,
December 5, 1961 (no. 494),
National Security Files, Box
313, JFK Library.

375 Robert Kennedy strongly
opposed: Schlesinger, *Robert
Kennedy,* pp. 603–5.

375 "I can feel the cold wind
. . .": Ibid., p. 604.

375 correct decision: Ibid.,
p. 605.

376 Reviewing Congo policy:
Rusk to JFK, Feb. 1, 1961.
National Security Files, Box
27–28, JFK Library.

377 under suspicious
circumstances: According to
the Senate Intelligence
Committee Report in 1975,
the CIA had been actively
plotting against Lumumba
and had delivered poison in
an abortive attempt to kill
him in Léopoldville.
Madeleine G. Kalb, "The
C.I.A. and Lumumba," *New
York Times Magazine,*
Aug. 2, 1981, pp. 32–34.

377 would oppose any
government: *New York
Times,* Feb. 16, 1961, p. 14.

377 two main dangers: Madeleine
G. Kalb, *The Congo Cables*

page

(Macmillan, 1982), pp. 258–
280.

377 "extremely upset"
. . ."infuriated": Brian
Urquhart, *Hammarskjöld*
(Knopf, 1972), p. 575.

377 Hammarskjöld was killed:
The details are recounted in
Kalb, *Congo Cables,*
pp. 287–99.

378 he wrote a memorandum:
Rusk to JFK, Nov. 11, 1961
(Item 3). National Security
Files, Box 27–28, JFK
Library.

378 limited U.N. military action:
Rusk to JFK, Dec. 9, 1961,
ibid.

380 left the situation to George
Ball: Ball, *The Past
Has Another Pattern,*
p. 258.

383 "Racial discrimination . . .":
U.S. Congress, Senate,
Committee on Commerce,
*Civil Rights—Public
Accommodations, Part I,*
88th Cong., 1st sess. (July 10,
1963), p. 58.

383 "packed with tourists . . .":
Time, July 13, 1963,
p. 10.

CHAPTER 13

page

384 "dangled like . . .": *Time,*
March 31, 1961, p. 8.

386 William Bundy, at the time:
William Bundy interview,
Jan.10, 1985.

386 "a solemn treaty . . .":
SEATO treaty, Article IV.

386 vote of 82 to 1: *Department
of State Bulletin,* Sept. 12,
1966, p. 379.

387 In a note to the British in

page

September 1964: State
Department file, Box 926.

388 Realizing the sensitive
nature: Cohen, *Dean Rusk,*
p. 166.

389 most of the weapons: *Time,*
Jan. 20, 1961, p. 29.

389 "a sort of Buddhist
Falstaff": *Time,* March 17,
1961, p. 21.

390 Of the 2 million: Ibid.

390 "Of course not": *Time,*
Feb. 3, 1961, p. 26.

390 His plan, set forth: Rusk to
JFK, undated memorandum
and circular. Kennedy
Papers, POF, Box 121, JFK
Library.

390 to include Souvanna
Phouma: Rusk to JFK,
memo of March 1, 1961.
Ibid.

391 Laos was to become neutral:
U.S. Congress, Senate,
Committee on Foreign
Relations, Executive
Sessions, 87th Cong., 2d
sess. (1962), p. 643.

392 "Diem is extremely sensitive
. . .": U.S. Congress,
Senate, Committee on
Foreign Relations, *The U.S.
Government and the
Vietnam War,* part 2, p. 15.

393 "question for the future":
New York Times, May 5,
1961, p. 1.

393 He cabled Kennedy: The
unpublished cable is
discussed in *Time,* July 5,
1971, p. 10.

394 "will not exceed . . .":
Senator Gravel Edition,
Pentagon Papers, vol. 2
(Boston: Beacon Press),
pp. 108–9.

394 "galvanize" the Vietnamese:

page

Cable from JFK to Nolting,
Department of Defense
Edition, *Pentagon Papers,*
Vol. 11, pp. 400–5.

395 "There can be peace . . .":
New York Times, March 2,
1962, p. 6.

395 He pointed to the growing:
New York Times, July 9,
1962, p. 1.

397 "losing horse": Barbara
Tuchman, *The March of
Folly* (Knopf, 1984), pp. 296–
297.

398 working on a cable: See Ball,
*The Past Has Another
Pattern,* p. 371, and
Hilsman, *To Move a Nation,*
pp. 483–94.

398 "situation in which power
. . .": Senator Gravel
Edition, *Pentagon Papers,*
vol. 2, pp. 234–35.

398 cautious approval: Ball, *The
Past Has Another Pattern,*
p. 372. Hilsman, *To Make a
Nation,* p. 488, says Rusk
added a sentence offering
South Vietnamese military
leaders direct support in any
interim period of breakdown
of the central government,
but Rusk vehemently denies
this.

398 "If Rusk and Gilpatrick . . .":
Ball, *The Past Has Another
Pattern,* p. 371.

399 The President also had
doubts: Senator Gravel
Edition, *Pentagon Papers,*
vol. 2, p. 235

399 "existing directive": U.S.
Congress, Senate,
Committee on Foreign
Relations, *The U.S.
Government and the
Vietnam War,* part 2, p. 153.

page

399   another approach to Diem:
       Senator Gravel Edition,
       Pentagon Papers, vol. 2,
       p. 239.

399   "bone and muscle": U.S.
       Congress, Senate,
       Committee on Foreign
       Relations, *The U.S.
       Government and the
       Vietnam War,* part 2,
       p. 159.

399   "without a policy . . .":
       Senator Gravel Edition,
       Pentagon Papers, vol. 2,
       p. 240.

399   "largely speculative": Ibid.,
       p. 241

399   "a secure and indepen-
       dent . . .": Rusk to Lodge,
       Sept. 12, 1963. National
       Security Files, Box 316–317,
       JFK Library.

400   "progress". . ."sound":
       U.S. Congress, Senate,
       Committee on Foreign
       Relations, *The U.S.
       Government and the
       Vietnam War,* part 2,
       p. 185.

400   At an October 5 meeting:
       Senator Gravel Edition,
       Pentagon Papers, vol. 2,
       p. 767.

400   "not to thwart . . .": Ibid,
       p. 769.

400   "that it's really the
       generals . . .": William J.
       Rust, *Kennedy in Vietnam*
       (Scribner's, 1985), p. 192.

400   "green light": U. Alexis
       Johnson, *The Right Hand of
       Power* (Prentice-Hall, 1984),
       p. 412.

400   There was fear: U.S.
       Congress, Senate,
       Committee on Foreign
       Relations, *The U.S.

page

       Government and the
       Vietnam War,* part 2,
       pp. 197–99.

401   "superb handling of a . . .":
       Rusk to Lodge, Deptel 722,
       Nov. 4, 1963, National
       Security Files, Box 200–201,
       JFK Library.

401   "first step forward . . .":
       Rusk circular, Deptel 841,
       Nov. 4, 1963, National
       Security Files, Box 208, JFK
       Library.

401   "cause for concern":
       Review of the Political
       Situation in South Vietnam,
       Nov. 15, 1962, National
       Security Files, Box 204, JFK
       Library.

401   "organize an in-depth
       study . . .": Rust, *Kennedy
       in Vietnam,* p. 2.

403   "There was absolutely no
       doubt . . .": *Time,* Dec. 6,
       1963, p. 26.

403   "May God give you . . .":
       State Department file, Box
       928.

403   "If this is true": Pierre
       Salinger, *With Kennedy*
       (Doubleday, 1966), p. 10.

404   He testified: U.S. Congress,
       *Hearings Before the
       President's Commission on
       the Assassination of
       President Kennedy,* vol. 5,
       pp. 365–67.

404   "On behalf of President
       Johnson . . .": *Department
       of State Bulletin,* June 7,
       1965, pp. 897–98.

CHAPTER 14
page

411   "Some of the people . . .":
       Sam Houston Johnson, *My

page

Brother Lyndon (Cowles Book Co., 1970), p. 117.

411 Johnson's instant recognition: Ibid., p. 129.

412 first meeting with the National Security Council: NSC Meetings Files, vols. 1–3, 12/5/63–7/27/65, National Security Files, Box 1, LBJ Library.

413 most important high-level meeting: See David C. Humphrey, "Tuesday Lunch at the Johnson White House: A Preliminary Assessment," *Diplomatic History,* Winter 1984, pp. 81–101.

413 "had great faith . . .": Cohen, *Dean Rusk,* p. 219.

415 "I thank the Lord . . .": LBJ to Rusk, Feb. 9, 1966. White House Central Files, Dean Rusk, LBJ Library.

415 the dog jumped: Interview of James Greenfield, journalist and former Rusk aide, by Richard Rusk, June 25, 1986.

415 Kennedy also made the rounds: Ibid.

415 initiated without the knowledge: Ball, *The Past Has Another Pattern,* p. 371.

416 "a wonderful man . . .": Interview of Emory Kobesio B. Y. Swank by Richard Rusk, June 1986. Emory Swank served as special assistant to the Secretary of State.

416 "His idea of relaxation": James Greenfield interview.

416 letter of February 21, 1964: Galbraith to LBJ. White House Central Files, Confidential Files, FG 105

page

Department of State 1964, LBJ Library.

417 "President Kennedy isn't the President . . .": Eric F. Goldman, *The Tragedy of Lyndon Johnson* (Knopf, 1969).

419 "Castro communism . . .": *Miami Herald,* May 17, 1964, *Now* magazine, p. 5.

419 sent George Ball to forestall: Ball, *The Past Has Another Pattern,* pp. 337–59.

420 "unrealistic nationalism": *Washington Post,* May 10, 1964, p. 1.

421 In December 1963: Hilsman, *To Move a Nation,* p. 355.

421 In April 1964: *New York Times,* April 18, 1964, p. 1.

422 "Your Secretary of State very much needs a rest": Bundy to LBJ, June 24, 1964, National Security Files, Memos to the President from McGeorge Bundy, vol. 5, LBJ Library.

422 Johnson reaffirmed the American commitment: "The U.S. Government and the Vietnam War," U.S. Congress, Senate, 98th Cong., 2d sess. (December 1984), p. 209.

422 troop rotations were juggled: Senator Gravel Edition, *Pentagon Papers,* vol. 2, p. 303.

423 to the time of Woodrow Wilson: Rusk harked back to a statement made by Woodrow Wilson in 1917 when talking about the main task of the American state in the international arena: "The right is more precious than

page

peace, and we shall fight for
the things we have always
carried nearest to our hearts
—for democracy, for the
right of those who submit to
authority to have a voice in
their own government, for
the rights and liberties of
small nations, for a universal
dominion of right by such a
concert of free peoples as
shall bring peace and safety
to all nations and make the
world itself at last free."
*Department of State
Bulletin,* June 4, 1962,
p. 897.

423 "We have no desire . . .":
*Department of State
Bulletin,* Jan. 11, 1965,
pp. 34, 38.

423 "I do not believe . . .":
*Department of State
Bulletin,* April 14, 1966,
p. 516.

423 "The idea in the
minds . . .": Interview of
Dean Rusk by Paige E.
Mulhollan, LBJ Library,
Sept. 26, 1969.

424 "Try and imagine . . .":
*Department of State
Bulletin,* Oct. 14, 1963,
p. 572.

424 "In Korea the international
community . . .":
*Department of State
Bulletin,* March 19, 1962,
p. 450.

424 "We fought the Korean
War . . .": *Department of
State Bulletin,* Jan. 23, 1967,
pp. 127, 130.

425 "I do believe . . .":
*Department of State
Bulletin,* Sept. 25, 1967, pp.

page

387–88. See also ibid., May
31, 1963, p. 731.

425 "When we speak of . . .":
*Department of State
Bulletin,* Nov. 4, 1968,
p. 631.

425 "These men in Hanoi . . .":
Ibid., p. 472.

426 Hanoi was supplying
leadership: These were the
CIA reports of the time as
stated in William Bundy's
unpublished manuscript on
Vietnam, pp. 12–24.

426 "a sober view . . .":
Summary Record of National
Security Council Meeting,
March 5, 1964, National
Security Files, NSC
Meetings File, Box 1, LBJ
Library.

426 "As compared to the
cost . . .": Summary Record
of National Security Council
Meeting, April 19, 1964,
National Security Files, NSC
Meetings File, Box 1, LBJ
Library.

427 "No, no, no!": Interview of
Gus Peleuses, security man
for Dean Rusk, by Richard
Rusk, March 1985.

428 "Is there any way . . .":
Rusk to Lodge, May 21,
1964. Cable 2027, National
Security Files, Country File:
Vietnam, LBJ Library.

428 "steady progress": *New
York Times,* Sept. 10, 1964,
p. 1.

428 There was a growing belief:
George Ball interview, Oct.
24, 1986.

429 Later investigation has cast
doubt: For accounts of the
investigation of the Gulf of

page

Tonkin incidents, see
especially U.S. Congress,
Hearing on February 20,
1968, *The 1964 Incidents,*
90th Cong., 2d sess. (1968);
Senator Gravel Edition,
Pentagon Papers, vol. 5;
Joseph C. Goulden, *Truth Is
the First Casualty* (Rand
McNally, 1969); and Eugene
C. Windchy, *Tonkin Gulf*
(Doubleday, 1971). See also
"Hanoi Attack in Tonkin
Gulf: Evidence Indicates It
Didn't Happen,"
*International Herald
Tribune,* May 8, 1985, p. 8;
and U.S. Congress, Senate,
*The U.S. Government and
the Vietnam War,* part 2,
Committee on Foreign
Relations, 98th Cong., 2d
sess. (December 1984).

430 "We believe that present
OPLAN . . .": Rusk to
Taylor, Aug. 3, 1964. Cable
336, National Security Files,
Country File: Vietnam, LBJ
Library.

431 "I'll go to my grave . . .":
Interview of Carl Rowan
by Richard Rusk, March
1985.

431 "Hell, those dumb . . .":
Ball, *The Past Has Another
Pattern,* p. 379.

433 the story of the Alamo:
George Ball interview.

433 policy hiatus: William
Bundy's unpublished
manuscript on Vietnam, pp.
14-10 to 14-14.

433 "we are not concealing
anything . . .": *New
York Times,* Oct. 9, 1964,
p. 1.

page

434 a rare personal memorandum
to the President: State
Department file, Box 928.

CHAPTER 15

page

437 "We refuse to be anti-
Communist": *Time,* April 28,
1967, p. 26.

439 "talking nonsense":
*Department of State
Bulletin,* May 10, 1965.

440 "No more niceties . . .":
William C. Westmoreland, *A
Soldier Reports* (Doubleday,
1976), p. 140.

440 meeting with the President:
Senator Gravel Edition,
Pentagon Papers, vol. 4, p.
310.

440 decision was debated: U.S.
Congress, Senate,
Committee on Foreign
Relations, *The U.S.
Government and the
Vietnam War,* part 3, 1965–
1966, pp. 187–246; William
Bundy's unpublished
manuscript on Vietnam,
chapters 24–27; Ball, *The
Past Has Another Pattern,*
pp. 399–403. A transcript of
notes on the meeting of July
21, 1965, held in the White
House Cabinet Room at
10:40 A.M. is in Meeting
Notes file, Box 1, LBJ
Library.

441 of "greater weight": William
Bundy's unpublished
manuscript on Vietnam,
p. 27-11.

441 "The central objective . . .":
Senator Gravel Edition,

page

Pentagon Papers, vol. 4,
p. 407.

441 "So Dean Rusk . . .":
William Bundy's unpublished
manuscript on Vietnam,
p. 27-12.

441 "Westerners can ever
win . . .": Transcript of
meeting of July 21, 1965,
Meeting Notes file, Box 1,
LBJ Library.

445 his reticence and reserve:
Joseph Kraft, "The
Enigma of Dean Rusk,"
Harper's, July 1965,
p. 100.

446 "no Secretary of State . . .":
Washington Post, March 2,
1966, p. A-17.

446 "Rusk's persistence . . .":
Charlotte Observer, Aug. 22,
1965, p. 12-A.

446 another difficult crisis: See
*Dominican Action, 1965:
Intervention or
Cooperation?,* Center for
Strategic Studies,
Georgetown University,
Special Report Series No. 2,
July 1966; also recounted in
interview with Tapley
Bennett, U.S. Ambassador
to the Dominican Republic in
1965, Feb. 7, 1985. See also
Tad Szulc, *Dominican Diary*
(Delacorte Press, 1965); Dan
Kurzman, *Santo Domingo:
Revolt of the Damned*
(Putnam's, 1965); and
Theodore Draper, "The
Dominican Crisis, a Case
Study in American Policy,"
Commentary, December
1965, pp. 30–33.

449 asked the OAS Council:
Department of State

page

Bulletin, June 14, 1965,
p. 941.

452 He advised Johnson to
rebuff: Rusk to LBJ, June
24, 1965. Box 7, Confidential
Files: Vietnam (Situation in)
1965–66, LBJ Library.

456 "Phase A–Phase B"
formula: U.S. Congress,
Senate, Committee on
Foreign Relations, *The U.S.
Government and the Vietnam
War,* part 3, 1965–1966,
pp. 528–31.

457 stop the bombing of North
Vietnam: This episode is
recounted in Wallace Thies,
When Governments Collide
(University of California
Press, 1979); Chester L.
Cooper, *The Lost Crusade*
(Dodd, Mead, 1970); and
George Herring, ed., *The
Secret Diplomacy of the
Vietnam War* (University
of Texas Press, 1983),
pp. 431ff.

458 "historic opportunity . . .":
Harold Wilson, *The Labour
Government, 1964–1970*
(Weidenfeld & Nicolson,
1971), p. 365.

460 At a speech on December 6:
*Department of State
Bulletin,* Jan. 1, 1968,
pp. 1–5.

461 ended aid to Egypt:
Washington Post, Feb. 1,
1965, p. A2.

462 Then unexpectedly, on May
19: *New York Times,* May
20, 1967, p. 1.

462 Strait of Tiran: *New York
Times,* May 23, 1967, p. 1.

462 Rusk was not seriously
advocating intervention: For

page

Rusk's role in the Six-Day War, see Steven L. Spiegel, *The Other Arab-Israeli Conflict* (University of Chicago Press, 1985), pp. 140ff.

463 "We are astonished . . .": State Department file, Box 927.

463 an angry note to Eban: Ibid.

CHAPTER 16

page

466 Quaker man: *New York Times,* Nov. 3, 1965, p. 1.

466 He wrote to Congressman John A. Blatnik: State Department file, Box 927.

467 note to the U.S. Embassy in New Delhi: Ibid.

468 "beached whale": *Time,* Feb. 9, 1968, p. 15.

469 grave decisions with respect to Vietnam: The events of March 1968 are recounted in a number of studies. See Isaacson and Thomas, *The Wise Men,* ch. 22; George Christian, *The President Steps Down* (Macmillan, 1970); Herbert Y. Schandler, *The Unmaking of a President* (Princeton University Press, 1977); Lyndon Johnson, *Vantage Point* (Holt, Rinehart and Winston, 1971); Townsend Hoopes, "LBJ's Account of March, 1968," *New Republic,* March 4, 1970, and *Limits of Intervention* (David McKay, 1969); Harry McPherson, *A Political Education* (Little, Brown, 1972); Maxwell Taylor, *Swords and*

page

Plowshares (W. W. Norton, 1972); Lady Bird Johnson, *White House Diary* (Holt, Rinehart and Winston, 1970); Hubert Humphrey, *The Education of a Public Man* (Doubleday, 1976); Marvin Kalb and Elie Abel, *Roots of Involvement* (W. W. Norton, 1971); Cooper, *Lost Crusade;* Peter Braestrup, *Big Story* (Westview Press, 1977); Clark Clifford, "A Vietnam Reappraisal," *Foreign Affairs,* July 1969; Clark Dougan, *The Vietnam Experience* (Boston Publishing Co., 1983).

472 "Rusk had the best understanding . . .": Johnson, *Vantage Point,* p. 410.

473 "We need some good news . . .": LBJ Library, Meetings from March 1968 through November 1968, Tom Johnson's Notes of Meetings: CBS Subpoena Releases, LBJ Library.

473 "I've got to get me . . .": Dougan, *Vietnam Experience,* p. 80.

474 "Mr. President, I believe . . .": McPherson, *A Political Education,* p. 432.

476 "take care of it": Johnson, *Vantage Point,* p. 418.

477 "The President . . . cannot give that speech": Kalb and Abel, *Roots of Involvement,* p. 249.

477 "In the morning the whole tone . . .": Interview of Clark Clifford by Richard Rusk, March 1985.

page

478 "indicated he did not
want . . .": Johnson,
Vantage Point, p. 420.

480 talked him out of it: Cohen,
Dean Rusk, p. 313.

482 "our two countries share a
common interest . . .":
State Department file,
Box 972.

484 Rusk had no advance
warning: See George Urban,
"The Invasion of
Czechoslovakia, 1968: The
View from Washington. A
Conversation with Eugene
Rostow," *Washington
Quarterly,* vol. 2, no. 1
(Winter 1979), pp. 106–20.

485 "talking past each other":
Life, Nov. 15, 1968, pp. 84a–
97.

485 a new chance for peace: The
events of October 1968 are
recounted in a number of
sources. See Henry
Brandon, *Anatomy of Error*
(Gambit, 1969); Christian,
The President Steps Down;
Cooper, *Lost Crusade;* Phil
G. Goulding, *Confirm or
Deny* (Harper & Row, 1970);
Henry F. Graff, *The Tuesday
Cabinet* (Prentice-Hall,
1970); Kalb and Abel, *Roots
of Involvement; New York
Times,* Nov. 11, 1968, pp. 1,
20ff; Taylor, *Swords and
Plowshares;* Jack Valenti, *A
Very Human President* (W.
W. Norton, 1975); Theodore
White, *The Making of the
President 1968* (Atheneum,
1969).

485 "particularly noncombative":
White, *The Making of the
President,* p. 377.

486 had to be "unconditional":
Brandon, *Anatomy of Error,*
p. 148.

486 He had grander plans:
Christian, *The President
Steps Down,* p. 79.

487 "MUST have day
certain . . .": State
Department file, Box 927.

487 Humphrey *had* to win:
Richard Holbrooke (a Rusk
family friend who was a
Foreign Service officer and
chief aide to Harriman and
Vance) interview, February
1968.

487 On October 27 the North
Vietnamese: *New York
Times,* Nov. 11, 1968,
p. 1.

487 "as long as we
recognize . . .": Christian,
The President Steps Down,
p. 88.

488 Rusk received a message
from Thieu: Ibid., p. 89.

489 "credibility in
stopping . . .": *New York
Times,* Nov. 3, 1968, p. 1.

489 "Nixon is going to
win . . .": Johnson, *Vantage
Point,* p. 521.

489 Rusk and Clifford both
counseled: Valenti, *A
Very Human President,*
p. 375.

490 "Like any GI in a foxhole":
Peter Lisagor, "Dean Rusk:
Reflections After Eight
Years," *Charlotte News,*
June 24, 1968.

490 "The man who has served
me most . . .": LBJ to Mrs.
Rusk, Dec. 9, 1968. White
House Central Files: Dean
Rusk, LBJ Library.

page

491   "this decade's man of the ages": Christian, *The President Steps Down,* p. 116.

EPILOGUE

page

493   ". . . out of a job": *New York Times,* Dec. 10, 1969, p. 21.

page

498   briefing presidential candidate George Wallace: State Department file, Box 927.

498   "We must protect Dobrynin on this": State Department file, Box 924.

R E F E R E N C E S
A N D   S O U R C E S

ARCHIVES

John F. Kennedy Library, Boston: Memos to and from Dean Rusk from the National Security Files; Presidential Office Files; private papers donations; Oral History Collection.

Lyndon B. Johnson Library, Austin: Memos to and from Dean Rusk from the National Security Files; Presidential Office Files; White House Central Files; Oral History Collection.

National Archives, Washington, D.C.: Memos to and from Dean Rusk to supplement the *FRUS* collection.

Princeton University Library, Princeton, N.J.: Hamilton Fish Armstrong Papers; Allen Dulles Papers; John Foster Dulles Papers; Louis Fischer Papers; James F. Forrestal Diaries; Raymond B. Fosdick Papers; Arthur Krock Papers; David Lawrence Papers; David E. Lilienthal Papers; Livingston T. Merchant Papers; David A. Morse Papers; Karl Lott Rankin Papers; Adlai Stevenson Papers; Jacob Viner Papers; Whiting Willaver Papers.

U.S. Department of State, Washington, D.C.: Secretary of State Office Files, 1961–69.

BOOKS

Abel, Elie. *The Missile Crisis*. Philadelphia: J. B. Lippincott, 1966.

Acheson, Dean G. *Present at the Creation: My Years in the State Department*. New York: W. W. Norton, 1969.

———. *This Vast External Realm*. New York: W. W. Norton, 1973.

Adams, John G. *Without Precedent*. New York: W. W. Norton, 1983.

Adler, Selig. *The Uncertain Giant: 1921–41 American Foreign Policy Between the Wars*. New York: Macmillan, 1965.

Allison, Graham. *Essence of Decision*. Boston: Little, Brown, 1971.

Ambrose, Stephen E. *Rise to Globalism*. New York: Penguin Books, 1983.

Armstrong, Hamilton Fish. *Fifty Years of Foreign Affairs*. New York: Praeger, 1972.

Ball, George. *The Past Has Another Pattern*. New York: W. W. Norton, 1982.

Barber, James David. *The Presidential Character: Predicting Performance in the White House*. Englewood Cliffs, N.J.: Prentice-Hall, 1985.

Barnet, Richard. *The Alliance: America-Europe-Japan—Makers of the Postwar World*. New York: Simon and Schuster, 1983.

———. *Intervention and Revolution*. New York: World Publishing Co., 1968.

Barnett, David Dean. *Dixie Mission: The United States Army Observer Group in Yenan, 1944*. Berkeley: Center for Chinese Studies, University of California, 1970.

Bell, Jack. *The Johnson Treatment*. New York: Harper & Row, 1965.

Berle, Beatrice. *Navigating the Rapids, 1918–1971*. New York: Harcourt Brace Jovanovich, 1973.

Berman, Larry. *Planning a Tragedy: The Americanization of the War in Vietnam*. New York: W. W. Norton, 1982.

Bernstein, Barton J., and Allen J. Mutusow. *The Truman Administration: A Documentary History*. New York: Harper & Row, 1966.

Bloomfield, Lincoln P. *In Search of American Foreign Policy*. London: Oxford University Press, 1974.

Blum, Robert. *The United States and China in World Affairs*. New York: McGraw-Hill, 1966.

Bohlen, Charles. *The Transformation of American Foreign Policy*. New York: W. W. Norton, 1969.

———. *Witness to History, 1929–1969*. New York: W. W. Norton, 1973.

Borg, Dorothy, and Waldo Heinrichs, eds. *Uncertain Years: Chinese-American Relations 1947–1950*. New York: Columbia University Press, 1980.

Bornet, Vaughn Davis. *The Presidency of Lyndon B. Johnson*. Lawrence: University of Kansas Press, 1983.

Bowles, Chester. *The Conscience of a Liberal*. New York: Harper & Row, 1962.

———. *Promises to Keep*. New York: Harper & Row, 1971.

Braestrup, Peter. *Big Story*. Boulder, Colo.: Westview Press, 1977.

Brandon, Henry. *Anatomy of Error: The Inside Story of the Asian War on the Potomac, 1954–1969*. Boston: Gambit, 1969.

Brown, Seyom. *Faces of Power*. New York: Columbia University Press, 1983.

Brune, Lester H. *The Missile Crisis of October 1962*. Claremont, Calif.: Regina Books, 1985.

Buckley, William. *McCarthy and His Enemies*. Chicago: Regnery, 1954.

Bundy, McGeorge, ed. *The Pattern of Responsibility*. Cambridge, Mass.: Riverside Press, 1951.

Caputo, Philip. *A Rumor of War*. New York: Holt, Rinehart and Winston, 1977.

Catudal, Honoré Marc, Jr. *The Diplomacy of the Quadripartite Agreement on Berlin*. Berlin: Berlin Verlag, 1978.

Chase, Harold W., and Allen H. Lerman, eds. *Kennedy and the Press*. New York: Thomas Y. Crowell, 1965.

Chayes, Abram. *The Cuban Missile Crisis*. London: Oxford University Press, 1974.

China White Paper August 1949. Stanford, Calif.: Stanford University Press, 1949.

Christian, George. *The President Steps Down*. New York: Macmillan, 1970.

Cleveland, Harlan. *NATO: The Transatlantic Bargain*. New York: Harper & Row, 1970.

Clinch, Nancy Gager. *The Kennedy Neurosis*. New York: Grosset & Dunlap, 1973.

Cohen, Bernard C. *The Political Process and Foreign Policy: The Making of the Japanese Peace Settlement*. Princeton, N.J.: Princeton University Press, 1957.

Cohen, Michael. *Palestine and the Great Powes, 1945–1948*. Princeton, N.J.: Princeton University Press, 1982.

Cohen, Warren I. *Dean Rusk*. Totowa, N.J.: Cooper Square Publishers, 1980.

Cooper, Chester L. *The Lost Crusade: America in Vietnam*. New York: Dodd, Mead, 1970.

Council on Foreign Relations. *The United States in World Affairs 1945–1947*. New York: Harper and Brothers, 1947.

———. *The United States in World Affairs 1947–1948*. New York: Harper and Brothers, 1948.

———. *The United States in World Affairs 1948–1949*. New York: Harper and Brothers, 1949.

———. *The United States in World Affairs 1951*. New York: Harper and Brothers, 1951.

Darby, Phillip. *British Defense Policy East of the Suez 1947–1948*. London: Oxford University Press, 1973.

Davids, Jules. *The United States in World Affairs, 1964*. New York: Harper & Row, 1965.

Davies, John Paton. *Dragon by the Tail*. New York: W. W. Norton, 1972.

Destler, I. M., Leslie H. Gelb, and Anthony Lake. *Our Own Worst Enemy?* New York: Simon and Schuster, 1984.

Divine, Robert A. *The Cuban Missile Crisis*. Chicago: Quadrangle Books, 1971.

———. *Exploring the Johnson Years*. Austin: University of Texas Press, 1981.

———. *American Foreign Policy Since 1945*. New York: John Wiley & Sons, 1975.

Documents on Germany 1944–1985. Department of State, Publication No. 9446.

Donald, Aida DiPace, ed. *John F. Kennedy and the New Frontier*. New York: Hill and Wang, 1966.

Donovan, Robert J. *Conflict and Crisis: The Presidency of Harry S Truman 1945–1948*. New York: W. W. Norton, 1977.

———. *Tumultuous Years: The Presidency of Harry S Truman 1949–1953*. New York: W. W. Norton, 1982.

Dougan, Clark. *Nineteen Sixty-eight*. Boston: Boston Publishing Co., 1983.

Draper, Theodore. *The Dominican Revolt*. New York: Commentary, 1968.

Dulles, Eleanor Lansing. *American Foreign Policy in the Making*. New York: Harper & Row, 1968.

Dulles, Foster R. *American Policy Toward Communist China 1949–1969*. New York: Thomas Y. Crowell, 1972.

Fairlie, Henry. *The Kennedy Promise*. New York: Doubleday, 1973.

Falkowski, Lawrence S. *Presidents, Secretaries of State, and Crises in U.S. Foreign Relations*. Boulder, Colo.: Westview Press, 1978.

Feld, Werner J. *American Foreign Policy: Aspirations and Reality*. New York: John Wiley & Sons, 1984.

Ferrell, Robert H. *America in a Divided World 1945–1972*. New York: Harper & Row, 1975.

FitzSimons, Louise. *The Kennedy Doctrine*. New York: Random House, 1972.

Fosdick, Raymond. *The Story of the Rockefeller Foundation*. New York: Harper, 1952.

Foster, H. Schuyler. *Activism Replaces Isolationism: U.S. Public Attitudes 1940–1975*. Washington, D.C.: Foxhall Press, 1983.

Franck, Thomas M. *Nation Against Nation*. London: Oxford University Press, 1985.

Fulbright, James William. *The Crippled Giant*. New York: Random House, 1972.

Gaddis, John W. *The United States and the Origins of the Cold War 1941–1947*. New York: Columbia University Press, 1972.

George, Alexander L., and Richard Smoke. *Deterrence in American Foreign Policy*. New York: Columbia University Press, 1974.

Geyelin, Philip. *Lyndon B. Johnson and the World*. New York: Praeger, 1966.

Gittings, John. *The World and China 1922–1978*. London: Eyre Methuen, 1974.

Goldman, Eric F. *The Tragedy of Lyndon Johnson*. New York: Knopf, 1969.

Goodman, Allen E. *The Lost Peace: America's Search for a Negotiated Settlement of the Vietnam War*. Stanford, Calif.: Hoover Institution Press, 1978.

Goulden, Joseph C. *Korea: The Untold Story of the War*. New York: Times Books, 1982.

———. *Truth Is the First Casualty*. Chicago: Rand McNally, 1969.

Goulding, Phil G. *Confirm or Deny*. New York: Harper & Row, 1970.

Graff, Henry F. *The Tuesday Cabinet*. Englewood Cliffs, N.J.: Prentice-Hall, 1970.

Grantham, Dewey W. *The United States Since 1945*. New York: McGraw-Hill, 1976.

Gravel, Sen. Mike, ed. *The Pentagon Papers*. Boston: Beacon Press, 1971.

Gromyko, Anatoli Andreievich. *Through Russian Eyes: President Kennedy's 1036 Days*. Washington, D.C.: International Library, 1973.

Gurtov, Melvin, and Ray Maghroori. *Roots of Failure: United States Policy in the Third World*. Westport, Conn.: Greenwood Press, 1984.

Halberstam, David. *The Best and the Brightest*. New York: Penguin Books, 1972.

Halle, Louis J. *The Cold War as History*. London: Chatto & Windus, 1967.

Heller, Deane, and David Heller. *The Kennedy Cabinet*. New York: Books for Libraries Press, 1961.

Heller, Francis H. *The Korean War: A Twenty-five Year Perspective*. Lawrence, Kans.: Lawrence Press, 1977.

Heren, Louis. *No Hail, No Farewell*. New York: Harper & Row, 1970.

Herring, George, ed. *The Secret Diplomacy of the Vietnam War: The Negotiating Volumes of the Pentagon Papers*. Austin: University of Texas Press, 1983.

Higgins, Trumbull. *Korea and the Fall of MacArthur*. New York: Oxford University Press, 1960.

Hilsman, Roger. *To Move a Nation*. New York: Doubleday, 1967.

Hochman, Stanley. *Yesterday and Today*. New York: McGraw-Hill, 1979.

Hoffmann, Stanley. *Gulliver's Troubles, or the Setting of American Foreign Policy*. New York: McGraw-Hill, 1968.

Home, Alec Douglas-. *The Way the Wind Blows*. London: Collins, 1976.

Hoopes, Townsend. *The Limits of Intervention: An Inside Account of How the Johnson Policy of Escalation in Vietnam Was Reversed*. New York: David McKay, 1969.

Humphrey, Hubert H. *The Education of a Public Man*. New York: Doubleday, 1976.

Isaacson, Walter, and Evan Thomas. *The Wise Men*. New York: Simon and Schuster, 1986.

Jackson, Henry F. *From the Congo to Soweto*. New York: William Morrow, 1982.

Jackson, Sen. Henry M., ed. *The Secretary of State and the Ambassador: Jackson Subcommittee Papers on the Conduct of American Foreign Policy*. New York: Praeger, 1964.

James, D. Clayton. *The Years of MacArthur*. Boston: Houghton Mifflin, 1970.

Jessup, Philip C. *The Birth of Nations*. New York: Columbia University Press, 1974.

Johnson, Haynes. *The Bay of Pigs*. New York: W. W. Norton, 1964.

Johnson, Lady Bird. *A White House Diary*. New York: Holt, Rinehart and Winston, 1970.

Johnson, Lyndon Baines. *The Vantage Point: Perspectives on the Presidency 1963–1964*. New York: Holt, Rinehart and Winston, 1971.

Johnson, Sam Houston. *My Brother Lyndon*. New York: Cowles Book Co., 1970.

Johnson, U. Alexis, with Jef Olivarius McAllister. *The Right Hand of Power*. Englewood Cliffs, N.J.: Prentice-Hall, 1984.

Jones, Joseph M., *The Fifteen Weeks*. New York: Viking, 1955.

Jonsson, Christopher. *Superpower: Comparing American and Soviet Foreign Policy*. New York: St. Martin's Press, 1984.

Kalb, Madeleine G. *The Congo Cables: The Cold War in Africa—From Eisenhower to Kennedy*. New York: Macmillan, 1982.

Kalb, Marvin, and Elie Abel. *Roots of Involvement: The U.S. in Asia 1784–1971*. New York: W. W. Norton, 1971.

Karnow, Stanley. *Vietnam*. New York: Viking, 1983.

Kegley, Charles W., Jr. *American Foreign Policy: Pattern and Process*. New York: St. Martin's Press, 1982.

Kennan, George F. *American Diplomacy 1900–1950*. Chicago: University of Chicago Press, 1951.

———. *Memoirs 1925–1950*. Boston: Little, Brown, 1967.

———. *The Nuclear Delusion*. New York: Pantheon Books, 1982.

———. *Realities of American Foreign Policy*. Princeton, N.J.: Princeton University Press, 1954.

Kennedy, Robert F. *Thirteen Days*. New York: W. W. Norton, 1969.

Kern, Montague; Patricia W. Levering; and Ralph B. Levering. *The Kennedy Crises*. Chapel Hill: University of North Carolina Press, 1983.

Kluckhohn, Frank L. *Lyndon's Legacy: A Candid Look at the President's Policymakers*. New York: Dorin-Adair Co., 1964.

Kolko, Joyce, and Gabriel Kolko. *The Limits of Power: The World and United States Foreign Policy 1945–54*. New York: Harper & Row, 1972.

Kraft, Joseph. *Profiles in Power: A Washington Insight*. New York: New American Library, 1966.

Kraslow, David, and Stuart H. Loory. *The Secret Search for Peace in Vietnam*. New York: Random House, 1968.

Kuklick, Bruce. *American Policy and the Division of Germany*. Ithaca, N.Y.: Cornell University Press, 1972.

Kulski, W. W. *The Soviet Union in World Affairs*. Syracuse, N.Y.: Syracuse University Press, 1973.

Kurzman, Dan. *Santo Domingo: Revolt of the Damned*. New York: Putnam's, 1965.

———. *Genesis 1948*. New York: World Press, 1970.

Kwitny, Jonathan. *Endless Enemies*. New York: Congdon and Weed, 1984.

Lash, Joseph P. *Dag Hammarskjöld*. New York: Doubleday, 1961.

Levering, Ralph B. *The Cold War, 1945–1972*. Arlington Heights, Ill.: Harlan Davidson, 1982.

Lilienthal, David E. *The Atomic Energy Years 1945–1950*. New York: Harper & Row, 1964.

Louis, William R. *The British Empire in the Middle East, 1945–1951*. London: Oxford University Press, 1984.

————, and Robert W. Stookey, eds. *The End of the Palestine Mandate*. Austin: University of Texas Press, 1985.

Lowenthal, Abraham F. *The Dominican Intervention*. Cambridge, Mass.: Harvard University Press, 1972.

Macmillan, Harold. *At the End of the Day, 1961–1963*. New York: Harper & Row, 1973.

————. *Pointing the Way, 1959–1961*. New York: Harper & Row, 1972.

McLellan, David S. *Dean Acheson: The State Department Years*. New York: Dodd, Mead, 1976.

McPherson, Harry. *A Political Education*. Boston: Little, Brown, 1972.

Manchester, William. *American Caesar: Douglas MacArthur 1886–1964*. Boston: Little, Brown, 1978.

————. *The Glory and the Dream*. Boston: Little, Brown, 1974.

Martin, John Bartlow. *Overtaken by Events: The Dominican Crisis from the Fall of Trujillo to the Civil War*. New York: Doubleday, 1966.

May, Ernest R. *Lessons of the Past*. New York: Oxford University Press, 1973.

Mee, Charles L., Jr. *The Marshall Plan: The Launching of the Pax Americana*. New York: Simon and Schuster, 1984.

Millis, Walter, ed. *The Forrestal Diaries*. New York: Viking, 1951.

Miroff, Bruce. *Pragmatic Illusions*. New York: David McKay, 1976.

Moore, John Hammond. *The American Alliance: Australia, New Zealand and the United States*. Sydney, Australia: Cassell, 1970.

Morgenthau, Hans J. *Politics Among Nations*. New York: Knopf, 1948.

Morris, Eric. *Blockade: Berlin and the Cold War*. London: Hamish Hamilton, 1973.

Mosley, Leonard. *Marshall: Hero for Our Times*. New York: Hearst Books, 1982.

Nash, Henry T. *American Foreign Policy*. Homewood, Ill.: Dorsey Press, 1973.

Oberdorfer, Don. *Tet!* New York: Doubleday, 1971.

O'Neill, William. *Coming Apart*. Chicago: Quadrangle Books, 1971.

Opotowsky, Stan. *The Kennedy Government*. New York: E. P. Dutton, 1961.

Paige, Glenn D. *The Korean Decision*. New York: Free Press, 1968.

Parmet, Herbert S. *Eisenhower and the American Crusades*. New York: Macmillan, 1972.

————. *JFK: The Presidency of John F. Kennedy*. New York: Dial Press, 1983.

Paul, Roland A. *American Military Commitments Abroad*. New Brunswick, N.J.: Rutgers University Press, 1973.

Price, Harry Bayard. *The Marshall Plan and Its Memory*. Ithaca, N.Y.: Cornell University Press, 1955.

Reese, Trevor R. *Australia, New Zealand, and the United States: A Survey of International Relations 1941–1968*. London: Oxford University Press, 1969.

Richardson, James L. *Germany and the Atlantic Alliance*. Cambridge, Mass.: Harvard University Press, 1966.

Roberts, Chalmers M. *First Rough Draft: A Journalist's Journal of Our Times*. New York: Praeger, 1973.

Roberts, Charles. *LBJ's Inner Circle*. New York: Delacorte Press, 1965.

Rostow, Walt Whitman. *The Diffusion of Power*. New York: Macmillan, 1972.

Rubin, Barry. *Secrets of State*. New York: Oxford University Press, 1985.

Rusk, Dean. *The Winds of Freedom*. Edited by E. K. Lindley. Boston: Beacon Press, 1963.

Rust, William J. *Kennedy in Vietnam*. New York: Scribner's, 1985.

Salinger, Pierre. *With Kennedy*. New York: Doubleday, 1966.

Sandusky, Michael C. *America's Parallel*. Alexandria, Va.: Old Dominion Press, 1983.

Schandler, Herbert Y. *The Unmaking of a President*. Princeton, N.J.: Princeton University Press, 1977.

Schick, Jack M. *The Berlin Crisis 1958–1962*. Philadelphia: University of Pennsylvania Press, 1971.

Schlesinger, Arthur M., Jr. *Robert Kennedy and His Times*. New York: Ballantine Books, 1978.

———. *A Thousand Days*. Cambridge, Mass.: Riverside Press, 1965.

Seaborg, Glenn T. *Kennedy, Khrushchev, and the Test Ban*. Berkeley: University of California Press, 1981.

Serfaty, Simon. *American Foreign Policy in a Hostile World*. New York: Praeger, 1984.

Shlaim, Avi. *The United States and the Berlin Blockade, 1948–1949*. Berkeley: University of California Press, 1983.

Sidey, Hugh. *John F. Kennedy, President*. New York: Atheneum, 1964.

———. *A Very Personal Presidency*. New York: Atheneum, 1968.

Simmons, Robert M. *The Strained Alliance*. New York: Free Press, 1975.

Slater, Jerome. *Intervention and Negotiation*. New York: Harper & Row, 1970.

Slusser, Robert M. *The Berlin Crisis of 1961*. Baltimore: Johns Hopkins University Press, 1973.

Smith, Jean Edward. *The Defense of Berlin*. Baltimore: Johns Hopkins University Press, 1963.

Sobel, Robert, ed. *Biographical Directory of the United States Executive Branch 1774–1977*. Westport, Conn.: Greenwood Press, 1977.

Soldberg, Carl. *Hubert Humphrey*. New York: W. W. Norton, 1984.

Sorensen, Theodore C. *Kennedy*. New York: Harper & Row, 1965.

———. *The Kennedy Legacy*. New York: Macmillan, 1969.

Spanier, John. *American Foreign Policy Since World War II*. New York: Praeger, 1977.

———. *The Truman–MacArthur Controversy and the Korean War*. Cambridge, Mass.: Belknap Press, 1959.

Spiegel, Steven L. *The Other Arab-Israeli Conflict*. Chicago: University of Chicago Press, 1985.

Stebbins, Richard P. *The United States in World Affairs, 1949*. New York: Harper & Row, 1950.

Steinberg, Alfred. *Sam Johnson's Boy*. New York: Macmillan, 1968.

Stillman, Edmund, and William Pfaff. *Power and Impotence: The Failure of America's Foreign Policy*. New York: Random House, 1966.

Sulzberger, Cyrus. *The Last of the Giants*. New York: Macmillan, 1970.

Szulc, Tad. *Dominican Diary*. New York: Delacorte Press, 1965.

Tanzer, Lester, ed. *The Kennedy Circle*. Washington, D.C.: Robert B. Bruce, 1961.

Taylor, Alastair M. *Indonesian Independence and the United Nations*. London: Stevens, 1960.

Taylor, Maxwell D. *Swords and Plowshares*. New York: W. W. Norton, 1972.

Thies, Wallace. *When Governments Collide*. Berkeley: University of California Press, 1979.

Thompson, Kenneth W., ed. *Traditions and Values: American Diplomacy, 1945 to the Present*. Washington, D.C.: University Press of America, 1984.

Truman, Harry S. *Memoirs: Years of Trial and Hope, 1946–1952*. New York: Doubleday, 1956.

———. *Years of Decisions*. New York: Doubleday, 1955.

Truman, Margaret. *Harry S Truman*. New York: William Morrow, 1973.

Tuchman, Barbara. *The March of Folly*. New York: Knopf, 1984.

———. *Stilwell and the American Experience in China*. New York: Macmillan, 1971.

Urquhart, Brian. *Hammarskjöld*. New York: Knopf, 1972.

U.S. Department of State. *Foreign Relations of the United States*. Series of volumes that include declassified cables and papers from each year or major international conference, usually published twenty years later. Washington, D.C.: Government Printing Office.

The U.S. Government and the Vietnam War: Parts I and II, 1945–1961. Committee on Foreign Relations, U.S. Senate, April and December, 1984.

Valenti, Jack. *A Very Human President*. New York: W. W. Norton, 1975.

Van Ness, Peter. *Revolution and Chinese Foreign Policy*. Berkeley: University of California Press, 1970.

The Vietnam Hearings. New York: Vintage Books, 1966.

Walton, Richard J. *Cold War and Counter-Revolution*. Baltimore: Penguin Books, 1973.

Weigley, Russell F. *The American Way of War*. New York: Macmillan, 1973.

Weintal, Edward, and Charles Bartlett. *Facing the Brink*. New York: Scribner's, 1967.

Weissman, Stephen R. *American Foreign Policy in the Congo*. Ithaca, N.Y.: Cornell University Press, 1974.

Westmoreland, William C. *A Soldier Reports*. New York: Doubleday, 1976.

White, Theodore. *The Making of a President*. New York: Atheneum, 1965.

———. *The Making of the President 1968*. New York: Atheneum, 1969.

Whiting, Allen S. *China Crosses the Yalu*. New York: Macmillan, 1960.

Wicker, Tom. *JFK and LBJ*. Baltimore: Penguin Books, 1970.

Wilson, Harold. *The Labour Government, 1964–1970: A Personal Record*. London: Weidenfeld & Nicolson, 1971.

Windchy, Eugene G. *Tonkin Gulf*. New York: Doubleday, 1971.

Windsor, Philip. *City on Leave*. London: Chatto & Windus, 1963.

Wyden, Peter. *Bay of Pigs: The Untold Story*. New York: Simon and Schuster, 1979.

Yergin, Daniel. *Shattered Peace*. Boston: Houghton Mifflin, 1977.

Yost, Charles W. *History and Memory*. New York: W. W. Norton, 1980.

ARTICLES

Alsop, Stewart. "Mr. Dove and Mr. Hawk." *Saturday Evening Post*, June 18, 1966, p. 18.

———. "Trouble with the State Department." *Saturday Evening Post*, March 3, 1962, p. 11.

Anderson, Jack. "Johnson and Rusk: How Well Do They Get Along?" *Parade*, Feb. 9, 1964, p. 8.

Ard, John. "Dean Rusk on the Record: Part One." *Presbyterian Survey Atlanta*, Nov. 30, 1970, p. 5.

———, and Ben Hartley. "Dean Rusk: Part Two." *Presbyterian Survey Atlanta*, Dec. 7, 1970, p. 2.

Ascoli, M. "On Hawks and Doves." *Reporter*, March 24, 1966, p. 24.

"Bitter Pen of Arthur M." *National Review*, Aug. 10, 1965, p. 680.

Brewin, Bob. "Dean Rusk Under Oath." *Village Voice*, April 16, 1985.

Campbell, A. "Mild Mr. Rusk." *New Republic*, April 11, 1964, p. 13.

"Change and Chatter." *Time*, July 16, 1965, p. 16.

Clifford, Clark M. "A Viet Nam Appraisal." *Foreign Affairs*, July 1969, p. 601.

"Coping with a World Plunged in Revolution." *Business World*, March 25, 1961, p. 104.

Crawford, K. "Dull Old Dean." *Newsweek*, Aug. 16, 1965, p. 28.

———. "Indispensables." *Newsweek*, Nov. 13, 1967, p. 42.

"Credibility of Commitment." *Time*, Dec. 24, 1965, p. 9.

Davis, T. N. "Of Many Things: Concerning A. Schlesinger's Recollections." *America*, Aug. 7, 1965, p. 124.

"Dean Rusk at Cornell." *Nation*, April 24, 1967, p. 516.

"Demonstration." *New Yorker*, Nov. 25, 1967, p. 52.

"Diplomat for Today's Issues," *Newsweek*, July 9, 1962, p. 21.

"Eagle Has Two Claws." *Time*, Dec. 26, 1966, p. 8.

"Empty Chair." *Newsweek*, Feb. 22, 1965, p. 21.

"Energy: A New Cause of War Coming Down the Road." *U.S. News & World Report*, June 27, 1977, p. 43.

"Exhaustive, Explicit and Enough." *Time*, Feb. 25, 1966, p. 22.

Frankel, M. "President's Just-a-Minute Men." *New York Times Magazine*, Sept. 12, 1965, p. 48.

"Get Rusk Movement: Is It Aimed at LBJ?" *U.S. News & World Report,* Nov. 20, 1967, p. 51.

"Goodbye, Mr. Rusk." *New Republic,* Jan. 18, 1969, p. 7.

Greenfield, M. "Byzantium on the Potomac." *Reporter,* Aug. 12, 1965, p. 10.

Griffith, Thomas. "It's News, But Is It Reality?" *Time,* May 27, 1985, p. 67.

"Growing Dissent." *Newsweek,* March 25, 1968, p. 33.

Halperin, Morton H. "Why Bureaucrats Play Games." *Foreign Policy,* Spring 1971, p. 70.

Henry, John B. "February 1968." *Foreign Policy,* Fall 1971, p. 3.

———, and William Epinosa. "The Tragedy of Dean Rusk." *Foreign Policy,* Fall 1972, p. 166.

"Honor Without Profit." *Time,* Sept. 7, 1970, p. 8.

Hoopes, Townsend. "LBJ's Account of March 1968." *New Republic,* March 14, 1970, p. 17.

"How About It, Mr. Rusk?" *New Republic,* Dec. 23, 1967, p. 4.

"How Two Officials Fared in South America." *U.S. News & World Report,* Nov. 29, 1965, p. 19.

"International Cop? Concerning Statements." *Newsweek,* Sept. 12, 1966, p. 23.

Karnow, Stanley. "Dean Rusk's Debut." *Reporter,* April 27, 1961, p. 37.

Kenworthy, E. W. "Evolution of Our No. 1 Diplomat." *New York Times Magazine,* March 18, 1962, p. 31.

Kraft, Joseph. "Comeback of the State Department." *Harper's,* November 1961, p. 45.

———. "The Dean Rusk Show." *New York Times Magazine,* March 24, 1968, p. 34.

———. "The Enigma of Dean Rusk." *Harper's,* July 1965, p. 100.

Lippmann, Walter. "Secretary Misunderstood." *Newsweek,* Nov. 6, 1967, p. 23.

McRee, Janelle Jones. "Georgia Profiles: David Dean Rusk," *Georgia Journal,* April/May 1984, p. 22.

Masters, R. D. "Rusk's Francophobia: de Gaulle and NATO." *Commonweal,* July 8, 1966, p. 431.

"Meet Dean Rusk, Early Dove." *Time,* July 5, 1971, p. 10.

"Messenger." *Newsweek,* July 18, 1966, p. 34.

Moskin, J. R. "Dean Rusk: Cool Man in a Hot World." *Look,* Sept. 6, 1966, p. 14.

"Musings from State." *Time,* Jan. 24, 1964, p. 14.

"Myth of Influence." *Nation,* Nov. 2, 1974, p. 420.

"Name of the Game: Question of Shift in Personnel." *Time,* March 15, 1963, p. 20.

"Neutral and Neutralist." *National Review,* Jan. 28, 1961, p. 39.

"New Horizons." *Newsweek,* Oct. 23, 1968, p. 27.

"The New Team at State." *New Republic,* Dec. 19, 1960, p. 3.

Nordan, David. "The View from Home." *Atlanta Magazine,* October 1982.

"Notes on a Native Son." *Atlanta Magazine,* October 1965.

"Now It's Time to Be Professor Rusk." *U.S. News & World Report,* Jan. 12, 1970, p. 10.

"On Camera." *Nation,* Feb. 19, 1968, p. 228.

"Perfect Format: Talks with Visiting Statesmen at U.S. Mission Building." *Time,* Oct. 4, 1963, p. 39.

"Professor Rusk." *Nation,* Jan. 12, 1970, p. 5.

"Professor Rusk's Problems." *Time,* Jan. 5, 1970, p. 19.

"Quiet Man." *Time,* Dec. 6, 1963, p. 24.

"The Quiet New Man at State." *Readers' Digest,* March 1961.

"The Real Dean Rusk." *Nation,* Oct. 30, 1967, p. 419.

"Report on Washington." *Atlantic,* November 1964, p. 10.

"Room at the Top." *Newsweek,* May 23, 1966, p. 30.

Rovere, R. H. "Letter from Washington." *New Yorker,* June 12, 1965, p. 143.

"Rusk Doctrine." *New Republic,* March 5, 1966, p. 5.

"Rusk Goes Home: Appointment at the University of Georgia." *Newsweek,* Jan. 12, 1970, p. 43.

"Rusk—New Tempo." *Newsweek,* Feb. 6, 1961, p. 19.

"Rusk Rebuts Policy Critics." *Senior Scholastic,* May 6, 1965, p. 17.

"Rusk's Reply: Reaction to Arthur Schlesinger, Jr.'s Attack." *Time,* Aug. 13, 1965, p. 16.

"Rusk to the Stand." *New Republic,* March 16, 1968, p. 4.

"Rusk Warns Allies: Do More for Defense." *U.S. News & World Report,* Nov. 11, 1963, p. 26.

Schlesinger, Arthur M., Jr. "How the State Department Baffled Him: Excerpts from *A Thousand Days.*" *Life,* July 30, 1965, p. 18.

"Secretary Rusk: Close-up of Washington's Busiest Man." *U.S. News & World Report,* Sept. 11, 1961, p. 52.

"Senators and the Secretary." *New Republic,* March 23, 1968, p. 8.

Shannon, W. V. "Dean Rusk and the President." *Commonweal,* March 29, 1963, p. 5.

Sidey, Hugh. "New Respect for the Old Dino." *Life,* July 23, 1971, p. 4.

———. "Vietnam and the Two Lonely Men." *Life,* Oct. 11, 1968, p. 6.

Sievers, H. J. "Sec. Rusk Grows in Stature." *America,* Feb. 10, 1968, p. 178.

Simpson, S. "Rusk Enigma: Who Runs the State Department?" *Nation,* March 6, 1967, p. 294.

Smith, B. "Quarterback of the Cabinet." *Saturday Evening Post,* July 22, 1961, p. 26.

Smith, Loran. "Dean Rusk: A Prophet in his Own Land." *Atlanta Journal and Constitution Magazine,* Sept. 10, 1978, p. 46.

"Standoff." *Time,* March 22, 1968, p. 20.

Stillman, Edward. "Dean Rusk: In the American Grain." *Commentary,* May 1968, p. 31.

"String Runs Out." *Time,* Feb. 4, 1966, p. 21.

Stupak, Ronald J. "Dean Rusk on International Relations: An Analysis of His Philosophical Perceptions." *Australian Outlook,* April 1981, p. 18.

"Table Talk at the Waldorf." *Time,* Sept. 29, 1961, p. 15.

"Talking and Balking." *Newsweek,* Aug. 21, 1961, p. 29.

"Talking to Tito: Rusk's Courtesy Call." *Time,* May 10, 1963, p. 27.

Thomson, James C., Jr. "On the Making of U.S. China Policy, 1961–69: A Study in Bureaucratic Politics." *China Quarterly,* January/March 1972, p. 220.

"Up from Dominoes." *Commonweal,* Oct. 27, 1967, p. 101.

Vandenbroucke, Lucien S. "The Decision to Land at the Bay of Pigs." *Political Science Quarterly,* Fall 1984.

Viorst, Martin. "Incidentally, Who Is Dean Rusk?" *Esquire,* April 1968, p. 98.

"The War." *Time,* Feb. 4, 1966, p. 21.

"What Liberty Means." *Newsweek,* Nov. 29, 1965, p. 26.

White, T. H. "Does He Drive or Is He Driven?" *Life,* June 8, 1962, p. 72.

———. "Why Dean Rusk Feels We Can't Lose." *Reader's Digest,* September 1962, p. 63.

"Whose History?" *New Republic,* March 12, 1966.

"Why U.S. Is in Trouble in the World." *U.S. News & World Report,* Jan. 25, 1965, p. 52.

Willey, F., and E. Shannon. "Comeback of Dean Rusk." *Newsweek,* Nov. 22, 1976, p. 60.

Willis, David K. "A Man Who Has Not Changed." *Christian Science Monitor,* Jan. 17, 1969.

DISSERTATIONS AND ACADEMIC PAPERS

Gutierrez, G. G. "Dean Rusk and Southeast Asia: An Operational Code Analysis." Paper presented at the 1973 Annual Meeting of the American Political Science Association, New Orleans, September 1973.

Henry, John Bronaugh. "March 1968: Continuity or Change?" Harvard College, April 1971.

Stueber, Frederick G. "Dean Rusk, East Asia, and the Kennedy Years." Williams College, April 1975.

DEAN RUSK SPEECHES, STATEMENTS, AND ARTICLES

The Stake of Business in American Foreign Policy, address of 10/10/49. *Department of State Bulletin (DSB)* 21:630–33, Oct. 24, 1949.

The United Nations and American Security, address of 10/21/49. *DSB* 21:652–57, Oct. 31, 1949.

Universal, Regional and Bilateral Patterns of International Organization, address of 2/15/50. *DSB* 22:526–32, April 3, 1950.

Security Problems in Far East Areas, address of 11/15/50. *DSB* 23:889–94, Dec. 4, 1950.

The Case Against Communist Aggression in Korea, address of 11/5/51. *DSB* 25:818–21, Nov. 19, 1951.

Underlying Principles of Far Eastern Policy, address of 11/6/51. *DSB* 25:821–24, Nov. 19, 1951.

"The President." *Foreign Affairs,* April 1960, pp. 353–69.

Views of Dean Rusk—Next Secretary of State (based on address). *U.S. News & World Report,* Dec. 26, 1960, pp. 64–70.

Secretary cites value of privacy for use of diplomatic channels, statement of 1/23/61. *DSB* 44:214, Feb. 13, 1961.

Mohandas K. Gandhi honored as "Champion of Liberty," remarks of 1/26/61. *DSB* 44:262, Feb. 20, 1961.

Secretary Rusk's news conference of 2/6/61. *DSB* 44:296–304, Feb. 27, 1961.

Secretary Rusk interviewed on "Today" show, 2/9/61. *DSB* 44:305–9, Feb. 27, 1961.

The Organization for Economic Cooperation and Development, address of 2/13/61. *DSB* 44:323–26, March 6, 1961.

Statement on German American relations, 2/16/61. *DSB* 44:334, March 6, 1961.

A Fresh Look at the Formulation of Foreign Policy, address of 2/20/61. *DSB* 44:395–99, March 20, 1961.

The Role of the Foreign Service, remarks at luncheon of American Foreign Service Association, 2/23/61. Reprinted in *Winds of Freedom,* p. 70.

Strengthening of U.S. defense, statement of 2/28/61. *DSB* 44:399, March 20, 1961.

United States foreign policy in a period of change, interview of Rusk by Robert Kee on BBC television, 3/6/61. *DSB* 44:439–44, March 27, 1961.

Secretary Rusk's news conference of 3/9/61. *DSB* 44:431–39, March 27, 1961.

Rusk-Gromyko meeting statement, 3/18/61. *DSB* 44:479, April 3, 1961.

Seventh SEATO meeting of Council of Ministers, 3/19/61. *DSB* 44:547, April 17, 1961.

Charter Day address, Berkeley, 3/20/61. *DSB* 44:515, April 10, 1961.

Secretary Rusk news conference at the University of California, Berkeley, 3/20/61. *DSB* 44:519–24, April 10, 1961.

Welcoming remarks to Adenauer, *DSB* 44: 623, May 1, 1961

Building an international community: science and scholarship, address of 4/7/61. *DSB* 44:624, May 1, 1961.

Bataan and Corregidor, remarks at exercises commemorating Bataan Day, 4/9/61. Reprinted in *Winds of Freedom,* pp. 327–29.

Rockefeller Public Service Awards, 4/11/61. *DSB* 44:640, May 1, 1961.

Secretary Rusk's news conference of 4/17/61. *DSB* 44:686–91, May 8, 1961.

The community of science and scholarship, major portion of remarks at Emory University after receiving honorary LL.D., 4/20/61. Reprinted in *Winds of Freedom,* pp. 315–17.

Secretary Rusk and Korean foreign minister meet to exchange views, 4/25/61. *DSB* 44:711, May 15, 1961.

CENTO holds ninth ministerial meeting, 4/25/61. *DSB* 44:778, May 22, 1961.

Welcoming Greek Prime Minister Karamanlis, 4/26/61. *DSB* 44:724, May 15, 1961.

Welcoming remarks to Adenauer. *DSB* 44:623, May 1, 1961.

Charting a new course in foreign aid, 5/3/61. *DSB* 44:747, May 22, 1961.

Annual dinner address before the Chamber of Commerce of the U.S., Washington, D.C., 5/3/61. *Mexican-American Review,* July 1961, p. 95.

Secretary Rusk's news conference of 5/4/61. *DSB* 44:756–63, May 22, 1961.

NATO holds ministerial meeting at Oslo, 5/10/61. *DSB* 44:800, May 29, 1961.

United States outlines program to insure genuine neutrality for Laos, statement of 5/17/61. *DSB* 44:844–88, June 5, 1961.

Department supports desegregation in interstate bus facilities, letter from Rusk to Robert Kennedy, 5/29/61. *DSB* 44:975, June 19, 1961.

Building the frontiers of freedom, 5/31/61. *DSB* 44:947–55, June 19, 1961.

A plan for international development, 6/7/61, *DSB* 44:1000–8, June 26, 1961.

Foreign aid, an opportunity in a crucial year, 6/15/61. *DSB* 45:3–10, July 3, 1961.

Secretary Rusk's news conference of 6/22/61. *DSB* 45:51–57, July 10, 1961.

Secretary Rusk's news conference at Chicago, 6/27/61. *DSB* 49:109-15, July 17, 1961.

Secretary Rusk interviewed on "At the Source," transcript of CBS-TV program, 6/29/61. *DSB* 45:145–51, July 24, 1961.

The Underlying Crisis: Coercion vs. Choice, address of 7/10/61. *DSB* 45: 175–83, July 31, 1961.

U.S. replies to Soviet "troika" proposal, 7/14/61. *DSB* 45:183, July 31, 1961.

Letter urging Congress to support President's aid proposals, 7/18/61. *DSB* 45:253, Aug. 7, 1961.

Secretary Rusk interviewed on "Editor's Choice," 7/23/61. *DSB* 45:282–288, Aug. 21, 1961.

Secretary Rusk's news conference of 7/27/61. *DSB* 45:275–81, Aug. 21, 1961.

Secretary holds European talks on current world problems, 8/3/61. *DSB* 45:361, Aug. 28, 1961.

President urges approval of atomic cooperation agreement with France, letter from Rusk to JFK, 8/3/61. *DSB* 45:557, Oct. 2, 1961.

Travel restrictions in Berlin, 8/13/61. *DSB* 45:362, Aug. 28, 1961.

Creating a U.S. disarmament agency for world peace and security, 8/14/61. *DSB* 45:411, Sept. 4, 1961.

Secretary Rusk interviewed on "Meet the Press," 8/20/61. *DSB* 45:434–39, Sept. 11, 1961.

The Importance of Foreign Aid in Today's World, address of 8/21/61. *DSB* 45:451, Sept. 11, 1961.

Joint news conference of Secretary Rusk and Secretary of the Treasury Douglas Dillon, 8/22/61. *DSB* 45:441, Sept. 11, 1961.

Role of Department of State in National Security Affairs, 8/24/61. *DSB* 45:455, Sept. 11, 1961.

Secretary Rusk supports creation of U.S. disarmament agency, 8/25/61. *DSB* 45:492, Sept. 18, 1961.

Seventh anniversary of SEATO, 9/6/61. *DSB* 45:528, Sept. 25, 1961.

The current danger, 9/8/61. *DSB* 45:507, Sept. 25, 1961.

Secretary Rusk greets International Navigation Congress, 9/11/61. *DSB* 45:563, Oct. 2, 1961.

Four Central Threads of U.S. Foreign Policy, address of 9/22/61. *DSB* 45:625–30, Oct. 16, 1961.

The obligation to understand the American system of government, 9/25/61. *DSB* 45:630, Oct. 16, 1961.

Rusk welcomes inception of OECD, 9/29/61. *DSB* 45:655, Oct. 16, 1961.

U.S. Foreign Policy: Four Major Issues, address of 10/11/61. *DSB* 45:702, Oct. 30, 1961.

Secretary Rusk interviewed on "Prospects of Mankind," 10/14/61. *DSB* 45:708, Oct. 30, 1961.

Economic growth and investment in education, 10/16/61. *DSB* 45:820, Nov. 13, 1961.

Secretary Rusk's news conference of 10/18/61. *DSB* 45:746–52, Nov. 6, 1961.

Secretary Rusk interviewed on "Issues and Answers," 10/22/61. *DSB* 45:801–7, Nov. 13, 1961.

Secretary Rusk interviewed on "Voice of America," taped on 10/24/61. *DSB* 45:845–50, Nov. 20, 1961.

Departure statement for Japan, 10/30/61. *DSB* 45:890, Nov. 27, 1961.

The importance of Japan, portion of opening statement at meeting of Joint U.S.-Japan Committee on Trade and Economic Affairs, 11/2/61. Reprinted in *Winds of Freedom,* pp. 212-15.

Our Continuing Interest in Korea, reply to welcoming address of Prime Minister of Korea, 11/4/61. Reprinted in *Winds of Freedom,* pp. 215-16.

Secretary Rusk's news conference of 11/17/61. *DSB* 45:918–25, Dec. 4, 1961.

U.S. considers measures on Dominican Republic, 11/18/61. *DSB* 45:931, Dec. 4, 1961.

International economic and social development, 11/30/61. *DSB* 46:18, Jan. 1, 1962.

Education—do it right, remarks at National Conference on International Social and Economic Development, 12/1/61. Reprinted in *Winds of Freedom,* pp. 320–21.

Secretary Rusk's news conference of 12/8/61. *DSB* 45:1053–59, Dec. 26, 1961.

Two lectures reprinted in *The Role of the Foundation in American Life* (Claremont University College, Claremont, Calif., 1961).

Secretary Rusk sends greetings to Republic of the Philippines, 12/29/61. *DSB* 46:175, Jan. 29, 1962.

Some issues of contemporary history, 12/30/61. *DSB* 46:83, Jan. 15, 1962.

Secretary Rusk interviewed on Hearst Metrotone/Telenews, 1/1/62. *DSB* 46:126, Jan. 22, 1962.

Secretary Rusk interviewed on "Reporters' Roundup," 1/7/62. *DSB* 46:123–26, Jan. 22, 1962.

Secretary Rusk interviewed on NBC-TV program "J.F.K. Report," 1/12/62. *DSB* 46:164–68, Jan. 29, 1962.

Secretary Rusk's news conference of 1/18/62. *DSB* 46:199, Feb. 5, 1962.

United States policy in the Congo, statement of 1/18/62 before the Senate Subcommittee on African Affairs. *DSB* 46:216–18, Feb. 5, 1962.

U.S. Trade Policy—Challenge and Opportunity, address of 1/19/62. *DSB* 46:195–99, Feb. 5, 1962.

Secretary Rusk interviewed on "Today" show, 1/22/62. *DSB* 46:241, Feb. 12, 1962.

Dean Rusk Tells Where U.S. Is Headed in Today's World, interview in *U.S. News & World Report,* Jan. 29, 1962, pp. 52–62.

American republics unite to halt spread of communism in Western hemisphere, Rusk's statement on departing for Punta del Este, 1/20/62. *DSB* 46:271, Feb. 19, 1962.

Secretary Rusk's news conference of 2/1/62. *DSB* 46:284, Feb. 19, 1962.

Report to nation on Punta del Este conference, 2/2/62. *DSB* 46:267, Feb. 19, 1962.

Status of U.S. trade relations with Yugoslavia and Cuba, statement before the House Select Committee on Export Control, 2/5/62. *DSB* 46:346, Feb. 26, 1962.

Statement on U.N. bonds, 2/6/62. *DSB* 46:312, Feb. 26, 1962.

Secretary Rusk interviewed on "Washington Viewpoint" radio program, 2/12/62. *DSB* 46:358–63, March 5, 1962.

U.S.-Japan committee called model for scientific cooperation, 2/14/62. *DSB* 46:425, March 12, 1962.

VOA in Lao and Thai, 2/17/62. *DSB* 46:377, March 5, 1962.

Trade and Aid—Essentials of Free World Leadership, address of 2/21/62. *DSB* 46:403–9, March 12, 1962.

America's goal—a community of free nations, 2/22/62. *DSB* 46:448, March 19, 1962.

Rusk greets VOA on 20th anniversary, 2/26/62. *DSB* 46:510, March 26, 1962.

The Future of Germany, excerpts from transcript of interview on German television, 2/28/62. Reprinted in *Winds of Freedom,* p. 171.

News conference of 3/1/62. *DSB* 46:455, March 19, 1962.

Secretary Rusk interviewed on "Eyewitness to History," 3/2/62. *DSB* 46:464, March 19, 1962.

The realities of foreign policy, 3/6/62. *DSB* 46:487–94, March 26, 1962.

Rusk and Thai foreign minister discuss matters of mutual concern, 3/6/62. *DSB* 46:498, March 26, 1962.

U.S. outlines initial proposals of program for general and complete disarmament, statement before the 18-nation disarmament committee in Geneva, 3/15/62. *DSB* 46:531–36, April 2, 1962.

U.S. urges Soviet Union to join in ending nuclear weapon tests, 3/23/62. *DSB* 46:571, April 9, 1962.

U.S. proposes patterns for future work of disarmament conference, 3/27/62. *DSB* 46:618, April 16, 1962.

The foreign aid program for fiscal year 1963, 4/5/62. *DSB* 46:659, April 23, 1962.

Pan American Day 1962, 4/13/62. *DSB* 46:703, April 30, 1962.

The Alliance for Progress in the context of world affairs, 4/25/62. *DSB* 46:787–94, May 14, 1962.

Secretary Rusk's news conference of 4/26/62. *DSB* 46:795–802, May 14, 1962.

Secretary Rusk attends CENTO, NATO, and ANZUS meetings, texts of communiqués released after each meeting, statements and news conference by Mr. Rusk, and announcements of the principal members of the U.S. delegations: Central Treaty Organization, London, 4/30–5/1/62; North Atlantic Council, Athens, 5/4–6; CBS interview of Secretary Rusk, Athens, 5/6; Australia–New Zealand–United States Council, Canberra, 5/8–9. *DSB* 46:859–71, May 28, 1962.

Secretary Rusk speaks in Australia and New Zealand following ANZUS meeting, texts of addresses made at parliamentary dinners at Canberra and Wellington, 5/9 and 5/10/62. *DSB* 46:936–50, June 11, 1962.

The U.S. and Mexico—partners in a common task, 5/14/62. *DSB* 46:919, June 4, 1962.

America's destiny in the building of a world community, 5/17/62. *DSB* 46:895, June 4, 1962; also published by Tennessee University in *Government and World Crisis,* a collection of lectures given in May 1962.

Trade and the Atlantic partnership, text of remarks made by JFK before the Conference on Trade Policy in Washington on 5/17/62 together with keynote remarks made by Secretary Rusk. *DSB* 46:906–11, June 4, 1962.

Dulles Library of Diplomatic History dedicated at Princeton. *DSB* 46:923, June 4, 1963.

New frontiers of science, space and foreign policy, 5/25/62. *DSB* 46:931, June 11, 1962.

Secretary Rusk's news conference of 5/31/62. *DSB* 46:970–76, June 18, 1962.

Deploring restrictions by Senate on foreign aid, 6/6/62. *DSB* 47:25, July 2, 1962.

Secretary Rusk interviewed on "Press Conference USA," 6/12/62. *DSB* 47:53, July 9, 1962.

Disarmament and arms control, 6/16/62. *DSB* 47:3–7, July 2, 1962.

U.S. again calls for action on drafting of disarmament treaty, 6/25/62. *DSB* 47:243, Aug. 13, 1962.

Department supports U.N. loan legislation, 7/2/62. *DSB* 47:142, July 23, 1962.

Secretary Rusk interviewed on "Issues and Answers," 7/8/62. *DSB* 47:179–85, July 30, 1962.

Secretary Rusk's news conference of 7/12/62. *DSB* 47:171–79, July 30, 1962.

Secretary Rusk holds talks with European leaders, departure statement, 7/18/62. *DSB* 47:96, July 16, 1962.

Tenth anniversary of Fulbright agreement, press release, 7/18/62. *DSB* 47:221, Aug. 6, 1962.

Remarks at the Plenary Session of the International Conference on Laos at Geneva, 7/21/62. Reprinted in *Winds of Freedom,* p. 191.

Foreign policy aspects of space communications, statement of 8/6/62. *DSB* 47:315–19, Aug. 27, 1962.

Department reports on developments on Warsaw Convention, Hague Protocol letter, Secretary Rusk to Senator Fulbright, 8/9/62. *DSB* 47:362, Sept. 3, 1962.

Winning a worldwide victory for freedom, 8/13/62. *DSB* 47:343, Sept. 3, 1962.

Secretary Rusk hopes for greater cooperation in space field, 8/15/62. *DSB* 47:348, Sept. 3, 1962.

Excerpts from interview on "Washington Conversation," 9/2/62. Reprinted in *Winds of Freedom,* p. 193.

Eighth anniversary of SEATO, 9/7/62. *DSB* 47:451, Sept. 24, 1962.

JFK and DR urge restoration of foreign aid funds, 9/19/62. *DSB* 47:518, Oct. 8, 1962.

Five goals of U.S. foreign policy, 9/24/62. *DSB* 47:547, Oct. 15, 1962.

Government of Algeria recognized by U.S., 9/29/62. *DSB* 47:560, Oct. 15, 1962.

Secretary discusses Cuban situation on "News and Comment," transcript of interview of 9/30/62. *DSB* 47:595–98, Oct. 22, 1962.

Conference on middle-level manpower to meet in Puerto Rico, statement of 10/7/62. *DSB* 47:628, Oct. 22, 1962.

United States presents facilities at Fort McNair to inter-American defense college, 10/9/62. *DSB* 47:642, Oct. 29, 1962.

Trade investment and U.S. foreign policy, 10/19/62. *DSB* 47:683, Nov. 5, 1962.

American republics act to halt Soviet threat to hemisphere, statement at a special meeting of the Council of OAS, 10/23/62. *DSB* 47:720–23, Nov. 12, 1962.

Discussions resumed with Japan on economic aid to Ryukyus. *DSB* 47:770, Nov. 19, 1962.

Basic Issues Underlying the Present Crisis, address of 11/20/62. *DSB* 47:867–73, Dec. 10, 1962.

Changing patterns in world affairs, transcript of television interview on "CBS Reports," in which Secretary Rusk answered questions put to him by David Schoenbrun, 11/28/62. *DSB* 47:907–17, Dec. 17, 1962.

Rusk remarks to F. M. Ohira after the Japan-U.S. Committee on Trade and Economic Affairs. *DSB* 47:959, Dec. 24, 1962.

Secretary Rusk's news conference of 12/10/62. *DSB* 47:994–1001, Dec. 31, 1962.

Secretary Rusk expresses appreciation to Venezuela for quarantine action, 12/14/62. *DSB* 47:993, Dec. 31, 1962.

Secretary discusses Berlin, transcript of filmed interview with Secretary Rusk by John Steele on 12/28/62 and broadcast on Time-Life stations on 1/12/63. *DSB* 48:135–37, Jan. 28, 1963.

Secretary Rusk interviewed on "Today" show, 1/21/63. *DSB* 48:202, Feb. 11, 1963.

Secretary Rusk interviewed on "Meet the Press," 1/27/63. *DSB* 48:244–250, Feb. 18, 1963.

Secretary Rusk's news conference of 2/1/63. *DSB* 48:235–43, Feb. 18, 1963.

The Road Ahead, address of 2/13/63. *DSB* 48:311–16, March 4, 1963.

Secretary Rusk holds press and radio news briefing at Los Angeles, 2/13/63. *DSB* 48:361–68, March 11, 1963.

The United Nations in the Fight for Freedom, address of 2/22/63. *DSB* 48:393–98, March 18, 1963.

Security and Freedom: A Free World Responsibility, address of 2/26/63. *DSB* 48:383, March 18, 1963.

Secretary Rusk's news conference of 3/8/63. *DSB* 48:432–39, March 25, 1963.

U.S. efforts to achieve safeguarded test ban treaty, statement of 3/11/63. *DSB* 48:485–89, April 1, 1963.

Secretary Rusk addresses Advertising Council, 3/12/63. *DSB* 48:467–75, April 1, 1963.

U.S. supports full membership for Japan in OECD, 3/28/63. *DSB* 48:522, April 15, 1963.

The foreign aid program, statement of 4/5/63. *DSB* 48:664–72, April 29, 1963.

Secretary interviewed on GFWC (General Federation of Women's Clubs) TV program, 4/12/63. *DSB* 48:698, May 6, 1963.

Some current issues on U.S. foreign policy, 4/18/63. *DSB* 48:679, May 6, 1963.

Secretary replies to allegations on aid shipments, letter of 4/19/63. *DSB* 48:685, May 6, 1963.

The Stake in Viet-Nam, address of 4/22/63. *DSB* 48:727–35, May 13, 1963.

U.S. and U.K. sign agreement on sale of Polaris missiles, 4/25/63. *DSB* 48:976, June 24, 1963.

Secretary Rusk's news conference of 5/29/63. *DSB* 48:931–38, June 17, 1963.

U.S. seeks solution to problem of tuna fishing off Ecuador. *DSB* 48:976, June 24, 1963.

The foreign aid program for 1964, statement of 6/11/63. *DSB* 49:19–28, July 1, 1963.

Fulfilling our basic commitments as a nation, statement of 7/10/63. *DSB* 49:154–59, July 29, 1963.

The State of the North Atlantic Alliance, address of 7/12/63. *DSB* 49:190–198, Aug. 5, 1963.

Rusk and Harriman discuss Nuclear Test Ban Treaty. *DSB* 49:240, Aug. 12, 1963.

Rusk discusses appropriation request before Senate committee, 7/16/63. *DSB* 49:260, Aug. 12, 1963.

The Kennedy Round—progress and promise, 7/17/63. *DSB* 49:291, Aug. 19, 1963.

Nuclear Test Ban Treaty signed at Moscow, 8/5/63. *DSB* 49:314, Aug. 26, 1963.

The Nuclear Test Ban Treaty: symbol of a new course, statement of 8/12/63. *DSB* 49:350–56, Sept. 2, 1963.

Secretary Rusk's news conference on 8/16/63. *DSB* 49:356–64, Sept. 2, 1963.

Ninth anniversary of SEATO, 9/6/63. *DSB* 49:465, Sept. 23, 1963.

Unfinished Business, address of 9/10/63. *DSB* 49:490–96, Sept. 30, 1963.

White House holds conference on export expansion, texts of three addresses made on 9/17/63 by JFK, Dean Rusk, and Christian Herter. *DSB* 49:595–605, Oct. 14, 1963.

Dedication of church center for the U.N., address of 9/22/63. *DSB* 49:570, Oct. 14, 1963.

U.S. stops aid to Dominican Republic and Honduras, 10/4/63. *DSB* 49:624, Oct. 21, 1963.

The Age of the Rights of Man, address of 10/12/63. *DSB* 49:654, Oct. 28, 1963.

International Educational and Cultural Exchanges: A Look Back and a Look Ahead, address of 10/24/63. *DSB* 49:742–44, Nov. 11, 1963.

Toward a New Dimension in the Atlantic Partnership, address of 10/27/63. *DSB* 49:726–31, Nov. 11, 1963.

Secretary Rusk's news conference of 11/8/63. *DSB* 49:810–17, Nov. 25, 1963.

The Gettysburg Address and our commitment to freedom, 11/17/63. *DSB* 49:842, Dec. 2, 1963.

Foreign Policy and the American Citizen, address of 12/10/63. *DSB* 49:990–996, Dec. 30, 1963.

Secretary Rusk would upgrade country desk officers [in the State Department]; excerpts from testimony before Senate Subcommittee on National Security Staffing and Operations, 12/11/63, Department of State News Letter, February 1964, pp. 2–4.

President Johnson and Secretary Rusk urge full appropriation for foreign aid, statement by Secretary Rusk of 12/12/63. *DSB* 49:999–1004, Dec. 30, 1963.

Impressions of President Kennedy, 12/18/63 ("CBS Reports" program). *DSB* 50:4–5, Jan. 6, 1964.

Secretary Rusk discusses the outlook for 1964 on Japanese television, 12/28/63. *DSB* 50:40–46, Jan. 13, 1964.

Secretary Rusk's news conference of 1/2/64. *DSB* 50:81–89, Jan. 20, 1964.

The first twenty-five years of the United Nations: from San Francisco to the 1970's. *DSB* 50:112–19, Jan. 27, 1964.

The making of foreign policy, transcript of a television interview of Rusk by Professor Eric Frederick Goldman of Princeton, filmed on 1/11/64. 50:164–176, Feb. 3, 1964.

The Present Prospect, address of 1/22/64. *DSB* 50:190–95, Feb. 10, 1964.

The United States and Japan: Common Interests in the Building of a Peaceful World, address of 1/28/64. *DSB* 50:230–35, Feb. 17, 1964.

Parliamentary Government and the Alliance for Progress, address of 2/5/64. *DSB* 50:305–7, Feb. 24, 1964.

Secretary Rusk's news conference of 2/7/64. *DSB* 50:274–84, Feb. 24, 1964.

Secretary Rusk interviewed on Voice of America, transcript of 2/14/64 for release 2/15/64 on the Voice of America program "Press Conference, USA." *DSB* 50:330–36, March 2, 1964.

Why We Treat Different Communist Countries Differently, address of 2/25/64. *DSB* 50:390–96, March 16, 1964.

Education for Citizenship in the Modern World, address before American Association of School Administrators. *DSB* 50:358–64, March 9, 1964.

Secretary Rusk's news conference of 2/27/64. *DSB* 50:403–9, March 16, 1964.

The community of interest between the U.S. and Mexico, remarks of 3/5/64. *DSB* 50:449–50, March 23, 1964.

Secretary Rusk's news conference of 3/6/64. *DSB* 50:439–46, March 23, 1964.

Your Stake in Foreign Aid, address of 3/6/64. *DSB* 50:434–38, March 23, 1964.

Equal employment opportunity, remarks at DOS, 3/12/64. *DSB* 50:629–31, April 20, 1964.

East-West trade, statement before the Senate Committee on Foreign Relations, 3/13/64. *DSB* 50:474–84, March 30, 1964.

The Toilsome Path to Peace, address of 3/19/64. *DSB* 50:530–35, April 6, 1964.

The foreign assistance program, statement before the House Committee on Foreign Affairs, 3/23/64. Department of State News Letter, April 1964, pp. 2–3, and *DSB* 50:595–601, April 13, 1964.

Secretary Rusk's news conference of 3/27/64. *DSB* 50:570–76, April 13, 1964.

Secretary Rusk's news conference of 4/3/64. *DSB* 50:608–14, April 20, 1964.

The Atlantic Alliance, address of 4/7/64. *DSB* 50:650–55, April 27, 1964.

SEATO Council of Ministers meets at Manila, statement of 4/13/64. *DSB* 50:690–92, May 4, 1964.

Arrival and return statements (in/from Taipei and Saigon), 4/16–4/20/64. *DSB* 50:694–97, May 4, 1964.

The Situation in the Western Pacific, address of 4/25/64. *DSB* 50:732–37, May 11, 1964.

Central Treaty Organization in Washington, address of 4/28/64. *DSB* 50:766–68, May 18, 1964.

Department of State budget request for fiscal 1965, statement before Senate Appropriations Subcommittee, 4/28/64. *DSB* 50:836–43, May 25, 1964.

Atlantic and European Unity, address in Brussels, 5/9/64. *DSB* 50:810–15, May 25, 1964.

Secretary Rusk on the BBC program "Encounter," 5/10/64. *DSB* 50:816–822, May 25, 1964.

North Atlantic Council meets at The Hague, statement of 5/12/64. *DSB* 50:850–52, June 1, 1964.

Laos and Viet-Nam—A Prescription for Peace, address of 5/22/64. *DSB* 50:886–91, June 8, 1964.

The National Interest—1964, address of 6/7/64. *DSB* 50:955–58, June 22, 1964.

Why Laos Is Critically Important, address of 6/14/64. *DSB* 51:3–5, July 6, 1964.

U.S.-Japan Science Committee concludes fourth meeting, remarks by Rusk, 6/23/64. *DSB* 51:61–62, July 13, 1964.

Secretary Rusk's news conference of 7/1/64. *DSB* 51:82–88, July 20, 1964.

Foreign policy aspects of U.S. immigration laws, statement of 7/2/64. *DSB* 51:98–101, July 20, 1964.

The Universal Appeal of the Declaration of Independence, address of 7/4/64. *DSB* 51:74–77, July 20, 1964.

Secretary Rusk interviewed on German television, transcript of interview between Rusk and Gerd Ruge of the All-German television network, 7/9/64. *DSB* 51:106–8, July 27, 1964.

U.S., New Zealand, and Australia reaffirm ties of friendship, remarks at a dinner on 7/17/64. *DSB* 51:194–97, Aug. 10, 1964.

OAS approves Rio Treaty measures against Castro regime, statement of 7/22/64. *DSB* 51:174–79, Aug. 10, 1964.

Some thoughts on the conduct of foreign policy, remarks of 7/23/64. *DSB* 51:185–88, Aug. 10, 1964.

Secretary Rusk interviewed on "Issues and Answers," 7/26/64. *DSB* 51:231–37, Aug. 17, 1964.

Secretary Rusk's news conference of 7/31/64. *DSB* 51:221–28, Aug. 17, 1964.

Department of State urges Congress to revise immigration laws, statement of 7/31/64. *DSB* 51:276–80, Aug. 24, 1964.

The Pursuit of Peace, address of 8/2/64. *DSB* 51:214–18, Aug. 17, 1964.

Secretary Rusk discusses Asian situation on NBC program, interview of 8/5/64. *DSB* 51:268–70, Aug. 24, 1964.

Statements by Secretary Rusk and Secretary McNamara at joint session of Senate Foreign Relations and Armed Services Committees, 8/6/64. *DSB* 51:267–68, Aug. 24, 1964.

Freedom in the Postwar World, address of 8/29/64. *DSB* 51:268–70, Aug. 24, 1964.

Secretary Rusk interviewed on "Meet the Press," 8/30/64. *DSB* 51:394–400, Sept. 21, 1964.

Tenth anniversary of SEATO, statement of 9/5/64. *DSB* 51:362–67, Sept. 14, 1964.

Secretary Rusk's news conference of 9/10/64. *DSB* 51:426–32, Sept. 28, 1964.

Teaching the Fundamentals on International Understanding, address of 9/8/64. *DSB* 51:437–441, Sept. 28, 1964.

Toward Victory for Freedom, address of 9/14/64. *DSB* 51:463–68, Oct. 5, 1964.

Secretary Rusk's news conference of 9/14/64. *DSB* 51:468–72, Oct. 5, 1964.

Freedom and Development, address before the American Negro Leadership Conference on Africa, 9/25/64. *DSB* 51:498–503, Oct. 12, 1964.

U.S. comments on Peiping's nuclear capacity. *DSB* 51:542–44, Oct. 19, 1964.

President Johnson proclaims 1965 as International Cooperation Year, remarks by Secretary Rusk, 10/2/64. *DSB* 51:557, Oct. 29, 1964.

Trade, Investment, and Peace, address of 10/5/64. *DSB* 51:570–75, Oct. 26, 1964.

Secretary Rusk's news conference of 10/8/64. *DSB* 51:575–81, Oct. 26, 1964.

Science and Development in Chile, address of 10/9/64. *DSB* 51:634–37, Nov. 2, 1964.

Man and Nature, address of 10/12/64. *DSB* 51:618–21, Nov. 2, 1964.

Mr. Rusk and Mr. William Bundy interviewed on Red China's nuclear testing, transcripts of 10/16/64. *DSB* 51:614–17, Nov. 2, 1964.

The Marine Corps and the Foreign Service: A Working Partnership, address of 10/16/64. *DSB* 51:643–45, Nov. 2, 1964.

Secretary Rusk discusses world developments on "Issues and Answers," 10/18/64. *DSB* 51:654–60, Nov. 9, 1964.

Toward the Brotherhood of Man, address of 10/19/64. *DSB* 51:650–52, Nov. 9, 1964.

Mixed-manned demonstration ship visits Washington, remarks of 10/20/64. *DSB* 51:661–62, Nov. 9, 1964.

Secretary discusses mainland China in television interview, 11/11/64. *DSB* 51:771–72, Nov. 30, 1964.

The role of international law in world affairs, remarks of 11/14/64. *DSB* 51:802–3, Dec. 7, 1964.

Trade and the Atlantic Partnership, address of 11/16/64. *DSB* 51:766–71, Nov. 30, 1964.

Message from Secretary Rusk to Jomo Kenyatta (during U.S. cooperation with Belgium in rescue of hostages from the Congo), 11/16/64. *DSB* 51:838–839, Dec. 14, 1964.

The trade union movement and social progress in the western hemisphere, 11/23/64. *DSB* 51:849–52, Dec. 14, 1964.

Statement by Rusk upon arrival at NATO ministerial meeting, 12/13/64. *DSB* 52:2, Jan. 4, 1965.

Secretary Rusk's news conference of 12/23/64. *DSB* 52:34–41, Jan. 11, 1965.

Policy, Persistence, and Patience, interview of 1/3/65. Department of State *General Foreign Policy Series* 191.

An interview with Secretary Rusk, transcript of NBC's "A Conversation with Dean Rusk," 1/3/65. *DSB* 52:62–74, Jan. 18, 1965.

The Secretary reports on Viet-Nam, excerpts from a television interview, 1/5/65. Department of State News Letter, January 1965, pp. 5–6.

The United States Navy, Watchdog of Peace, address of 1/23/65. *DSB* 52:165–67, Feb. 8, 1965.

Foreign policy aspects of proposals to revise immigration law, statement before House Immigration and Naturalization Subcommittee, 2/24/65. *DSB* 52:384–88, March 15, 1965.

Secretary Rusk's news conference of 2/25/65. *DSB* 52:362–71, March 15, 1965.

Some Fundamentals of American Policy, address of 3/4/65. *DSB* 52:398–403, March 22, 1965.

Our Atlantic Policy, address of 3/6/65. *DSB* 52:427–31, March 22, 1965.

Secretary Rusk discusses Viet-Nam situation, transcript of "Face the Nation" program, 3/7/65. *DSB* 52:442, March 29, 1965.

The foreign assistance program for 1966, statement of 3/9/65. *DSB* 52:482–488, April 5, 1965.

Secretary regrets that Soviets do not support Viet-Nam accords, statement of 3/19/65. *DSB* 52:489, April 5, 1965.

International Visitors and the American Society, address of 3/19/65. *DSB* 52:588–92, April 19, 1965.

Secretary Rusk discusses use of tear gas in Viet-Nam, statement of 3/24/65. *DSB* 52:528–32, April 12, 1965.

Secretary Rusk discusses Viet-Nam situation, transcript of BBC interview, 4/2/65. *DSB* 52:569–71, April 19, 1965; also printed in *U.S. News & World Report,* April 19, 1965, pp. 79–80.

Secretary rules out suspension of U.S. raids on North Viet-Nam, statement of 4/7/65. *DSB* 52:685–87, May 3, 1965.

Central Treaty Organization in Tehran, statement by Rusk, 4/7/65. *DSB* 52:685–87, May 3, 1965.

Korean Foreign Minister holds talks with Secretary Rusk, joint statement, 4/17/65. *DSB* 52:651, May 3, 1965.

The Reform of Our Basic Immigration Law, address of 4/19/65. *DSB* 52:806–9, May 24, 1965.

The Control of Force in International Relations, address of 4/23/65. *DSB* 52:694–701, May 10, 1965.

U.S. willing to participate in conference on Cambodia, 4/25/65. *DSB* 2:711–712, May 10, 1965.

Secretary urges ratification of U.N. charter amendments, statement of 4/28/65. *DSB* 52:827–30, May 24, 1965.

Secretary discusses situation in Dominican Republic, transcript of interview of Secretary Rusk by John Hightower of Associated Press. *DSB* 52:842–844, May 31, 1965.

U.S. unwilling to maintain consular relations with Cambodia, letter to Cambodian foreign minister, 5/6/65. *DSB* 52:853–54, May 31, 1965.

Secretary Rusk to Ambassador Columbo re "Act of Santo Domingo," letter of 5/7/65. *DSB* 52:868, May 31, 1965.

Memorial to President Kennedy at Runnymede, remarks of 5/14/65. *DSB* 52:897–98, June 7, 1965.

Tenth anniversary of signing of Austrian State Treaty, remarks of 5/15/65. *DSB* 52:898, June 7, 1965.

Secretary Rusk's news conference of 5/26/65. *DSB* 52:938–47, June 14, 1965.

Secretary discusses Dominican situation on NBC-TV, transcript of an interview with Rusk by John Chancellor, 5/28/65. *DSB* 52:947–49, June 14, 1965.

Guidelines of U.S. Foreign Policy, commencement address, 6/8/65. *DSB* 52:1030–34, June 28, 1965.

The Alliance for Progress: A Partnership of Mutual Help, address of 6/10/65. *DSB* 53:2–5, July 5, 1965.

Secretary Rusk reviews efforts to reach peaceful settlement in Southeast Asia, 6/18/65. *DSB* 53:5–12, July 5, 1965.

Viet-Nam: Four Steps to Peace, address of 6/23/65. *DSB* 53:50–55, July 12, 1965.

Secretary discusses Viet-Nam on USIA television, transcript of an interview of Rusk by members of the international press, 6/24/65. *DSB* 53:105–10, July 19, 1965.

Building a Decent World Order, address of 7/5/65. *DSB* 53:27–31, July 5, 1965.

Secretary talks about Viet-Nam on "Issues and Answers," transcript of an interview with Rusk on ABC, 7/11/65. *DSB* 53:183–90, Aug. 2, 1965.

U.S.-Japan cabinet committee of trade and economic affairs holds fourth meeting in Washington, opening remarks, 7/12/65. *DSB* 53:242–43, Aug. 9, 1965.

President Johnson and Secretary Rusk pay tribute to Ambassador Stevenson, 7/14/65. *DSB* 53:229, Aug. 9, 1965.

Consular convention with the Soviet Union, statement of 7/30/65. *DSB* 53:375–78, Aug. 30, 1965.

Secretary Rusk's news conference of 8/2/65. *DSB* 53:302–10, Aug. 23, 1965.

Political and military aspects of U.S. policy in Viet-Nam, transcript of a television interview with Rusk and McNamara on CBS, 8/9/65. *DSB* 53:342–356, Aug. 30, 1965.

U.S. continues to abide by Geneva conventions of 1949 in Viet-Nam, letter to president of International Committee of the Red Cross, 8/10/65. *DSB* 53:447, Sept. 13, 1965.

U.S. recognizes Singapore as sovereign, independent state, message from Rusk, 8/11/65. *DSB* 53:357, Aug. 30, 1965.

Viet-Nam: winning the peace; transcript of an interview with Rusk, Arthur Goldberg, and McGeorge Bundy, 8/23/65. *DSB* 53:431–44, Sept. 13, 1965.

Secretary Rusk's news conference of 8/27/65. *DSB* 53:481–86, Sept. 20, 1965.

Secretary discusses U.S. policy in Viet-Nam on Belgian TV, transcript of an interview recorded 9/1/65. *DSB* 53:512–14, Sept. 27, 1965.

Eleventh anniversary of SEATO, statement by Rusk, 9/4/65. *DSB* 53:536–537, Sept. 27, 1965.

The Anatomy of Foreign Policy Decisions, address of 9/7/65. *DSB* 53:502–509, Sept. 27, 1965.

Secretary Rusk appears on NBC's "American White Paper," transcript, 9/7/65. *DSB* 53:509–12, Sept. 27, 1965.

Notes on a Native Son: Secretary of State Dean Rusk recalls a boyhood spent in modest circumstances but rich in love, laughter, and learning (interview). *Atlanta Magazine,* October 1965, p. 40.

The Unseen Search for Peace, George Huntington Williams memorial lecture, 10/16/65. *DSB* 53:690–99, Nov. 1, 1965.

Secretary Rusk's news conference of 11/5/65. *DSB* 53:854–62, Nov. 29, 1965.

Mr. Rusk, Mr. McNamara discuss Rhodesia, Rio meeting, Viet-Nam, news conference in Austin, Texas, 11/11/65. *DSB* 53:894–96, Dec. 6, 1965.

The Common Quest for Freedom and Prosperity in the American Republics, address of 11/22/65. *DSB* 53:985ff, Dec. 20, 1965.

Secretary Rusk's news conference of 11/26/65. *DSB* 53:930–39, Dec. 13, 1965.

Secretary Rusk's news conference of 12/9/65. *DSB* 53:1006–13, Dec. 27, 1965.

U.S.-Italian exchange on North Viet-Nam contacts released, Rusk to Fanfani to Rusk, 12/4/65. *DSB* 54:11–13, Jan. 3, 1966.

Secretary Rusk discusses Viet-Nam on Canadian TV, filmed on 12/30/65. *DSB* 54:86–89, Jan. 17, 1966.

Secretary Rusk and Vietnamese Premier restate basic positions, joint communiqué, Saigon, 1/16/65. *DSB* 54:155–56, Jan. 31, 1966.

Secretary Rusk's news conference of 1/21/66. *DSB* 54:189–97, Feb. 7, 1966.

Secretary Rusk's news conference of 1/31/66. *DSB* 54:223–29, Feb. 14, 1966.

The Chain of Common Interest Uniting the United States and Mexico, address of 2/10/66. *DSB* 54:365–67, March 7, 1966.

As Told by Secretary Rusk—Why U.S. Fights Viet-Nam, text of a statement of 2/18/66. *U.S. News & World Report,* Feb. 28, 1966, p. 60.

Nonproliferation of nuclear weapons, statement of 2/23/66. *DSB* 54:406–410, March 14, 1966.

Food for Freedom Act of 1966, statements before the House Committee on Agriculture, 2/25 and 3/7/66. *DSB* 54:496–503, March 28, 1966.

Secretary gets new responsibility for conduct of foreign affairs, announcement and message, 3/4/66. *DSB* 54:506–9, March 28, 1966.

Keeping Our Commitment to Peace, address of 3/14/66. *DSB* 54:514–21, April 4, 1966.

United States policy toward Communist China, statement of 3/16/66. *DSB* 54:686–95, May 2, 1966.

The heart of the problem: The U.S. commitment in Viet-Nam, fundamental issues, statements by Rusk and Gen. Maxwell Taylor before the Senate Committee on Foreign Relations, broadcast over nationwide TV. 3/17 and 3/18/66. *DSB* 54:346–62, March 7, 1966.

The foreign assistance program for 1967, statement of 3/17/66. *DSB* 54:628–634, April 18, 1966.

Secretary Rusk appears on "Face the Nation," transcript of interview, 3/20/66. *DSB* 54:565–70, April 11, 1966.

Secretary Rusk reviews U.S. commitment to freedom in Southeast Asia, excerpts from address before the Council on Foreign Relations, 3/24/66. Department of State News Letter, June 1966, p. 4.

Secretary Rusk's news conference of 3/25/66. *DSB* 54:557–64, April 11, 1966.

How the Secretary of State apportions his time: study prepared in the Bureau of Public Affairs, together with a portion of an interview with Rusk on 4/3/66 on "Open End" in which he discussed his working day. *DSB* 54:651–54, April 25, 1966.

Secretary Rusk answers questions on NATO issues and Viet-Nam, interview by *Paris-Match* magazine for publication in the 4/16/66 issue. *DSB* 54:695–99, May 2, 1966.

CENTO meets at Ankara, statement of 4/20/66. *DSB* 54:775, May 16, 1966.

U.S. position on nuclear sharing reaffirmed by Secretary Rusk, statement of 4/27/66. *DSB* 54:768, May 16, 1966.

Secretary comments on Peiping's militancy in Southeast Asia, transcript of ABC's "Red China: Year of the Gun?" 4/27/66. *DSB* 54:772–74, May 16, 1966.

Background of U.S. policy in Southeast Asia, statement of 5/9/66. *DSB* 54:830–34, May 30, 1966.

Secretary Rusk's news conference of 5/17/66. *DSB* 54:882–87, June 6, 1966.

Organizing the Peace for Man's Survival, address of 5/24/66. *DSB* 54:926–934, June 13, 1966.

Secretary Rusk's news conference of 5/27/66. *DSB* 54:918–25, June 13, 1966.

North Atlantic Council meets at Brussels, statement of 6/4/66. *DSB* 54:1001, June 27, 1966.

Where NATO stands, statement of 6/13/66. *DSB* 54:998–1001, June 27, 1966.

Progress Toward a Decent World Order, address of 6/14/66. *DSB* 55:44–49, July 11, 1966.

A report on the NATO meeting at Brussels, statement before the Subcommittee on National Security and International Operations of the Senate Committee on Government Operations, 6/16/66. *DSB* 55:7–9, July 4, 1966.

Secretary Rusk meets with Asian leaders, statements, press conferences, texts of communiqués and pertinent documents concerning his trip to Australia, Formosa, Japan, and Korea, 6/26–7/9/66. *DSB* 55:169–84, Aug. 1, 1966.

Secretary Rusk's news conference of 7/12/66. *DSB* 55:162–68, Aug. 1, 1966.

Review of United States refugee policy, statement of 7/14/66. *DSB* 55:235–240, Aug. 15, 1966.

The world food and population crisis, statement of 7/20/66. *DSB* 55:199–202, Aug. 8, 1966.

Secretary Rusk's news conference of 8/5/66. *DSB* 55:258–65, Aug. 22, 1966.

U.S. marks third anniversary of limited test ban treaty, 8/6/66. *DSB* 55:413–424, Sept. 19, 1966.

The Goal of a Reliable Peace: A Survey of Free World Progress, address of 8/22/66. *DSB* 55:362–68, Sept. 12, 1966.

International defense commitments of the United States, statement of 8/25/66. *DSB* 55:377–81, Sept. 12, 1966.

A review of United States foreign and military policy, 8/25/66. *DSB* 55:413–424, Sept. 19, 1966.

Twelfth anniversary of SEATO, statement of 9/8/66. *DSB* 55:454–55, Sept. 26, 1966.

Secretary Rusk's news conference of 9/16/66. *DSB* 55:478–83, Oct. 3, 1966.

The Outlook for Freedom, address of 9/21/66. *DSB* 55:586–90, Oct. 17, 1966.

Requirements for Organizing the Peace, address of 10/12/66. *DSB* 55:658–663, Oct. 31, 1966.

The University Campus and Foreign Policy, address of 11/14/66. *DSB* 55:914–18, Dec. 19, 1966.

The future of the Pacific Community, address of 11/15/66. *DSB* 55:838–43, Dec. 5, 1966.

Secretary Rusk's news conference of 11/18/66. *DSB* 55:844–51, Dec. 5, 1966.

Reports by Secretary Rusk, Secretary McNamara, and Mr. John McCloy, remarks of the president and the three officials at a press briefing at the LBJ Ranch, 11/23/66. *Weekly Compilation Presidential Documents* 2:1719–23, Nov. 28, 1966.

Secretary Rusk, Secretary McNamara, Mr. McCloy meet with President Johnson, 11/23/66. *DSB* 55:919, Dec. 19, 1966.

Secretary Rusk's news conference of 12/21/66. *DSB* 56:42–48, Jan. 9, 1967.

Secretary Rusk discusses prospects for 1967 on "Face the Nation," transcript of an interview on Viet-Nam war and the possibilities for peace, 1/1/67. *DSB* 56:126–32, Jan. 23, 1967.

Secretary Rusk redefines United States policy on Viet-Nam for student leaders, texts of a letter from Secretary Rusk of 1/4/67 to 100 student leaders and the students' letter of 12/29/66 addressed to President Johnson. *DSB* 56:133–37, Jan. 23, 1967.

Secretary Rusk interviewed on "Today" show, 1/12/67. *DSB* 56:168–72, Jan. 30, 1967.

Secretary Rusk urges congressional support for consular convention with the Soviet Union, statement of 1/23/67. *DSB* 56:247–50, Feb. 13, 1967.

Science and Foreign Affairs, address of 1/24/67. *DSB* 56:238–42, Feb. 13, 1967.

Building a Durable Peace, address of 1/26/67. *DSB* 56:269–73, Feb. 20, 1967.

Outer Space Treaty signed by three nations at White House ceremony, statement of 1/27/67. *DSB* 56:266, Feb. 20, 1967.

Secretary Rusk discusses Viet-Nam in interview for British television, 1/31/67. *DSB* 61:274–84, Feb. 20, 1967.

Secretary Rusk's news conference of 2/9/67. *DSB* 56:317–22, Feb. 27, 1967.

Secretary Rusk discusses European affairs and Viet-Nam, interview for German television for broadcast on 2/12/67. *DSB* 56:358–65, March 6, 1967.

Secretary Rusk and Secretary McNamara discuss developments in Latin America and Viet-Nam, transcript of joint press conference, 2/28/67. *DSB* 56:464–66, March 20, 1967.

Secretary Rusk comments on Hanoi's attitude, statement of 3/2/67. *DSB* 56:516, March 27, 1967.

Secretary Rusk and Ambassador Goldberg urge Senate approval of Outer Space Treaty, statements of 3/7/67. *DSB* 56:600–12, April 10, 1967.

Thailand grants U.S. permission to use U Tapao air base, statement of 3/22/67. *DSB* 56:597–98, April 10, 1967.

Secretary Rusk's news conference of 3/28/67. *DSB* 56:618–24, April 17, 1967.

Secretary Rusk discusses Punta del Este conference on "Meet the Press," 4/16/67. *DSB* 56:722–28, May 8, 1967.

SEATO council reaffirms resolve to repel aggression, opening statement of 4/18/67. *DSB* 56:742–44, May 15, 1967.

White House luncheon for General Westmoreland, remarks of the President, General Westmoreland, and Secretary Rusk, 4/28/67. *Weekly Compilation Presidential Documents* 3:674–79, May 8, 1967.

The Role of the United States in World Affairs, address of 5/1/67. *DSB* 56:770–73, May 22, 1967.

The foreign assistance program for 1968, statement of 5/4/67. *DSB* 56:826–833, May 29, 1967.

A conversation with Dean Rusk, transcript of interview from the Department of State, 5/5/67. *DSB* 56:774–88, May 22, 1967.

Our Foreign Policy Commitments to Assure a Peaceful Future, address of 5/18/67. *DSB* 56:874–79, June 12, 1967.

Address by Rusk at international conference on water for peace, 5/31/67. *DSB* 56:904–7, June 19, 1967.

The situation in the Near East, statement at news briefing at the White House, 6/5/67. *DSB* 56:949–51, June 26, 1967.

Secretary Rusk replies to questions on Viet-Nam for Swedish newspaper, 7/1/67. *DSB* 57:91, July 24, 1967.

The Road to a Lasting Peace, address of 7/6/67. *DSB* 57:87–91, July 24, 1967.

The foreign assistance program, statement of 7/14/67. *DSB* 57:185, Aug. 14, 1967.

Secretary Rusk's news conference of 7/19/67. *DSB* 57:159–67, Aug. 7, 1967.

The Central Purpose of United States Foreign Policy, address of 8/5/67. *DSB* 57:251–55, Aug. 28, 1967.

American Purposes and the Pursuit of Human Dignity (American presence in Southeast Asia and role in the Vietnamese conflict), address of 8/29/67. *DSB* 57:343–49, Sept. 18, 1967.

Secretary Rusk's news conference of 9/8/67. *DSB* 57:383–90, Sept. 25, 1967.

Thirteenth anniversary of SEATO, 9/8/67. *DSB* 57:391, Sept. 25, 1967.

Secretary Rusk and Ambassador Bunker discuss Viet-Nam in TV and radio interviews, 9/10/67. *DSB* 57:411–21, Oct. 2, 1967.

OAS foreign ministers take steps against Cuban subversion, statements of 9/23/67. *DSB* 57:490–93, Oct. 16, 1967.

Secretary Rusk's news conference of 10/2/67. *DSB* 57:555–64, Oct. 30, 1967.

White House ceremony marks entry into force of Outer Space Treaty, statement of 10/10/67. *DSB* 57:566, Oct. 30, 1967.

Rusk news conference of 10/12/67. *Congressional Quarterly, Weekly Report,* 25:2127–32, Oct. 20, 1967.

Secretary Rusk discusses Viet-Nam in interview for foreign television, transcript of 10/16/67. *DSB* 57:595–602, Nov. 6, 1967.

Our Purpose Is Peace. *Reader's Digest,* December 1967, p. 59; also in *DSB* 57:801–7, Dec. 11, 1967.

The price of protectionism, statement before Senate Finance Committee. *DSB* 57:634–38, Nov. 13, 1967.

Firmness and restraint in Viet-Nam, excerpt from address of 10/30/67. *DSB* 57:703–5, Nov. 27, 1967.

The Political Future of the Family of Man, address of 11/14/67. *DSB* 57:735–74, Dec. 4, 1967.

Secretary Rusk urges appropriation of full amount authorized under the Foreign Assistance Act, statement before Senate Committee on Appropriations, 11/29/67. *DSB* 57:801–7, Dec. 11, 1967.

The World in Our Living Room, *Time,* Dec. 17, 1967, p. 18.

The American Interest in Europe, address to the United Italian-American Labor Council, 12/2/67. *DSB* 57:855–59, Dec. 25, 1967.

1967—A Progress Report, address of 12/6/67. *DSB* 58:1–5, Jan. 1, 1968.

Secretary Rusk's news conference of 1/4/68. *DSB* 58:116–24, Jan. 22, 1968.

The crisis in Korea, news briefing, 1/24/68. *DSB* 58:190–93, Feb. 12, 1968.

Share in Freedom, address of 1/10/68. *DSB* 58:228–31, Feb. 19, 1968.

Mclean's Interviews Dean Rusk on the War in Viet-Nam, *Maclean's,* February 1968, pp. 9ff; also in *DSB* 58:206–9, Feb. 12, 1968.

Secretary Rusk interviewed by members of the U.S. Student Press Association, 2/2/68. *DSB* 58:346–56, March 11, 1968.

Secretary Rusk and Secretary McNamara discuss Korea and Viet-Nam on "Meet the Press," 2/4/68. *DSB* 58:261–72, Feb. 26, 1968.

Our Concern for Peace in East Asia, address of 2/10/68. *DSB* 58:301–4, March 4, 1968.

Secretary Rusk reports on Hanoi's rejections of U.S. peace proposals, statement of 2/14/68. *DSB* 58:305, March 4, 1968.

Secretary Rusk commends actions of Marine security guards of American Embassy in Saigon, remarks of 2/16/68. *DSB* 58:357–58, March 11, 1968.

Rusk vs. Senators: The War Explained; excerpts from hearing of the Senate Foreign Relations Committee, 3/11 and 3/12/68. *U.S. News & World Report,* March 25, 1968, pp. 74–78.

The foreign aid program for fiscal 1969, statement before Senate Foreign Relations Committee, 3/11/68. *DSB* 58:445–48, April 1, 1968.

SEATO council of ministers meet at Wellington, statement of 4/2/68. *DSB* 58:515–18, April 22, 1968.

The Business of Building a Peace, address of 4/17/68. *DSB* 58:579–83, May 6, 1968.

U.S. suggests suitable sites for Viet-Nam negotiations, statement of 4/18/68. *DSB* 58:577–78, May 6, 1968.

Gaining the Full Measure of the Benefits of the Atom, address of 5/2/68. *DSB* 58:632–34, May 20, 1968.

U.S. economic and military assistance program for fiscal year 1969, statement before House Foreign Affairs Committee, 5/2/68. *DSB* 58:724–729, June 3, 1968.

Consolidating the Rule of Law in International Affairs, address at University of Georgia, 5/4/68. *DSB* 58:669–73, May 27, 1968.

Secretary Rusk interviewed for Japanese magazine, transcript of interview for publication in July issue of *Bungei Shunju* of Tokyo, 5/17/68. *DSB* 58:821–825, June 24, 1968.

Liberal trade policy and the U.S. national interest, statement before House Committee on Ways and Means, 6/10/68. *DSB* 59:50–53, July 8, 1968.

United States and Soviet Union exchange ratification of consular convention, statement of 6/13/68. *DSB* 59:39, July 8, 1968.

Secretary Rusk's news conference of 6/21/68. *DSB* 59:33–38, July 8, 1968.

Secretary Rusk discusses Berlin situation with Bonn officials, 6/27/68. *DSB* 59:74–75, July 15, 1968.

Nuclear Nonproliferation Treaty transmitted to the Senate for advice and consent to ratification, statement before Senate Committee on Foreign Relations, 7/10/68. *DSB* 59:131–34, July 29, 1968.

Secretary Rusk interviewed for *Yomiuri* newspaper (Tokyo), 7/29/68. *DSB* 59:214–17, Aug. 26, 1968.

Rusk's Analysis: Hanoi Pushes Build-up, Still Scorns Peace, summary of news conference of 7/30/68. *U.S. News & World Report,* Aug. 12, 1968, p. 8.

Secretary Rusk's news conference of 7/30/68. *DSB* 59:185–92, Aug. 19, 1968.

Cabinet report on Czechoslovakia and Vietnam, press briefing following cabinet meeting on 8/22/68. *Weekly Compilation Presidential Documents* 4:1263–65, Aug. 26, 1968.

Soviet intervention in Czechoslovakia, news conference, 8/22/68. *DSB* 59:261–63, Sept. 9, 1968.

Fourteenth anniversary of SEATO, 9/8/68. *DSB* 59:334–35, Sept. 30, 1968.

Some Myths and Misconceptions about U.S. Foreign Policy, address of 9/12/68. *DSB* 59:350–56, Oct. 7, 1968; a.k.a. Communist Aggression, address in *Vital Speeches* 35:2–6, Oct. 15, 1968.

Twenty Years in Perspective, address of 9/25/68. *DSB* 59:373–76, Oct. 14, 1968.

Department urges appropriation of full amount authorized for foreign assistance programs, statement before Senate Committee on Appropriations, 9/26/68. *DSB* 59:419–24, Oct. 21, 1968.

U.S. War Policy, the Official Word, excerpts from address, 10/2/68. *U.S. News & World Report,* Oct. 14, 1968, pp. 20ff.

The rights of men and nations. *DSB* 59:405–10, Oct. 21, 1968.

Secretary Rusk interviewed on "Issues and Answers," 10/6/68. *DSB* 59:471–80, Nov. 4, 1968.

Transformation in Asia and the Pacific, address of 10/7/68. *DSB* 59:461–66, Nov. 4, 1968.

Secretary Rusk opens press briefing room, transcript of remarks, 10/10/68. *DSB* 59:480–82, Nov. 4, 1968.

Secretary Rusk's news conference of 11/1/68. *DSB* 59:520–25, Nov. 18, 1968.

Secretary Rusk interviewed on "Face the Nation," 12/1/68. *DSB* 59:645–650, Dec. 23, 1968.

The human landscape, opening remarks at science convention, 12/9/68. *DSB* 60:127–28, Feb. 10, 1969.

Crew of U.S.S. *Pueblo* released at Panmunjom, statement 12/22/68, *DSB* 60:2, Jan. 6, 1969.

Death of Trygve Lie, statement of 12/30/68. *DSB* 60:78, Jan. 27, 1969.

Rusk Looks Back Over Eight Years at a News Conference, 1/3/69. *U.S. News & World Report,* Jan. 20, 1969, p. 55.

Secretary Rusk's news conference of 1/3/69. *DSB* 60:45–52, Jan. 20, 1969.

Reception honoring Secretary of State Dean Rusk: the President's remarks upon presenting the Medal of Freedom to Secretary Rusk, with the Secretary's response, 1/16/69. *Weekly Compilation Presidential Documents* 5:113–116, Jan. 20, 1969.

Mr. Secretary on the Eve of Emeritus, interview, *Life,* Jan. 17, 1969, pp. 56–62B.

Policy Is About the Future, address, March 11, 1969, *Owens-Corning Lectures 1968–69,* Denison University, Granville, Ohio, pp. 3–17.

Interview with Ben Hartley and John Ard, *Survey,* Dec. 7, 1970, pp. 2–8.

The 25th U.N. General Assembly and the Use of Force, *Georgia Journal of International Law: The Legal Regulation of the Use of Force,* April 1971, pp. 19–35.

Interview of Secretary Rusk, 7/2/71. *U.S. News & World Report,* July 19, 1971, pp. 68–76.

Michael Reisman's *Nullity and Revision:* The Review and Enforcement of International Judgments and Awards, book review by Dean Rusk, *Vanderbilt Journal of Transnational Law,* vol. 5, no. 2 (Spring 1972), pp. 575–80.

Perspectives on European Unification, Symposium on Expansion of the Common Market. *Law and Contemporary Problems* (Duke University), Spring 1972, pp. 221–27.

Diplomacy and National Power, lecture at the National War College, Washington, D.C., Sept. 11, 1972. Transcript available at the University of Georgia Library, Dean Rusk Collection.

Prospective Issues in U.S.-Chinese Relations, lecture. Reprinted in *China's Open Wall,* edited by Festus Justin Viser (Memphis State University Press, 1972).

The Prospects for Peace in a Strange, New World, lecture, 5/4/73. American Experience Program, University of Pittsburgh, 17 pp.

Dean Rusk's Views of the Washington Press Corps, *Seminar,* December 1973, pp. 4–8.

The Revisionist Historians, transcript of PBS "Firing Line" program, telecast on 1/27/74.

Viewpoint: International Conference on the Law of the Sea, by Dean Rusk. *UGA Research Reporter,* Spring 1973, p. 10.

Pinchhitter, by Dean Rusk. *The Bulletin,* May/June 1974, p. 21.

The American Revolution and the Future, lecture, 6/17/74. Institute for Public Policy Research, Washington, D.C.

Necessity Impels the South to Think International, excerpts from address at annual meeting of Southern Growth Policies Board. *Southern Living,* November 1974, p. 44a.

The Future of International Politics. Furman University Bulletin, *Life in the Year 2000: A Symposium,* J. Daniel Cover, ed., vol. 22, no. 2 (December 1974), pp. 42–49.

Integrity as a Basis of Effective Diplomacy, summary of address. *Intellect* 104:75, September 1975.

Some Untold Truths, excerpts from address. *New Directions* (Howard University magazine), vol. 6, no. 2 (April 1977), pp. 7–10.

Commencement Address, University of Georgia, June 10, 1977.

Eight experts size up U.S. future in a dangerous world: "Energy—A New Cause of War Coming Down the Road." *U.S. News & World Report,* June 27, 1977, pp. 43–44.

Informal remarks at the Georgia Federation of Democratic Women, 12/8/77, 11pp.

The Interdependence of All Peoples, by Dean Rusk. *Top Management Report,* International Management and Development Institute, Washington, D.C., 1977.

American Security in the Long Perspective, lecture. *Program for the National Security of the U.S.,* April 20, 1978, pp. 8–14.

Professional Leadership, address of 5/2/78. *Vital Speeches* 44:642–44, Aug. 15, 1978.

Excerpt from testimony on treaty-making procedures, 4/11/79. *Congressional Digest* 58:171ff, June 1979.

Professional Leadership: Art or Science? *Leadership in a Dynamic Society,* Frank E. Fuzmits, ed. (Indianapolis: Bobbs-Merrill, 1979).

An Overview: American Foreign Policy in the 80's, address. Washington Seminar LTV Corporation, 1980, pp. 12–24.

Lecture to the Academic Convocation of Kennan Professors, 6/1/80, Chapel Hill, N.C.

The Super Powers—Détente and Confrontation, address to 1980 Kiwanis International Convention, 6/25/80, Anaheim, Calif.

Dean Rusk on U.S. Foreign Policy. Interview by Andrew Power in *Macrocosm: The Public Affairs Review,* vol. 1, Spring 1981, pp. 4–5.

The Classics in a Nuclear World. *The Classical Outlook,* vol. 59, no. 1 (October–November 1981).

Nuclear Advice from One Who Has Been There, by Dean Rusk. *Washington Post*, Oct. 1, 1981.

A Personal Reflection on International Covenants on Human Rights. *Hofstra Law Review,* vol. 9, no. 2 (Winter 1981), pp. 515–22.

Tensions in International Trade and Foreign Policy Under President Reagan. *Public Law Forum,* symposium, St. Louis University School of Law, vol. 1, 1981.

Foreign Policy in the Eighties: The President and the International Environment. *The Virginia Papers on the Presidency,* vol. 5, Kenneth Thompson, ed. (University Press of America, 1981), pp. 35–54.

Can Business Contribute More to Development?, keynote address by Dean Rusk. Center for Global Policy Studies publication, University of Georgia, July 1982.

A New Secretary of State: At the Pleasure of the President. *Washington Post,* July 18, 1982.

Diplomacy and International Trade: Emphasis on Agricultural Commodities. *Journal of Agribusiness,* vol. 1, no. 1 (February 1983), pp. 13–16.

Lecture, 4/5/83. J. W. Fanning lecture series, Georgia Center for Continuing Education, pp. 3–13.

Response by the Honorable Dean Rusk to the Presentation of the Honorary Doctorate of Laws, Hampden-Sydney College, 10/14/83, Fall Convocation.

Men of the Year: Some Practical and Realistic Advice. *Time,* Jan. 2, 1984, pp. 38–40.

State Department According to Rusk, excerpts from remarks. *New York Times,* Feb. 11, 1984.

In Praise of Consensus: Reflections Upon the American Constitution. *The Ferdinand Phinizy Lectures,* University of Georgia, 1984, pp. 1–23.

CONGRESSIONAL TESTIMONY BY DEAN RUSK

Foreign relations, House Committee, 1951–1956 executive session transcripts, 83d Cong., House.

Technical aid to underdeveloped nations, programs review, 84th Cong., Senate.

National security programs, administrative effectiveness review, 86th Cong., Senate.

Communicational satellite system development and impact on foreign relations, 87th Cong., Senate.

Communism in Cuba and application of Monroe Doctrine, 87th Cong., Senate.

Establishment of Disarmament Agency for World Peace and Security, 87th Cong., Senate.

Export control programs administration, investigation, 87th Cong., House.

Foreign aid programs, Fiscal Year 1962 appropriations, 87th Cong., House and Senate.

Foreign aid programs, Fiscal Year 1962 authorization, 87th Cong., House.

Foreign aid programs, Fiscal Year 1962 authorization and reorganization, 87th Cong., House.

Foreign aid programs, Fiscal Year 1963 appropriations, 87th Cong., House and Senate.

Foreign aid programs, Fiscal Year 1963 authorization, 87th Cong., House and Senate.

International development and security programs, implementation, 87th Cong., Senate.

National Security Council role in national security planning, 87th Cong., Senate.

Nomination to be Secretary, State Department, 87th Cong., Senate.

Nuclear arms control policies, effect on military preparedness investigation, 87th Cong., Senate.

State and Justice Departments, Judiciary, and related agencies program. Fiscal Year 1962 appropriations, 87th Cong., Senate.

State Department programs, Fiscal Year 1962 appropriations, 87th Cong., House.

State Department programs, Fiscal Year 1963 appropriations, 87th Cong., House.

U.N. bonds, U.S. purchase authorizations, 87th Cong., Senate.

U.S. Disarmament Agency for World Peace and Security, establishment of, 87th Cong., House.

Diplomatic corps role in foreign policy development and administration, 88th Cong., Senate.

East-West trade, foreign policy implications review, 88th Cong., Senate.

Foreign aid programs, Fiscal Year 1964 appropriations, 88th Cong., House and Senate.

Foreign aid programs, Fiscal Year 1964 authorization, 88th Cong., House and Senate.

Foreign aid programs, Fiscal Year 1965 appropriations, 88th Cong., House and Senate.

Foreign aid programs, Fiscal Year 1965 authorization, 88th Cong., House and Senate.

Immigration, national quota system, gradual elimination, 88th Cong., House.

International Development Association, U.S. participation increase, 88th Cong., House.

Nuclear test ban proposals, effect on national security, 88th Cong., Senate.

Nuclear Test Ban Treaty, ratification, 88th Cong., Senate.

Public accommodations, nondiscriminatory access guarantee, 88th Cong., Senate.

State and Justice Departments, Judiciary, and related agencies programs, Fiscal Year 1965 appropriations, 88th Cong., Senate.

State and Justice Departments programs, Fiscal Year 1964 appropriations, 88th Cong., Senate.

State Department programs, Fiscal Year 1964 appropriations, 88th Cong., House.

State Department programs, Fiscal Year 1965 appropriations, 88th Cong., House.

Vietnamese Tonkin Gulf attack on U.S. vessels, military response authorizations, 88th Cong., Senate.

Army social science research, effect on foreign policy, Project Camelot, 89th Cong., House.

China and Vietnam, foreign and military policy of U.S., analysis, 89th Cong., House.

Establishment of Food for Freedom program and commodity reserves program, 89th Cong., Senate.

Foreign aid programs, Fiscal Year 1966 appropriations, 89th Cong., House and Senate.

Foreign aid programs, Fiscal Year 1966 authorization, 89th Cong., House and Senate.

Foreign aid programs, Fiscal Year 1966 supplemental authorization, 89th Cong., House.

Foreign aid programs, Fiscal Year 1967 appropriations, 89th Cong., House and Senate.

Foreign aid programs, Fiscal Year 1967 authorization, 89th Cong., House.

Foreign aid programs, Fiscal Years 1967–71 authorizations, 89th Cong., Senate.

Foreign aid to Vietnam, Fiscal Year 1966 authorization supplemental, 89th Cong., Senate.

France withdrawal from NATO, 89th Cong., House.

France withdrawal from NATO, effect on NATO structure and administration, 89th Cong., Senate.

Immigration, national origins quota system, termination, 89th Cong., House and Senate.

India emergency food relief, 89th Cong., Senate.

Military commitments of U.S., overview of Vietnam Conflict impact, 89th Cong., Senate.

Nuclear weapons nonproliferation, Senate resolution commending President's actions, 89th Cong., Senate.

Refugee policy revision, political and military aspects, 89th Cong., Senate.

Sino-Soviet dispute, impact on Vietnam Conflict, 89th Cong., House.

Soviet-U.S. consular convention, 89th Cong., Senate.

State Department programs, Fiscal Year 1966 appropriations, 89th Cong., House.

State Department programs, Fiscal Year 1967 appropriations, 89th Cong., House.

State Department security, and passport policy, investigation, 89th Cong., Senate.

State Department security investigation, Otepka case, 89th Cong., Senate.

State, Justice, and Commerce Departments, Judiciary, and related agencies, Fiscal Year 1967 appropriations, 89th Cong., Senate.

State, Justice, and Commerce Departments, the Judiciary, and related agencies, Fiscal Year 1966 appropriations, 89th Cong., Senate.

U.N. Security Council and Economic and Social Council membership increase, 89th Cong., Senate.

World hunger and agricultural production, 89th Cong., House.

ABM deployment and arms sales to foreign countries, 90th Cong., Senate.

Consular Convention with Soviet Union, diplomats' and tourists' rights, 90th Cong., Senate.

European troops, balanced reduction of Soviet and U.S. forces, Senate support resolution, 90th Cong., Senate.

Foreign aid programs and related agencies, Fiscal Year 1969 appropriations, 90th Cong., House.

Foreign aid programs, Fiscal Year 1968 appropriations, 90th Cong., House and Senate.

Foreign aid programs, Fiscal Year 1968 authorization, 90th Cong., House and Senate.

Foreign aid programs, Fiscal Year 1969 appropriations, 90th Cong., Senate.

Foreign aid programs, Fiscal Year 1969 authorization, 90th Cong., House.

Foreign aid to Vietnam, Fiscal Year 1968 authorization, 90th Cong., Senate.

GATT Kennedy Round results, implementation, 90th Cong., House.

Government, science, and international policy seminar proceedings, 90th Cong., House.

Import quotas revision, 90th Cong., Senate.

Latin American Common Market establishment, congressional support, 90th Cong., House.

Latin American summit conference, Punta del Este, 1967, 90th Cong., Senate.

Nuclear Non-Proliferation Treaty, Senate advice and consent, 90th Cong., Senate.

State Department programs, Fiscal Year 1968 appropriations, 90th Cong., House.

State Department programs, Fiscal Year 1969 appropriations, 90th Cong., House.

State, Justice, and Commerce Departments, Judiciary, and related agencies, Fiscal Year 1968 appropriations, 90th Cong., Senate.

State, Justice, and Commerce Departments, Judiciary, and related agencies, Fiscal Year 1969 appropriations, 90th Cong., Senate.

Treaty on Outer Space, ratification, 90th Cong., Senate.

Executive privilege, withholding of information from Congress, 1972, Senate.

National security policy and world power alignment, 1972, House.

Law of the Sea conference, U.S. preparations, 1973, House.

Dr. Kissinger's role in wiretapping, inquiry, 1974, Senate.

Arms Control and Disarmament Agency operations overview, 1975, House.

Soviet-U.S. détente, trade and nuclear arms reduction, problems and prospects, 1975, Senate.

Warrantless wiretapping of government officials and newsmen, 1975, Senate.

Government warrantless surveillance prohibition, 1976, House.

Intelligence agencies oversight by Congress, 1976, Senate.

Korean armistice talks of 1951, 1976, Senate.

Nomination of Philip C. Jessup to be U.N. General Assembly delegate in 1951, 1976, Senate.

OAS Charter development issues, 1949–50 hearings transcript, 1976, Senate.

Palestine refugees relief, 1949–50 hearings transcript, 1976, Senate.

Foreign policy options, 1977, Senate.

Mutual Defense Assistance Act inclusion of Korea, Philippines, China in 1950, 1977, House.

Panama Canal treaties ratification, 1978, House and Senate.

Export controls and foreign policy, 1979, Senate.

Treaties termination by presidential and congressional concurrence, 1979, Senate.

Export licensing and control programs, extension and revision, 1980, House.

House Foreign Affairs Committee executive sessions, 1951, Korean War peace negotiations, 1981, House.

House Foreign Affairs Committee executive sessions, 1952, U.S.-Japan treaty negotiations, 1981, House.

Executive sessions of the Senate Foreign Relations Committee (Historical Series) of the 87th Cong., 1st sess., in 1961, made public April 1984.

Executive sessions of the Senate Foreign Relations Committee together with joint sessions with the Senate Armed Services Committee (Historical Series) of the 87th Cong., 2d sess., in 1962, made public April 1986.